SPORT LEADERSHIP
in the 21st Century

John F. Borland
Assistant Professor
Department of Sport Management and Recreation
Springfield College
Springfield, MA

Gregory M. Kane
Assistant Professor
Department of Health and Physical Education
Eastern Connecticut State University
Willimantic, CT

Laura J. Burton
Associate Professor
Department of Educational Leadership
University of Connecticut
Storrs, CT

JONES & BARTLETT
LEARNING

World Headquarters
Jones & Bartlett Learning
5 Wall Street
Burlington, MA 01803
978-443-5000
info@jblearning.com
www.jblearning.com

Jones & Bartlett Learning books and products are available through most bookstores and online booksellers. To contact Jones & Bartlett Learning directly, call 800-832-0034, fax 978-443-8000, or visit our website, www.jblearning.com.

Substantial discounts on bulk quantities of Jones & Bartlett Learning publications are available to corporations, professional associations, and other qualified organizations. For details and specific discount information, contact the special sales department at Jones & Bartlett Learning via the above contact information or send an email to specialsales@jblearning.com.

Production Credits

Executive Publisher: William Brottmiller
Publisher: Cathy L. Esperti
Acquisitions Editor: Ryan Angel
Associate Editor: Kayla Dos Santos
Associate Director of Production: Julie C. Bolduc
Production Manager: Susan Beckett
Senior Marketing Manager: Andrea DeFronzo
Art Development Editor: Joanna Lundeen

VP, Manufacturing and Inventory Control: Therese Connell
Composition: Cenveo Publisher Services
Cover Design: Scott Moden
Photo Research and Permissions Coordinator: Lauren Miller
Cover Image: © Taras Kushnir/ShutterStock, Inc.
Printing and Binding: Edwards Brothers Malloy
Cover Printing: Edwards Brothers Malloy

To order this product, use ISBN: 978-1-284-03415-8

Library of Congress Cataloging-in-Publication Data
Unavailable at time of printing

ISBN: 978-1-4496-9086-1

6048

Printed in the United States of America
18 17 16 15 14   10 9 8 7 6 5 4 3 2 1

BRIEF CONTENTS

CONTENTS

4   The Necessary Skills Set   65

Mauro Palmero
Ming Li

8 Forging Significant Change   149
Jon Welty Peachey
Janelle E. Wells

9 Fostering Innovation   169
Larena Hoeber
Orland Hoeber

12 Shepherding Sport for Development Organizations   225

Jennifer Bruening
Nadia Moreno
Brooke Page Rosenbauer

13 Addressing the Gender Gap in Sport   245

Heidi Grappendorf

14   Lingering Issues in Race and Leadership   263
Jacqueline McDowell
Algerian Hart
Emmett Gill

15   Positioning the Organization Through Branding   287
John F. Borland
Sungho Cho

16 Leading Athletes with Disabilities   307

Mary A. Hums
Eli Wolff
David Legg

17 Leadership on a Global Scale   327

James J. Zhang
Kenny K. Chen
Jay J. Kim

PREFACE

Sport Leadership in the 21st Century fills a gap in the current offerings of sport management textbooks. There are few textbooks available to students, professors, and practitioners that focus on sport leadership. Many sport management professors have relied on books that discuss leadership in general, forcing them to teach sport management students from a general leadership perspective, outside the context of sport. We believe the sport management community deserves a book that examines leadership in various sport contexts, which is why we hope *Sport Leadership in the 21st Century* will serve as a significant contribution to our discipline and signal the importance of sport leadership instruction in academic programs.

The text defines leadership this way:

Leadership is an influence relationship aimed at moving organizations or groups of people toward an imagined future that depends upon alignment of values and establishment of mutual purposes.

The significance of this conceptualization of leadership is its ability to capture three important elements: influence, future, and mutuality. In sport organizations, there will always be a need for leaders to influence and motivate employees in positive ways to work toward organizational goals and future success. With the aging and retirement of the Baby Boomer generation, millennials are moving into organizations. These young people do not have the seasoned leadership experience of the people retiring. They may not know how to best influence their leaders and learn leadership concepts. Academic departments can address this need for leadership knowledge. We feel that this leadership definition—and this textbook—can give them a leg up. Furthermore, sport organizations—whether for-profit or not-for-profit—have the desire to be successful well into the future. This success is measured in the ability to reach established organizational goals. These organizations need people who can imagine what that successful future may look like through analyses of internal and external factors. Finally, no leader can do it alone. Leaders must establish mutual benefits for organization and employees and help followers understand the value of work not only from an organizational standpoint but from a personal standpoint. Leaders, if transformational, can establish mutual purposes by articulating how an organization's success connects to the personal success of individual employees.

Because we believe leadership is a complex activity, this book is intended for upper-level under-graduate sport management students and sport management graduate students who are interested in learning about or leading sport organizations in the 21st century. Entry-level employees and other sport practitioners will also benefit from reading this book. Our purpose in constructing this textbook is to provide foundational instruction on the establishment of leadership in sport management. This instruction is imparted through case studies, interviews with leaders in the sport industry, discussion questions that build critical thinking skills, and relevant chapter content that relies strongly on leadership research and current sport industry examples of leadership.

In many cases, the research utilized in these chapters is drawn from other disciplines, including psychology, business, sociology, and, of course, management. The chapter contributors have deftly "connected the dots," using the available research on leadership and tying it to sport, particularly in cases where specific sport leadership research was not available. Students will have to make these same connections after they graduate as good (and bad) leadership ideas can come from varying sources. Similar leadership concepts have been woven throughout the chapters by design, as we believe the repetition of these concepts will allow readers to recognize the most important information regarding leadership. An overview of some chapters and concepts is below:

- Chapter 2, *Understanding the Difference Between Leadership and Management*, is a breakthrough chapter. Readers are walked through the different research perspectives of management and leadership, culminating in a definition that summarizes leadership's most important activities. The goal of this chapter is to distinguish leadership from management, breaking from the thought that leadership is simply a management function. This is crucial because we believe that although the two functions of leadership and management are complementary, they demand different mindsets entirely.

- Chapter 3, *Transformational, Transactional, and Servant Leadership*, examines the characteristics of transformational leadership. Transformational leadership is a concept that finds its way into many chapters because it connects to many other concepts, such as brand building and organizational change. The goal of this chapter was to distinguish between different types of leadership so readers can connect their own experiences with leaders to their personal development in leadership. In other words, what kind of leader do you want to be? The information in this chapter helps answer that question.

- Chapter 4, *The Necessary Skills Set*, discusses the expertise that leaders need to develop to successfully shepherd organizations. The information in Chapter 4 is paramount because of its ability to form a baseline of understanding about what leadership entails. What skills really need to be developed by students? Once students understand those skills, they, with the help of faculty and mentors, can methodically work toward developing the skills early on and not later in their careers.

- Chapter 6, *Applying a Principled and Ethical Approach to Sport Leadership*, provides a comprehensive account of the importance of having leaders who exercise values and principles in their stewardship of 21st-century sport organizations. The contributors provide several examples, both historic and current, documenting unethical behavior, and they suggest alternative pathways leaders can choose to make better decisions. We believe leadership and ethics go hand in hand, and ethical leadership is a crucial competency for 21st-century leaders, particularly in sport, and particularly given many of the high-profile examples of poor ethical leadership seen in sport at all levels.

Other prevalent leadership concepts covered in the textbook include the difference between autocratic and democratic leadership; the different sources of leadership power; the four components of transformational leadership; the importance of self-reflection seen through the concepts of self-awareness and self-regulation; information about how leaders can "resonate" with and motivate employees; leadership models to make decisions about ethical dilemmas; integrative and strategic thinking; organizational change; innovation; crisis communication; team leadership; the use of sport for development and peace; the continued pattern of gender and racial discrimination in leadership positions; the emerging importance of branding; leading athletes with disabilities; a global perspective on leadership; and developing leadership as a student.

Although this list is not exhaustive, it highlights the key concepts, competencies, and areas of knowledge that future leaders need to understand to lead in the 21st century. If read closely, students can glean and begin to develop valuable leadership tools from this textbook to help them not only emerge as leaders but shepherd organizations to successfully fulfill missions and strategic visions.

The textbook relies heavily on industry perspectives in the form of case studies and interviews with leaders in the sport industry. These featured pieces bring more voices into each chapter, infusing real world experiences into the often static classroom experience. We believe sport management students need both the theoretical and practical pieces. We have tried to create a balance in this textbook with an introductory chapter that delves into the importance of the theoretical development of leadership in the 20th century. The remaining chapters are also rich in researched knowledge about best practices in leadership. The case studies and interviews allow readers to apply these theories and leadership paradigms. We have included case studies that range from the strategic leadership of the American Hockey League (Chapter 7, *Strategy and Leadership*) to the difficult decisions sport management students must consider when selecting an internship (Chapter 18, *Real World Applications and Career Paths*). Furthermore, industry interviews include information from the brave new world of social media (Chapter 5, *Communication that Motivates and Resonates*) to how leaders of athletes with disabilities can hasten their full integration into media coverage and Olympics governance structures (Chapter 16, *Leading Athletes with Disabilities*).

HOW TO USE THIS BOOK

Each chapter of *Sport Leadership in the 21st Century* includes a number of pedagogical elements designed to aid in the mastery of the material, including case studies, key terms, and discussion questions. The following explanations outline these key resources that will assist in your study time and help you grasp the key concepts at hand.

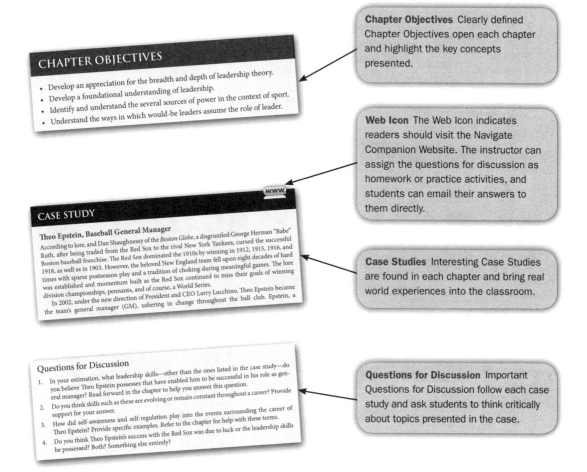

Chapter Objectives Clearly defined Chapter Objectives open each chapter and highlight the key concepts presented.

CHAPTER OBJECTIVES

- Develop an appreciation for the breadth and depth of leadership theory.
- Develop a foundational understanding of leadership.
- Identify and understand the several sources of power in the context of sport.
- Understand the ways in which would-be leaders assume the role of leader.

Web Icon The Web Icon indicates readers should visit the Navigate Companion Website. The instructor can assign the questions for discussion as homework or practice activities, and students can email their answers to them directly.

CASE STUDY

Theo Epstein, Baseball General Manager

According to lore, and Dan Shaughnessy of the *Boston Globe*, a disgruntled George Herman "Babe" Ruth, after being traded from the Red Sox to the rival New York Yankees, cursed the successful Boston baseball franchise. The Red Sox dominated the 1910s by winning in 1912, 1915, 1916, and 1918, as well as in 1903. However, the beloved New England team fell upon eight decades of hard times with sparse postseason play and a tradition of choking during meaningful games. The lore was established and momentum built as the Red Sox continued to miss their goals of winning division championships, pennants, and of course, a World Series.

In 2002, under the new direction of President and CEO Larry Lucchino, Theo Epstein became the team's general manager (GM), ushering in change throughout the ball club. Epstein, a

Case Studies Interesting Case Studies are found in each chapter and bring real world experiences into the classroom.

Questions for Discussion

1. In your estimation, what leadership skills—other than the ones listed in the case study—do you believe Theo Epstein possesses that have enabled him to be successful in his role as general manager? Read forward in the chapter to help you answer this question.
2. Do you think skills such as these are evolving or remain constant throughout a career? Provide support for your answer.
3. How did self-awareness and self-regulation play into the events surrounding the career of Theo Epstein? Provide specific examples. Refer to the chapter for help with these terms.
4. Do you think Theo Epstein's success with the Red Sox was due to luck or the leadership skills he possessed? Both? Something else entirely?

Questions for Discussion Important Questions for Discussion follow each case study and ask students to think critically about topics presented in the case.

INTRODUCTION

Thoughts on leadership and the qualities of a leader have existed for thousands of years, and many of these ideas have passed the test of time. Ancient Chinese philosopher and military tactician Sun Tzu is credited with several written works on leadership, most notably *The Art of War*, and after more than 2,000 years his leadership philosophy and tactics are still employed by military leaders. Tzu's teachings are also finding an audience among contemporary business managers. In 2000, *Sun Tzu and the Art of Business* was published, connecting Tzu's thinking to modern business strategy. Like Tzu, today's leaders need to be adept at sizing up their competition and looking for perceived weaknesses they can exploit to gain a marketplace advantage—if, indeed, this is one of their organization's goals. Emanating from ancient Greece, Plato's *Republic* discussed the qualities of

Introduction A thorough Introduction sets the stage for each chapter and weaves the topics discussed in the related case study.

LEADERSHIP PERSPECTIVE

Kevin DeShazo is the founder of Fieldhouse Media, an organization that provides social media education to student-athletes and coaches. The company also provides social media monitoring for athletic departments through its FieldTrack software, which helps to facilitate education and promote compliance with an athletic department's social media policy.

Kevin DeShazo.
Courtesy of Kevin DeShazo

Q: What challenges does social media create for leaders of athletic departments and coaches?
It has created numerous challenges, the biggest being that social media gives student-athletes an outlet to share their unfiltered thoughts to a global audience. They're 18–22 years old, and firing

Leadership Perspective Leadership Perspective boxes include engaging interviews with leaders in the sport industry who discuss interesting experiences and best practices in leadership.

DISCUSSION QUESTIONS

1. What are the differences among autocratic, democratic, and laissez-faire communication/leadership styles? Can you think of leaders in sport who personify each style of communication through their leadership?
2. In what ways can an autocratic communication style be successful in sport? Are there sports where a particular communication style is more accepted than another?
3. What are the advantages to collegiate athletic departments educating student-athletes about social media? Do you agree that banning or restricting social media use is an appropriate strategy? Explain your thoughts.

Discussion Questions Additional Discussion Questions close out each chapter and are ideal for homework assignments and in-class discussion. As with the Case Studies, the Web Icon indicates readers should visit the Navigate Companion Website. The instructor can assign the Discussion Questions as homework or practice activities, and students can email their answers to them directly.

ACKNOWLEDGMENTS

We received significant assistance in putting together this textbook. We relied on contributors from research colleges as well as teaching colleges. Some of our contributors are practitioners working in the field, which made them uniquely qualified to find and use content in the chapters that confirmed their leadership ideas and experiences. In particular, Chapter 12, *Shepherding Sport for Development Organizations*, the three contributors are practitioners in the sport-for-development field. In addition to founding and managing Husky Sport with the help of her graduate students, Jennifer Bruening is also a sport management professor at the University of Connecticut. In Chapter 12, she teamed with Nadia Moreno and Brooke Page Rosenbauer, who develop programming for A Ganar, a youth workforce development program that utilizes soccer and other team sports to help youth in Latin America and the Caribbean, ages 16–24, find jobs. In order for our discipline to grow, we need to form more of these practitioner–professor relationships and shine the light on professors acting as practitioners. Chapter 12 is a result of such a collaboration. This is only one example of the valuable information put forth by the diversity of contributors to this book. We thank all the contributors for their efforts and patience during the editorial process. As editors, we learned a lot about sport leadership from the insights of the collaborators, and we thank them for finding time for this project in their already busy schedules. We believe we have chosen the best people in our field to contribute to this textbook on sport leadership.

Furthermore, we would like to thank the prospectus and chapter reviewers for helping guide the topic selection process. Because putting together a sport leadership textbook was uncharted waters for us, the reviewers' insights provided a compass and allowed us to pick what appeared to be the most relevant topic areas. We also thank everyone at Jones & Bartlett Learning for their patience. The steadfastness of Acquisitions Editor Megan Turner and Associate Editor Kayla Dos Santos was greatly appreciated as we learned the process of putting a book together for the first time. They were, in fact, the teachers and we were the students.

ABOUT THE AUTHORS

AUTHORS

John F. Borland, PhD

John F. Borland is an assistant professor in the Sport Management and Recreation Department at Springfield College, where he teaches courses in sport communication, facilities, and event management. He serves as the department's internship coordinator and is co-advisor to the school's sport management club. He was a newspaper copy editor for nine years prior to obtaining master's and doctoral degrees in sport management. His research interests include sport for development and gender and race in sport. His work has been published in *Sport Management Review, International Journal of Sport Communication,* and *International Journal of Sport Management.*

Gregory M. Kane, PhD

Gregory M. Kane is an assistant professor in the Department of Health and Physical Education at Eastern Connecticut State University. After completing graduate degrees in exercise physiology (MA) and sport management (PhD), he went on to teach courses in sport sociology, research methodology in sport, and leadership and problem solving in sport. In addition, Dr. Kane has presented both nationally and internationally on the pedagogy and assessment methods of leadership. Currently, Dr. Kane is advisor to several clubs, including the sport management club, and serves as president of the University Senate.

Laura J. Burton, PhD

Laura J. Burton is an associate professor of sport management in the Department of Educational Leadership in the Neag School of Education at the University of Connecticut. She teaches courses in management, event management, and sport psychology at the undergraduate and graduate levels. Her research interests focus on the underrepresentation of minority groups in leadership positions within sport organizations and how organizational culture and leadership influence change processes within sport organizations. Dr. Burton serves on the editorial boards of *Sport Management Education Journal* and *Women in Sport & Physical Activity Journal.*

CONTRIBUTORS

Peter Bachiochi, PhD
Department of Psychology
Eastern Connecticut State University
Willimantic, CT

Blair Browning, PhD
Department of Communication
Baylor University
Waco, TX

Jennifer Bruening, PhD
Sport Management Program
University of Connecticut
Storrs, CT

Kenneth K. Chen
Department of Kinesiology
University of Georgia
Athens, GA

Sungho Cho, JD/PhD
School of Human Movement, Sport,
    and Leisure Studies
Bowling Green State University
Bowling Green, OH

Zachary J. Damon, MBA
Sport Management Department
Texas A&M University
College Station, TX

Wendi Everton, PhD
Department of Psychology
Eastern Connecticut State University
Willimantic, CT

Emmett Gill, PhD
Department of Social Work
North Carolina Central University
Durham, NC

Heidi Grappendorf, PhD
Department of Parks, Recreation,
    and Tourism Management

North Carolina State University
Raleigh, NC

Meg G. Hancock, PhD
Sport Administration in the Health and Sport
    Sciences Department
University of Louisville
Louisville, KY

Maylon T. Hanold, EdD
Center for the Study of Sport and Exercise
Seattle University
Seattle, WA

Algerian Hart, PhD
Department of Kinesiology
Western Illinois University
Macomb, IL

Larena Hoeber, PhD
Department of Kinesiology
University of Regina
Regina, SK Canada

Orland Hoeber, PhD
Department of Computer Science
University of Regina
Regina, SK Canada

Mary A. Hums, PhD
Department of Health and Sport Sciences
University of Louisville
Louisville, KY

Jay J. Kim
Sport Management and Policy Program
University of Georgia
Athens, GA

David Legg, PhD
Department of Physical Education
    and Recreation
Mount Royal University
Calgary, AB Canada

Ming Li, EdD
Center for International Studies
Western Michigan University
Kalamazoo, MI

Timothy Liptrap, EdD
Sport Management Department
Nichols College
Dudley, MA

Kevin McAllister, EdD
Department of Health, Physical Education,
    and Recreation
Springfield College
Springfield, MA

Jacqueline McDowell, PhD
Department of Recreation, Sport, and Tourism
University of Illinois at Urbana-Champaign
Champaign, IL

Nadia Moreno, BA
A Ganar Program
Partners of the Americas
Washington, DC

Mauro Palmero, PhD
Department of Kinesiology
East Tennessee State University
Johnson City, TN

Brooke Page Rosenbauer, MS
A Ganar Program
Partners of the Americas
Washington, DC

Jimmy Sanderson, PhD
Department of Communication Studies
Clemson University
Clemson, SC

Pete Schroeder, EdD
Department of Health, Exercise,
    and Sports Sciences
University of the Pacific
Stockton, CA

Janelle E. Wells, PhD
Department of Sport Management
Florida State University
Tallahassee, FL

Jon Welty Peachey, PhD
Department of Recreation, Sport, and Tourism
University of Illinois at Urbana-Champaign
Champaign, IL

James J. Zhang, PhD
Department of Kinesiology
University of Georgia
Athens, GA

Reviewers

Donald E. Cragen, PhD
Business Department Chair
Thomas College
Waterville, ME

Brooke E. Forester, PhD
Health, Physical Education, Leisure Services
University of South Alabama
Mobile, AL

Susan Hastings-Bishop, PhD
Recreation, Leisure Services, and Wellness
Ferris State University
Big Rapids, MI

Christopher M. Keshock, PhD
Health, Physical Education, Leisure Studies
University of South Alabama
Mobile, AL

William J. Kuchler, EdD
Department of Sport Management
Methodist University
Fayetteville, NC

Ryan Suchanek, BS
Department of Sport Management
Cushing Academy
Ashburnham, MA

CHAPTER 1

LEADERSHIP THEORIES

Gregory M. Kane

CHAPTER OBJECTIVES

- Develop an appreciation for the breadth and depth of leadership theory.
- Develop a foundational understanding of leadership.
- Identify and understand the several sources of power in the context of sport.
- Understand the ways in which would-be leaders assume the role of leader.

CASE STUDY

Yvon Chouinard, Founder of Patagonia

Established in 1973 by Yvon Chouinard, Patagonia is one of the most successful and environmentally conscious sporting goods suppliers in the world. The company posts more than $500 million in annual revenue while spending little on marketing, donating 1% of its total sales to the environment, and actively telling its customers not to buy its products unless they really need its products (Welch, 2013). The company's brand remains strong and respected, as does customer loyalty to its products. In recent years, Patagonia has outsold its targeted customer base—not its intention—by creating high-quality, highly functional products that have wide appeal.

Chouinard developed Patagonia out of a love for outdoor adventure and performance. The company was built from a small rock climbing manufacturing operation out of the back of his car into the company it is today. Central to Chouinard's philosophy is the idea that products need to make sense, and thus need to be tested; creativity is encouraged at Patagonia. He does this by

(continues)

implementing a unique leadership style that perpetuates throughout the entire company. Thus, he sees himself as one who initiates and facilitates change (Chouinard, 2005).

One way Chouinard fosters change is by bringing in ideas from outside the company. "Most people hate change—it's threatening. I thrive on it," he says. "I do that by holding all-company forums. We wire in our Reno, Nevada, warehouse and offices in Europe and Japan. I encourage people to ask questions then and there or to come see me in my office whenever" (Welch, 2013, para. 9). Furthermore, Chouinard developed the *5-15 Report*, which requires employees to spend 15 minutes a week writing a report to their managers on their challenges, ideas, and work. Managers then spend 5 minutes reviewing these, create a summary, and communicate this feedback to the executives and CEO. Employees are encouraged to communicate their feelings and suggestions, creating an internal culture of transparency. This vision has transformed the company (Buchanan, 2013).

Another way Chouinard develops creativity and sets the tone for his company's culture is by developing a nurturing workplace environment. One way he does this is by subsidizing daily lunches, which allow for more social connection. "Not only are we feeding our employees good food, but we are building a community, too. Socializing is important" (Welch, 2013, para. 25). Furthermore, in 1981 Chouinard developed an onsite childcare facility to relieve some of the pressures of work–family conflict. Employees can pop in to see their children throughout the day, freeing themselves from pressures felt by distance from their children, and thus allowing employees to be free to create (Chouinard, 2005).

Chouinard's style of leadership is evident in his philosophy of how to find the right employees. "I purposely try to hire people who are really self-motivated and good at what they do, and then I just leave them alone" (Welch, 2013, para. 1). In addition to finding the right people, Chouinard has tried to provide the right organizational culture—beyond lunches and day care for employees' children—for those ideal employees. In his autobiography, *Let My People Go Surfing*, Chouinard notes that he strives to put more joy into the workplace. He wants work to be enjoyable on a daily basis for his employees. He has encouraged a relaxed dress code and promotes flex time so employees have the freedom to enjoy personal pursuits or stay at home to care for a sick child. Ultimately, he has said he wants to blur the demarcation line between work and play and family (Chouinard, 2006).

Questions for Discussion

1. Can you describe the types of leadership behavior that Patagonia's founder Chouinard displays? You will have to review this chapter for assistance.

2. What traits does Chouinard possess that allow him to be an effective leader? Use examples from the case study to support your answer.

3. How does Chouinard use his power as a leader to maintain success at Patagonia? How would Chouinard define success for his company?

4. In your view, can Chouinard's style of leadership sustain Patagonia in the future? Explain why or why not.

5. If Chouinard were to step down as the leader of the company, do you think Patagonia would continue to be the same type of company and sustain the success it has had under Chouinard's leadership?

INTRODUCTION

Thoughts on leadership and the qualities of a leader have existed for thousands of years, and many of these ideas have passed the test of time. Ancient Chinese philosopher and military tactician Sun Tzu is credited with several written works on leadership, most notably *The Art of War*, and after more than 2,000 years his leadership philosophy and tactics are still employed by military leaders. Tzu's teachings are also finding an audience among contemporary business managers. In 2000, *Sun Tzu and the Art of Business* was published, connecting Tzu's thinking to modern business strategy. Like Tzu, today's leaders need to be adept at sizing up their competition and looking for perceived weaknesses they can exploit to gain a marketplace advantage—if, indeed, this is one of their organization's goals. Emanating from ancient Greece, Plato's *Republic* discussed the qualities of a just man and how these are needed for idealistic leadership in a just city-state (Brickhouse & Smith, 2009). Some leaders in sport are revered and respected because of their sense of fairness and impact on their organizations. Dan Rooney, chairman of the Pittsburgh Steelers, who is credited with suggesting the NFL's Rooney Rule that has attempted to pave the way for more diversity in hiring head coaches, comes to mind when considering Plato's sense of fairness. Although this text is predominantly focused on leadership in contemporary times—the 21st century—and equipping future leaders of sport with the skills and perspectives needed to lead both for-profit and not-for-profit sport organizations, it is crucial and instructive to glimpse the evolution of leadership and its theoretical development. Today's leaders have much to learn from past leaders and past theories of leadership because organizational challenges encountered today are often variations on situations encountered in the past.

Theories of leadership are a useful way for students learning about leadership to compare different perspectives at different points in history in different contexts. Furthermore, theories offer frameworks of analysis by providing explanations as to why certain relationships exist between units (e.g., leader and follower) in the empirical—or observed—world. *Leadership* is a prolific area of study with several theories, many reaching back decades. For students who may have little formal education in leadership concepts, this chapter serves as an introduction. It is certain that you have observed leaders in society and sport, on your campus, or even at your places of work; it is quite possible that you, as a sport management student, have already engaged in leadership opportunities on campus, in your community, in a group project in class, or at a sporting event where you have volunteered or worked. This chapter serves as a primer as to what is going on between leaders and followers with regard to leadership styles and sources of power. The mechanisms for leadership ascendancy are also discussed. Finally, some of the prominent leadership theories of the 19th and 20th centuries are briefly explained. The theories included in this chapter are likely to reappear again in your further study of leadership and were carefully selected for their contribution to the development of leadership thinking for the 21st century.

LEADER AND LEADERSHIP DEFINED

In his seminal work, *Handbook of Leadership* (1974), Ralph Stogdill writes a brief account of the origins of the words *"leader"* and "leadership." This account is repeated in Bass's (1981) revision of Stogdill's original work. It appears as though "lead" and "leader" have been part of European languages since about 1300. The notable exception is French, in which the word "leader" had no clear translation even into the late 20th century (Blondel, 1987). It is not until Webster's *An American Dictionary of the English Language* from 1828 that a definition of "leadership" appears.

Likewise, in Europe, the word "leadership" did not appear until the first half of the 19th century in writings about political influence and control of the British Parliament (Bass, 1981). Curiously, *Webster's* omitted any definition of "leadership" from subsequent dictionaries until 1965, when several definitions are listed in the third edition of the *New International Dictionary of the English Language.*

The foundational starting point in the study of leadership is an understanding of the parts that make up the word. The word "leadership" can be broken down into three parts: *lead*, *-er*, and *-ship*. The first part, *lead*, is likely derived from the Middle English *lede*, which means to come first or go first (Dictionary.com, n.d.a). The use of *-er* denotes one who performs a task or is employed in a role, such as baker—one who bakes (Dictionary.com, n.d.b). Therefore, a leader is someone who is employed in a role in which they are at the forefront of a group; thus, the one who defines the path. The use of *-ship* denotes a skill or craft, as in the word "scholarship" (Dictionary.com, n.d.c). Based on this interpretation, leadership is the skill set needed in the craft of defining the path for a group by one who is in employed in such a position.

A more modern interpretation of leadership is less concrete. Similar to the idea that there is no single model of the perfect leader, there is no perfect definition of leadership. However, there are some common elements to oft-quoted leadership definitions. Northouse (2012) defines leadership as a "process whereby an individual influences a group of individuals to achieve a common goal" (p. 5). Russell (2005) suggests leadership is the "interpersonal influence exercised by a person or persons, through the process of communication, toward the attainment of an organization's goals" (p. 16). Furthermore, Rue and Byars (2009) define leadership as "the ability to influence people to willingly follow one's guidance or adhere to one's decisions" (p. 465).

There appears to be some similarities among these definitions. Influence is a common element in all the definitions; goal setting and a relationship between the leader and the group being led are also alluded to in the definitions. The operational definition for this leadership text must then consider these important elements agreed upon by leadership scholars. The definition this text will use throughout, developed through a closer examination of the differences between leadership and management and aligned well with the three definitions presented in the previous paragraph, is:

> Leadership is an influence relationship aimed at moving organizations or groups of people toward an imagined future that depends upon alignment of values and establishment of mutual purposes.

This definition builds on the works of others and includes several important ideas. First, leadership is more than just a role. It is the behaviors one exhibits in this role. Some scholars have referred to leadership as a process; however, this loses the human element, the person-centered approach at investigating leadership. Leadership is interactive and dynamic, calling upon both actions and mannerisms to influence followers or subordinates. Second, power is an essential component of leadership in that it will alter the type of influence one has with one's followers (i.e., the group). Finally, alignment between leaders and followers on values and mutual purposes—or outcomes that benefit both the organization and the people involved—is necessary for leadership to be successful. Followers need to understand why a certain action is required.

POWER

An appreciation of power enables an effective leader to influence a group to achieve common goals. Thus, *power* is a condition that allows for influence over a group or individual and provides the ability to change another person's behavior, actions, or attitude (Raven, 2008). Therefore, a leader is in a state (power) to offer guidance, direction, incentive, or punishment to his or her subordinates. ("Subordinates" and "followers" are used interchangeably throughout this chapter.) Drawing upon this power allows the leader to obtain the desired goals by motivating the group.

In their seminal work, French and Raven (1959) discuss the five sources of leader power—reward, coercive, legitimate, referent, and expert—and how they relate to social systems. These provide a framework for this discussion of power and leadership in sport. A sixth source of power—informational power—was identified after the French and Raven work (Raven, 1992; Raven, Schwarzwald, & Koslowsky, 1998).

Reward

Reward power is the state or condition in which a leader has the ability or authority to provide rewards to subordinates. In this instance, the leader is able to motivate the group to perform based on the promise of some type of reward. This would be the carrot that motivates the mule to move forward in the famous carrot-or-stick approach to motivation. The reward provides an incentive for production. In sport, this is a common tactic for motivating a team or group. For example, a marketing/sales director may reward an employee with a bonus based on going above and beyond a quota for group ticket sales. This power is especially effective if the employees themselves are motivated extrinsically (i.e., motivated by salary, vacations, pay bonuses, or promotions). The National Hockey League (NHL) instituted a performance-based pay system in 2009 that largely avoided guaranteed salary increases in favor of bonuses based on a league employee's fulfillment of annual goals. The system works this way: Before the start of a season, each league employee compiles a list of goals they hope to accomplish for the year, and the employee's ability to meet those goals determines the size of the pay bonus he or she can receive at the end of the season (Mickle, 2009).

Coercive

Similar to reward power in that a leader has the ability to give something, with *coercive power* the leader distributes punishments. This would be the stick in the carrot-or-stick approach. Coercive power is the condition in which a leader has the ability to distribute negative consequence as the result of failing to meet expectations. In the previous NHL example, not fulfilling the goals a league employee sets forth means not receiving a salary bonus at the end of the season. This power is often used in sport. Given the competitive marketplace in sport, failure to reach revenue quotas or organizational goals tends to mean longer work hours or, if profits are not achieved over several quarters, a company staff "restructuring" plan that leads to layoffs can occur. The threat of punishment becomes the motivating factor to obtaining goals.

Legitimate

Legitimate power is rooted in the rights, responsibilities, and values of cultural groups. Social structure and learned hierarchy establish an order in which those at the top are awarded privileges and duties that those at the bottom follow. By now in your sport management studies you have likely encountered an organizational chart, which shows the progression of power from the top (e.g., an athletic director) to the bottom (intern). This implicit respect and acknowledgment of different levels of job titles provides an opportunity for power to influence interactions among members of the organization. Legitimate power is present when social and cultural norms exist that provide one with the right to influence others. Put another way, legitimate power is the power of a formal position or title. A general manager, an athletic director, or a league commissioner has implicit power that is associated with his or her position in the organization. Those within the group recognize that these people have a leadership role because of the title/role they possess.

Referent

Often compared to charisma, with *referent power* the relationship between a leader and a subordinate is based on the personal qualities and characteristics exhibited by the leader. In this instance, the leader commands such a presence of personality that group members are compelled to follow. The late Bill Veeck, who owned three baseball teams and created many of the tenets on which modern-day sport marketing and customer service are based, had a commanding presence of personality. Veeck's propensity for needling baseball's conservative governance between the 1940s and 1980s with his off-the-wall promotions provided him many loyal supporters. It was Veeck's enthusiasm and ingenuity that compelled his employees to line up behind him (Dickson, 2012). Furthermore, with referent power, the subordinate receives satisfaction by avoiding "discomfort" by complying with the wishes of the leader. The notion of avoiding discomfort applies less to Veeck, who welcomed new ideas, and more to the late George Steinbrenner, who owned the New York Yankees from 1973 to 2010. He maintained a large presence in the Yankees organization through his authoritarian leadership. His referent power was apparent by his nickname, "The Boss."

Expert Power

Power that is derived from having great knowledge, skill, or expertise is said to be *expert power*. This power materializes when a subordinate is in a position of need, and the leader has desired information. A relationship is created in which the needs of the subordinate are satisfied while the leader provides some type of service. For example, a sport information director has desired knowledge that an intern or an assistant sport information director desires. Thus, a relationship is created that satisfies the needs of both leader and subordinate. It is not necessary for this relationship to be a formal one; rather, this association may be created when a situation arises in which expertise or knowledge is needed. One sees a doctor for his or her expertise, visits a personal trainer to learn his or her skills, or enrolls in a course to seek the professor's knowledge.

Informational Power

Finally, *informational power* refers to a leader explaining to a subordinate how a job or task should be done differently. The leader puts forth persuasive reasons why the suggested change would be a more effective way of doing things (Raven, 2008). The subordinate agrees that the way described by the leader is better and changes his or her behavior accordingly. The information provided by the leader seems to be congruent in addressing the issue, thus influencing the supervisee's attitude or behavior (Gabel, 2011). Informational power may seem similar to expert power, but expert power refers more to a leader's accumulated knowledge, skills, and expertise whereas informational power is isolated to a single situation. A new baseball scout may seek to create a mentee/mentor relationship with the team's general manager (GM) so he can take advantage of the GM's expertise honed through 20 years of work (expert power). In contrast, that same GM can suggest to his scouts new ways of doing work through new sources of information. Oakland Athletics General Manager Billy Beane recommended that his scouts use different information to look for undervalued players who had a knack for getting on base and scoring runs (informational power) (Lewis, 2004) rather than the old-school way of scouting that places value on possession of the five tools of baseball: hitting for average, hitting for power, fielding, throwing, and base running.

It must be noted that although the six sources of power have been identified in different contexts, they can exist simultaneously within an individual. An athletic director can exhibit more than one source of power: (1) having the ability to reward coaches with contract renewals, (2) being able to punish with termination, (3) having the power that is embedded within the group from their title, (4) having charisma, (5) having expertise in coaching and administration, and (6) going to conferences and talking to fellow athletic directors to acquire new information on how to change job functions. The sources of power need not be mutually exclusive; rather, they enable a leader to draw upon power to meet a particular circumstance. The effective leader uses these sources of power dynamically as the need changes for different leadership styles.

FIGURE 1.1 **Interaction between leader, subordinate/group, and environment impact leadership style.**

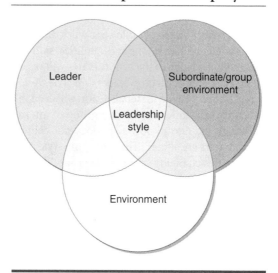

THE DYNAMICS OF LEADERSHIP STYLES

The leader, whether they are leading one or many, amateurs or pros, children, teens, or adults, will find that no two situations are the same. As such, the leadership style must also change to fit the needs of the situation. Imagine the coaching style of Division I basketball coaches and how that style must change if they are coaching their son's or daughter's youth basketball team. Likewise, administrators of a top flight, highly competitive Division I program may lead their program differently than a competitive Division III program that emphasizes student-athlete development over competition. What elements might alter leadership styles? When might a leader consider changing leadership style?

There are three elements to weigh when considering a leadership style: the leader, the subordinates, and the situation [environment] (Mondy,

Holmes, & Flippo, 1980), as depicted in **Figure 1.1**. The interaction between the leader, the subordinate/group, and the environment will impact the resulting leadership style. Thus, leadership styles are dynamic and depend upon the characteristics of these three variables.

Up until this point we have discussed power as part of the leader's role. The leader is also a person with experiences, skills, and needs that are unique to that individual. Therefore, individual leadership styles can change as the leader's experiences change, as they gain skills, or as their personal needs change. Using Billy Beane of the Oakland A's again as an example, his leadership style changed as rival American League teams' payrolls ballooned and his team's payroll stayed relatively low in comparison. He sought more information about player assessment and asked his scouts to adjust their thinking to the Athletics' financial realities (Lewis, 2004). Thus, leadership styles need not be static; they can change as the leader matures, takes on new responsibilities, or self-evaluates and deems change as being necessary.

The subordinates or followers will contribute to the leadership style. The ages, abilities, skill levels, and knowledge of the subordinates will necessitate an alteration in one's leadership style. A GM for a Minor League Baseball team will lead his executive staff differently than a group of interns. Although the GM's knowledge does not change, the followers are altered. The leadership style must adapt to this changing subordinate group. The language that a leader uses will change, the emphasis on development of followers may change, and the skill-directed activities may change. Effective leaders evaluate and adjust their leadership to meet the needs of subordinates.

Likewise, the situation in which the leader is attempting to lead will exert an influence on the leadership style. Factors like the type of organization (e.g., not-for-profit or for-profit), the group's goals, and the actions of the group will influence the leadership style; for example, a difference in leadership style is needed for leading a recreational sport league versus a Division I athletic department, and each group of participants are not the only consideration. Leadership styles, in this situation, must reflect differences in levels of organization, commitment to competition, and drive for success.

PATHS TO LEADERSHIP

The savvy individual who seeks a leadership role will be aware of the ways in which they can rise to this position. Understanding the route to achieving leadership status empowers an individual with a plan for action. Thus, having a firm understanding of the ways one might assume the role of leader becomes important. According to Shivers

(1980), four paths exist: appointment, election, emergence, and charisma. Taking on leadership roles early on—particularly while you are still in school—can help put you in a position to take advantage of one of these four paths later in your career.

Appointment

In sport contexts, individuals are often appointed to positions of leadership. As in the case where a marketing director may appoint a team leader on an account, appointment to the leadership position is a common occurrence. Interestingly, there are unique relationships that exist with this method of leadership attainment. A person is selected because he or she is thought to possess some qualities that align with those who are making the appointment. For instance, a marketing director may appoint a team leader because they have proven themselves in the past. Appointment suggests a relationship, responsibility, and perhaps shared values between the person who is selected and those who appointed him or her.

Election

The elected leader assumes a leadership role as the result of a process, formal or otherwise, that identifies an individual by popular decision. In this case, the elected leader has appealed to the electorate, those people who are designated as having the right to vote, and received a majority of votes. This can exist in a formal environment such as the election of a new league commissioner by a vote of team owners. As in the appointment situation, a relationship is then developed with the electorate, in this case the team owners. Popularity existed and so a responsibility to those who elected the leader may be present. Often, this relationship between the owners and commissioner causes a rift between the commissioner and players union during times of labor strife (i.e., lockouts and player strikes). This is a time when a leader has many followers and has to rely on different leadership styles to work with opposing sides.

Emergence

The *emergent leader* is said to spontaneously rise from a group that is in need of leadership. For example, imagine a pick-up basketball game in which there are no captains. No captains are appointed; none is elected from the group. Yet, teams need to be balanced, the informal rules need to be agreed upon, and the game needs to be initiated. What follows is the process of emergent leadership. Someone possesses certain qualities, in this case perhaps experience, communication, problem-solving abilities, and the ability to take control of the situation. Thus, they have become the emergent leader. Children in informal play environments naturally engage in this type of leadership role process often, with the two best players emerging as the leaders. Not to be confused with dictatorships, where leaders use force to achieve their leadership goals, emergent leadership matches a person's abilities, skills, and knowledge to the needs of the situation. Emergent leadership is sometimes seen in group projects in sport management classes. Nobody is elected leader, but often a person with high standards for the quality of work to be submitted emerges as a guiding force.

Charisma

Charisma is the metaphysical force of one's personality that compels others to follow. Some people possess characteristics that are likable and entertaining, and have a belief that they are infallible, thus making them attractive to others. This attraction provides for an avenue to leadership. The relationship that is developed is complacency (i.e., self-satisfaction), based on both the avoidance of displeasing the charismatic leader and the potential of pleasing the leader. Although this form of assuming the role of the leader is well-established and commonly observed, it should be noted that this form of leadership depends on the strength of the leader's personality, not their knowledge, experience, or skill. This form of leadership can be dangerous to wield and even more dangerous to follow (Raelin, 2003). Simply having charisma is not enough; leaders must also possess substance in the form of knowledge and skills and the ability to form meaningful relationships with subordinates. Charismatic leaders cannot do it all on their own. The values shared between leaders and followers must be mutually beneficial.

LEADERSHIP THEORIES

The theoretical underpinnings of leadership have had a distinctive history. Sun Tzu, Socrates, Plato, Lao Tzu, St. Thomas Aquinas, Niccolo Machiavelli, and Mahatma Gandhi are some of the classical names in the literature. Throughout the ages, leadership theories and philosophies moved from a focus on religious, military, and political matters, to behavioral, optimal performance, and capitalist-like movements. The following are selected theories, and their brief histories and philosophies.

Great Man Theory

The *great man theory* of leadership was a popular 19th-century belief that leaders are born, not made. According to this theory, popularized by Scottish writer Thomas Carlyle in the 1840s, leaders are both born with leader characteristics and born out of social, political, or economic circumstance. Thus, it was the innate qualities of the individual that allowed for their rise to leadership positions. The middle of the 20th century saw this theory fall from favor as behavioral theories began to take over. However, some held onto this belief. In 1980, Indiana basketball coach Bobby Knight (now a basketball analyst on ESPN) said, "The first thing you people need to know about leadership is that most of you simply don't have it in you" (Organ, 1996, p. 1). Contrary to the great man theory is the idea that individuals can develop knowledge, skills, and behaviors of leadership.

Bobby Knight coached college basketball from 1965 to 2000, amassing 902 victories.
© John Swart/AP Images

Trait Theory

In the 20th century, a systematic approach to studying leadership abilities emerged. Studies identified certain characteristics that might predispose someone as a great leader. These "traits" or factors were identified by comparing leaders and followers, and by identifying the characteristics an effective leader possesses. In his meta-analysis of 124 leadership studies, Stogdill (1948) identified five factors that predispose leadership effectiveness: capacity, achievement, responsibility, participation, and status. Over the passing decades others have contributed to the literature by offering their own meta-analyses (Lord, De Vader, & Alliger, 1986; Mann, 1959; Stogdill, 1974). Northouse (2012) reduced many of these

analyses into five major leadership traits: intelligence, self-confidence, determination, integrity, and sociability. Leadership studies at two Midwest universities also laid some of the groundwork to ascertain leader traits.

THE OHIO STATE STUDIES

The Ohio State Studies, initiated in 1945 and continuing into the 1950s, represented a turning point in the investigation of leadership behaviors (Stogdill & Coons, 1957). Despite early pressure to simply look at case studies of successful leadership, the Ohio State Studies took a quantitative approach to investigating leadership (Shartle, 1979). Although criticized for their lack of theory development, the Ohio State Studies were successful in developing a multidimensional approach to leadership. Central to these studies were two dimensions of leadership behavior: initiating structure and consideration. Initiating structure refers to developing goals, outlining tasks, and setting expectations; consideration refers to leader–subordinate relations and fellowship. This extensive body of research led to leadership measurements such as the Leadership Behavior Description Questionnaire-Form XII (LBDQ-Form XII) (Stogdill, 1963) and, later, the Leadership Scale for Sports (LSS) (Chelladurai & Saleh, 1980).

THE UNIVERSITY OF MICHIGAN STUDIES

Ohio State's gridiron rival to the north, the University of Michigan, also took a behavioral approach to identifying leadership qualities in the 1950s. However, unlike the Ohio State Studies, greater theory-based explanations of leader behavior were developed. Most importantly, the studies created a continuum of employee orientation/production orientation leadership behaviors. Whereas one end of the continuum was anchored by employee orientation—the leader's focus on creating a strong relationship with subordinates—the other end was anchored by production orientation—the leader's focus on the specific tasks and skills needed to complete the job (Bowers & Seashore, 1966).

LIKERT'S SYSTEM OF MANAGEMENT

Perhaps outshined by the scale that bears his name (Likert Scale), Rensis Likert's system of management was an important contribution to the research and application of leadership theory and motivation. Like the foundational University of Michigan Studies, a continuum was developed from *autocratic* to *participative* (Likert, 1961). The four classifications follow:

1. *Exploitive authoritative:* This type of leadership is exemplified by the leader who has little trust in his or her subordinates, and thus makes all the decisions for the group. The group in this environment is motivated by threats and coercion.
2. *Benevolent authoritative:* Again, the leader has relatively low trust in his or her subordinates and makes decisions for the group. However, in this situation the leader uses a system of rewards to motivate the subordinates.
3. *Consultative:* The leader has an enhanced level of trust in the subordinates and thus calls upon them to aid in decision making. The group is motivated in their ability to be involved with decision making.
4. *Participative team:* The leader displays a high degree of trust in the subordinates. Responsibility for success rests throughout the organization and motivation rests with achievement.

Situational Theory

Based on the work of Hersey and Blanchard (1969), situational leadership theory, later called *situational leadership*, suggested that leadership styles were dependent upon the environment or "situation" in which a leader needs to act. This theory implies that leadership styles need to change as the situation and needs of the subordinates change. Essential to this is the idea that there are two dimensions that coexist to change the leader's behavior: supportive behavior and directive behavior (Blanchard, Zigarmi, & Nelson, 1993). Supportive behavior refers to showing socio-emotional concern for subordinates whereas directive behavior refers to the need for leaders to delegate tasks and watch over subordinates. Hersey and Blanchard (1982) note that these behaviors change depending on the skills and maturity of the workforce. If subordinates are mature and responsible, a large amount of supportive and directive behaviors may not be needed. The leader plays more of a background role, only providing socio-emotional support when necessary. But for a group of subordinates that is insecure, immature, or lacks experience, more supportive and directive behaviors are needed until they grow and gain experience.

LEWIN, LIPPITT, AND WHITE STUDIES

In 1939, Lewin, Lippitt, and White created their highly regarded foundational work on "social climate" (Lewin, Lippitt, & White, 1939). This groundbreaking social science investigation focused on leadership behaviors in boys' hobby clubs (Edginton, Hudson, Scholl, & Lauzon, 2011). The authors developed an interesting experimental stimulus that the boys would be exposed to during their 3-month investigation. Three leadership styles exposed the children to a variety of situational circumstances that resulted in behavior changes in the boys. The three leadership styles were *authoritarian*, *democratic*, and *laissez-faire* (Lewin et al., 1939).

Authoritarian leadership was exemplified by a dictator-like style. All the boys' activities were organized and directed by the leader. Praise and criticism were given to each individual, and the leader did not openly engage the group. This style of leadership led to enhanced levels of aggression, boys seeking approval and attention from the leader, and domination within the peer group. This reaction was significant enough that a "scapegoat" role resulted within the group, and boys opted out of the investigation (Lewin et al., 1939, p. 278).

Democratic leadership was characterized by the leader facilitating the group's activities in consultation with the group. Thus, the activities of the group were discussed and decided upon by full group input. The leader was "objective" and frequently participated in the activities of the group. Group members could choose whom they worked with and what tasks each would do. This leadership style resulted in interactions between the boys that were "friendly" and more "spontaneous" (Lewin et al., 1939, p. 277). Furthermore, boys under this type of leadership style developed and exercised collective planning and individual decision making.

The laissez-faire style of leadership was the last group investigated. This style was characterized by lack of adult participation. Thus, all group decisions were generated by the boys, and they only interacted with the leader when technical questions arose. Furthermore, little to no praise or criticism was offered by the leader. The outcome of this environment was less productive than the other groups. However, in the absence of a leader, the group maintained its productivity, unlike in the authoritarian lead group.

The Lewin, Lippitt, and White studies remain an important and classic contribution to leadership theory. The lasting impact of their research is seen in modern applications of Lewinian theory to economics (Diamond, 1992), mathematics, biology, and social psychology (Scheidlinger, 1994).

BLAKE AND MOUTON'S MANAGERIAL GRID

First developed in the 1960s, the managerial grid has been through many iterations (Blake & Mouton, 1964, 1978, 1985, 1994). It is widely accepted as a critical and important analysis of leadership behavior. It is similar in some respects to the Ohio State Studies, which combined a focus on tasks and a focus on the relationship with the subordinate. However, the managerial grid

develops these concepts further by quantifying the degree to which the focus is on tasks or "concern for production/results," and the focus is on the relationship with the subordinate or "concern for people." The one to nine scale in **Figure 1.2** allows for discernment among the various responses regarding concern for production or people, where one represents a low concern and nine represents a high concern. Blake and McCanse (1991) postulated there were five leadership types:

1.1—Impoverished Management: Emphasizes a situation in which there is both low concern for results and low concern about people. The apathetic nature of this leader results in behavior that is withdrawn from subordinates and indifferent to success.

1.9—Country Club Management: This combination of low concern for results with high concern for people results in a leader who is more interested in pleasing people than in the performance of tasks. This leader attempts to create an environment that is friendly and welcoming.

9.1—Authority-Compliance Management: This represents a high concern for results but a low concern for people. This controlling leadership style is characterized by dictating instructions to subordinates in a way that does not show concern or compassion.

5.5—Middle of the Road Management: This style of compromise is evident in leaders who balance concern for results with satisfying relationships. The group is functioning; however, there is potential for greater success.

9.9—Team Management: Great emphasis is placed on production and on people. This optimal balance of developing human relationships and effective results attainment provides for the most satisfying work environment.

FIGURE 1.2 **The Managerial Grid.**

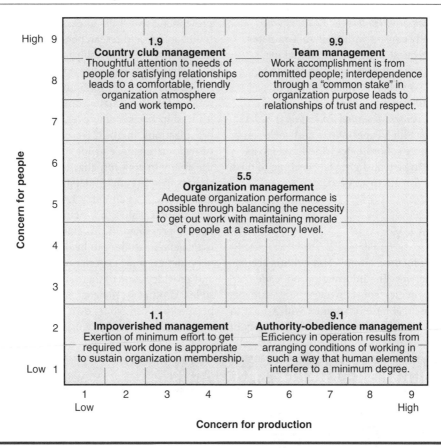

Source: Reproduced from Blake, R. Moulton, J. (1964). *The Managerial Grid: The Key to Leadership Excellence.* Houston, TX: Gulf Publishing Company.

PATH–GOAL THEORY OF LEADERSHIP

Inspired by the work of Georgopoulous, Mahoney, and Jones (1957) and later Evans (1970), House (1971) developed the motivation-rich *path–goal theory.* The theory was later refined into the theory we have come to understand today (House, 1996). According to the theory, leaders will change the path to attaining a goal based on the motivation of their subordinates. Chelladurai and

Saleh (1980) confirm the need for motivational factors similar to path–goal theory for coaching in the Leadership Scale for Sports. House (House & Mitchell, 1974) examined four approaches:

1. *Directive leadership:* Characterized by leaders who set clear expectations and goals for their subordinates. Thus, it is fundamentally satisfying to have clear and obtainable goals in which to achieve.

2. *Supportive leadership:* Exemplified by leaders who show concern for the

well-being of subordinates. This supportive behavior motivates the subordinates to achieve through mutual respect.

3. *Participative leadership:* Leaders who actively consult with their subordinates and request shared decision making. Buy-in is achieved with this leadership style, as well as satisfaction with the consultation.

4. *Achievement-oriented leadership:* Leaders who set high expectations and goals can motivate subordinates to achieve. Goals need to be realistic yet far reaching to push subordinates to succeed.

Summary

This chapter focused on pre–21st-century leadership perspectives. The information on leadership presented provides sport management students with a theoretical base of support with which to confidently begin their journey into the study of leadership. Understanding the evolution of leadership theories and ideas from Sun Tzu and Plato up to Blake and McCanse provides future sport professionals with the understanding of how long philosophers and researchers have considered the importance of leadership. Undoubtedly, given the competitive nature of sport business and the difficulties not-for-profit and for-profit organizations face to remain competitive and solvent, leadership has become even more important for organizations in the 21st century. This chapter provides students learning about leadership with the ability to conceptualize leader–follower experiences in sport and understand what it might be like for them as an entry-level employee as they pursue internships and their first jobs. The information presented in this chapter allows the sport management student to begin to reflect on his or her practical sport experiences—as they happen—and provide scope to their exposure to leadership styles. Ultimately, the goal is to develop reflective perspectives on your own leadership abilities, styles, and behaviors as you develop them.

LEADERSHIP PERSPECTIVE

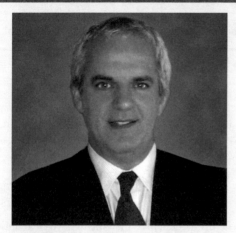

Frank Russo.
Courtesy of Frank Russo

Frank Russo is the Senior Vice President of Business Development and Client Relations for Global Spectrum, one of the world's foremost providers of management, marketing, and venue operations.

Q: What is your role in leadership?

My primary role is to develop new business for the company. I lead a team of people to respond to RFPs (requests for proposals) typically issued by city-, county-, or state-owned universities to manage arenas, stadiums, convention centers, multipurpose complexes, fairgrounds, and ice rinks. We manage 117 facilities, which represent 85 different clients. Therefore, we operate multiple venues for a number of clients. The other part of my job is to make sure that we maintain strong client relations, on an ongoing basis, so that they renew our contracts. In addition, I sit on the executive committee of Global Spectrum. But, my primary role for the company is to develop new business and to keep the business that we currently have.

Q: What skills are required to be an effective leader?

They say that knowledge is power, and I believe that you may come in cold but your learning technique must be quick and effective. You must have the ability to earn respect as a leader. The way you treat people will come back to you. I think you need to have a clear and honest recognition of your own skills. By doing so, you can recognize where you are lacking and can hire people to do what you can't do, rather than hire people to be just like you. Communication skills are critical and an openness to listen to people throughout the organization, top and bottom. For me it is much more important to listen and understand what our clients want.

Q: What ways/techniques have you developed that allow you to be most effective?

I was a history major in college and I learned to research, organize, coordinate, and create a battle plan. So whether you are doing a history paper, or you are preparing to respond to an RFP at the Cleveland Convention Center, a lot of it is very similar. You must be connecting the dots, creating the story, and then selling it. Whether you want to get an *A* in history or a management contract in Cleveland, you should have your resources focused on that objective. So, research, communication, staying updated in the industry, being aware of what your competition is doing, how to improve upon that, and how to offer a better "mousetrap" are all critical skills because you are always competing. Sometimes you are competing against others, but when you have a contract with a client, you can also be competing with yourself, especially when you are dealing with the government. For example, if you are worth $250,000, then someone comes along and says that they can do the job for $95,000, you are suddenly worth only $94,000. So we are constantly working to demonstrate our value to each client in relation to the fees they are paying us. I need to convey to the client why it is in their best interest to have us as their facility manager. This shows the client that sometimes the lowest price isn't always the best price.

Q: Are there any technologies that you find important with respect to leadership? What technologies should undergraduates be aware of or develop proficiency in?

Of course, having basic computer skills is essential. You should use those skills to be quick, efficient, and done in an organized fashion. You should be able to handle the complex nature of a multipurpose event center, through a computerized booking system, and be able to juggle those events, while making sure they are running on schedule, and in a timely fashion, as promised on their contract.

In a way, I think the business should change so that you can back off technology and have more face-to-face time, more conversation, and a little more personal time to recharge yourself. Recharging is important because you could be on duty for 24 hours a day. I think the biggest problem with technology is the inability to turn it off, sit down, be quiet, listen, and concentrate so that you can focus on listening and understanding the problem. A handwritten letter can go a long way in developing a relationship.

Q: What lessons would you give to students to be future leaders?

If I could go back to college, I would love to have the opportunity to take classes where I learned as opposed to simply studying for tests. That is my number one regret and my number one wish. In that context, I encourage our interns to take the tasks assigned with enthusiasm, ask questions, and learn the basics of the business they are interning for. Learning how to contribute, as opposed to getting in a comfort zone and just blending in, is also good advice. You should take a broad view and definition of your job. It may be just an internship, but I want the intern who will show initiative, and constantly ask what can they do, and create an impression that is lasting. Eventually, that will lead to me giving them more to do and then pay more attention to them.

Having awareness and an openness to talk to your boss is important. If I am not doing anything, I want my intern to observe that and come into my office, talk to me, and ask me good questions. You should not be intimidated because you are an intern. Don't be quiet about something that you suggest improving. Make suggestions, ask questions, and insert yourself into the operations of management.

Q: Anything else you would like to add?

I think it is important for students to get involved with their professional organization; for us it is IAVM (International Association of Venue Managers). They have an annual conference, where students work as volunteers. The IAVM offers great internship opportunities and networking opportunities. The IAVM has regional conferences, arena manager conferences, convention center conferences, theater boot camp, and a lot of opportunities for students to work as interns to help the IAVM at those conferences. They also offer student memberships that also provide students with certain publications, which is a very useful way to get more information about future careers.

KEY TERMS

authoritarian

autocratic

charisma

coercive power

democratic

emergent leader

expert power

great man theory

informational power

laissez-faire

leader

leadership

legitimate power

participative

path–goal theory

power

referent power

reward power

situational leadership

theories

DISCUSSION QUESTIONS

1. What role might power play in the leadership of a Major League Baseball team? A Minor League Baseball team? A Division I athletic department? Look at the six sources of power and compare and contrast the different scenarios.
2. Think about the six major professional team sport leagues in the United States (the WNBA, NHL, MLS, MLB, NFL, and NBA). What ways exist in which one might assume the role of a leader (i.e., commissioner, coach, general manager, club president, players' representative)?
3. Pick a leader in sport or business whom you admire and would like to model yourself after. What type of leadership style do they exhibit based on the managerial grid shown in Figure 1.2?
4. What traits do you possess at this moment that you feel will enable you to become an effective leader?
5. What sources of power do you have as a sport management student? Think about your dream leadership job in sport. What sources of power will you need in that job?

For a full suite of assignments and additional learning activities, use the access code found in the front of your book. If you do not have an access code, you can obtain one at **www.jblearning.com**.

REFERENCES

Bass, B. M. (1981). *Stogdill's handbook of leadership*. New York: Free Press.

Blake, R. R., & McCanse, A. A. (1991). *Leadership dilemmas—Grid solutions*. Houston, TX: Gulf.

Blake, R. R., & Mouton, J. S. (1964). *The managerial grid: The key to leadership excellence*. Houston, TX: Gulf.

Blake, R. R., & Mouton, J. S. (1978). *The new managerial grid: Strategic new insights into a proven system for increasing organization productivity and individual effectiveness, plus a revealing examination of how your managerial style can affect your mental and physical health*. Houston, TX: Gulf.

Blake, R. R., & Mouton, J. S. (1985). *The managerial grid III: A new look at the classic that has boosted productivity and profits for thousands of corporations worldwide*. Houston, TX: Gulf.

Blake, R. R., & Mouton, J. S. (1994). *The managerial grid*. Houston, TX: Gulf.

Blanchard, K. H., Zigarmi, D., & Nelson, R. B. (1993). Situational leadership after 25 years: A retrospective. *Journal of Leadership and Organizational Studies, 1*(1), 21–36.

Blondel, J. (1987). *Political leadership*. Beverly Hills, CA: Sage.

Bowers, D. G., & Seashore, S. E. (1966). Predicting organizational effectiveness with a four-factor theory of leadership. *Administrative Science Quarterly, 11*(2), 238–263.

Brickhouse, T., & Smith, N. D. (2009). Plato (427–347 BCE). *Internet Encyclopedia of Philosophy*. Retrieved from http://www.iep.utm.edu/plato

Buchanan, L. (2013, March 18). How Patagonia's roving CEO stays in the loop. Retrieved from http://www.inc.com/leigh-buchanan/patagonia-founder-yvon-chouinard-15five.html

Chelladurai, P., & Saleh, S. (1980). Dimensions of leader behavior in sports: Development of a leadership scale. *Journal of Sport Psychology, 2*(1), 34–45.

Chouinard, Y. (2005). Let my people go surfing. Retrieved from http://www.patagonia.com/us/patagonia.go?assetid=5625

Chouinard, Y. (2006). *Let my people go surfing: The education of a reluctant businessman.* London: Penguin Group.

Diamond, G. A. (1992). Field theory and rational choice: A Lewinian approach to modeling motivation. *Journal of Social Issues, 48*(2), 79–94.

Dickson, P. (2012). *Bill Veeck: Baseball's greatest maverick.* New York: Walker.

Dictionary.com. (n.d.a). lead. Retrieved from http://dictionary.reference.com/browse/lead

Dictionary.com. (n.d.b). -er. Retrieved from http://dictionary.reference.com/browse/-er

Dictionary.com. (n.d.c). -ship. Retrieved from http://dictionary.reference.com/browse/-ship

Edginton, C. R., Hudson, S. D., Scholl, K. G., & Lauzon, L. (2011). *Leadership for recreation, parks, and leisure services.* Champaign, IL: Sagamore.

Evans, M. G. (1970). The effects of supervisory behavior on the path-goal relationship. *Organizational Behavior and Human Performance, 5*(3), 277–298.

French, J. R. P., & Raven, B. H. (1959). The basis of social power. In D. Cartwrite (Ed.), *Studies in social power* (pp. 150–167). Ann Arbor, MI: Institute for Social Research.

Gabel, S. (2011). The medical director and the use of power: Limits, challenges and opportunities. *Psychiatric Quarterly, 82*(3), 221–228.

Georgopoulous, B. S., Mahoney, G. M., & Jones, N. W. (1957). A path-goal approach to productivity. *Journal of Applied Psychology, 41*(1), 345–353.

Hersey, P., & Blanchard, K. H. (1969). Life cycle theory of leadership. *Training and Development Journal, 23*(5), 26–34.

Hersey, P., & Blanchard, K. H. (1982). Leadership style: Attitudes and behaviors. *Training and Development Journal, 36*(5), 50–52.

House, R. J. (1971). A path goal theory of leader effectiveness. *Administrative Science Quarterly, 16*(3), 321–339.

House, R. J. (1996). Path-goal theory of leadership: Lessons, legacy, and a reformulated theory. *Leadership Quarterly, 7*(3), 323–352.

House, R. J., & Mitchell, T. T. (1974). Path-goal theory of leadership. *Journal of Contemporary Business, 3,* 81–97.

Lewin, K., Lippitt, R., & White, R. K. (1939). Patterns of aggressive behavior in experimentally created "social climates." *Journal of Social Psychology, 10*(2), 269–299.

Lewis, M. (2004). *Moneyball.* New York: W.W. Norton.

Likert, R. (1961). *New patterns of management.* New York: McGraw-Hill.

Lord, R. G., De Vader, C. L., & Alliger, G. M. (1986). A meta-analysis of the relation between personality traits and leadership perceptions: An application of validity generalization procedures. *Journal of Applied Psychology, 71*(3), 402–410.

Mann, R. D. (1959). A review of the relationships between personality and performance in small groups. *Psychological Bulletin, 56*(4), 241–270. doi: 10.1037/h0044587

Mickle, T. (2009, November 23). NHL starting performance-based pay system. *Street and Smith's SportsBusiness Journal.* Retrieved from http://www.sportsbusinessdaily.com/Journal/Issues/2009/11/20091123/This-Weeks-News/NHL-Starting-Performance-Based-Pay-System.aspx?hl=rewards%20system%20employee&sc=0

Mondy, R. W., Holmes, E. B., & Flippo, E. B. (1980). *Management: Concepts and practices.* Newton, MA: Allyn and Bacon.

Northouse, P. G. (2012). *Leadership: Theory and practice.* Thousand Oaks, CA: Sage.

Organ, D. W. (1996). Leadership: The great man theory revisited. *Business Horizons, 39*(3), 1–4. doi: 10.1016/s0007-6813(96)90001-4

Raelin, J. A. (2003). The myth of charismatic leaders. *Training and Development, 57*(3), 46–51.

Raven, B. H. (1992). A power/interaction model of interpersonal influence: French and Raven thirty years later. *Journal of Social Behavior and Personality, 7*(2), 217–244.

Raven, B. H. (2008). The bases of power and the power/interaction model of interpersonal influence. *Analyses of Social Issues and Public Policy, 8*(1), 1–22.

Raven, B. H., Schwarzwald, J., & Koslowsky, M. (1998). Conceptualizing and measuring a power/interaction model of interpersonal influence. *Journal of Applied Social Psychology, 28*(4), 307–332.

Rue, L. W., & Byars, L. L. (2009). *Management: Skills and application.* New York: McGraw-Hill/Irwin.

Russell, R. V. (2005). *Leadership in recreation* (3rd ed.). New York: McGraw-Hill.

Scheidlinger, S. (1994). The Lewin, Lippitt and White study of leadership and "social climates" revisited. *International Journal of Group Psychotherapy, 44*(1), 123–127.

Shartle, C. L. (1979). Early years of the Ohio State University leadership studies. *Journal of Management, 5*(2), 127–134.

Shivers, J. S. (1980). *Recreational leadership: Group dynamics and interpersonal behavior.* Hightstown, NJ: Princeton Book Company.

Stogdill, R. M. (1948). Personal factors associated with leadership: A survey of the literature. *Journal of Psychology, 25*(1), 35–71. doi: 10.1080/00223980.1948.9917362

Stogdill, R. M. (1963). *Manual for the leader behavior description questionnaire—Form XII.* Columbus: Ohio State University, Bureau of Business Research.

Stogdill, R. M. (1974). *Handbook of leadership: A survey of theory and research.* New York: Free Press.

Stogdill, R. M., & Coons, A. E. (1957). *Leader behavior: Its description and management.* Columbus, OH: Ohio State University, Bureau of Business Research.

Welch, L. (2013, March 12). The way I work: Yvon Chouinard, Patagonia. Retrieved from http://www.inc.com/magazine/201303/liz-welch/the-way-I-work-yvon-chouinard-patagonia.html

CHAPTER 2

UNDERSTANDING THE DIFFERENCE BETWEEN LEADERSHIP AND MANAGEMENT

Maylon T. Hanold

CHAPTER OBJECTIVES

- Understand the origins and conceptual evolution of management and leadership.
- Understand the perceived similarities between leadership and management.
- Differentiate between leadership and management.
- Identify tools important to both managers and leaders in sport.
- Develop a working definition of leadership.

CASE STUDY

USA Canoe/Kayak

When explaining the interplay between leadership and management, it is not surprising that Joe Jacobi, chief executive officer (CEO) of USA Canoe/Kayak, the national governing body for the Olympic sports of flatwater sprint and whitewater slalom as well as the Paralympic sport of paracanoe, might use a boat analogy.

> I'm a Stephen Covey guy. . . . Leading is setting the destination on the map, where the boat needs to go. Management is operating the boat to get it there. . . . I believe in the destination of where we are going. I can also see having gone through a positive period with USA Canoe/Kayak after going through a real negative one that even if I didn't fully agree with every little part of the destination, I can definitely see the importance of operating the ship to go on that course and doing it the right way. I think that is a big part of the integrity of an

(continues)

organization and defining those roles between leadership and management. In our case, we had "managers" that are a big part of setting the destination as well. And that is a different hat for sure, setting the course on the map and actually steering the ship to go down that course. (J. Jacobi, personal communication, March 28, 2013)

In December 2011, USA Canoe/Kayak (USA C/K) announced its move from Charlotte, North Carolina, to the boathouse district in Oklahoma City, Oklahoma, where voters approved a 1-cent sales tax in 2009 to finance a $60 million kayaking and canoeing complex. The move to Oklahoma City has allowed USA C/K to be the only Olympic sport based in Oklahoma; it also showed the commitment of Oklahoma City leaders to change the national perception that Oklahomans live in a dust bowl (Team USA, 2012).

USA C/K's move encompasses several aspects of leadership discussed in this chapter: adapting to change, understanding mutual purposes, and creating a vision and strategy. CEO Jacobi credits the leadership of board chairman Bob Lally, who oversaw strategic planning sessions in November 2011 that helped transform USA C/K from simply paying lip service to its goals and mission to making those goals and mission part of the language of the organization. When key stakeholders of USA C/K meet now, they discuss their progress with regard to their five goals:

1. Generate the resources needed for USA Canoe/Kayak to achieve its mission and goals.
2. Develop new and innovative paths of access to competitive paddle sports that expand our base of participation.
3. Win medals at premier international events.
4. Set high standards for performance and sport culture, founded in a strategy and structure that coordinates, collaborates, and empowers leadership at all levels of our sport.
5. Expand global presence and influence.

It is USA C/K's adherence to these goals that allows it to formulate strategy going forward. Jacobi has said that each goal comes with four to six strategies—along with tactics—for achieving the goals (J. Jacobi, personal communication, March 28, 2013). This is a classic case of management and leadership working together. The nuts-and-bolts aspect of talking through and formulating strategies, goals, and tactics for an organization falls under management tasks in that it informs how employees do their work in the present. However, these strategies, goals, and tactics allow leaders to establish and articulate what an organization really values. These values—which have to be lived by the organization and its employees and not simply spoken—signal to outside organizations what mutual benefits can be obtained from partnerships. USA C/K now has two strong partners in the Oklahoma City Boathouse District and the American Canoe Association. These partners have positioned the organization to build its base of participants through its Paddle Now! grassroots initiative.

Questions for Discussion

1. Using one organization from professional sport and one from collegiate sport, can you identify organizational activities that would differentiate between management and leadership based on Jacobi's quoting of Covey?

2. What do strategies, tactics, and goals mean to you, and how would you differentiate them? Again, use a couple of sport organizations as context.

3. USA C/K has five organizational goals it follows. Can you think of two more that the organization could add? Feel free to look at the organization's website: http://www.teamusa.org/USA-Canoe-Kayak.

4. Read the chapter to learn about the differences between management and leadership. Based on what you know, what management functions are likely to take place at USA C/K? What leadership functions can be expected?

INTRODUCTION

Because the focus of this text is on leadership within the sport management field, it is crucial to distinguish between the two concepts of leadership and management to understand perceived differences and similarities. Since Zaleznik's classic article, "Managers and Leaders: Are They Different?" in the *Harvard Business Review* in 1977, the debate about whether management and leadership are distinct activities continues. Research exploring the differences between management and leadership has grown considerably (Bennis, 2009; Kotter, 1990a; Macoby, 2000; Perloff, 2007; Toor, 2011; Weathersby, 1999; Yukl, 1989; Zimmerman, 2001). Although the debate is far from over, there tend to be three major assumptions present in current research. First, management and leadership are essentially the same because attempts to distinguish the two remain vague and confusing, and thus, impractical (Mangham & Pye, 1991). The second view of management and leadership acknowledges that the two concepts are intertwined, but believes they are distinct on some levels. Scholars have described the relationship such that (1) leadership is a form of management in that it is good or excellent management, and (2) leadership is a function of management. The final approach considers management and leadership as distinct with respect to what they are, how they are conceptualized, and the functions they serve.

Despite the different views, this text takes the position that *management* and *leadership* are different. Before moving on to why we consider management and leadership to be discrete activities, it is instructive to review the development of leadership studies. To this end, we begin the chapter with the two prominent ways that management and leadership have historically been associated with each other. Then, we consider how management and leadership are distinct activities and why it is important to see them this way. Finally, we examine the differences in detail and offer examples from the sport management literature and recent research to show the differences.

HISTORICAL PERSPECTIVE: MANAGEMENT VERSUS LEADERSHIP

Manager and management have a history grounded in the industrial revolution when factory owners were interested in maximizing profits by making sure that work processes in place were streamlined, rational, and consistent. Efficiency and control were paramount. Management theory grew out of these concerns. Although defined in many different ways, management has consistently been about organizing people to achieve organizational goals using limited resources (Chelladurai, 2009). Three distinct phases characterize the meanings of management and the function of managers.

The first phase was called the *scientific management movement*. Essentially codified in 1911 with the publication of *The Principles of Scientific Management* by Frederick Taylor, management in this context was about motivating employees through extrinsic rewards to perform prescribed, efficient movements. It was entirely focused on the work of organizations with little regard for either the psychological or sociological concerns of employees. A reaction to this work-centered approach marked the second phase. This phase, called the *human relations movement*, took place during the late 1920s and early 1930s. In this movement, management became more concerned with motivating workers intrinsically. Finally, the last phase, organizational behavior, considers efficiency and human relations aspects to examine organizational success.

Unlike management, leadership study has not been defined by movements, or defined much at all. Although the word "leadership" appeared in English dictionaries in the early 17th century (Rost, 1993), it was not until Webster's *An American Dictionary of the English Language* in 1828 that a definition of leadership appeared in this country. Webster omitted any definition of leadership from its dictionaries until 1965, when several definitions were listed in the third edition of the *New International Dictionary of the English Language*. Furthermore, formal studies of leadership appeared only sparingly in the 19th century, but more prominently in the latter half of the 20th century.

Leadership and Management as Synonymous

The strong presence of management as a concept early in the 20th century coupled with the absence of the word "leadership" from dictionaries may simply reflect the lack of perceived need to distinguish the two concepts. Rost (1993) explains this lack of clear distinction as a natural and logical result of the historical context:

> They [scholars and practitioners] were reflecting the reality as they saw it. Their perception of leadership as management was the reality they perceived in the industrial era in which they lived and worked. They did not distinguish between leadership and management because in their minds there was no need to do so. They were one phenomenon. (pp. 92–93)

Indeed, the 1925 *Thesaurus Dictionary* by March and March listed synonyms for "take the lead" as "leading-following, management" and a synonym for "leader" as "manager."

With the onset of the human relations phase of management, more scholars became interested in identifying what was lacking in scientific management and needed in order to attend to the human side of organizations. As a result, the concept of leadership, although simply defined in dictionaries, began to be framed as a more human-oriented skill. Notably, there was a shift from the idea of a leader as someone who controls and directs to one who influences. Schenk (1928), a prominent voice in this shift, says, "Leadership is the management of men by persuasion and inspiration rather than the direct or implied threat of coercion" (p. 111). Although leadership appears to take on a form of its own, it is clear from this definition that leadership is never clearly disassociated from management.

As the concept of leadership developed during the second half of the 20th century, leadership studies, articles, and books abounded. However, what is more remarkable is that despite clearly writing about leadership, scholars often failed to provide specific definitions of leadership (Rost, 1993). Furthermore, two trends indicate the extent to which leadership and management were thought of as indistinguishable. First, throughout the

1980s, leadership was defined as achieving organizational goals, resulting in confusion between management and leadership. Many scholars from fields such as education, the military, business, feminist research, and political science included the idea of achieving organizational goals within either their definitions or notions of leadership (Hersey & Blanchard, 1988; Hollander, 1985; Jago, 1982; Segal, 1981; Sergiovanni, 1984). Dating back to the 19th century, there has been consistent agreement among management scholars and practitioners that management is the process of achieving organizational goals. Thus, leadership scholars who insist on organizational goals being accomplished as an indication of leadership create confusion because two distinct words have been given the same characteristics. Second, several scholars during the 1980s overtly conceded the indistinguishable qualities of leadership and management. For example, Kuhn and Beam (1982) concede, "The term leadership is already applied so widely to formal executives, officers, squad leaders, and the like that we may simply accept it and say that leadership is the performance of the sponsor, or managerial, function . . ." (p. 381). Also, in Yukl's (1989) widely used textbook, he states, "The terms leader and manager are used interchangeably in this book" (p. 5). To reflect this perspective, Yukl employs the phrase "managerial leadership." Today, a significant number of scholars remain unsure as to whether the debate is useful because the distinctions between leader and manager remain obscure in practice and research (Mangham & Pye, 1991). Furthermore, current debates often demonstrate that "a common confusion remains that leadership and management are similar and that leaders and managers play similar roles [such that] sometimes leaders manage and sometimes managers lead" (Toor, 2011, p. 311). Northouse (2010) says that it makes sense for researchers to "treat the role of managers and leaders similarly and do not emphasize the differences between them" (p. 11).

Leadership and Management Overlap

The idea that leadership and management are distinct but still overlap is the most prominent idea in leadership research today. Two distinct views about how leadership and management overlap are common in the literature. The first view imagines leadership as a higher form of management; that is, leadership is management done well. The second view comes from the stance that management is what goes on in organizations. Leadership is simply an essential skill of managers. The logic that management subsumes leadership makes sense given the historical dominance of management study, the lack of a coherent leadership theory, and the ultimate concern that the majority of people occupy management positions by title or collective understanding. This way of thinking has experienced resurgence since the exponential growth of organizations (Kotterman, 2006).

LEADERSHIP AS EXCELLENT MANAGEMENT

Concurrent to the idea that management and leadership were synonymous, the concept of leadership as good management became increasingly prominent during the explosion of the leadership literature in the 1980s. Rost (1993) coined the phrase, "the industrial paradigm of leadership" (p. 94) to identify this development, which he considers to be the most important unifying factor among leadership literature through the 1980s. Upon review of hundreds of leadership articles, Rost noted that management and leadership were often described as being different in degree. What emerged during this time was an underlying sense that leadership could not possibly be just any kind of management. As a result, scholars and practitioners began to frame leadership as not simply management, but rather good or excellent management.

With the introduction of Burns's (1978) seminal work, *Leadership*, the idea of excellence became much more highly correlated to leadership as compared to management. Excellence was still tied to goal achievement, but goals could be achieved through transactional or transformational leadership, two terms that Burns used to describe two styles of leadership. Transactional leadership provides employees rewards (e.g., a paycheck) in return for goal accomplishment. *Transformational leadership* sparks an interest in excellence beyond focusing on work processes. Burns essentially introduces the idea that leadership should help organizations not only realize purposes, but also achieve excellence by bringing employees to a much higher state of being and, subsequently, performance. Katz and Kahn (1978) capture a similar sentiment with their articulation of leadership versus management. They say, "we consider the essence of organizational leadership to be the influential increment over and above mechanical compliance [management] with routine directives of the organization" (pp. 302–303). This expanded view of excellence or something "over and above" as tied to leadership solidifies the idea that "leadership is that which is done by excellent managers and management is that which is done by average managers" (Rost, 1993, p. 116).

In his famous book, *The Managerial Mystique: Restoring Leadership in Business,* Zaleznik (1989) gives considerable attention to leadership as people-oriented. He argues that leadership is different from management. He proposes, "the distinction is simply between a manager's attention to how things get done and a leader's to what the events and decisions mean to participants" (Zaleznik, 1978, p. 12). Zaleznik describes this quality as being more human related. He says, "managers relate to people according to the role they play . . . while leaders, who are concerned with ideas, relate in more intuitive and empathetic ways" (Zaleznik, 1978, p. 11). Despite his attempt to distinguish leadership and management, Zaleznik ultimately frames a leader as a great manager. He talks about the actions of an "effective manager," defining this person as a

leader. He contrasts this with "ineffective managers," who remain simply managers. Again, despite his efforts to distinguish leadership from management, Zaleznik's language choices reflect the view that leadership is excellent management.

Leadership as a Function of Management

Another position that grew out of the "leadership as good management" perspective during the 1970s and 1980s was that leadership was an essential management skill. Although leadership was beginning to be distinguished from management, it could not entirely disassociate itself from management. Thus, when leadership began to be framed as distinct, it naturally developed as a function of management. Mintzberg (1973), a prominent scholar on business management, developed a list of 10 managerial roles from his study of executives. Being a leader is listed as one of those roles, which reflects the dominant thinking at the time. Yukl (2002) sums up this major assumption of several decades by saying, "Most scholars seem to agree that success as a manager or administrator in modern organizations necessarily involves leading" (p. 6).

Leadership as a unique management skill came about because of a growing sense that leadership as simply good or excellent management was not capturing the qualitative differences between leadership and management. Of this particular period of time, Bryman (1992) notes that

> There was considerable disillusionment with leadership theory and research in the early 1980s. Part of the disillusionment was attributed to the fact that most models of leadership and measurement accounted for a relatively small percentage of variance in performance outcomes such as productivity and effectiveness. (p. 21)

These measures were focused on goal setting, providing direction and support, leader–follower exchange relationships, and behaviors based on "cost-benefit assumptions" (Bass, 1985, p. 5). In other words, trying to measure leadership as some excellent version of management was not necessarily accounting for differences in performances. The resultant conclusion was that leadership must be a separate skill of management.

This special skill became associated with Burns's (1978) transformational leadership. As noted earlier, these skills were more human focused, based in values, and relied on interpersonal skills. As Burns frames it, transformational leadership is more focused on vision, inspiration, higher purposes, and charisma. Despite being discussed as distinct and being concerned with people versus work processes, leadership was seen as a complementary skill, or rather a skill to be developed as a manager to be effective.

Such thinking is evidenced in the various ways scholars and practitioners have talked about these skills. Gomez-Mejia, Balkin, and Cardy (2005) note that leadership is "a management function in which motivating people to achieve higher purposes, perform to the best of their ability, and work with other people to do so" (p. 11) is a key aspect. While exploring the notion of charisma, Conger and Kanungo (1994) use language that maintains the idea that leadership is a management function. They say, "managers in a charismatic leadership role are also seen to be deploying innovative and unconventional means for achieving their visions" (p. 443), and that they are attempting to "operationalize the charismatic leadership role of managers in organizations" (p. 443). This particular relationship between management and leadership also appears often in practitioner articles. One such example comes from the domain of human resources. McLean (2005) remarks that despite the differences between leadership and management, "there is the argument that leadership is a facet of management and therefore cannot be separated" (p. 16). In these instances, the inclination to keep management and leadership closely bound together is readily apparent.

THE CASE FOR DIFFERENTIATING MANAGEMENT AND LEADERSHIP

Without the distinction between the activities of management and leadership, organizations could be set up for failure. Without differentiation, management tends to be denigrated and leadership exalted. Several scholars (Kotter, 1990a, 1990b; Rost, 1993) warn that this confusion leads people to think of leadership as the remedy for all organizational dilemmas. Kotter (1990a) maintains that this is a dangerous view because both management and leadership are needed. If there is strong leadership but weak management in a complex world, the result is "a) emphasis on long term but no short term plans, b) strong group culture without much specialization, structure or rules, c) inspired people who are not inclined to use control systems or problem solving disciplines" (p. 17). The converse is also true. Organizations with strong management but weak leadership have trouble moving in new directions when the environment necessitates a change. In other words, efficient systems of organization operations are not enough when those systems need to be reconsidered altogether. Furthermore, without clear articulation of the differences, the myth that people want to be led, not managed, gains ground. Yet, this myth does not match reality (Rost, 1993). People do like to be managed. They like order, clear expectations, and having a strong sense of how their work fits into accomplishing organizational goals. The act of ordering chaos is management. Organizations cannot thrive without this kind of order. In short, organizations need both leaders and managers.

Czarniawska-Joerges and Wolff (1991) believe that the distinction serves important cultural purposes. They argue that the terms "leadership" and "management" embody certain archetypes that have distinct meanings for cultures at specific points in time. Given that people operate based on shared understandings, clarity about the roles of managers and leaders is important. If an employee understands what is commonly accepted as typical activities of managers as opposed to leaders, they can more accurately discern their own feelings about their boss's relative strengths and weaknesses. These shared understandings allow for the culture to create itself in consistent ways. By eliminating confusion over the activities of management and leadership, organizational culture develops positively with fewer misunderstandings.

Furthermore, by clearly distinguishing management and leadership, it is possible to talk about good, bad, effective, ineffective, or mediocre management and leadership. In other words, distinguishing the two allows scholars and practitioners to recognize various levels of competency. When leadership is viewed as an excellent form of management, this distinction is impossible to make. In contrast, by distinguishing the two, not only can different skill sets be identified for each area, but also the competency with which they are done can also be evaluated. If those differences are not clearly articulated, confusion over the terms only brings about difficulties in performance assessments, hiring practices, and professional development. Simply put, misunderstandings about the differences, as culturally defined, ultimately hinder organizational practices. Distinction allows us to focus our efforts more clearly on developing people (Kotter, 1990b; Zacko-Smith, 2007). Organizations can more precisely assess relative strengths and weaknesses of people, focusing attention on developing the necessary skills or simply matching people to positions in which their strengths serve them well. As Kotter (1990b) puts it, "Once companies understand the fundamental difference between leadership and management, they can begin to groom their top people to provide both" (p. 104).

We stand in agreement with those who feel it is necessary to distinguish clearly between leadership and management in order to study, test, and develop the two skills within the sport industry. As such, we explore the conceptual, definitional, and functional differences between management and leadership in more detail.

CONCEPTUAL DIFFERENCES BETWEEN MANAGEMENT AND LEADERSHIP

Many scholars view management and leadership as distinct, but complementary activities, both of which are necessary for organizations to succeed. Reviewing the historical development of this idea, three aspects about management versus leadership surface. First, management deals with tangibles such as how to do work. In contrast, leadership operates on the level of intangibles such as establishing values and creating social worlds in which mutual purposes are co-created. Second, management works in the present whereas leadership is focused on the future. Third, management focuses on making complex systems run smoothly. Leadership involves moving an organization through change. Scholars who support the view that management and leadership are separate, different activities argue that both functions are needed for organizations to succeed.

One trend that has surfaced over the past 60 years regarding management and leadership is that management is a mechanistic process whereas leadership is a social process. Long before Zaleznik's (1977) classic article regarding the differences between management and leadership, various scholars have explored the idea that leadership is relational. Coming from an institutional leadership perspective, Selznick (1957) writes, "the task of building special values and a distinctive competence into the organization is a prime function of leadership" (p. 27). In this early account, Selznick points out a qualitative difference between management and leadership—namely, leadership is essentially a social phenomenon because establishing values is a social activity.

Continuing along this line of thinking, Hosking and Morley (1988) propose that leadership entails structuring not what people do, but what events and actions mean to people. Scholars who see leadership as clearly different from management assert that leadership is about constructing shared values and meanings (Drath, 2001) based on trust (Bennis & Nanus, 1985) and is entirely relational (Rost, 1993). Leadership is about how communities "construct one another, and become such things as leaders and followers" (Drath, 2001, p. xvi), whereas management is about the exercise of power and authority in accomplishing tasks (Rost, 1993).

A second theme that emerges in a review of the leadership literature is that management focuses on doing activities efficiently in the present moment, whereas leadership is future oriented and based in the notion of vision. Bennis (1977) posited that "leading is different from management; the difference between the two is crucial. I know many institutions that are very well managed and very poorly led" (p. 3). Further study of leadership prompted Bennis and Nanus (1985) to think that many organizations were overmanaged and underled. They conclude that many people in organizations

> excel in the ability to handle the daily routine, yet never question whether the routine should be done at all. . . . Managers are people who do things right and leaders are people who do the right thing. The difference may be summarized as activities of vision and judgment—effectiveness versus activities of mastering routines—efficiency. (p. 21)

The final theme that permeates the literature framing management and leadership as distinct has its roots in Burns's descriptions of transactional and transformational leadership. Burns's definition of transformational leadership marked an important step toward viewing management and leadership as fundamentally different. Although his definition of transformational

leadership is lengthy, the distinction between transactional and transformational leadership remains rather simple at its core. Transactional leadership is effective for maintaining the status quo whereas transformational leadership is needed to move organizations through change while focusing on the growth and development of people. Kotter (1990a, 1990b) takes this difference seriously and puts forth the most cogent argument for distinguishing management and leadership in his famous book, *A Force for Change: How Leadership Differs from Management* (1990a). Kotter succinctly frames the difference by saying that management is about coping with complexity and leadership is about coping with change. He aligns transactional activities with management and transformational actions with leadership. Kotter (1990b) maintains that "leadership and management are two distinctive and complementary systems of action. Each has its own function and characteristic activities" (p. 103). In other words, Kotter posits that management (transactional) and leadership (transformational) are essential for organizational success. **Table 2.1** summarizes these major trends between management and leadership as described in the literature.

DEFINING MANAGEMENT AND LEADERSHIP

Despite some clear trends regarding the differences between management and leadership, defining the two concepts has always been difficult. Scholars and practitioners shape various definitions based on the nuances they observe in real situations. Many attempts have been made to capture the essences of each. The following definitions of management exemplify some of the major characteristics associated with this concept:

> Management consists of the rational assessment of a situation and the systematic selection of goals and purposes (what is

TABLE 2.1 **Summary of Trending Differences Between Management and Leadership**

Management	Leadership	Source
Status Quo Versus Change		
Regulates existing systems	Seeks opportunities for change	Zaleznik (1978)
Accepts the status quo	Challenges the status quo	Bennis & Goldsmith (1997)
Works within current paradigms	Creates new paradigms	Covey, Merrill, & Merrill (1994)
Mechanistic Versus Social		
Focuses on how things get done	Focuses on what things mean to people	Zaleznik (1978)
Makes complex systems work efficiently	Helps people accept and move through change	Kotter (1990a)
Involves telling others what to do	Involves energizing people to take action	Bennis & Goldsmith (1997)
Relies on control	Relies on trust	Bennis & Nanus (1985)
Monitors results through methodical means to bridge performance gaps and solve problems	Inspires people to surmount obstacles by satisfying basic human needs	DuBrin (1995)
Efficiency Versus Vision		
Achieves efficiency and effectiveness within the organization's mission	Creates vision, sells vision, evaluates progress, and determines next steps	Perloff (2007)
Is a function consisting of planning, budgeting, evaluating, and facilitating	Is a relationship that is composed of identifying and selecting talent, motivating, coaching, and building trust	Macoby (2000)
Present Versus Future		
Consists of routine and structure that deal with the present	Is oriented toward the future	Perloff (2007)
Focuses on short-range goals, keeping an eye on the bottom line	Focuses on long-range goals, keeping an eye on the horizon	Bennis & Goldsmith (1997)

to be done?); the systematic development of strategies to achieve these goals; the marshalling of the required resources; the rational design, organization, direction and control of the activities required to attain the selected purposes; and, finally, the motivating and rewarding of people to do the work. (Levitt, 1976, p. 73)

Management is coordinating work activities so that they are completed efficiently and effectively with and through other people. (Robbins, Coulter, & Langton, 2006, p. 9)

Leadership definitions are surprisingly harder to find. Historically, scholars and practitioners tended to explain traits, behaviors, and characteristics of managers and leaders without offering a clear, succinct definition (Rost, 1993). Despite this lack, several scholars have tried to capture the essence of leadership in a definition. The following are a few that illustrate the most common qualities of leadership expressed in the literature.

A shift in paradigm is in order. (Bass, 1985, p. xiii) . . . . To sum up, we see the transformational leader as one who motivates us to do more than we originally expected. (p. 20)

Leadership is much more adequately seen as a *process of interaction*. This process includes everything that goes on in the group that contributes to its effectiveness. Leadership exists when group members deal with one another in ways that meet their needs and contribute to their goals. (Whitehead & Whitehead, 1986, pp. 74–75)

DEFINITIONAL DIFFERENCES BETWEEN MANAGEMENT AND LEADERSHIP

Despite some similarities between the concepts, important differences are evident. According to Rost (1993) there are four perceptible differences between the definitions of management and leadership. These differences extend from the idea that language matters (Lakoff, 2000). A review of these definitional differences illustrates how management and leadership are conceptually different. Furthermore, it establishes a clear picture of why both management and leadership are important to organizational success.

Authority Versus Influence Relationship

Management is a relationship between managers and those they guide based on positional authority. Authority is determined by organizational structures, job descriptions, and contractual agreements. When people use authority to get others to do things, management is happening. Certainly, directives given by a manager may be either coercive or noncoercive. Coercive simply means telling people what to do. This type of management is efficient and practical. These types of directives are usually task oriented and to the point. For instance, the manager of game-day logistics for a Minor League Baseball team will likely train employees by giving them very specific procedures to follow. A noncoercive form of authority may involve some kind of democratic decision making about how to improve procedures on game day. Managers who ask for feedback and seek ideas for improvements about game-day procedures before making changes are operating in a noncoercive way. In either instance, everyone involved accepts the nature of this authority, and the fundamental arrangement is top-down.

Leaders are also involved in a relationship, but they guide people based on influence. Influence is perhaps the most widely articulated characteristic of leadership, and it involves the idea of persuasion. Leaders influence others by wielding all different kinds of power sources other than authority (Rost, 1993). They utilize sources such as charisma, rational arguments, expression of vision and ideals, perceptions, and symbols to move people toward action. Influence never involves coercion and often leads to intrinsic motivation on the part of the followers. For example, John Wooden not only focused on the details of playing basketball, but also used vision and ideals through his Pyramid of Success to inspire his players to become their best.

Legendary basketball coach John Wooden's Pyramid of Success has inspired leaders to seek out the best in their followers.
© AP Images

Manager/Subordinate Versus Leader/Follower Relationship

Understanding who plays what role in management and leadership is needed to identify when one or the other is occurring. When managers use their authority to guide work, it is helpful to frame this as a manager/subordinate relationship. *Subordinate* is by no means a derogatory term, but rather an indicator that an authority/compliance act is occurring. Similarly, when the relationship changes to one involving influence, then it is useful to describe the people involved in that relationship as leaders and *followers*. Such distinctions are necessary to determine what prompted people to do work in both relationships. More importantly, it is essential to recognize that both management and leadership do not occur simply

because a manager directs and a leader articulates a vision. Without subordinates complying and followers being moved to action, neither management nor leadership exists. This language, which includes both subordinates and followers, ensures that management and leadership are recognized as relationships.

Given that sometimes managers lead and leaders manage, this framework also allows us to distinguish when each is happening. It also allows each to happen within the same person, simultaneously or at different times depending on the organizational context or goals to be achieved at the moment. As such, this language provides a road map to understanding complex behavior. These distinctions in language also inform the ways in which managers and leaders make sure they are doing the right thing at the right time. Finally, identifying areas for professional development becomes an easier task.

In reality, many sport organizations are understaffed. As a result, people frequently take on various tasks that require different skills. For instance, a university recreation department director needs to make sure procedures are followed for safety reasons, resources are used judiciously, and students benefit from the programs. When discussing safety procedures and resource allocation with their staff, recreation directors would most likely be in a manager/subordinate relationship. Alternately, inspiring the staff to make sure that every student experience is positive and informed by current thinking would entail few routine directives and more likely the use of power sources to inspire staff toward action.

Produce and Sell Goods/Services Versus Intend Real Changes

Managers and subordinates accomplish specific tasks and goals. This work is required for the organization to meet its most immediate goals. When people work together in the direct production or selling of goods or services, this work is management. Much of the work in sport event operations falls into this category and involves managers and subordinates. The work of creating operational plans, securing sponsorships, and confirming facility needs is guided by managers and done by subordinates.

In contrast, work directed toward intended change requires leadership. Organizations need to change in order to stay competitive and thrive with shifting demands, demographics, and cultural contexts. The intention of creating change is sufficient to identify whether leadership is happening. Otherwise, leadership could only be identified after the fact, which is not ideal for recognizing what needs to happen in real time. In sport event management, working toward improving an event from one year to the next would best be accomplished by leadership with leaders articulating a compelling vision such that followers become excited about potential improvements so that they are intrinsically motivated to action.

Coordinate Activities Versus Establish Mutual Purposes

One of the most important defining aspects of management is that it is about coordinating activities of the organization so that differentiation and integration happen smoothly. Coordination emerges out of rational thought processes aimed at knowing what work is to be done, how it should be divided, and how it comes together to accomplish the goals of the organization. In larger organizations people typically are focused on their immediate tasks and hold individual goals specific to their tasks. It is the coordination of these disparate goals that is the work of the manager. Negotiated agreements, routine exchanges, meetings to share information, and compromises are characteristic of when coordination takes places. When a university athletics department goes through the process of restructuring and creating a new organizational chart, the actual negotiation of job responsibilities and authority is management at work.

The work of leadership is defined as establishing mutual purposes, which is different from coordinating activities in that it entails bringing a community together around shared understandings about why the organization exists. This work is intangible in some ways because it does not involve direct negotiation over actions. Leadership happens when leaders and followers work together to generate and clarify the essential purpose of the organization, not the work that will be required to carry out that purpose. For this kind of work to be considered leadership, the three other criteria must also be met. In the case of a university athletics department, stepping back and setting the specific purposes of athletics within the larger mission of the university is a leadership activity as long as the leader is relying on influence, followers are involved, and some sort of changes are mutually agreed upon.

FUNCTIONAL DIFFERENCES BETWEEN MANAGEMENT AND LEADERSHIP

Despite definitional differences, it is evident that management and leadership are both involved with carrying out an organization's mission, attending to human relationships, making sure that people take actions toward the mission, and assuming responsibility for the success of the organization. What differs are the ways in which these organizational objectives are accomplished; that is, management and leadership have different functions within an organization. As Kotter (1990a) and Kotterman (2006) remind us, both functions are needed for an organization to fulfill its mission, objectives, and goals. Management is tactical and leadership is strategic (Kotterman, 2006). Kotter (1990a) noted that managers work at making the organizational systems work "efficiently and effectively hour after hour, day after day" (Kotter, 2012, para. 5). In contrast, leadership imagines and creates the systems and constantly looks toward the future (Kotter, 1990a). We now turn to the different functions in detail by looking at mission, human relationships, organizational processes, and key tasks.

Realization of Mission

MANAGEMENT PLANS AND BUDGETS

In order to realize its mission—or the organization's purpose—an organization must have plans in place about how to do so as well as allocate resources to the key activities outlined in those plans. Planning is a deductive process in which people decide what to do to get from A to B. This work entails setting specific goals and establishing measures to reach those goals. These types of goals are often called operational or *tactical goals* (Chelladurai, 2009) and are often found in strategic plans. As part of the realistic achievement of the mission, resources need to be allocated to accomplish these specific goals. Keeping track of the budget and making sure resources are used in ways that carry out the operational and tactical plans is the responsibility of management because this activity is part of the day-to-day agenda of an organization.

LEADERSHIP CREATES VISION AND STRATEGY

Ultimately, plans cannot be put in place or resources appropriately allocated without a clear vision and overall strategy about how an organization will fulfill its purpose. Understanding where an organization currently stands is part of the work of leadership. This is equivalent to knowing where A is when going from A to B. Establishing B is setting the overall direction of an organization. This is an inductive process that involves looking at industry patterns and relationships by asking questions such as who are our direct competitors, who is doing well, what kinds of things are they doing, and what are our strengths and weaknesses compared to them? This step involves many

people at different levels in order to gain accurate data. The next step involves establishing a *vision* in terms of what the company should be like. This includes ideas about organizational culture and business activity that are unique, desirable, and realistic. As Kotter (1990a) notes, a vision should be specific enough to provide something from which to plan but vague enough to remain relevant through changes and that would "encourage initiative" (p. 36). Whether a vision is desirable depends on the answer to the question, does it serve the needs of key constituents? Finally, leadership is responsible for determining a strategy based on all relevant data. This final step entails determining a sound strategy. In other words, what general implementation direction will the organization take that is realistic for achieving goals but not necessarily guaranteed? The vision and strategy concern moving toward something different, something not yet done before, but energizing and realistic. Although the leader is ultimately responsible for the vision and strategy, she or he seldom establishes these alone.

Human Relationships

MANAGEMENT IMPLEMENTS PLANS

Management is concerned with creating "human systems that can implement plans as precisely and efficiently as possible" (Kotter, 1990a, p. 49). Once plans and budget are in place, management is responsible for many of the human resource concerns such as creating organizational charts, establishing job descriptions, hiring the right people for the job, and ensuring progress toward goals. Organizational charts are about differentiation and integration. In other words, how will the work be divided and how will it be coordinated so that the mission is achieved? Specific job descriptions determine the details about the work assigned to specific people. At this level, management establishes what people do and delegates responsibility. Then, managers hire the right people to fulfill those needs. Ultimately, managers are responsible for telling people what to do. As noted earlier, telling is not always a negative thing. In fact, telling is necessary in many instances, but there are other, more democratic methods that a manager can employ to establish the specific means to carry out plans. In short, management connects and integrates people so that work gets done efficiently and effectively.

LEADERSHIP ALIGNS PEOPLE

Leadership connects and integrates people in different ways than management. One important function of leadership is to align people within and beyond the organization in order to achieve the mission. Kotter (1990a) defines alignment as " a condition in which a relevant group of people share a common understanding of a vision and a set of strategies, accept the validity of that direction, and are willing to work toward making it a reality" (p. 60). Whereas management is concerned with the orderly division and coordination of work, alignment involves connecting people in ways that are much less routine. Kotter explains that leaders establish informal networks, creating "spider-like" webs of relationships depending on needs and timing. Alignment also results from communicating the vision frequently and consistently. Although such a task seems simple, Jack Welch, former CEO of General Electric, admits that "communicating the vision and the atmosphere around the vision has been and is continuing to be, by far the toughest job we face" (Welch as cited in Kotter, p. 510). The goal of alignment is to link various visions so that people feel compelled to work together rather than compete with each other as they work to achieve their specific goals. The unity created through alignment is a powerful force that influences the creation of teams, coalitions, and partnerships made of people who believe in the mission (Kotterman, 2006). Often, organizations decide to decentralize and democratize so that

people have more control over how to implement that vision. Again, exactly how this happens is the work of management, but alignment of people allows management to happen in less coercive and more democratic ways. Finally, alignment results in organizational culture that is self-sustaining and directed toward achieving the mission.

Processes

MANAGEMENT OVERSEES

Another important function of management is to control the process and problem solve to make work more efficient, but still effective (Kotter, 1990a). It is about keeping things working smoothly, on time, on budget, and with quality. As Kotter reminds us, managers help people "complete routine jobs successfully, day after day" (p. 62). Controlling involves measuring processes such as return on investment (ROI), systems analyses, and satisfaction of those who are primarily served by the organization. Management is responsible for sustaining those processes, reducing variation, and anticipating short-term needs. Managers are responsible for making sure benchmarks and goals are in place so that people can see real progress toward goals and adjust when necessary. Although they can approach their work in a wide variety of ways, "managers take responsibility for those processes and are constantly seeking to improve them" (Kotterman, 2006, p. 15).

LEADERSHIP MOTIVATES

Leadership appeals to shared values, involves people, supports efforts, and recognizes successes in order to motivate people to do work. One way to describe leadership's role in getting work done is that unlike management, which is about getting people to do work based on control, leadership motivates people by "satisfying very basic human needs; for achievement, belonging, recognition, self-esteem, sense of control over one's life and

TABLE 2.2 **Summary of the Functions of Management and Leadership**

Organizational Aspects	Management	Leadership
Realization of mission	Plans and budgets (Kotter, 1990a)	Creates vision and strategy (Kotter, 1990a) Establishes organizational culture (Kotter, 1990a)
Human relationships	Implements structure • Organizes and staffs (Kotter, 1990a) • Delegates responsibility and authority (Kotterman, 2006)	Aligns people • Communicates vision • Influences creation of teams, coalitions, and partnerships made of people who believe in mission and vision (Kotterman, 2006) • Uses informal networks (Kotter, 1990a) • Creates and sustains organizational culture
Processes	Oversees • Controls and problem solves (Kotter, 1990a) • Monitors results (Kotterman, 2006)	Motivates (Kotter, 1990a) • Appeals to shared values • Involves people • Supports efforts • Recognizes successes

living up to one's ideals" (Kotter, 1990a, p. 63). This type of motivation includes articulating a vision that aligns with people's values; involving people in creating the control processes; offering support in the form of development, training, and feedback; and recognizing the efforts of others in some public fashion (Kotter, 1990a). **Table 2.2** summarizes the key tasks of leadership and management.

A WORKING DEFINITION OF LEADERSHIP

Clearly, the complex world needs both managers and leaders, but it is leadership that is essential to meet the demands of a rapidly changing world. As sport organizations grow and adapt to external forces and as technology improves—something sport observers have seen a lot of over the past decade—processes become so complex that management alone will not serve the organization well (Kotter, 1990a). Incremental improvements no

longer lead to a competitive advantage. Kotter's research shows that for organizations to gain a competitive advantage in the 21st century, leadership is required alongside good management. Searching for new directions, innovations, and services becomes even more important in the current environment.

Given the conceptual, definitional, and functional differences between management and leadership and the fact that this text takes the view that leadership is distinct from management, we offer the following definition of leadership:

Leadership is an influence relationship aimed at moving organizations or groups of people towards an imagined future that depends upon alignment of values and establishment of mutual purposes.

At its core, leadership is a dynamic process that involves developing and influencing relationships (Hosking & Morley, 1988; Rost, 1993). Leaders influence people such that they are inspired to do work, feel as though their values align with the organization, and become co-creators of organizational culture. Leaders know that their work is dynamic because it is based in the notion of possibility. They stay focused on the future and often take the view from 30,000 feet. From this vantage point, they are able to see a future that might be difficult to accomplish, but possible and realistic. They envision what the organizational culture might look like or what purposes will become important for long-term success. Leadership is about moving organizations or groups of people toward this imagined future. Leaders rely more on personal power such as friendship, loyalty, expertise, charisma, and dedication instead of positional power such as formal authority, rewards, punishments, and control of information. In doing so, leaders understand their work consists of establishing meanings for organizations and is extremely relational in nature. Good leaders embody the values of the organization and work hard to establish mutual purposes by appealing to shared values and being authentic in doing so.

SUMMARY

The concepts regarding management and leadership have evolved over many years. The industrial revolution marked a significant move toward organizing on a large scale. During this time efficiency was paramount, facilitating the definitional and functional overlap of management and leadership. Since that time, the work of organizations has diversified, bringing more attention to the concept of leadership. We maintain that new complexities in organizations and rapid environmental change require people in organizations to make the distinction between management and leadership. Articulating conceptual differences regarding the purposes of management and leadership provides an important way of thinking about how each contributes to the success of organizations. Specific definitional differences help people identify the distinct roles of managers and leaders and functional differences clarify overall tasks. Once distinctions are made, assessment of leadership and leadership development are more easily achieved.

LEADERSHIP PERSPECTIVE

Gina Gotch.
Courtesy of Gina Gotch

Gina Gotch is Vice President of Gear at Amer Sports, a publically traded sports equipment company with internationally recognized brands including Salomon, Wilson, Precor, Atomic, Suunto, Mavic, and Arc'teryx. Prior to Amer Sports, Gotch led teams through the design and production of apparel for Sugoi and Outdoor Research.

Q: What are some skills and attributes a good manager should possess?

For me, management is working toward a goal and organizing people or processes and taking steps to achieve a certain goal. In management, you have to already know the direction because you are working to get to that place. A manager needs to be super-consistent in how they deal with people and how they handle themselves. A manager is more technical and short-term focused. They make things happen today. They work within a defined timeframe and a set of parameters. I think a good manager considers their people and how they are motivated and how to get them to agree on a position, which isn't the same as being the leader on the project.

Q: What are some skills and attributes a good leader should possess?

Leadership is more about defining and heading up those goals. It is more of a "what you want to be" and management is more of how you get there. A leader doesn't have to be a leader with a specific title or position in a company as long as you help provide a direction or an idea. I mean some people may be in the middle of an organization, but they really help move people along with seeing what could be or how things could be different. You know, having an ability to lead by example and show the way things can be done rather than having accountability to make somebody change or do something different. I think a leader has a little more leeway in how they can act because they are expected to do things a little differently. A leader has to have the ability to see long-term, to think about things in broader terms and be more strategic—it's about setting priorities. At first, this means getting in small groups and face to face. I'm finding this is important and then doing what you say. That's a big thing at the leadership level. If you don't follow through on what you're going to do, it makes it difficult.

Q: In your experience, what are some of the pitfalls to avoid as a leader?

I've known some leaders who are very good at having a vision and what is needed to move the business forward and get other people inspired about an idea, but when it actually comes to communicating the specifics about how that's going to happen or what needs to happen, they sometimes just don't get how their message is coming across to others. For example, they might talk about an idea in an hour meeting, which at the end the decision is made, but they didn't leave time for feedback or the message was delivered poorly. Not being a good "people person" can affect your leadership in a negative way because it can get people to question what you're doing.

Q: How would you describe the relationship between management and leadership?

You are a better leader if you can manage. I don't think you need to be a leader to be a good manager. For example, if you are in a leadership position, I think you need to have some management skills, but if you are a manager, I don't think you need to be a good leader. You need to be really good at executing but not necessarily good at having a vision, but you need to be able to execute that vision. There are always good leaders throughout a business, but you need to have the managers in place to make sure that vision happens. To be a good manager you really have to understand what's the best message, like for some people, you need tell them all the good. Understanding how to change your message to match people you are talking to. I don't think a leader necessarily needs that. It helps, but as a leader you need to communicate big ideas to a broad audience. A manager needs that level of detail where there's a goal and follow-up to make sure the goal actually happens.

A leader simply needs to make sure people are headed in the right direction, but they themselves don't necessarily need to make sure that the details of that are happening.

Q: What does it take to move a company through change?

Sugoi was interesting because when I went there, part of my role was to transition from 100% factory in Canada to doing things offshore. It was really interesting—getting people to buy into and understand why they needed to change and then put a process in place to make sure that we *could* change. And there were a few steps to that. You know whenever you try to change something, there's often resistance. And we had to help people see that vision of how big we could be and how fast we were growing and how we could no longer produce in the same way that we had been because we just no longer had the capacity in Canada. Ultimately, it's really about drawing out people and their potential. When you're looking at the growth of people, I think it's a little bit of a mix between leadership and management. You really have to inspire them, which is the leadership part, but guidelines or rules help you manage them toward those goals. That management toward those goals is confidence building because they can see success.

Q: How do you move people through change?

It was a lot of time just talking to people about the opportunities for growth and how much bigger our company could be. Once people understood that, then being able to start the process that supported it and do things that bring that to life. We tried to get certain people who were interested in the idea, get them more involved, give them some responsibilities for projects. It was a really flat product structure but by finding a couple of leaders within the department who were on board with things moving forward and could see more of that future—giving them some extra responsibilities and holding them accountable. It really helped bring along the whole group to respond positively to the change. It gave them power to be part of the process rather than just be dragged along into it. They got to help define how it would work, give input with some changes concerning management. It really was about finding leaders within that flat organization and then putting them in positions of authority and giving them clear goals and responsibilities. It really helped turn the group around and made them much more a team to help them execute. More interestingly, this approach really helped develop some people into leaders. There were several women who were there as pattern makers. I remember one woman who would ask a question every time she changed one line on a pattern, but at the end of this process, she ended up being promoted to a product manager, actually making decisions about what products were going to be made.

KEY TERMS

followers

human relations movement

leadership

management

manager

scientific management movement

subordinates

tactical goals

transformational leadership

vision

DISCUSSION QUESTIONS

1. Is it possible for a manager to be a good leader and a leader to also be a good manager? Explain your answer.
2. If an organization has strong leadership and weak management, what problems can this cause? If an organization has weak leadership and capable management, what issues can arise?
3. Now that you know the definitions of management and leadership, give some thought to a former or current work situation. How would you describe the quality of leadership and management? Do you see aspects of both? Neither? One or the other? Give examples.
4. Researchers Bennis and Nanus (1985) wrote, "Managers are people who do things right, and leaders are people who do the right thing." How do you interpret this statement?
5. What characteristics of the sport business environment are likely to change in the future, thus requiring effective leadership of sport organizations?

For a full suite of assignments and additional learning activities, use the access code found in the front of your book. If you do not have an access code, you can obtain one at **www.jblearning.com**.

REFERENCES

Bass, B. M. (1985). *Leadership and performance beyond expectations*. New York: Free Press.

Bennis, W. (1977, March–April). Where have all the leaders gone? *Technological Review*, 3–12.

Bennis, W. (2009). *On becoming a leader* (4th ed.). Philadelphia, PA: Basic.

Bennis, W., & Goldsmith, J. (1997). *Learning to lead: A workbook on becoming a leader*. Reading, MA: Addison-Wesley.

Bennis, W., & Nanus, B. (1985). *Leaders: Their strategies for taking charge*. New York: Harper & Row.

Bryman, A. (1992). *Charisma and leadership in organizations*. London: Sage.

Burns, J. M. (1978). *Leadership*. New York: Harper & Row.

Chelladurai, P. (2009). *Managing organizations for sport and physical activity: A systems perspective*. Scottsdale, AZ: Holcomb Hathaway.

Conger, J. A., & Kanungo, R. N. (1994). Charismatic leadership in organizations: Perceived behavioral attributes and their measurement. *Journal of Organizational Behavior, 15*(5), 439–452.

Covey, S. R., Merrill, A. R., & Merrill, R. R. (1994). *First things first*. New York: Free Press.

Czarniawska-Joerges, B., & Wolff, R. (1991). Leaders, managers, entrepreneurs on and off the organizational stage. *Organization Studies, 12*(4), 529–546.

Drath, W. (2001). *The deep blue sea: Rethinking the source of leadership*. San Francisco, CA: Jossey-Bass.

DuBrin, A. J. (1995). *Leadership: Research, findings, practice, and skills*. Boston, MA: Houghton Mifflin.

Gomez-Mejia, L. R., Balkin, D. B., & Cardy, R. L. (2005). *Management: People, performance, change*. Boston, MA: McGraw-Hill Irwin.

Hersey, P., & Blanchard, K. (1988). *Management of organizational behavior: Utilizing human resources* (5th ed.). Englewood Cliffs, NJ: Prentice Hall.

Hollander, E. P. (1985). Leadership and power. In G. Lindzey & E. Aronson (Eds.), *Handbook of social psychology* (3rd ed., Vol. 2, pp. 485–537). New York: Random House.

Hosking, D. M., & Morley, I. E. (1988). The skills of leadership. In J. G. Hunt, B. R. Baliga, H. P. Dachler, & C. A. Schriesheim (Eds.), *Emerging leadership vistas* (pp. 89–106). Lexington, MA: Lexington Books.

Jago, A. G. (1982). Leadership: Perspectives in theory and research. *Management Science, 28*, 315–336.

Katz, D., & Kahn, R. L. (1978). *The social psychology of organizations* (2nd ed.). New York: Wiley.

Kotter, J. P. (1990a). *A force for change: How leadership differs from management.* New York: Free Press.

Kotter, J. P. (1990b). What leaders really do. *Harvard Business Review, 68*(3), 103–111.

Kotter, J. P. (2012, December 4). Change leadership. Retrieved from http://www.kotterinternational.com/our-principles/change-leadership

Kotterman, J. (2006). Leadership versus management: What's the difference? *Journal for Quality and Participation, 29*(2), 13–17.

Kuhn, A., & Beam, R. D. (1982). *The logic of organizations.* San Francisco, CA: Jossey-Bass.

Lakoff, R. (2000). *The language war.* Berkeley: University of California Press.

Levitt, T. (1976). Management and the postindustrial society. *Public Interest, 44*, 69–103.

Macoby, M. (2000). Understanding the difference between management and leadership. *Research-Technology Management, 43*(1), 57–59.

Mangham, I., & Pye, A. (1991). *The doing of managing.* Oxford, UK: Blackwell.

McLean, J. (2005). Management and leadership. *Manager: British Journal of Administrative Management, 49*(Oct./Nov.), 16.

Mintzberg, H. (1973). *The nature of managerial work.* New York: Harper & Row.

Northouse, P. G. (2010). *Leadership: Theory and practice.* Thousand Oaks, CA: Sage.

Perloff, R. (2007, July 14–15). *Managing and leading: The universal importance of, and differentiation between, two essential functions.* Presentation at Oxford University.

Robbins, S. P., Coulter, M., & Langton, N. (2006). *Management.* Toronto: Pearson/Prentice Hall.

Rost, J. C. (1993). *Leadership for the 21st century.* New York: Praeger.

Schenk, C. (1928). Leadership. *Infantry Journal, 33*, 111–122.

Segal, D. R. (1981). Leadership and management: Organizational theory. In R. H. Ruch & L. J. Korb (Eds.), *Military leadership* (pp. 41–69). Beverly Hills, CA: Sage.

Selznick, P. (1957). *Leadership in administration: A sociological interpretation.* Evanston, IL: Row, Peterson.

Sergiovanni, T. J. (1984). Leadership as cultural expression. In T. J. Sergiovanni & J. E. Corbally (Eds.), *Leadership and organizational culture* (pp. 105–114). Urbana: University of Illinois Press.

Taylor, F. W. (1967/1911). *The principles of scientific management.* New York: Norton.

Team USA. (2011, December 13). USA Canoe/Kayak announces relocation of its headquarters to Oklahoma City. Retrieved from http://www2.teamusa.org/USA-Canoe-Kayak/Features/2011/December/13/USA-Canoe-Kayak-Announces-Relocation-of-its-Headquarters-to-Oklahoma-City.aspx

Toor, S.-u.-R. (2011). Differentiating leadership from management: An empirical investigation of leaders and managers. *Leadership and Management in Engineering, 11*(4), 310–320.

Weathersby, G. (1999). Leadership vs. management. *Management Review, 88*(3), 5.

Whitehead, J. D., & Whitehead, M. A. (1986). *The emerging laity: Returning leadership to the faith community.* Garden City, NY: Doubleday.

Yukl, G. A. (1989). Managerial leadership: A review of theory and research. *Journal of Management, 15*(2), 251.

Yukl, G. A. (2002). *Leadership in organizations* (5th ed.). Upper Saddle River, NJ: Pearson/Prentice Hall.

Zacko-Smith, D. (2007). The leader label: Influencing perceptions, reality and practice, Kravis Leadership Institute. *Leadership Review, 7*, 75–88.

Zaleznik, A. (1977). Managers and leaders: Are they different? *Harvard Business Review, 55*(3), 67–78.

Zaleznik, A. (1978). Managers and leaders: Are they different? *McKinsey Quarterly*, (1), 2–22.

Zaleznik, A. (1989). *The managerial mystique: Restoring leadership in business.* New York: Harper Row.

Zimmerman, E. L. (2001). What's under the hood? The mechanics of leadership versus management. *Supervision, 62*(8), 10.

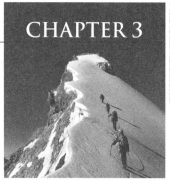

CHAPTER 3

TRANSFORMATIONAL, TRANSACTIONAL, AND SERVANT LEADERSHIP

Laura J. Burton
Jon Welty Peachey
Zachary J. Damon

CHAPTER OBJECTIVES

- Differentiate the leadership styles of transactional, transformational, and servant leadership.
- Identify contexts that are appropriate for each type of leadership style.
- Understand and describe the behaviors associated with transactional, transformational, and servant leadership.
- Describe organizational outcomes associated with each type of leadership style.
- Describe behaviors and characteristics associated with authentic leadership.

CASE STUDY

New Leader, New Style

Within this Division I athletic department, staff was in turmoil. Teams were losing and had been for several years, and morale was at an all-time low. According to many coaches and staff, the department was dysfunctional. Each functional area (e.g., compliance, marketing, operations) or team (e.g., football, field hockey, basketball) was operating in its own silo, on its own island, with little interaction among them. There was also little trust among athletic department employees. Many attributed this negativity to the culture and climate established by the athletic director, who was distant from employees. He established many rules and procedures in a hierarchal system, paying little attention to building relationships with staff or encouraging and inspiring staff in their efforts. As a consequence, he was not trusted by many staff.

(continues)

When this athletic director resigned for personal reasons, the president of the university had the opportunity to hire a new athletic director. The president sought an individual to provide the positive and visionary leadership necessary for the department to improve staff morale and overall performance of its teams. To this end, the president hired Mark as the new athletic director. Immediately upon taking the job, Mark moved his office from the back corner of the administrative suite into a central, visible location where everyone could have access to him. He had an open door policy where any employee or student-athlete could come to visit with him at any time, if he were not in a meeting or off-site. He kept the blinds raised in his office so staff and visitors would know when he was there if they needed to talk. Immediately after being hired as athletic director, Mark met with each employee in the department to talk about their goals and their hopes for the department, and to begin building quality relationships with them.

At the same time, he crafted a new vision for the athletic department. This vision described an athletic department where all activities and resources would be centered upon doing what was in the best interests of the student-athletes. If improving the welfare of student-athletes was the primary focus, Mark believed that performance objectives and winning on the field or court would follow. He held numerous staff meetings and public forums to promote this new vision and constantly reminded staff about its importance and how it should guide their day-to-day activities. The previous athletic director primarily attended only the revenue-producing sports of basketball and men's hockey. In contrast, Mark and his administrative team began attending as many home and away events as possible for all sports, not just revenue-producing sports, to show support for and to encourage all coaches and student-athletes. He was a visible supporter at these events. He also continued to meet with staff individually to inspire them in their efforts and encourage them to be creative in the pursuit of their objectives.

In the 2 years following Mark's appointment, trust among staff and between staff and the athletic administration increased, and morale improved tremendously. Many employees felt Mark truly cared about them and their program, wanted them to succeed, and would provide the support and encouragement necessary for success. For example, one head coach of 19 years commented on Mark's leadership: "I think that the coaches . . . feel again very much supported by the administration. More so than any time I've been here. I like the idea of the athletic department being a community that cares about one another and supports each other." In addition, the turnover rate decreased for the department because staff felt inspired by Mark and were aligned with his new vision, which made the work climate extremely positive. As a result of Mark's leadership and improved morale and climate, 2 years after Mark's appointment, the athletic teams were having one of their most successful years in the history of the university.

Questions for Discussion

1. How would you describe Mark's leadership in his role as athletic director? Read and review the chapter before answering this. Provide specific examples from the case study to support your answer.

2. Why do you think the athletic teams had one of their most successful years in the university's history after 2 years under Mark's leadership?

3. In what ways did Mark's leadership influence employees of the athletic department? Do these employee outcomes align with previous work in sport management examining the influence of leadership behavior?

4. What advice would you provide to Mark in regard to leadership that will enable him to continue successfully leading this athletic department into the future?

INTRODUCTION

Most scholars agree that there is a relationship between leadership and an organization's success or failure (Klimoski & Koles, 2001). At the most basic level, leaders will establish the direction of an organization by developing a vision of the future, and then, after forming influential relationships, will align people by communicating this vision and inspiring them to overcome any obstacles (Robbins & Judge, 2003). Leaders are individual actors who display personal behaviors. For the purposes of this chapter, we take a bifurcated view of these individual behaviors, distinguishing between relations- and task-oriented foci (Foels, Driskell, Mullen, & Salas, 2000). Relationship-oriented leaders focus primarily upon organizing, supporting, and developing employees, whereas task-oriented leaders engage in defining work and roles required of employees in pursuit of organizational objectives.

What makes for an effective 21st-century leader? Murray and Mann (2006) suggest that leaders must delegate and nurture, empower subordinates, relate to all people within the organization, encourage ownership, pursue learning opportunities for all members, build teamwork, and have fun at their jobs. Leadership experts Kouzes and Posner (1993) opine that highly effective leaders must inspire a shared vision, model the way for employees, enable others to act, encourage the heart or build relationships, and challenge the process. Twenty-first–century leaders must pay attention to relationship building and participatory decision making. As a result, over the past

20 years, a majority of the research in management, and also in other fields, including sport management, has examined the transformational style of leadership (Antonakis, 2012).

The following sections of this chapter will explore *transformational* and *transactional leadership*, how these leadership behaviors are measured, and importantly, how transformational leadership has been studied in sport management. We will also describe *servant leadership*, an area of leadership that is gaining more interest within the context of sport management. Servant leadership as a leadership behavior will be described and a model to understand how servant leadership may work will also be presented. We will also explore new developments in how servant leadership is measured and discuss the application of servant leadership within sport management. Finally, authentic leadership, and its emphasis on the leader's journey, will be discussed. After reading this chapter, we hope that students considering careers in sport management will understand the different behaviors and characteristics associated with different types of leadership so that they can begin to develop these leadership tendencies while working toward their sport management degrees.

TRANSFORMATIONAL AND TRANSACTIONAL LEADERSHIP

James MacGregor Burns (1978) was the first to introduce the concepts of transformational and transactional leadership. Burns was interested in understanding what leaders and followers offered one another. Transformational leaders try to motivate followers to change or to transform themselves. Transformational leaders are responsive to the individual needs of followers, inspire followers, and align the goals of the organization, leader, group, and individuals. Transformational leaders—given their interest in the growth of their followers—set challenging expectations for them. In contrast, transactional leaders try to motivate their followers by exchanging resources, offering payment for doing work. Within transformational leadership, followers identify with the needs of the leader, and leaders will motivate their followers to achieve more than the followers believe is possible (Bass, 2008). A transactional leader is expected to give subordinates something they desire in exchange for something the leader wants (Kuhnert & Lewis, 1987). Transactional leaders emphasize exchanges made between leaders and followers (Bass, 2008). Whereas transactional leadership is viewed as similar to "old" approaches to leadership, focused on role and task requirements, transformational leadership is seen as a "new" approach focused on the charisma and vision of leaders (Antonakis, 2012; Bryman, 1992; Doherty, 1997). The model of transformational–transactional leadership developed by Bass (1985) is presented in **Figure 3.1** as the Full Range Leadership Model (Avolio & Bass, 1991) and includes the concepts of transformational, transactional, and laissez-faire leadership. Each leadership type is discussed in this chapter.

Transformational Leadership

Based on the work of Burns (1978) and Kuhnert and Lewis (1987) in the development of transformational leadership, and the concept of charismatic leadership as developed by House (1977), Bass (1985) advanced a more refined model of transformational leadership. He describes leaders as those who inspire followers to achieve extraordinary outcomes while also helping to develop the individual leadership skills of their followers (Bass, 2008). Mentor-coaches such as Pat Summitt, Mike Krzyzewski, and Tony Dungy have created coaching lineages that indicate their ability to equip their assistant coaches and former players with leadership skills. Transformational leadership is visionary and appeals to the higher order psychological needs of employees of feeling valued and worthwhile in the organization (Bryman, 1992). Transformational leaders understand that these needs, along with esteem needs that recognize a follower's unique contributions, are necessary to distinguish themselves from transactional leaders.

Transformational leadership has four dimensions: (1) *idealized influence* (behaviors of leaders and attributes of leaders), (2) *inspirational motivation*, (3) *intellectual stimulation*, and (4) *individualized consideration* (Bass & Riggio, 2006). Idealized influence has two elements: the charismatic behaviors of the leader and the elements of leadership that are attributed to the leader by his or her followers. It is also described as the emotional component of leadership (Antonakis, 2012; Northouse, 2012). Leaders are trusted, admired, and respected by their followers, because these leaders often demonstrate high levels of moral and ethical behavior (Bass & Riggio, 2006). As a result, leaders are highly respected by their followers and, in turn, followers seek to emulate the leaders' behaviors. As noted by Northouse (2012), "the charisma factor describes people who are special and who make others want to follow the vision they put forward" (p. 192). For example, followers may view an intercollegiate athletic director as trustworthy, honest, and charismatic, attributes that would then engender respect and pride among athletic department employees who may, in turn, seek to emulate these behaviors. This athletic director may also be an excellent communicator, consistently conveying the values and mission of intercollegiate athletics to employees and other stakeholders.

FIGURE 3.1 **The Full Range Leadership Model.**

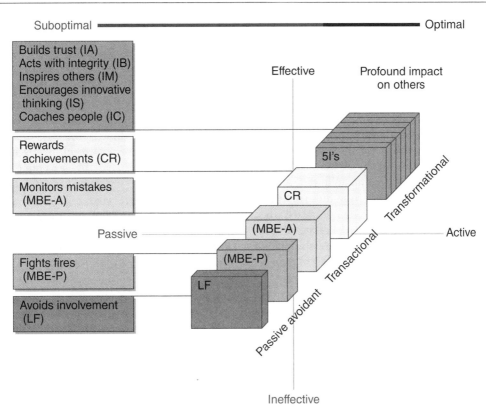

Source: Reproduced from Avolio, B. J., & Bass, B. M. (1991). *Full-range leadership development*. Binghamton, NY: Bass, Avolio & Associates.

Inspirational motivation captures how leaders will set high expectations for followers and motivate and inspire their followers to meet these high expectations. Leaders set clear expectations for their followers and demonstrate they are committed to these shared goals. Leaders will display enthusiasm and optimism to help followers meet these high expectations, and provide support to help followers achieve more than they would in their own self-interest (Bass & Riggio, 2006). An intercollegiate athletic director may serve as a "cheerleader" during times when the teams are not doing well or when athletic departments have suffered sanctions, and keep the department—particularly the marketing specialists who have to encourage spectators to still attend games—excited about future possibilities. This cheerleading can inspire employees to give their best efforts to the department, even in a year when performance is suffering and perceptions about athletics might be negative. When the University of Connecticut named Warde Manuel its new athletic director in early 2012, he came to a department whose storied men's basketball team faced a postseason ban due to a low academic progress rating only a year removed from winning the NCAA Tournament. This scenario created an opportunity for Manuel to utilize inspirational motivation.

Intellectual stimulation describes the processes leaders will use to stimulate followers to be creative and innovative. In addition, leaders will encourage followers to question assumptions and challenge the way things are done within an organization. Followers are encouraged to think on their own and leaders provide an open environment where all ideas are encouraged, and followers are not criticized if their ideas differ from those of leaders (Bass & Riggio, 2006). This is demonstrated when a director of marketing in intercollegiate athletics provides opportunities for graduate assistants and interns to develop and carry out plans to increase attendance at football games. Furthermore, an intercollegiate athletic director demonstrating intellectual stimulation will encourage employees to think creatively to solve problems, welcome innovative suggestions from staff, and encourage risk taking from followers in pursuit of department objectives. This creative problem solving is sometimes seen in adaptive sports for athletes with disabilities. One of the difficulties in disabled sports is addressing the fact that the limited number of participants in a particular sport will also have a wide variety of disabilities. To manage these sports, leaders of these organizations employ disability points. Athletes are given a point rating based on the degree of their disability. Teams in volleyball and wheelchair basketball can only have a set amount of points on the court at any time.

Finally, individualized consideration captures how leaders create a supportive environment, paying attention to their followers' needs for growth and achievement. Leaders recognize followers' needs and desires and provide environments that support these differences. Leaders designate tasks to followers in an effort to develop followers'

leadership skills. In addition, leaders serve as advisors or mentors to help support followers as they carry out their assigned tasks (Northouse, 2012).

Transactional Leadership

A transactional leader motivates by contract and reward, promising followers rewards for good performance and focusing on rules and procedures (Bass, 1990). Transactional leadership includes the following four dimensions: (1) *contingent reward*, (2) *active management* by exception, (3) *passive management* by exception, and (4) *laissez-faire*. Using contingent rewards, leaders assign tasks for followers to fulfill with the understanding that a reward will be provided to the followers after successful completion of the task. Leaders try to gain agreement from the followers regarding what tasks must be completed and the reward for completing the tasks. An example of contingent reward would be a fitness club manager establishing a minimum number of new membership sales in conjunction with input from staff of the fitness club. When the staff meets that sales goal, they will receive a previously agreed upon performance bonus. Given the large percentage of sales jobs in the sport management field, it would not be surprising to find that contingent reward is a prevalent leadership technique.

Active management by exception occurs when leaders look for mistakes or deviations from normal standards when monitoring followers' work. Leaders then take actions to correct mistakes that are noticed. An example of management by exception would be when a facility manager reviews an event risk management plan developed by her staff member and makes changes to the plan prior to its implementation during the event. Or, when the facility manager inspects the setup for a basketball game, notices chairs and tables that are not set up correctly, and takes action to rectify the situation.

Leaders following passive management by exception wait for mistakes or deviations from normal standards. Only after these standards have not been met will the leader intervene to address the problem. Both active and passive management by exception use more negative reinforcement behaviors, in comparison to the positive reinforcement behaviors followed in contingent reward. Using the same example of a facility manager, if following passive management by exception, this leader would wait until an accident occurred during the event as a result of the faulty risk management plan before making changes to the plan. The facility manager would also not correct the faulty setup at the basketball game but would wait until a problem occurred before corrections were made. Figure 3.1 explains the contrast between active and passive leadership through the Full Range Leadership Model (Avolio & Bass, 1991).

Laissez-faire leadership is the absence of leadership. Leaders do not make necessary decisions and actions are not taken. An example of this type of leadership would be an athletic director who calls no meetings with his leadership team, has no strategic plan for the department, and has little contact with the athletic department staff.

Transformational Leadership in Sport Management

Research has shown that leaders who demonstrate transformational leadership are considered to be more effective by followers when compared to leaders using transactional or laissez-faire leadership behavior. Employees report more job satisfaction when led by transformational leaders (Judge & Piccolo, 2004). In addition, transformational leadership was more effective in achieving increased employee work-team performance and effectiveness than transactional leadership (Stewart, 2006), and studies have shown that transformational leadership leads to higher quality relationships with employees (Krishnan, 2005;

Lee, 2004; Tse & Lam, 2008). Transformational leadership has also been shown to improve the performance of both employees working in groups and employees working alone (Strang, 2005; Wang & Huang, 2009). Employees working for transformational leaders are also less likely to leave their jobs (Martin & Epitropaki, 2001; Tse & Lam, 2008). This is an important point given the high cost of replacing employees with regard to job training and interviewing. In addition, transformational leaders have been shown to be more effective than transactional leaders in guiding and implementing significant organizational change (Eisenbach, Watson, & Pillai, 1999). Finally, some work has also suggested employees evaluate female leaders more favorably than male leaders when female leaders demonstrate transformational rather than transactional leadership behaviors. This more favorable evaluation of women as transformational leaders is linked to the view that this type of leadership is congruent with nurturing and communal characteristics that are associated with women. In contrast, male leaders are expected to exhibit more transactional leadership qualities (Eagly & Carli, 2003; Powell, Butterfield, & Bartol, 2008).

Within sport management, researchers have found that, overall, transformational leadership is associated with more positive outcomes for sport organizations. A study with NCAA Division II head coaches revealed that although transactional leadership positively affected followers' behavior and action toward organizational goals, transformational leadership more broadly impacted followers' behavior in a positive manner beyond the effects of transactional leadership (Kim, 2009). Also, Division III athletic directors believed leaders demonstrating transformational leadership motivated extra effort among followers. In addition, these athletic directors believed employees would be more satisfied working for transformational leaders. Transformational leadership was preferred overall, regardless of whether this style was displayed by a male or female leader (Burton & Welty Peachey, 2009; Welty Peachey & Burton, 2011). Leaders who demonstrated charisma and individualized consideration dimensions of transformational leadership were considered most effective. However, leaders who demonstrated passive management by exception and laissez-faire behaviors, characteristics of transactional leadership, were seen as least effective (Burton & Welty Peachey, 2009; Doherty & Danylchuk, 1996).

When intercollegiate coaches evaluated athletic directors, they indicated that their levels of job satisfaction were positively related to athletic directors demonstrating transformational leadership (Choi, Sagas, Park, & Cunningham, 2007; Yusof & Mohd Shah, 2008). Intercollegiate coaches were also less likely to consider leaving their jobs when working for athletic directors demonstrating transformational leadership (Wells & Welty Peachey, 2011). Also, transformational leadership of the athletic director resulted in higher levels of employee commitment to the athletic department. Employees reported feeling more attached to and more involved in the athletic department. Employees also reported feeling a closer sense of identification with the athletic department (Kent & Chelladurai, 2001). In addition, although transformational leadership of the athletic director was positively related to organizational commitment of department employees, it was even more strongly related to commitment to the supervisor (the athletic director) than to the organization (Andrew, Kim, Stoll, & Todd, 2011).

Transformational leadership is critical to successfully guiding and leading organizational change in sport organizations (Amis, Slack, & Hinings, 2004; Welty Peachey, Bruening, & Burton, 2011) in the 21st century. Employees and stakeholders of an organization typically resist organizational change, whether it is a change in leadership or new marketing initiatives. Transformational leaders are generally considered to have the qualities and skills necessary to help overcome employee resistance to change (Phelan, 2005; Slack & Hinings, 1992). Transformational leaders are active in the change process, visible to employees, and good communicators. They have the ability to align employees around a new vision. These leadership behaviors all serve to mitigate employee resistance. Transformational leaders also serve as "cheerleaders" during organizational change, which can motivate and inspire followers to embrace new ideas and routines (Ott, 1996).

Within a Division I athletic department, Welty Peachey, Bruening, and Burton (2011) found that transformational leadership of the athletic director was a major factor in organizational change success and in mitigating resistance and ambivalence to change among employees over time. In another study, Welty Peachey and Burton (2012) discovered that Division I athletic directors displaying transformational leadership during organizational culture change were perceived by their employees as more effective and better able to stimulate extra effort than transactional leaders. Also, employees were more satisfied with transformational leaders. In the campus recreation department setting, leaders demonstrating more transformational leadership were able to implement culture-building activities and change the culture more effectively than those leaders demonstrating less transformational leadership (Weese, 1995). In a study of Canadian YMCA organizations, leaders demonstrating more transformational leadership behaviors also produced more positive organizational change outcomes than leaders displaying less transformational leadership (Wallace & Weese, 1995). Furthermore, employees perceived transformational leaders, compared to transactional leaders, as managing major structural realignment more effectively in Canada's National Sport Organizations (Amis et al., 2004; Slack & Hinings, 1992). Transformational leadership was an essential ingredient for changing team cultures within professional sport franchises in the United States

(Frontiera, 2010). Finally, Division I college head coaches who demonstrated transformational leadership were able to change team cultures by articulating and reinforcing shared visions and values (Schroeder, 2010).

A study of YMCA organizations in Canada showed that transformational leadership had a positive effect on organizational change behavior.
© Kevin Wolf/AP Images

SERVANT LEADERSHIP

Servant leadership focuses on the interaction between leader and follower and emphasizes how leaders can be attentive to the needs of followers, show concern for their followers, and nurture and emphasize the needs of their followers. Servant leaders place the interests, needs, and aspirations of others before their own (Greenleaf, 1977). The primary objective of the servant leader is first to serve, and then to lead.

Servant leadership is different than other approaches to leadership because it emphasizes the ideal of service in the relationship between leader and follower (van Dierendonck, 2011). Servant leadership is a people-centered approach to leadership that also includes an ethical and moral component (Sendjaya, Sarros, & Santora, 2008). In addition, whereas transformational leadership emphasizes leading for organizational objectives, servant leadership gives greater emphasis to serving followers (Stone, Russell, & Patterson, 2004). Given the increasing interest in corporate social responsibility within sport organizations (both in the United States and internationally), servant leadership is an appealing and relevant form of leadership to examine within sport. Also, as national and international professional sport organizations and intercollegiate athletic departments suffer ethical breaches, servant leadership offers a needed perspective on leadership.

Although there is currently no consensus on a definition or theoretical framework for servant leadership, Robert K. Greenleaf is widely credited with the development of the concept of servant leadership and has written extensively about it. The most popular servant leadership definition comes from his writings (1977):

> It begins with the natural feeling that one wants to serve . . . The difference [is] the care taken . . . to make sure that other people's highest priority needs are being served. The best test . . . is: Do those served grow as persons? Do they . . . become healthier, wiser, freer, more autonomous, and more likely themselves to become servants? And, what is the effect on the least privileged in society? Will they benefit, or at least not be further deprived? (p. 13)

Greenleaf credits the formation of the concept of servant leadership to *Journey to the East*, a novel by Hermann Hesse (1956). In this story of a band of men on a mythical journey, Hesse describes a servant, Leo, who works for the group. Leo does menial chores for the men but also sustains the men through his songs and his spirit. Leo is an extraordinary presence in the group. When Leo disappears, the group falls into disarray and the journey ends. Later, the men come to know that Leo, whom they had known as a servant, was actually a great and noble leader (Greenleaf, 1977).

With servant leadership, serving and leading become interchangeable, because being a leader implies a person serves, and being a servant allows a person to lead (van Dierendonck, 2011). Servant leaders are defined by the character they display while serving others (Parris & Welty Peachey, 2012). Greenleaf (1977) noted that servant leadership is demonstrated whenever those served by

such leaders are positively transformed in multiple dimensions (e.g., emotionally, intellectually, socially, and spiritually) into servant leaders themselves (Sendjaya et al., 2008).

A challenge to the study of servant leadership has been how to take the writings of Greenleaf and attempt to develop a theory to explain this concept of leadership. To build a theory of servant leadership, scholars have made numerous attempts to describe and classify the characteristics of servant leadership (van Dierendonck, 2011). Spears (2002) attempted to describe the characteristics of leadership in an effort to clarify servant leadership for practitioners (Northouse, 2012). The 10 characteristics of servant leadership as identified by Spears are included in **Table 3.1.**

TABLE 3.1 **Characteristics of Servant Leadership**

Characteristic	Description
Listening	Servant leaders communicate by listening first.
Empathy	Servant leaders demonstrate that they understand what followers are thinking and feeling.
Healing	Servant leaders—in caring for followers—help them to overcome personal problems.
Awareness	Servant leaders are attuned to and receptive to their social, physical, and political environments—and are therefore able to understand the greater context of situations.
Persuasion	Servant leaders influence change through clear and persistent communication that is nonjudgmental.
Conceptualization	Servant leaders are visionary—thinking about the long-term objectives of the organization and responding to problems in creative ways.
Foresight	Servant leaders have the ability to reasonably predict what is going to occur in the future.
Stewardship	Servant leaders take up the responsibilities of leading followers and the organization.
Commitment to growth	Servant leaders make a commitment to each follower, helping each person grow personally and professionally.
Building community	Servant leaders foster community, allowing followers to feel a part of something greater than themselves.

Source: Data from Spears, L. C. (2002). Tracing the past, present, and future of servant leadership. In L. C. Spears, M. Lawrence, & K. Blanchard (Eds.), *Focus on leadership: Servant-leadership for the twenty-first century* (pp. 1–10). New York: John Wiley and Sons.

Model of Servant Leadership

In an effort to develop a more complete understanding of servant leadership, van Dierendonck (2011) provides a model to better understand and explain the complexities of this concept. This model of servant leadership takes into account antecedents to leadership behavior, the interaction of leader and follower, and the outcomes of servant leader behavior. The antecedent conditions, or existing conditions, that influence servant leadership behavior include the context and culture of the organization, the attributes of the leader, and the receptivity of followers (van Dierendonck, 2011). Servant leadership could best support the mission of intercollegiate athletics, which is to serve the needs of student-athletes (Burton & Welty Peachey, 2013). The middle part of the model describes a set of behaviors that characterize servant leadership, the leader/follower relationship, and the climate created by the leader. The final section of the model includes the outcomes associated with servant leadership, which include follower performance and growth, organizational performance, and societal impact.

Antecedent Conditions

CONTEXT AND CULTURE OF THE ORGANIZATION

The behaviors of a servant leader are influenced by the context and culture of the organization. As an example, a professional sport organization would foster a highly competitive context, and would support a norm of competition among its employees. A recreation-based sport organization would more likely foster a cooperative environment, and support collaboration among employees. These different norms could influence how servant leadership is performed in those organizations (Northouse, 2012). In addition, the culture in which the organization operates can also influence servant leadership. In a more collective culture (e.g., Japan), where the benefits to the group are valued above the interests of the individual, servant leadership would be more common. This may be quite different from a more individualistic culture (e.g., the United States), where individual accountability and effort are encouraged over the accountability of the group. In this type of culture servant leadership may be challenged.

LEADER ATTRIBUTES

Each leader brings individual needs and qualities to the relationship with followers. These individual needs and qualities influence the process of servant leadership. Effective leaders, regardless of style of leadership, have a desire for power. Within the context of servant leadership, leaders would seek out a positive use of power; that is, servant leaders would desire power as a means to help others and care for others. In addition, individual traits such as emotional intelligence, self-determination, and moral development will have an influence on the behaviors of servant leaders (van Dierendonck, 2011).

Characteristics

Six characteristics of servant leadership, which are similar to those described by Spears (2002) earlier in Table 3.1, are included in the model of servant leadership (van Dierendonck, 2011).

1. *Developing people:* Servant leaders foster an empowering attitude in followers, which generates self-confidence and provides followers with a sense of personal power. This type of leadership behavior encourages information sharing with followers, encourages self-directed decision making, and provides support and coaching for innovative performance. Servant leaders fundamentally believe in the intrinsic value possessed by each follower, recognizing and acknowledging each person's abilities and what the person can learn (Greenleaf, 1998).

2. *Humility:* Servant leaders acknowledge that they can benefit from the expertise of others, and therefore actively seek out the contributions of followers. Servant leaders put their own accomplishments and talents in perspective. Demonstrating humility, the servant leader puts followers' interests first, provides them with support, and facilitates their performance. A servant leader also demonstrates humility by retreating into the background when a task has been successfully accomplished.

3. *Authenticity:* Servant leaders demonstrate authenticity by being true to oneself, both in public and in private. Authenticity is about expressing oneself in ways that are consistent with inner feelings and thoughts. A servant leader demonstrates authenticity by being honest, doing what was promised, and showing vulnerability.

4. *Interpersonal acceptance:* Servant leaders are able to create an environment in which followers feel safe and trust that they are able to make mistakes and still feel that they will be accepted. Servant leaders understand the perspectives of others, and are able to "walk in another's shoes." Servant leaders show empathy, compassion, and forgiveness even when confronted with arguments, personal offenses, or mistakes.

5. *Providing direction:* Servant leaders clearly demonstrate to followers what is expected of them. Within the context of servant leadership, leaders provide an appropriate amount of accountability for followers. Also, leaders customize directions based on followers' abilities, needs, and input. This type of leading allows for new ways of getting things accomplished and creates new ways to meet old problems, with consistent reliance on values and convictions when accomplishing tasks.

6. *Stewardship:* Servant leaders are willing to take responsibility for the entire organization and put the interests of the organization over and above their own self-interests. Servant leaders act as role models and caretakers. By acting as role models and setting an example for followers, leaders can inspire others to act in the common interests of all. The characteristics of stewardship are closely linked to the concepts of teamwork, social responsibility, and loyalty.

Servant Leader/Follower Relationship

An important component of the model of servant leadership is an understanding of the quality of the relationship between the servant leader and the follower. Servant leaders will build this high-quality relationship with followers by striving for consensus among their followers. They will use persuasion through consultation, appeals, and use of explanation. When fostering such a relationship, a servant leader will voluntarily lead followers "because they are persuaded that the leader's path is the right one for them" (Greenleaf, 1998, p. 44).

In addition, a safe psychological climate is necessary to foster the servant leader and follower relationship. Servant leaders focus on empowerment of followers so that followers feel safe to use their knowledge, make mistakes, reflect on their actions, and continuously learn and develop. In order for this to occur, interpersonal trust within a safe psychological climate is necessary.

Outcomes

Follower growth and development are central outcomes to a model of servant leadership. Followers' *self-actualization* is an expected outcome in the model of servant leadership. Self-actualization refers to continuous development of oneself and the realization of one's potential. An additional expected outcome of servant leadership is a positive attitude toward work, which would include job satisfaction, organizational commitment, and engagement. Another expected outcome is the potential development of servant leader behaviors in followers. When followers are cared for and empowered by servant leaders, they begin treating others this way (Northouse, 2012).

Organizational performance can also be impacted by servant leadership, and is therefore another outcome of the servant leadership model. Sustainable business practices and corporate social responsibility may be better served in an organization led by a servant leader. Organizations with a focus on corporate social responsibility will practice ethical behavior, care for people, recognize their responsibilities outside of the organization, and emphasize creativity in business practices. These characteristics are closely linked to servant leaders (Hind, Wilson, & Lenssen, 2009).

Contrasting Servant and Transformational Leadership

Although there appear to be similarities between the behaviors of transformational leaders and servant leaders, the primary distinction between these leadership styles is servant leaders emphasize the personal growth of their followers first, while also contributing to the community. In addition, servant leaders hope to inspire their followers to enact servant leadership behaviors. Servant leaders set the following priorities in their leadership focus: followers first, organizations second, their own needs last (Graham, 1991). In contrast, the role of the transformational leader is to inspire followers in an effort to pursue the goals and objectives of the organization (Sendjaya et al., 2008). **Table 3.2** summarizes transactional, transformational, and servant leadership differences.

Servant Leadership in Sport Management

In contrast to the extensive amount of research examining transformational leadership in sport management, there has been minimal work examining servant leadership in sport. However, this area appears to be gaining the interest of researchers, as noted by an increase in presentations regarding servant leadership at the 2012 and 2013 North American Society for Sport Management research conferences. One area of research in sport that has noted the benefits of servant leadership is within the sport psychology literature, specifically examining coaches' use of servant leadership.

There has been a noted shift in the understanding of effective coaching behavior, as athletes seek out coaches offering more democratic approaches to leading, greater empowerment of athletes, and a shift away from autocratic fear-based models of coaching (Hammermeister et al., 2008). If the primary objective and motivation for coaches is success for their athletes, coaching offers an interesting context for the study of servant leadership (Hammermeister et al., 2008). Outcomes noted by coaches who adopt servant leadership behaviors included athletes who were more intrinsically motivated, demonstrated more mental toughness, and were more satisfied with their sport experiences (Hammermeister et al., 2008; Rieke, Hammermeister, & Chase, 2008). In addition, athletes playing for coaches with servant leader characteristics also performed better as a team and individually when compared to athletes playing for non–servant leader coaches (Rieke et al., 2008).

In the management context of sport, new research has explored the characteristics and behaviors of the leader of a nonprofit sport organization who demonstrated servant leadership. The servant leadership demonstrated by this leader influenced the development of long-term volunteers, who then went on to become servant

TABLE 3.2 **Transactional, Transformational, and Servant Leadership Behaviors**

Transactional	Transformational	Servant
Contingent reward • Provide external reward after successful completion of task Active management by exception • Takes corrective action when mistakes are noticed Passive management by exception • Only takes corrective action after mistakes occur Laissez-faire • No decision making, no actions taken	Idealized influence • Demonstrate high levels of moral and ethical behavior • Inspire followers to emulate ethical and moral behavior Inspirational motivation • Set high expectations and motivate followers to meet those expectations Intellectual stimulation • Encourage creativity and innovation in addressing challenges Individualized consideration • Create a supportive environment serving followers' needs for growth and development	Empower and develop • Share information with followers and encourage self-direction Humility • Put followers' interests first, provide support, and facilitate their performance Authenticity • Express oneself in ways consistent with inner thoughts and feelings Interpersonal acceptance • Demonstrate empathy, compassion, and forgiveness to followers Providing direction • Customize directions to followers' needs, abilities, and input • Provide an appropriate amount of accountability Stewardship • Take responsibility for entire organization—inspire followers to act in the common interest for all

Sources: Data from Bass, B. M., & Riggio, R. E. (2006). *Transformational leadership.* Mahwah, NJ: Lawrence Erlbaum Associates; Spears, L. C. (2002). Tracing the past, present, and future of servant leadership. In L. C. Spears, M. Lawrence, & K. Blanchard (Eds.), *Focus on leadership: Servant-leadership for the twenty-first century* (pp. 1–10). New York: John Wiley and Sons; van Dierendonck, D. (2011). Servant leadership: A review and syntheses. *Journal of Management, 27,* 1228–1261.

leaders (Parris & Welty Peachey, 2013). Within the context of nonprofit sport organizations, servant leaders can positively influence the motivation of their volunteers by developing a shared vision to serve others, building a loving and open community, and creating a context in which followers can become servant leaders (Parris & Welty Peachey, 2013). Because there is little additional research within sport management exploring the concept of servant leadership, there appear to be many opportunities for scholars to better understand the influences of such behavior on organizational outcomes and employee outcomes within the context of sport organizations. Another area garnering interest within sport management research is exploring ways in which servant leadership can be measured (Trail, Hanold, & Cuevas, 2012). The development of a valid and reliable instrument to study servant leadership in sport will be necessary to advance our understanding of the influence of this type of leadership in sport organizations.

AUTHENTIC LEADERSHIP

A final area of leadership prevalent in the research—*authentic leadership*—is concentrated more on the leader and his or her own journey and self-concept (Shamir & Eilam, 2005). This differs from the previously mentioned leadership styles in that the emphasis is on the leader instead of the follower or the organization. The internal focus of authentic leadership is included in the definition given by Avolio, Gardner, Walumbwa, Luthans, and May (2004): "We conceive of authentic leaders as persons who have achieved high levels of authenticity in that they know who they are, what they believe and value, and they act upon those values and beliefs while transparently interacting with others" (p. 802). Through knowing oneself, the authentic leader is able to transfer his or her qualities onto followers, thus helping them grow. Through the process of transferring the personal identification trait of the authentic leader, leaders are also able to increase their followers' performance (Avolio et al., 2004).

May, Chan, Hodges, and Avolio (2003) suggest authentic leadership as a possible answer to the unethical and inauthentic leadership behaviors seen within the corporate landscape of the United States. The same can be said in the sport context as numerous scandals continue to involve poor behavior and unethical decisions by those in leadership positions. Although authentic leadership can trace its roots back to transformational leadership, May et al. (2003) point out that "authentic leaders are not necessarily transformational, visionary, or charismatic leaders. But . . . will be the ones who take a stand that changes the course of history for others" (p. 248).

SUMMARY

One of the most widely studied leadership behaviors in sport management is transformational leadership. Leaders who demonstrate transformational leadership are responsive to the individual needs of their followers by empowering them and by aligning the goals of the organization, the leader, the group, and the individual (Bass, 2008). Transformational leaders are visionary and appeal to the higher order psychological needs of employees for feeling valued and worthwhile in the organization (Bryman, 1992). In contrast, transactional leaders motivate followers by contract and reward. Transactional leaders focus on rules and procedures and promise followers rewards for good performance (Bass, 1990).

Research in sport management has found that transformational leaders are considered more effective leaders, achieve better outcomes for their organizations, create greater employee commitment and satisfaction, and are better able to lead organizations through significant change.

Servant leadership is related to transformational leadership, but is a distinct form of leadership. Servant leaders first serve their followers, and empower followers, but not for organizational objectives. Servant leaders emphasize the personal growth of their followers first. In contrast, transformational leaders also want to empower followers, but they do so in order to better serve the objectives of the organization. There is growing interest in the use of servant leadership both in business and in sport management contexts, and as scholars continue to develop and refine valid and reliable measures of servant leadership, the influence of servant leadership in sport management will continue to develop.

Another new leadership construct is authentic leadership, which focuses on the beliefs and values of the leader, and transferring those values to followers. Through knowing oneself, the authentic leader is able to transfer his or her values to others in the organization.

LEADERSHIP PERSPECTIVE

Ryan Ivey is the Athletic Director for Texas A&M University Commerce and has served in that capacity for less than 1 year. Prior to his time at Texas A&M Commerce, he worked as associate athletic director at McNeese State University. He has identified as a servant leader and has utilized this leadership style during his brief tenure at Commerce.

Ryan Ivey.
Courtesy of Ryan Ivey

Q: Within the leadership literature, there are studies to support multiple types of leadership behavior as beneficial to organizational outcomes. As an athletic director, can you discuss the benefits of employing transactional leadership behaviors within your program? In what types of situations is transactional leadership behavior most helpful to athletic department employees and to athletic department organizational outcomes? When is it detrimental to athletic department employees and to athletic department organizational outcomes?

Transactional leadership, using a "chain of command" style, provides stability and clear communication to all employees. This can be especially important in a high profile organization. When employees know who leaders are and who is responsible, it can facilitate solving problems when issues arise. I see transactional leadership as most beneficial in crisis situations; when there are issues on campus, that is when that type of leadership behavior is most important. I also see transactional leadership being important when conducting performance evaluations, identifying compensation and bonuses, evaluating win–loss, APR (academic progress rate) scores, and so on. I also see the benefit of that leadership style to help foster rules compliance.

Q: As a follow-up to the first question—consider the behaviors associated with transformational leadership. Again, can you discuss the benefits of employing transformational leadership behaviors within your program? In what types of situations is transformational leadership behavior most helpful to athletic department employees and to athletic department

organizational outcomes? When is it detrimental to athletic department employees and to athletic department organizational outcomes?

I believe that transformational leadership is beneficial in providing better communication among leaders and employees. I also believe transformational leadership helps to develop better relationships between leaders and employees, and helps employees to develop creativity and collaboration with their colleagues. Transformational leaders can also provide inspiration and motivation for staff, and help to build trustworthiness with employees by leading in a more transparent fashion. Transformational leaders have passion about their organizations and share that passion with their employees. They do not try to force goals on employees, but instead try to get employees involved in the decision-making process. Transformational leadership is best used when you are trying to begin a new program or change an existing program. It is important to provide members of the organization with a voice in the change process.

Q: You have identified yourself as a servant leader. Can you explain your understanding of servant leadership and describe why you would consider yourself to be a servant leader?

As a servant leader, I tell our coaches my job is to serve the coaches and student-athletes. It is my job as the leader of the athletic department to do things to make their lives easier so they can have success. This isn't about me. My job as the leader of the department is to be sure that all employees have the resources necessary to help best support our student-athletes. To help them compete academically, socially, engage in campus life, compete in athletics, and engage in the community. It is important to let your employees know that this is really who I am, and you can come to me if you need something. It is important as a servant leader to be approachable; to listen to what your employees need, to be empathetic, and to understand the lives of student-athletes. As a servant leader in athletics, you need to know who you are and what you need to do to be a better person. You need to make a commitment to grow with your employees, engage them, and foster their abilities. Let them know that we are all in this together, that we are there to support one another and most importantly to serve one another.

Q: What are the benefits to servant leadership? What are the challenges?

The primary benefit is that leading is bigger than being about one person. You get more as a servant leader and by serving others than by having your employees serve you. Servant leadership is beneficial to the entire organization, because it improves the climate and culture that is fostered in your organization. Servant leadership also fosters loyalty in your employees. It can make it difficult for someone to leave your organization. Servant leadership can permeate the culture of the organization. Your employees will want to be a part of your organization, fight with you, demonstrate transparency and accountability, and loyalty. Employees don't want to disappoint you because of what you've done for them as a servant leader.

The major challenge to servant leadership is that you get to a point where you can be taken advantage of if people in your organization don't share your value systems. They can take advantage for their own personal gain. As a servant leader, you need to balance that challenge and you have to be sure that you are strong enough to make the difficult decisions. If you need to let people go, that is difficult but it is necessary.

Q: Considering the future of college athletics, what type(s) of leadership style(s) do you think will best meet the needs/challenges facing athletic directors?

I think personally it is servant leadership. With the way the college landscape is changing—it isn't about the money—conference realignment, those decisions weren't made in the best interest of the student-athlete. At the highest level—that is a farm system—but let's call it that. Let's be honest about what is going on. For all the bad that may come from college athletics, there is a lot of good that is also happening. Let's get back to the core of what we do and who we are. There is something special about being a part of college athletics and helping student-athletes grow. As leaders we have an opportunity to make a difference in the lives of student-athletes and employees, and in the larger world of college athletics.

KEY TERMS

active management

authentic leadership

contingent reward

idealized influence

individualized consideration

inspirational motivation

intellectual stimulation

laissez-faire

passive management

self-actualization

servant leadership

stewardship

transactional leadership

transformational leadership

DISCUSSION QUESTIONS

1. Considering the leadership theories presented in this chapter, identify a leader in the field of sport and describe whether he or she uses transactional, transformational, servant, or authentic leadership.
2. Given the scandals facing professional sport (e.g., use of performance enhancing drugs, illegal behavior by coaches and athletes), what type of leadership could best support organizations that are trying to move past such scandals? Use information from the chapter to support your answer.
3. Describe the most significant differences between transformational and servant leadership.
4. Why would a leader want to utilize authentic leadership behaviors in a sport organization?
5. Which type of leadership behavior do you think is best to utilize within a sport organization? Provide details from the chapter to support your answer.

For a full suite of assignments and additional learning activities, use the access code found in the front of your book. If you do not have an access code, you can obtain one at **www.jblearning.com**.

References

Amis, J., Slack, T., & Hinings, C. R. (2004). Strategic change and the role of interests, power and organizational capacity. *Journal of Sport Management, 18,* 158–198.

Andrew, D. P. S., Kim, S., Stoll, J. A., & Todd, S. Y. (2011). To what extent does transformational leadership affect employees? An exploratory analysis of a collegiate athletic department. *Applied Research in Coaching and Athletics Annual, 26,* 178–207.

Antonakis, J. (2012). Transformational and charismatic leadership. In D. V. Day & J. Antonakis (Eds.), *The nature of leadership* (2nd ed., pp. 256–288). Thousand Oaks, CA: Sage.

Avolio, B. J., & Bass, B. M. (1991). *Full-range leadership development.* Binghamton, NY: Bass, Avolio & Associates.

Avolio, B. J., Gardner, W. L., Walumbwa, F. O., Luthans, F., & May, D. R. (2004). Unlocking the mask: A look at the process by which authentic leaders impact follower attitudes and behaviors. *Leadership Quarterly, 15*(6), 801–823.

Bass, B. M. (1985). *Leadership and performance beyond expectations.* New York: Free Press.

Bass, B. M. (1990). *Bass and Stogdill's handbook of leadership: Theory, research and management applications* (3rd ed.). New York: Free Press.

Bass, B. M. (2008). Development and identification of leaders and leadership. In B. M. Bass & R. Bass (Eds.), *The Bass handbook of leadership: Theory, research and managerial applications* (4th ed., pp. 1051–1158). New York: Free Press.

Bass, B. M., & Riggio, R. E. (2006). *Transformational leadership.* Mahwah, NJ: Lawrence Erlbaum Associates.

Bryman, A. (1992). *Charisma and leadership in organizations.* Newbury Park, CA: Sage.

Burns, J. M. (1978). *Leadership: Transformational leadership, transactional leadership.* New York: Harper & Row.

Burton, L., & Welty Peachey, J. (2009). Transactional or transformational? Leadership preferences of Division III athletic administrators. *Journal of Intercollegiate Sport, 2*(2), 245–259.

Burton, L. J., & Welty Peachey, J. (2013). The call for servant leadership in intercollegiate athletics. *Quest, 65*(3), 354–371.

Choi, J., Sagas, M., Park, S., & Cunningham, G. B. (2007). Transformational leadership in collegiate coaching: The effects of transformational leadership on job satisfaction, organizational commitment, and organizational citizenship behavior. *International Journal of Sport Management, 8*(4), 427–446.

Doherty, A. J. (1997). The effect of leader characteristics on the perceived transformational/transactional leadership and impact of interuniversity athletic administrators. *Journal of Sport Management, 11*(3), 275–285.

Doherty, A. J., & Danylchuk, K. E. (1996). Transformational and transactional leadership in interuniversity athletics management. *Journal of Sport Management, 10*(3), 292–309.

Eagly, A. H., & Carli, L. L. (2003). Finding gender advantage and disadvantage: Systematic research integration is the solution. *Leadership Quarterly, 14,* 851–859.

Eisenback, R., Watson, K., & Pillai, R. (1999). Transformational leadership in the context of organizational change. *Journal of Organizational Change Management, 12*(2), 80–89.

Foels, R., Driskell, J. E., Mullen, B., & Salas, E. (2000). The effects of democratic leadership on group member satisfaction: An integration. *Small Group Research, 31*(6), 676–701.

Frontiera, J. (2010). Leadership and organizational culture transformation in professional sport. *Journal of Leadership and Organizational Studies, 17*(1), 71–86.

Graham, J. W. (1991). Servant leadership in organizations: Inspirational and moral. *Leadership Quarterly, 2,* 105–119.

Greenleaf, R. K. (1977). *Servant leadership: A journey into the nature of legitimate power and greatness.* New York: Paulist Press.

Greenleaf, R. K. (1998). *The power of servant-leadership.* San Francisco: Berrett-Koehler.

Hammermeister, J., Burton, D., Pickering, M., Chase, M., Westre, K., & Baldwin, N. (2008). Servant-leadership in sports: A concept whose time has arrived. *International Journal of Servant-Leadership, 4,* 185–215.

Hesse, H. (1956). *Journey to the east.* London, UK: Owen.

Hind, P., Wilson, A., & Lenssen, G. (2009). Developing leaders for sustainable business. *Corporate Governance, 9,* 7–20.

House, R. J. (1977). A 1976 theory of charismatic leadership effectiveness. In J. G. Hunt & L. L. Larson (Eds.), *Leadership: The cutting edge* (pp. 189–207). Carbondale: Southern Illinois University.

Judge, T. A., & Piccolo, R. F. (2004). Transformational and transactional leadership: A meta-analytic test of their relative validity. *Journal of Applied Psychology, 89*(5), 755–767.

Kent, A., & Chelladurai, P. (2001). Perceived transformational leadership, organizational commitment, and citizenship behavior: A case study in intercollegiate athletics. *Journal of Sport Management, 15*(2), 135–159.

Kim, H. (2009). *Transformational and transactional leadership of athletic directors and their impact on organizational outcomes perceived by head coaches at NCAA Division II intercollegiate institutions* (doctoral dissertation). Retrieved from ProQuest Dissertations and Theses database. AAT 3393209.

Klimoski, R. J., & Koles, K. L. K. (2001). The chief executive officer and top management team interface. In S. J. Zaccaro & R. J. Klimoski (Eds.), *The nature of organizational leadership: Understanding the performance imperatives confronting today's leaders* (pp. 219–269). San Francisco, CA: Jossey-Bass.

Kouzes, J. M., & Posner, B. Z. (1993). *Credibility: How leaders gain and lose it, why people demand it.* San Francisco, CA: Jossey-Bass.

Krishnan, V. R. (2005). Leader-member exchange, transformational leadership, and value system congruence. *Electronic Journal of Business Ethics and Organizational Studies, 10*(1), 14–21.

Kuhnert, K. W., & Lewis, P. (1987). Transactional and transformational leadership: A constructive/deconstructive analysis. *Academy of Management Review, 12*(4), 117–130.

Lee, J. (2004). Effects of leadership and leader-member exchange on commitment. *Leadership and Organization Development Journal, 26,* 655–672.

Martin, R., & Epitropaki, O. (2001). Role of organizational identification on implicit leadership theories (ILTS), transformational leadership and work attitudes. *Group Process and Intergroup Relations, 4,* 247–262.

May, D. R., Chan, A. Y. L., Hodges, T. D., & Avolio, B. J. (2003). Developing the moral component of authentic leadership. *Organizational Dynamics, 32*(3), 247–260.

Murray, M., & Mann, B. (2006). Leadership effectiveness. In J. Williams (Ed.), *Applied sport psychology: Personal growth to peak performance* (pp. 109–139). New York: McGraw-Hill.

Northouse, P. G. (2012). *Leadership: Theory and practice.* Thousand Oaks, CA: Sage.

Ott, J. (1996). *Classic readings in OB* (2nd ed.). Belmont, CA: Wadsworth.

Parris, D. L., & Welty Peachey, J. (2012). Building a legacy of volunteers through servant leadership: A case study of a cause-related sporting event. *Nonprofit Management and Leadership, 23*(2), 259–276.

Parris, D. L., & Welty Peachey, J. (2013). A systematic literature review of servant leadership theory in organizational contexts. *Journal of Business Ethics, 113,* 377–393.

Phelan, M. (2005). Cultural revitalization movements in organizational change management. *Journal of Change Management, 5*(1), 47–56.

Powell, G. N., Butterfield, D. A., & Bartol, K. M. (2008). Leader evaluations: A new female advantage? *Gender in Management: An International Journal, 23,* 156–174.

Rieke, M., Hammermeister, J., & Chase, M. (2008). Servant leadership in sport: A new paradigm for effective coaching behavior. *International Journal of Sports Science and Coaching, 3,* 227–239.

Robbins, S. P., & Judge, T. A. (2003). *Organizational behavior.* Upper Saddle River, NJ: Pearson Education.

Shamir, B., & Eilam, G. (2005). "What's your story?" A life-stories approach to authentic leadership development. *Leadership Quarterly, 16*(3), 395–417.

Schroeder, P. J. (2010). Changing team culture: The perspectives of ten successful head coaches. *Journal of Sport Behavior, 32*(4), 63–88.

Sendjaya, S., Sarros, J. C., & Santora, J. C. (2008). Defining and measuring servant leadership behaviour in organizations. *Journal of Management Studies, 45,* 402–424.

Slack, T., & Hinings, C. R. (1992). Understanding change in national sport organizations: An integration of theoretical perspectives. *Journal of Sport Management, 6,* 114–132.

Spears, L. C. (2002). Tracing the past, present, and future of servant leadership. In L. C. Spears, M. Lawrence, & K. Blanchard (Eds.), *Focus on leadership: Servant-leadership for the twenty-first century* (pp. 1–10). New York: John Wiley and Sons.

Stewart, G. L. (2006). A meta-analytic review of relationships between team design features and team performance. *Journal of Management*, *32*(1), 29–55.

Stone, A. G., Russell, R. F., & Patterson, K. (2004). Transformational versus servant leadership: A difference in leader focus. *Leadership and Organization Development Journal, 25*, 349–361.

Strang, K. D. (2005). Examining effective and ineffective transformational project leadership. *Team Performance Management*, *11*(3/4), 68–103.

Trail, G., Hanold, M., & Cuevas, K. (2012, June). *Servant leadership in sport*. Paper presented at the North American Society for Sport Management Annual Conference, Seattle, WA.

Tse, H. H., & Lam, W. (2008, August). *Transformational leadership and turnover: The roles of LMX and organizational commitment*. Paper presented at the Academy of Management Meeting, Anaheim, CA.

van Dierendonck, D. (2011). Servant leadership: A review and syntheses. *Journal of Management, 37*(4), 1228–1261.

Wallace, M., & Weese, J. (1995). Leadership, organizational culture and job satisfaction in Canadian YMCA organizations. *Journal of Sport Management*, *9*, 182–193.

Wang, Y. S., & Huang, T. C. (2009). The relationship of transformational leadership with group cohesiveness and emotional intelligence. *Social Behavior and Personality: An International Journal*, *37*(3), 379–392.

Weese, W. J. (1995). Leadership and organizational culture: An investigation of Big Ten and Mid-American Conference campus recreation administrations. *Journal of Sport Management, 9*, 119–134.

Wells, J. E., & Welty Peachey, J. (2011). Turnover intentions: Do leadership behaviors and satisfaction with the leader matter? *Team Performance Management*, *17*(1/2), 23–40.

Welty Peachey, J., Bruening, J., & Burton, L. (2011). Transformational leadership of change: Success through valuing relationships. *Journal of Contemporary Athletics*, *5*(2), 127–152.

Welty Peachey, J., & Burton, L. (2011). Male or female? Exploring perceptions of leader effectiveness and a (potential) female leadership advantage with intercollegiate athletic directors. *Sex Roles*, *64*(5/6), 416–425.

Welty Peachey, J., & Burton, L. (2012). Transactional or transformational leaders in intercollegiate athletics? Examining the influence of leader gender and subordinate gender on evaluation of leaders during organizational culture change. *International Journal of Sport Management*, *13*, 1–28.

Yusof, A., & Mohd Shah, P. (2008). Transformational leadership and leadership substitutes in sports: Implications on coaches' job satisfaction. *International Bulletin of Business Administration*, *3*, 17–29.

CHAPTER 4

THE NECESSARY SKILLS SET

Mauro Palmero
Ming Li

CHAPTER OBJECTIVES

- Identify crucial leadership skills that could be utilized in a given sport organizational context.
- Understand which skills are needed to implement an organization's vision.
- Develop recommendations regarding how to acquire leadership skills.
- Establish an understanding of important leadership competencies that will be further developed in later chapters.

CASE STUDY

Theo Epstein, Baseball General Manager

According to lore, and Dan Shaughnessy of the *Boston Globe*, a disgruntled George Herman "Babe" Ruth, after being traded from the Red Sox to the rival New York Yankees, cursed the successful Boston baseball franchise. The Red Sox dominated the 1910s by winning in 1912, 1915, 1916, and 1918, as well as in 1903. However, the beloved New England team fell upon eight decades of hard times with sparse postseason play and a tradition of choking during meaningful games. The lore was established and momentum built as the Red Sox continued to miss their goals of winning division championships, pennants, and of course, a World Series.

In 2002, under the new direction of President and CEO Larry Lucchino, Theo Epstein became the team's general manager (GM), ushering in change throughout the ball club. Epstein, a

(continues)

Massachusetts native and Yale graduate, served as sports editor for the college newspaper during his Yale days and later in public relations for the San Diego Padres under Lucchino's leadership. Epstein quickly moved up through the ranks by proving himself competent while simultaneously earning a juris doctorate from the University of San Diego School of Law.

Epstein was appointed Red Sox general manager in late 2002 at age 28, the youngest GM in baseball history. This early career included two World Series titles (2004 and 2007) and six postseason appearances. In 2007, he received the Carl Maddox Sport Management Award; in 2008, he received the Major League Executive of the Year award; in 2009, he was named Executive of the Decade by *Sporting News*; and also in 2009, *Sports Illustrated* ranked Epstein the third-best general manager of the decade.

During his tenure, Epstein amassed great praise for his skills at leading a team. In particular, he has been said to have had three important skills—developing team chemistry, retaining assets, and vision (MacPherson, 2013).

On team chemistry:

> When asked about working for an organization that is constantly under the microscope with the pressure to succeed, Epstein said, "Any potential conflict or any bad fit really gets amplified here" (MacPherson, 2013, para. 14). As a leader of baseball operations, it's my responsibility to manage [the pressure] and to be true to our own philosophies and to put the best team on the field and build the best organization so we can succeed year in and year out. Our successes were probably well documented, so any failings have to be attributed directly to us in baseball operations. (Speier, 2012, para. 16)

On retaining assets:

> Had we been completely true to our baseball philosophy that we set out and believed in and followed, we probably wouldn't have made certain moves that we made anyway, moves that, as I look back on them, they were probably moves too much of convenience, of placating elements that shouldn't have been important. (Speier, 2012, para. 23)

On possessing vision:

> I think in a big market, the daily struggle is how to balance the here and now with legitimate plans for the future. It's a difficult thing to reconcile . . . You have to start thinking about now at the expense of the future sometimes. (Speier, 2012, para. 20)

After disappointing 2010 and 2011 seasons, Epstein left the Red Sox for the Chicago Cubs. "I think I had some degree of self-awareness and that led me to the decision to put a cap on my time in that role with the Red Sox, because it would have been really hard to navigate it and still be happy," Epstein said. "Changing environment is a really helpful tool to get the best out of oneself in a lot of different ways. Professionally and personally, it was definitely time for me" (Speier, 2012). Since his departure, many have questioned whether Epstein's success as a young general manager was due to his skill as a leader or simply luck.

Questions for Discussion

1. In your estimation, what leadership skills—other than the ones listed in the case study—do you believe Theo Epstein possesses that have enabled him to be successful in his role as general manager? Read forward in the chapter to help you answer this question.

2. Do you think skills such as these are evolving or remain constant throughout a career? Provide support for your answer.

3. How did self-awareness and self-regulation play into the events surrounding the career of Theo Epstein? Provide specific examples. Refer to the chapter for help with these terms.

4. Do you think Theo Epstein's success with the Red Sox was due to luck or the leadership skills he possessed? Both? Something else entirely?

INTRODUCTION

The ever-changing nature of today's sport industry imposes high demands on sport organizations, which trickle down to sport leaders and their followers. Sport organizations are charged with branding themselves to create lifelong relationships with customers, consistently providing customers with excellent customer service, diversification of revenue, empowering and retaining employees, strategic planning, creative marketing, innovation, and corporate social responsibility, just to name a few organizational functions. To become or remain successful at all the necessary activities they must engage in, sport organizations must recruit, develop, and rely on leaders who develop and consistently display expertise in building and implementing a vision (including hiring the right people to assemble the best possible working team); the interpersonal skills of communication, empathy, and motivation; coping with crises and conflict; and addressing and forging change. To get a job and succeed in the industry, sport leaders (rookies and veterans) must strive to develop those skills through formal education, on-the-job training, and various professional development initiatives offered by professional associations.

Given the absence of sport management research specifically related to leadership skills, this chapter presents information drawn mainly from other disciplines, such as business and psychology. It is important to indicate that the skills set described here is not associated with a single specific leadership type or leader. If you ask 10 different sport leaders what the most important leadership skills are, you are likely to get a variety of answers. The authors' intent was to provide readers with a set of leadership skills drawn from the best features of each leadership type and that can be used by any leader, working for any sport organization, to achieve success. Different leadership styles and skills will be needed in different organizational cultures, but there are some common, core areas that each leadership style needs to embrace. To that end, four areas will be covered in this chapter that demand a development of skills: crafting a vision, communication, coping with crisis and conflict, and addressing and forging change. Within each area, the authors discuss several different subskills needed for success in the four main areas. **Table 4.1** shows the leadership

TABLE 4.1 Leadership Skills Required of Sport Leaders

Leadership Skills	Subsets
Implement a vision	Conceptualization Foresight Stewardship Understanding the organization's capability to succeed Matching the right people with the job/project Recognizing the team's capability to succeed Providing followers with an identity
Communication	Listening Emotional intelligence Self-awareness and self-regulation Building community
Motivation	Commitment to followers' growth Delegating responsibility and empowerment
Crisis and conflict	Calming tense situations Problem solving Empathy
Address and forge change	Communicating change Involving followers, promoting teamwork

skills recommended for sport leaders, broken down by the main areas and the subskills for each area. This table also serves as an outline for this chapter. The sum of these skills—and others—can lead to the construction of credibility, which is the foundation of leadership (Kouzes & Posner, 2002).

IMPLEMENT A VISION

No matter what type of leadership style you prefer—transactional, transformational, servant, or authentic; a combination of them; or a different leadership style entirely—understanding how to enact a vision for an organization is crucial. A *vision* is an idea for future success or direction, and serves as a foundation from which a sport organization moves forward. Organizations need leaders who not only can create a vision, but also implement it. To do so, these leaders must be able to conceive a vision, foresee its effects, and identify the organization's chance of success. In addition, they act with the best interest of the organization in mind (stewardship), and attempt to assemble a group of motivated and capable individuals to carry out the implementation of the idea. Kouzes and Posner (2002) point out that this vision should be a shared vision. In particular, 21st-century sport leaders need to be forward thinking and imagine the possibilities for their organization. Kevin Plank of Under Armour is one such leader.

When Plank started Under Armour, he first identified a need for performance apparel that would be moisture wicking and provide athletes with muscle support. He then created a vision for his innovative company. From his vision, superior apparel was created that is not only light, but also can keep athletes cool and dry. Plank's foresight put his company in the best position to claim a piece of the sport apparel market untapped by other traditional brands. His unique vision made major competing brands follow his lead, including Nike, Adidas, and Reebok. Now that Under Armour has had success, its vision is simple: "To empower athletes everywhere" (Under Armour, 2013). This vision shows the global reach Under Armour pursues with its apparel.

Conceptualization

Conceptualization is the process by which leaders (alone or assisted by other members of the organization) evaluate the sport industry's environment, trends, dynamics, and shifts in perceived value or expectations, and attempt to set a future direction for the organization (vision). In one of your sport management classes, you may have already heard the acronym "SWOT." The "O" and "T" of the SWOT represent opportunities and threats. The "S" and "W" represent strengths and weaknesses. The conceptualization function asks leaders to assess an organization's external threats and opportunities. This analysis encourages organizations to size up the competition and take calculated risks. When Plank of Under Armour analyzed the environment, he realized there were no products available like the ones he envisioned. He saw a need, or opportunity, and filled it. A good sport leader must be able to put forth an idea for a vision, analyze it, and work toward it. A vision affects a wide range of performance measures, promotes change, guides strategic planning, motivates individuals, and supports the criteria used for recruiting talent and making decisions within a context (Anzalone, 2007). A vision must be well articulated with a corresponding strategic plan. To achieve effectiveness, a leader must strike a balance between the organization's vision and mission—the organization's overall purpose—and the coordination of individual and/or group task execution (Slack & Parent, 2006; Zaccaro & Banks, 2004). A leader must have the ability to promote the changes called for by the vision so that the organization can gain and/or maximize its competitive advantage.

Foresight

Foresight is a competency that allows sport leaders to learn from past and present situations and project possible consequences a decision made today may have in the future. Their focus is on anticipating those influencing factors that may either assist organizations in achieving their desired results or, conversely, hold them back. In other words, foresight is not predicting or envisioning the future. It is, instead, weighing pros and cons, and evaluating different courses of action before making a decision. If leaders pay attention to trends and

understand how mistakes have been made in the past in their organization and by their competitors, these pros and cons can be identified more readily. Foresight enables leaders to deal with the inevitable variations that will occur as the future unfolds (Anzalone, 2007; Hammett, 2004; Spears, 2010). Sport retail firms such as Nike and Adidas are global companies, and they expect to sell their products in as many countries as possible as the 21st century continues. Knowing which products will gain popularity with international consumers and which markets to tap takes foresight. Colors and design of apparel are important matters for research and design departments to determine for different countries and global regions. Understanding trends such as population growth and increases in disposable income in certain countries will allow Nike and its competitors to weigh the pros and cons of each strategic decision that works toward vision.

Stewardship

In addition to foresight, *stewardship* is central to carrying out a vision's implementation. Stewardship is making decisions with the best interest of the organization in mind to achieve its strategic goals and objectives. By doing so, sport leaders create a sense of responsibility in followers for the long-term survival and success of the organization with which they are affiliated. Leaders incite and develop stewardship in their followers through various relational, contextual, and motivational supportive leadership behaviors (Hernandez, 2008). For example, a ticket sales director at a Division I athletic department takes advantage of daily interactions with his sales representatives to educate them on the department's culture (contextual support) and to show through his actions (relational support) how to put the best interests of the athletic department in every sales transaction. The same ticket sales director uses each sales milestone achieved to celebrate group and individual performance (motivational support). In addition, leaders assist followers in developing self-determination; that is, followers choose to initiate and regulate their own actions in a way that supports the continuation of successful work behavior and processes. It is important to emphasize that stewardship does not support mediocre performance. Because stewardship is primarily built upon trust, leaders, followers, and stakeholders expect everyone involved will deliver their best performance in service of the current and future well-being of the organization. Transformational and servant leaders have the ability to form this trust with followers because their focus on stewardship demonstrates high levels of integrity and ethical behavior (Bass & Riggio, 2006) in addition to creating a supportive environment for followers through individualized consideration.

Understanding the Organization's Capability to Succeed

To effectively implement a vision, sport leaders cannot rely only on foresight and stewardship. They have to be able to ensure that their vision is compatible with the organization's capability to succeed. Effective leaders need to be skilled not just in assessing people, but also in the honest assessment of the abilities (strengths) and shortcomings (weaknesses) of their organization as a whole. Leaders' internal assessments let them know how resources, processes, and values affect what an organization can and cannot do. Many sport organizations, particularly nonprofits, work with small staffs. The use of interns, part-time employees, and volunteers in sport has become prevalent; this practice puts pressure on leaders to assess their organization's human resources and the organization's ability to succeed.

When asked what their organization can realistically achieve, leaders frequently look for the answer in their organization's resources, including people, equipment, technologies, available revenue, product designs, information, brands, and relationships with suppliers, distributors, and customers (Christensen & Overdorf, 2000). Having access to abundant, high-quality resources increases an organization's chances of coping with change and achieving success. However, existing resources are not the only factor affecting an organization's capability to succeed. The organization's processes and the way leaders and followers interact, coordinate efforts, communicate, and make decisions when transforming resources into products and services are actions that also help determine an organization's ability to succeed. Another crucial factor related to an organization's capability to succeed is the extent to which followers embrace organizational values. Such values should be not only the foundation upon which all decisions are made within an organization, but also used by followers at every level to prioritize their tasks. Referring again to Under Armour, one of the organization's values is to call positive attention to the work of men and women in the U.S. military. The company's "Protect This House" campaign has been geared toward recognition of veterans and the Wounded Warrior Project.

Matching the Right People with the Job/Project

One of the central characteristics of an effective leader is his or her ability to "identify the right person for the right job and to train employees to succeed at the jobs they're given" (Christensen & Overdorf, 2000, p.1). Leaders do not always have the chance to assemble their own team. Many times, they must work with the group that is given to them when they join an organization. When assembling a team, leaders are normally interested in the members' technical and interpersonal skills that are relevant to the group's tasks, the distribution of power among the members, and the member diversity within the group (Mealiea &

Baltazar, 2005). Another valuable leadership skill related to group/team assembly is the ability to attract and retain people who are both passionate about their work/organization and highly motivated (Gilley, Dixon, & Gilley, 2008). Although there is little research in the area, retention, job satisfaction, and leadership appeal appear to be congruent with the transformational and servant styles of leadership.

Recognizing the Team's Capability to Succeed

After sport leaders assemble their teams, they must recognize and monitor the team's capability to succeed. As they monitor the team's performance, they must make appropriate changes to remove identified deficiencies as soon as possible—procrastination may compromise a team and organization's performance.

To be successful in this process, a leader must look for the existence of some important characteristics in their working group. The members of the group need to understand (as a group and individually) what they are doing and why, and to share the responsibility of achieving the goal with the leader. Diversity of styles and behavior, and sharing of knowledge, experience, and emotional support among the members should be embraced and encouraged. The group leader also must listen to group members and allow all members to express their opinions and preferences. All members must be empowered to participate in the process of assessing their performance and changing goals (if necessary) (Mealiea & Baltazar, 2005).

To measure the potential for success of a group of ushers working in a concert at a basketball arena, the director of operations must assess the ushers' levels of understanding of the goal in providing the best possible experience to patrons. In addition to articulating that vision to the followers, the director also needs to assess the ushers'

levels of knowledge on the type of act that will perform at the concert, and the characteristics, demographics, and psychographics of the crowd attending the concert. Each usher individually must display a deep knowledge of the physical characteristics of the seating section assigned to them and the specific policies applicable to the event in regard to what fans can and cannot do; they also must demonstrate a readiness to enforce those policies. The ushers must also display a deep level of willingness to share previous experiences and awareness of known new issues. In addition, the ushers must be allowed to provide the organization's leadership with their feedback and suggestions for solving identified problems and improving their performance.

Providing Followers with an Identity

After the team has been assembled, sport leaders must work to create an identity for followers and inspire them to perform their best. A *follower* usually bases his or her identity on the extent to which he or she sees him- or herself as a member of a group, and on his or her assessment of the significance of such membership (Avolio & Gardner, 2005). To create followers' identification and commitment, leaders must play the role of mentors and "model the way" for their followers (Kouzes & Posner, 2002). Such mentorship is based on conveying to followers the team's purpose, the followers' roles in relation to that purpose, and clear norms of social interaction so as to promote future performance and satisfaction.

As followers incorporate values and beliefs conveyed to them by a leader, their perceptions of themselves change and develop over time. Such perception changes cause followers to become more transparent with their leader, which consequently influences the leader's development. The follower and leader influence each other's development as their relationship evolves. Once an authentic relationship is built upon openness, transparency, loyalty, and trust between a leader and followers, all the people involved in the relationship will incorporate their respective roles into their respective identities.

COMMUNICATION

Effective sport leaders lead through effective communication. This essential interpersonal skill serves to "enable, foster and create the understanding necessary to encourage others to follow a leader" (Barrett, 2006, p. 385). Effective communication uses the full range of communication skills to overcome interferences—or "noise," as communication researchers may refer to it—and to create and deliver the leader's message. Leaders must not only be able to write and speak well—take note of the comments from Minor League Baseball President Patrick O'Conner in the interview at the end of this chapter—but also use listening, emotional intelligence, and self-awareness to connect to followers. Effective communication transmits behavioral intent from the leaders to their followers, thus building trust. Leaders' communication must be congruent with their actions. Communication that is not validated by actions undermines followers' motivation and trust, and is viewed as insincere and manipulative (Mayfield & Mayfield, 2002). In other words, say what you will do and do what you say.

A new general manager for a local Minor League Baseball team probably was hired because of the ability to articulate a vision for the team and the ability to convey a clear idea on how things needed to change to either continue the team's success with regard to revenue and customer service or to send the team on the path to achieve success. To achieve success, it is probably not a good idea to just use the legitimate power of the GM position and demand things get done the GM's way. The GM has to "sell" ideas through

words and actions. However, to do well, the GM needs to listen to followers' concerns, and incorporate a few of their suggestions into the vision. A new GM also may want to connect with followers by understanding their concerns, and by showing concern. This can relate to their emotions. With such a connection in place, the GM will be able—through good words and deeds—to make the followers feel part of the "team." By communicating effectively with followers and creating a good sense of community, the GM will be able to motivate and engage followers to do more and with more efficiency, whatever task is at hand—even the toughest ones.

Listening

Leaders must have a deep knowledge about not only themselves, but also their followers. Knowing followers means understanding what concerns them, excites them, or reduces their enthusiasm, and how they feel about the organization's mission and vision. A leader's ability to listen effectively is essential to achieving the desired level of knowledge about their followers. To do so, leaders must actively listen. *Active listening* involves paying attention, withholding judgment (have an open mind and hold criticism), reflecting (use paraphrasing to confirm understanding), clarifying (doublecheck any issue that is ambiguous or unclear by using probe questions), summarizing (restate core themes), and sharing (introduce ideas, feelings, and suggestions) (Alimo-Metcalfe & Alban-Metcalfe, 2001; Anzalone, 2007; Hoppe, 2007). This technique is particularly effective for newly hired leaders. Pete Bevacqua, the new CEO of the PGA of America, made listening a priority when he took over in early 2013: "The real focus in the first few weeks has been to learn the business and the staff. I've spent time in every department just listening and meeting people, hearing the story of what they do. I'm not trying to come in like I've got it all figured out" (Smith, 2013, para. 8).

Pete Bevacqua made listening a priority when he took over as CEO of the PGA of America in 2013.
© Steve Jennings/WireImage/Getty Images

Through active listening, leaders can identify and deal with areas of confusion and uncertainty, show that they care for followers' concerns and needs, and acquire valuable information to improve communication with followers. One aspect of servant leadership is how it emphasizes how leaders are attentive to the needs of followers, show concern for them, and nurture and emphasize their needs.

Emotional Intelligence

Emotional intelligence is essentially the leader's ability to understand and manage their and their followers' emotions as they interact and work together. Emotionally intelligent leaders are confident in their ability to manage and influence life events, enhancing their ability to support, stimulate, and motivate followers (Brown & Moshavi, 2005; George, 2000). They effectively identify

and understand followers' emotions and are able to connect on a personal level by showing their own emotions. They also can predict emotional reactions and influence behavior by managing emotions. Along with active listening, emotional intelligence helps leaders manage followers' interactions and emotional responses, especially when there is a crisis or conflict.

When professional sport leagues go through labor disputes, it is common for team personnel to be threatened with furlough (temporary layoff from work until the labor dispute is resolved). These are times of high uncertainty and confusion, and emotions can be prevalent. For instance, a director of sales for a professional sport team under such circumstances must do his or her best to keep the sales team together, and maintain its focus and drive for the work that needs to be done when the league resumes normal activities. To do so, he or she needs to rely on active listening and emotional intelligence to show that he or she acknowledges, understands, and cares for everyone's concerns and troubles so as to establish honest and trustworthy communication during tough times.

Self-Awareness and Self-Regulation

Effective leaders must make regular evaluations of themselves on both personal and professional levels to achieve *self-awareness*. Although this may not seem like a communication skill, intrapersonal communication—or communicating with oneself through self-assessment—can create self-awareness. We talk privately to ourselves more than we talk openly to anyone else. Self-awareness is a continuous process whereby leaders acquire understanding of their talents, strengths, sense of purpose, core values, beliefs, desires, knowledge, experience, and capabilities (Avolio & Gardner, 2005). Through self-awareness, leaders can keep a pulse on their overall effectiveness and their relationship with their followers. Leaders' concerns should not be only with followers' perceptions of their leadership effectiveness. They should also make sure they are doing everything in their power to help followers succeed, instead of micromanaging them.

As leaders assess their leadership abilities and performance, they acquire understanding of themselves at personal and professional levels. They then must use such knowledge to regulate their actions. *Self-regulation* encompasses leaders' ability to control and adjust their actions. To do so, leaders use their morals and values and check for discrepancies between these standards and their actions'/decisions' actual or potential outcomes (Gardner, Avolio, Luthans, May, & Walumbwa, 2005). The control acquired through self-awareness and self-regulation allows leaders to be authentic in their actions, to earn followers' trust, and to enhance communication within the organization.

Building Community

A leader's knowledge of self and ability to control his or her actions, combined with good use of active listening and emotional intelligence, creates a positive rapport with followers. Commonly displayed by servant leaders, positive rapport allows leaders to build a community with their followers by consulting frequently and listening carefully to them. Such a sense of community allows the leader to get things done through persuasion, not by the power of their position or coercion. It also enhances a leader's ability to articulate and communicate his or her plan to lead the organization forward. The combination of these features fosters trust and reliability between leaders and followers, and makes everyone feel proud to belong to a team.

MOTIVATION

Motivation is directly affected by the quality of the experience a follower has within an organization and with its leadership. Job satisfaction, perceived equity, and organizational commitment are key

factors to make followers' experiences positive (Gilley et al., 2008). However, because sport leaders influence those factors, their ability to persuade and influence others to work in a common direction is imperative.

Carrot-and-stick leadership is based on extrinsic motivation—if the follower does what the leader wants, he or she reaps an external benefit such as higher pay, more vacation, or a job promotion. This is the "carrot" that is dangled in front of them. If the follower does not fulfill a leader's request, he or she gets the "stick" in the form of some sort of punishment, whether it is lower pay, being fired, or a "chewing out" session. Daniel Pink's *Drive* refers to this leadership as Type X behavior, based on McGregor's work (McGregor, 1985). But, as Ryan and Deci (2000) learned, human beings have an inner drive to be autonomous, self-determined, and connected to one another. Type I behavior, in contrast to Type X, suggests followers are less concerned with external rewards that a work activity can provide than with the inherent satisfaction of the activity itself (Pink, 2009). Furthermore, Pink reported that leaders who wanted to tap into intrinsic motivation should provide conditions that allow for autonomy, mastery, and purpose in their organizations. Autonomy means "acting with choice" (Pink, 2009, p. 90); mastery refers to the desire to get better at something that matters for your organization; and purpose refers to connecting followers' place in an organization to something bigger than themselves (Pink, 2009). It is important for leaders to realize that external rewards such as pay, vacation, and job promotions are not going to motivate everyone.

Let's imagine that you are the YMCA's new regional director and that your organization has a history of high turnover, low job satisfaction, and low motivation. To solve the problem, you could propose to give substantial raises to everyone in the organization. But this is neither feasible, realistic, nor advisable given the earlier discussion of intrinsic motivation. So what do you do? Your first step will be to sell yourself as an effective, trustworthy, and empathetic leader by creating conditions to allow employees autonomy, mastery, and purpose. That will give you the power to positively influence your staff members. You will also have to invest time and resources in your staff's professional development through classes, coaching, and mentoring. By presenting those opportunities to your employees, you show them that you care for their needs and aspirations, and make them feel appreciated. Furthermore, you will also have to assign meaningful responsibilities (according to their capabilities) and empower them to make decisions on their own, without micromanaging them. Also, consider giving them a new task to perform and master that will get their creative juices flowing.

Commitment to Followers' Growth

By neglecting to invest time and resources in followers' development, leaders and organizations may learn the hard way that underappreciated and underdeveloped followers have no motivation to perform well and be productive. Thus, effective leaders must actively develop their followers' potential. They must pay close attention to each follower's needs and aspirations, and create new opportunities for development. It is also important that the organization invests time and financial resources on the coaching and mentoring of its followers (Gilley et al., 2008). When leaders interact with followers with respect and provide appropriate opportunities for growth, they enhance followers' engagement and commitment to the organization. Engaged followers have high levels of identification with their leaders, and are more likely to feel satisfied with and enthusiastic about work.

Delegating Responsibility and Empowerment

It is not beneficial to leaders/organizations to invest time and resources in their followers' development if they do not delegate significant responsibilities to their followers and empower them to carry out such responsibilities. The responsibilities delegated must be compatible with each follower's capability and experience. Along with delegating, leaders must provide support and empower followers to act autonomously. *Empowerment* is based on purpose: Everyone is free to do whatever they believe is appropriate as long as it is in accordance with the organization's vision, goals, and policies (Hernandez, 2008). Although empowered followers have the freedom to make their own decisions (autonomy), to a certain extent, they must be held accountable for their results. Depending on positive results, delegated responsibility, empowerment, and accountability can greatly foster followers' growth and improve motivation.

CRISIS AND CONFLICT

Leaders will, at one point in their careers, or at several points, face crisis and conflict situations. To successfully deal with these situations, leaders must keep a level head in tense situations, solve complex problems, express empathy, and heal frustrated feelings among followers. Such abilities cannot prevent teams and organizations from facing crisis and conflict, but can certainly help leaders guide followers through them.

Assume you are the CEO for a road race event organizing company. During your last event, many things went wrong, with hot temperatures and shortage of water supplies forcing the event to be cancelled halfway through the race. Not only is your organization's reputation at stake, but also there is a lot of finger pointing going on inside your organization. What is your next move? As you take the necessary actions to rehabilitate your company's image, you will have to calm the tense internal situation you have. You will have to first hold back your judgment while employing active listening skills to learn what exactly happened before you make your decision. (You may need to terminate a few people in the process.) After all the fires are put out, you need to work hard on showing empathy to your employees and starting to rebuild relationships within your organization and possibly with your customers. Your main goal should be to grow back the staff members' confidence and motivate them to work on improving their performance, which is immensely helpful as you try to recover your organization from such a debacle.

Calm Tense Situations

Hopefully, by the time a crisis/conflict strikes, leaders have established good communication, trust, and respect with and among their followers. Otherwise, they will have a harder time calming tense situations. In those situations, the goal is to regain control and prevent further damage. A leader's approach must be based on fair treatment and active listening to all parties involved in the issue. They should also hold their judgment and problem-solving actions (at least initially) to take the pressure off the issue and prevent the situation from escalating to something even worse (Hoppe, 2007). In addition, showing empathy is a key factor in these circumstances. When leaders can properly calm down tense situations, they can increase the chance of healing the affected relationship quickly and effectively, and help the team and organization return to the pursuit of their goals and objectives sooner.

Problem Solving

After calming a tense situation, leaders can start addressing the identified problem(s). Problem solving has a significant impact on all aspects of leadership. Regardless of the type of issue that leaders are dealing with, they will have to make decisions on how to solve the problem at hand. Effective leadership behavior fundamentally

depends upon the leader's ability to solve a large range of problems that arise daily in organizations. Problem solving is about choosing the best available strategies (at the best possible time and place) to effectively influence followers' behavior toward resolving the issue that prevents the team/organization from achieving its goals and objectives (Mumford, Zaccaro, Hardin, Jacobs, & Fleishman, 2000). Leaders must also be aware that the best initial course of action may be no action at all in some crisis/conflict situations.

Because today's organizations are characterized by complexity, conflict, and change, leaders must deal with all kinds of ill-defined social problems (Mumford et al., 2000). These are problems that have no clear right or wrong answers and can be solved in different ways. The first issue that leaders face in problem solving is to clearly define what the problems are. Another issue is that sometimes the problems are new and unique, which makes it difficult to obtain accurate, timely, and relevant information due to a lack of precedent. In addition, leaders must solve problems under the pressures of short time and high demands. As a result, they must often solve multiple, rapidly unfolding problems, choosing workable solutions rather than taking time to find the best available solution.

Empathy

In difficult times, followers look up to their leaders for support and guidance. The first thing a leader must do is to provide followers with *empathy*. Leaders display empathy by showing their understanding and consideration of and respect for followers' troubles, and the feelings and emotions generated by a conflict/crisis situation (Anzalone, 2007). They show that they can relate to the experience themselves. By sharing their emotions, followers and leaders establish a bond that helps facilitate and expedite the healing process that individuals and teams must go through after facing crisis and conflict. Leaders should show empathy to followers even when crisis and conflict are not present. Although leaders may not be able to prevent undesirable situations from occurring, by showing empathy they certainly will improve the chance that the team and individuals will endure those situations successfully.

Address and Forge Change

Due to the quickly changing world we live in and our need to keep up with the changes of our globalized world, organizations have become complex, conflict prone, and change driven. Within such an environment, leaders must be capable of adjusting to change in order to be effective and maintain their jobs (Mumford et al., 2000). Thus, leaders must learn to deal with uncertainty. They also must provide their followers with the support they need to cope with the uncertainty and guide them through a constant state of change.

To address and forge change, sport leaders must be able to appropriately communicate change. They must involve and support followers by promoting teamwork and collaboration. They do so by being flexible, earning followers' trust, and displaying dependability and good judgment (Gilley et al., 2008). This entire process is based on honest feedback to and consistent coaching of followers.

Let's look at a hypothetical situation in which you are the director of tickets sales for a major league professional sport team. Because of the team's long-lasting losing record, your organization has been selling discounted tickets to try to increase attendance. Recently, team ownership demanded that you no longer sell discounted tickets. Your sales workforce is not happy about that because they perceive the change will make achieving sales goals almost impossible. What do you do? You will have to clearly communicate what the change entails and convince your staff members that the change is a doable and positive one. As you develop strategies to implement the proposed change, you must deeply involve your team members in the process. By doing so, it is

likely that members of the sales team will buy into the change and work like a true team to accomplish the plan that was devised by the group.

COMMUNICATE CHANGE

Leaders' ability to effectively address and forge change is significantly affected by their abilities to appropriately communicate change and motivate followers to implement it (Gilley et al., 2008). To communicate change appropriately, leaders should first specify the nature of the change and explain the reasons behind it. Next, information about the change is dispersed throughout the entire organization in a timely manner. Following the initial communication, direct supervisors should explain the scope of the change and its implications (including how success will be measured and rewarded) to followers at each level. Finally, leaders should consider followers' responses to the change and address issues that arise (Mayfield & Mayfield, 2002).

INVOLVE FOLLOWERS, PROMOTE TEAMWORK

Followers' involvement and support are critical to successfully addressing and forging change. To involve followers in that process, leaders need to allow followers to meaningfully participate in the process of implementing change, and demonstrate their confidence in the employee's ability to be successful on the job (Zaccaro & Banks, 2004). The first step is to include followers in the process of implementing change by linking followers' self-concepts to values and outcomes articulated in the change plan. In other words, leaders explain the reasons for change and allow followers to help develop the steps to be taken to implement the proposed change. Next, leaders must convince followers they are capable of performing their jobs successfully under the new circumstances. A high level of anxiety is common when change comes. Leaders must assure followers that they can handle change, embrace it, and be optimistic about their future performance. In addition to boosting followers' confidence, leaders must strive to become models for organizational change. The followers will keep a close eye on their leaders' behaviors related to change. Thus, leaders must display the same confidence and positive attitude toward change that they expect from their followers.

After leaders successfully enlist followers' involvement, they must create an environment conducive to collaboration. Working teams must allow members who have diverse skills and backgrounds to effectively communicate and constructively challenge each other's ideas. Effective teamwork and collaboration cannot occur when a hostile work environment, unrealistic expectations, poor communication, poor training, and coercive control are present. Thus, leaders must maintain open communication, share leadership, clearly define roles and work assignments, and value team diversity to successfully promote effective teamwork and collaboration (Gilley et al., 2008).

Leaders who successfully involve followers and promote teamwork when going through change display specific qualities that greatly influence the entire change process. Such qualities include flexibility, ability to earn followers' trust, good judgment, and ability to reward (Zaccaro & Banks, 2004). When addressing change, leaders may not have full control over the situation, so they must be flexible and able to quickly change focus and priorities to successfully guide followers through the process. Followers deal better with change and uncertainty when they work under leaders whom they trust. Trustworthy leaders are fair, dependable, keep commitments, take responsibility for their actions, and empathize with their followers. Due to the uncertainty and stress generated by change, followers greatly benefit from leaders who exercise good judgment. Their decisions are supported by logical, factual information, and consideration of followers' perceptions, views, and emotions. Throughout the change process, leaders should encourage followers' involvement and

collaboration. Followers respond well while being rewarded for incremental change. Such rewards are commonly based on organizational needs and followers' performance.

SUMMARY

Everyone wants to lead and, above all, be a good leader. But, how can you get there? As a sport management student, the time is now to start honing your leadership skills so that you can be effective in some or all of the four general areas discussed in this chapter. Effective undergraduate sport management programs will provide you with good leadership content to help you grasp the basics of good leadership skills. You should consider taking leadership classes in other fields (e.g., business, marketing, and communications) if they are offered at your school, or consider an online course. This chapter drew from research literature other than sport, and that interdisciplinary approach can be effective for sport business leaders in the 21st century because good ideas about leadership can come from anywhere. Being part of or creating the leadership in a sport management club within your sport management program is a great window of opportunity for you not only to enhance your leadership skills, but also to gain field experience and improve your resume. Attending or helping organize student conferences, leadership symposiums, and seminars at your institutions are also great opportunities to learn and enhance your leadership skills. Those are experiences by which you can observe and learn how others lead. Once you have read this chapter and understand the four general areas discussed here along with the many subskills, you will be able to make connections from this chapter to leadership experiences as they arise.

It is never too early to think about internships. Obtaining internships at organizations known to do a good job mentoring students is a good way to develop leadership skills. Because not all sport organizations do a good job mentoring interns, it is a good idea to do some research before you decide which internships you will apply for. You should go to the organization's website and try to find out what interns actually do and what the mentoring opportunities are. You can also contact the person responsible for the internship program and ask about the interns' responsibilities and mentoring opportunities. If possible, talk to interns who have worked there.

Finally, membership in professional sport management associations such as the North American Society for Sport Management (NASSM), International Association of Venue Managers (IAVM), Sport and Recreation Law Association (SRLA), Sport Marketing Association (SMA), and National Association of Collegiate Directors of Athletics (NACDA) is also a great avenue to acquire leadership skills. Many professional organizations provide members with access to leadership books, articles, classes, seminars, webinars, and conferences. In addition, such associations provide members with access to field best practices and networking opportunities.

LEADERSHIP PERSPECTIVE

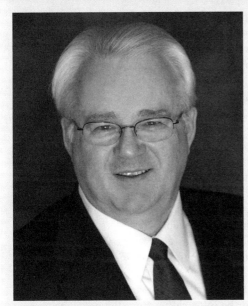

Patrick O'Conner.
Courtesy of Patrick O'Conner

Patrick O'Conner has spent 31 years in professional baseball, including the last 20 in the Minor League Baseball (MiLB) office. He joined the Minor League Baseball staff in May 1993 as Chief Operating Officer and added the title of Vice President, Administration in December 1995. O'Conner was elected the 11th president of Minor League Baseball in December 2007. He was re-elected for a second term in December 2011.

Q: How important is it for an organization like Minor League Baseball to have a vision? How does it influence your daily operations?

It is critically important to have a vision as a core element of a business plan or management team approach. What we have here is a living and breathing entity. It is very important to have a vision and try to envision, predict, and position your company to deal with the challenges that lie ahead of you. It is much more important to be proactive than reactive. It is important to be visionary. What it does on a daily basis for us is to empower a certain element of our staff to deal with today, to execute the vision and plan that was prepared months or years ago. It allows another portion of the staff to look out into the future. When I took my current job, my predecessor who I had worked alongside for 15 years told me: You are going to get paid for what happens in 1 year, 3 years, and 5 years. When you get 1 year out, you will move further ahead of the company. The best asset I can provide as CEO is to keep the company in what we call "deja vu moments." When we get there physically, we have already done it in our minds, in our business, and in our psyche. So we are in the position to effectively deal with various issues that we face. Having a vision is important, but equally important is to check the vision. You don't let it set in stone. Without a vision, you tend to get complacent, tend to get stagnant, and tend to lose whatever edge and assets you have in the market. Eventually, you will lose your market share.

Q: How do you persuade and influence your subordinates in Minor League Baseball to work in a common direction?

It is multifaceted. One way is that you don't have people that work for you; you have people that work with you. There is some distinction between them. If people around you feel that, (1) you are open to suggestions, and (2) their input is not only welcome but solicited and mandatory, they will come prepared to participate. It is much easier to come to a consensus. You need to empower your subordinates. Our discussion is more often about the decision-making process not the decision. You have to empower people to be aggressive. You have to empower people to do what they think needs to be done. You need to empower people to get together and collaborate among themselves. When you do all that, at the end of day, they have a better understanding of why we are doing something and what we are doing, and they are more likely get behind it. That is what we try to do here. We effectively call it the inner circle. It is the people who discuss critical issues facing the company. It is the group that maps strategies. I tell them what they are responsible for is keeping me informed of what has been done, not always coming to check in to see if it is OK to do it. This system ensures that we are operating from a position of consensus within our own ranks. There are so many overlaps to leadership. It starts from the notion, "people don't work for me, but they work with me." There is a general management philosophy that we try to use to govern all of our clubs. I am a firm believer that to manage down or govern from the top down, the information has to come from the bottom up. If you are not the boots on the ground, you would be better talking to the boots on the ground. Often when things didn't work well in an organization, it's because the management didn't enlist the support, the help, and the information from the people who were asked to execute the plan.

Q: How do you deal with a crisis when it occurs? What are the strategies that you used to employ to cope with it?

Whatever you do, don't let your subordinates see you sweat. I think there are a couple of things about this issue. One is that if you know what you are doing and are prepared for every conceivable alternative or every conceivable action or reaction, then you won't be prone to panic. It goes back to the "deja vu moments." Have we thought this through well enough to know most or all of the alternatives? Sometimes, we get caught by surprise. There is a really easy four-step process: first, you need to determine if it is truly a crisis. Then you evaluate the level of crisis and assess what is at stake and what assets are in place. After that, you do a thorough investigation on what your options are, what outcomes you are seeking, and what the options are to get to the outcomes. Finally, you need to implement the chosen option. If you answered the first two questions [note: the first and second interview questions] in a way where people have been brought into the solutions and the process, they will react to a "crisis" in a timely manner. There are a few "don'ts" in crisis management. We don't lay blame. There is plenty of time for that. We don't point fingers. We only assess the problem. We will have that conversation later. There is no finger pointing and blame assessment in crisis management. You simply assess the situation and all the options to get you to the desirable conclusion. Along the way, you need to include your staff as well as human and financial resources, as part of the assessment and investigation process, and plan all the elements. And lastly, but most importantly, you deal with the problem in a calm and orderly fashion.

Q: How critical is the ability to forge or adjust to change?

As it is said, the only thing that never changes is change. You are going to have change. Your best plan can fall short because of external forces and changes beyond your control. We have a saying in baseball: It is a game of adjustments. That applies on the field. If the pitcher tries to get you out on a curve ball, you better adjust your approach or he is going to get you out. If the batter is prone to hit the ball to the right field, you need to adjust to move your outfielder to the right-field side of the diamond. Business is also a game of adjustments. Change is constant. The speed in which change occurs is unbelievably quick now because of technology, and because it is so easy to access information. It is a much more volatile environment and prone to change. It occurs much more quickly. You have to heighten your sense of being on top of your game. But at the core is communication and being able to deal with people. Being able to deal with change may be the second most important thing in the business world today. You need to deal with people in order to address change. People are more important than the change itself. If you are unable and unwilling to deal with change, you basically lack a vision. You will become stagnant. You will become old news.

Q: Among all the leadership skills, which one is the most critical for a sport executive to possess?

Communication is the most critical skill. It is writing and verbal communication. When you look at virtually every aspect of what business is, it is managing people and managing human resources. All physical resources eventually have to be managed by people. It is communication dealing with your constituents, dealing with your clients, the media, and the public. In every aspect of what you are doing, if you cannot communicate effectively, you cannot effectively address, explain, and get people to buy in to your vision. If you cannot communicate effectively, you won't be able to effectively deal with people. If you cannot communicate effectively, your crisis management will fall short. No matter how well you are prepared, how smart you are, and how thorough you are, if you cannot communicate the crisis management actions, you are going to fall short. If you cannot communicate with people and cannot explain the change that you are encountering and soon to encounter, you will not be able to manage them effectively. If you cannot effectively provide communication with written and verbal skills, all your assets will be underutilized.

KEY TERMS

active listening
conceptualization
emotional intelligence
empathy
empowerment
follower

foresight
motivation
self-awareness
self-regulation
stewardship
vision

DISCUSSION QUESTIONS

1. Of all the skills and abilities that the authors deemed important, which ones seem most important to acquire given the ever-changing nature of 21st-century sport leadership? Why?
2. Why are a leader's personal values and beliefs so important to the conceptualization, foresight, and stewardship needed in establishing a vision for a sport organization?
3. Which leaders in sport do you feel embody many of the skills discussed in this chapter? In pairs or groups of three, list at least five sport leaders.
4. Are self-awareness and self-regulation prevalent leadership skills among today's sport leaders, or are sport leaders more likely to act first and think later?
5. Which leadership opportunities are available to you on campus and/or in your hometown? List at least five opportunities.

For a full suite of assignments and additional learning activities, use the access code found in the front of your book. If you do not have an access code, you can obtain one at **www.jblearning.com**.

REFERENCES

Alimo-Metcalfe, B., & Alban-Metcalfe, R. J. (2001). The development of a new transformational leadership questionnaire. *Journal of Occupational and Organizational Psychology, 74*, 1–27.

Anzalone, F. M. (2007). Servant leadership: A new model for Law Library leaders. *Law Library Journal, 99*(4), 794–812.

Avolio, B. J., & Gardner, W. (2005). Authentic leadership development: Getting to the root of positive forms of leadership. *Leadership Quarterly, 16*, 315–338.

Barrett, D. (2006). Strong communication skills: A must for today's leaders. *Handbook of Business Strategies, 7*(1), 385–390.

Bass, B. M., & Riggio, R. E. (2006). *Transformational leadership* (2nd ed.). Mahwah, NJ: Lawrence Erlbaum Associates.

Brown, W. F., & Moshavi, D. (2005). Transformational leadership and emotional intelligence: A potential pathway for an increased understanding of interpersonal influence. *Journal of Organizational Behavior, 26*, 867–871.

Christensen, C. M., & Overdorf, M. (2000). Meeting the challenge of disruptive change. *Harvard Business Review, 78*(2), 67–76.

Gardner, W. L., Avolio, B. J., Luthans, F., May, D. R., & Walumbwa, F. (2005). "Can you see the real me?" A self-based model of authentic leader and follower development. *Leadership Quarterly, 16*, 343–372.

George, J. M. (2000). Emotions and leadership: The role of emotional intelligence. *Human Relations, 53*, 1027–1055.

Gilley, A., Dixon, P., & Gilley, J. W. (2008). Characteristics of leadership effectiveness: Implementing change and driving innovation in organizations. *Human Resource Development Quarterly, 19*(2), 153–169.

Hammett, P. (2004). Strategic foresight: A critical leadership competency. *Leadership Advance Online, 4*, 1–7.

Hernandez, M. (2008). Promoting stewardship behavior in organizations: A leadership model. *Journal of Business Ethics, 80*, 121–128.

Hoppe, M. H. (2007). Lending an ear: Why leaders must learn to listen actively. *Leadership in Action, 27*(4), 11–14.

Kouzes, J. M., & Posner, B. Z. (2002). *The leadership challenge* (3rd ed.). San Francisco, CA: Jossey-Bass.

MacPherson, B. (2013, April 22). Team building with Billy Beane and Theo Epstein. Retrieved from http://blogs.providencejournal.com/sports/red-sox/2013/04/team-building-with-billy-beane-and-theo-epstein.html

Mayfield, J., & Mayfield, M. (2002). Leader communication strategies: Critical paths to improving employee commitment. *American Business Review, 20*(2), 89–94.

McGregor, D. (1985). *The human side of enterprise: The 25th anniversary printing.* New York: McGraw-Hill.

Mealiea, L., & Baltazar, R. (2005). A strategic guide for building effective teams. *Public Personnel Management, 34*(2), 141–160.

Mumford, M. D., Zaccaro, S. J., Hardin, F. D., Jacobs, T. O., & Fleishman, E. A. (2000). Leadership skills for a changing world: Solving complex social problems. *Leadership Quarterly, 11*(1), 11–35.

Pink, D. H. (2009). *Drive: The surprising truth about what motivates us.* New York: Riverhead Trade.

Ryan, R. M., & Deci, E. L. (2000). Self-determination theory and the facilitation of intrinsic motivation, social development, and well-being. *American Psychologist, 55*(1), 58–68.

Slack, T., & Parent, M. M. (2006). *Understanding sport: The application of organization theory* (2nd ed.). Champaign, IL: Human Kinetics.

Smith, M. (2013, January 21). Poised, and dressed, for success at PGA America. *Street and Smith's SportsBusiness Journal.* Retrieved from http://www.sportsbusinessdaily.com/Journal/Issues/2013/01/21/Leagues-and-Governing-Bodies/Bevacqua.aspx?hl=leader%20listen&sc=0

Spears, L. C. (2010). Character and servant leadership: Ten characteristics of effective, caring leaders. *Journal of Virtues and Leadership, 1*(1), 25–30.

Speier, A. (2012, April 13). How success bred a monster: Theo Epstein considers his Red Sox legacy. Retrieved from http://www.weei.com/sports/boston/baseball/red-sox/alex-speier/2012/06/13/how-success-bred-monster-theo-epstein-consider

Under Armour. (2013). Mission & values. Retrieved from http://www.underarmour.jobs/our-mission.asp

Zaccaro, S. J., & Banks, D. (2004). Leader visioning and adaptability: Bridging the gap between research and practice on developing the ability to manage change. *Human Resource Management, 43*(4), 367–380.

CHAPTER 5

COMMUNICATION THAT MOTIVATES AND RESONATES

James Sanderson
Blair Browning

CHAPTER OBJECTIVES

- Recognize and understand the importance of communication skills in leadership.
- Understand and differentiate the different leadership communication styles.
- Recognize the importance of motivation in the workplace and how motivation and communication interact.
- Demonstrate the ability to recognize instances in sport organizations when strong communication is needed to motivate employees.

CASE STUDY

New Jersey Devils' Mission Control

It is no secret that the use of social media has expanded greatly as the marketing and communication departments of professional sport teams attempt to engage and communicate with fans in memorable and exciting ways. Measurable statistics like the number of followers on Twitter and the number of "likes" on Facebook let sponsors and advertisers know the level of fan engagement with a team. In February 2011, the New Jersey Devils of the National Hockey League launched Mission Control, a digital command center specially outfitted with the latest in technology. The command center, converted from a storage closet, is in the executive offices of the Prudential Center, and it is operated by 25 fans known as the Devils Generals (334 fans applied for the open positions). The fans serve as a "sounding board" (Boudevin, 2013, para. 7) for fans like them.

(continues)

Devils management has asked the Devils Generals what kind of content the Devils should be sharing with its fans via social media. The Generals, who are volunteers, manage the team's social media efforts, including Facebook, Twitter, and the Devils Army Blog. Devils leadership believes that real fans operating the Devils social media efforts have a better chance to resonate—or communicate effectively and memorably—with fellow fans. The Devils employ a simple and effective communication strategy. Fellow fans communicate better with other fans because of the common traits they share. The strategy is working. When Mission Control launched in 2011, the team had 5,000 Twitter followers. In February 2013, more than 145,154 people followed the team. At the beginning of the 2011–2012 season, the team had 56,700 Facebook followers. In February 2013, it had 327,390 Facebook "likes." As of February 2013, the Devils were 14th in the National Hockey League in the number of Twitter followers and 15th in Facebook fans and the team ranked No. 1 in fan engagement, which measures how often fans comment on, like, or share social media posts (Boudevin, 2013).

This heightened level of direct communication *from* fans *to* fans has ramifications for sponsorship acquisition and the business side of the Devils. According to *SportsBusiness Journal*, leadership at the Devils began to monetize the social media program 1 year after its launch (Dreier, 2012). Rich Krezwick, president of Devils Area Entertainment, said he has seen the business opportunities that fan-to-fan communication can have for sponsorship sales: "Mission Control has been our lead in sales meetings, not just a throw-in" (Dreier, 2012, para. 2). In 2012, the Devils signed new partnerships with Pfister Energy, T-Mobile, the New Jersey Division of Travel and Tourism, and the New Jersey Lottery. Each of the partnerships is connected in some way to the team's social media hub, Mission Control. The lottery partnership brings with it a title sponsorship of the team's online fantasy game, where users follow player stats during the season. The Travel and Tourism division sponsors a fan-generated photo mosaic where fans submit photos of their favorite destinations in the state (Dreier, 2012).

Fan-to-fan interaction and monetization of fan engagement are only two areas of burgeoning opportunity for marketing departments of professional sport organizations. Using the global positioning systems embedded in many wireless devices, location-based "check-in" platforms are used to unlock marketing offers, help drive ticket sales, and deepen fan connections (Fisher, 2011). Here's how it works: On sites such as Facebook and Twitter, users post what they are doing. It is also possible, using a mobile app, to "check in" and post where they are in the world. Sport executives clearly see the benefit of this technology. If the marketing team for a professional baseball team knows where a fan is placed in the stadium, and members of the team's marketing department know something about that fan's purchasing behavior, they can send him or her offers that are highly specific regarding merchandise, food, or tickets.

Questions for Discussion

1. What are some of the obvious advantages of having fans operate the social media correspondence with fellow fans for a professional sport team?
2. The marketing leadership for the Devils is putting a lot of faith in unpaid employees to reach out to fans. Is there any downside to this strategy?

3. Look at the Facebook and Twitter pages for the Devils. Other than some of the fan-engagement techniques utilized by the Devils Generals on these pages, can you think of other ways Facebook and Twitter can engage fans?
4. What other social-media platforms should professional sport teams be using?
5. Given what was said about check-in platforms, at some point, is there ever a danger of over-communication with fans?

INTRODUCTION

Every stakeholder—whether a customer or an employee—brings different kinds and levels of motivation to bear in his or her relationship with a sport organization, so it is imperative that leaders in sport recognize the value of memorable and effective communication in obtaining desired outcomes from these stakeholders. Communication skills must be nurtured by leaders, evaluated, and adjusted. It is not enough to motivate someone one time; one must continually manufacture an "a-ha" moment to inspire the stakeholder. Communication must resonate and "stick" with the stakeholder to ensure staying power and the ability to motivate. In other words, structuring communication in a way that will achieve buy-in from key stakeholders is more likely to yield sustainable results compared to one-time or scripted messages.

In sport, the importance of realizing, forging, fostering, and maintaining relationships cannot be underestimated. In sport management academic programs, professors impress upon students that sport management is a relationship enterprise, and the more people they meet, the better off they will be when looking for an internship and a job and also moving up in an organization once they have a job. As a leader of a sport organization, whether it is a for-profit or not-for-profit, it is important to forge and foster relationships with both internal stakeholders (followers) and external stakeholders (customers). Because we believe effective communication is such an important skill for sport management students to hone, this chapter will provide information in four primary areas: (1) communication models, (2) different styles of leadership and how communication interacts with that style, (3) explicating how communication motivates employees in sport organizations, and (4) identifying future communication challenges for sport leaders.

This book's definition of leadership includes "moving people towards an imagined future." A leader cannot do that through telepathy. Substantive communication must take place between leaders and followers as well as organizations and customers to move people toward that imagined future.

MODELS OF COMMUNICATION

Communication is the process of transferring information from a sender to a receiver (Thill & Bovee, 2007) through an exchange process whereby information can be shared a multitude of ways, including via a blog, via Twitter, through a presentation, in an employee review meeting, or even through informal chatting near the coffee machine—or more likely these days texting over a cell phone. The Shannon-Weaver Model of Communication shown in **Figure 5.1** illustrates the process of communication and the steps involved (Weaver & Shannon, 1949). By looking at this model, it is easy to see how effective motivation can be thwarted. If the *transmitter* (leader)

FIGURE 5.1 **Shannon-Weaver Model of Communication.**

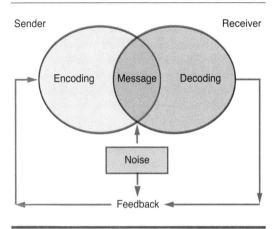

Berlo's theory of communication—although still linear (i.e., sender sends a message, receiver hopefully gets it, but there is little opportunity for feedback)—further refines the Shannon-Weaver model by reducing the number of terms to source, *message*, channel, and receiver. The model identifies important criteria for creating a meaningful message (Berlo, 1960). For a message to resonate between source and receiver, they both must possess similar communication skills. For example, if a sport marketer from a Minor League Baseball team visits an introductory sport management class to give a talk on effective marketing, she would not be able to use much industry jargon (e.g., segmentation, target marketing, ambush marketing, demographics, psychographics) because the students may not be familiar with these words. The information would likely come across as confusing and insignificant. So, it would behoove the class instructor to speak with the marketer beforehand and let her know the level of instruction needed for the talk.

Looking again at Berlo's model in **Figure 5.2,** the source must encode the message through the techniques of content, code, treatment, elements, and structure (Berlo, 1960). Referring again to the sport marketer/classroom example, our speaker must have an overall theme to her message (*content*)—in this case, to help new sport management students understand what effective marketing looks like for a Minor League Baseball team. She might say, "Effective marketing allows our organization to create demand for our products. This will be the main focal point of our talk today." *Code* refers to the form in which the message is sent. Obviously, the messages are sent verbally, but what kind of language is used? Does the speaker use contemporary words and phrases that are likely to resonate with 18-year-old students or language that is likely to resonate only with fellow marketing experts? *Treatment* refers to how the message is conveyed. Does our marketer convey her messages in an unimportant way or does

and the *receiver* (employee or customer) are not on the same *frequency*, "*noise*" is likely to disrupt the intended meaning of the message. For example, the general manager of a Minor League Baseball team may want his staff to increase growth in new fans coming to the ballpark. The leader calls together the sales staff and suggests more cold calls, more word-of-mouth recruiting in towns near the ballpark, and the advertising of more promotions. However, unless the leader recommends how this three-pronged strategy works together or how the work can be delegated among staff members, the message becomes muddled and loses its meaning. The noise here is the lack of specificity and clear direction. In some cases, it is difficult for leaders and subordinates to bridge the gap between different visions of the organization, and shared meaning becomes impossible.

Effective communication occurs when the information shared is understood by both parties.

FIGURE 5.2 **Berlo's SMCR Model of Communication.**

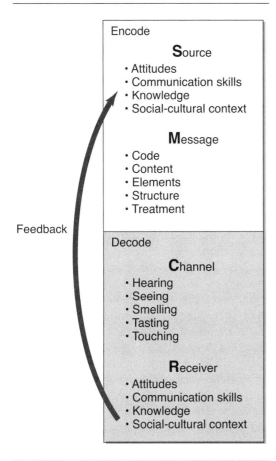

while the message is being conveyed, such as hand movements and body movements. Finally, *structure* refers to how the message is arranged. Is there any organization to the talk? Does the speaker provide examples of effective marketing before she defines what effective marketing is? Does she give a historical analysis of marketing to lay the groundwork? This encoding process needs to take into account the receiver's communication skills. If the receiver does not have similar communication skills as the source, the message may not be completely understood.

LEADERSHIP/ COMMUNICATION STYLES

Definitions of leadership involve an influence relationship. But how does a leader achieve and cultivate this "influence relationship"? Leadership is not formulaic and cannot be scripted in a manner where one style will fit all situations. Because leaders are dealing with different stakeholders from week to week and year to year, a uniform leadership style is not realistic. Certainly, there are styles that individuals are more comfortable using, but this does not mean that they are unable to strategically implement a different style when it is required. Whereas some leadership approaches focus on the leader's traits, personality characteristics, or skills and capabilities, the style approach is unique because it "emphasizes the behavior of the leader" (Northouse, 2012, p. 75).

"My way or the highway." "He's a player's coach." "He's a floor general or a coach on the floor/field." These statements are all well-known and frequently used in the domain of athletics, but they also serve as excellent descriptors of the three main leadership styles described by Lewin, Lippitt, and White (1939): (1) *autocratic*, (2) *democratic*, and (3) *laissez-faire*. In the following section, these leadership styles will be connected to communication approaches in which

she convey the crucial nature of marketing as the backbone of every sport organization? Is she authoritative or casual about her message? Does she use a PowerPoint presentation or a video? Is the information conveyed in an interesting and creative fashion? *Elements* of message encoding refer to other forms of communication seen leaders communicate with internal stakeholders, or followers. Furthermore, a new approach—"sticky" communication—will be discussed as a more contemporary approach to communication. These styles of leadership certainly are not unique to athletics; examples of each of these styles can readily be found in other environments.

Autocratic: "My Way or the Highway"

Lewin et al. (1939) noted that under an autocratic leader, the authority figure decides all policy determinations, techniques, and activity steps. Also called authoritarian leaders, these individuals provide clear expectations for tasks, and the boundaries between leader and follower are clearly delineated. Authoritarian leaders make decisions independently with little or no input from the rest of the group. A pastor who has a hand in everything from preaching the sermon to selecting specific music for worship, or former Ford and Chrysler CEO Lee Iacocca, a renowned autocratic leader, would be examples of this type of leader. Perhaps more than any other vocation, autocratic leaders within sport have always been plentiful. Immediately, George Steinbrenner, the late owner of the New York Yankees, comes to mind. Steinbrenner's tenure was marked by a multitude of manager changes. Steinbrenner was also known universally as "The Boss." During his tenure as owner, Steinbrenner regularly butted heads with his managers, firing them frequently and often not consulting them on what was needed on the field as far as talent. Although Steinbrenner's involvement diminished through the years, this excerpt from Dick Schaap's book, *Steinbrenner*, covers Steinbrenner's all-encompassing leadership style and how it affected his communication approach with his subordinates:

> Steinbrenner's involvement drove [Manager Billy] Martin mad. Martin hated Steinbrenner coming to him with stacks of statistics, telling

him, based on the statistics, who should be in the lineup, and who should be pitching. . . . He hated Steinbrenner's questioning every move he made that backfired, every pinch-hitter who failed, every relief pitcher who struggled. (Schaap, 1982, p. 198)

Steinbrenner's leadership style leaned toward complete control.

As a result of the term "authoritarian," what quickly comes to mind with this style—particularly in sport—is a leader who barks orders at employees and asks for little input to organizational decision making. It paints a picture of someone who demands maximum effort and if he or she does not receive it, the guilty party will quickly find themselves on the unwelcome end of a tongue lashing. Also, an authoritarian leader may communicate their complete control over an organization by acquiring several titles. For example, Jerry Jones is the owner, president, and general manager of the Dallas Cowboys. Given that Jones holds the three most prominent management titles, there may be little room for debate about player personnel and the future direction of the franchise. It can safely be said that Steinbrenner led with a rigid, top-down communication style in which his decisions were not easily questioned. Although it is difficult to know whether Jones possesses the same in-your-face style as Steinbrenner did because we are not privy to behind-closed-doors meetings at the Cowboys headquarters, Jones, and only Jones, is the face of the Cowboys organization.

So, a fair question to ask is this: How does this autocratic style motivate employees? The answer lies in the "bottom line" nature of sports. Many sport organizations are results-driven enterprises, and anything that enables them to achieve their desired success is deemed to be worth it. For example, many professional sport organizations have two important goals: win championships and earn profits. However, yelling at a salesperson or a marketer without purpose would be noise—a message that may be received but is not understood completely. Talking directly and constructively to help an individual maximize his or her talents, particularly talents that are underdeveloped, could possibly lead to successful outcomes.

This concept is embodied by Baylor University women's basketball coach, Kim Mulkey, the only woman to have won a national championship and a gold medal as a player, and national championships as an assistant coach and as a head coach (the latter two at Baylor in 2005 and 2011). Coaching one of, if not the most dominant woman players in history, Brittany Griner, as well as an All-American point guard, Odyssey Sims, Mulkey had to adapt her leadership of this veteran and talented squad in 2012. After soundly defeating Tennessee, Mulkey stated, "What I have to do with this bunch is motivate them. I have to get on them, aggravate them, love them, laugh at them, get mad at them. Whatever it takes" (Voepel, 2012, para. 25). Though certainly not for everyone, the autocratic style is results-driven and can produce exemplary results. Indeed, Lewin et al. (1939) wrote, "Is not democratic group life more pleasant, but authoritarianism more efficient?" (p. 271). Mulkey's approach seems to bridge the autocratic and democratic styles because it shows concern for people, while still driving decisions from the top. Yet, all of the things she may do with her players are for one explicit goal—to get them to play together and win. As Mulkey said, "Whatever it takes." Additionally, Turman and Schrodt (2004) discovered that when coaches' autocratic leadership was moderated by positive feedback, athletes indicated they experienced higher levels of affective learning.

People are the tools necessary to achieve tasks; although this sounds removed, cold, and calculated, it is precisely what Lewin et al. (1939) meant by authoritarianism being "more efficient." After all, Steinbrenner's Yankees teams did win five World Series titles during his 33-year tenure as owner, which would be the envy of any team in Major League Baseball. Autocratic leadership, when mixed with other constructs, can yield optimal results. This suggests that involvement and communication between leaders and followers can net positive results, and this accounts for why some leaders subscribe to the need to communicate and obtain input from followers.

Democratic or Participative

The democratic style of leadership, at times also known as *participative leadership*, enables a more open style predicated on two-way communication—a dialogue rather than a monologue. It is the potential for shared understanding that Duarte (2010) had in mind when suggesting that a speaker find a similar frequency as his or her audience. Lewin et al. (1939) stated, "All policies are a matter of group discussion and decision, encouraged and assisted by the leader" (p. 373). Whereas autocratic is more direct in style, the democratic style has more of a team and supportive approach. Blake and Mouton (1964) examined leadership from the perspective of concern for people and concern for production. Their category of "authority-compliance" aligns with the autocratic style because it notes high concern toward task achievement and a low amount of concern toward the people trying to complete the task. In contrast, a leader equaling out these concern levels by showing high concern for both production and people results in the category of "team management," which corresponds to the democratic style. Indeed, Northouse (2012) observed that this style "places a strong emphasis on both tasks and interpersonal relationships" (p. 81). This type of participatory leadership has helped Major League Soccer (MLS) become a fledgling league that has expanded from 12 teams in 2006 to 19 teams during the 2013 season. Some observers credit the stewardship of

MLS Commissioner Don Garber and his ability to create a consensus among teams and owners about the direction of the league. In separate interviews with AOL Fanhouse and *Street and Smith's SportsBusiness Journal*, Garber is depicted as a commissioner who is open to new ideas, is willing to listen to anyone, and understands the importance of creating harmony among key stakeholders (Mickle, 2009; Straus, 2011).

> I need to create consensus. I need to marshal all the different points of view on any issue. Whether it's an issue about a television contract, . . . about the formation of [Soccer United Marketing], or the folding of teams, our playoff format or our salary budgets, I need to take all the information that exists and all the opinions that exist, many of them differing, and try to move it to the middle to create consensus. (Straus, 2011, para. 63)

Garber likely employs some of both the autocratic and democratic leadership styles. He said he understands that he is the "public face of the league" (Straus, 2011, para. 67), but he has stakeholders that he is beholden to, such as the MLS board of directors and team owners, so dialogue is required to allow MLS to continue to grow.

The leader–follower relationship can be tenuous. A leader who values the interpersonal side may deflect threats to both the organization's cohesiveness and to a follower specifically by engaging in self-handicapping (Carron, Prapavessis, & Grove, 1994). Hardy, Eys, and Carron (2005) noted self-handicapping is employed, "to represent the strategies people use to proactively protect their self-esteem by providing excuses for forthcoming events by adopting or advocating impediments to success" (p. 168). For instance, a marketing and sales director with an inexperienced sales staff may keep some criticisms at bay by constantly reminding the general manager that his or her staff lacks experience. Attributing

employees' mistakes to youth or inexperience to subdue criticism resonates with a democratic style because of the value placed on relationships.

Consider also legendary UCLA basketball coach John Wooden, whose teams won 10 national championships in 12 years and included two of the greatest collegiate players of all time: Lew Alcindor (Kareem Abdul-Jabbar) and Bill Walton. Wooden had a clear focus for how he wanted tasks accomplished, but he also showed concern for player relationships. To be clear, democratic leadership does not mean that leaders get walked on by their subordinates; it simply means that they value relationships as much as tasks. When Wooden was queried about whether he had double standards toward some of the star players on his team, Walton spoke for him. On an *Outside the Lines* report on ESPN, Walton told Jeremy Schaap that Wooden would say, "'Double standard, what are you talking about? I've got twelve standards— one for each player on the team'" (Schaap, 2005). Wooden's philosophy speaks to the delicate balance that democratic leaders strive to achieve. With regard to tasks, Wooden knew exactly what he wanted his followers to do and how he wanted them to do it, but with regard to people, he knew that he needed to adapt to his players rather than expecting and perhaps demanding that his players adapt to him. Wooden understood that each person is wired differently.

Whereas an autocratic leader would communicate to a follower, "I'm the leader, so you adapt to me," the democratic leader is willing to communicate to his followers interpersonally in that he or she believes that such efforts will help his or her followers accomplish the tasks the leader desires. For example, in a study of collegiate athletes, Amorose and Horn (2000) discovered that high levels of intrinsic motivation were associated with athletes who perceived their coaches' leadership and instruction/communication style to be high in democratic and low in autocratic. Similarly, Hollembeak and Amorose (2005) found that democratic behavior from coaches positively affected athletes' autonomy, and therefore intrinsic motivation, whereas autocratic behavior yielded the opposite effect. They suggested that coaches who develop a more democratic style, which includes soliciting input from athletes and adopting some of their recommendations, are likely to have athletes with greater intrinsic motivation. Leadership that allows input from followers can lead to autonomy for those followers, Pink (2009) notes. When a leader communicates to followers that more self-direction is needed for an organization to be successful, followers feel as if they are "acting with choice" (p. 90). This outcome enables leader messages to resonate with followers, enabling goals to coalesce and producing a harmonious work environment.

A hallmark of democratic leadership is its value of participation and communication with followers. However, in some situations, a leader delegates decision-making authority to subordinates and the leader is less conspicuous in making these decisions, although he or she is still involved to some degree.

Laissez-Faire

Most sport organizations do not experience the laissez-faire leadership style in its truest sense—the complete absence of a leader. However, there are some examples that speak to this type of style, albeit indirectly. Peyton Manning has been in the public eye for nearly two decades as a premier quarterback at the high school, collegiate, and professional levels. Fans are used to seeing Manning with the Indianapolis Colts and now the Denver Broncos arrive at the line of scrimmage and strategically perform before the ball is snapped. Manning famously assesses the defense, and then steps back from the line to call an audible (change the play) because of the gaps he observes in the defensive coverage. As the play clock ticks down, it is up to Manning at this point to call the right play based on what he sees in the defense. Although the coach may initially call the play from the sideline, Manning has earned the trust to adapt on the fly.

Manning serves as the field general; this transformation is not unique to the quarterback position. On the defensive side of the ball, the duty of altering play calls often falls into the hands of the middle linebacker. On the basketball court, it is typically the point guard and in baseball, the catcher is often tasked with everything from shifting the defensive alignment of teammates on the field to calling pitches. Not all coaches are comfortable surrendering this control, but players at these key positions are often empowered to make big decisions like those just listed as they occur in real time. They each serve as a leader on the field or floor and the leader off the field of play delegates these responsibilities because of trust, which reflects a healthy leader–follower relationship. These behaviors encompass what Lewin et al. (1939) described as laissez-faire leadership in that there is, "Complete freedom for group or individual decision . . ." (p. 273).

Turning to the world of sport management, specifically event management, it is not possible for the top executives of a minor league hockey team to oversee every facet of management of a regular season game. The executives have to rely on their employees to be leaders in their own right and make decisions on the fly. From the moment the doors are open to the arena, a minor league hockey game is a flurry of activities that include selling tickets, greeting customers, organizing promotions on the concourse and on the ice before the game and during intermissions, and keeping the arena clean and safe for patrons. Decisions need to be made about how to manage these activities smoothly. Leaders empower capable employees to make these decisions by communicating the task and then letting the employee carry it out.

Effective communication is needed to lead teams of followers in managing events successfully.
Courtesy of John Borland

Although laissez-faire leadership is frequently associated with the complete absence of a leader, the previous examples demonstrate that there are situational episodes in which laissez-faire leadership is appropriate. Although these incidents are unique to game situations, the more traditional sense of laissez-faire leadership—the literal absence or a void in leadership that has been created through a variety of circumstances—also manifests in sport. These events range from a leader no longer wanting to lead; to a leader knowing their term is up and, as a lame duck, not wanting to make any decisions that will impact a future or their legacy; to a leader being cognizant that their leadership is temporary. This state of transitory leadership affects how the leader communicates and how motivated the employees ultimately are in carrying out the organization's vision.

Sticky Communication

The past few sections have discussed some common communication styles of leaders that have stood the test of time. But, because we are well into the second decade of the 21st century, more contemporary thoughts on communication and leadership have emerged with more emphasis on the receiver of the communication. In sport business, where team victories and gate receipts are at stake, meaning that millions of dollars hang in the balance, organizational communication must benefit both leaders and followers (Daft, 2003). With the ease and frequency of communication so prevalent thanks to social media, the quality of communication between leaders and followers has now come into focus, leading to different conceptualizations of communication put forth by contemporary scholars. For communication to have a long-lasting effect, or for it to "stick," it must fully resonate with an audience. "*Resonance* occurs when an object's natural vibration frequency responds to an external stimulus of the same frequency" (Duarte, 2010, p. 4). In her book *Resonate*, Duarte discusses the importance of getting to know one's audience and understanding what is truly important to them. You cannot communicate well with a key stakeholder, whether it is an employee or a sponsor, until you truly understand the stakeholder's needs and wants. As you can see, the older, linear model of communication of Shannon-Weaver falls by the wayside in favor of the idea that the deliverer of a message needs to better understand the receiver of a message before noise can truly be avoided. When one has learned about the audience through marketing research (if it is a customer) or active listening (if it is an employee or a customer), it is much easier to communicate to them on their level, or their "frequency," as Duarte puts it. Furthermore, Duarte (2010) notes that a successful presentation of ideas must understand the hearts and minds of the audience to which the communication is geared. If a servant or transformational leader truly has a follower's best interests at heart and either want to serve the follower above all else or transform the follower to reach a higher level of productivity, it is important to understand the follower's needs to improve communication between the two. This understanding can be done simply by listening.

In the case study that opened the chapter, the New Jersey Devils' leadership understands that using fans to manage the Devils' social media platforms strikes a chord with fellow Devils fans who are contributing content to the Devils' social media platforms and reading what is being contributed by the Devils Generals. The Devils Generals "resonate" with the legion of fans following the Devils. Resonation defined differently, and perhaps more simply than Duarte's "frequency" conceptualization, can be seen in Malcolm Gladwell's bestselling book, *The Tipping Point* (2002), in which it

is referred to as *stickiness*. Gladwell noted that the messenger (for example, a general manager of a baseball team) is not the only thing that matters in helping a message spread:

> . . . the content of the message matters too. And the specific quality that a message needs to be successful is the quality of "stickiness." Is the message . . . memorable? Is it so memorable, in fact, that it can create change, that it can spur someone to action? (p. 92)

Any sport leader would jump at the chance to uncover the secret formula that would enable their messages to both resonate and motivate their employees and convince external stakeholders to do business with their organizations. Unfortunately, no perfect algorithm exists that will produce this winning combination across any situation; again, internal and external stakeholders have different levels of motivation. Nevertheless, there are communication strategies that leaders can employ to accomplish these designs.

MOTIVATING WITH MEMORABLE MESSAGES

Duarte (2010) referenced the importance of people being on the same frequency when communicating with one another. In particular, she suggests creating common ground with your audience and, more boldly, "get to the know hero" (Duarte, 2010, p. 55). Although she was speaking more about getting to know your audience before giving a formal presentation to them, her communication ideas can be utilized for day-to-day communication between managers and for communication from leaders about an organization's vision. This leads to a pressing question: What communication techniques do leaders use to achieve this frequency and motivate their followers? *Motivation* is often achieved by framing a message so that subordinates interpret it in such a way that they see it in their self-interest to perform the tasks that leaders think will help the organization survive and thrive. Although it is true that motivation also can be internal, even conscientious self-starters required someone to select them in the first place. Leadership is evident throughout all aspects of an organization, ranging from the assembly of the team (who is hired or recruited), to putting team members in the best positions to succeed and matching their talents with other team members, to conceptualizing the right goals that this particular team is capable of achieving. Although people may perform well because they are intrinsically motivated, the leader still has to place that person on the team in the first place and facilitate a situation that enables them to maximize their talent. Motivation, like leadership, is not formulaic, but whether it is based on incentivizing or an inspirational speech, the message must be memorable.

Stohl (1986) defined a memorable message as a message that individuals remember for a long period of time that had a major influence on their life. Barge and Schlueter (2004) used the notion of memorable messages to explore what kinds of messages new members attuned to during organizational entry and how those messages "would influence the way they construct their relationship with an organization" (p. 234). This research applies seamlessly in sports, for example, when considering the recruitment of a new sport management graduate to an organization. Every leader wants to offer some type of message that will stay with the individual and that will ultimately influence their transition to the new organization. A message that is memorable to one person may not be so to another, which creates a difficult task for leaders. One new employee may be motivated by messages about extrinsic rewards, such as salary, benefits, and prestige, whereas another new employee might be more intrinsically motivated and hopes to hear messages about

self-directedness and the impact an organization can have on its community. More than likely, new employees will possess both intrinsic and extrinsic motivations.

In their best-selling book, *Freakonomics*, Levitt and Dubner (2005) wrote that all individuals respond to economic, moral, and/or social incentives. These incentives are forms of communication. Whether Major League Baseball (MLB) pitcher Zack Greinke ever wanted to live in Los Angeles probably became a moot point when the Dodgers offered him a 6-year contract worth a guaranteed $147 million with the potential to have it increase to $158 million. *Economic incentives* are powerful, and not just for the individuals signing lucrative contracts. It is common for players and coaches to have incentives in their contracts that are activated based on performance (e.g., number of games played, reaching a certain bowl game or the NCAA tournament). For most people, economic incentives are quite motivating. Of course, they do not come without problems because they could increase selfishness, which leaders then have to manage. Although it is unlikely to happen, it would be interesting to see sport agents negotiate collective goals as incentives into contracts.

Moral incentives can be powerful as well, because employees may want to work for an organization with which they share similar beliefs. It may simply be that a leader has painted such a bold and audacious vision for the organization that it requires faith to believe in this vision and that incentive can be powerful as employees come together to make it happen. The 2012–13 National Football League (NFL) season saw the debut of a rookie head coach and rookie quarterback with the Indianapolis Colts, Chuck Pagano and Andrew Luck, respectively. Pagano was diagnosed with leukemia in the fifth week of the season and had to leave the team, prompting responses that ranged from players (and even a couple of cheerleaders) shaving their heads in solidarity to the launch of wristbands that said "Chuck Strong."

About a month later, in week 9 of the NFL season, Pagano made his first trip back to the stadium and met with the team, where he said the following:

> I got circumstances. You guys understand it. I understand it. It's already beat. It's already beat. My vision that I'm living is to see two more daughters get married, dance at their weddings and then hoist that Lombardi several times. I'm dancing at two more weddings and we're hoisting that trophy together. (Smith, 2012)

All-Pro Colts receiver Reggie Wayne said the room was very teary-eyed and that there was not a player in the locker room who was not going to give everything they had to get Pagano a "W" that day (Smith, 2012). Motivation cannot be manufactured, and when it truly inspires and transforms people the results are amazing. The 2011 Colts team went 2–14, but the 2012 version went 11–5 and qualified for the postseason, a visible indicator that they responded to the motivation they received from their coach.

Finally, Levitt and Dubner (2005) discuss *social incentives*, which typically consist of things that make us feel liked, respected, or appreciated. They also could entail the camaraderie of the team that a leader oversees. For example, in perhaps the most (in)famous case of National Basketball Association (NBA) off-season free agency, the Miami Heat lured the two biggest free agents, LeBron James and Chris Bosh, to join perennial All-Star and friend, Dwyane Wade. Although many believed that this tilted the axis of power in the NBA too much to one team, the players' salaries all fit within the salary cap. However, working with one's friends, where the employee knows that he or she is well liked, respected, and appreciated, could certainly provide a strong social incentive.

Social incentives are powerful (McLaren, 2002). Sometimes, the motivating factor can be that a person feels they fit in and once that cohesion is experienced, they believe they can conquer the world. Yet, Carless and DePaola (2000) have argued that task cohesion is more important than social cohesion. They stated, "Improved group performance is more likely to accrue from targeting behaviors that enhance commitment to the group task rather than behavior that increases people's liking for one another" (p. 72). This hammers home the fact that a leader has to wear many hats; finding the right message to reach the right team members can be a difficult task, but it is why they have been chosen for the role—leaders lead.

FUTURE CHALLENGES

One leadership style cannot be used for every situation and every person. This may have worked in the past when media coverage was more regional, but in today's media environment where incidents can instantly become national news and players have access to social media channels with sizeable audiences who can exponentially retransmit messages, sport leaders must be more reflective in their leadership. This is not to suggest that players and others in sport organizations should not be held accountable, but rather that sport leaders must be cognizant that their decisions extend well beyond their immediate circle, and it is more difficult to cover up problems.

With respect to sport leaders, it is clear that cover-up is not an option. Sooner or later, incidents will come to light (consider the fallout at Rutgers University over its men's head basketball coach in April 2013), and no longer can fear of bad publicity in the present be considered an acceptable exchange for the reality of bad publicity in the future. Leaders in sport organizations must be accountable and take the necessary steps to confront and address a crisis. Clearly, this is not an easy task, and yet, being a leader requires rising to meet challenges in less than desirable circumstances. Sport leaders who proactively address issues, while perhaps taking some lumps, will be much better off than those who elect to conceal problems in the hope that the incident will not be discovered. *Not* communicating something important, such as a violation of ethics, can lead to lawsuits and a broken image, as cyclist Lance Armstrong, baseball player Ryan Braun, and other athletes who have been linked to performance-enhancing drugs have discovered. Armstrong is an appropriate example here because he was seen by many as the leader of the Livestrong movement to fight cancer and the leader of the U.S. Postal Service's cycling team. Indeed, such an approach is naïve, because it is extremely difficult for sensitive information to stay under wraps in today's media era.

The technological environment in which we live also highlights another challenge that sport leaders face—social media. Social media has become a dominant force in sports (Sanderson, 2011a) and has greatly changed sport organizations' ability to control information. Whereas all sports have been affected to various degrees by social media, collegiate athletics represent a unique venue. Social media is a primary communicative avenue utilized by college students, and student-athletes are no different than their peers in their desire to utilize these platforms. Yet, the content of many college students' social media postings can become problematic, and this extends to student-athletes as well. As a result, coaches and athletic administrators have taken a variety of approaches in dealing with social media, including restricting and prohibiting its use and contracting with third-party vendors to monitor student-athletes' social media postings. In perhaps the most extreme case, Old Dominion head football coach Bobby Wilder has implemented a policy that bans players from using Twitter for the entire time they are on scholarship (Minium, 2012).

Interestingly, research indicates that leadership with regard to social media in collegiate athletics is lacking (Sanderson, 2011b). Many athletic departments either do not have social media policies, rely on ambiguous policies, or do not educate student-athletes about social media, a remarkable stance considering education is the primary mission of the institution.

Sport leaders face more challenges than those discussed in this chapter. However, we believe that it is paramount that sport leaders be assertive in meeting and addressing challenges, rather than concealing these problems, and that sport leaders embrace and lead with respect to technological changes, particularly collegiate athletics. Sport leaders are under a microscope more than ever, and it is imperative that leaders adapt to their followers, yet still retain accountability for their decisions.

Finally, sport leaders, particularly coaches, must be mindful of *power* and *influence*, and use these in positive and productive ways. Richmond and McCroskey (1984) defined power as "an individual's capacity to influence another person to do something he/she would not have done had he/she not been influenced" (p. 125). Coaches and other sport leaders use power as a vehicle for influence. Sport leaders who use their power as a vehicle toward accomplishment will find themselves in a productive and harmonious environment, where they work in concert with their followers to accomplish collective goals. But power and influence can be taken too far—so far, in fact, that leaders hoard information and do not feel the need to communicate decisions to followers. This lack of transparency has been seen time and again in both college and professional sport.

SUMMARY

This chapter discussed different leadership/communication styles in sport and the role of forms of motivation in leading people to achieve and accomplish goals. It forged a path from the first communication models of the mid-20th century, including some popular leadership styles that are still prevalent, to newer, more contemporary ways of thinking about communication and motivation. Furthermore, the authors explicated some of the challenges that sport leaders face with regard to the instantaneous nature of communication. As sport management students read this chapter, there are some important takeaways:

- Try to understand your audience before communicating with them because this understanding will make it easier to come up with messages that are "sticky."
- Although you are likely savvy regarding the newest forms of technology and ways to communicate quickly, your co-workers may not be (including your boss), so be

sure to understand how people want to be communicated with.

- Honesty is the best policy when communicating bad news about something that has gone wrong in an organization. Make sure the message that you send out from top leadership to external stakeholders is consistent.
- Continue to hone your oral and writing skills because both are likely to be invaluable as you enter the workplace and move into leadership roles.

Although the way we communicate has become more efficient in the 21st century, substantive communication is as important as ever.

LEADERSHIP PERSPECTIVE

Kevin DeShazo.
Courtesy of Kevin DeShazo

Kevin DeShazo is the founder of Fieldhouse Media, an organization that provides social media education to student-athletes and coaches. The company also provides social media monitoring for athletic departments through its FieldTrack software, which helps to facilitate education and promote compliance with an athletic department's social media policy.

Q: What challenges does social media create for leaders of athletic departments and coaches?

It has created numerous challenges, the biggest being that social media gives student-athletes an outlet to share their unfiltered thoughts to a global audience. They're 18–22 years old, and firing off a tweet or Facebook post without thinking can lead to some serious repercussions—both for the individual and for the department. The challenge comes in how do you allow them the freedom to use these tools that the world is using to communicate, while limiting the risk involved? That comes through education. Education can help individuals avoid costly mistakes, as well as give them a foundation and strategy on how to use it in a positive, purposeful way.

Q: A popular decision by leaders of collegiate athletic programs is to restrict or ban student-athletes from using some social media platforms, primarily Twitter. Is this an effective strategy? Why or why not?

It is a horrible strategy. For one, they ban Twitter but allow Facebook. If they're saying something inappropriate on Twitter, they're saying something inappropriate on Facebook. Secondly, there's no tangible benefit to banning it. Social media use has no impact on an athletic event. Turner Gill banned Twitter while at Kansas and the football team won two games. Oklahoma State allowed players to tweet, and won 11 games including a BCS game. Coaches want to eliminate distractions, but social media is not a distraction unless your players are tweeting in practice or during games—if that's the case, the coach has bigger problems. There's also the issue of the players making new accounts and not telling coaches. They're not just going to sit around and not use a platform that all of their friends are using. They'll get around it. We saw South Carolina players posting to Twitter from Instagram. Not technically "tweeting," but still getting their message out. We have to acknowledge that these platforms are here and do what colleges were intended to do—educate.

Q: Some athletic directors and coaches restrict/prohibit student-athletes from using social media, yet use these tools themselves or promote their use for other stakeholders. Does this create a leadership disconnect?

This is a big issue in collegiate athletics. Coaches will ban it, yet use it themselves or allow their staff to use it. Many times they'll use social media in recruiting, then ban the kids once they're on campus. What example does that set? That shows a lack of trust, which drives a wedge between players and coach. There needs to be some consistency and some trust. And, of course, some education for all involved.

Q: In your view, what qualities separate those administrators and coaches who embrace social media from those who do not?

Wow. Great question. For one, a willingness to change. To realize that times and people change, and coaches have to adjust. That doesn't mean they change their coaching style, but their leadership style and tactics have to adapt. Those who love to learn seem to be more open to social media. They may or may not be comfortable with it, but they know it's a part of today's world and they can't ignore it, so they spend time trying to figure out what it's all about. The bigger difference is in education. Those who embrace it have educated themselves and have experienced the good of social media. Those who don't embrace it typically have no idea what "the tweeter" is.

Q: How can embracing social media have positive outcomes for leaders in collegiate athletics?

There is so much good it can bring to a program. You have the opportunity to directly reach a large amount of people who are specifically interested in your program—as well as general sport fans. Social media allows them to feel a greater sense of attachment and ownership. This leads to more engaged, passionate fans, which leads to butts in seats and dollars spent. You can promote your teams/players/coaches on a global scale, gaining attention in places that could lead to new recruits and/or new people applying for the university. The ROI [return on investment] is tremendously higher than spending thousands of dollars on marketing campaigns, given that social media only costs time.

KEY TERMS

autocratic

communication

democratic

economic incentives

frequency

influence

laissez-faire

message

moral incentives

motivation

noise

participative leadership

power

receiver

resonance

social incentives

stickiness

transmitter

DISCUSSION QUESTIONS

1. What are the differences among autocratic, democratic, and laissez-faire communication/leadership styles? Can you think of leaders in sport who personify each style of communication through their leadership?
2. In what ways can an autocratic communication style be successful in sport? Are there sports where a particular communication style is more accepted than another?
3. What are the advantages to collegiate athletic departments educating student-athletes about social media? Do you agree that banning or restricting social media use is an appropriate strategy? Explain your thoughts.
4. After the Texas Rangers were eliminated from the 2012 MLB postseason, Rangers President Nolan Ryan publicly criticized star player Josh Hamilton for trying to quit smokeless tobacco during the season, and insinuated that was the reason Hamilton's performance diminished over the season. Based on what you have learned in this chapter, do you think this was a good leadership communications strategy? Explain your answer.
5. What are some of the future challenges you see for leaders and their communication strategies within sport organizations?

For a full suite of assignments and additional learning activities, use the access code found in the front of your book. If you do not have an access code, you can obtain one at **www.jblearning.com**.

References

Amorose, A. J., & Horn, T. S. (2000). Intrinsic motivation: Relationships with collegiate athletes' gender, scholarship status, and perceptions of their coaches' behavior. *Journal of Sport and Exercise Psychology, 22,* 63–84.

Barge, J. K., & Schlueter, D. W. (2004). Memorable messages and newcomer socialization. *Western Journal of Communication, 68,* 233–256.

Berlo, D. K. (1960). *The process of communication.* New York: Holt, Rinehart and Winston.

Blake, R. R., & Mouton, J. S. (1964). *The managerial grid: The key to leadership excellence.* Houston, TX: Gulf.

Boudevin, J. (2013, February). Mission control takes over Prudential Center's social media. *Venues Today.* Retrieved from http://www.venuestoday.com/news /detail/mission-control-expands-0220

Carless, S. A., & DePaola, C. (2000). The measurement of cohesion in work teams. *Small Group Research, 31,* 71–88.

Carron, A. V., Prapavessis, H., & Grove, J. R. (1994). Group effects and self-handicapping. *Journal of Sport and Exercise Psychology, 16,* 246–258.

Daft, R. L. (2003). *Organization, theory and design.* Independence, KY: South-Western College.

Dreier, F. (2012, January 9). Devils' social hub starts to pay off. *Street and Smith's SportsBusiness Journal.* Retrieved from http://www.sportsbusinessdaily. com/Journal/Issues/2012/01/09/Franchises/Devils. aspx?hl=Mission%20Control%20Devils&sc=0

Duarte, N. (2010). *Resonate: Present visual stories that transform audiences.* Hoboken, NJ: Wiley.

Fisher, E. (2011, November 28). Checking out check-in platforms: As location-based apps catch on with consumers, marketers map out ways to use the technology to find new business. *Street and Smith's SportsBusiness Journal.* Retrieved from http://www .sportsbusinessdaily.com/Journal/Issues/2011/11/28 /In-Depth/Lead.aspx?hl=check-in&sc=0

Gladwell, M. (2002). *The tipping point: How little things can make a big difference.* New York: Little, Brown and Company.

Hardy, J., Eys, M. A., & Carron, A. V. (2005). Exploring the potential disadvantages of high cohesion in sports. *Small Group Research, 36,* 166–187.

Hollembeak, J., & Amorose, A. J. (2005). Perceived coaching behaviors and college athletes' intrinsic motivation: A test of self-determination theory. *Journal of Applied Sports Psychology, 17,* 20–36.

Levitt, S. D., & Dubner, S. J. (2005). *Freakonomics: A rogue economist explores the hidden side of everything.* New York: Harper Collins.

Lewin, K., Lippit, R., & White, R. K. (1939). Patterns of aggressive behavior in experimentally created social climates. *Journal of Social Psychology, 10,* 271–301.

McLaren, B. (2002). *More ready than you realize: Evangelism as dance in the postmodern matrix.* Grand Rapids, MI: Zondervan.

Mickle, T. (2009, March 16). How Dan Garber helped MLS get its game on. *Street and Smith's SportsBusiness Journal.* Retrieved from http:// www.sportsbusinessdaily.com/Journal/ Issues/2009/03/20090316/SBJ-In-Depth/ How-Don-Garber-Helped-MLS-Get-Its-Game-On .aspx?hl=democratic%20leadership&sc=0

Minium, H. (2012, September 15). ODU football Twitter ban among most restrictive in U.S. Retrieved from http:// hamptonroads.com/2012/09/odu-football-twitter- ban-among-most-restrictive-us

Northouse, P. G. (2013). *Leadership: Theory and practice* (6th ed.). London, UK: Sage.

Pink, D. H. (2009). *Drive: The surprising truth about what motivates us.* New York: Riverhead Trade.

Richmond, V. P., & McCroskey, J. C. (1984). Power in the classroom II: Power and learning. *Communication Education, 33,* 125–136.

Sanderson, J. (2011a). *It's a whole new ball game: How social media is changing sports.* New York: Hampton Press.

Sanderson, J. (2011b). To tweet or not to tweet . . .: Exploring Division I athletic departments' social media policies. *International Journal of Sport Communication, 4,* 492–513.

Schaap, D. (1982). *Steinbrenner!* New York: Avon.

Schaap, J. (2005). Interview with John Wooden and former UCLA players. Retrieved from http://www.youtube .com/watch?v=_sgLFGf8UTA

Smith, S. (2012). Colts coach Chuck Pagano gives emotional speech in 1st trip back to stadium since leukemia diagnosis. Retrieved from http://www.cbsnews .com/8301-400_162-57545174/colts-coach-chuck- pagano-gives-emotional-speech-in-1st-trip-back-to- stadium-since-leukemia-diagnosis/

Stohl, C. (1986). The role of memorable messages in the process of organizational socialization. *Communication Quarterly, 34,* 231–249.

Straus, B. (2011, February 25). MLS commissioner Don Garber: Soccer's steward sits down with FanHouse. *AOL News.* Retrieved from http://www.aolnews.com/2011/02/25/mls-commissioner-don-garber-american-soccers-steward-sits-down/

Thill, J. V., & Bovee, C. L. (2007). *Excellence in business communication* (8th ed.). Upper Saddle River, NJ: Prentice Hall.

Turman, P. D., & Schrodt, P. (2004). New avenues for instructional communication research: Relationships among coaches' leadership behaviors and athletes' affective learning. *Communication Research Reports, 21,* 130–143.

Voepel, M. (2012, December 19). Baylor devours Lady Vols. Retrieved from http://espn.go.com/womens-college-basketball/story/_/id/8761112/women-college-basketball-baylor-lady-bears-devour-tennessee-lady-vols

Weaver, W., & Shannon, C. E. (1949). *The mathematical theory of communication.* Urbana: University of Illinois Press.

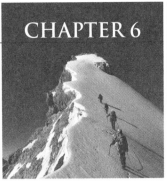

CHAPTER 6

APPLYING A PRINCIPLED AND ETHICAL APPROACH TO SPORT LEADERSHIP

Meg G. Hancock
Mary A. Hums

CHAPTER OBJECTIVES

- Demonstrate an understanding of a historical grounding of ethics in the sport industry.
- Discuss ethics and ethical decision making within the context of sport and sport organizations.
- Recognize chronic and emerging ethical issues in sport at various levels.
- Establish a framework for becoming an ethical leader.

CASE STUDY

Donor Gifts and Athletic Departments

The majority of Division I athletic departments' expenses substantially outweigh revenues, and as the cost to compete continues to rise (Knight Commission on Intercollegiate Athletics, 2010), university presidents and intercollegiate athletic directors will continue to seek out donations from wealthy alumni/ae, athletic boosters, and major corporations. Donations to university athletic departments have not been without controversy. One recent example occurred when Florida Atlantic University (FAU) announced an agreement in which GEO Group, the second largest for-profit prison operator, to donate $6 million over the next 12 years in exchange for the opportunity to name a soon-to-be-constructed football stadium for the FAU athletic program (Myerberg, 2013). The controversy began soon after FAU made the announcement. Student groups and

(continues)

community organizers protested the naming rights deal based on reports citing the company for numerous corruption and abuse allegations at its prison facilities (Myerberg, 2013). The U.S. Occupational Safety and Health Administration (OSHA) cited the company for violations at its prisons, but the company has contested those findings (Ostrowski, 2012). After the initial protests, the university leadership indicated it would stand behind the naming rights deal. However, only days later, following mounting pressure by student groups and community organizers, the university announced that the gift by GEO Groups would be withdrawn (Vasquez, 2013).

This is not the only example of controversy surrounding donor gifts to support university athletics. There have been concerns raised that athletic departments can be influenced by donors when those donors are providing significant amounts of financial support. Phil Knight, the founder of Nike and graduate of the University of Oregon, has given large sums of money in support of the University of Oregon's athletic programs (Sharp, 2011). There have been questions raised regarding whether the size of the donations, over $300 million to both the university and the athletic department, has resulted in Knight having influence over decision making within the athletic department (Rosenberg, 2011). A similar situation has also developed at the University of Maryland. Kevin Plank, the founder of Under Armour and graduate of the university, has provided $1.7 million in financial support to the University of Maryland athletic department since 2007 (Barker, 2011).

For the near term, it does not appear that expenses for college athletic departments will be declining. Therefore, the necessity for leaders in intercollegiate athletics to seek out the financial support of wealthy donors will continue. However, given the potential for controversial partnerships or for questions regarding the influence of boosters, athletic directors and other leaders in intercollegiate sport must follow ethical decision-making principles when considering donor-supported funding for university athletic programs. In addition, athletic directors must recognize the potential ethical issues that may arise when accepting substantial financial contributions in support of athletics.

Questions for Discussion

1. An important part of the ethical decision-making process is to first recognize an ethical dilemma. Considering the examples provided in this section, why would donations of large sums of money by wealthy athletic supporters or by owners of controversial companies lead to potential ethical issues for leaders in intercollegiate athletics?

2. What situational factors in intercollegiate athletics can provide athletic directors with the tools to successfully navigate an ethical dilemma? Read through the chapter to help answer this question.

3. Explain how you could use the ethical decision-making model described in the chapter to avoid entering into the same type of controversy over naming rights that was described in the case study.

INTRODUCTION

A recent study of professional sport teams, leagues, and federations valued the global sport industry at $480–$620 billion (A.T. Kearney, 2012). Plunkett Research estimated the size of the sport industry in the United States alone to be $435 billion. Even more astonishingly, the sport industry is growing faster than the gross domestic products in Brazil, Russia, India, and China as well as markets in North America and Europe (A.T. Kearney, 2012). In the United States, the "Big Four" professional sport leagues—Major League Baseball, the National Basketball Association, the National Football League, and the National Hockey League—combined accrue $23 billion in gate, media, and sponsorship revenues annually. Of the 32 NFL teams, 20 are valued at over $1 billion (Ozanian, 2012). On the intercollegiate level, sport revenue for the National Collegiate Athletic Association (NCAA) reached over three-quarters of a billion dollars (Plunkett Research, 2012). Media rights negotiations between the Big 12 Conference, ABC/ESPN, and Fox in 2012 resulted in a deal worth $2.6 billion over 13 years (McMurphy, 2012). Mathematically, the deal equates to $20 million per school per year. The International Olympic Committee (IOC) expects to pass $4 billion in global broadcast revenues for the 2014 and 2016 Olympic Games contracts (Mickle, 2012).

We are all keenly aware of the monetary magnitude of the sport industry. This industry is not alone in piling up billions of dollars or euros in revenues annually. However, we must also be keenly aware that with financial success come opportunities for pitfalls, missteps, and temptations along the way.

The National Business Ethics Survey (NBES) found that the most profitable companies were at a greater risk for unethical behavior and employee misconduct. The study found only 62% of employees were confident in the ethical decision making of their immediate supervisors and top-level

management. Moreover, nearly one-third of the employees surveyed said their supervisors did not model ethical behavior. The survey also indicated an increase in the percentage of employees who perceived pressure to compromise personal and professional standards, experienced retaliation after reporting misconduct (whistle-blowing), and perceived a weak organizational culture of ethics (Ethics Resource Center, 2012).

Although the NBES was not specific to the sport industry, it is important to consider that as sport continues to grow on a national and global scale, many youth, intercollegiate, professional, and international sport organizations may face similar ethical challenges. In 2010, Ohio State was given the moniker "Tattoo U" when football players were found to have exchanged team memorabilia for free tattoos. Also from 2002–2010, 73 current and former players on the University of Miami football team were implicated in a scandal that alleged that a booster provided players with, among other things, cash and prostitutes (Robinson, 2011). Finally, in what were perceived to be two of the most egregious scandals in college sport since Southern Methodist University received the "death penalty" from the NCAA for providing football student-athletes with impermissible benefits. A year later, Penn State defensive coordinator Jerry Sandusky was indicted and charged with the sexual abuse of eight boys over 15 years. Athletic Director Tim Curley resigned when allegations of abuse surfaced. Head football coach Joe Paterno and university president Graham Spanier were subsequently fired.

Lest we forget, NFL scandals have also made headlines in recent years, including "SpyGate" (New England Patriots), "Bounty-gate" (New Orleans Saints), Michael Vick's incarceration for dog fighting, and Plaxico Burress's self-inflicted gunshot wound from an unregistered handgun. Major League Baseball is rife with allegations of performance-enhancing drug use (see Barry Bonds, Mark McGwire, Manny Ramirez, and Melky Cabrera). Scandals even arise in youth leagues. In 2001, Danny Almonte and the Rolando Paulino All-Stars were stripped of their Little League World Series wins because Almonte was found to be 2 years older than Little League rules permitted (Malley, 2011). Incidents of violence involving parents at youth sporting events also persist. Then there was the seemingly infallible Tiger Woods and allegations of rampant adultery. In 2012, the U.S. Anti-Doping Agency and the International Cycling Union both stripped Lance Armstrong of seven Tour de France victories and instituted a lifetime ban amid allegations of performance-enhancing drug use.

In short, the domain of sport has suffered from questionable ethical practices if not downright unethical behavior. Although many of the aforementioned examples focus on athletes, this chapter will focus on the sport leader. We begin with a historical grounding of ethics in the sport industry, followed by a section on ethics and ethical decision making within the context of sport and sport organizations. We offer information regarding chronic and emerging ethical issues in sport at various levels. The chapter concludes with a framework for becoming an ethical leader.

HISTORICAL BACKGROUND

The modern sport industry evolved around 150 years ago in England. Since then, nearly every segment of the sport industry has encountered and addressed the unsavory and questionable behavior of players, coaches, and administrators. Money, or a bottom line approach, has significantly influenced the decision-making process in sport. Consider the development of the club system to better manage the growing complexities of gambling in the thoroughbred racing industry to ensure fair and honest racing (Crosset & Hums, 2012b). Then came the Black Sox Scandal of 1919, after which, in 1921, Major League Baseball (MLB) banned eight players for intentionally

losing games during the 1919 World Series in exchange for promises of large sums of money (Malley, 2011). In 2008, National Basketball Association (NBA) referee Tim Donaghy was sent to prison after it was revealed he not only bet on NBA games, but also may have been involved in the orchestration of a small-time gambling ring affiliated with organized crime.

Eight Chicago White Sox players conspired with gamblers to throw the World Series in 1919. The players were banned from Major League Baseball in 1921.
Courtesy of *The Sporting News*

Social issues have also contributed to the complexities of ethical decision making. In 1947, Jackie Robinson was the first baseball player to break Major League Baseball's color barrier. To put this into perspective, it would be another 7 years before the U.S. Supreme Court declared segregation unconstitutional. Pierre de Coubertin, the father of the modern Olympic Games, claimed: "An Olympiad with females would be impractical, uninteresting, unaesthetic, and improper" (Boulongne, 2000, p. 23). Although de Coubertin felt the inclusion of female athletes was "uninteresting," a number of scientists and medical doctors felt women's participation in sport was downright unhealthy, positing that physical activity could inhibit a woman's reproductive capability. Today, more women participate in sport than ever before. However, gender fraud, medical conditions such as hyperandrogeny, and the participation of transgender athletes have served as catalysts for policy (re)formation, such as sex testing by national and international sport governing bodies.

Historically, violence and the health and safety of athletes have led to intense ethical debate. Recently, the inclusion of athletes with disabilities has taken center stage in the United States and in countries around the world. Regardless of level or industry segment, you, as a sport management professional, will encounter situations that will require you to consider your personal values and the values of others. In these moments, you may begin to consider which behaviors or decisions are ethical versus those that are not. This chapter is designed to help you gain a better understanding of your own ethics and the ethics of others, ethical dilemmas, and ethical decision-making models.

ETHICS AND ETHICAL DILEMMAS

In our experience, few questions in a classroom cause students to shrink into their seats more than a discussion on ethics. A class that has been responsive and talkative all semester suddenly becomes eerily quiet. After a few seconds of silence, we pose the question again, "What is ethics?" More silence, then a muffled voice comes from the corner of the room, "The difference between right and wrong." The greatest consternation among students occurs in the debate around what or who determines right and wrong, as well as the context in which those determinations are made. *Ethics* is, in essence, the difference between right and wrong, but the difference is rarely so black and white. Perhaps the response, or lack thereof, reflects the "grey zone where clear-cut right versus wrong answers may not always exist" (Sims, 1992, p. 506).

Ethics and sport are perfect examples of the "grey zone"; they seem inherently contradictory (Volkwein, 1995). In one breath, we espouse the value of sport in teaching character, good sporting conduct, healthy lifestyles, and the importance of teamwork. In the next breath, we may cheer for a team whose players, coaching staff, and owner have been accused of orchestrating a bounty system in which players receive rewards for injuring opposing players. Think about it: When you learned about the New Orleans Saints' bounty system, what were your initial reactions? Some of you may have reacted with outrage, whereas others may have taken the stance of "every other team does it, the Saints just got caught."

DeSensi and Rosenberg (1996) suggested the contradiction between sport and ethical behavior stems from a capitalistic, "win at all costs" mentality, which has "misguided or misdirected individual thoughts and actions" (p. 5). Perhaps another reason many students become uneasy when discussing ethics is because the word seems to elicit the perception of judgment grounded in personal values. Ethics is, in fact, the "systematic study of *values* guiding our decision making" (Crosset & Hums, 2012a). More simply, ethics is moral principles that govern decisions and behavior. *Morals*, then, are the enactment of ethical principles. It is important to understand the foundation of ethical philosophies (Malloy & Zackus, 1995) so that you, as a sport professional, can (1) identify your personal biases and (2) identify the personal biases of employees and stakeholders. Each tradition is briefly explained in the following sections.

Philosophical Traditions

Two dominant philosophies are perceived to govern ethical decision making and behavior—*teleology* and *deontology*. Teleology suggests decisions can be judged good or bad, right or wrong based on the consequences of those decisions (DeSensi & Rosenberg, 1996). In other words, the fundamental principle of teleology is for the outcome of a decision to result in the greatest good for the most people (Volkwein, 1995). In 1972, the federal government passed Title IX, which outlawed sex discrimination in educational institutions receiving federal financial assistance. The intention of Title IX was to provide women equal opportunity, equal access, and fair treatment in educational settings. Increased athletic participation was a by-product of Title IX. Less than 300,000 women participated in interscholastic sport in 1972 compared to 3.6 million men (National Federation of State High School Associations [NFHS], 2012). Today, over 3.2 million women participate compared to 4.4 million men (NFHS, 2012). From a teleologist's perspective, Title IX passage was a "good" decision because it positively impacted the lives of millions of young women and men.

A second philosophical approach, deontology, contends the right decisions are those that are in accord with conduct, duties, or rules agreed upon by a community or society (DeSensi & Rosenberg, 1996). Repercussions of decisions are of no consequence because the decision was grounded in principle (Malloy & Zakus, 1995). Consider the case of Elijah Earnhart, the 6-foot, 300-pound 12-year-old who wanted to play Pee Wee football. During a preseason weigh-in, Earnhart was deemed "too big to play" because he exceeded the 135-pound weight limit set by the Pee Wee Football Association (PWFA). Ultimately, Earnhart was denied the opportunity to play. The PWFA president explained, "Rules are rules" (Ray, 2012). Rules are the principles that guide the governance of the PWFA.

As a sport manager, rarely will you find yourself or your staff members declaring allegiance to teleology or deontology. You may discover some of your staff making decisions for the "greater good" whereas others will make decisions based on principle. Although ethical traditions may help us understand the philosophies that guide decision-making behavior, they do little to help us identify and respond to ethical dilemmas.

Ethical Dilemmas

According to Volkwein (1995, p. 311), an *ethical dilemma* or moral dilemma exists "whenever an action is involved." More specifically, a dilemma exists when the action has the potential to harm or benefit others (Jones, 1991). The action must also be considered within the context of a community and the social norms to which that community subscribes. Social context is important because it defines what is legal and morally acceptable in a given community.

Sport managers encounter ethical dilemmas from youth to professional levels regarding issues pertaining to equity, diversity, competitive fairness, legal matters, personnel, and, more recently, technology and the use of social media (DeSensi & Rosenberg, 1996; Hutchens, 2011). On a daily basis, sport managers encounter myriad ethical dilemmas, some more unusual than others. The following section addresses current and emerging ethical issues in youth and interscholastic sport, intercollegiate athletics, professional sport, and sport internationally. As you read through each section, consider some of the ethical dilemmas you think leaders in sport might encounter.

YOUTH SPORT

For the purpose of this section, youth sport includes young men and women participating in recreational and interscholastic athletics. In a 2004 report compiled by Hedstrom and Gould, the Institute for the Study of Youth Sports (ISYS) documented critical issues influencing youth participation in sport, which included participation and retention, health and safety concerns, and equity. In addition to these current issues, the sport leader would be remiss if he or she failed to acknowledge the emerging presence of youth with disabilities. The participation and retention of youth in recreational sport has been identified as a concern because recent data confirms the number of youth participating in sport is on the decline. Consider this: Over 35 million youth participate in sport each year. That number drops to 7.5 million by the time students reach high school (National Center for Sports Safety [NCSS], 2012). The decline has been attributed to cost of participation, lack of interest, poor experiences with peers, poor experiences with coaches, and lack of opportunity (for girls) (NCSS, 2012).

Although health and safety issues (e.g., nutrition, training errors, lack of qualified coaching) have long been a concern of youth sport managers, several recent highly publicized events have brought attention to hazardous playing conditions and the growing rate of injuries due to overuse or inadequate equipment. Heat-related illnesses and lightning strikes, in particular, have claimed the lives of youth athletes and spectators. A study by the National Center for Sports Safety (NCSS, 2012) found that nearly 3.5 million children age 14 or under receive medical treatment for sport injuries each year. Additionally, the NCSS reported, "injuries associated with sports and recreational activities account for 21 percent of all traumatic brain injuries among children in the United States" (para. 4). Between 1982 and 2002, 256 athletes died while participating in high school sport (NCSS, 2012).

One of the challenges faced by youth sport leaders is hiring knowledgeable coaches who can also exercise sound judgment about playing conditions. Hedstrom and Gould (2004) contend finding quality coaches is critical to enhancing the experience of youth, while also ensuring health and safety. Unfortunately, the pool of qualified youth sport coaches is relatively shallow (Hedstrom & Gould, 2004), and most recreational and interscholastic programs offer little training.

Training may also require financial commitment from the coach, prohibiting some people from being involved.

Some ethical dilemmas are more complicated than others. Regardless of the dilemma, the decision has consequences—positive and negative—for those involved. Let's go back to the example of Elijah Earnhart, the boy deemed "too big" to play Pee Wee football. The president of the PWFA was faced with an ethical dilemma—to let Earnhart play despite his size or to ban him because of his size. The president's statement, "Rules are rules," seems simplistic and may reflect the PWFA president's ethical philosophy; however, it is important to recognize this ethical dilemma has repercussions for a number of individuals—players, coaches, and parents. Imagine, for a moment, you are Elijah. How do you feel about being banned from Pee Wee football? Imagine you are the parent of a child on a team opposing Elijah's. How do you feel about his ban? As the president of the PWFA, how would you go about making the decision? Would you consider what benefits the greater good? Do you stick to the rules? What factors would play into the decision-making process? Not sure where to begin? The following section offers suggestions on ethical decision making.

INTERCOLLEGIATE ATHLETICS

Intercollegiate athletics has a history dating to the 1800s, and has been marred by the questionable behavior and decisions of players, coaches, fans, and administrators. The National Collegiate Athletic Association (NCAA) was founded in 1906 to "protect young people from the dangerous and exploitive athletics practices of the time" (NCAA, 2012b, para. 1). A report by the Carnegie Foundation issued in 1929 condemned colleges and universities for "academic abuses, recruiting abuses, payments to student athletes, and the commercialization of athletics" (Barr, 2012, p. 165). Not surprisingly, many issues organized intercollegiate sport faced over 150 years ago persist today. Intercollegiate athletic departments, conferences, and the NCAA continue to wrestle with topics such as student-athlete health and safety, "pay for play" and extra benefits, the commercialization of sport, and equity (racial, gender, and disability).

Student-athlete health and safety has been identified as an area of concern for the NCAA and intercollegiate athletic programs. The recent deaths of current and retired NFL football players O.J. Murdock, Junior Seau, Ray Easterling, and Dave Duerson brought to light the profound effects of repetitive head injuries. Additionally, a study on young athletes ages 15 to 24 found the majority of concussions occurred in football, women's soccer, wrestling, and women's basketball; the concussion rate of girls was nearly twice as high as that of boys (Marar, McIlvain, Fields, & Comstock, 2012). Subsequently, the NCAA developed a partnership with the Centers for Disease Control and Prevention (CDC) to ensure student-athletes are "properly protected from and treated for concussions" (NCAA, 2012a, para. 1). Although the NCAA and CDC have taken steps to educate administrators, student-athletes, and coaches, we all know examples of student-athletes competing with concussions or other injuries. Many student-athletes feel pressure to compete regardless of injury, so how can intercollegiate athletic administrators monitor injuries? Should administrators intervene if it may mean the team loses a star athlete or a game? What if the star athlete in question has a potential professional career in sport? Should he or she be required to sit out a contest where scouts are present?

Perhaps the issue of student-athlete health and safety is a product of the "win-at-all-costs" mentality of a multi-million-dollar sport industry. In 2011, the NCAA reported revenues in excess of $838 million, which included an initial $617 million payout from a 14-year, $10.8 billion contract with Turner Broadcasting and CBS Sports (NCAA, 2012c). Although the revenues of the NCAA are still shy of professional sport organizations and leagues, the amount of revenue generated has created concern about the commercialization of college sport as well as the benefits—or lack thereof—afforded to student-athletes. Other companies, like EA Sports, have profited to the sum of millions from using the likenesses of NCAA student-athletes. As top-tier college programs such as Ohio State, Miami, and North Carolina continue to recover from "extra benefit" scandals, coaches and administrators debate whether such benefits would be eliminated if student-athletes were paid for their performance. Given the profitability of college sport, administrators must grapple with questions, including: Should student-athletes be paid? If so, which student-athletes and how much? Does paying some student-athletes and not others create issues of equity among all student-athletes?

The ethical dilemmas in college athletics are plentiful and plague intercollegiate administrators, coaches, student-athletes, and fans. Thus, it is important for leaders in sport to consider the scope of their decisions. Who is involved? Who is affected? And, at what cost to the person(s) and organization? How can you make the best decision? Finally, it is important to consider that your decision might have repercussions for industry segments other than your own.

PROFESSIONAL SPORT

The world of professional sport is also littered with ethical dilemmas, whether on the field or in the front office. In North American professional sport, the "Bounty-gate" scandal in New Orleans, where players were allegedly offered monetary rewards for targeting and injuring specific opponents in the NFL, resulted in not only players being sanctioned, but also front office staff (Nagler, 2012). Were the sanctions too harsh? Too lenient? The debate continues. One question was how involved and informed the front office was of this questionable player behavior.

A completely different ethical dilemma facing people in the front offices of professional sport franchises deals with the current state of the economy. It has become evident that the sport industry is not recession-proof. As money gets tight, owners and general managers must make decisions about laying off front office employees. Workforce questions in a tight economy become even more complicated in the face of labor disputes. The 2012 NHL lockout resulted in actions like those taken by the St. Louis Blues, which laid off employees and forced other employees to work fewer hours (Logan, 2012). The ethical dilemma here is: Which employees are deemed expendable and which can remain? What happens to employee benefits during this time? One more ethical issue deals with the front office controlling players' ability to express their opinions. Major League Baseball's Miami Marlins Manager Ozzie Guillen created a firestorm of controversy by making public comments praising Cuba's Fidel Castro. The team responded by suspending him for five games (Thompson & Macur, 2012).

In another case, Brendon Ayanbadejo of the NFL's Baltimore Ravens was publicly criticized by a Maryland state legislator after the player publicly supported same-sex marriage. The legislator called on the Ravens ownership to silence Ayanbadejo; ownership refused (Klemko, 2012). These are two very different examples of team management weighing in on the ethical dilemma of what opinions an employee should be able to publicly express. Similar dilemmas exist in intercollegiate athletics with regard to student-athletes' use of Twitter.

INTERNATIONAL SPORT

There may be no industry more global than sport, and that scope brings with it some interesting situations. First of all, sport managers working in an international environment will work with people from different cultures, and different cultures may deal with ethical issues differently. For example,

Sholtens and Dam (2007) found there were significant differences in ethical policies among firms headquartered in different countries. This means that sport managers working in a diverse workplace will need to be cognizant of this and also respectful of it. For example, although some people may feel that not allowing women the opportunity to compete in the Olympic Games is discriminatory, others may feel just the opposite (Al Nafjan, 2012). These are two dichotomous views, and sport managers need to be aware of them. Issues will vary in importance depending on where one lives and works.

Some of the most discussed ethical issues internationally revolve around the world's most popular sport—football (soccer). The president of the international federation governing football, Sepp Blatter of FIFA, has been a lightning rod for the organization's allegations of corruption and a lax approach to racism on the pitch (Associated Press, 2012; Murphy, 2011). Match fixing by players and referees seems commonplace and sometimes part of the culture of the sport. Officials are finally starting to step up and take concerted actions to try and rein in this blot on the sport's character (Bang, 2012). Another issue clouded with ethical questions is the awarding of the location of the World Cup, the sport's flagship event. The recent awarding of the 2022 World Cup to Qatar has sparked controversy over a voting scandal (Sale, 2012).

The Olympic and Paralympic Games are not without their own ethical dilemmas. Every time the Olympic and Paralympic Games—or almost any other international major multisport event for that matter—are staged, a host city will need to build new sport facilities. Often, this results in the displacement of people living where the new construction takes place. In Beijing, nearly 1.5 million people were to be displaced during preparations for the 2008 Summer Olympic and Paralympic Games (Bulman, 2007). The Games in Seoul, Barcelona, and Athens also resulted in displacements. Already, there is word that the 2016 Games in Rio de Janeiro will see many people having to move due to forced evictions (Zirin, 2012).

ETHICAL DECISION MAKING

Every day, leaders and managers in sport are faced with ethical dilemmas that require decision making. As a student still learning about the sport industry, you are likely to be less familiar with certain ethical dilemmas than senior-level administrators are. The purpose of this chapter is not to make you aware of every ethical dilemma in sport, but rather to prepare you to identify and address ethical dilemmas in a manner that is congruent with the law and values in a sport organization and the larger sport community. Many *ethical decision-making models* are out there for your consideration, but the critical factor in each is the initial recognition that an ethical dilemma exists. Once the dilemma is identified, the decision-making process can commence. Ethical decision making is complex and includes the consideration of multiple factors (Beu, Buckley, & Harvey, 2003). When engaging in ethical decision making, Cooke (1991) offers five cautionary points (pp. 250–251):

1. Decision making is a process of reasoning through an actual or potential dilemma.
2. Reasonable people may disagree about which ethical course of action is appropriate.
3. Not all ethical situations are clear cut.
4. There are seldom "quick fixes" to an ethical dilemma.
5. Sound management practice requires the assessment of all relevant information.

When resolving ethical dilemmas, a number of variables have the potential to impact the decision maker and, thus, the decision itself. As Cooke (1991) points out, decision making is a process of reasoning. Reasoning is the process of making a fair decision (Crosset & Hums, 2012a). Furthermore, people you perceive to be reasonable (i.e., of sound judgment) may disagree. This disagreement is, in part, due to their personal values and experiences, ethical foundations, and moral principles. It is important for you, the sport manager, to identify and understand variables so as to reduce bias as you try to reach a final decision (Cooke, 1991). Variables influencing the decision-making process happen at two levels: individual and situational (Sims, 1992; Sinha & Mishra, 2011).

Individual

Individual factors include demographics, personality, and cognitive moral development. As sport becomes more global, populations of athletes, coaches, and administrators become more diverse. Gender, age, race, cultural variables (e.g., birth nation, religion, political and religious affiliations), and sexual orientation are but a few demographic factors that influence our ethical philosophies, moral actions, and ethical decision making (Beu et al., 2003; Kuntz, Kuntz, Elenkov, & Nabirukhina, 2012). For example, studies have shown that women and people of color are underrepresented in all levels of coaching and sport management (Acosta & Carpenter, 2010; Lapchick, 2011). The underrepresentation of these groups has been attributed to discriminatory hiring practices; white, male-dominated organizational structures; and stereotypes about women and people of color. When it comes to hiring practices, women and people of color may be more sensitive to ethical issues and dilemmas due to the personal relevance of their experience (Kuntz et al., 2012).

As another variable, everyone brings his or her own individual personality to the workplace. Over the years, psychologists have defined personality in various ways. For the purpose of understanding personality as it applies to ethical behavior, personality is defined as "a pattern of relatively permanent traits, dispositions, or characteristics that give some consistency to people's behavior" (Lefton, Brandon, Boyes, & Ogden, 2005, p. 14). Personality is shaped by heredity as well as environmental influences such as family and social groups, culture, and behavior in specific situations (Chelladurai, 2006).

Cognitive moral development (CMD) also has been identified as an individual factor that has the potential to affect ethical decision making. CMD is an active process in which people learn that a behavior is right or wrong. Although multiple theories of CMD exist, the most important component to CMD is acknowledging that social, cultural, and demographic variables aid in the formation of what behaviors people perceive to be "right" and "wrong." Thus, when presented with an ethical dilemma, reasonable people may use different cognitive processes to resolve it (Beu et al., 2003).

In sum, the way people perceive a situation may be determined by their experience as a member of a particular demographic group, their cognitive development, and/or their personality. Thus, it is important for a sport manager to recognize how these variables affect the ethical decision-making process.

Situational Factors

Situational factors are, perhaps, the most important and difficult factors to navigate because they account for the interaction among organizations, the law, and the social norms of a community. Organization factors include the structure, culture, and socialization practices of a given company, business, or team (Jones, 1991). Thus, organization factors play a critical role in ethical decision making and behavior. In other words, these factors may influence otherwise reasonable people to make poor ethical decisions and engage in unethical conduct.

Structure represents the division of labor in an organization. Additionally, structure establishes the formal and informal flow of communication through the organization. The manner in which information about the organization is communicated is critical to establishing an organizational culture. *Organizational culture* is established by communicating an organization's mission, goals, values, employee attitudes, and policies. Many organizations establish a code of ethics or an *ethical code of conduct*. These codes are sets of rules in an organization that guide behavior. As suggested by Helin and Sanstrom (2007), the mere existence of an ethical code of conduct does not ensure ethical behavior. Furthermore, "not everyone in an organization has a moral orientation or is willing to do the right thing" (Komives, Lucas, & McMahon, 2007, p. 181). To be effective, a code of conduct should be a part of organizational culture and, ideally, the behavior of the people at all levels of an organization should reflect this code.

Socialization is the process of integrating a person into a particular environment. It requires introducing employees to organizational rules and expectations, culture, and behavior. The socialization process is a critical organizational factor to consider. As a leader of a sport organization, it is important to consider how information about organizational goals, codes of conduct, and expectations are communicated, as well as who is engaged in communicating such information.

Other situational factors beyond the sport organization itself include external forces that have the potential to significantly impact your sport organization. External forces may include the economy, government and law, the use of technology, social and media perception, competition, and fan behaviors. When external forces affect your organization, they also affect how you make decisions within and about your organization and employees. Although external forces affect the decision-making process in terms of what and how information is considered, it is up to the sport manager to ensure decisions remain ethical.

To illustrate, in the late 1990s Nike was the most profitable sporting goods organization in the world. Associated with top-name athletes like Michael Jordan, Bo Jackson, Deion Sanders, and Tiger Woods, Nike soon found itself embroiled in controversy over child labor issues, toxic work environments, and substandard working wages in factories overseas. Its labor practices with regard to workers in developing countries were put under the microscope. Nike's image was tarnished in the media, which affected consumers' perception of the organization.

The Ethics Resource Center (2012) found that companies behave differently during economic difficulties in that managers and employees tend to make more ethical decisions. It is not clear why decisions are more ethical at this time. It could be assumed, however, that people make more ethical decisions in a time of uncertainty because they perceive ethical behavior is important to retaining their jobs. Conversely, the Center also found that ethical behavior declines during periods of economic growth. So what does that mean for a growing and profitable industry like sport? Does it mean that in times of economic growth, people in organizations are less ethical? No, but it does illustrate the importance of understanding how an external force, like the economy, has the potential to affect ethical decision making.

Individual and situational variables have the potential to affect the ethical decision-making process. Given the myriad of factors, how can one person make sense of it all? First, it is important to understand that one person cannot make sense of it all. If anything, that is where ethical decision making goes wrong. Remember the discussion on how individual factors like race, gender, culture, age, and experience affect how we perceive issues? Ethical decision making requires social interaction with other people (Cottone & Claus, 2000). More importantly, it should include interaction with people who share perspectives, experiences, knowledge bases, and backgrounds different from your own. Once you have those people in the room and the ethical issue has been identified, the decision-making process can begin.

Ethical Decision-Making Models

Now that you have an understanding of factors to consider when making an ethical decision, let's turn our attention to applying what you know. Please note, ethical decision-making models do not make ethical decisions; instead, they describe a process for examining a situation (Cottone & Claus, 2000). There are hundreds of ethical decision-making models that cannot possibly be addressed in this chapter. Instead, we will focus on two types of decision-making models—issue-contingent (Jones, 1991) and practice-based (Hums & MacLean, 2008).

ISSUE-CONTINGENT

The issue-contingent model (Jones, 1991) shown in **Figure 6.1** is different from practically based models. Issue-contingent ethical decision making places more emphasis on identifying the characteristics of an ethical dilemma. The foundation of the issue-contingent model is the concept of moral intensity. Moral intensity is a multidimensional construct composed of five components: magnitude of consequences, social consensus, probability of effect, temporal immediacy, and proximity. Intensity varies from issue to issue; therefore, it is contingent on a situation.

Think back to the discussion on ethical philosophies. Remember teleology—a decision should benefit the most people? *Magnitude of consequences* is just that—how many people will benefit from or be harmed by the decision. For some ethical dilemmas, the magnitude of consequences of the corresponding decision may be minimal; for others, the consequences could be extensive. *Social consensus* is the amount of agreement in an organization or community that the proposed decision is "good" or "bad" *Probability of effect* is the likelihood that the

FIGURE 6.1 **Ethical decision making by individuals in organizations: An issue-contingent model.**

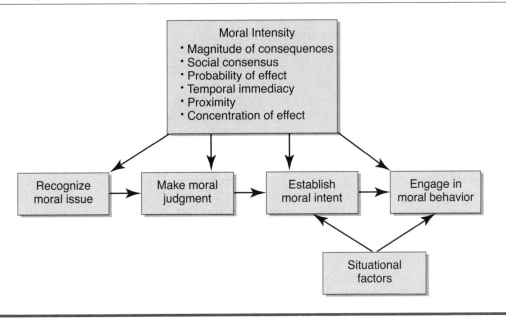

Source: Reproduced from Jones, T. M. (1991). Ethical decision making by individuals in organizations: An issue-contingent model. *Academy of Management Review, 16*(2), 366–395.

decision will result in the benefit or harm of a group or individual, as predicted. The time that elapses between the point at which an ethical decision is made and when the consequences resulting from the decision surface is *temporal immediacy*. Depending on the situation, some decisions must be made and executed in a short period of time, whereas other decisions occur over a span of weeks, months, or even years. Similarly, some decisions will result in immediately observable consequences; other consequences may unfold over time. *Proximity* is the "feeling of nearness (social, cultural, psychological, or physical)" (Jones, 1991, p. 376) the decision maker(s) has for individuals who could be affected by the decision.

Moral intensity is the manner in which a decision maker considers an ethical dilemma. A key factor in understanding moral intensity, however, is the decision maker's ability to recognize the moral element of their decision (Jones, 1991). In other words, as a sport manager, it is important to recognize that your decision will affect other people and you have a choice when addressing an ethical dilemma. Rarely will you encounter a situation in which there is only one course of action. It is possible you may feel as though there is no "right" or "good" decision. If you feel that way, remember that you have a choice, and you are responsible for the consequences of that choice. This is known as a *moral judgment*. When you make a moral judgment, all of the factors (i.e., individual, organizational, industry) influencing the decision-making process are in play. The moral judgment is your understanding of what is "right" and "wrong" within a given context.

Finally, moral intent is a person's intention to act on a particular decision. A sport manager may choose a "right" judgment about how to handle an ethical dilemma. However, several factors such as pressure from a supervisor, career advancement, or negative media perception may prevent the decision maker from implementing the "right" decision. For example, many unethical decisions were made during the Penn State sex abuse scandal. According to reports, Joe Paterno, Tim Curley (then athletic director), and university president Graham Spanier settled on a plan of action for addressing sex abuse allegations against Jerry Sandusky. That plan included reporting the offense to an outside law enforcement agency. Curley then contacted Spanier via email and indicated that, following a discussion with Paterno, the two decided it would be best to handle the matter internally. The three men agreed not to report the "shower incident" to authorities despite the acknowledgment that failure to report such an egregious observation would leave the Penn State athletic department "vulnerable" (Balingit, 2012).

The Penn State case tells us that moral intent does not equal moral behavior. Moral behavior is engaging in a "right" or "good" plan of action to solve an ethical dilemma. One example of moral behavior would be Jeff Long's (Athletic Director, University of Arkansas) decision to fire head football coach Bobby Petrino. While at Arkansas, Petrino returned the team to prominence in the Southeastern Conference, including an appearance in a BCS bowl his second season. Despite his on-field success, Long said Petrino "engaged in a pattern of misleading and manipulative behavior" (ESPN, 2012, para. 4), which included covering up an affair with a staff member.

The components of moral intensity, when combined with moral judgment, moral intent, and moral behavior, are effective guides for identifying an ethical dilemma. Now that you understand how to identify a dilemma, the following section provides a simple, practice-based model for addressing the issue.

PRACTICE-BASED

We make personal and business decisions every day when we gather and analyze information and then act upon that information. These decisions can be as simple as where to park at work or as complicated as who a sport organization chooses to lay off in hard times. To an extent, all business decisions are ethical decisions to a greater or lesser degree. A critical element of ethical decision making is having a framework to guide you through ethical dilemmas. One such model suggested by Zinn (1993) has been modified for use in the sport industry (Hancock & Hums, 2011; Hums & McLean, 2008) and includes the following steps:

1. Identify the correct problem to solve.
2. Gather all pertinent information.
3. Explore codes of conduct relevant to one's profession or to this particular dilemma.
4. Examine one's own personal values and beliefs.
5. Consult with peers or other individuals in the industry who may have experienced similar situations.
6. List decision options.
7. Look for a win–win situation if at all possible.
8. Ask the question, "How would my family feel if my decision, and how and why I arrived at my decision, were posted on the Internet tomorrow?"
9. Sleep on it.
10. Make the best decision possible, knowing it may not be perfect.
11. Evaluate the decision over time.

Let's step through this model with an example. You are the athletic director at an NCAA

Division II school. Your men's basketball coach is well known among Division II circles and has done a good job carrying out the mission of Division II athletics. The coach has an excellent win/loss record, but, more importantly, he has been skillful at developing young men and helping them understand that getting an education is more important than success on the basketball court. He has often talked to his players about the evils of alcohol and drugs. The coach has asked to meet privately with you in your office. Because you are a strong supporter of the basketball team, the coach knows you well and trusts you. But what he has to say comes as a surprise. He tells you, "I have been going to Alcoholics Anonymous meetings secretly for the past 2 months because I'm pretty sure I have a drinking problem." Becoming visibly emotional, he pleads with you, "I needed to tell someone so I came to you . . . but please don't tell the president [of the university]. I could lose my job and be disgraced. Everything I worked for would be gone." You are definitely on the horns of an ethical dilemma.

Let's identify the problem first, which in this case, is what to do with the information the coach has just shared. Next, you need to gather as much information as possible about how the coach came to believe he had a drinking problem, the school's culture and the culture of the athletic department, who may know and not know already, and laws about confidentiality. Codes of conduct that may be of help would include clauses dealing with confidentiality or treatment of people with alcoholism.

Next, you need to examine your personal values and beliefs. Perhaps you harbor certain feelings about people with alcohol addiction, perhaps you know and trust the president of the college much more than the coach does, or perhaps you know someone who also has an alcohol addiction. All those factors may enter your mind when making your decision. Although you can know and name those values and beliefs, you may need

to step back from them to examine the whole picture. After looking into your own values and beliefs, you need to reach out and consult others whose judgment you trust and respect such as other athletic directors or even friends. Sit down and make a list of decision options, including who needs to know about his condition, not telling the president, or telling the president.

This decision is complex and involves some heavy issues and personal information. It must be made rationally and fairly. You may think your decision will never see the light of day, but in this world of social media, your decision and what went into it may show up anywhere. How would your family feel about how you decided on a course of action? When possible, sleep on your decision. What this really means is take as much time as you possibly can to make your decision. Ethical decisions must not be made too hastily, yet the reality of an athletic director's life is that the decision must be made in a timely fashion. After that, make what you perceive to be the best decision possible. Finally, you will need to evaluate the decision. This will take time, but you will need to look back and see how your decision played out in the long run.

An ethical decision-making model like this can help a sport manager make some sense from the chaos that often surrounds an ethical dilemma. Situations requiring ethical decision making are never simple or straightforward. Having a structure to follow helps one map out the best decision possible.

BECOMING AN ETHICAL LEADER

You have no doubt heard the adage, "What is popular is not always right. What is right is not always popular." Managing ethical issues effectively requires that sport administrators and employees know how to recognize and deal with ethical dilemmas in their everyday work lives (Sims, 1992). As we have discussed, you will have to identify ethical dilemmas and engage in ethical decision-making processes that require an awareness of personal and professional values, situational contexts, and consequences. For those decisions, you will be either reviled or revered. Thus, it is important that as an ethical leader you are fair, honest, and trustworthy.

Whether you supervise yourself or a staff of 100, it is up to you to construct the ethics and morals that will guide your conduct and, hopefully, the conduct of others. As previously discussed, a code of ethics is one way to establish a culture of ethics in an organization. Additionally, the ethical leader must empower employees to identify and report unethical behavior. For example, in 2006, Anucha Browne Sanders said she was fired from her job with the New York Knicks after she filed a sexual harassment lawsuit against the president of basketball operations and NBA legend, Isiah Thomas. In college athletics, administrators and coaches have lost their jobs after reporting episodes of discrimination, harassment, or other questionable behaviors by school officials. A code of ethics and a well-defined reporting structure can help mitigate unethical behavior.

Unethical behavior undermines the *integrity* of organizational culture and has the potential to negatively impact how people perceive the organization. One need look no farther than the public criticism Nike has had to handle over the years because of its labor practices around the world. Those who contend that in 2012 the NFL was attempting "union busting" in regards to the officials lock-out certainly saw the league take a public hit when 70,000 calls flooded NFL headquarters on the day after a non-union replacement referee crew made a game-altering call.

As an ethical leader, it is important to understand why unethical behavior occurs in sport organizations. Sims (1992) attributes unethical behavior to four factors. First, people engage in unethical behavior because it is rewarded. Second, the values of top-level management are not congruent with organizational values. The ethical climate of an organization is "the shared set of understandings about what is correct behavior and how ethical issues will be handled" (Sims, 1992, p. 510). Third, an organization appears ethical, but moral actions suggest otherwise. Finally, an ethical climate cannot exist in an organization where unethical behavior is justified. One way unethical behavior is justified is when it goes unreported. The Ethics Resource Center (2012) offered several reasons employees may not report misconduct: (1) the belief that no corrective action would take place; (2) reporting was not confidential; (3) fear of retaliation from co-workers, supervisors, or upper management; and (4) not knowing who to contact.

As an ethical leader, it is your responsibility to ensure your employees are comfortable reporting unethical behavior, while also encouraging ethical conduct. Ethical leadership is important because it increases employees' satisfaction with their supervisors, job attitudes, and optimism about the future of the organization (Piccolo, Greenbaum, & Eissa, 2012). It is also positively related to higher levels of trust in management and co-workers (Piccolo et al., 2012). Piccolo et al. (2012) offer five suggestions for an ethical approach to leadership:

1. Broaden an employee's evaluation criteria.
2. Craft policies, processes, and stories that highlight ethical commitment and foster an ethical culture.
3. Model ethical behavior.
4. Publicly celebrate wins that are not exclusively financial in nature.
5. Provide employees more autonomy in the workplace and the opportunity to see their work as significant beyond the bottom line.

As the economic growth of sport continues, ethical dilemmas and decision-making processes will become more complex. As an ethical sport leader in the 21st century, you must address current ethical issues, but also anticipate potential dilemmas and decisions within the sport industry and respective organizations. It is important to promote an ethical climate and organizational culture. Set ethical standards for yourself, your employees, and your organization. Model those standards and expect your employees to model them for each other. Your decisions will not be easy, and they will not always be popular.

SUMMARY

The sport industry is rife with ethical dilemmas. As a sport manager, it is up to you to recognize and address ethical issues that affect you, your employees, and your organization. To be an ethical leader, you must first be able to identify ethical dilemmas, and then employ an ethical decision-making strategy. Regardless of the scope, your decision will impact multiple stakeholders—employees, fans, sponsors, donors, parents, athletes, and community members. When appropriate, engage your stakeholders to help you determine the best course of action for your organization. You will be held responsible and accountable for the consequences—positive and negative—of your decisions and ethical actions. Finally, it is important to consider that the ethical decisions you make as a sport manager not only have immediate consequences for those involved, but also may play a key role in the future of your organization and the sport industry.

LEADERSHIP PERSPECTIVE

Peter Roby.
Courtesy of Peter Roby

Peter Roby has been the Athletic Director for Northeastern University in Boston, Massachusetts, since 2007. Prior to his time as leader of the athletic department, Peter served as the Director of Northeastern's Center for Sport and Society.

Q: What skills are required of leaders of sport organizations to best address ethical issues?

Whether you are a leader in business, a leader in sports, or most simply, a person in your community, you have to be committed to leading a life of integrity. I have made a distinction between leadership and management—managers make sure people do things right and leaders make sure people do the right thing.

When someone tells me they want to be a leader—the first question I ask is, "Why do you want to lead?" You need to be able to answer that question first. If the answer is about ego (glory, spotlight, fame, excitement of sport), then ego will guide the decisions you make. We make decisions as leaders that are guided by why we want to be a leader. It is so important that we recognize why we want to lead because that will guide our decisions. If you are being guided by how to best serve the organization you are leading—and not being guided by ego—then you will make decisions that are best for the organization and not decisions that are only best for you.

As a leader you must be committed to living a life of integrity. As a leader you have to ask who's interests are you putting first. You should not be putting your own interests first. We make decisions as leaders that are guided by why we want to be leaders. It is important to know why you are leading and how we are best representing the interests of those we are leading. If you are conscious of your actions as a leader and recognize that what you do drives the culture of your organization, then you are leading.

Q: How can leaders of sport organizations develop and improve their ethical decision-making skills?

You must concentrate on critical thinking skills and not only responding to stimuli and information without being thoughtful. Students face those decisions in their college life—they have to think about how they want to be perceived by others on campus—the decisions they make around going out at night, how you represent yourself, and if you're a student-athlete, how are you representing yourself and your college/university.

Students have to make decisions based on their goals; they have to make choices in support of those goals. If you want to be respected, you can't make bad decisions. If you want to be a leader, you have to make decisions that put you in a positive light with your peers. Leaders must be respectful, truthful, consistent, and empathetic. Leaders must live those things every day. If you live that way on a consistent basis, you can improve your ethical decision making.

Q: In your opinion, what are the most significant ethical issues facing leaders in intercollegiate sport?

I believe the most significant challenge we face is that we must be clear about what business we are in within college athletics. With the changes that have been made with conference realignment and colleges now focusing on athletics as a means of revenue generation, we risk losing sight of the business we are in, which is the youth development business. We cannot lose sight of the fact that we are in the youth development business and that we are not in the revenue generating business. When focus is on revenue, leaders' behavior can shift and we can make decisions that can come at the expense of the athlete.

I also see a lack of loyalty and a lack of traditional rivalries in college athletics today. Again, we have lost sight of the "greater good" and ironically, as institutions we make decisions based on only institutional interest ahead of the collective interests of all institutions.

Q: Do you believe that leaders in intercollegiate sport are facing more significant ethical issues today than leaders of previous generations of intercollegiate sport?

I believe ethical issues are more significant now than they were for previous generations of leaders in intercollegiate sport. As the cost of higher education increases, so do the demands on colleges to satisfy multiple competing priorities. Leaders of colleges have looked to intercollegiate sport as a place to generate revenue to help meet those increasing costs.

As a result of the exposure colleges receive and the potential for revenue generation from athletics, the recognition of sport as an important co-curricular activity is being lost. Intercollegiate sport has now become a place where everything is magnified. There is intense pressure. People are quick to lose their jobs if teams are not successful. People are quick to jump from job to job without any sense of loyalty.

DISCUSSION QUESTIONS

1. Aside from the examples provided in the chapter, discuss two or three current ethical scandals (youth, intercollegiate, professional, or international) that need to be addressed by leaders in the field.
2. Can you provide examples (other than the example provided in the chapter) within sport that followed the philosophy of teleology in ethical decision making? Can you provide examples that followed the philosophy of deontology in ethical decision making?
3. Ethical decision-making models take into account both individual-level factors and situational factors to help explain how an individual moves through the process of making a decision regarding an ethical dilemma. Consider your individual-level factors and describe how these factors can influence how you make a decision regarding an ethical dilemma.
4. Describe some of the similarities and differences you note when reviewing the two models of ethical decision making included in the chapter (i.e., issue-contingent model and practice-based model).
5. What can you do to improve your skills as a leader to best support ethical decision making? Use information from the chapter to support your answer.

KEY TERMS

cognitive moral development (CMD)
deontology
ethical code of conduct
ethical decision-making models
ethical dilemma
ethics
integrity
magnitude of consequences
moral intensity
moral judgment

morals
organizational culture
probability of effect
proximity
situational factors
social consensus
teleology
temporal immediacy
values

For a full suite of assignments and additional learning activities, use the access code found in the front of your book. If you do not have an access code, you can obtain one at **www.jblearning.com**.

References

Acosta, R. V., & Carpenter, L. J. (2010). Women in intercollegiate sport: A longitudinal study—33-year update, 1972–2010. Retrieved from http://www.acostacarpenter.org

Al Nafjan, E. (2012). The Olympic triumph of Saudi Arabian women. Retrieved from http://www.guardian.co.uk/commentisfree/2012/jul/31/olympic-triumph-saudi-arabian-women

Associated Press. (2012). FIFA meets to appoint prosecutor to examine World Cup winning bids. Retrieved from http://www.guardian.co.uk/football/2012/jul/16/fifa-prosecutor-world-cup-bids

A.T. Kearney (2012). The sports market. Retrieved from http://www.atkearney.com/paper/-/asset_publisher/dVxv4Hz2h8bS/content/the-sports-market/10192

Balingit, M. (2012, June 12). Ex-PSU president Spanier's emails on Sandusky surface. Retrieved from http://www.post-gazette.com/state/2012/06/12/Ex-PSU-president-Spanier-s-emails-on-Sandusky-surface/stories/201206120204

Bang, S. (2012). Report recommends European cooperation against match-fixing. Retrieved from http://www.playthegame.org/news/detailed/report-recommends-european-cooperation-against-match-fixing-5377.html

Barker, J. (2011). Under Armour's Kevin Plank an important source of funds for Maryland. Retrieved from http://articles.baltimoresun.com/2011-04-09/sports/bs-sp-terps-kevin-plank-0410-20110409_1_maryland-athletics-maryland-special-teams-ralph-friedgen

Barr, C. A. (2012). Collegiate sport. In L. P. Masteralexis, C. A. Barr, & M. A. Hums (Eds.), *Principles and practice of sport management* (4th ed., pp. 163–186). Sudbury, MA: Jones & Bartlett Learning.

Beu, D. S., Buckley, M. R., & Harvey, M. G. (2003). Ethical decision-making: A multidimensional construct. *Business Ethics: A European Review, 12*(1), 88–107.

Boulongne, Y. (2000). Pierre de Coubertin and women's sport. *Olympic Review, 26*(31), 21–26.

Bulman, E. (2007, June 5). Rights group: 1.5 million people displaced by preparations for 2008 Beijing Games. Retrieved from http://www.usatoday.com/sports/olympics/2007-06-05-3431055449_x.htm

Chelladurai, P. (2006). *Human resource management in sport and recreation* (2nd ed.). Champaign, IL: Human Kinetics.

Cooke, R. A. (1991). Danger signs of unethical behavior: How to determine if your firm is at ethical risk. *Journal of Business Ethics, 10*(4), 249–253.

Cottone, R. R., & Claus, R. E. (2000). Ethical decision-making models: A review of the literature. *Journal of Counseling and Development, 78,* 275–283.

Crosset, T. W., & Hums, M. A. (2012a). Ethical principles applied to sport management. In L. P. Masteralexis, C. A. Barr, & M. A. Hums (Eds.), *Principles and practice of sport management* (4th ed., pp. 121–140). Sudbury, MA: Jones & Bartlett Learning.

Crosset, T. W., & Hums, M. A. (2012b). History of sport management. In L. P. Masteralexis, C. A. Barr, & M. A. Hums (Eds.), *Principles and practice of sport management* (4th ed., pp. 3–25). Sudbury, MA: Jones & Bartlett Learning.

DeSensi, J. T., & Rosenberg, D. (1996). *Ethics in sport management.* Morgantown, WV: Fitness Information Technology.

ESPN. (2012, April 11). Arkansas fires Bobby Petrino. Retrieved from http://espn.go.com/college-football /story/_/id/7798429/arkansas-razorbacks-fire-bobby-petrino-coach

Ethics Resource Center. (2012). 2011 national business ethics survey: Workplace ethics in transition. Retrieved from http://www.ethics.org/nbes

Hancock, M., & Hums, M. A. (2011). Participation by transsexual and transgendered athletes: Ethical dilemmas needing ethical decision making skills. *ICSSPE Bulletin, 68.* Retrieved from http://www.icsspe.org

Hedstrom, R., & Gould, D. (2004). *Research in youth sports: Critical issues status.* East Lansing, MI: Institute for the Study of Youth Sports.

Helin, S., & Sandstrom, J. (2007). An inquiry into the study of corporate codes of ethics. *Journal of Business Ethics, 75,* 253–271.

Hums, M. A., & MacLean, J. C. (2008). *Governance and policy in sport organizations* (2nd ed.). Scottsdale, AZ: Holcomb Hathaway.

Hutchens, B. (2011). The acceleration of media sport culture. *Information Communication and Society, 14*(2), 237–257.

Jones, T. M. (1991). Ethical decision making by individuals in organizations: An issue-contingent model. *Academy of Management Review, 16*(2), 366–395.

Klemko, R. (2012, September 7). Brendon Ayanbadejo responds to delegate on gay marriage. *USA Today.* Retrieved from http://usatoday30.usatoday.com/ sports/football/nfl/ravens/story/2012-09-07/brendan-ayanbadejo-gay-marriage/57680822/1

Knight Commission on Intercollegiate Athletics. (2010). Restoring the balance: Dollars, values, and the future of college sports. Retrieved from http://www.knightcommission.org/restoringthebalance

Komives, S. R., Lucas, N., & McMahon, T. R. (2007). *Exploring leadership: For college students who want to make a difference* (2nd ed.). San Francisco, CA: Jossey-Bass.

Kuntz, J. C., Kuntz, J. R., Elenkov, D., & Nabirukhina, A. (2012). Characterizing ethical cases: A cross-cultural investigation of individual differences, organizational climate, and leadership in ethical decision-making. *Journal of Business Ethics, 113*(2). Retrieved from http://link.springer.com/article/10.1007/s10551-012-1306-6?null

Lapchick, R. (2011). 2010 racial and gender report card. Retrieved from http://www.tidesport.org/racialgenderreportcard.html

Lefton, L. A., Brandon, L., Boyes, M. C., & Ogden, N. A. (2005). *Psychology* (2nd ed.). Toronto, ON: Pearson, Allyn and Bacon.

Logan, T. (2012, September 25). St. Louis Blues lay off 20 employees as NHL lock-out drags on. Retrieved from http://www.stltoday.com/sports/hockey/professional/st-louis-blues-lay-off-employees-as-nhl-lockout-drags/article_4e156e8c-0743-11e2-be33-0019bb30f31a.html

Malley, B. (2011, September 27). The 20 biggest scandals in sports history. Retrieved from http://bleacherreport.com/articles/854416-the-20-biggest-scandals-in-sports-history

Malloy, D. C., & Zakus, D. H. (1995). Ethical decision making in sport administration: A theoretical inquiry into substance and form. *Journal of Sport Management, 9,* 36–58.

Marar, M., McIlvain, N. M., Fields, S. K., & Comstock, D. R. (2012). Epidemiology of concussions among United States high school athletes in 20 sports. *American Journal of Sports Medicine, 40*(4), 747–755.

McMurphy, B. (2012, September 7). Big 12 strikes new media deal. Retrieved from http://espn.go.com/college-sports/story/_/id/8346345/big-12-announces-media-deal-abc-espn-fox

Mickle, T. (2012, August 6). Revamped sales strategy helps IOC boost media rights fees. *Street and Smith's SportsBusiness Daily Global Journal.* Retrieved from http://www.sportsbusinessdaily.com/SB-Blogs/Olympics/London-Olympics/2012/08/iocrevenue.aspx

Murphy, C. (2011, November 18). FIFA chief Blatter: There is no on-field racism in football. Retrieved from http://edition.cnn.com/2011/11/16/sport/football/football-blatter-fifa-racism/index.html

Myerberg, P. (2013, February 20). FAU sells stadium naming rights to for-profit prison operator. *USA Today.* Retrieved from http://www.usatoday.com/story/gameon/2013/02/20/florida-atlantic-geo-group-stadium-naming-rights/1933013/

Nagler, A. (2012, May 2). Roger Goodell uses punishment of Bountygate leaders to send strong message. *Los Angeles Times.* Retrieved from http://bleacherreport.com/articles/1169468-nfl-roger-goodell-uses-punishment-of-bountygate-leaders-to-send-strong-message

National Center for Sports Safety. (2012). Sports injury facts. Retrieved from http://www.sportssafety.org/content/ResourcesNews/SportsSafetyInformation.aspx

National Collegiate Athletic Association. (2012a). Concussions. Retrieved from http://www.ncaa.org/wps/wcm/myconnect/public/ncaa/health+and+safety/concussion+homepage/concussion+landing+page

National Collegiate Athletic Association. (2012b). History. Retrieved from http://www.ncaa.org/wps/wcm/connect/public/ncaa/about+the+ncaa/history

National Collegiate Athletic Association. (2012c). National Collegiate Athletic Association and subsidiaries consolidated financial statement. Retrieved from http://www.ncaa.org/wps/wcm/myconnect/public/ncaa/finances/ncaa+consolidated+financial+statements

National Federation of State High School Associations. (2012). 2011–2012 high school athletics participation survey results. Retrieved from http://www.nfhs.org/content.aspx?id=3282

Ostrowski, J. (2012, August 25). Dogged by complaints, prison operator GEO Group keeps growing. Retrieved from http://www.palmbeachpost.com/news/news/dogged-by-complaints-prison-operator-geo-group-kee/nRHZ8/

Ozanian, M. (2012, September 5). Dallas Cowboys leads NFL with $2.1 billion valuation. Retrieved from http://www.forbes.com/sites/mikeozanian/2012/09/05/dallas-cowboys-lead-nfl-with-2-1-billion-valuation

Piccolo, R. F., Greenbaum, R., & Eissa, G. (2012). Ethical leadership and core job characteristics: Designing jobs for well-being. In N. Reilly, M. J. Sirgy, & C. A. Gorman (Eds.), *Work and quality of life: Ethical practices in organizations.* New York: Springer.

Plunkett Research. (2012). Sports industry overview. Retrieved from http://www.plunkettresearch.com/sports-recreation-leisure-market-research/industry-statistics

Ray, R. (2012, August 13). Boy, 12, ruled too big to play football. Retrieved from http://www.myfoxdfw.com/story/19266464/boy-12-ruled-too-big-to-play-football

Robinson, C. (2011, August 16). Renegade Miami football booster spells out illicit benefits to players. Retrieved from http://sports.yahoo.com/news/renegade-miami-football-booster-spells-213700753--spt.html

Rosenberg, M. (2011, January 7). Nike's Phil Knight has branded Oregon into national power. Retrieved from http://sportsillustrated.cnn.com/2011/writers/michael_rosenberg/01/06/oregon.knight/index.html#ixzz2Z34XdLBV

Sale, C. (2012, March 27). FIFA urged to look at World Cup vote. Retrieved from http://www.dailymail.co.uk/sport/article-2121334/Charles-Sale-FIFA-urged-look-World-Cup-vote.html

Sharp, A. (2011, November 22). Is Nike's influence on the University of Oregon football team bordering on interference? Retrieved from http://www.businessinsider.com/nike-influence-university-of-oregon-football-interference-2011-11

Sholtens, B., & Dam, L. (2007). Cultural values and international differences in business ethics. *Journal of Business Ethics.* 75(3), 273-284.

Sims, R. R. (1992). The challenge of ethical behavior in organizations. *Journal of Business Ethics, 11*(7), 505–513.

Sinha, A. K., & Mishra, S. K. (2011). Factors affecting ethical decision making in a corporate setting. *Purushartha, 4*(1), 135–154.

Thompson, E., & Macur, J. (2012, April 10). In Miami winning clearly isn't the only thing. Retrieved from http://www.nytimes.com/2012/04/11/sports/baseball/marlins-suspend-manager-for-5-games-over-comments-on-castro.html?_r=0

Vasquez, M. (2013, April 1). Prison firm withdraws gift to name FAU football stadium. Retrieved from http://www.miamiherald.com/2013/04/01/3318361/prison-firm-withdraws-gift-to.html

Volkwein, K. A. (1995). Ethics and top-level sport: A paradox? *International Review for the Sociology of Sport, 30,* 311–320.

Zinn, L. M. (1993). Do the right thing: Ethical decision making in professional and business practice. *Adult Learning, 5*(7–8), 27.

Zirin, D. (2012, September 17). Letter from Rio: Save Armando's house from the Olympics. *The Nation.* Retrieved from http://www.thenation.com/blog/169975/letter-rio-save-armandos-house-olympics

CHAPTER 7

STRATEGY AND LEADERSHIP

Kevin McAllister

CHAPTER OBJECTIVES

- Understand the main characteristics of strategic leadership.
- Understand and differentiate mission and vision within the context of leadership.
- Explain the thought processes of strategic leaders.
- Understand the importance of integrative thinking in strategy.

CASE STUDY

American Hockey League's Strategic Turnaround

In 1994, despite 50 years of continuous operation, the American Hockey League (AHL) was at a critical phase. Its membership profile featured a number of very small markets and some poorly capitalized teams, and it was facing aggressive competition from the International Hockey League, which had attracted major U.S. markets with much deeper ownership. The two leagues were competing for the same player base and National Hockey League (NHL) affiliation agreements. In advance of the 1994–95 season, the long-serving (28 years) president of the AHL, Jack Butterfield, retired and the board of governors selected Dave Andrews, the former general manager of the Cape Breton Oilers, to become the next president and chief executive officer (CEO).

When Andrews took over, the league immediately launched a strategic plan based on a thorough threat and opportunity analysis. Competent marketing and communications executives

(continues)

were recruited and a strong push was made to build a new and energetic AHL brand through international showcase events and strengthened media relations and broadcast opportunities. The strategy included aggressively pursuing expansion into new markets with stronger ownership, and refocusing the AHL's on-ice product on younger players, high NHL draft picks, and a new commitment to develop players for the NHL and its teams. Seven years later the International Hockey League ceased operations and its top six markets and ownership groups were absorbed by the AHL. Since then, the AHL has increased its membership to 30 teams, all with NHL affiliations. It has expanded its market across all of the United States and Canada and is now considered the premier professional hockey developmental league in the United States and Canada. League revenues have grown from $25 million to $125 million annually and more than 90% of NHL players, coaches, and officials have passed through the AHL. Recently, the league celebrated its 75th anniversary, a milestone that may not have been foreseeable in the 1980s and 1990s.

So how did the AHL turn this troubling situation around? How did the league develop strategy that led to its current conditions? What type of leadership was necessary to turn it around? How does a league "right the ship" in the face of significant challenges and fiscal straits? The simple answer for the AHL was a change of leadership; but that doesn't explain why the league underwent a significant turnaround. The more complex answer is that the new leader of the AHL demonstrated strategic leadership. Sport commissioners or league presidents have to demonstrate the qualities of leadership necessary to convince numerous partners and stakeholders that the leader's course of action will be successful; this can be a daunting task if success has been limited in the past and the current stakeholders need to be convinced before any new stakeholders can be introduced. A league has to convince its current players, owners, spectators, corporate partners, and media outlets that there is a viable plan for the future before future partners can be courted and invited to support its ongoing vision. According to Andrews, strategic leadership is the requisite leadership type necessary to envision, plan, direct, motivate, and execute a successful governance strategy. These type of leaders need to develop trust by selling and delivering on "brighter days to come." This is not easy when most sport team owners prioritize their own businesses well ahead of the collective success of the league. How does a leader in this situation sell the collective interests of a league, often over the individual interests of the voters? He or she demonstrates strategic leadership.

Questions for Discussion

1.   When Dave Andrews took the helm as president and CEO of the AHL, he initiated several initiatives to strengthen the league. Which initiatives do you feel were most significant in strengthening the league?

2.   Using the Internet, find the AHL website. Identify the key stakeholders with whom Dave Andrews and his corporate team must build trust to keep the league running successfully. Which stakeholders are most important to Andrews's team? Why?

3. Can you think of examples of other professional leagues that thrived following a change in leadership at the top or leagues that struggled after a change in leadership? Cite the reasons for success/struggle following the change in leadership. You will likely have to engage in research to answer this question.

4. How has the leadership in Major League Baseball (MLB), the NHL, the National Football League (NFL), the National Basketball Association (NBA), and the Barclays (English) Premier League sold the importance of their respective leagues' collective interest over the interest of individual franchises? Do some research to find concrete examples from each league.

INTRODUCTION

William Hulbert understood that for a professional sport league to function successfully, it needed to be run on sound business principles and authority needed to rest with the league and not with a loose association of teams. When he took over leadership of the National League of Professional Baseball Players in 1876, he told baseball team owners that their teams had to be in good financial health in order to compete in the National League (Crosset & Hums, 2012). Ever since Hulbert's decree, sport and business have been inextricably linked in the United States, and that link has endured today in the several professional leagues in the United States. This marriage of sport with business has not always been true in Europe. Hamil and Walters (2010) examined the financial performance of teams in the English Premier League in the 1990s and 2000s. Collectively, these teams did not turn a profit, relying instead on securing unsustainable debt to pay highly skilled players. The owners of these teams did not want to be relegated to lower divisional play where the opportunities for better sponsorship and the ability to attract skilled players (and therefore not only improve the team but also draw more spectators) diminished significantly. Hulbert would not have allowed these organizations to field teams in his National League in the late 19th century. Similarly, the American Hockey League (discussed

in the case study that opened this chapter) has been successful since 1994 because of a recommitment to its fiscal responsibilities under the leadership of Commissioner Dave Andrews and his executive team.

From Hulbert to Andrews, the strategic thinking of leaders is paramount in the success of sport's governing bodies and the ability of the governing body to sustain a successful league through a strong, centralized leadership. As this chapter will illustrate, strategy and leadership are virtually inseparable. What will be important for sport management students to understand is *how* and *why* the two concepts are inextricably linked. This chapter uses sport management, business, and education research to provide a comprehensive examination of the origins of strategy along with contemporary thinking on strategic leadership and what leads to and constitutes strategic success. Students should understand the building blocks for strategic thinking—mission, vision, goals, core values—and appreciate how leaders are involved in the process of implementing strategic thinking. Additionally, students will learn about BHAGs (big hairy audacious goals), Level 5 leadership, and the ability to manage paradoxes by integrating more than one strategic goal through "Genius of the AND." Ultimately, the author develops a definition of strategic leadership. Understanding this definition, how it applies to sport, and the marriage between strategy and leadership is a crucial competency for the 21st-century sport leader.

WHAT IS STRATEGY?

There is no one easy definition for *strategy*. The term *strategy* comes from the Greek word *general* (Montgomery, 2012b), the leader of the military. The dialectical connection between strategy and leader ensures that those who develop strategy for their organizations are leaders, and this connection has special meaning in the business of sport. Business experts have deliberated about strategy as one of the most important components of successful business for many years (Russell-Walling, 2007), specifically referencing the term *corporate strategy* in the 1960s. Many of these corporate strategists compare their strategic thinking to famous military strategies, including Sun Tzu's principles for strategy in the *The Art of War* written around 500 BC, or Von Clauswitz's *Principles of War* from 1812 (Mintzberg, Lampel, Quinn, & Ghoshal, 2003). It is not surprising that business strategists referenced these military strategists because the main premise behind both business and military strategy is an attempt to "defeat" competition. In each strategy type, there is a common theme about understanding the opposition while developing a long-term plan to defeat the opposition; this is easily relatable to sport.

Strategy is conceived by leaders for organizations via a thorough examination of mission, vision, goals, and core values. As Christensen, Allworth, and Dillon (2012) explain, "strategy is what you want to achieve and how you will get there" (p. 22). Sport managers superficially understand this simplified definition because many have played a sport where strategy is employed on the playing field to describe how one team attempts to beat another. Consequently, students of sport believe they have an understanding about how to implement strategy (again, from the on-field analogy) as an organized approach to play-calling

designed to exploit the weaknesses of the other team while ensuring that their own team has the right personnel to accomplish this.

In business, strategy often is defined as a means of creating competitive advantage or superior performance (Harvard Business Essentials (HBE) on Strategy, 2005; Magretta, 2012; Porter, 1998). Organizations develop business strategy to create a distinct difference from their competition by developing a plan of action designed to exploit that difference or advantage. Businesses cannot create effective strategy without first understanding their own position relative to the industry or competition, in order to make choices designed to create *differentiation* (Mintzberg et al., 2003; HBE on Strategy, 2005) in the marketplace. In other words, what sets Under Armour apart from Nike in the athletic apparel industry? Who is the industry leader? Is the trailing company making gains? Furthermore, Montgomery (2012b) explains that "strategy is a company's campaign in the marketplace" (p. 10), once again referencing and mixing business and military euphemisms. In the battle for customers, companies such as Nike and Under Armour need to supply and introduce new apparel via attention-getting marketing campaigns that tap into customer wants and needs. Their marketing approaches are visible expressions emphasizing how each company differs from the other.

Much as Covey (2004) explains in *The 7 Habits of Highly Effective People*, the first order for any business is to "know itself" relative to the industry and then develop a plan to distinguish the business from the competition, thereby creating its niche and advantage. Students can begin to learn how organizations "know" themselves by examining the usual foundation of any organization: its mission and vision.

MISSION AND VISION

It is important to understand how organizational leaders begin the strategic process. Leaders often begin to develop strategy based on a clear *mission*. This oft-used term is actually difficult to define because there are many subtle differences among the definitions of what a mission is. Huff, Floyd, Sherman, and Terjesen (2008) discuss mission as the explicit or outward description of the five key components of strategy: what is done, how it is done, by whom, for whom, and why those people value the organization. This is a business-focused definition of mission. Fried (2005) simply refers to mission as the end result of the organization incorporating the organization's goals and objectives successfully. Although this last definition could be applied to those missions encompassing strategy related to sport organizations, the reference to goals and objectives is a little too simplistic to define the term *mission*.

In Angelica's (2001) discussion of nonprofits' missions and mission statements, he defines them as lasting statements about the purpose of the organization that guide future direction. Additionally, Chappelet and Bayle (2005) describe mission as a reason for the organization to exist. Hums and MacLean (2008) suggest a mission statement should explain what the organization is about and what it does, and these two things should be communicated through the organization's purpose and values. Taking into account all the definitions, the definition of mission is a description of what the organization is or represents, some indication or reference to values or purpose, while providing some direction to both internal and external customers about the organization's important objectives. These varied definitions also demonstrate some of the complexities leaders need to address early in the strategy development process. It is difficult to begin strategy with a mission when there are numerous iterations and explanations about what a mission should be or what it should say about an organization. Even the mission length is a difficulty. Some seem to suggest a long, developed mission, whereas others suggest simple, concise themes.

In her book, *The Strategist*, Montgomery (2012b) addresses this concern directly. She posits

that the term *mission* has become overused and, subsequently, confused. Leaders are in an uncomfortable position because a confusing message about what the business or organization represents can have a significantly negative impact on both the internal and external customers of the organization. The internal staff cannot develop a good product or service, nor can the staff sell it if they are uncertain about what they are creating. The customer is not going to buy into a product or service that has little or confusing value. Subsequently, Montgomery (2012b) uses the term *purpose* in place of mission; this is a term that describes how the organization creates uniqueness and value in basic terms. Collins and Porras (2004) use the term *core values* or core ideology to describe a basic set of clearly stated operating principles, which are not necessarily about profitability. Core principles need to be authentic and aligned throughout the organization.

For the Amateur Athletic Association, its core purpose is to address amateur or grassroots-level sport rather than focusing on elite athletes competing at the professional, Olympic, or World Championship level. These elite priorities fall squarely with the U.S. Olympic Committee and affiliated sport national governing bodies (NGBs). Additionally, professional sport governing organizations highlight the importance of competitive advantage and professionalism, as the NFL, NBA, MLB, and NHL each compete with each other to some degree. Collins and Porras (2004) argue core values should not be focused on profitability, because a properly aligned business strategy that consistently follows the organization's ideology creates value in the mind of the customer, and is therefore successful. Here, it is important for the organization to be authentic in its message to all stakeholders, internal and external, rather than focus on making money. In this definition, it is easier for nonprofits to carry out their stated purposes instead of focusing on how to stay in the black. **Table 7.1** contains a sample of mission statements.

TABLE 7.1 **Mission Statements of Sport Organizations**

U.S. Olympic Committee

To support U.S. Olympic and Paralympic athletes in achieving sustained competitive excellence and preserve the Olympic ideals, and thereby inspire all Americans.

National Basketball Association

Our mission is to be the most successful and respected sports league in the world guided by two principles: We will grow and celebrate the game of basketball; we understand the popularity and visibility of our teams, players, and league obligate us to demonstrate leadership in social responsibility.

U.S. Soccer

To make soccer, in all its forms, a preeminent sport in the United States and to continue the development of soccer at all recreational and competitive levels.

National Collegiate Athletic Association

Our mission is to be an integral part of higher education and to focus on the development of our student-athletes.

Source: Data from NCAA. (n.d.). Office of the president. Retrieved from http://www.ncaa.org/wps/wcm/connect/public/ncaa/ncaa+president/on+the+mark; U.S. Soccer. (n.d.). U.S. soccer celebrating 100 years. Retrieved from http://m.ussoccer.com/About/About-Home.aspx; Blann, F. W., & Armstrong, K. L. (2011). Sport marketing. In P. M. Pedersen, J. B. Parks, J. Quarterman, & L. Thibault (Eds.), *Contemporary sport management* (p. 254). Champaign, IL: Human Kinetics; Team USA. (n.d.). USOC mission statement. Retrieved from http://support.teamusa.org/site/PageServer?pagename=about_USOC

Another important ingredient associated with strategy is *vision.* This is another term that has many definitions and attributed terms, such as visionary and vision statement. The term can be attributed to both people (most notably in transformational leadership or visionary discussions) and businesses. The basic definition of vision is the long-term (3 to 5 years) idea about where the organization wants to be, but this does not indicate the subtleties and complexities that experts imply when they define the term. For example, Huff et al. (2008) use the term "compelling image" (p. 7) to describe vision. In this strategic management definition, the authors indicate that vision is an educated exercise in an organization's future aspirations; that is, vision describes where the company should be or what the company should represent in the not-too-distant future.

Angelica (2001) expands this by describing a vision statement as that which inspires the organization. The vision should describe how the world will be served and how the organization will play a role in that servitude. This definition impacts nonprofits and their priority to serve a community

or social need over the business goal of differentiation. However, both for-profit and nonprofit organizations need to have a basic understanding about their desired future. Also, the idea that a vision will *inspire* the members of the organization, as Angelica indicates, is a major component of transformational leadership (Chelladurai, 2001; Slack & Parent, 2006).

As associated with strategy, both mission and vision are important. One describes what the organization values or does, and the other describes the organization's picture of the future. These terms also highlight the differences between good managers and good leaders. The mission describes those who are good at problem solving (Parke, 2012) or who are specialized (Watkins, 2012) in their responsibilities to achieving what the organization accomplishes. The vision describes how leaders or the broad generalists (Watkins, 2012) prepare the organization for the challenges or priorities (Parke, 2012) of the future. As such, some of the elements that make up good visions are also what set great leaders apart from managers. Watkins (2012) highlighted several key components that separate leaders from managers. One of the important challenges for managers promoted into leadership roles is to move from the mission-driven specialist problem solver to the generalist who understands the integration necessary among all departments to achieve the organization's long-term goals. This might mean that the leader is also able to provide cross-departmental communication that allows different departments to be able to communicate with each other to achieve the organizational goals. As this suggests, leaders need to be the ones to integrate the departments' or subunits' "collective knowledge" (p. 68). In doing so, Watkins (2012) describes how leaders are long-term strategists rather than daily results-driven tacticians (managers). With a vision to the future, leaders do not always see their work in metrics-driven daily activity; instead, they focus on future results that occur as an outcome of collective work of organizational units. This requires the leader to be more of an architect, seeing and communicating the potential final result as a result of aligning all departments and units collectively. For students learning about strategic

leadership, Watkins's discussion will be important later in the chapter.

The Chinese Olympic Committee (COC) appears to understand the connection between mission and vision. China's Olympic gymnasts, divers, and many other athletes are the best in the world. The COC seemingly attempted to expand its Olympic dominance in many summer sports to the Winter Olympic sports. It appears that the COC wants to be first or second in certain winter sports as part of its Olympic strategy, because it has moved into aerial ski competition and other sports that rely on skills that have made its summer sport athletes successful. This is all in an attempt to dominate not only the Summer Olympic medal count, but to compete for the Winter Olympic medal count as well. Although Chinese leaders set the direction and long-term vision of Olympic dominance, the mission-driven managers carry out those responsibilities in coaching, logistics, and managing the program. Again, there is a distinct difference between those who can see and set the future, and those who are responsible for carrying out the responsibilities of achieving the vision.

The Chinese Olympic Committee has employed a deliberate strategy to improve the standing of its athletes at both the Summer and Winter Olympic Games.
© claudio zaccherini/ShutterStock, Inc.

STRATEGY DEVELOPMENT

Because the implementation of effective strategy is dependent on a thorough understanding of the marketplace and the "self" of the organization within the marketplace—which should be made apparent through the organization's mission and vision—students of strategy can begin to understand the intricacies and difficulties of purposeful planning that can lead to strategy development. This planning is based on understanding the marketplace and keeping in mind the organization's mission and vision. The planning takes the form of businesses researching their customers' wants and needs, forecasting their customers' future wants and needs, and understanding the buying power consumers hold relative to the business's product or service. Proper planning requires business leaders to have a thorough analysis of the competitors and substitutes: who/what they are, where they are relative to the business and others, and what they are likely to do in the marketplace to compete with other businesses (Magretta, 2012; Porter, 1998). When the Lancaster (PA) Barnstormers, a minor league baseball team that plays in the Atlantic League of Professional Baseball, considers how it will sell tickets for its 72 home dates every season, its leadership must consider the other entertainment and leisure options the region's citizens can access and then market and price its baseball games accordingly. Good business strategy follows from an internal and external analysis of those business components that influence or will be influenced by planned action of a business (HBE on Strategy, 2005). The Barnstormers must consider their internal components—inviting baseball stadium, exciting promotions, no affiliation with Major League Baseball, just to name a few—and external components—community pride, weather, economy—and make assertions about their potential customer base and what patrons may want and need before purchasing a ticket.

Sport governance researchers have turned to Mintzberg's five P's of strategy when explicating strategy development (Chappelet & Bayle, 2005; Hums & MacLean, 2008). These P's (plan, ploy, pattern, position, perspective) highlight the key elements of strategy by addressing the long-term planning necessary to "outwit" or outperform competitors, as evidenced by a design of actions taken to do so. This is accomplished by understanding the location of the business within the environment (geographic, economic, political) and the business's perception of its place within that environment (Minztberg et al., 2003). Through the use of Mintzberg's work, sport organizations initiate *strategy development* as a deliberate planning for the future to achieve an organization's goals, while also allowing for the dual and sometimes competing goals that are important to governing organizations and, particularly, national governing bodies (NGBs). The first competing goal (Winand, Zintz, Bayle, & Robinson, 2010) is the paradox of trying to fund strategy for elite athletes or to improve grassroots efforts. Although not as important in the United States, many governing bodies worldwide have to be concerned about another paradox: whether to receive funding from public or private sources. Most sports, particularly nonmainstream sports, have to decide on the paradox regarding a dependence on volunteer staff or hired professionals.

Despite the common paradoxes and regardless of a business strategy, NGBs have a distinct responsibility to oversee or protect the best interests of the sport (Yasser, McCurdy, Goplerud, & Weston, 2003). For example, football and hockey governing bodies currently are developing policy to address one of the most significant concerns the sports have faced recently: concussions. Because of lawsuits from former players concerned about the dangerous conditions of football, and the long-term threat to football from parents who do not want their children to play because of health concerns, the NFL and USA Football should consider policies and guidelines that protect the future of the sport. These governing bodies develop strategy to sustain a future or to have permanence

(Chelladurai, 2001), which is not immediately apparent to those who do not recognize the seriousness of the concussion problem. This, however, is just a small glimpse of the challenges and concerns that sport governing bodies address when they develop strategy.

Achieving Strategic Focus

By now, it should be obvious that planning and developing strategy for an organization is a complex process, regardless of whether the organization is strictly a business organization, a sport business organization, or a sport governing body. How, then, do these organizations focus on strategy? Birshan and Kar (2012) outline three tips. First, an organization should contextualize strategy relative to its distinct industry. In other words, Jones & Bartlett Learning (the publisher of this text) competing against other academic publishers develops different strategies than the NFL's campaign to supplant MLB as "America's Sport." The formula for selling products (books versus tickets) or creating loyal customers is different for each organization. This is not to say that the organizations could not learn anything from one another, but they reside in different industries. The economics of the industry, general operating principles of the industry, and distinct operating principles unique to sport are all important influencers to developing business strategies for teams. Teams are successful when they capture market resources from substitute entertainment.

Second, effective strategists also address or identify future industry-related changes or disruptions (Birshan & Kar, 2012). A common concern is what will be the next generation of smartphone technology because teams that do not make effective use of social media will fail to capture markets of new generation consumers who demand instant information and access to the experience. Traditional sport business success depended on putting fans in the stands or getting them watching through the traditional medium of television.

If consumers are not in the stands or in front of a screen, how can sport businesses attract future consumers from different demographics who access information differently? To address future industry changes, the AHL constantly performs *SWOT analyses* (strengths, weaknesses, opportunities, and threats) on the hockey industry. The league makes itself aware of threats (e.g., poor economy) and opportunities (e.g., increased use of social media) that may negatively or positively impact league operations. At one point there was an opportunity to merge with the International Hockey League, which benefited the AHL in the late 1990s and early 2000s. It provided the AHL with more NHL affiliates and greater reach in markets that were previously unavailable. Another threat has been the concussion issue for the league, and there have been a number of rule changes and product improvements to address this concern. Consistent vigilance and research allow the league to seize opportunities and reduce the potential threats.

Finally, communication among those in the strategic process is paramount (Birshan & Kar, 2012) in maintaining strategic focus. Usually, there is no dearth of information or data available to the strategy team, but it is important that they communicate effectively about interpreting the data to fully understand the issues facing the business. For a team, knowing which of the following—group sales, walk-up sales, season ticket sales, or corporate sponsor sales—is important to help support the team's chosen strategy. More and more, sport organizations are hiring employees for the sole purpose of sifting through this data of key performance indicators, looking for ebbs and flows and reasons for valleys and peaks in sales and overall revenue production. The business must also coordinate consistent efforts among the various sales points in a way that reinforces the most important contributor (i.e., group sales) while improving the lowest performing (i.e., walk-up sales). The AHL has introduced a team businesses services department. The primary function of this group of people is to communicate and train all teams about best practices for this sales breakdown. The only way this is possible is by sharing and communicating team financials among the members of the league. Without this sharing of information, organizations may concentrate their efforts on consumers, who may not be the most profitable or cost-effective consumers for the business and subsequently the league.

Another reason effective communication is important is due to the numerous stakeholders who impact strategy development (Huff et al., 2008). Huff and colleagues argue that strategy is developed with many stakeholders in mind. Some stakeholders have a supportive orientation whereas others oppose what the organization is attempting to accomplish. In sport there are many stakeholders who are important, including fans, owners, players, corporate partners, media, supportive governing bodies (feeder systems), and communities most affected by the teams and the competition. Astute strategy leaders in sport should take the position that the most influential stakeholders need to be brought in, and, if possible, made a part of the decision-making process. Only strategists with exceptional skills can communicate well with all stakeholders in a way that does not negatively impact the strategic direction of the organization.

One final important component of strategic focus is an emphasis on *sustainability* (Porter, 2011). Once the organization has achieved a competitive advantage, it has to position itself to maintain its advantage. Many organizations rest once this advantage has been achieved, assuming that because the organization performs similar activities better than its rivals, this is sufficient and will continue unabated. Being effective is not the same as sustainability over time. The AHL has existed for 75 years, longer than many businesses. It has sustained itself over time despite threats and cultural shifts that the league has faced. Contrast this with failed startups such as the Women's United Soccer Association (WUSA), which lasted just two

seasons, and the United States Football League (USFL), which lasted three seasons. Another example of sustainability is the U.S. Olympic team. The U.S. team has been at or near the top of the medal counts over the past couple Olympic Games, although its dominancy has been challenged by the Chinese team with its concentrated, top-down approach to training across all sports, including their Paralympians. During the London Paralympics, the Chinese team won more gold medals than the next two countries combined. This competitive advantage occurred despite the fact that the country did not even field a team with athletes with disabilities before 2008. Now every country is chasing the Chinese because not only did the country develop a sustainable advantage, but it appears poised to maintain it.

THINKING STRATEGICALLY

In the 1980s and 1990s, many businesspeople worried (for good reason) that Japanese business leaders had overtaken American ingenuity. One of the reasons that the Japanese were successful in their strategic thinking was demonstrated in the classic work by Kenichi Ohmae (1982), *The Mind of a Strategist*. Whereas Watkins used analogies to explain the differences between leaders and managers, Ohmae argued that the secret to good visionary thinking was to focus on a couple of key elements. These elements included avoiding the *tunnel vision* that pressures to perform inevitably bring. Tunnel-visioned leaders tend to believe that there is an "all or nothing" thinking to accomplishing a goal or thinking about the future. This is similar to Mintzberg and colleagues' (2003) discussion of emergent strategy. As the environment or economic conditions change, these situations impact the strategy of the organization. It is important, therefore, to be flexible enough to understand that there may be more than one path to achieving goals or strategic direction. As organizations evolve along the strategic continuum, opportunities come up that should be taken. Those who have a narrow understanding of vision and cannot recognize the opportunities for what they are will not be able to implement successful strategy decisions. The secret is to see the opportunities and take advantage of them, something that the daily, isolated managers cannot always see in their limited responsibilities.

As all of this suggests, strategic visionaries should be flexible (Ohmae, 1982), while constantly assessing the options or opportunities that arise. Ohmae is not saying that strategists are so flexible that they follow *any* emergent path. What is important to understand is that no strategy is perfect, and leaders need to find a critical balance between staying the course and taking advantage of the real opportunity that is available based on the information or data that is available. Shavinina (2011) refers to this as flexibility of the mental space, or expanded boundaries of thinking about the future, the vision, or the opportunities that are potentially available. Despite the ability to see beyond the typical boundaries of ideas, leaders are also able to maintain a proper perspective, something that perfectionists or those with tunnel vision cannot. Finally, an important guideline for good visionaries is to focus on the proper measures of success—something that can be stated simply but has complex applications. Montgomery (2012b) refers to this as "staying agile." Strategic leaders need to have the flexibility of thought that allows them to be "open to reinterpreting what your business is about" (p. 139). Her concern is that leaders have the responsibility to make choices about an organization's direction but will sometimes back themselves into an unassailable corner if they do not keep emerging opportunities as possibilities. Tunnel vision is the bane of strategic thinking and flexibility; the agile opportunist will see potential, possibly when others will not because of the limited, daily operations-thinking of managers.

In *Built to Last*, Collins and Porras (2004) proselytize that trial and error is often an important path to building lasting organizations. Leaders who fail to recognize inflexible strategies that do not adapt to the changing environment will probably not be successful. Successful leaders build organizational structures and cultures designed to improve the learning and adaptive capabilities of the organization. Leaders with a combination of adopting trial-and-error methods and specific knowledge about how the industry operates can move their organization strategically forward. In Major League Baseball, there is a desire to equip ballparks with Wi-Fi capabilities so that thousands of fans can use their cell phones to access the Internet while watching baseball games. The San Francisco Giants, with relatively new AT&T Park, provide universal Wi-Fi via an LTE network capable of accommodating 4G devices, but it did not happen overnight. It took 8 years of stops and starts to complete. The team started with 130 access points in 2004, and settled on 800 access points in 2012. The move has been a boon for Giants players competing for All-Star votes (Hoornstra, 2013) because fans can vote in the stadium when reminded to by Giants personnel. "Prior to 2012, honestly, we didn't feel comfortable pointing to fans and saying, 'Pull out your devices and vote right now,'" said Bill Schlough, the Giants' senior vice president and chief information officer. "That, in a stadium full of 44,000 people, is a large risk" (Hoornstra, 2013, para. 22). If the new technology can be this successful for the Giants, the trial can dictate how the rest of the league could utilize technology for future success. It is well known that social media and current technology can improve the experience of attending sporting events, but there is still a risk that this new and future technology will not provide an adequate return on investment to justify the expense.

Role of BHAGs in Strategic Thinking

Strategy leaders who are willing to take risks are important in the sport industry, regardless of profit motives. Montgomery (2012a) suggests that too many companies rely on a clinical, isolated formula to determine success without addressing the role of the leader in this process. She refers to the strategic process as a mystery (Montgomery, 2008), and states that the chief strategists' responsibility is to unravel the mystery, connecting a human element to the process. There is something special about these types of leaders that sets them apart from others. These people are what Ohmae (1982) refers to as "bold thinkers"—people who are able to distinguish between the minutiae of daily problem solving and the complexities of future possibilities. These types are not just setting goals or taking advantage of opportunities; these are risk takers setting what Collins and Porras (2004) refer to as *BHAGs*, or big hairy audacious goals.

According to Collins and Porras (2004), BHAGs are goals so compelling that they engage the entire organization emotionally and passionately. This is not a goal that says, "Our goal is to be successful" (generic and uncompelling), it is "Our goal is to top the medal count at the 2012 London Paralympics" when there was not even a Paralympic program 8 years prior to the 2012 Games. These are goals that take a high level of commitment from the entire organization to be accomplished despite the high risk of failure that also accompanies these goals. These are bold goals to the insiders but unrealistic to outsiders. Most people outside NASA probably thought landing a man on the moon was unachievable. Or those outside of China thought creating an unparalleled Paralympic program was not possible in a country where there was little recognition for people with disabilities let alone athletes with disabilities.

For any organization to be successful in its BHAGs, Collins and others believe there are some important characteristics. Goals always have to be clear and measurable, but BHAGs also have to reflect the core operating values of the organization. Also, these BHAGs need to keep the organization moving forward, or stimulate progress. Because a BHAG is so audacious, the organization will fail if the entire organization does not commit

to its measurable success. There are significant risks involved in achieving these goals. For the Chinese Paralympic leaders, there were significant financial risks to achieving the 2012 goals and serious social risks, yet the entire organization aligned and compelled itself to be successful.

Collins and Porras (2004) cautioned leaders about the degree of risk associated with BHAGs. There is no magic wand or generic formula for creating and subsequently achieving these goals and, in fact, the authors discuss the trial-and-error method of determining BHAGs for many of the organizations they studied before each settled on the correct one. The other term the authors use is "opportunistic" rather than "great idea." They suggest that persistence, and even luck at times, are important determinants of success. From a business perspective, persistence and risk over time is not a formula that is seen as acceptable. The authors are concerned that most business strategy is usually focused on the yearly goals (which is inappropriate because vision encompasses 3- to 5-year periods). In their research, the great businesses were the ones that had a timeless commitment to values and opportunities rather than a yearly short-term focus on achievement. Often, the businesses researched by Collins and his team chose the wrong path at times in their strategic history because they took risks, but managed to return to their core purpose and values, again taking a chance on an opportunity over time. Because Olympic success is measured over 4-year increments, it is a little easier for NGBs to think and act over time. Also, there are clear results defining success at the elite level; however, there is a tremendous risk involved in long-term strategic planning, particularly when there is little success in the short term. Despite the lengthy efforts of Sport Canada to improve its medal count at the Winter Olympics, many were calling the Vancouver Games a failure at the midpoint of the 2010 Winter Olympics primarily because Canadian athletes had not won enough medals, particularly gold. Eventually, Canadian athletes "owned the podium," punctuated by the Canadian men's and women's hockey teams defeating the U.S. teams.

STRATEGIC LEADERSHIP

What, then, are the important traits of leadership necessary to fully understand the nature of strategy, understand the requisite components of strategy, embrace flexible and integrative thinking, and understand how to create legitimate BHAGs to inspire the organization? How do leaders develop organizational alignment when strategy and vision are achieved in the future? Strategy and leadership seem to be synonymous, but is it enough to say so in order to ensure that students of leadership understand the complexities that the previous discussions about strategy have been attempting to provide? Essentially there is one more question to be answered: What does leadership for the long term look like? You have gotten many clues already if you have read this chapter closely.

Boal and Hooijberg (2001) reviewed important research addressing *strategic leadership* from the previous decades, and highlighted some of the significant features of strategic leadership. Strategic leaders are those at the pinnacle of the organizational structure, who are responsible for goal-setting integration of the entire organization. In their estimation, important characteristics of strategic leaders include these leaders' ability to learn, assimilate information, and then apply what they have learned to new opportunities. In addition to their own leadership capacity, these types of leaders create organizational cultures that can learn as well; leaders should support learning from mistakes. Most organizational leaders do not tolerate mistakes at all, and although no organization can tolerate repeated mistakes, a culture that recognizes mistakes will occur is important. Ultimately, it is not being overly concerned about

making mistakes, but recognizing and using the mistakes as a learning process for improvement that is unique, and a hallmark of good leadership for strategy.

Strategic Leadership in Education

Interestingly, the term *strategic leadership* is not usually found in sport or sport business literature. In fact, a library database search of the term usually turns up research about strategic leadership in education, as in Quong and Walker's 2010 work on the seven principles of strategic leadership. Here the authors discuss the strategic efforts of school leaders to improve their schools while recognizing the numerous stakeholders who will need to support the vision of these leaders, much as Huff et al. (2009) confer in strategic management. Not surprisingly, Quong and Walker describe principles that include leaders who are vision and future oriented, who use evidence-based practices and benchmarks to determine success, and who simply find ways to get things done. Surprisingly, the authors discuss strategic leaders as those who are fit, both physically and mentally, which involves a "reputation for being resourceful" (p. 29). Their premise is those who can manage their own health can manage to find new opportunities for the school, while making good partners with all stakeholders. Strategic leaders are able to get everyone to share a vision for the future, while also managing conflict among the group. In the end, strategic leaders do all of this ethically, doing what is best for the students, the families, the schools, and the community. A strategic leader can see the future, gets everyone on board, and does it right.

In their discussion of educational strategic leadership, Davies and Davies (2010) provide advice for those moving from lower-level administrative positions into senior leadership positions. They recommend taking a very broad, long-term approach to setting the vision or moral purpose, while being able to articulate strategic planning into action, similar to some attributes of transformational leadership, discussed next. Much as Quong and Walker (2010) do, the Davies discuss building consensus among all stakeholders, but also reframe Mintzberg's emerging strategy, because strategic leaders are the ones who scan for future challenges and opportunities that might arise. Much of their research is devoted to assisting those moving from lower-level management to senior-level leadership positions. Both of the education-based authors placed more emphasis on the moral responsibilities to do the "right thing." However, there is a consistent message for both educational and business strategic leaders: Have a firm vision of the future while building consensus.

With moral responsibilities as a component of visions for the future, much of the educational research sounds like a description of *transformational leadership*. Chelladurai's (2001) summary of Bass's 1985 work refers to transformational leadership as being used by leaders who are able to articulate a new vision and order for an organization, convince others of that vision, and support those who work to achieve that vision. Slack and Parent (2006) reviewed Tichy and Devanna's (1986) transformational leadership study of CEOs, which probably served as the foundation for some of the educational strategic leadership studies. Parent and Slack reinforce Quong and Walker's (2010) explanation about how strategic leaders recognize the opportunities on the horizon and work to build consensus throughout the organization, while managing the process of change and challenge to the status quo. Both transformational leaders and strategic leaders are adept at articulating a vision and building an organizational commitment to achieving it.

Some students may believe that strategic leaders are *charismatic leaders,* those who are able to motivate and inspire others through bold visions and unique ideas (Roberto, 2011). They seemingly take risks regardless of the costs to themselves, but are able to inspire others through their indifferent risks to themselves. There is a downside to *charismatic leadership* and strategy, however. Roberto (2011) cautions that the bold, confident aspirations often lead to arrogance, which can lead to an inflated sense of infallibility. As a result, charismatic leaders sometimes stop listening to others or start taking personal credit for group decisions, thereby alienating themselves from their leadership team. Even more problematic is that these types of leaders can be prone to impulsive behaviors instead of what Collins (2001) refers to as rigorous adherence to facts and data. Roberto's biggest concern about charisma is that it often leads to selfish, unjustified decision making. Strategy and leadership are not about the individual; they involve the entire team of senior management and organizational alignment.

Level Five Leadership

There is one other leadership style associated with strategy, namely Collins's (2001) Level Five leader, which he describes as a leader who can lead a good company to become a great company. There are some interesting characteristics about this type of leader, particularly the fearlessness and unwavering resolve these leaders exhibit when committing to a course of action or strategy. Collins describes these leaders as a study in duality. They are often modest and humble, yet fearless and willful. They do not call attention to themselves, preferring to let the business speak for itself, rather than depend on a "cult of personality" (think charismatic) that many people have been criticized for in sport, including the late Al Davis and Jerry Jones. One reason Collins argues that these leaders demonstrate humility is because they are willing to ask questions and engage in dialogue rather than develop their own interpretation of the data or environment without input from others. These types of leaders do not succumb to the downfalls of charismatic leadership despite their bold risk taking associated with BHAGs. Level Five leaders create an environment in which everyone has the opportunity to be heard, which increases morale and the sense of empowerment that is often diminished when other leaders coerce results.

Collins (2001) also believes these leaders review mistakes and breakdowns without blaming employees. This creates an environment in which everyone wants to improve, because everyone understands the "red flags" of information that leaders refuse to ignore. This is a special type of leader who can be humble enough to not have every answer but is determined enough to fully research appropriate solutions to overcome mistakes. He or she is also a lifelong learner, as discussed by Boal and Hooijberg (2001). These Level Five leaders seem willing to allow the mistakes humans are noted for as long as there is a beneficial change in activity; again, they empower followers to learn from mistakes because they are not afraid to take some risks.

Integrative Thinking: Genius of the AND

One of the most underdiscussed traits of strategic leadership is the idea of cognitive complexity, or what Collins and Porras (2004) refer to as the *Genius of the AND* (p. 43). Leaders who demonstrate this genius are able to examine two potentially opposed thoughts and make sense of them. Many see the business world as an "either–or" situation. Either this is the only path to success or this other path is the way to success. A leader can be bold or conservative, promote change or stay the course. Often, business breakthroughs have occurred because good leaders have the ability to do both. As discussed earlier by Winand, Zintz, Bayle, and Robinson (2010, from Cameron, 1986), strategic performance is often based on mission paradoxes or contradictions. Should a national governing body pursue a strategy to develop elite athletes or develop its grassroots efforts to build

the feeder system? Should the organization pursue public sources of revenue or private sources? A "Genius of the AND" strategic leader has the ability to reconcile these and determine a vision and action plan that achieves both. USA Track and Field and USA Swimming have demonstrated that they can have success at the Olympic level over a succession of Olympics (the elite), which has occurred over time, indicating that there is also a feeder system that produces quality replacements to keep the organizations at the highest level of elite competition.

Martin (2007) calls this *integrative thinking* or opposable thinking—the ability to hold two opposing ideas or issues in your mind while determining the right course of action. Martin also cautions against thinking about a problem as an "either–or" situation and offers four ways that integrative thinking can be developed in leaders. The first is to *determine salience* by addressing *any and all* relevant factors rather than excluding potentially important ones simply because people cannot handle so many points of information. This can be messy. Second, leaders *determine causality* by exhaustively examining how relevant factors of decision making impact each other. Leaders then *envision the decision architecture* by visualizing what decisions need to be made and in what order after determining the previous factors, essentially understanding and visualizing the big picture. They are then able to *achieve resolution*, understanding that the outcome of the decisions does not have to come with unwanted tradeoffs (although sometimes it does), but still easing the tensions that inevitably result from others that fear those tradeoffs.

Martin's (2007) discussion of integrative thinking indicates that leaders are able to overcome overconfidence or are able to sift through the amount of data that organizations generate. They have the unique capability to understand what is important and what is not, what will cause what, and the decision-making process necessary to achieve success. They do not mind the "messiness" of change and embrace these opportunities rather than ignore or avoid them. Boal and Hooijberg (2001) argue that to develop these types of skills, strategic leaders must have the capacity to learn and change. These cognitive abilities can be developed, but the strategic leader has to have the ability to understand that they do not know everything and have to continuously adapt to the changing environment.

One final piece to understanding strategic leaders is clarifying the leaders' vision of the team. Although most students want to focus on the one person who deftly leads a company to success, it is never one person who does it all. Most people probably expect that the top-level team should all have the same views, when in fact many leaders do not want everyone thinking the same way. In an interview with *McKinsey Quarterly* (2010), Anne Mulcahy of Xerox discussed how she expects what she refers to as "internal critics," or people willing to question and provide feedback about a leader's decision making (para. 22). She wants to hear feedback and actively creates a culture designed to examine all opportunities because her top team has the courage to question or provide feedback that people do not want to hear. Good leaders recognize the value and importance of having the right team to achieve success in strategy. Most of the experts on the team comment at some point, and many say some things that most would expect them to say and some things others might not expect.

Summary

Strategic leadership is a complex idea incorporating the important elements of strategic planning and focus with the long-term vision and attributes of specific types of leaders. They are architects at the head of the organization surrounded by a diverse team. The strategic leader is the one who can envision the future and possess the motivational and communication abilities to get support from a range of diverse and divergent stakeholders. They get everyone to share that vision. These leaders have the ability to make the complex simple through their integrative thinking and their understanding of the AND, and they need to be unyielding in their pursuit of their organizational goals, developed through their relentless understanding and research of the industry in which they operate. This is particularly important for the many paradoxes that governing bodies face in sport. They recognize the value of the team and the risks involved in making decisions, but they appreciate and are willing to take those risks more so than others. They also learn and improve from mistakes. In sport, strategic leadership describes the type of leader necessary to take a 50-year-old league, the AHL, on the verge of dissolution, and make it the most successful professional developmental hockey league in North America. Strategic leaders are the people who can convince all stakeholders that there is a brighter tomorrow, and get a team together to execute and produce.

LEADERSHIP PERSPECTIVE

Laurie Turner is Director of Athletics at Pacific Lutheran University, a Division III private liberal arts university located in the Pacific Northwest. She oversees 20 intercollegiate sport programs, the intramurals program, club sports, and all of the athletic and recreational facilities.

Laurie Turner.
Courtesy of Laurie Turner

Q: How do you see vision, strategy, and leadership?

I see leadership as kind of sitting back sometimes and reflecting on the bigger picture, looking at, are we really going in the direction we thought we were going? Strategy comes from reviewing assessments and issues that are out there. For instance, if our goal is to win championships, then I need to be able to say, this is what the competition's doing; this is how many full-time coaches they have, these are their responsibilities, this is how much fundraising they have to do, and this is what we have to do. So it's really evaluating what like institutions are doing as well as institutions that we would like to be compared to and seeing where we are in comparison. Then, my role is providing a realistic vision for our coaches. That vision matches the vision of PLU, and the mission statement of the university feeds into that. So I provide vision from a conceptual perspective as well as really working with the coaches in terms of their day-to-day operations, getting them to see how that fits into all the financial pieces. My work is to look long term and to work with my coaches so that they have that vision, too, so that it actually happens at multiple levels. But, you have to have the management piece, because without that you don't really know what has to be done. You can't empower your people at a level where they can be successful if you have no comprehension of what it takes to get that work done.

Q: Describe a situation in which you have had to articulate a strategy for athletics to the larger community.

This is the first year that our enrollment is down since the economic downturn. We've been able to hold on until now, but I kept telling them we're in trouble, it's going to catch up, because higher education is going to get more expensive and we haven't maintained our facilities and it's going to be much more competitive. But as an institution, we sat back and said, "OK, we've met our enrollment, everything's good." So now, it's not panic, but we really have to look at our facilities and when a student comes to consider PLU, how do the old buildings and outdoor spaces affect our ability to attract the 17-year-old students? Knowing that, and seeing that as the big picture, how can I as a leader in athletics say, "OK, here is a time to talk about our front porch and how you can use athletics to benefit the university." We've made some progress. We just had a field dedication with a synthetic surface, but it's taken a long time to get there. We've done some improvements to our baseball field. We've done some improvements to our swimming pool.

Q: How do you enact forward thinking as a leader?

I try to empower all my coaches to be leaders and so that's kind of a leadership style and how I see each one of them reviewing their entire program. I tell them, for example, you are the CEO of women's basketball and these are my expectations and these are the university's expectations. I need them to be a leader in what they are doing, in the tasks they do, and in being on the cutting edge. I want them to do the research and ask, "Is there a better way to get these things done?" The expectation from our student-athletes and parents is that we need to be excellent in everything we do, even if we have limitations in our resources, which we do. That can't be the stopping point in how we do our work—really trying to be innovative in that regard. It is always about being forward thinking and being progressive as the environment changes. We have monthly meetings with coaches. We have development opportunities to educate our coaches so that they have the information they need to continue to do their job well. And it goes beyond coaching. I think giving people the tools to be able to articulate a larger message about PLU athletics and not just care about their own individual sport is important.

Q: How would you describe your relationship with your coaches?

Moving from a head coach to being an athletic director, I traded in a team of athletes for a team of coaches, so my style is very much as a mentor or collaborator with them. Once in a while they get called into the principal's office so to speak, but they see that I value collaboration. If they have an issue and they're not really sure how to handle it, or they have a student-athlete in student conduct, they will seek me out for advice. I see it being a flat organization where I work with them. I work with them through their challenges rather than dictating to them what they should do. It's really working together on the goals they have and figuring out how to achieve our objectives. That's a difference in philosophy from the more traditional way of leading, which was more authoritarian, because I'm asking them to think in terms of how they can help themselves achieve a certain goal rather than having a sense of entitlement and a certain expectation. It's about getting people to see where they could have helped facilitate moving in the direction they want to go and where they may have collaborated with others to make their own goals achievable.

Q: What is your strength as a leader?

I am pretty balanced. Yes, I'm passionate about things, but I'm capable of sitting back and listening without becoming defensive. For instance, I remember colleagues getting all upset about how much football got [resources], and it's not that I approve of that, but at least I understand why it's that way, and that helps me see what it will take to make changes in those areas. A strength is being able to have that balance and be a good listener. People will usually walk out of the office, and they may not get what they want, but they know that I've listened and that I will try to do the best I can to help. I'm also really direct. Even if I believe something should happen, I will say that's just not going to happen in the next 5 years. It's about living in reality, knowing what I know, and knowing the environment.

Interview conducted by Maylon Hanold.

KEY TERMS

achieve resolution
BHAGs
charismatic leaders
charismatic leadership
core values
determine causality
determine salience
differentiation
envision the decision architecture
Genius of the AND

integrative thinking
mission
strategic leadership
strategy
strategy development
sustainability
SWOT analyses
transformational leadership
tunnel vision
vision

DISCUSSION QUESTIONS

1. Now that you have a firm grasp on strategic leadership, can you think of leaders in professional sport who have had the ability to set a course for their organization? Name a leader and explain the vision.
2. What do William Hulbert and sustainability have in common, and what does it have to do with strategic leadership?
3. In groups of four or five, select a sport organization, assume roles in its leadership structure, and suggest some BHAGs that the organization should pursue in the future to differentiate itself from its competitors.
4. In those same groups, suggest some organizations who have used BHAGs to achieve a competitive advantage. Who are the organizations and what are the BHAGs?
5. The author talks about integrative thinking or "the ability to hold two opposing ideas or issues in their mind while determining the right course of action." Why is this approach to strategic thinking important for sport organizations in the 21st century?
6. How does Level Five leadership improve and enhance the charismatic and transformational approaches to strategic leadership?

www

For a full suite of assignments and additional learning activities, use the access code found in the front of your book. If you do not have an access code, you can obtain one at **www.jblearning.com.**

REFERENCES

Angelica, E. (2001). *Crafting effective mission and vision statements.* Saint Paul, MN: Fieldstone Alliance.

Bass, B. M. (1985). *Leadership and performance beyond expectations.* New York: NY: Free Press.

Birshan, M., & Kar, J. (2012). Becoming more strategic: Three tips for any executive. *McKinsey Quarterly.* Retrieved from http://www.mckinseyquarterly.com/Becoming_more_strategic_Three_tips_for _any_executive_2992

Blann, F. W., & Armstrong, K. L. (2011). Sport marketing. In P. M. Pedersen, J. B. Parks, J. Quarterman, & L. Thibault (Eds.), *Contemporary sport management* (p. 254). Champaign, IL: Human Kinetics.

Boal, K. B., & Hooijberg, R. (2001). Strategic leadership research moving on. *Leadership Quarterly, 11*(4), 515–549.

Cameron, K. S. (1986). Effectiveness as paradox: Consensus and conflict in conceptions of organizational effectiveness. *Management Science, 32*(5), 539–553.

Chappelet, J., & Bayle, E. (2005). *Strategic and performance management of Olympic sport organizations.* Champaign, IL: Human Kinetics.

Chelladurai, P. (2001). *Managing organizations for sport and physical activity: A systems perspective.* Scottsdale, AZ: Holcomb Hathaway.

Christensen, C. M., Allworth, J., & Dillon, K. (2012). *How will you measure your life?* New York: HarperCollins.

Collins, J. (2001). *Good to great: Why some companies make the leap . . . and others don't.* New York: HarperCollins.

Collins, J., & Porras, J. I. (2004). *Built to last: Successful habits of visionary companies.* New York: HarperCollins.

Covey, S. (2004). *The 7 habits of highly effective people: Powerful lessons in personal change.* New York: Free Press.

Crosset, T. W., & Hums, M. A. (2012). History of sport management. In L. P. Masteralexis, C. A. Barr, & M. A. Hums (Eds.), *Principles and practice of sport management* (pp. 3–25). Sudbury, MA: Jones & Bartlett Learning.

Davies, B. J., & Davies, B. (2010). The nature and dimensions of strategic leadership. *International Studies in Educational Administration, 38*(1), 5–21.

Fried, G. (2005). *Managing sport facilities.* Champaign, IL: Human Kinetics.

Hamil, S., & Walters, G. (2010). Financial performance in English professional football: An inconvenient truth. *Soccer and Society, 11*(4), 354–372.

Harvard Business Essentials on Strategy. (2005). *Create and implement the best strategy for your business.* Boston, MA: Harvard Business School.

Hoornstra, J. T. (2013, July 2). MLB: Dodgers can't dial up All-Star votes with wi-fi woes. *LA Daily News.* Retrieved http://www.dailybulletin.com/ci_23587094/mlb-dodgers-cant-dial-up-all-star-votes

Huff, A. S., Floyd, S. W., Sherman, H. D., & Terjesen, S. (2008). *Strategic management: Logic and action.* Hoboken, NJ: John Wiley & Sons.

Hums, M. A., & MacLean, J. C. (2008). *Governance and policy in sport organizations* (2nd ed.). Scottsdale, AZ: Holcomb Hathaway.

Magretta, J. (2012). *Understanding Michael Porter: The essential guide to competition and strategy.* Boston, MA: Harvard Business School.

Martin, R. (2007). How successful leaders think. *Harvard Business Review, 85*(6), 60–67.

McKinsey Quarterly. (2010). How we do it: Three executives reflect on strategic decision making. *McKinsey Quarterly, 2,* 46–57.

Mintzberg, H., Lampel, J., Quinn, J. B., & Ghoshal, S. (2003). *The strategy process: Concepts, context, cases.* Upper Saddle River, NJ: Prentice Hall.

Montgomery, C. A. (2008). Putting leadership back into strategy. *Harvard Business Review, 86*(1), 54–60.

Montgomery, C. A. (2012a, July). How strategists lead. *McKinsey Quarterly.* Retrieved from http://www.mckinseyquarterly.com/How_strategists_lead_2993

Montgomery, C. A. (2012b). *The strategist: Be the leader your business needs.* New York: HarperCollins.

National Collegiate Athletic Association. (n.d.). Office of the president. Retrieved from http://www.ncaa.org/wps/wcm/connect/public/ncaa/ncaa+president/on+the+mark

Ohmae, K. (1982). *The mind of the strategist: The art of Japanese business.* New York: McGraw-Hill.

Parke, C. (2012). Preparation meets strategic planning: Organizations without a vision for the future won't get there. *Industrial Engineer, 44*(1), 44–48.

Porter, M. E. (1998). *Competitive strategy: Techniques for analyzing industries and competitors.* New York: Free Press.

Porter, M. E. (2011). What's strategy? In *HBR's 10 must reads: The essentials* (pp. 181–218). Boston, MA: Harvard Business Review Press.

Quong, T., & Walker, A. (2010). Seven principles of strategic leadership. *International Studies in Educational Administration, 38*(1), 22–34.

Roberto, M. A. (2011). *Transformation leadership: How leaders change teams, companies, and organizations.* Chantilly, VA: The Teaching Company.

Russell-Walling, E. (2007). *50 management ideas you really need to know.* London, UK: Quercus.

Shavinina, L. V. (2011). Discovering a unique talent: On the nature of individual innovation leadership. *Talent Development and Excellence, 3*(2), 165–185.

Slack, T., & Parent, M. M. (2006). *Understanding sport organizations: The application of organization theory* (2nd ed.). Champaign. IL: Human Kinetics.

Team USA. (n.d.). USOC mission statement. Retrieved from http://support.teamusa.org/site/PageServer?pagename=about_USOC

Tichy, N. M., & Devanna, M. A. (1986). *The transformational leader.* New York: John Wiley & Sons.

U.S. Soccer. (n.d.). U.S. soccer celebrating 100 years. Retrieved from http://m.ussoccer.com/About/About-Home.aspx

Watkins, M. D. (2012). How managers become leaders: The seven seismic shifts of perspective and responsibility. *Harvard Business Review, 90*(6), 64–72.

Winand, M., Zintz, T., Bayle, E., & Robinson, L. (2010). Organizational performance of Olympic sport governing bodies: Dealing with measurement and priorities. *Managing Leisure, 15*, 279–307.

Yasser, R., McCurdy, J. R., Goplerud, C. P., & Weston, M. A. (2003). *Sports law: Cases and materials* (5th ed.). Cincinnati, OH: Anderson.

CHAPTER 8

FORGING SIGNIFICANT CHANGE

Jon Welty Peachey
Janelle E. Wells

CHAPTER OBJECTIVES

- Define the concept of organizational change.
- Describe the factors that may contribute to resistance to and acceptance of organizational change.
- Describe how organizational change is realized differently at the individual, group, and organizational level.
- Identify the steps in organizational change.

CASE STUDY

Football at Georgia State

In 2006, the Georgia State University Athletics Department contracted with national consulting firm C.H. Johnson Consulting, Inc., to conduct a feasibility study to see if the school should consider adding a Division IAA football program. The athletic department was interested in knowing what direct and indirect impacts adding a football program would have on the university and the athletic department (C.H. Johnson Consulting, 2006). The firm's study report noted: "A football program requires enthusiasm and passion for the effort. This is too large of a financial, staffing, and time commitment to attempt if the Georgia State community does not have the steadfastness to see it through" (C.H. Johnson Consulting, 2006, Sec. 2, p. 3). The report further discussed the

(continues)

importance of adding new staff members and embarking on development and marketing strategies that would attract the interest of donors and the corporate community at large. If Georgia State (a member of the Sun Belt Conference, which puts Georgia State football at the FBS [Football Bowl Subdivision] level, rather than FCS [Football Championship Subdivison]) brought football into the athletics equation, it would mark a significant organizational change for the school and the athletic department. Ultimately, the decision would come down to money: how much the school needed to raise to cover all the new scholarships to support an 85-person squad; how much was needed to put the team on the field given the costs associated with facilities and equipment; how much it would cost to add women's teams to maintain Title IX equity; and finally, how much revenue and prestige could be brought in by having a football program. The athletic director at the time, Mary McElroy, announced the findings from the consulting report and said more information needed to be gathered through town-hall meetings with the community and university (Georgia State University, 2006). Georgia State did eventually decide to add football, and the planning process started in 2008 when Bill Curry was hired as head coach (Georgia State, 2008). Georgia State kicked off the 2010 season with a 41–7 win over Shorter College and ended its first season with a 6–5 record.

By all accounts, adding football represented a significant organizational change for Georgia State. Football is a popular sport in the southern part of the United States, so many observers thought the change was appropriate and would put GSU on the map, athletically speaking. Georgia, Florida, and Texas are important areas of recruiting for college coaches from big-time programs. So, given that high school players are available to play college football, C.H. Johnson Consulting reasoned in its report to Georgia State that "there would be ample opportunities to recruit successfully and field a successful team" (C.H. Johnson Consulting, 2006, Sec. 3, p. 3). Despite this, even putting a successful team on the field would not necessarily bring monetary success. The sport marketplace in metropolitan Atlanta is a crowded one. Many sport entities, including the football teams at the University of Georgia and Georgia Tech University, the Georgia Force (arena football), the Atlanta Hawks, the Atlanta Braves, and the Atlanta Falcons, are vying for media attention, sponsorship attention, and ticket sales. Georgia State has four seasons under its belt and is embarking on what it hopes is a bright future in football. The program needs to develop a strong base of support among students and alumni as well as overall institutional support. Georgia State has never been perceived as a "big-time" athletics school. By adding football, it has taken one big step in that direction, and it did so in a measured way, taking the time to consult with experts and getting its leaders involved.

Questions for Discussion

1. Hofstra and Northeastern Universities eliminated football programs in the recent past. Which move do you think would lead to more resistance among students, student-athletes, and athletic department personnel: adding football or cutting it? First, identify the college or university you are considering and then explain your position. Also, discuss the factors in each case that informed your position.

2. If you were athletic director at Georgia State when discussions about adding football were ongoing, what would you say to current athletic department employees to get them on board with adding football? What resistance would you anticipate?

3. Reading ahead in the chapter, the author talks about four environmental constraints for change agents. Which constraints can be applied to the idea of adding a Division IAA football program to Georgia State?

4. Which type of leader—transformational or transactional—is best suited to initiate the change discussed in the case study? Support your answer by connecting the details from the chapter to the details in the case study.

INTRODUCTION

Organizations in many industry sectors, including sport, are recognizing that it is no longer sufficient to conduct business as usual in the 21st century. The pace of organizational change continues to increase exponentially in today's turbulent, challenging, and unpredictable economic climate. For sport organizations to survive and grow, they must adapt quickly and nimbly to changes in strategy, size, environment, and technology (Slack & Parent, 2006). Large-scale organizational change initiatives, or transformational change, have become commonplace in the sport industry, with continuous change models more the norm than the exception. Sport organizations are constantly reorganizing, restructuring, attempting to change the organization's culture, revisioning strategy, revamping policies and procedures, or replacing key leaders and other personnel as a result of various external and internal pressures. In the opening case study, administrators at Georgia State examined the school's external environment—other schools and their successful football programs—and saw that adding football was a way to elevate the school's athletic profile and add students to yearly enrollment totals, as it has done for many other schools.

Successful organizational change is difficult to accomplish because stakeholders typically resist change efforts (O'Toole, 1996) or will be ambivalent, or unsure, about the changes (Welty Peachey & Bruening, 2012b). Research has identified three key barriers to effective change in organizations: lack of management visibility and support, inadequate skills of management, and employee resistance (Jick & Peiperl, 2003). Initiating change can be a competitive, hostile activity, benefiting some while injuring others. Many organizational change efforts fail and end up generating recalcitrance, building resentment, and fostering dissatisfaction. To many stakeholders, change suggests loss of control and increased uncertainty, and poses a threat to traditional procedures, values, and status levels (Turnley & Feldman, 1998).

To overcome resistance, the leadership style and behavior of change agents, or those leading and guiding change, become vitally important. The leadership demonstrated by the change agent, how he or she works with different stakeholder groups within and outside of the sport organization, and the change processes undertaken by the change agent all play an important role in gaining widespread acceptance of transformational change. In fact, certain types of leadership behavior are critical for fostering change acceptance, mitigating resistance, and securing the success of transformational change over time (Welty Peachey, Bruening, & Burton, 2011). When Peter Roby took over as athletic director at

Northeastern University in Boston, he was faced with the difficult reality of needing to discontinue the football program in order to better serve student-athletes and achieve financial objectives for the athletic department. Of course, the thought of dropping football sparked widespread resistance from various stakeholders, including student-athletes, football alumni, athletic department coaches and staff, students, donors, and other community stakeholders. Three years after taking the helm, Roby did decide to discontinue football. Although resistance to this transformational change was high at the beginning, over time, Roby's transformational leadership style, open and honest communication, and strategic thinking about how to best implement this change garnered more and more support, to the point where a year after the program was dropped, the voices of dissatisfaction with the decision were minimal. Roby's transformational leadership was a key factor leading to change success.

In this chapter, we begin by providing a historical context for organizational change, where we define organizational change, introduce the different types and driving forces of organizational change, and give examples of transformational change in the sport industry. Next, we provide an overview of responses to organizational change. In this section, we examine the individual, group, organizational, and process factors that can lead to resistance or acceptance of change, and also discuss the environmental constraints that can make leading change challenging. We then elaborate on ambivalence as a first response to organizational change. Following, we address leadership and organizational change, where we review various leadership styles and their association with change implementation success. The final section covers the change implementation process and examines leadership strategies that can be employed for overcoming resistance and ambivalence and marshaling support for organizational change.

NATURE OF ORGANIZATIONAL CHANGE

No matter the size of an organization, change can have a ripple effect (Miles, 2001). Organizational change may be a foreseen or unforeseen response to an internal or external force, and perceived as either continuous or episodic (Weick & Quinn, 1999). Continuous change emerges incrementally without end, whereas episodic change is infrequent and possibly radical (Weick & Quinn, 1999). Whether the organizational change is broad or narrow in scope, or continuous or episodic, scholars agree the rate of change is increasing (Quinn, 2004). To survive, organizations may be required to exchange tradition for uncharted territories to move into the future. As they progress down this unfamiliar path, sport organizations may experience three types of change: developmental, transitional, or transformational (Appelbaum et al., 2008).

An organizational change in which natural growth occurs is referred to as *developmental change* (Appelbaum et al., 2008); this includes simple modifications to a sport organization's policy and procedures manual. As an organization slowly evolves, it moves through the most common change, *transitional change*, to improve the current state gradually (Want, 2003). An example of transitional change is when a sport organization reallocates office space among employees or allows more employees to work from home. Unfortunately, if several challenges occur simultaneously, transitional change may not suffice quickly enough for organizations. Thus, organizations are forced to make possibly unknown, radical alterations, which are defined as transformational change (Schneider, 1987). *Transformational change* efforts, the focus of this chapter, question the current assumptions and reject the current paradigm (Kuhn, 1970). Ending the football program at Northeastern was a transformational change. Although transformational change can be disruptive in nature, when executed successfully it is competitive and differentiating (Denning, 2005). When a leader-driven transformational change occurs, drastically different strategies are formulated and modifications of the organization's structure and culture may occur.

Whether broad or narrow in scope, change can be prompted by internal or external pressures, which are responded to proactively or reactively by organizations. Specifically, external environmental forces including, but not limited to, reduced revenue, enhanced competition, and unsatisfied customers have increased the pace of organizational change (Attaran, 2004). When a change is employed to avoid a crisis, it is known as a *proactive change*; when the change is a response to a situation, it is referred to as a *reactive change*. Change triggered by a crisis, such as downsizing for financial reasons, may require a transformational change that may result in resistance to the unknown future state of the organization.

In sport, organizational change may be experienced in performance or management domains. A highly visible performance change can occur on a sport team when the coach's strategy shifts to gain competitive advantage. However, this chapter is concerned with change in the management domain, which Slack and Parent (2006) categorize into four functional areas for sport organizations: people, productivity, structure/system, and technology.

RESPONSES TO ORGANIZATIONAL CHANGE

Stakeholders in sport organizations will have varied responses to change due to a number of individual, group, organizational, process, and environmental factors. By far, most of the research in this area has centered upon resistance and how to overcome resistance in order to enable change success. Recently, researchers have suggested that ambivalence may be the initial response to

organizational change by many stakeholders. Of course, some stakeholders will accept transformational change from its inception, whereas others will grow to accept change, or parts of the change, over time. In this section, we review these common responses to organizational change— *resistance*, *acceptance*, and *ambivalence*. Skilled leaders must understand the nature of these responses, when and why they come about, and employ strategic leadership strategies in order to work with these responses and enable successful change.

Resistance and Acceptance

Resistance is a tridimensional negative attitude toward change that includes affective, behavioral, and cognitive components (Oreg, 2006). Some sources of resistance may have their strongest impact on stakeholders' emotions, others may more directly influence behaviors, and still other resistance sources may influence what stakeholders think about the change. Many organizational change efforts fail which may foster resentment toward leaders, result in stakeholder resistance to future change, and lead to discontent toward leaders and the organization.

In fact, when confronted with organizational change, stakeholders are less concerned with what the change actually is and will look like than with how they will personally adapt to it. They do not see this as resistance, but as survival. In essence, stakeholders resist change that exceeds their coping capabilities (Jick & Peiperl, 2003). In addition, managers often try to avoid resistance because it can have negative consequences for the organization (Oreg, 2006), such as lower levels of job satisfaction and organizational commitment among employees, as well as greater intentions to leave the organization (Rush, Schoel, & Barnard, 1995; Wanberg & Banas, 2000).

INDIVIDUAL LEVEL

There are many reasons why individuals resist change. Personality dispositions play a role in resistance to change. For example, individuals high in agreeableness who are trusting, forgiving, caring, altruistic, and have cooperative values (Costa & McCrae, 1992) will be more accepting of change than individuals who are manipulative, self-centered, suspicious, and ruthless (Vakola, Tsausk, & Nikolaou, 2004). Individuals open to new experiences will be creative, innovative, imaginative, reflective, and untraditional, whereas individuals low in openness will be conventional, have narrow interests, and be unanalytical (Costa & McCrae, 1992). Individuals more open to new experiences tend to also be more accepting of change. Sport management students looking to succeed in the sport industry would do well to adopt this adventurous spirit of possibility because change is necessary for organizational success. Neuroticism represents individual differences in adjustment and emotional stability (Costa & McCrae, 1992). Individuals high in neuroticism experience negative emotions such as anxiety, hostility, depression, self-consciousness, impulsiveness, and vulnerability. Not surprisingly, individuals lower in neuroticism have been found to be more accepting of organizational change (Oreg, 2003).

Outside of personality dispositions, stakeholders will resist change due to the perceived impact that change may have on them, both professionally and personally. Stakeholders' views of change often depend on how they see their own work and home situations impacted by it, and to what degree the change program aligns with what they most value in their working lives. Consequently, there will be less resistance if stakeholders' interests are met and they see ways in which they will benefit from the change. For instance, in a major restructuring of the Canadian Intercollegiate Athletics Conferences, a study found that different perceptions of the impact of this organizational change on personal goals, interests, and values led to disagreements, conflict, and resistance to the implementation of the change process (Hill & Kikulis, 1999). Within the sport industry, it has

been suggested that if goals relating to power, money, prestige, convenience, job security, or professional competence are threatened as a result of proposed organizational change, then the change will be resisted, even in situations where the change is good for the organization as a whole (Slack & Parent, 2006).

In addition, if a stakeholder has had prior negative experiences with organizational change, he or she may resist change more than if prior experiences were more positive (Jick & Peiperl, 2003). Finally, there are also indications that stakeholders will resist change if they believe that the values being espoused through the organizational change conflict with their personal values or beliefs. At a Division I institution going through major transformational change, for instance, this was the case among some coaches who did not believe that the student-centered philosophy being promoted by the new athletic director aligned with their old-school attitudes about coaching, and thus this new philosophy change was highly resisted by these coaches (Welty Peachey & Bruening, 2012a).

GROUP LEVEL

In a sport organization pursuing transformational change, existing subunits (e.g., departments or divisions) may gain or lose power and autonomy, or even be restructured or disbanded entirely. Other subunits may have their roles in the organization reconfigured, with employees either gaining or losing responsibility. Additionally, work routines and tasks will likely be influenced either positively or negatively by change. Reallocation of resources will lead to resistance among group members of subunits, depending on how much group/team roles and functioning are negatively impacted by change. If subunits stand to gain power/prestige and experience increased intrinsic job satisfaction and rewards as a result of the change, they will likely offer support more readily than if a subunit stands to lose power/prestige and other resources that affect the job satisfaction of its members. Also, if a subunit perceives a threat to its continued existence as a result of proposed change, resistance from members of that subunit is expected. Conversely, if a subunit does not perceive a threat to its existence, that subunit may embrace change to a greater degree (Oreg, 2006). For example, if a sport organization is considering outsourcing its marketing activities, this transformational change will be resisted by the organization's marketing department, because group members will likely lose their jobs due to the change.

ORGANIZATIONAL LEVEL

One organizational-level variable that can have an influence on resistance or acceptance of transformational change is the leadership displayed by the change agent. The organizational change phenomenon is complex and requires skillful leadership to successfully guide and implement change in order to mitigate resistance and realize organizational benefits and outcomes. The importance of leadership to the change management process is underscored by the fact that change, by definition, requires creating a new system and then institutionalizing these new approaches (Kotter, 1995). Good leaders have a vision for the organization and know how to achieve that vision (Banutu-Gomez & Banutu-Gomez, 2007).

Managerial support for change and fostering trust in their actions among employees is essential. For example, lack of managerial support for organizational change initiatives can lead to increased levels of resistance among stakeholders. However, if stakeholders believe that managers support the change initiatives, this will build trust and establish credibility, lessening resistance (Meyer, Srinivas, Lal, & Topolnytsky, 2007). But if trust is broken during the change process, stakeholders will resist change efforts more. Thus, leadership displayed by change agents and other managers is critical to the success of transformational change. In fact, some leadership styles, such

as transformational leadership, are better suited to guiding transformational change and mitigating resistance than other leadership styles. The relationship among leadership styles, resistance, and organizational change success is discussed in more detail in the Leadership and Organizational Change section, which follows our discussion on ambivalence.

In addition to leadership, another organizational-level variable that can influence responses to change is organizational culture. *Organizational culture*, as defined by Schein (1996) is "the set of shared, taken-for-granted implicit assumptions that a group holds and that determines how it perceives, thinks about, and reacts to its various environments" (p. 236). In layperson's terms, organizational culture is "the way we do things around here." From 2008 to 2012, Scott O'Neill, president of Madison Square Garden Sports, changed the way the popular entertainment facility did things. He instituted a more aggressive sales culture predicated on improvements in service and creativity. He instilled a greater emphasis on revenue development, raising ticket prices for the Knicks and Rangers and creating two job positions/titles directly concerned with revenue development—executive vice president of revenue performance and executive vice president of business development and operations (Lombardo, 2012). Scholars have noted the connection between leadership and organizational culture, and whether organizational culture is a source of resistance to or acceptance of change (Rashid, Sambasivan, & Rahman, 2004). It is suggested that organizational culture is created by leaders and that "the only thing of real importance that leaders do is to create and manage culture" (Schein, 1988, p. 2). To this end, scholars have examined types of organizational cultures that best support organizational change and mitigate resistance. Generally, organizational cultures with flexible structures and supportive climates are more conducive to change acceptance than mechanistic structures characterized by many hierarchal levels, inflexibility, and high formality and rules (Harper & Utley, 2001; Welty Peachey et al., 2011).

CHANGE PROCESS

Leaders must also pay attention to change process factors of active participation, communication, and pace of change in order to mitigate resistance and facilitate acceptance of transformational change. With regard to participation, even in the midst of crisis, employee involvement in decision making and problem solving will generate support for change (Carroll & Hatakenaka, 2001). Participation by stakeholders from all levels of the organization in the change process is critical to implementation success and mitigating resistance. Employees who are active participants in the change process will resist change less than employees who do not actively engage and participate in the process (Lines, 2004; Welty Peachey et al., 2011). This is instructive for leaders in that they should encourage active participation from followers. In addition to participation, effective communication strategies will lessen stakeholder resistance to change (Elving, 2005; Welty Peachey et al., 2011); stakeholders who are informed about the reasons for change and provided with consistent communication on change efforts will resist change less than stakeholders who have change thrust upon them in a top-down manner with little communication. Furthermore, if employees do not receive adequate and timely information about changes taking place in the organization, they will engage in sensemaking on their own, which will lead to cynicism about change and ultimately resistance (Reichers, Wanous, & Austin, 1997).

Finally, change agents must pay attention to the pace at which change is introduced into the organization. Some research has shown that the most effective transformational changes are initiated rapidly throughout the organization (Nadler & Tushman, 1988). If transformational change is implemented more gradually, it runs the risk of being sabotaged by internal politics, structures, culture, and the organizational history and status quo, thus fostering resistance. However, others have argued that rapidly implementing widespread, revolutionary change across an organization is not the most effective method for engaging in transformational change, nor an accurate depiction of how it occurs (Child & Smith, 1987). Additionally, there is ambiguity in terms of the order in which different parts of an organization should be transformed. Some scholars suggest change should be initiated rapidly throughout the entire organization to overcome initial inertia and prevent resistance from building up among organizational members (Romanelli & Tushman, 1994). Others have argued that change should take place first in an organization's most central functional elements (Hinings & Greenwood, 1988), whereas others suggest transformational change is more successful when peripheral elements of an organization are changed first (Beer, Eisenstat, & Spector, 1990).

ENVIRONMENTAL CONSTRAINTS

Leaders who are change agents can be faced with a number of environmental constraints when attempting to lead transformational change. First, change agents must pay attention to the resources and facilities that are available to support the transformational change. Physical, financial, and human resources must be sufficient to support the change initiatives, or the change program runs the risk of failing and generating stakeholder resistance. For example, in one Division I intercollegiate athletic program going through transformational change to a more student–athlete–centered philosophy, stakeholders resisted change if they did not perceive the resources of the department or university to be sufficient to support the change initiative (Welty Peachey & Bruening, 2011). Second, internal politics of the organization can undermine change initiatives and foster resistance. Sport organizations have many different stakeholders, from players, employees, coaches, and management to fans, boosters, donors, and community leaders. Different stakeholders will have different agendas and interests, and may not support changes that are deemed to go against their agendas. For instance, at the Division I athletic department mentioned previously, the success of athletics brought about by the organizational changes sparked jealousy on the part of other institutional stakeholders who were not happy that athletics was receiving more attention and institutional support. These were political constraints that the athletic director had to navigate daily as he charted a new course for the department (Welty Peachey & Bruening, 2011).

A third constraint faced by change agents in sport organizations is organizational history and tradition. Sport organizations will have traditions, histories, policies, and procedures in place that create expected ways to operate on the part of various stakeholders. When changes go against these rich traditions and histories, they can be resisted by stakeholders who do not wish to deviate from how things have always been done. At the intercollegiate athletic department described previously, for instance, some of the longer tenured staff resisted change because the changes were forcing these individuals to do things differently and move them out of their comfortable routines (Welty Peachey & Bruening, 2011). Finally, stakeholder concerns for legitimacy of the sport organization are another constraint change agents face as they lead transformational change. Recently, there have been instances of Division I intercollegiate athletic programs discontinuing football (e.g., Hofstra, Northeastern University, University of the Pacific), and this transformational change was likely resisted vehemently by many stakeholder groups who believed dropping the football program would undermine the foundation of what made a Division I athletic department legitimate—having a competitive and visible football program (Welty Peachey & Bruening, 2011).

Major League Baseball and its owners' refusal to banish the color line until 1947 deeply illustrates the reluctance of a sport organization to go against tradition.
© Everett Collection Inc/Alamy

Ambivalence

Although most of the focus on responses to transformational change has centered upon resistance and acceptance, recent research has suggested that ambivalence may actually be the most prevalent initial type of response among stakeholders (Piderit, 2000; Welty Peachey & Bruening, 2012b). Ambivalence connotes the mixed evaluations or motives that individuals experience with respect to attitude objects (i.e., the idea, issue, or object about which an employee has a feeling or belief) in their social environments (Sparks, Harris, & Lockwood, 2004). In this vein, it might be difficult for an individual to form an immediate opinion about transformational change. Instead, she or he may take some time to decide whether to welcome or reject change. For instance, a sport organization employee might not know immediately how he or she feels, or what he or she believes, about new changes being implemented in the organization. Full judgment might be reserved until the employee can ascertain how the changes will personally impact him or her, his or her subunit, work routines and roles, and the organization as a whole. In fact, in one Division I intercollegiate athletic department going through transformational change, ambivalence was the typical response among many stakeholders (Welty Peachey & Bruening, 2012b). The new athletic director enacted major changes to the department's philosophy, strategy, resource allocations, and ways coaches should treat student-athletes, but many stakeholders, particularly longer-tenured individuals who had seen changes come and go before, adopted a wait-and-see attitude. They wanted to see how they would be personally affected, and how the changes would impact organizational performance, before giving full support.

LEADERSHIP AND ORGANIZATIONAL CHANGE

Leaders are critical to the success of transformational change and to overcoming stakeholder resistance and ambivalence. Next, we review different types of leadership styles and their relationship with transformational change.

Transformational and Transactional Leadership

By now, these two types of leadership should be well known to you. Change and leadership research has shown certain leadership qualities are more appropriate for specific types of change. For instance, transformational leaders are better suited for nonroutine situations where adaptation is the goal (Pawar & Eastman, 1997). Conversely, when an organization is centered on maintaining

progress, transactional leaders who emphasize a reward-based system for task completion may be a better fit (Bass, 1995). As such, in relatively stable work environments, transactional leadership is used when both the leader and the group members are satisfied with their purpose and process (Chelladurai, 1999). Group members have a set of needs and desires, and the leader distributes rewards or punishments in exchange for followers' compliance or resistance.

A transactional ticket office manager initiating new ticket sales procedures may reward employees in the form of bonuses for the amount of sales each employee brings the organization. The ticket manager may exercise his or her influence by setting challenging goals, assisting goal achievement by enhancing group members' abilities, and supporting the group members' efforts (House, 1971). Specifically, the ticket manager may guide employees on how to obtain new business, set challenging goals, and provide support. In contrast, a transformational ticket office manager faced with a financial hardship and reduced employee benefits, such as the loss of complimentary athletic tickets, may need to influence major change in organization members' attitudes and assumptions while building commitment to the organization's new mission and strategies (Yukl & Van Fleet, 1992).

Transformational leadership (Bass, 1985) has been portrayed as one of the most effective leadership styles when change is prominent (Burke et al., 2006; Mumford, Scott, Gaddis, & Strange, 2002). According to Tichy and Devanna (1990), transformational leaders follow a process whereby they recognize the need for change, create a new vision, and then institutionalize the change. During the initial phase of organizational change, developing a vision and inspiring employees toward the vision are major facets of transformational leadership used to set the direction of change and assemble resources for change (Kotter, 1995).

Transformational leaders explicitly engage employees' attention to the vision and instill confidence to achieve expectations (Bass, 1985; Bono & Judge, 2003). By articulating a clear vision and demonstrating enthusiasm, transformational leaders inspire and motivate their employees to work hard (Bass, 1985). Also, when the leader models the expected behavior required to institutionalize the change, he or she emulates what Kotter (1996) argues is "the way things are done around here." In addition, through the use of charisma, transformational leaders are able to commit employees to their vision (Bass, 1998; Podsakoff, MacKenzie, Moorman, & Fetter, 1990). Specifically, research on transformational leaders has revealed how influential they are on followers' affective experiences (e.g., Bono & Ilies, 2006). First, by being enthusiastic and optimistic about change and confident in themselves and their employees, transformational leaders affect the feelings of their employees. Second, the individualized consideration provided by transformational leaders (Bass, 1990; Bono & Judge, 2003) has helped alleviate their employees' fear or resentment of organizational change (Kiefer, 2005).

Leadership begins with an executive officer of an organization and filters to lower levels through empowerment. In the context of sport, the status, image, and profitability of the National Basketball Association (NBA) has been largely attributed to a transformational leader, Commissioner David Stern. Owners bought into his vision, and the image of the NBA was transformed. Similarly, Billie Jean King, the founder of the Women's Sports Foundation in 1974, transformed the perception of women through sport. However, transformational leaders may not be confined to large organizations with hierarchical organizational structures. An example is the hiring of a new coach for an athletic team. This new hire may transform the values, aspirations, and beliefs of the team.

Not only are transactional and transformational leadership important for managing change, but, depending on the timeframe of change, so are participative and authoritative leaders. Thus, it is important to understand that different leadership styles need to be used in different situations.

Participative Leadership

Similar to transformational leadership, participative leadership is referred to as a change-oriented style and is linked to stimulating positive outcomes in employees (de Poel, Stoker, & van der Zee, 2012; Kahai, Sosik, & Avolio, 2004; Spreitzer, 2007). If time and resources are allotted, participative leaders are able to actively engage their workgroup followers to share in the decision-making process (Somech, 2003). Numerous studies have revealed positive associations between participative leadership and employee outcomes, such as increased effectiveness, increased job satisfaction, and lower conflict (Burke et al., 2006; Kotlyar & Karakowsky, 2006; Lovelace, Shapiro, & Weingart, 2001; Williams, 1998), which may contribute to the success of participative leadership during transformational change.

Autocratic Leadership

Finally, when time is limited, the use of an autocratic leadership style is appropriate during change. Dictated by the leader's information, an autocratic leader personally makes a decision with little input from followers (Chelladurai, 1999). Because the leader and the group are unable to take the time to engage in participative decision making, the leader must make the decision. In order for the decision to be effectively executed by the group, the members must understand and accept the leader's autocratic decision (Chelladurai, 1999). For example, if a sport leader is facing a crisis-ridden predicament, such as immediate dissolution of the organization due to financial loss, a directive stance may be necessary to implement a transformational change. This way, the leader communicates the urgency of the situation, as well as engages and motivates stakeholders accordingly (Pascale, Millemann, & Gioja, 2000).

CHANGE IMPLEMENTATION

Regardless of the leadership style of the change agent, many sport organizations are insufficiently prepared for implementing change and mistakenly view implementation as a step-by-step, linear process. In reality, implementing change is a messy proposition. Before beginning a change implementation process, it is important for change agents to consider the nature of resistance and ambivalence, and how these responses can be used to gain widespread stakeholder support over time.

Encouraging Resistance and Ambivalence

Resistance is often viewed by management as dysfunctional to the organization. This one-sided story neglects the fact that resistance can be a resource during change, and leaders acting as change agents often contribute to resistance through their own actions and inactions, most notably through breach of agreements and failure to restore trust. Breaches in trust can occur when there are changes to the allocation and distribution of resources, the processes and procedures through which these reallocations are made, or the ways in which individuals in power relate to those with less power or authority. This often takes place in transformational change, and change agents will ultimately be more successful in leading change if they repair damaged relationships first (Reichers et al., 1997). It is crucial for change agents to realize that stakeholder resistance is often based on valid concerns and should be something an organization uses to improve itself.

Contrary to popular thought, resistance can actually be an asset to the organization during change rather than an indicator of dysfunction. A continued challenge for change agents is to get new conversations heard and spoken about often enough that they take root and grow. This is where resistance can be of value, because it keeps the topic in play and at the forefront of conversations, giving stakeholders from all levels in the organization an opportunity to participate in the conversation and offer feedback (Caruth, Middlebrook, & Rachel, 1985). This feedback gives change agents data to improve the change process and adjust the pace, scope, and sequencing of change (Ford, Ford, & D'Amelio, 2008). Thus, paradoxically, resistance could be a factor in the ultimate success of change. In addition, change agents may wish to foster ambivalent attitudes toward change rather than discourage them. Ambivalence may provide a basis for motivating new action, rather than a continuation of old, stale routines (Piderit, 2000).

Change Implementation Steps

After change agents acknowledge that resistance and ambivalence can be assets to guiding successful transformational change, careful thought must be given to the change implementation process in order to gain widespread support from stakeholders throughout the sport organization. One helpful guide for change implementation has been developed by Jick and Pieperl (2003). These steps for implementing transformational change and gaining widespread stakeholder support are outlined in **Table 8.1**.

First, change agents in sport organizations must analyze the organization and determine the forces driving change and the organization's need for change. A study of the organization's history of change should be commenced, and traditional barriers to change identified. If these barriers are not addressed, patterns of resistance are likely to reoccur. Second, a shared vision among all stakeholders in the sport organization should be created so that stakeholders understand the need for change and the implications this will have for their roles. The formulation of vision needs to begin at the top of the organization and then be translated and disseminated effectively throughout the organization through good communication and

---

TABLE 8.1 **Change Implementation Steps**

---

1. Analyze the organization and determine the need for change.

2. Create a shared vision.

3. Examine organizational history and tradition, and separate from the past if needed.

4. Create a sense of urgency for change.

5. Exhibit strong leadership.

6. Line up informal leaders in the organization who can work as advocates for change.

7. Design an implementation plan.

8. Develop enabling structures.

9. Pay attention to communication and participation.

10. Reinforce and institutionalize change.

Source: Data from Jick, T., & Peiperl, M. (2003). *Managing change: Cases and concepts* (2nd ed.). New York: McGraw-Hill.

---

information-sharing strategies. As mentioned previously, a transformational leader is well-suited to create this shared vision for change and gain its acceptance throughout the sport organization.

Third, change agents must address past organizational history and traditions, and make a concerted effort to separate from them if warranted. However, traditions in sport organizations do provide stability and a frame of reference amidst the chaos of change, so change agents must recognize the value of heritage as an anchor in change, reinforcing the positive aspects of this heritage but disengaging from elements of the organizational history that will impede effective change. Fourth, change agents should create a sense of urgency and need for action, without appearing to fabricate a crisis. This sense of urgency is essential for aligning stakeholders at all levels of the organization. Also, it is critical that middle managers understand the need for change, because they

will likely be the ones communicating and reinforcing changes to front-line staff. Thus, frequent and consistent communication is needed between change agents and implementers of change.

Fifth, a strong leader is needed to envision and guide change. Leadership plays a critical role in creating an organization's vision, motivating employees to embrace the vision for change, and designing organizational structure, policies, and procedures that reinforce the desired change and discourage old and stale practices. It must also be noted that leadership of change can be distributed to teams of leaders initiating change (change leader teams), which have the advantage of combining multiple skill sets of various leaders in the implementation of change. Sixth, change agents should obtain broad-based support for transformational change throughout the sport organization. This support must come not only from managers and change agents, but also from recipients of change who will carry out the vision. Change agents should first focus on lining up support from informal leaders in an organization who will be receptive to change and can then work as advocates for change in their respective areas.

Seventh, an actual implementation plan needs to be created to map out the change effort, listing timelines and dates by which the organization hopes to achieve its goals. The change process is not something that is done without careful thought and must be guided by a detailed and thorough map of how to get to the end result. It is also important that the plan maintains a level of flexibility to environmental contingencies that may develop and be broken into steps so as not to overburden stakeholders with multiple demands, which could lead to overload and burnout. This leads to the eighth recommendation, which is that enabling structures must be developed to facilitate and support the changes. These structures can encompass workshops for stakeholders and training as to how to function within a new environment, and also include creative reward structures for stakeholders who embrace the changes. Also, small accomplishments along the way should be celebrated when working toward achievement of hard and specific goals, to foster motivation and adherence to the implementation plan.

Ninth, as mentioned previously, change agents must pay attention to communication and participation processes when guiding change. They should communicate early and often about the change process, and be as transparent and honest as possible about the ramifications and benefits for the organization as a whole, and for stakeholders individually. It is recommended that stakeholders at all levels of an organization being affected by change have involvement in the planning and implementation process. Finally, it is important to reinforce and evaluate the change program continuously throughout the process.

Summary

In this chapter, we have focused on forging transformational change in sport organizations. We began by providing an overview of the nature of change and forces driving change in the sport industry, which was followed by a discussion of factors influencing and constraining the three most common responses to transformational change: resistance, acceptance, and ambivalence. We then reviewed various leadership styles and their association with change outcomes, primarily looking at transactional, transformational, participative, and autocratic leadership. Because transformational change is dynamic and situational, the most appropriate leadership style must match the type of change and its context. We concluded by presenting a specific 10-point plan for change implementation to guide change agents leading transformational change.

Transformational change is a continuous process in the 21st-century sport industry. Sport leaders will need to recognize how their leadership contributes to or hinders the success of transformational change, develop implementation strategies that take into account the varied interests of myriad stakeholders, and garner support from these stakeholders in order for change to be successful. We hope this chapter was illustrative and informative as to the importance of leadership in forging significant change.

LEADERSHIP PERSPECTIVE

After graduating from the University of Florida with a BS in Public Relations from the College of Journalism, former football letterman Phil Pharr began working at Gator Boosters in 1981. Three decades later, he has experienced several organizational changes and has recently been promoted to executive director of Gator Boosters. In this position, he is responsible for all facets of the organization. This includes, but is not limited to, generating and cultivating donor relationships, coordinating fundraising efforts for facility/endowment projects, budgeting, and strategizing with the University of Florida's Athletic Association and Foundation.

Phil Pharr.
Courtesy of Phil Pharr

Q: Describe some of the biggest organizational changes you have encountered with your organization over the past three decades.

The first is the growth of the Gator Boosters staff. In 1981, there were four and a half full-time employees. Today, we have 13. Second, the level of professionalism has continued to increase. Third, the increasing annual ceiling [annual fundraising goal] has refocused our attention to major gifts, endowments, and capital improvements. Lastly, the role of the Gator Boosters board of directors has increased.

Q: Of those changes you just mentioned, let's focus on one to analyze. Were there any major obstacles or challenges that the organization had to overcome to implement the change?

With the changing demographic of boosters, unstable economy, fan experience expectations, and media, our strategy has evolved. Recently, we have engaged in a new approach with the University of Florida's Foundations to meet the increasing annual ceiling.

Q: How did employees respond to the organizational change? Why do you think they responded this way?

Incredibly well. Believe me, there was nervous apprehension, but it was an opportunity to grow as an organization and individually. We are a very unique organization and consider ourselves to be one of the best in our field, but we also know we can always raise the bar to be better.

Q: What strategies were employed by leadership to guide the organization through the change? (I'm assuming that buy-in was achieved.)

I realized a long time ago that you make everyone unhappy by trying to make everyone happy; therefore, it was important for me to be as transparent as possible. We are all aware this is a work in progress, so there is constant motion and we have to be more fluid.

Q: With your recent promotion, what key leadership strategies do you expect to employ to direct the organization through future changes?

To be as transparent as possible and to take advantage of resources that are available at the Foundation. In addition, we will continue being more professional with our approach in every aspect of the business.

KEY TERMS

acceptance
ambivalence
developmental change
organizational culture
proactive change

reactive change
resistance
transformational change
transitional change

DISCUSSION QUESTIONS

1. Some of the chapter examples focused on the deletion of a college football program. Who would resist such a move? List stakeholders who might resist this change. In your view, what reasons would they have for resisting such a move?
2. Referring to Question 1, put yourself in the position of an athletic director. What arguments can you make that will counter some of the resistance you expect to encounter?
3. Under the leadership of Roger Goodell, the National Football League has undergone much change with regard to rules and safety. What changes have you seen, and has there been any resistance to these changes? Finally, why has the NFL undergone such organizational change?
4. Suppose a Triple A minor league baseball team is moving from one city to another and has only 6 months to complete the move. Which leadership style or styles should the team's president employ to hasten acceptance of this change and get employees moving in the same direction? Is quelling all resistance a good idea? Why or why not?
5. Using the change implementation process, which steps seem most important for the commissioner of the American Hockey League if he wanted to outlaw fighting in league games?

For a full suite of assignments and additional learning activities, use the access code found in the front of your book. If you do not have an access code, you can obtain one at **www.jblearning.com.**

REFERENCES

Appelbaum, S. H., Mitraud, A., Gailleur, J., Iacovella, M., Gerbasi, R., & Ivanova, V. (2008). The impact of organizational change, structure and leadership on employee turnover: A case study. *Journal of Business Case Studies, 4*(1), 21–38.

Attaran, M. (2004). Exploring the relationship between informational technology and business process reengineering. *Information and Management, 41,* 585–596.

Banutu-Gomez, M. B., & Banutu-Gomez, S. M. T. (2007). Leadership and organizational change in a competitive environment. *Business Renaissance Quarterly, 2*(2), 69–91.

Bass, B. M. (1985). *Leadership and performance beyond expectations.* New York: Free Press.

Bass, B. M. (1990). *Bass and Stogdill's handbook of leadership* (3rd ed.). New York: Free Press.

Bass, B. M. (1995). Transformational leadership redux. *Leadership Quarterly, 6,* 463–478.

Bass, B. M. (1998). *Transformational leadership: Industry, military, and educational impact.* Mahwah, NJ: Erlbaum.

Beer, M., Eisenstat, R. A., & Spector, B. (1990). *The critical path to corporate renewal.* Boston, MA: Harvard Business School Press.

Bono, J. E., & Ilies, R. (2006). Charisma, positive emotions and mood contagion. *Leadership Quarterly, 17,* 317–334.

Bono, J. E., & Judge, T. A. (2003). Self-concordance at work: Toward understanding the motivational effects of transformational leaders. *Academy of Management Journal, 46*(5), 554–571.

Burke, C. S., Stagl, K. C., Klein, C., Goodwin, G. F., Salas, E., & Halpin, S. M. (2006). What type of leadership behaviors are functional in teams? A meta-analysis. *Leadership Quarterly, 17,* 288–307.

Carroll, J. S., & Hatakenaka, S. (2001). Driving organizational change in the midst of crisis. *Sloan Management Review, 42*(3), 70–79.

Caruth, D., Middlebrook, B., & Rachel, F. (1985). Overcoming resistance to change. *S.A.M. Advanced Management Journal, 50*(3), 23–27.

Chelladurai, P. (1999). *Human resource management in sport and recreation.* Champaign, IL: Human Kinetics.

Child, J., & Smith, C. (1987). The context and process of organizational transformation: Cadbury Ltd. in its sector. *Journal of Management Studies, 24*(6), 565–593.

C.H. Johnson Consulting. (2006, November). Football program strategy assessment. Retrieved from http://www.georgiastatesports.com/pdf2/53118. pdf?&ATCLID=695518&SPSID=53686&SPID= 5679&DB_OEM_ID=12700

Costa, P. T., Jr., & McCrae, R. R. (1992). *Revised NEO personality inventory (NEO-PI-R) and NEO five factor inventory (NEO-FFI) professional manual.* Odessa, FL: PAR.

Denning, S. (2005). Transformational innovation. *Strategy and Leadership, 33*(3), 11–16.

de Poel, F. M., Stoker, J. I., & van der Zee, K. I. (2012). Climate control? The relationship between leadership, climate for change, and work outcomes. *International Journal of Human Resource Management, 23*(4), 694–713.

Elving, J. L. W. (2005). The role of communication in organizational change. *Corporate Communications, 10*(2), 129–139.

Ford, J. D., Ford, L. W., & D'Amelio, A. (2008). Resistance to change: The rest of the story. *Academy of Management Review, 33*(2), 363–377.

Georgia State University. (2006). Athletics Director Mary McElroy's open letter to the Georgia State University community on the football feasibility study. Retrieved from http://www2.gsu.edu/~wwwexa/news/archive /2006/06_1121-football.htm

Georgia State University. (2008). Bill Curry named head football coach. Retrieved from http://www .georgiastatesports.com/ViewArticle.dbml? DB_OEM_ID=12700&ATCLID=1480110

Harper, G., & Utley, D. (2001). Organizational culture and successful information technology implementation. *European Management Journal, 13,* 11–16.

Hill, L., & Kikulis, L. M. (1999). Contemplating restructuring: A case study of strategic decision-making in interuniversity athletic conferences. *Journal of Sport Management, 13,* 18–44.

Hinings, C. R., & Greenwood, R. (1988). *The dynamics of strategic change.* Oxford, England: Basil Blackwood.

House, R. J. (1971). A path-goal theory of leader effectiveness. *Administrative Science Quarterly, 16,* 321–338.

Jick, T., & Peiperl, M. (2003). *Managing change: Cases and concepts* (2nd ed.). New York: McGraw-Hill.

Kahai, S. S., Sosik, J. J., & Avolio, B. J. (2004). Effects of participative and directive leadership in electronic groups. *Group and Organization Management, 29,* 67–105.

Kiefer, T. (2005). Feeling bad: Antecedents and consequences of negative emotions in ongoing change. *Journal of Organizational Behavior, 26*(8), 875–897.

Kotlyar, I., & Karakowsky, L. (2006). Leading conflict? Linkages between leader behaviors and group conflict. *Small Group Research, 37,* 377–403.

Kotter, J. P. (1995). Leading change: Why transformational efforts fail. *Harvard Business Review, 73*(2), 59–67.

Kotter, J. P. (1996). *Leading change.* Boston, MA: Harvard Business School Press.

Kuhn, T. S. (1970). *The structure of scientific revolutions* (2nd ed.). Chicago, IL: University of Chicago Press.

Lines, R. (2004). Influence of participants in strategic change: Resistance, organizational commitment and change goal achievement. *Journal of Organizational Change Management, 4*(3), 193–215.

Lombardo, J. (2012, September 10). Unexpected exit for MSG's change agent. *Street and Smith's SportsBusiness Journal.* Retrieved from http://www.sportsbusinessdaily .com/Journal/Issues/2012/09/10/Franchises/ONeil .aspx?hl=Organizational%20change&sc=0

Lovelace, K., Shapiro, D. L., & Weingart, L. R. (2001). Maximizing cross-functional new product teams' innovativeness and constraint adherence: A conflict communications perspective. *Academy of Management Journal, 44,* 779–793.

Meyer, J. P., Srinivas, E. S., Lal, J. B., & Topolnytsky, L. (2007). Employee commitment and support for organizational change: Test of the three-component model in two cultures. *Journal of Occupational and Organizational Psychology, 80,* 185–211.

Miles, R. M. (2001). Accelerating corporate transformations by rapidly engaging all employees. *Organizational Dynamics, 29,* 313–321.

Mumford, M. D., Scott, G. M., Gaddis, B., & Strange, J. M. (2002). Leading creative people. *Leadership Quarterly, 13,* 705–750.

Nadler, D. A., & Tushman, M. L. (1988). *Competing by design.* New York: Oxford University Press.

Oreg, S. (2003). Resistance to change: Developing an individual difference measure. *Journal of Applied Psychology, 88*(4), 587–604.

Oreg, S. (2006). Personality, context and resistance to organizational change. *European Journal of Work and Organizational Psychology, 15*(1), 73–101.

O'Toole, J. (1996). *Leading change: The argument for values-based leadership.* New York: Ballantine.

Pascale, R., Millemann, M., & Gioja, L. (2000). *Surfing the edge of chaos.* New York: Crown Business.

Pawar, B. S., & Eastman, K. K. (1997). The nature and implications of contextual influences on transformational leadership: A conceptual examination. *Academy of Management Review, 22,* 80–109.

Piderit, S. K. (2000). Rethinking resistance and recognizing ambivalence: A multidimensional view of attitudes toward organizational change. *Academy of Management Review, 25*(4), 783–794.

Podsakoff, P. M., MacKenzie, S. B., Moorman, R. H., & Fetter, R. (1990). Transformational leader behaviors, and their effects on followers' trust in leader, satisfaction, and organizational citizenship behaviors. *Leadership Quarterly, 1,* 107–142.

Quinn, R. E. (2004). *Building the bridge as you walk on it.* San Francisco, CA: Jossey-Bass.

Rashid, Z., Sambasivan, M., & Rahman, A. (2004). The influence of organizational culture on attitudes towards organizational change. *Leadership and Organization Development Journal, 25,* 161–179.

Reichers, A. E., Wanous, J. P., & Austin, J. T. (1997). Understanding and managing cynicism about organizational change. *Academy of Management Executive, 11*(1), 48–59.

Romanelli, E., & Tushman, M. (1994). Organizational transformation as punctuated equilibrium: An empirical test. *Academy of Management Journal, 37,* 1141–1166.

Rush, M. C., Schoel, W. A., & Barnard, S. M. (1995). Psychological resiliency in the public sector: "Hardiness" and pressure for change. *Journal of Vocational Behavior, 46,* 17–39.

Schein, E. H. (1988). *Organizational culture and leadership.* San Francisco, CA: Jossey-Bass.

Schein, E. H. (1996). Culture: The missing concept in organization studies. *Administrative Science Quarterly, 41,* 229–240.

Schneider, B. (1987). The people make the place. *Personal Psychology, 40*, 437–453.

Slack, T., & Parent, M. (2006). *Understanding sport organizations: The application of organization theory* (2nd ed.). Champaign, IL: Human Kinetics.

Somech, A. (2003). Relationships of participative leadership with relational demography variables: A multi-level perspective. *Journal of Organizational Behavior, 24*, 1003–1018.

Sparks, P., Harris, P. R., & Lockwood, N. (2004). Predictors and predictive effects of ambivalence. *British Journal of Social Psychology, 43*, 371–383.

Spreitzer, G. M. (2007). Giving peace a chance: Organizational leadership, empowerment, and peace. *Journal of Organizational Behavior, 28*, 1077–1095.

Tichy, N. M., & Devanna, M. A. (1990). *The transformational leader.* New York: John Wiley.

Turnley, W. H., & Feldman, D. C. (1998). Psychological contract violations during corporate restructuring. *Human Resource Management, 37*(1), 71–83.

Vakola, M., Tsausk, I., & Nikolaou, I. (2004). The role of emotional intelligence and personality variance on attitudes toward organizational change. *Journal of Managerial Psychology, 19*, 88–111.

Wanberg, C. R., & Banas, J. T. (2000). Predictors and outcomes of openness to changes in a reorganizing workplace. *Journal of Applied Psychology, 85*(1), 132–142.

Want, J. (2003). When worlds collide: Corporate culture—Illuminating the black hole. *Journal of Business Strategy, 24*, 14–22.

Weick, K. E., & Quinn, R. E. (1999). Organizational change and development. *Annual Review of Psychology, 50*, 361–386.

Welty Peachey, J., & Bruening, J. (2011). An examination of environmental forces driving and constraining organizational change in a Football Championship Subdivision intercollegiate athletic department. *Sport Management Review, 14*(2), 202–219.

Welty Peachey, J., & Bruening, J. (2012a). Are your values mine? Exploring the influence of value congruence on responses to change in a Division I intercollegiate athletics department. *Journal of Intercollegiate Sport, 5*(2), 127–152.

Welty Peachey, J., & Bruening, J. (2012b). Investigating ambivalence towards organizational change in a Football Championship Subdivision intercollegiate athletic department. *Sport Management Review, 15*, 171–186.

Welty Peachey, J., Bruening, J., & Burton, L. (2011). Transformational leadership of change: Success through valuing relationships. *Journal of Contemporary Athletics, 5*(2), 127–152.

Williams, T. (1998). Job satisfaction in teams. *International Journal of Human Resource Management, 9*, 782–799.

Yukl, G. A., & Van Fleet, D. D. (1992). Theory and research on leadership in organization. In M. D. Dunnette & L. M. Hough (Eds.), *Handbook of industrial and organizational psychology* (2nd ed., pp. 147–197). Chicago, IL: Rand McNally.

CHAPTER 9

FOSTERING INNOVATION

Larena Hoeber
Orland Hoeber

CHAPTER OBJECTIVES

- Define the concept of innovation in the context of sport organizations.
- Describe the relationship between leadership and innovation and describe how leadership supports innovation from the managerial, organizational, and environmental perspectives.
- Demonstrate an understanding for how organizational structure, culture, size, and complexity provide support for the innovation process in sport organizations.
- Identify the managerial determinants (age, level and amount of education, tenure in the organization and position, and variety of background and experience) necessary to foster innovation in sport organizations.

CASE STUDY

Innovation Saves the Data for CSO

During her time as executive director of a nonprofit, community-based sport organization (CSO) in a mid-sized city in Canada, Sarah recognized ongoing problems in the reporting of soccer scores and statistics in their adult soccer league (175 teams with over 2,500 players). The reporting of scores and statistics was based on paper sheets that were completed by team captains and then submitted to the referees working that game. Staff members would then enter postgame data. This process was time consuming and often resulted in errors in data entry. Sarah recognized that

(continues)

implementing an online system to manage postgame data would reduce paper, release staff from tedious data entry that took up to 4 hours each Monday, and improve data entry errors. The online system would also improve player access to game information and help staff and referees with league rule enforcement.

Sarah sought out the services of a local software development and web services company to develop an electronic game sheet (EGS). The company was asked to source the hardware components, write custom software for the devices, develop the procedures for uploading the results of each game over the wireless network, and create the website software for the game, team, and individual statistics. Members of this web services company were also participants in the adult soccer league for which the EGS was being developed. Implementation of the EGS resulted in referees having the ability to check players in prior to the start of the game by swiping their player ID cards through a handheld device that would automatically check their eligibility to play in the game. Information regarding goals and penalties was entered into the handheld system at the end of each game. Up-to-date game information was synchronized over the wireless network and was then available on the league website. The resulting system reduced staff time and errors, and improved enforcement of league rules.

Sarah was instrumental in first recognizing that a new system was required to address game-day data entry for the adult soccer league. Sarah made sure the board of directors for the CSO knew there were issues with the old paper version of game data statistics, and she provided research and pricing to support the move to an electronic version of game day data entry. She worked to ensure that the board of directors did not ignore this proposal. When the EGS system was approved, Sarah worked closely with her staff, key team contacts in the adult league, and referees to be sure everyone was comfortable with the system. Referees for the league noted that her communication with them was an important part of the successful implementation of the new system. Once the new system was in place, Sarah handed over maintenance of the EGS to her staff. They were responsible for synchronizing information and assisting referees with proper use of the system. This transfer empowered staff members to take ownership of the EGS and be sure it was addressing the needs of the soccer league.

Staff members and referees working for the CSO noted that Sarah's strategic leadership skills were instrumental in adopting this innovation. Sarah noted that it was important to have a big-picture approach to using technology in the organization and also be willing to take risks on new and unproven systems. She envisioned use of the new EGS system to improve the efficiency of the organization, because she knew that if this new technology worked, it would give the staff more time to focus on important work within the CSO instead of taking time to complete menial data entry. Sarah demonstrated a proactive, visionary style of leadership. The board of directors also showed leadership skills in allowing Sarah to pursue this new innovation. Board members saw the benefits of using technology in the CSO and were supportive of Sarah's willingness to pursue the use of new technology to improve the adult soccer league. This support was instrumental in the decision to adopt the EGS system.

Questions for Discussion

1. What leadership skills were necessary for Sarah to successfully lobby for adoption of the EGS system?
2. What challenges might Sarah have had to overcome to be sure that the EGS system was implemented successfully?
3. Why is it important for leaders to recognize innovation in organizational operations?
4. Identify an innovation in sport that was successfully implemented by the leader of that organization.

INTRODUCTION

Innovation has been, and continues to be, of interest to many organizations because of its connection to competitiveness, effectiveness, growth, and survival (Damanpour & Schneider, 2006; Hage, 1999; Tidd, 2001; Wolfe, 1994; Zahra & Covin, 1994). Despite the wealth of research and interest in this topic (see, for example, Crossan & Apaydin, 2010; Hage, 1999; Wolfe, 1994), there is still some confusion about the definition of innovation.

One commonly accepted definition of innovation is "any idea, practice, or material artifact perceived as new by the relevant unit of adoption" (Zaltman, Duncan, & Holbek, 1973, p. 10). This definition recognizes that "newness" is defined by the context in which the innovation is occurring. Innovations can be identified as new based on their frame of reference at the group, organizational, industry, and global levels (Crossan & Apaydin, 2010; Johannessen, Olsen, & Lumpkin, 2001). The group level refers to subsections, divisions, or departments within an organization. Using a professional sport team as an example, the marketing department could be the first one to use a new internal communication platform. If a firm or company is using something new relative to other firms or companies in the same industry, this would be considered an innovation at the

organizational level. An example of this might be a sport team that is the first to use smart cards to track spectator purchases. Innovations at the industry level are ones that distinguish one industry from another. An example of this is when one sport league begins using a new social media platform, which is later used by other sport leagues. Innovations at the global level are inventions that are new to the world. For example, 3D filming and 24/7 specialty channel broadcasting were first introduced in the sport sector.

There is some debate if every "new" idea is an innovation. Some argue that the term *innovation* is overused (Kwon, 2012). If everyone is claiming to be innovative, how do the innovative organizations or leaders stand out? People generally agree upon newness (or improvement) at the global level—that is, something that has never been seen before in the world and results in improvements in performance or experience. We agree that there is much to be learned from these innovations (which can also be referred to as inventions); however, global-level innovations are relatively rare. It is more common that we see innovations at the group, organizational, or industry levels. These innovations can represent a minor or incremental change from the status quo, such as the redevelopment of an existing program for a new target market or demographic; for example, a swim club could offer a learn-to-swim program to persons with a physical disability. Innovations can reflect fundamental or radical shifts from the status quo. The introduction of instant replay in televised sports radically changed how viewers experienced the game, as well as how these games were officiated and perceived.

Another area of confusion with respect to innovation is that there are different forms of innovation. Products or goods are the more visible forms of innovation; however, innovations can also be in the form of services, processes, structures, or systems (Damanpour, 1996; Wolfe, 1994). For example, a local, nonprofit sport club could introduce babysitting as a new service, online membership registration as a new process for tracking members, or hire professional staff, thus changing the club's structure. **Table 9.1** lists some service and process innovations identified by presidents of community sport organizations in Canada (Hoeber et al., 2009).

Given the breadth of research on innovation and the variation of definitions that people use to understand this concept, we turned to a definition based on an in-depth review of research. Baregheh, Rowley, and Sambrook (2009) defined innovation as "the multi-stage process whereby organizations transform ideas into new/improved products, service[s] or processes, in order to advance, compete and differentiate themselves successfully in their marketplace" (p. 1334).

For the purpose of this chapter, we will highlight innovations at all levels, recognizing that some organizations strive to be cutting edge and ahead of the pack, and others need to innovate in order to survive within their industry. We will examine both the role of leaders in innovative organizations (e.g., how do leaders encourage innovation within their organizations) and leading organizations within the sport field. Conceptualization is a key skill for leaders. Conceptualization is the

TABLE 9.1 **Service and Process Innovations in Community Sport Organizations**

Sport	Service Innovations	Process Innovations
Curling	• New game format (e.g., "pick-up" curling) • Online newsletters • New membership payment options	• Targeting new potential members (youth, new immigrants, students) • Establishing a succession plan for board members
Soccer	• New leagues for women, different age groups • Creation of websites	• Establishing partnerships for developing facilities • New board positions • Adopting a database program
Swimming	• Programs for persons with disabilities, First Nations youth • Live Internet streaming of meets	• Creation of paid staff positions • Establishing sponsorship packages
Ultimate Frisbee	• New tournaments • Supporting charities	• Paying volunteers • "Carbon flip" to start the game • Polling the members

Source: Data from Hoeber, L., Doherty, A., Hoeber, O., Wolfe, R., Misener, K., & Cummings-Vickaryous, B. (2009). *An exploration of the nature of innovations in community sport organizations.* North American Society for Sport Management 24th Annual Conference. May 27–30, Columbia, SC.

process by which leaders evaluate the sport industry's environment, trends, dynamics, and shifts in perceived value or expectations, and attempt to set a future direction for the organization (vision). If leaders are truly examining their organizations' external environments, innovation can play an important role in making operations run more efficiently and improving both the spectator and participant experience in sport.

HISTORICAL GROUNDING

The sport industry offers an interesting arena for examining innovation. Sport organizations are characterized by passion and commitment to the product (Babiak & Wolfe, 2009). This passion can be a deterrent to innovation if it is tied to strong feelings of nostalgia, tradition, and history (Smith & Shilbury, 2004; Thiel & Mayer, 2009; Wolfe, Wright, & Smart, 2006) or it can result in key stakeholders becoming deeply committed to the innovations the organization undertakes. Golf is an interesting example of both a commitment to tradition and openness to change. On the one hand, some golf clubs have remained loyal to their traditional approaches to restricted membership and course maintenance, which may contribute to negative public images, at the expense of including a wider range of members or adopting more environmentally friendly maintenance procedures. On the other hand, professional and recreational golfers demand cutting-edge innovations with their golf equipment to improve performance in areas like accuracy and swing speed.

It is also interesting to examine innovations in the sport industry because it includes sectors that produce tangible goods, as well as sectors that provide services. Within the sporting goods sector, improvements in manufacturing, materials, and processes result in tangible differences in products that can be experienced by customers and clients. These improvements can result in improved athletic performance, which translates into competitive advantages. Thus, innovation is key for success in the sporting goods sector. As **Table 9.2** indicates, there are numerous examples of such innovations that run the gamut from new fabrics in sport apparel and swim gear to innovations in ice hockey, football, and skiing.

A large sector of the sport industry focuses on services, which includes sport media. This

TABLE 9.2 **Sample of Sporting Goods Innovations**

Sport	Product Innovation	Purpose
Running	Wick-away fabrics	Keep athletes cool; reduce chance of overheating
Ice hockey	Composite sticks (carbon fiber, graphite, fiberglass)	Lighter stick; more accurate shots; more consistency in performance
Swimming	Sharkskin swim suits	Reduce resistance in the water
Football	Air bladders in helmets	Stabilize athletes' heads; reduce chance of concussions
Downhill skiing	Avalanche safety vests and backpacks	Increase survival rates in avalanches

particular segment of the sport services sector is reliant on innovations in technology and communications to reach a wider or more specific audience and to provide a better viewing and/or listening experience for spectators. Broadcasting of sporting events has been the catalyst for innovations in televised media. For example, 3D sport broadcasting was introduced at the 2010 FIFA World Cup (Host Broadcast Services, n.d.). Other broadcasting innovations include using banners and graphics over live televised coverage, virtual images such as the yellow first-down line in football, and the Hawk-Eye ball-tracking system used in tennis (shown in **Figure 9.1**). (See **Table 9.3** for more examples of technological innovations in sport broadcasting.) Other sport media innovations include on-demand programming and live streaming of events on the Internet.

Not all sport media innovations have been successful. In 1996, Fox Sports introduced the FoxTrax, a tracking system to follow the puck in ice hockey games. This tracking system involved adding a "blue glow" to the puck so viewers could better see the puck on the ice, and a "comet tail" to indicate speed (Cavallaro, 1997). There were mixed reactions to this technological innovation (see Cavallaro, 1997; Mason, 2002), with some of the more vocal opposition coming from established hockey fans who saw the innovation as a compromise to the integrity of the game. It was last used in 1998.

Training is another area of the sport service sector in which innovations are important and visible. Here, coaches, athletes, and sport organizations use innovations in technology and sport psychology to gain competitive advantages. ESPN recently published an overview of the top technological innovations in the 2012 Summer Olympics, many of which relate to training and competition (Curtis, 2012). These included Dartfish software, a high-speed camera system that athletes like Usain Bolt use to pinpoint areas of improvement. Also recently, with the help of a software company, the U.S. Ski and Snowboard Association (USSA) created an athlete-management system that allows athletes to record everything from the number of hours they sleep to the number of sets they do in the weight room. The information is recorded in a phone app and shared with USSA coaches and the organization's high-performance teams. In addition, the software system assigns athletes a training regimen from 6,500 available exercises (Mickle, 2013).

It is more difficult to identify innovations in some sport services, such as professional sport leagues or sport governing bodies, because they may be internal processes and structures that are less obvious to the general public, or intentionally protected as trade secrets. However, Wolfe and colleagues' (2006) discussion of the use of sabermetrics to assess human resources in Major League Baseball, Sheridan's (2007) assessment of Wimbeldon's revised seeding system, and Caza's (2000) case study of context receptivity to

FIGURE 9.1 **Hawk-Eye is a computer tracking system used in numerous sports, such as cricket and tennis, to visually track the trajectory of the ball.**

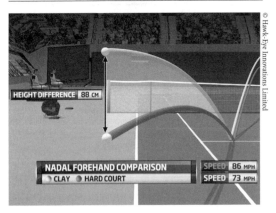

© Hawk-Eye Innovations Limited

TABLE 9.3 **Technological Innovations in Sport Broadcasting**

Sport/Event	Area of Innovation	Examples
Summer Olympics	Timing	• Official automatic timing provided by Omega, the lone manufacturer of stopwatches: Los Angeles (1932) • Electronic automated timing: Tokyo (1964)
	Televised broadcasts	• First televised broadcasts: Berlin (1936) • First televised home broadcasts: London (1948)
	Virtual imaging	• Virtual lines on swimming lanes to indicate record times: Sydney (2000)
Baseball	Cameras	• Centerfield cameras: Chicago (1951) • Slow motion cameras: ABC and NBC (1984)
	Graphics	• Electronic character graphics (1970s) • Pictoral graphics: Fox (1990s)
	Digital television	• High-definition transmission (1997)
Football	Television	• Instant replay: CBS (1963) • Virtual imaging 1st and 10 line: ESPN (1998)
Motor sports	Graphics	• Highlight lead car: (2000s) • Virtual dashboard (2000s)

Source: Data from IEEE Global History Network. (n.d.a). Technological innovations and the Summer Olympic Games. Retrieved from http://www.ieeeghn.org/wiki/index.php/Technological_Innovations_and_the_Summer_Olympic_Games; IEEE Global History Network. (n.d.b). Technological innovations in sports broadcasting. Retrieved from http://www.ieeeghn.org/wiki/index.php/Technological_Innovations_in_Sports_Broadcasting

innovations in a provincial boxing association illustrate innovations within these types of sport organizations.

DETERMINANTS OF INNOVATION

Organizational innovativeness is one of the main streams of research in innovation studies (Wolfe, 1994). In this stream, researchers are interested in identifying the determinants that help an organization be innovative. There is an extensive body of literature on the determinants of organizational innovativeness (Wolfe, 1994). Here, a determinant is defined as any activity, process, or condition that either supports or opposes the ability of an organization to innovate. These determinants can be grouped into three levels of analysis: managerial, organizational, and environmental (Damanpour & Schneider, 2006). *Managerial determinants* relate to the support and attitude of top managers and leaders toward innovation. *Organizational determinants* relate to the internal environment, including the structure, culture, size, and complexity of the organization. *Environmental determinants* are those that exist in the context outside of the organization (e.g., social, political, economic, and cultural contexts) that facilitate innovation or act as a barrier to innovation.

For the purpose of this text, we highlight how leadership supports innovation from these three levels of determinants (managerial, organizational, environmental). First, we examine managerial characteristics that support innovation. Second, we consider how leaders can foster innovation within the organization. Third, we examine how leaders embrace environmental determinants (when they work in support of innovation) or manage them (when they work against innovation).

Managerial Determinants

Leadership is a critical element in fostering organizational innovation because it is the leaders in an organization who have the opportunity to offer support and guidance when innovations are developed or proposed, and to create an environment that is conducive to implementing innovations (Crossan & Apaydin, 2010). Damanpour and Schneider (2006) suggest "top managers heavily influence organizational capabilities by establishing organizational culture, motivating and enabling managers and employees, and building capacity for change and innovation" (p. 220). Management has the ability to develop and maintain an environment that fosters innovation and to provide the necessary resources to implement it. This support can be exhibited by presidents, executive officers, departmental managers, and/or board members (Crossan & Apaydin, 2010).

We often think of leadership support for innovation happening in a top-down approach (Daft, 1978). So what distinguishes top managers who support innovation from those who do not? Some of the individual, managerial factors that contribute to innovation include favorable attitudes toward innovation such as acceptance of risk, tolerance of ambiguity, openness to or tolerance of change, originality, proactiveness, and independence (Crossan & Apaydin, 2010; Damanpour & Schneider, 2006, 2009). Leaders are instrumental in getting buy-in for change from skeptical

employees. Innovation can equate to transformational change in organizations. Consider all the workplaces that computerized operations in the late 20th century. Also, consider how global companies now use a variety of teleconferencing and videoconferencing devices like Skype to connect with key stakeholders spread around the world. If sport leaders favor innovation, it is likely they will be open to new ideas and direct resources to pursuing and implementing innovations. This is done with the hope that these innovations will result in a competitive advantage. Owners of the Seattle Sounders, a Major League Soccer (MLS) team, exhibit some of these characteristics. From the inception of the team, the owners decided to manage the team democratically, allowing fans a significant say in the operation of the team. Fans decided the name of the team, and regularly have a say in the general management of the team. A membership council meets with the front office of the team three times a year (Gaschk, 2008). This membership system was proposed by the actor Drew Carey, one of the owners of the Seattle Sounders.

Managerial demographics are also key determinants of innovation (Crossan & Apaydin, 2010; Damanpour & Schneider, 2006). Demographics such as age, level and amount of education (more education), tenure in the organization and position (less tenure; newer to the organization), and variety of background and experience have been connected with innovation. With respect to age, it is expected that younger managers will support and develop more innovations because they are receptive to new ideas, and for technological innovations, they are familiar and comfortable with technology (Berry, Berry, & Foster, 1998; Damanpour & Schneider, 2006). In contrast, older managers may be less willing to pursue innovations because they are committed to the status quo (Damanpour & Schneider, 2006). In a case study of the adoption and implementation of a technological innovation in a community sport organization, the youthfulness of the board was viewed as a facilitator of innovation because they were open to technology and willing to try something new (Hoeber & Hoeber, 2012).

Sometimes, leadership for innovation rests with one individual, referred to as an *innovation champion* (Damanpour & Schneider, 2006; Wolfe, 1994; Wolfe et al., 2006). These are individuals, at any level in the organization, who propose, develop, advocate, and in some cases implement innovations. A high profile example of an innovation champion in professional sport is Billy Beane, the general manager of the Oakland Athletics, a Major League Baseball team. His adoption of sabermetrics, a system to assess baseball players' skills that emphasized past performances and unconventional statistics (Wolfe et al., 2006), challenged the conventional system used by scouts. Beane turned to sabermetrics because he had limited financial resources to recruit expensive players who were highly rated on traditional skills, like hitting power or arm strength. Sabermetrics allowed Beane and the A's to scout players with undervalued talents, like on-base percentage. Although there was some hesitation by A's ownership to adopt this approach, Beane "had the necessary energy, commitment, and organizational power" (Wolfe et al., 2006, p. 117), characteristics associated with innovation champions, to ensure sabermetrics was adopted by the team. His use of this human-resource management innovation provided him with a competitive advantage, because he was able to recruit quality players at low salaries. This is an example of the need for sport leaders, even if they are questioned, to challenge the "old school" system or ways of thinking.

Caza's (2000) case study of proposed innovations in a regional boxing association highlighted the importance of innovation champions. One innovation, the athlete ranking system, was implemented in part because the vice president of operations, a volunteer board member, built support for it through consultation and discussion with members. A second innovation, the adoption of a computerized scoring system, lacked leadership commitment from a volunteer board member and ultimately was abandoned.

Organizational Determinants

Innovation is not always initiated or actively supported by top managers. Rather, innovation can arise from a bottom-up or shared approach (Daft, 1978); that is, innovation can be fostered and developed within the organization. Leaders still play an important role in this approach, through the establishment of structures and cultures that promote innovation within the organization.

Large, complex organizations are seen as conducive to innovation because they have formal structures and systems in place to support the innovation process. One of the key structures is research and development departments, which are specifically tasked with creating innovations. Many large sporting goods manufacturing companies, like Nike and Under Armour, rely on research and development (R & D) departments to establish cutting-edge innovations that will translate into competitive advantages.

Leaders are instrumental in establishing an organizational culture that supports risk taking, openness to change, and forward thinking by their employees, members, and board members (Igira, 2008; Jaskyte, 2004). Leaders can establish this culture through stated organizational values and discourses. Although Nike has an R & D department, it also has a stated commitment to innovation. As such, employees in all areas of the organizations are encouraged to suggest and develop innovation. Thus, Nike can reap the benefits of innovations in fabrics, materials, and design, as well as in the areas of supply chain management, marketing, and workplace environments.

In the sport industry, innovations are sometimes proposed and initiated by *boundary spanners* (Daft, 1978). These are members or quasi-members who are involved in multiple domains (e.g., work in the private sector, volunteer for a nonprofit sport club) and bring ideas into an organization. These boundary spanners can include athletes, coaches, customers, volunteers, or board members. Franke and Shah (2003) studied the development and diffusion of product innovations in amateur sport communities. They found a "community-based innovation system" (Franke & Shah, 2003, p. 169) in which the sport participants (i.e., users) developed product innovations, which were readily shared within the sport communities. These individuals are participants in the sport as well as members of other communities and industries, and thus can bring ideas from a variety of sources to the sport. Boundary spanners are also an important source of innovation in nonprofit sport organizations, which are governed by a volunteer board of directors. These individuals represent many different sectors in society (e.g., education, marketing, business, law) and can use their knowledge and expertise from these other sectors as a source of new ideas for the sport organization.

Environmental Determinants

Innovations can develop as a result of pressures and opportunities from the environment. Leaders play a vital role in recognizing and capitalizing on opportunities to do something different or to keep up with competitors, and in managing negative pressures in the environment by turning to innovation (Damanpour & Schneider, 2006).

Leaders can identify opportunities for innovation within their market or industry. These opportunities can arise from changing demands of their members or clients, innovations being adopted by competitors in their sector, or external stakeholders (e.g., suppliers, funders, sponsors) sharing ideas. Under Armour is known for its focus on innovation and entrepreneurship. The company currently has a section on its website to encourage people outside of its organization to submit ideas, a practice referred to as "open sourcing." Under Armour is capitalizing on the creativity of others and their willingness to share their ideas. In doing so, they are expanding their options for sources of new ideas beyond their employees.

Not all innovations need to be copied, but nevertheless, leaders must be aware of what their competitors are doing to gain competitive advantages. Social media is an innovation that more sport teams are adopting because they see how other sport teams and other companies, outside the sport industry, are benefiting from it. It is difficult to know which professional team or which leader was the first to use Facebook and Twitter, but it is clear that teams recognize the value of these for marketing and communicating with customers, and for public and community relations.

Leaders must also monitor the social, political, economic, and cultural environments in which the organization operates, because changes and shifts in these environments may mitigate the need to be innovative. To illustrate, golf course operators need to be aware of changes in the political and social environments regarding the use of pesticides. If new municipal legislation is enacted banning the use of pesticides, golf courses in the municipality need to consider new procedures for turf maintenance. Consumer demands for online interactions is a significant societal trend that leaders in all areas of the sport industry must attend to, and respond with innovations in areas such as communications, purchasing, and broadcasting. Another major area of consideration for leaders is demographic changes in society, including an aging population, immigration, and reductions in family sizes, as well as shifts in societal attitudes about sexuality, disability, and multiculturalism. Leaders can address these environmental shifts through the adoption and implementation of innovative services and products. Toronto is recognized as the most multicultural city in Canada, and one of the most multicultural in the world, with almost half of its population in

2006 being foreign-born (City of Toronto, n.d.). The South Asian and Chinese communities are two of the largest visible minorities in the city. In response to this shift in the population, the National Basketball Association's Toronto Raptors began broadcasting their games in Punjabi in 2009, and in Mandarin in 2012 (National Basketball Association, 2009, 2012).

SUMMARY

The goal of this chapter has been to formalize the concept of innovation, and discuss it from the perspective of managerial, organizational, and environmental determinants in the context of sport organizations. Regardless of the driving force behind innovation, the leaders in a sport organization play a critical role in not only directly supporting the undertaking of an innovation, but also fostering an environment that is supportive and open to both internal and external sources of innovative practices.

Although technological innovation within the sporting goods sector is easy to identify, innovation is also occurring within the service sector of sport, as well as in the internal operational processes, structures, and systems of many sport organizations. Such innovation spans the professional/recreational divide, and may occur within both the product domain (sporting goods sector) and the process domain (sport organizations/teams). Supporting innovations in these contexts is a crucial role for sport leaders.

LEADERSHIP PERSPECTIVE

Richard Krezwick.
Courtesy of Richard Krezwick

Richard Krezwick was president of Devils Area Entertainment between 2009 and 2013 and was responsible for all operational aspects of the Prudential Center, overseeing the overall programming and management of the arena that hosts the New Jersey Devils along with Seton Hall University's NCAA Division I men's basketball. The venue is also host to many concerts, family shows, and athletic events. Before coming to New Jersey, Krezwick worked with AEG as the vice president of regional operations following 10 years as president of Boston's FleetCenter.

Q: When I say the word *innovation* with regard to sport and, more specifically, sport facilities and event management, what does that word mean to you?

It's multifaceted, cutting edge technology, both within the brand and within the facility, new fan experience touch points, inventive and engaging business platforms, making the facility more than just about the game, but a true entertainment destination. It's being creative on how we provide our product to our fans; bringing them closer to the game and entertainment by providing them unique access and utilizing technology.

Q: In your mind, where do new ideas or innovation come from?

It comes from everywhere: our fans, our staff, and even other industries. For example, we have leather-back plush seats similar to something you would see in a luxury movie theater or high-end automobile. We often look at everything to see if it's something we can bring to our arena or facility to enhance our fan experience. Innovation is truly everywhere; the key is interpreting it to our industry.

Q: What kinds of innovations would patrons notice while walking through the Prudential Center or attending an event there? Why is innovation so important for customer satisfaction?

On our main concourse, fans will not see any permanent signage. All of our sponsor messages are run on large screens that look similar to iPhones. The content is more dynamic so fans notice it, and its more cost effective to add/subtract messages, not to mention that we don't have hard printing costs. It also gives our partners flexibility to change messages quickly and efficiently. It's important technology that saves us money and is better for the consumer and the sponsor.

Q: How, as an important leader for Devils Arena Entertainment, have you created an environment among employees and fellow executives that is conducive to fostering the development of innovation and implementing innovations in the facility, its events, and the organization?

We dedicated our time, resources, and staffing to help set ourselves ahead of the curve with the creation of "Mission Control," and it's something we've fully integrated throughout our organization. We were the first in professional sport to have this type of digital command center. We empower our most socially and digital savvy fans through our Devils Generals and Rock Reporters programs to extend our reach through our social media channels. It's become engrained into our culture and into everything we do.

Q: In the future, where do you see innovation heading with regard to live entertainment?

I wish I knew already, but I feel all signs point to mobile. Giving fans things like real-time photos and updates from backstage or the locker room, to a way in which you can purchase merchandise like a tour T-shirt without missing the encore are all things we will start to see in the future. I think we will see advancements in e-tickets and more secure ways for fans to attend events. We do everything with our phones already, I can see them playing a bigger part in the way we consume live entertainment. I have no doubt the live entertainment industry will continue to test the limits of how we can give more to the fans that attend shows and events.

KEY TERMS

boundary spanners
environmental determinants
innovation
innovation champion

managerial determinants
organizational determinants
organizational innovativeness

DISCUSSION QUESTIONS

1. Explain the concept of innovation within a sport organization. Aside from those listed in the chapter, what other examples of innovation have had an impact on the success of a sport organization or sport league?
2. Organizational innovativeness is contingent on three levels of determinants. What are these determinants and how do they relate to organizational innovation?
3. Why are the demographic characteristics of a manager important determinants of organizational innovativeness?
4. Innovation can be a top-down, bottom-up, or shared approach. Describe each of these approaches to innovation and how leaders can support each approach.
5. If you were the marketing manager for a minor-league baseball team, what steps would you take as a leader to be sure that your organization fosters innovation with regard to in-game promotions? What would be your most significant challenges as you attempted to foster innovation in your organization?

For a full suite of assignments and additional learning activities, use the access code found in the front of your book. If you do not have an access code, you can obtain one at **www.jblearning.com**.

REFERENCES

Babiak, K., & Wolfe, R. (2009). Determinants of corporate social responsibility in professional sport: Internal and external factors. *Journal of Sport Management, 23*(6), 717–742.

Baregheh, A., Rowley, J., & Sambrook, S. (2009). Towards a multidisciplinary definition of innovation. *Management Decision, 47*(8), 1323–1339. doi: 10.1108/00251740910984578

Berry, F. S., Berry, W. D., & Foster, S. K. (1998). The determinants of success in implementing an expert system in state government. *Public Administration Review, 58*(4), 295–305.

Cavallaro, R. (1997). The FoxTrax hockey puck tracking system. *IEEE Computer Graphics and Applications, 17*(2), 6–12. doi: 10.1109/38.574652

Caza, A. (2000). Context receptivity: Innovation in an amateur sport organization. *Journal of Sport Management, 14*, 227–242. Retrieved from http://hk.humankinetics.com.libproxy.uregina.ca:2048/JSM/bissues.cfm

City of Toronto. (n.d.). Toronto's racial diversity. Retrieved from http://www.toronto.ca/toronto_facts/diversity.htm

Crossan, M., & Apaydin, M. (2010). A multi-dimensional framework of organizational innovation: A systematic review of the literature. *Journal of Management Studies, 47*(6), 1154–1191. doi: 10.1111/j.1467-6486.2009.00880.x

Curtis, C. (2012, August 13). Top tech innovations from the 2012 Olympics. Retrieved from http://espn.go.com/blog/playbook/tech/post/_/id/1603/top-tech-innovations-from-2012-olympics

Daft, R. L. (1978). A dual-core of organizational innovation. *Academy Management Journal, 21*(2), 193–210. doi: 10.2307/255754

Damanpour, F. (1996). Organizational complexity and innovation: Developing and testing multiple contingency models. *Management Science, 42*(5), 693–716.

Damanpour, F., & Schneider, M. (2006). Phases of the adoption of innovation in organizations: Effects of environment, organization and top managers. *British Journal of Management, 17*, 215–236. doi:10.1111/j.1467-8551.2006.00498.x

Damanpour, F., & Schneider, M. (2009). Characteristics of innovation and innovation adoption in public organizations: Assessing the role of managers. *Journal of Public Administration Research and Theory, 19*(3), 495–522. doi: 10.1093/jopart/mun021

Franke, N., & Shah, S. (2003). How communities support innovative activities: An exploration of assistance and sharing among end users. *Research Policy, 32*(1), 157–178.

Gaschk, M. (2008, May 16). Sounders FC owner caters to fans. *Seattle PI.* Retrieved from http://www.seattlepi.com/sports/article/Sounders-FC-owner-caters-to-fans-1273654.php

Hage, J. T. (1999). Organizational innovation and organizational change. *Annual Review of Sociology, 25*, 597–622.

Hoeber, L., Doherty, A., Hoeber, O., Wolfe, R., Misener, K., & Cummings-Vickaryous, B. (2009). *An exploration of the nature of innovations in community sport organizations.* North American Society for Sport Management 24th Annual Conference. May 27–30, Columbia, SC.

Hoeber, L., & Hoeber, O. (2012). Determinants of an innovation process: A case study of technological innovation in a community sport organization. *Journal of Sport Management, 26*(3), 213–223.

Host Broadcast Services. (n.d.). 2010 FIFA World Cup South Africa. Retrieved from http://www.hbs.tv/past-hbs-missions/2010-fifa-world-cup-south-africatm.html

IEEE Global History Network. (n.d.a). Technological innovations and the Summer Olympic Games. Retrieved from http://www.ieeeghn.org/wiki/index.php/Technological_Innovations_and_the_Summer_Olympic_Games

IEEE Global History Network. (n.d.b). Technological innovations in sports broadcasting. Retrieved from http://www.ieeeghn.org/wiki/index.php/Technological_Innovations_in_Sports_Broadcasting

Igira, F. (2008). The situatedness of work practices and organizational culture: Implications for information systems innovation uptake. *Journal of Information Technology, 23*, 79–88. doi:10.1057/palgrave.jit.2000132

Jaskyte, K. (2004). Transformational leadership, organizational culture, and innovativeness in non-profit organizations. *Nonprofit Management and Leadership, 15*(2), 153–168. doi: 10.1002/nml.59

Johannessen, J. A., Olsen, B., & Lumpkin, G. (2001). Innovation as newness: What is new, how new, and new to whom? *European Journal of Innovation Management, 4*(1), 20–31.

Kwon, L. (2012, May 23). You call that innovation? *Wall Street Journal,* B1.

Mason, D. (2002). "Get the puck outta here!" Media transnationalism and Canadian identity. *Journal of Sport and Social Issues, 26*(2), 140–167. doi: 10.1177/0193723502262003

Mickle, T. (2013, July 22). Idea innovators: Troy Flanagan, high performance director, U.S. Ski and Snowboard Association. *Street & Smith's SportsBusiness Journal.* Retrieved from http://www.sportsbusinessdaily.com/Journal/Issues/2013/07/22/Idea-Innovators/Troy-Flanagan.aspx

National Basketball Association. (2009, November 20). Raptors to broadcast CBC games in Punjabi. Retrieved from http://www.nba.com/raptors/news/raptors_punjabi_112009.html

National Basketball Association. (2012). Raptors to broadcast game in Mandarin. Retrieved from http://www.nba.com/raptors/news/raptors-broadcast-game-mandarin

Sheridan, H. (2007). Evaluating technical and technological innovations in sport: Why fair play isn't enough. *Journal of Sport and Social Issues, 31*(2), 179–194. doi: 10.1177/0193723507300485

Smith, A., & Shilbury, D. (2004). Mapping cultural dimensions in Australian sporting organizations. *Sport Management Review, 7*, 133–165. doi:10.1016/S1441-3523(04)70048-0

Thiel, A., & Mayer, J. (2009). Characteristics of voluntary sports clubs management: A sociological perspective. *European Sport Management Quarterly, 9*(1), 81–98. doi: 10.1080/16184740802461744

Tidd, J. (2001). Innovation management in context: Environment, organization and performance. *International Journal of Management Reviews, 3*(3), 169–183. doi: 10.1111/1468-2370.00062

Wolfe, R. (1994). Organizational innovation: Review, critique, and suggested research directions. *Journal of Management Studies, 31*, 405–431. doi: 10.1111/j.1467-6486.1994.tb00624.x

Wolfe, R., Wright, P., & Smart, D. (2006). Radical HRM innovation and competitive advantage: The *Moneyball* story. *Human Resource Management, 45*, 111–126. doi: 10.1002/hrm.20100

Zahra, S., & Covin, J. (1994). The financial implications of fit between competitive strategy and innovation types and sources. *Journal of High Technology Management Research, 5*(2), 183–211. doi: 10.1016/1047-8310(94)90002-7

Zaltman, G., Duncan, R., & Holbek, J. (1973). *Innovations and organizations.* New York: Wiley.

HANDLING CRISIS AND CONFLICT

Peter Schroeder

CHAPTER OBJECTIVES

- Demonstrate an understanding of the importance of crisis containment.
- Understand the importance of leadership in times of organizational crises.
- Understand the impact of social media with regard to crises in sport.
- Describe the steps needed to form a crisis plan, carry it out, and evaluate it.

CASE STUDY

Reforming Colorado Football

The University of Colorado football program ended the 20th century with great success, but also with widespread allegations of sexual assault. The first of several accusations involving Colorado football players or recruits surfaced in December 1997 (Associated Press, 2004b). The events occurred just over a year before Gary Barnett took the job as the Colorado head football coach in 1999 (Associated Press, 2004b). Over the next 6 years, several Colorado students claimed they had been raped by Colorado football players and recruits at parties. Anne Gilmore and Lisa Simpson filed separate lawsuits in 2002 and 2003 for rape allegations (Sander, 2007). In 2004, Monique Gillaspie filed a suit for rape, and Katie Hnida, former Colorado kicker, alleged she had been raped by a Colorado player in 1999 (Associated Press, 2004b; Sander, 2007).

(*continues*)

In response to Hnida's allegations, Barnett said, "It was obvious Katie was not very good. She was awful. You know what guys do? They respect your ability. You can be 90 years old, but if you can go out and play, they'll respect you. Katie was not only a girl, she was terrible. OK? There's no other way to say it" (Associated Press, 2004a).

After hearing these comments, Colorado placed Barnett on paid leave (Associated Press, 2004b). During the 2004 off-season, Colorado self-imposed recruiting restrictions that eliminated player hosts and most on-campus visits during the football season (Associated Press, 2004a). An investigative panel created by the Colorado Board of Regents criticized university officials for not monitoring the recruiting process of the athletics program. After reviewing the allegations, the Colorado attorney general's office decided against filing charges; however, Gilmore and Simpson combined lawsuits and took their case to the U.S. Court of Appeals. Judges in the 10th Circuit determined that Athletic Director Dick Tharp and Barnett fostered unsuitable and potentially unlawful behavior by athletes and recruits (Sander, 2007). Tharp resigned from the athletic director position but stated that his resignation "should not in any way be construed as an admission to having engaged in any activity of wrongdoing. When completely investigated, the record will show that I performed my duties responsibly and in the best interests of the Department of Athletics and the University of Colorado" (Dodge, 2004b). Richard Byyny, Colorado chancellor, and university president Elizabeth Hoffman also resigned after receiving widespread criticism for not firing Coach Barnett (Dodge, 2004a; Sander, 2007). In December 2005, Barnett resigned after reaching an agreement for a $3 million settlement with Colorado (Sander, 2007).

The lawsuit involving Gilmore and Simpson was settled for $2.85 million. Under the terms of the decision, Colorado was also required to create a Title IX advisor position and add another part-time counselor for victim advocacy. Following the case, associate vice president for university relations, Ken McConnellogue, stated, "We're in an entirely different place than when this first came up. We have new people in 11 of our top 12 leadership positions, and we've enacted a series of reforms in our intercollegiate athletic programs and in our student services" (Sander, 2007, p. A20).

Questions for Discussion

1. Re-read the case study and assess the allegations versus what the University of Colorado did to remedy the crisis situation. In the end, do you feel the university did enough?

2. What do you think of Colorado's decision to put Barnett on paid administrative leave rather than firing him? What would you have done?

3. After Barnett was fired, Tom Lucero, a member of the school's board of regents, said Barnett had become emblematic of the scandal surrounding the football program (ESPN, 2005). In your view, should the football coach be held responsible if some of his players commit crimes?

4. The 21st century thus far has seen a lot of high-profile crises involving college football programs (Miami, Ohio State, North Carolina). In your view, how can the leadership of athletic departments do a better job of preventing wrongdoing by coaches and student-athletes and, thus, prevent crises?

INTRODUCTION

Crisis situations have become common in 21st-century sport. Seemingly every day the news features stories of athletes, coaches, teams, universities, or leagues creating controversy. The events creating controversies not only seem more common, but also have become more egregious. Therefore, it is imperative that leaders in sport maintain a skill set that enables them to handle crisis and conflict. The absence of these skills during a crisis can destroy organizational cultures, cost leaders their jobs, and create widespread public disillusionment (Lawson, 2007). For example, as described in the case study, a sexual assault scandal in the football program at the University of Colorado led to the resignation or dismissal of its chancellor, president, athletic director, and football coach. Conversely, with strong leadership, sport organizations can emerge from crises stronger in purpose, reputation, and support. Oklahoma State's response to the deaths of 10 members of its men's basketball traveling party left the victims' families feeling "overwhelmed with the generosity" (Paterson et al., 2007, p. 267).

Crises can arise from things as simple as photos or tweets to actions as grave as child molestation or murder. To persist through such difficulties, sport leaders and managers must diligently prepare for public relations crises and have the courage and intuition to execute crisis communication plans. This chapter will offer such insights. It will begin by defining and characterizing public relations crises, including the dynamic role of social media in crises. Next, steps to prepare for public relations crises will be provided. Strategies for dealing with crises will be offered, as will techniques for assessing these strategies. Sport management students reading this chapter should place these strategies in the context of how an organization's collective leadership should respond. The chapter is more focused on the collective rather than an individual leader, because it takes more than one person to defuse crisis situations.

CHARACTERIZING CRISES

Management and leadership of sport organizations are unlike those of any other businesses or corporations. Its laborers, athletes and coaches, are incredibly visible and often adored (and sometimes hated) by millions of fans. Not surprisingly, media coverage of these individuals and their teams is unparalleled. Furthermore, sport managers lack control over these individuals who form the core elements of their product (Mullin, Hardy, & Sutton, 2007). What results is an environment in which situations regularly arise that can negatively affect sport organizations. However, not all of these incidents actually constitute crises.

To become a *crisis*, an event must be "a major occurrence with a potentially negative outcome affecting the organization, company, or industry, as well as its public, products, services or good name" (Fearn-Banks, 2011, p. 2). There are three major elements that enable sport managers to know if they need to move into crisis mode (Horine, 1999; Stoldt, Dittmore, & Branvold, 2006). Crises are sudden. Although many types of crises can be anticipated, the timing of them cannot. Second, the incident must result in some damage to the sport organization. This usually comes in the form of a diminished brand image among its key publics or financial losses. The damage does not have to destroy the organization, but it must be significant enough to impede its future functioning (Fearn-Banks, 2011). Disruption is the third aspect of a crisis. Crises move organizations from their core processes and force them to focus on crisis management.

The illegal bounty program run by the New Orleans Saints illustrates each aspect well. The program began in 2009, but the story broke in March 2012. In terms of damages, the bounty scandal harmed the goodwill developed by the Saints' Super Bowl victory and positive contributions to the rejuvenation of New Orleans. In addition, the National Football League (NFL) fined the Saints $500,000, revoked two draft picks, and suspended several players and coaches. As a result, the normal operations for the Saints were disrupted. The Saints had to supply NFL investigators with over 18,000 organizational documents, and the team had to determine how to temporarily restructure its coaching staff and roster in the wake of the league's punishments (King 2012; Klemko, 2012).

To best prepare for and manage such crises, it is imperative to understand their life cycles. Walaski (2011) presents four stages of a crisis that begins with the prodromal phase. In this phase, clues and signals about the impending crisis emerge if the organization is alert or has detection systems in place. Second, the crisis breakout occurs. This is the single pivotal event when organizational disruption begins. Crisis breakout does not always occur with the initial misstep. Sometimes the mishandling of a minor problem can initiate the breakout. For example, when Ohio State's football players illegally exchanged memorabilia for tattoos in 2010, it was a manageable misstep. The crisis breakout occurred when the media learned that the head coach hid the information for 9 months (Robinson & Wetzel, 2011). The chronic phase develops as the organization uses various strategies to handle the crisis. When done effectively, the organization can shorten this phase, but the converse can occur when a crisis is mismanaged. Finally, resolution signals the end of the crisis as the organization has minimized its damaging effects or it has been naturally resolved.

Social Media and Crises

Crisis life cycles have been drastically altered by changes in the way people consume information. Rather than relying on traditional forms of media—television, newspapers, radio—people have turned increasingly to Internet sites that allow interaction between users to gather information (Ingram, 2010; Smith, 2011). Social media are largely responsible for the changes in crisis life cycles. Social networking sites, like Facebook and Twitter, fall under the umbrella of social media.

Although such sites are driven primarily by relationships, they are just as powerful as other forms of social media during a crisis (Shih, 2011).

This power is evident in several ways. First, social media sites can create news. According to the Pew Internet and American Life Project (Patrick, 2010), 73% of Americans get news from social media sites. This trend is due in part to the fact that such sites facilitate passive consumption of information. In other words, users do not have to search for information; it is delivered to them in their preferred format (Giblin, 2011).

Second, social media sites can break news. In some cases, bloggers and users of Twitter are finding and sharing crisis information before traditional journalists (Liu, 2010). Social media do not feature a "strict and lengthy editorial process" (Liu, p. 29; Baron, 2006), so information is often disseminated quickly and with little editorial oversight. Social media posters and users are driven by speed, not the traditional journalistic standards of proximity, accuracy, and objectivity.

Third, social media sites can become news. This is particularly true in sport, where athletes, coaches, and even owners use social media sites as a way to release information directly to their fans and the public. Because this information is unedited, journalists and reporters use this information to create or improve their own stories in a process called "media catching" (Waters, Tindall, & Morton, 2010). ESPN's *SportsCenter* often features tweets from athletes and fans during its broadcasts. Although Twitter is the most prominent source cited in media catching, posts on other social media sites can also become news. A video posted on YouTube of a New York Giants player hazing a teammate became a national news story in which head coach Tom Coughlin begrudged the existence of social media (Monkovic, 2012).

Fourth, social media sites can accelerate and amplify the news. Information now travels at such fast rates that Qualman (2009) has suggested that information is not shared by word of mouth, it is shared by "world-of-mouth." Mobile communication devices enable individuals to create, upload, and disperse information virtually anywhere in the world. Once the information reaches social media sites, amplification begins. When the information is received by users, they can choose to share it with a network of friends. This can happen with incredible speed. "Likes," "tweets per second," and "views" are all common statistics that can demonstrate how amplified a story has become, and sport stories are among the most tweeted in history (Hernandez, 2012).

Finally, social media sites can shape the meaning of crises. These sites cover news more subjectively than traditional media outlets (Liu, 2010). Often this means that organizations can face harsh criticism in cyberspace (Gannon, 2011). The amplification of such criticism adds significant stress to sport organizations during crises. On the other hand, the space provided by social media sites for users to respond, repost, like, and link enables them to alter the framing of a crisis through online discussion (Kelleher, 2009).

CRISIS COMMUNICATION

Whether a crisis emerges from traditional media outlets or social media, sport managers are responsible for managing information during such situations. This is referred to as *crisis communication*. Crisis communication falls under the broad umbrella of crisis management. Although sport managers may be involved in various aspects of crisis management, leaders are most often responsible for preparing, executing, and evaluating a *crisis communication plan*. It is these three skills of crisis communication—strong preparation, precise execution, and continual evaluation—that will be the focus of this section.

Preparing for Crises

To best meet the challenges posed by crises and ensure effective leadership, sport organizations must create *crisis management plans*. The creation processes and resulting plans will vary by organizational type, size, and possible crises. However, there are several common tools and techniques that can be used by all types of sport organizations (Walaski, 2011). These are forecasting, prioritizing, and plan development.

Crisis management planning begins with *forecasting* (Rollo & Zdziarski, 2007; Stoldt et al., 2006). Forecasting is the process of predicting which types of crises are likely to occur in a particular sport organization. For example, intercollegiate athletic departments would be wise to prepare for National Collegiate Athletic Association (NCAA) violations, whereas professional franchises are more apt to prepare for difficulties stemming from franchise relocation. The forecasting process should not simply be left to an organization's public relations specialists (Rollo & Zdziarski, 2007). Leaders such as coaches, athletic directors, and general managers along with other employees including agents, scouts, and even campus police/security can be included in the identification of risk areas for sport organizations and athletes. Employees lower in the organizational hierarchy may hear or see things that can foretell crises; such input must be encouraged for thorough forecasting. Additionally, internal and external sources of data can assist in this process. Looking at a sport organization's past problems, email records, or financial records can provide clues about prospective misfortunes. Externally, the negative events that happen to peer organizations and the public discourse in traditional or social media outlets can also help predict crises.

Because planning for every possible crisis is implausible, sport organizations must prioritize their plans. Prioritization is based on two factors: likelihood and impact (Rollo & Zdziarski, 2007; Walaski, 2011). The more likely the occurrence of a particular crisis, the more attention it should be given in the planning process, as depicted in the general risk matrix in **Figure 10.1**. For example, all sport organizations should have steps to deal

FIGURE 10.1 **General risk matrix.**

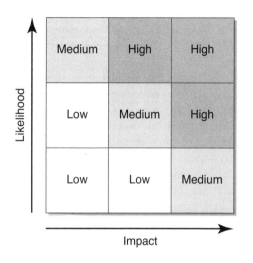

with a coach or athlete getting arrested for driving under the influence (DUI), due to its frequency of occurrence. Similarly, if a crisis will have a major impact on the sport organization, then it too must be included in the crisis plan. Although the crashing of a team plane is unlikely to occur, its impact would be so significant that plans must be made for these types of catastrophic events.

CRISIS COMMUNICATION PLAN DEVELOPMENT

Crisis communication plans are developed as part of an overall crisis management plan. Before beginning the creation of a crisis communication plan, several steps must be taken. First, the sport organization must ensure that senior management supports the development of the plan and is willing to implement it when needed (Stoldt et al., 2006; Walaski, 2011). Second, the members of a sport organization must acknowledge that the plan is a foundation, not a "how-to" document. It is to serve as the resource for key information (e.g., lines of communication, partners, experts) but cannot address all the possibilities that arise from

a crisis (Reynolds, 2002; Walaski, 2011). Finally, leaders and managers must put together the right mix of people to create the crisis management plan. The group of people involved in forecasting crises is a good starting point for plan development. However, the addition of legal counsel, public relations staff, human resources, or student affairs administrators might be required depending on the type of sport organization.

Once these steps have been taken, the development of the plan can begin. Crisis management plans have several components. Walaski (2011) notes that although crisis management plans come in numerous forms, "a review of several formats reveals many common elements and few differences" (p. 129). The shared elements are outlined in the following sections.

Purpose and Scope

Typically, crisis management plans serve a dual purpose: to anticipate and prevent crises and to aid in effectively responding once crises occur (Walaski, 2011). However, it is imperative for the sport organization to define what it means by a "crisis." Some organizations are willing to accept more risk before invoking the plan, whereas others quickly implement crisis strategies. A clear definition of *crisis* and "the characteristics and attributes that are meaningful" (Rollo & Zdziarski, 2007, pp. 78–79) will aid the organization in activating the plan, developing a response team, and executing protocols during the crisis. The purpose of the plan should also list the likely crises and the unique responses to each (e.g., injury vs. arrest) (Walaski, 2011).

Activation

The *activation* step of a crisis management plan should identify who will put the plan in motion and how this will be done (Walaski, 2011). In sport organizations, all employees should be able to activate the plan (Stoldt et al., 2006). There are many different kinds of crises (e.g., athlete arrests, fan violence, rule violations), so restricting activation only to executives could prevent the organization from quickly responding to or properly dealing with the media. With respect to the Penn State scandal, for example, had janitors or assistant coaches felt capable of activating the crisis plan, some of the damage to the victims and university could have been avoided (Johnson & Marklein, 2012).

In other cases, the crisis plan is activated automatically if a specific sequence of events has occurred (Rollo & Zdziarski, 2007). When an athlete suffers a severe injury, the medical staff responds immediately, and their response initiates other levels of crisis management by the facility manager, a media relations staffer, a coach, and an administrator. Due to the extensive interrelationships needed to activate crisis management plans, keeping employee contact information current is critical (Stoldt et al., 2006).

Responders and Authority

The third step of the plan's development is defining the *response team* and the *lines of communication* within the team. In most cases, the athletic director, sports information director, and university counsel (or their equivalents in other sport organizations) will serve on the response team. However, the composition of the response team can be adjusted based on the nature of the crisis. For moderate crises, top-level administrators (e.g., president, owner) do not need to be involved. If there are public questions about the eligibility of a college athlete, the response team might include the assistant athletic director for compliance instead of the athletic director. However, if the crisis involves a prominent NFL quarterback committing a felony, the president and owner of the team might be added to the response team due to the organizational significance of the problem. Regardless of the membership of the response team, it must establish clear lines of authority. These lines increase the speed of the response, minimize cross-departmental conflict, and empower those implementing the plan with decision-making authority (Rollo & Zdziarski, 2007). Although top executives are not always on response teams, the lines of authority must

include them in case the crisis snowballs and they must become involved (Rollo & Zdziarski, 2007).

Internal Communication

The most important group needing information in the wake of crises is members of the organization tasked with its response (Fearn-Banks, 2011). This communication should consist of three things (Fearn-Banks, 2011). First, members of the sport organization must know what happened. Although not all of the details must be shared, the responders must have enough information to communicate effectively with the segment of the public to which they have been assigned. Second, responders must be reminded of their responsibility in the plan and ordered to execute it. Finally, members of the response team should be instructed about what they are not allowed to do or say. Often, members of key publics (e.g., families, media) are frantically attempting to find out information, and responders must know whom to direct such individuals to for information. If key information is leaked, the sport organization can lose control of the crisis response.

Definition of Key Publics

Crisis management plans should establish who must be informed during the crisis response. The *key publics* will vary significantly according to the type of crisis, but those most affected should be given the most consideration. Typically, employees, the media, and customers are critical publics, but in some cases, governing bodies, families, owners, shareholders, or university administrators will comprise a key public (Carter & Rovell, 2003; Lawson, 2007). The key publics should also be prioritized so that information is shared in an order that protects the organization and is fair to each group. When 10 members of an Oklahoma State basketball traveling party died in a plane crash on January 27, 2001, university administrators were informed first. Then, support staff from the university and athletic department were informed to develop a response. Once that was developed, the families of the victims were notified (Paterson et al., 2007). A news conference with the media was not held until 3 days later (news9.com, 2001).

External Communication Philosophy and Policies

Due to the intense media coverage of crises in sport, crisis management plans must include guidelines for organizations about how to communicate with external publics. Selflessness must be at the core of such philosophies. Sport organizations must put the interests of others above their own and recognize that short-term financial loss is sometimes needed to ensure the organization's survival (Walaski, 2011). Stoldt et al. (2006) advise that victims' families be prioritized and information be released as quickly as possible because "silence creates a void that feeds negative speculation" (Hessert, 2006, p. 34). Instead of avoiding the media, sport organizations should attempt to be *the* source of information during crises. This can reaffirm the public's belief in the sport organization and minimize the role of other, potentially adversarial, sources during the crisis. Such recommendations are important given the rapid pace of information transmission created by social media. Savvy sport organizations incorporate social media into their external communication philosophies. By using websites like Facebook and Twitter to disseminate information during a crisis, sport organizations can maintain their status as the main source of information and build public credibility in their responses (Gannon, 2011; Kelleher, 2009; Vorvoreanu, 2009). Gannon (2011) suggests that organizations gain credibility from their publics by responding with such techniques.

Spokesperson Identification

Clarifying who will be the lead spokesperson during a crisis is a critical part of an external communication strategy. "Spokespersons do not just read a statement; perceptually they are the statement" (Lawson, 2007, p. 112). Therefore, the spokesperson should have strong public speaking skills and the ability to deal calmly with intense questions. The spokesperson should work closely with public relations staffers who work behind the scenes to gather information, craft messages, and prepare for crises (Lawson, 2007). The individual chosen should also reflect the gravity of a crisis. This was evident in two separate crises at Texas A&M University. When 12 students died in the construction of a pregame bonfire at Texas A&M in 1999, the university president publicly represented the university (Paterson et al., 2007). However, when the Texas A&M football coach was mired in a booster scandal, the athletic director disseminated the information (Associated Press, 2007).

When 12 students died in the construction of a pregame bonfire at Texas A&M in 1999, the university president publicly represented the university and was an integral part of activating the crisis management plan.
© Bryan College Station Eagle, Stuart Villanueva/AP Images

EXECUTING THE CRISIS COMMUNICATION PLAN

As outlined previously, creating the crisis communication plan is a detailed process that best situates the sport organization to respond effectively to crises. However, for the sport organization to maintain financial stability and credibility with its publics, crisis plans must be executed effectively. Effective plan execution begins rapidly. The risk of inaction is far greater than making an early mistake (Combs, 1999; Lawson, 2007). Publics can interpret silence as confusion within an organization or, worse yet, guilt. In fact, with the speed of digital media, the information void may be filled with inaccurate or unflattering information from other sources. To combat this, sport organizations must know how to craft appropriate messages, remain disciplined with the messages, and use the correct channels for those messages.

Creating Key Messages

When a sport organization is threatened by a crisis, key messages must be "crafted to repair the damage" (Sanderson, 2008, p. 248; Walton & Williams, 2011). Researchers have identified five types of key messages during crises: denial, evasion of responsibility, reducing offensiveness, corrective action, and mortification (Benoit, 2006; Sanderson, 2008; Walton & Williams, 2011). **Table 10.1** shows examples of the key messages. Although the first three are often used in sport, such strategies have led to unsatisfactory results (Benoit & Hanczor, 1994; Sanderson, 2008; Walton & Williams, 2011). Instead, the mortification and corrective action strategies have the highest potential for positive outcomes. These types of messages provide the sport organization with a solid starting point for such responses, all of which can be adapted to various types of crises.

First, the sport organization must acknowledge the crisis with genuine concern. Failing to respond in a timely fashion can communicate a number of things to the key publics, but it is often perceived as a lack of concern. Minimizing the importance of the crisis with an inappropriate response can also alienate key publics and potentially exacerbate the crisis (Walaski, 2011; Walton & Williams, 2011). (See the Colorado case study at the beginning of the chapter.) Once the crisis has been acknowledged, the next step for leaders and managers in the sport organization is to discuss its level of responsibility. This can entail the organization explaining its role in creating the crisis or simply explaining what happened and how the organization was involved. Although admitting a role in the crisis is often uncomfortable, the organization may earn psychological credit from its publics for honesty, and the admission helps establish the sport organization as the main source of information on the crisis (Walaski, 2011). The third aspect of message creation is to outline corrective actions or a plan for improvement. Such plans provide tangible evidence of the sport organization's concern and allow publics to envision a better future. These actions should be taken even if they are costly to the sport organization. Oklahoma State's plan to offer full scholarships to family members of the victims of the basketball plane crash is a prototypical response (Paterson et al., 2007).

MESSAGE DISCIPLINE

When creating any of these messages, it is critical for the sport organization to create and deliver them in a disciplined manner. Media outlets thirst for knowledge about crises, especially those in sport. Staying disciplined provides the sport organization with the best opportunity to be seen as a credible source of information and to bring timely closure to a crisis. Such discipline starts with the collaborative work between public relations and the senior members of the crisis response team to craft key messages.

Key messages consist of statements about the organization's position that can be used as sound bites by various types of media outlets (Stoldt

TABLE 10.1 Benoit's Image Repair Strategies Applied to Sport

Strategy	Definition	Sport Example
Denial		
Simple denial	Did not perform act	Sammy Sosa denies taking steroids.
Shift blame	Another performed the act	Officials covered up policing errors by blaming the rowdy fans for the deaths of 96 Liverpool soccer fans in the Hillsborough disaster.
Evade Responsibility		
Provocation	Responded to another's act	Alex Rodriguez blamed pressure from his large contract with the Texas Rangers for his use of performance-enhancing drugs.
Defeasibility	Lack of information or ability	Barry Bonds admitted using cream and clear substances, but claimed he did not know they were performance-enhancing drugs.
Accident	Mishap	Prior to committing suicide, Junior Seau blamed a car accident on falling asleep.
Good intentions	Meant well	After a woman was raped by two University of Iowa football players in 2007, the athletic department told the victim that the case could be better handled if she kept it within their jurisdiction.
Reduce Offensiveness		
Bolstering	Stress positive traits	Commissioner David Stern emphasized that the NBA used the Tim Donaghy betting scandal as "an opportunity to get better."
Minimization	Act less harmful than believed	Kobe Bryant stated that he believes his alleged sexual assault of a hotel employee in Eagle, Colorado, was consensual.
Differentiation	Act less harmful than similar acts	After tweeting an unfounded critique of an NFL player, Maurice Jones-Drew said, " I didn't commit a crime."
Transcendence	More important values	After rookie Dez Bryant refused to carry a veteran's pads, NFL players justified hazing as a tradition of initiation.
Attack accuser	Reduce accuser's credibility	Ryan Braun cited Major League Baseball's (MLB's) flawed testing procedures when he tested positive for performance-enhancing drugs.
Compensation	Reimburse victim	Following a plane crash that killed 10 people associated with the Oklahoma State basketball team, the university offered full scholarships to family members of the victims.
Corrective Action	Plan to repair/ prevent recurrence	The International Skating Union conducted an internal assessment to correct judging flaws that resulted in outrage over judging in the 2002 Winter Olympics.
Mortification	Apologize, express remorse for acts	MLB umpire Jim Joyce tearfully apologized for missing a call that would have allowed Armando Galarraga to pitch a perfect game.

Source: Data from Benoit, W. L. (2006). President Bush's image repair effort on *Meet the Press*: The complexities of defeasibility. *Journal of Applied Communication, 34*(3), 285–306.

TABLE 10.2 Key Messages from Texas A&M Following Bonfire Collapse

1. Concern for the parents of the injured and dead students

2. Facts about the bonfire tradition

3. Facts about the bonfire accident

4. An understanding of and appreciation for the "Aggie Spirit" and the "specialness" of the Texas A&M family

Source: Reproduced from Fearn-Banks, K. (2011). *Crisis communication: A casebook approach* (4th ed.) New York: Routledge.

et al., 2006). They form the centerpiece of responses to media inquiries and are repeated often (see **Table 10.2**). The content of key messages should be underscored with a focus on objectivity. Key messages must be truthful and informative (Fearn-Banks, 2011). Any attempts to use talking points as a distraction will likely result in an expansion of the crisis when the truth is inevitably discovered. The use of clear, common terminology avoids confusion and frustration for key publics not familiar with the jargon in the industry (Walaski, 2011). Words that have overtly negative connotations (e.g., looting, riot) can also instigate needless emotion during a crisis (Fearn-Banks, 2011). Speculation should not be included in statements because it leads to more questions about the future, which the spokesperson cannot answer. Blame is also unadvisable in key messages (Fearn-Banks, 2011). Determining the root causes of a crisis is often a lengthy process, and assigning blame early on may ultimately embarrass the sport organization.

Preparing to deliver key messages is a second way to enhance discipline during a crisis response. Several authors recommend practicing the delivery of media statements and mock question-and-answer sessions to adhere to the intended messages (Lawson, 2007; Walaski, 2011).

Providing speakers with message maps or talking points is another way to ensure speakers do not veer from the organization's core message (Walaski, 2011). Sharing key messages with important representatives of the organization or the crisis response team improves the consistency of the organization's external communication. Although it is not advisable to have multiple voices during a response, sometimes the expertise or status of an organizational representative is essential. Sharing the key messages with them ensures that the organization's "voice" is consistent (Walaski, 2011).

MEDIUM SELECTION

The mediums through which information is shared during a crisis are growing in complexity. Undoubtedly, the best means of conveying information, especially with those most affected by the crisis, is personal communication. When appropriate, these interactions should include high-ranking and/or visible representatives of the sport organization. These meetings are often fraught with emotion, but they can help victims begin to move through the healing process. News conferences and media interviews featuring the spokesperson and selected officials are common in crises. When appearing in these mediums, the following guidelines can help speakers effectively communicate key messages (Fearn-Banks, 2011; Stoldt et al., 2006; Walaski, 2011):

- Listen to the entire question before answering.
- Only discuss what you have expertise to discuss.
- Remain polite and informative.
- Understand the reporter's job and treat them as an ally.
- Deliver information in a calm, positive manner.
- Look the questioner in the eye.
- Convey appropriate emotions and avoid humor.
- Use common language.

Although traditional media outlets are still important, the use of blogs and social media websites like Facebook and Twitter constitute a "significant change in the ways in which audiences communicate with each other and require organizations to adapt their message methods" (Walaski, 2011, p. 85). Social media allow information to be disseminated more rapidly and broaden the reach of information to publics. However, the distinct advantage to using social media during crisis communications is that it opens up new options.

Social media can be used to develop relationships with key publics before crises occur. By engaging in the regular use of social media prior to a crisis, organizations can build social capital with its publics that can have benefits when a crisis hits (Gannon, 2011). *Social capital* essentially refers to the accumulation of resources generated by the network of relationships among people (Bourdieu & Wacquant, 1992; Coleman, 1988). Sport organizations can use social media to develop networks and the resulting resources that will prove beneficial during crises. When authentic networks are developed, publics are more likely to seek information directly from the organization as opposed to other sources. Publics are also more likely to support the sport organization and trust its communications (Gannon, 2011).

A second advantage of social media during crises is the interactivity it enhances. Interactivity has always been at the core of public relations, but social media enable this to occur with more speed and authenticity. Applications like Viralheat and Radian6 make it easy for organizations to listen to online public discourse during a crisis. However, publics now expect more than listening; they expect true interactivity. Such interactivity mandates that organizations not only listen, but also converse and alter organizational behavior (Vorvoreanu, 2009). During a crisis, this becomes imperative. The sport organization can reassure its publics and increase trust in its response by allowing publics to comment on blogs and Facebook pages or by responding to tweets (Gannon, 2011).

The human voice provided by social media is a third benefit of its inclusion in crisis communications. News conferences and news releases have a formal feel, but social media provide a medium that taps into emotion. Whether through pictures, videos, tweets, or responses to them, social media enable sport organizations to empathize with their publics in a language and format familiar and accessible to them. Once again, "this human face can potentially win back the goodwill of the public" (Gannon, 2011, p. 92).

CRISIS CONCLUSION AND EVALUATION

Determining the conclusion of a crisis is difficult. Just as sport organizations do not control the causes of a crisis, neither can they mandate when it ends. If a crisis is defined as any event that poses a threat to the financial stability of an organization or its credibility with constituents, then there are several ways to determine when a crisis is wrapping up. Internal sources of data can be a first place to determine if the organization is still under the threat of damage. Sport organizations can examine records such as ticket sales, merchandise sales, funds raised, academic records, retention rates, win/loss records, or graduation rates to determine if each has returned to a precrisis level. External sources of data can also provide indications about the conclusion of the crisis. Changes in media coverage, television ratings, and social media chatter can all provide confirmation that a sport organization's efforts to respond to a crisis have been effective.

That said, public declarations that a crisis is over are dangerous. First, the sport organization cannot really control whether the crisis is over. Publics determine when they are willing to forgive athletes or coaches, if they are ready to move on from a tragedy, or when they are no longer concerned about the events that ignited the crisis. Premature declarations reek of insensitivity and can further alienate key publics. More troubling is when a sport organization declares that a crisis is over only to have outside (e.g., media or NCAA) investigations deepen the crisis.

This was the case for Ohio State's Athletics Department in December 2010. On December 23, Ohio State athletics director Gene Smith accepted sanctions by the NCAA for violations committed by its players who illegally exchanged memorabilia for tattoos. At the time, Smith indicated that OSU had first learned of the impermissible activities on December 8. However, media investigations broadened this relatively minor crisis when it became clear head coach Jim Tressel knew about the scandal in April 2010 and subsequently lied about it (Robinson & Wetzel, 2011).

Whenever the sport organization has determined it can move beyond such crises and get back to normal operations, the crisis communications plan must be evaluated. This evaluation will help the sport organization improve its prevention, planning, and responses for future crises (Fearn-Banks, 2011). Finding the correct timing for the evaluation can be tricky (Johnston, 2007). It is often wise to wait a few weeks before beginning the evaluation because this allows reports to be written and filed and emotions surrounding a crisis to subside. However, waiting much longer may result in inaccurate or skewed recollections of those involved.

A good starting place for evaluation is to reconstitute the team that helped develop the crisis plan. This group has the most intimate knowledge of the plan's execution, and it can use the evaluation as a means for debriefing from the emotion of the crisis (Johnston, 2007). The evaluation should also incorporate feedback from the members of the organization who were on the front lines of the crisis response to determine the practices that were most effective for dealing with the various stakeholders during the crisis (Fearn-Banks, 2011). In addition, the group can retroactively collect data from the same types of media used to determine the end of a crisis (i.e.,

written reports, editorials, social media chatter) to assess various aspects of the crisis response. Using this data, evaluations can be broken down into three major areas: transparency, listening, and clarity (Hyer & Covello, 2005). The following questions were adapted from Hyer and Covello to assist in the assessment process.

In evaluating the transparency of crisis communication, the following questions should be asked:

- Was the sport organization open and candid with the media?
- Was bad news first revealed by the sport organization?
- Was the plan activated promptly?
- In the event of uncertainty, was the sport organization willing to find the information and get back to the reporter in the appropriate timeframe?
- When in doubt, did the sport organization lean toward sharing more information, not less?
- Did the sport organization engage in speculation?
- Did the sport organization disclose information as soon as possible? Fill information voids? Minimize or exaggerate the crisis? Discuss uncertainties, strengths, and weaknesses—including those identified by other sources?

With regard to evaluating organizational listening during a crisis, the following questions are important:

- Were the correct publics targeted by the sport organization?
- Did the sport organization empathize with the publics?
- Was every important group listened to?
- Were assumptions made about what stakeholders wanted during the crisis?
- Was the validity of people's emotions acknowledged?

- Did the sport organization use words, gestures, and actions to respond to those emotions?
- Did the sport organization use social media outlets that encourage listening feedback, participation, and dialogue?
- Was sensitivity to local norms considered?
- Were corrections made following any errors?
- Was additional information provided if requested?

Finally, in evaluating clarity after a crisis, the following should be asked:

- Was communication at the appropriate level for your publics?
- Were the appropriate mediums for communicating messages used?
- Was an appropriate spokesperson selected to communicate the organization's key messages?
- Was the spokesperson prepared for interactions with various publics?
- Did the spokesperson and organization stay focused on key messages?
- Was nontechnical language used?
- Did the sport organization have all possible information throughout the response?
- Did the sport organization promise only that which could be delivered and then follow through?

Once the applicable questions are answered, the last step is to develop the report. The report should focus on three major elements (Johnston, 2007). First, the timeline of the events should focus on the facts of the crisis: (1) What happened? (2) When did it happen? (3) Who was involved? The second section should document the crisis, explaining how the events happened and why they happened. Finally, the report must offer recommendations. These should be specific and identify specific groups that can respond to the recommendation. Each aspect of the report should be supported by appendices featuring evidence and references. To close the evaluation loop, it is important for the evaluation committee to follow up on the recommendations to ensure that they are being instituted (Johnston, 2007).

CULTURE CHANGE

A detailed discussion about a change in organizational culture following a crisis is beyond the scope of this chapter. However, when the crisis is significantly more harmful to the sport organization and results from clear faults within the organization, a crisis communication plan is not enough. In such instances, wholesale culture change is often required for the organization to regain its publics' confidence. Culture change moves beyond the superficial—donating money to a cause or removing the name from a building—and uses a multifaceted process to alter the basic assumptions upon which an organization acts, behaves, and makes decisions. Altering the culture for the better takes leadership.

Suffice to say, it is not uncommon for an organization to act in complete contrast with its stated beliefs and values (Bolman & Deal, 2003; Schein, 2004). At the deepest level of culture, basic assumptions are the true premise for organizational behavior. They provide a subconscious, almost thoughtless, guide for members to react to the environment. Ultimately, basic assumptions provide members of an organizational culture with the "mental maps" that define, "what to pay attention to, what things mean, how to react emotionally to what is going on" (Schein, 2004, p. 32).

Changing such assumptions, especially those in some athletic department cultures, is a complex process that can take 10–15 years (Schein, 2004). Cultural change involves three phases: unfreezing, cognitive restructuring, and refreezing

(Schein, 2004). Unfreezing begins by acknowledging the status of an existing culture (Hatch, 2000; Schein, 2004; Trice & Beyer, 1993). In young or rigid organizational cultures, only incremental leader actions may be needed, but in cultures damaged by crises, a combination of tactics is often required to complete a wholesale turnaround (Hatch, 2000; Schein, 2004; Trice & Beyer, 1993). The key to starting this change is that leaders must demonstrate the cultural dysfunction to the culture's members. Only when the *members* believe that the organization's culture led to the crisis will they become open to cultural change (Schein, 2004). Schein contends that this unfreezing process is best accomplished by presenting enough disconfirming data to create anxiety or guilt in members. Crises can facilitate cultural change because, "crises heighten anxiety, and the need to reduce anxiety is a powerful motivator" (Schein, 2004, p. 254) for change.

Once the members of a culture buy into the need for cultural change, cognitive restructuring begins. For leaders, a foundational step in this phase is to establish a vision for the culture's new direction. This gives members of the culture the "psychological safety" (Schein, 2004, p. 322) that enables them to overcome the fear and uncertainty created by crises. Furthermore, visions increase motivation and commitment among followers by providing a common purpose and a sense of importance to their work.

In cognitive restructuring, leaders use a variety of tactics to create a shift in an organizational culture's values and assumptions (Major, 2000; Schein, 2004; Trice & Beyer, 1993). Schein (2004) identifies five primary mechanisms used to create deep cultural changes. A first technique for leaders is to change what they pay attention to, measure, and control. The extent to which leaders become involved in, ask questions about, or comment on certain aspects of the organization can guide members toward new values and assumptions. Second, role modeling and teaching can be used to alter culture. Formal means (i.e., orientations, trainings, handbooks) can superficially alter the cultural artifacts, but informal techniques (i.e., dress, language, demeanor) are often more potent for deeper cultural change. Resource allocation is a third means for conveying new cultural assumptions. Allotting additional resources to a particular aspect of an organization or adding a department in response to a crisis clearly communicates important shifts in culture. Fourth, altering an organization's personnel can change culture rapidly and visibly. Often, crises in sport lead to the dismissal of coaches and administrators, and the values and assumptions of the individuals selected as replacements convey clear messages about the organization's direction. Lastly, leaders can reward organizational members for behaviors consistent with new cultural assumptions or punish them for contrasting actions. In administering such feedback, the magnitude and consistency of the feedback carry significant cultural weight (Sathe & Davidson, 2000).

Cultural change cannot be complete until the new cultural assumptions have been institutionalized, or what Schein (2004) refers to as "refreezing" (p. 328). Refreezing necessitates that leaders reinforce the new assumptions and demonstrate clearly that the new culture is being used in the daily operation of the organization. The internal and external data sources used to evaluate the crisis communication plan can provide clues that the new culture is moving in the right direction. However, the truest indication that a sport organization's cultural change efforts have taken hold is when the "new way of doing things" just becomes "the way we do things."

SUMMARY

Crisis situations are common in sport and can arise from a variety of sources. Crises can threaten the financial stability of a sport organization or damage its credibility with various key publics. Therefore, it is imperative that sport managers and leaders have extensive knowledge of crisis communication. This begins by forecasting for potential crises and prioritizing those that are most likely and damaging. Crisis communication plans must be developed to deal with such events. These plans provide an extensive framework for communicating with key publics during the crisis. When using the plan, sport organizations must create key messages, communicate them with discipline, and select the right mediums of communication—which now include social media. Although determining the conclusion of a crisis is difficult, a thorough wrap-up of the plan should include an evaluation to improve responses to subsequent crises. This can be a lengthy process, but one that may prevent future crises from occurring.

LEADERSHIP PERSPECTIVE

Lynn King.
Courtesy of Lynn King

Lynn King was the athletic director at the University of the Pacific from 2000 to 2011. Before that, he was the athletic director at Drake University for 10 years. The following interview, conducted by the author, recounts an incident of sexual assault in 2008 involving four student-athletes. Three student-athletes on the men's basketball team were accused and subsequently found guilty by a school judicial board of assaulting a female basketball player. King talks about how his department reacted to the crisis situation.

Q: When the sexual assault happened, what was your first reaction? Who did you call first?

Well, my first reaction was, of course, I was shocked, and I was really just disappointed, but the very first call I made was to [the vice president for] student life and then the next call was to [the director of] public safety. Everything ran through student life. As did every other student, and that was, that's something that we are committed to and that's what we did and a lot of times if our student-athletes, like a drinking issue or whatever, they could get punished twice. So, they'd have to live with the department policy and what we would require them to do as well, but we worked hand and glove with judicial affairs on everything so I mean there wasn't even a question in my mind at all. You know, I got [the VP for student life] involved right away.

Q: Did the athletic department have policies and procedures for sexual assault? Or did it, at a certain level, just go right to . . . ?

At a certain level, it goes right over to student life. We, athletics, did not have written policies with regard to that. Our policy was that we work with the institution. We work through the institutional student life piece. I had seen enough of this where departments try to settle it internally, and that's an explosion waiting to happen. I go down a whole list of issues, but I mean that's what we did with everything. Everything. Even for the minor things, they'd still have consequences both in the department and possibly in their team, but they go right to judicial just like every other student goes right through judicial, and that was our expectation.

Q: Were the coaches surprised by the process?

No. I think, to be honest with you, they weren't surprised by the process at all. The coaches were actually very good. You know [the men's coach] was defensive of his guys, but not defensive in a way that says, "Hey, you got to treat them differently or special." He just wanted their rights, you know, they have rights too, and that's exactly the way we all approached it, as a matter of fact. So, no, the coaches were really actually very good to work with. It was actually [the women's coach] who brought it to us, because her assistant coach brought it up to her once the kids brought it up to the assistant coach, and the assistant coach brought it up to her, and then to us. But we brought [the men's coach] in right away and said this is what's going on. And he wanted to know the process, and he wanted to be involved in the process and he was actually the advocate for the guys, which is fine. [Author's note: Judicial affairs allows students to select an advocate for the process at University of the Pacific.] They can pick faculty or staff. So again, straight through student life policy, judicial policy is how we operated from start to finish.

Q: More generally, what role do you think leaders have to take in crisis-type situations?

Well, I think first of all you have to act. I mean you've got to, whether the word is "swiftly" or "succinctly," you've got to act. And what that means to me is you've got to have a plan. You have to know. You know, who would ever have thought? Did I ever think that was going to happen to me? No. Was I aware that those things happen? Yeah. And had I thought about it? You bet. So, I think maybe the most important thing is, out of the blocks: Know what the basic plan is and be committed to it. The fact that we took it immediately to student life and that we were going to move it to the student life process—the institutional process—was key, and you know, I looked to the institution to try to solve it, not the athletic department. The other way, it doesn't work. It just doesn't work. You try to solve it with the coaches, it doesn't work. And I understand Division I-A schools get all the power, and I get all that. But there is an ethical piece to this thing that I don't think you can ignore. And that is that they are students first. Number one. And you need to operate that way. So I think to be able to act swiftly, you have to be decisive. You have to be thoughtful, and you really have to consider all the, I think, all the constituents. I think you need to consider the rights of the accused. I think you definitely need to consider the rights of the victim, and then you have to take the teams into account, too. What's going on with those teams? How do you deal with that? So, I think those are the key things. I think what it really comes down to is forethought. Then it's just proactive leadership with regard to attempting to keep it in control. Just stay in control of the situation the best you can.

Q: What are your thoughts on social media use by student athletes? Did you have any policies in place when you were the AD?

We did, as a matter of fact. You know, I think a little bit before that, we'd had some Facebook pieces with, frankly, it was the women's volleyball team with compromising pictures. And so we did set some policy with regard to what our expectations were with student-athletes on social media. And, that was right at the start of Facebook. And we actually were monitoring Facebook also. And we had a time when individual coaches would require their student-athletes to friend them. . . . Now with Twitter and everything, our ability to control it is . . . if the same thing happened today, my discussion with the student-athletes might be a little bit different. It would be kind of the thing where I'd say this: All you do is cause more problems for yourself and the department if you're using social media. But I don't think you can mandate them not to do it unless it's something that can be really debilitative.

KEY TERMS

activation	key messages
crisis	key publics
crisis communication plan	lines of communication
crisis management plans	response team
forecasting	social capital

DISCUSSION QUESTIONS

1. The author discusses the role of social media in spreading news about a crisis as well as helping organizations give a "human voice" to dealing with crises. Is social media more of a help or a hindrance in controlling crises in sport? Explain.
2. Can you think of recent crises in sport in which the organization's reputation was tarnished? What happened that made the organization unable to recover quickly?
3. The author discusses the unfreezing, cognitive restructuring, and refreezing process of changing organizational culture. In your view, is it likely that Penn State's athletic department has completed this process? Why or why not?
4. Why is crisis evaluation such a key component of the crisis plan process?
5. Although not all crises are foreseeable, what crises are possible for a Major League Baseball organization? A youth hockey league? A high school soccer team? A college athletic department?

For a full suite of assignments and additional learning activities, use the access code found in the front of your book. If you do not have an access code, you can obtain one at **www.jblearning.com**.

REFERENCES

Associated Press. (2004a, February 18). School faces new sex assault allegation. *ESPN College Football.* Retrieved from http://sports.espn.go.com/ncf/news /story?id=1737416

Associated Press. (2004b, February 19). Timeline of events surrounding CU recruiting scandal. *USA Today.* Retrieved from http://www.usatoday.com/sports /college/football/big12/2004-02-19-timeline_x.htm

Associated Press. (2007, September 28). Franchione discontinues inside info newsletter for A&M boosters. *ESPN College Football.* Retrieved from http://sports .espn.go.com/ncf/news/story?id=3040891

Baron, G. (2006). *Now is too late: Survival in an era of instant news.* Bellingham, WA: Edens Veil Media.

Benoit, W. L. (2006). President Bush's image repair effort on *Meet the Press*: The complexities of defeasibility. *Journal of Applied Communication, 34*(3), 285–306.

Benoit, W. L., & Hanczor, R. S. (1994). The Tonya Harding controversy: An analysis of image restoration strategies. *Communication Quarterly, 42,* 416–433.

Bolman, L. G., & Deal, T. E. (2003). *Reframing organizations: Artistry, choice, and leadership* (3rd ed.). San Francisco, CA: Jossey-Bass.

Bourdieu, P., & Wacquant, L. J. D. (1992). *An invitation to reflexive sociology.* Chicago, IL: University of Chicago Press.

Carter, D., & Rovell, D. (2003). *On the ball.* Upper Saddle River, NJ: Prentice Hall.

Coleman, J. S. (1988). Social capital in the creation of human capital. *American Journal of Sociology, 94,* S95–S120.

Combs, W. T. (1999). *Ongoing crisis communications: Planning, managing, and responding.* Thousand Oaks, CA: Sage.

Dodge, J. (2004a). Byyny resigns as UCB chancellor. Retrieved from http://www.cu.edu/sg/messages/3992.html

Dodge, J. (2004b). Embattled AD Dick Tharp resigns. Retrieved from http://www.cu.edu/sg/messages/3929.html

ESPN. (2005, December 9). Barnett forced out, receives $3 million settlement. Retrieved from http://sports.espn .go.com/ncf/news/story?id=2252252

Fearn-Banks, K. (2011). *Crisis communication: A casebook approach* (4th ed.). New York: Routledge.

Gannon, P. J. (2011). *The impact of social media on crisis communication* (master's thesis). Stockton, CA: University of the Pacific.

Giblin, P. J. (2011). *Social media's impact on campus crisis communication plans* (master's thesis). Stockton, CA: University of the Pacific.

Hatch, M. J. (2000). The cultural dynamics of organizing and change. In N. M. Ashkanasy, C. P. M. Wildreon, & M. F. Peterson (Eds.), *Handbook of organizational culture and climate* (pp. 245–260). Thousand Oaks, CA: Sage.

Hernandez, B. A. (2012, February 12). Top 15 tweets per second record. *Mashable Social Media.* Retrieved from http://mashable.com/2012/02/06/tweets-per-second-records-twitter/

Hessert, K. (2006). Working as a sport public relations consultant. In G. C. Stoldt, S.W. Dittmore, & S. E. Branvold (Eds.), *Sport public relations: Managing organizational communication* (pp. 33–34). Champaign, IL: Human Kinetics.

Horine, L. (1999). *Administration of physical education and sport programs* (4th ed.). New York: McGraw-Hill.

Hyer, R., & Covello, V. (2005). *Effective communication during public health emergencies.* Geneva, Switzerland: World Health Organization.

Ingram, M. (2010, September 8). Like it or not, Twitter has become a news platform. *Gigaom.* Retrieved from http://gigaom.com/2010/09/08/like-it-or-not-twitter-has-become-a-media-outlet

Johnson, K., & Marklein, M. B. (2012, March 7). Freeh report blasts culture of Penn State. *USA Today.* Retrieved from http://usatoday30.usatoday.com/news/nation /story/2012-07-12/louis-freeh-report-penn-state-jerry-sandusky/56181956/1

Johnston, D. (2007). Crisis debriefing. In E. L. Zdziarski, N.W. Dunkel, J. M. Rollo, & Associates (Eds.), *Campus crisis management: A comprehensive guide to planning, prevention, response and recovery* (pp. 337–342). San Francisco, CA: John Wiley & Sons.

Kelleher, T. (2009). Conversational voice, communicated commitment, and public relations outcomes in interactive online communication. *Journal of Communication, 59*(1), 172–188.

King, P. (2012, March 12). Way out of bounds. *Sport Illustrated*. Retrieved from http://sportsillustrated.cnn.com/vault /article/magazine/MAG1195695/2/index.htm

Klemko, R. (2012, March 22). Sean Payton suspended; Saints fined for bounty program. *USA Today*. Retrieved from http://content.usatoday.com/communities/thehuddle /post/2012/03/sean-peyton-suspended-saints-fined- for-bounty-program/1#.UFF4we0Zfwx

Lawson, C. J. (2007). Crisis communication. In E. L. Zdziarski, N. W. Dunkel, J. M. Rollo, & Associates (Eds.), *Campus crisis management: A comprehensive guide to planning, prevention, response and recovery* (pp. 97–120). San Francisco, CA: John Wiley & Sons.

Liu, B. F. (2010). Distinguishing how elite newspapers and A-list bloggers cover crises: Insights for managing crises online. *Public Relations Review, 36*(1), 28–34.

Major, D. A. (2000). Effective newcomer socialization into high-performance organizational cultures. In N. M. Ashkanasy, C. P. M. Wildreon, & M. F. Peterson (Eds.), *Handbook of organizational culture and climate* (pp. 355–368). Thousand Oaks, CA: Sage.

Monkovic, T. (2012, August 20). For Giants, debate over a dunking. *New York Times*. Retrieved from http:// fifthdown.blogs.nytimes.com/2012/08/20/for-giants- debate-over-a-dunking/

Mullin, B. J., Hardy, S., & Sutton, W. (2007). *Sports marketing* (3rd ed.). Champaign, IL: Human Kinetics.

News9.com. (2001, January 30). Eddie Sutton, players hold news conference after plane crash tragedy. *9 Oklahoma's Own*. Retrieved from http://www.news9 .com/story/13878145/2001-osus-eddie-sutton-holds- news-conference-after-plane-crash-tragedy

Paterson, B. G., Bird, L. E., Burks, S. M., Washington, C. K., Ellet, T., & Daykin, A. (2007). Human crises. In E. L. Zdziarski, N. W. Dunkel, J. M. Rollo, & Associates (Eds.), *Campus crisis management: A comprehensive guide to planning, prevention, response and recovery* (pp. 255–282). San Francisco, CA: John Wiley & Sons.

Patrick, W. (2010). Social networks are major news source. *Technorati*. Retrieved from http://technorati.com/social- media/article/social-networks-are-major-news-source1

Qualman, E. (2009). *Socialnomics. How social media transform the way we live and do business*. Hoboken, NJ: John Wiley & Sons.

Reynolds, B. (2002). *Crisis and emergency risk communication*. Atlanta, GA: U.S. Centers for Disease Control and Prevention.

Robinson, C., & Wetzel, D. (2011, March 7). Tressel knew of gear scheme last April. *Yahoo! Sports*. Retrieved

from http://rivals.yahoo.com/ncaa/football/news; _ylt=AiaER_1lOaubLySDi4EYe4Q5nYcB?slug= ys-osuprobe030711

Rollo, J. M., & Zdziarski, E. L. (2007). Developing a crisis management plan. In E. L. Zdziarski, N. W. Dunkel, J. M. Rollo, & Associates (Eds.), *Campus crisis management: A comprehensive guide to planning, prevention, response and recovery* (pp. 73–95). San Francisco, CA: John Wiley & Sons.

Sander, L. (2007). U of Colorado at Boulder settles lawsuit over alleged rapes at football recruiting party for $2.85 million. *Chronicle of Higher Education*. Retrieved from http://www.titleix.info/Resources/Legal-Cases /Colorado-Lawsuit-Alleged-Rape-Football- Recruiting-Party.aspx

Sanderson, J. (2008). "How do you prove a negative?" Roger Clemens's image repair strategies in response to the Mitchell report. *International Journal of Sport Communication, 1*, 246–262.

Sathe, V., & Davidson, E. J. (2000). Toward a new conceptualization of culture change. In N. M. Ashkanasy, C. P. M. Wildreon, & M. F. Peterson (Eds.), *Handbook of organizational culture and climate* (pp. 279–296). Thousand Oaks, CA: Sage.

Schein, E. H. (2004). *Organizational culture and leadership* (3rd ed.). San Francisco, CA: Jossey-Bass.

Shih, C. (2011). *The Facebook era: Tapping online social networks to market, sell, and innovate*. Upper Saddle River, NJ: Prentice Hall.

Smith, A. (2011). The Internet and campaign 2010. *Pew Internet and American Life Project*. Retrieved from http://www.pewinternet.org/reports/2011/The- internet-and-campaign-2010.aspx

Stoldt, G. C., Dittmore, S. W., & Branvold, S. E. (2006). *Sport public relations: Managing organizational communication*. Champaign, IL: Human Kinetics.

Trice, H. M., & Beyer, J. M. (1993). *The cultures of work organizations*. Englewood Cliffs, NJ: Prentice Hall.

Vorvoreanu, M. (2009). Perceptions of corporations on Facebook: An analysis of Facebook social norms. *Journal of New Communications Research, 4*(1), 67–86.

Walaski, P. (2011). *Risk and crisis communications: Methods and messages*. Hoboken, NJ: John Wiley & Sons.

Walton, L. R., & Williams, K. D. (2011). World Wrestling Entertainment responds to the Chris Benoit tragedy: A case study. *Journal of Sport Communication, 4*, 99–114.

Waters, R. D., Tindall, N. T., & Morton, T. S. (2010). Media catching and the journalist public relations practitioner relationship: How social media are changing the practice of media relations. *Journal of Public Relations Research, 22*(3), 241–264.

CHAPTER 11

TEAM LEADERSHIP AND GROUP DYNAMICS

Peter Bachiochi
Wendi Everton

CHAPTER OBJECTIVES

- Develop an understanding of team leadership and group dynamics.
- Identify problems when working in a group.
- Describe the conditions in which teams operate successfully in sport organizations.
- Discuss current sport management examples of team leadership.

CASE STUDY

Team Leadership and the Boston Red Sox

In 2012, the Boston Red Sox experienced a collapse the likes of which few professional teams have ever experienced. The 2011 team, though narrowly missing the playoffs, compiled a 90–72 record. The 2012 team finished 69–93 and in last place in the American League East, 26 games behind the division-winning New York Yankees. The collapse was arguably a result of failures of leadership at every level (Silvia & Neslin, 2012). Although there were multiple situational factors at work such as critical injuries, senior management and team leaders played critical roles, too. The key people who were identified in the team's collapse were team owner John Henry, president and CEO Larry Lucchino, general manager Ben Cherington, and manager Bobby Valentine.

As a remedy for the poor end to the 2011 season—the team lost 18 of its final 24 games and was nosed out by the Tampa Bay Rays for the Wild Card slot—the Red Sox fired long-time manager Terry Francona and brought in Bobby Valentine to shake things up in the hope of returning

(continues)

the Red Sox to the playoffs, where they had not been since 2009. It was not long before Valentine started alienating fans and players. In April, he decided to do a regular radio stint on the New York–based "Michael Kay Show." Michael Kay is the TV voice of the New York Yankees. That same month, he criticized veteran player Kevin Youkilis's commitment, saying, "I don't think he's as physically or emotionally into the game as he has been in the past for some reason" (Edes, 2012, para. 4). Valentine followed this up by questioning the commitment of Josh Beckett, Carl Crawford, and Mike Aviles. Although Valentine may have been trying to motivate the players, his approach backfired. In June, fan favorite David Ortiz lamented that playing in Boston used to be fun, but "now, every day it's something new not related with baseball" (McDonald, 2012, para. 2).

Senior management had a role in the collapse. President Larry Lucchino sent a letter to rally season-ticket holders, talking about players and conspicuously not mentioning Valentine. However, in August, Red Sox owner John Henry gave Valentine his vote of confidence and general manager Ben Cherington took some of the responsibility for the poor team performance. This did not quell the situation as the strains between Valentine and several of his coaches came to light, culminating in the firing of the team's pitching coach.

The blame for the collapse cannot be placed entirely on leadership. Injuries decimated the Red Sox lineup, including wrist surgery for Carl Crawford, a shoulder injury to most valuable player (MVP) candidate Jacoby Ellsbury, and dozens of other injuries over the season. Pitcher John Lackey missed the entire 2012 season, recuperating from Tommy John surgery. Trades of key players also increased instability. Cornerstone player Kevin Youkilis was traded in June to the Chicago White Sox and a blockbuster trade sent Adrian Gonzalez, Josh Beckett, Carl Crawford, and Nick Punto to the Dodgers. The trade will save the Red Sox $261 million in contracts through 2018 (Associated Press, 2012) and was a sign that leadership was ready to make some big changes to fix a situation spiraling out of control. Beckett's departure was a welcome sign for Red Sox fans because his demeanor and rising earned run average (ERA) alienated Red Sox fans. Beckett was believed to be one of the players eating chicken and drinking beer in the clubhouse during games in the 2011 season.

Bad press also dogged the team. In September, owner John Henry denied that the team was for sale. Although he did not mention the coaching staff directly, Valentine said, "there are situations during the year where I didn't think it was all for one and one for all" (Abraham, 2012, para. 7). Valentine also said the Red Sox had the weakest roster "in the history of baseball" (Harrison, 2012, para. 3). At the end of the season, the statistics spoke for themselves. The Red Sox had their first losing season since 1997 and their first 90-loss season in 46 years. Valentine was fired in early October.

Questions for Discussion

1. Using Hill's team leadership model, explained in the chapter, which internal team leadership actions played a role in the Red Sox's 2012 collapse?
2. Which external team leadership actions played a role in the Red Sox's 2012 collapse?
3. How did the various leadership decisions impact the performance of the team?
4. What could team leaders have done differently at each stage of the season?

INTRODUCTION

As someone who follows sport, when you think of team leadership in sport the first people who probably come to mind are team captains, coaches, and star players. However, team leadership happens both during the game and away from the field and court. At game time, players and coaches are the key leaders, but away from the game, athletic directors, event directors, general managers, and team owners take action and make decisions that have lasting impact. The focus of this chapter will largely be on the leadership that happens away from the game, on the business side of the operations.

Several developments in the world of business and the world at large have raised the profile of teams in many organizations. Decades of downsizing have created greater spans of control, which have in turn created a greater reliance on teams to get work done. Constantly evolving technological advances (e.g., file sharing, online conferencing) have made it possible for teams to be more efficient and to work together from nearly anywhere. Similarly, the environment in which teams must work is growing more complex with "multiple stakeholders with sometimes clashing agendas, high information load, dynamic situational contingencies, and increased tempo of change" (Zaccaro, Rittman, & Marks, 2001, p. 452). In the world of professional sport, travel schedules, changing rosters, and constant press coverage introduce daily challenges to teams. These developments have also fundamentally changed the role of leaders in organizations, thus requiring a new combination of old skills, as well as the acquisition of some new skills.

To maximize the effectiveness of teams, organizations must understand that sometimes teams are not the correct approach for the task at hand. The failure of teams is often a function of using them at inappropriate times or for inappropriate tasks. Sometimes a situation calls for a decision to be made by an individual without consultation. This chapter will begin with some of the key group dynamics that could undermine or facilitate the

effectiveness of teams, followed by a typology of tasks that addresses when teams are most (or least) appropriate. Then, we will outline and close with coverage of models of team leadership that illustrate the delicate balance of the broad range of skills that team leaders must incorporate in both face-to-face team settings and virtual teams.

GROUP DECISION MAKING

Table 11.1 shows there are a variety of paths that groups can use to make decisions, and each path will have an impact on the potential for conflict within the group, the time it takes to make the decision, and how "included" group members feel. These decision styles can be placed on a continuum of group member input (Johnson & Johnson, 2000), from no group input at all (the leader makes the decision) to full and complete group input (group consensus).

The leader decides which process the group will use, but that decision must be thoughtful—leaders must weigh the amount of time the decision can take with the level of influence and conflict desired within the group. If the decision will have a large impact on the group, or if it must have the buy-in of the group for its implementation to be successful, the decision ought to include group input (Kerr & Tindale, 2004; Murnighan, 1981). For example, captains of sport teams typically are not chosen by the coach, but by team members. A captain chosen by the coach may or may not have the endorsement of the team, but if the team is allowed input (such as by using a voting technique), then the members are more likely to accept the outcome. Other decisions can be made by the group leader alone and will be accepted by the group, such as how practice sessions will be designed.

More inclusive decision-making strategies tend to increase group member interdependence and, therefore, group cohesion, while also increasing the social skills of individual members and individual accountability toward the end product (Wagner,

TABLE 11.1 **Decision-Making Pathways**

How Is the Decision Made?	Level of Influence Group Members Feel	Potential for Conflict Within Group	Time It Takes to Make Decision
Group leader alone makes decision	None	Low	Fast
Group leader assigns an expert from group to make decision	Limited	Low	Fast
Group leader consults with the group to receive input, and then makes decision	Somewhat	Low	Not as fast
Mathematical computations (such as an average)	Somewhat	Low	Fast
Voting	Somewhat	Low	Fast
Consensus	Full	High	Slow

Source: Data from Johnson, D. W., & Johnson, F. P. (2000). *Joining together: Group theory and group skills* (7th ed.). Boston: Allyn and Bacon.

1994). If these outcomes are desired, then leaders ought to include group members in decisions. In fact, most research indicates that groups produce output that is higher in quality than that produced by individuals (Kerr & Tindale, 2011; Larson, 2010). On the other hand, if the group members do not have enough knowledge about the topic, or if members lack maturity, then the decisions will not be of high quality and there may be few benefits for the group (Johnson & Johnson, 2000).

GROUPTHINK

It does not take much for a cohesive team with strong leadership to stray from the path of effective decision making. In 2003, when the Detroit Pistons took Serbian player Darko Milicic with the No. 2 pick in the National Basketball Association (NBA) Draft, it was not considered a surprise. Many scouts had lined up behind the drafting of Milicic, citing his versatility and potential. Milicic played three seasons in Detroit, averaging less than 2 points per game. Although it is likely

Milicic would have played much more on a less talented team (the Pistons won the NBA championship in 2004) and potentially developed into a better player, he has never become the superstar that many scouts predicted he would become. Why was Milicic so highly touted? Slate writer Jack Hamilton noted, "Darko was the dubious beneficiary of a hazy mixture of groupthinking and magical thinking, a pre-YouTube moment made of wishful scouting reports from distant lands . . ." (Hamilton, 2013, para. 3). Pistons general manager Joe Dumars admitted later that the team did not have much predraft information on Milicic. It appears Dumars was swept away by the groupthink of professional basketball scouts hoping for an infusion of European big men into the league. Media reports print what NBA scouts say and think, which can create a consensus that may affect a decision when little information is available. Groupthink can infect teams and negatively affect team leadership decision making.

Groupthink was coined and identified by Irving Janis (1972) during his research on a variety of poor decisions made by groups. For example, during World War II there were several warning signs that the Japanese were planning an attack on the United States (increased radio traffic, the presence of a Japanese submarine in Pearl Harbor the night before the attack), but these signs were ignored by commanders. If commanders had allowed reconnaissance flights, then the Japanese fleet would have been spotted and the attack on Pearl Harbor would not have been a surprise. The decision to not send reconnaissance flights had baffled historians for some time. Janis explained that the failure was because of groupthink.

Groupthink happens within cohesive groups with strong leaders, both of which are desirable characteristics for a group to have. Usually decisions made by such groups are high-quality decisions, but sometimes the group feels pressure to maintain cohesion and allegiance to the leader at the cost of good decision-making practices, which can result in bad decisions. Janis explains that groups operating with groupthink share similar characteristics. In addition to being highly cohesive and having strong, directive leadership, they tend to be isolated from outside group influences and experiencing a high-stress situation. Under these conditions, Janis says that a group is likely to have most or all of the eight symptoms of groupthink.

1. *Illusion of invulnerability* occurs when there is a collective agreement that the group is strong and invincible, so decisions tend to be risky. For instance, successful teams may acquire a player or coach known to be a lightning rod for controversy, assuming that the team cannot be hurt by the turbulence that accompanies such a player or coach.
2. *Collective rationalization* happens as the decision is being finalized, whereby group members create reasons for why the decision will work and do not seek out problems with the decision. Team members may focus exclusively on that

same lightning rod player's talent and ignore the controversy he or she creates.

3. *Stereotypes of outgroups* begin to occur that paint all within the group as having desirable and superior qualities and those outside the group (particularly those perceived as oppositional to the group) as having undesirable qualities.
4. Such stereotypes feed into the *belief in the inherent morality of the group*, wherein the group and its members are morally correct. For instance, the Dallas Cowboys are often called "America's Team," and this moniker may bring with it beliefs in the inherent superiority of the team and its management.
5. If people in the group disagree with the decision, a process begins to *place direct pressure on dissenters* so that comments that are perceived as critical are suppressed. There are likely people on a team who have reservations about acquiring a lightning rod–type player, but their thoughts are suppressed directly or indirectly.
6. This pressure will cause other group members to engage in *self-censorship* and not voice their own misgivings about the emerging decision.
7. Because multiple members are engaging in self-censorship, an *illusion of unanimity* emerges, and it appears that nobody in the group has misgivings about the decision (although multiple members do).
8. Finally, groups operating under groupthink have *self-appointed mind guards* who shield group members from controversial information coming from outside the group and who also suppress dissent within the group.

Given that bad decisions can occur under desirable circumstances (such as cohesion and strong leadership) as a result of groupthink, it is important for group leaders to take active steps to help prevent groupthink. Such steps are relatively easy to enact. For example, group cohesion differs from group conformity, so steps can be taken to reduce conformity without having an impact on cohesion. A cohesive group can set up systems to allow and foster dissent, worries, and doubts among members. The strong leader can purposefully not state his or her personal opinion on the topic. The leader can go further by creating a norm that would require formalizing pros and cons of every option, including the appointment of a "devil's advocate."

GROUP PRODUCTIVITY

As a sport management student, you have likely been involved in group projects in some of your courses. Faculty members hypothesize that you will likely work in teams in a professional environment, so it is a good idea to get experience in the classroom doing similar work. As you have probably learned, being in a group environment sometimes causes individuals to work more, but sometimes they work less. The social aspect of group work can be both a deterrent and a boon to productivity.

Social Facilitation

Being in a group can lead people to work harder. With *social facilitation* present, groups can provide support and encouragement to members that enable productivity. A long history of research has found that, compared to working alone, people perform a number of tasks better when in the presence of others. Triplett (1898) found that people will ride a bicycle faster when they are racing others than when they are timed. Other early studies confirmed this finding, but contradictory findings began to emerge as well. In some circumstances, being in the presence of others would impair performance (e.g., Allport, 1920; Burwitz & Newell, 1972). These contradictions were resolved by

Robert Zajonc (1965) with his discovery that being in the presence of others will cause performance to increase only if the task being done is either easy or well-learned (what he called a dominant response) (Weber & Hertel, 2007). If the task is not easy and/or is unfamiliar, being in the presence of others will impair performance compared to if one is working alone.

In an interesting test of this hypothesis, researchers surreptitiously watched bar patrons playing billiards. They watched long enough to detect whether players were skilled (they made at least two-thirds of their shots) or not skilled (they missed at least two-thirds of their shots). After making this determination, one of the researchers moved closer to the billiard table and made it obvious that they were watching the player. A second researcher then recorded what percentage of shots the player made. Those who had been initially identified as skilled increased their shot percentage on average from 71% to 80%; those who were unskilled decreased their shot percentage on average from 36% to 25% (Michaels, Blommel, Brocato, Linkous, & Rowe, 1982).

Social Loafing

Latané, Williams, and Harkins (1979) coined the phrase *social loafing* to describe circumstances in which people perform some group tasks with less effort than when they were performing the same task alone. The researchers had participants, as individuals, clap their hands and shout as loud as they could and measured the loudness of the noise using a decibel reader. These individuals were then put into differently sized groups and were asked to, in their group, clap their hands and shout as loud as they could. The amount of noise produced per person shrank more and more as group sizes increased. Social loafing is more possible in a group, however, when that group is performing particular tasks (such as additive tasks, described in Steiner's Typology of Tasks later in this chapter).

Group Size

There are other critical group dynamics that a leader must manage to maximize the productivity of the team once the decision to use teams has been made, such as the size of the group. Generally, smaller groups perform better compared to larger groups (Liden, Wayne, Jaworski, & Bennett, 2004), though more recent research shows these performance differences might be related to the amount of perceived social support, which, ironically, dissipates with larger groups (Mueller, 2012). Being in a group adds complexity to all things people do, and those leading groups must take these dynamics into consideration. The leader of a group sets the tone and structure of how a group will operate. The decisions he or she makes can either help the group be successful or hamper its functioning and performance, particularly in terms of group decision making and group productivity.

Working in a group adds complexity to all things people do, and those leading groups must consider these dynamics.
© Walter G. Arce/ShutterStock, Inc.

Given that several of these well-established (and very preventable) group dynamics can completely derail the effectiveness of a group, team leaders need to pay particular attention to each of them. It is also important to keep in mind that the terms *team* and *group* are often used interchangeably. Although every team is a group, not every group is a team. Teams have a level of interdependence (Salas, Dickinson, Converse, & Tannenbaum, 1992) that is not a quality of every group. Therefore, the group dynamics discussed apply to teams, but there are a number of factors unique to teams and to team leadership in particular.

ARE TEAMS ALWAYS BETTER?

How tasks are structured can have a big impact on how well (or poorly) the group functions. One of the most useful ways of looking at the impact of the nature of tasks on productivity is with Steiner's Typology of Tasks (Steiner, 1972). In his typology, Steiner outlines the tasks that are better suited for groups and those better suited for individuals. The first way to think about tasks is to determine whether they are divisible (i.e., the task can be broken up into distinct parts) or unitary (i.e., there is no way to break the task into parts). Generally, Steiner says, groups tend to do better with divisible tasks. Whether groups are superior to individuals with unitary tasks depends on a secondary *task typology*.

- *Additive tasks* are those where the group performance is summed, as in a tug-of-war rope-pulling competition. Additive tasks are more subject to shirking of duties (see social loafing), particularly if individual efforts are not tracked.
- *Disjunctive tasks* are those where the end product is a function of the best score of an individual member. In this type of task, for example, a group might be given a word puzzle to solve and the

group would choose to present the answer proposed by their best problem solver. In sport, whoever comes up with the best promotion idea for a theme night would represent the group's "best score."

- *Conjunctive tasks* are those where the end product is a function of the worst performer in the group (the weakest link). For example, a mountain-climbing team roped together is limited in its speed by its slowest member.

- *Compensatory tasks* are those tasks that use a mathematical averaging of all group members in order to produce the group's end product. For instance, team members may participate in the interviews and ratings of new applicants to the team. The ratings of all team members would be averaged to determine the new team member.

- *Discretionary tasks* are those where it is up to the group to decide how individual efforts are combined to create a final product. The group has full autonomy to design the task any way they wish. Therefore, discretionary tasks are a natural fit for teams, but a leader needs to consider the appropriateness of teams for other types of tasks.

HISTORICAL GROUNDING OF TEAM LEADERSHIP

Although teams have been used within organizations for as long as there have been organizations, a more concerted focus on team leadership has emerged only in the last several decades. In one of the earliest treatments of team leadership, McGrath (1962) laid out a core that has become a central element of most current models of team leadership: there is a boundary-spanning balance between internal team functions and external environmental monitoring/action. More specifically,

team leaders engage in internal diagnostic functions as well as external monitoring functions. Team leaders compare team performance to accepted standards, but also engage in forecasting to assess the potential effects of external conditions on the team. Based on this monitoring, team leaders also must make decisions about whether taking action is necessary. For instance, team leaders may need to make changes to team composition if the team is not performing at acceptable levels or may need to steer the team in a different direction to avert the negative effects of a volatile external environment.

These functions can be seen clearly in all professional sport leagues nearly every year as teams retool in response to trades, retirements, injuries, and other changes that are foreseen and unforeseen. The Miami Heat is a perfect example of a team that has gone through several roster changes, building around the centerpiece of Dwyane Wade in the hope of bringing a championship to Miami. However, it was not until it became clear that LeBron James was looking to leave Cleveland that the owners of the Heat pulled together the blockbuster deal that brought James and Chris Bosh to South Beach. They followed the approach that had worked so well for the Boston Celtics when the Celtics acquired Ray Allen (who later also went to the Heat) and Kevin Garnett to create the first Big Three, including Paul Pierce. In both cases, the owners of the teams saw internal weaknesses and external opportunities and built truly high-performing teams.

In a similar vein, Hackman and Walton (1986) described team leaders as monitors of and actors within a larger social system. They outlined the knowledge and skills needed by team leaders to manage teams most effectively. Specifically, team leaders must have basic knowledge of team processes, data-gathering skills, and diagnostic skills. Team leaders also need to have knowledge of change processes, negotiation skills, decision-making skills, and creativity to take appropriate action within the team.

Komaki, Desselles, and Bowman (1989) used a behavioral approach to study sailing team leaders. The researchers outlined the monitoring, feedback, and team coordination behaviors necessary to maintain team performance. In a related approach, Zenger, Musselwhite, Hurson, and Perrin (1994) found team leaders must engage in internal team-building functions such as building trust, inspiring teamwork, making the most of team differences, and creating a team identity. If you read the case study for the chapter, it is easy to see that the Boston Red Sox had little team identity or inspiration to work with one another. This is a far cry from the Francona-led 2004 team that was flush with camaraderie and dubbed itself the "Idiots." Team leaders also need to support team decisions, expand team capabilities, and foresee and influence change.

Consistent with early leadership studies, Kozlowski, Gully, McHugh, Salas, and Cannon-Bowers (1996) found decision-making team leaders serve two primary roles: developmental and task-contingent. The developmental role consists of behaviors such as defining social structure, coaching, and creating a cohesive whole. Head coaches serve these functions when they select their assistant coaches and team captains. If all those people are not on the same page, the team will not gel. The task-contingent role consists of behaviors such as goal setting, monitoring, providing feedback, and taking action to get the team back on track. Again, the assistant coaches are the network that the head coach manages to achieve the task of winning games. A meta-analysis by Burke et al. (2006) demonstrated that person-oriented team leader behaviors, especially empowerment, were the best predictors of perceived team effectiveness and actual team productivity. Boundary-spanning behaviors, a key function that team leaders serve to keep the team connected to and aware of the rest of the organization, were strongly connected to team effectiveness perceptions. Given that team leadership is an inherently social process, the conditions for team effectiveness need to be understood.

CONDITIONS FOR TEAM EFFECTIVENESS

Team leaders are particularly instrumental in establishing certain conditions for *team effectiveness* (Hackman & Walton, 1986). Hackman (2002) elaborated on these, emphasizing they are really necessary preconditions for teams to thrive and that team leaders play an integral role in developing and maintaining them. The five conditions also emphasize the complexity of team leadership as well as the balance among internal functions, external functions, and the boundary spanning necessary for the team to flourish. The sport organizations that foster these conditions create the context for management, as well as their teams, to thrive. These conditions could very well be the difference between good leadership and great leadership. These five conditions are being a real team, rather than a team in name only; having a compelling direction; having an enabling structure; maintaining a supportive organizational context; and having expert coaching.

A Real Team

All too often a group of people working on a task are called a team when they really are just a group of people working on a task. In order to be a real team, they first need to have a team task. The task must require a level of interdependence that can allow members to capitalize on the varied skills the team provides. Hackman (2002) identified co-acting groups, individuals that, although they work together, do not rely upon one another. In creating interest in a new season, members of the ticket and sales staff of a minor league hockey team will perform different mini-tasks that work toward the main task: selling tickets for the upcoming season. One employee might concentrate on acquiring group sales, one member might concentrate on selling season tickets, and yet another member might concentrate on the sale of luxury suites. The team must also be bounded, in that the membership of the team is clear. Given that team members often have other responsibilities, it is critical for a team leader to clarify roles and membership within the team. The team must also have clearly delimited authority. Teams can be manager-led, self-managing, self-designing, or self-governing, and each type has varying levels of authority. The level of team authority must be specified at its inception. Finally, a real team is stable over time. Dealing with the ongoing arrivals and departures of members can undermine the performance of the team (Hackman, 2002). This can be difficult in minor league sports because many ticketing and sales jobs are entry-level positions and employees are eager to leave for greener pastures.

This can also happen in collegiate sport. As assistant coaches move on to become head coaches, the internal task and relationship-management skills of the team leader are truly tested. Effective team leaders like Nick Saban at the University of Alabama expect their protégés to develop and move on. The head coaches who win on a consistent basis and build dynasties are effective at "reloading" and carrying on. They have a "system" that makes it easier for new coaches to join the team and to immediately contribute.

Compelling Direction

Decades of research on goal setting have established the importance of specific goals that motivate action (Locke & Latham, 2006). The benefits of a compelling direction are that it energizes, orients, and engages the team. Clear direction also serves as a compass, moral or otherwise, to orient the team members for the task at hand. This direction also engages every member of the team to play the role for which they were chosen. It helps to orchestrate the players who need to take the lead at certain points and those who need to wait for their turn in the process. Phil Jackson, called the "Zen Master," brought this clarity of focus to both the Chicago Bulls and the Los Angeles Lakers, resulting in multiple NBA championships for both teams.

Enabling Structure

Managers or leaders composing teams can make three big mistaken assumptions: assuming bigger is better, that similarity facilitates team process, and that everyone knows how to work as a team member (Hackman, 2002). Although the size of the team is a function of the complexity of the task, Steiner (1972) demonstrated that productivity does not improve in a linear fashion as group size increases, but rather levels off in predictable ways. For instance, as group size grows, social loafing becomes more likely. Similarly, as group size increases, process losses (coordination challenges, individual motivational decrements) increase. There is no optimal size for groups, but Hackman's research suggests that four- to six-member teams are sufficient for many tasks.

When managers compose teams with the first priority that members get along well together, the homogeneity that often results can doom those teams to mediocrity. Task-focused conflict can actually lead to more creative and improved decisions compared to homogeneous (similar characteristics) groups. Team composition needs to be a balance between too many similarities and too many differences (Hackman, 2002). The third element of an enabling structure involves interpersonal skills, because some people lack the basic skills to be effective team members. There are times to challenge others and times to cooperate, and team members that do too much of either bring down the team. High-profile athletes (e.g., Terrell Owens) can bring their talents to a team, but they often bring a level of dysfunction along with them. When the team cannot manage the dysfunction, the team ultimately fails.

Supportive Organizational Context

The environment in which teams operate can support or undermine the work of the team, and this all starts with reward systems. Most organizations have established human resources systems that typically reward individual performance. To optimize team performance, the reward system needs to provide *reinforcement* (not just rewards) that is contingent upon effective *team* performance. Rewards are viewed as valuable by the provider but not necessarily by the receiver, whereas reinforcement is something that will increase the likelihood of the desired behavior. Reinforcement, therefore, is contingent upon engaging in the behavior that makes the team more successful, and is provided in a timely manner. In other words, it is usually not a weekly paycheck. Player contracts with bonuses for postseason performance can achieve the right level of reinforcement.

Information systems must provide the information needed to the people who need it at the point in time when they need it. Information is power, and restricting it can hinder the performance of teams. Furthermore, an education system must provide the technical and group-process training that is necessary for teams to thrive. The constantly evolving context in which teams operate makes the timeliness of training absolutely essential as well. Although leaders develop the skills of their employees, leaders need regular training to stay sharp, too.

Expert Coaching

Team leaders also play a critical role in coaching team members. Although similar to coaching a team, expert coaching in this context is separate from what has been discussed previously. The focus is on developing the skill set of the team as well as the resources available to them. One key role of a team coach is to minimize process losses, those "inefficiencies or internal breakdowns" (Hackman, 2002, p. 169) that inhibit the team's performance given its resources and members. Although coaching may be thought of as focusing on interpersonal dynamics, great coaches attend to task performance as well. Coaches motivate effort levels, facilitate appropriate performance

strategies, and ensure the sharing of member knowledge and development of their skills. Effective team leaders are also not intimidated by high-performing contributors and embrace their role as the developer of their members.

The team leader is instrumental in establishing and/or maintaining these enabling conditions. Many of the team leader actions that are summarized in the model that follows illustrate the means by which leaders foster an environment within the team, as well as how they manage the external context in which the team must operate.

HILL'S MODEL FOR TEAM LEADERSHIP

Hill (2012) presents *Hill's model for team leadership* that integrates many of the components of existing models and research. The model in **Figure 11.1** begins with the leadership decisions that must be made, consistent with the work of McGrath (1962). Team leaders must decide whether events within or outside the team simply need to be monitored or if they require action. If action is required, does the situation call for a task-related or relational intervention? Finally, if action is required, is the focus internal or external? For instance, if team members are not cooperating, the team leader must first decide whether the situation is merely temporary and requires monitoring only or if the team members appear to be embroiled in a long-term debate. If action is required, Hill's model provides several avenues to pinpoint the correct action to be taken.

Internal Leadership Actions

Hill (2012) broke down internal actions into two categories: task and relational. The internal task actions include goal focusing, structuring for results, facilitating decisions, training, and maintaining standards. As Hackman and Walton (1986) mentioned, goals must be clear and motivating.

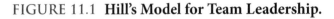

FIGURE 11.1 **Hill's Model for Team Leadership.**

Source: Reproduced from Hill, S. E. K. (2012). Team leadership. In P. G. Northouse, *Leadership: Theory and practice* (6th ed., pp. 287–318). Thousand Oaks, CA: Sage Publications.

A lack of cooperation among team members could be a sign that individual goals rather than team goals have taken prominence and the team leader may need to step in to refocus team members. Sometimes, a reminder of the team's mission may be all that is required. Structuring the team for results is a function of having the right number of team members, but also having the right balance of skills for the task(s) at hand. Particularly in sport organizations, an employee's success in some individual area of sport business may not be a clear indication of their potential for team performance. Individual achievers may not have the right skills to put the needs of the team first and for some, no amount of training will change that. Facilitating decisions is another essential task. Training for teams must be seen as ongoing and not simply a means of compensating for deficiencies. Given the changing environment in which teams operate, staying current depends on training. The last internal task action (although this list is not exhaustive) is maintaining standards. Team leaders play an essential role within the team of monitoring and maintaining performance levels. In this sense, the team leader plays the role of manager as well as evaluating team performance and addressing inadequate contributions by team members.

The internal relational leadership actions in Hill's model include coaching, collaborating, managing conflict, building commitment, satisfying needs, and modeling principles. In this model, coaching team members in interpersonal skills is the primary focus, but coaching could involve any number of team-related skills. Collaborating addresses the actions of the leader to involve members in the activities of the team. Managing conflict and power issues include actions to address the conflict that is nearly inevitable in team settings. Building commitment and esprit de corps can be accomplished through a wide variety of tactics, including formal recognition events or simple get-togethers. Satisfying individual member needs is something that often is forgotten in a team setting. Although the team and its goals are the primary focus, an effective team leader does not forget that the team is a collective of individuals who need differing levels of support. Modeling ethical and principled practices is also important to maintain perceptions of fairness.

External Leadership Actions

Hill's model also addresses the external leadership actions that are at the heart of the boundary-spanning nature of team leadership and the monitoring function described by McGrath (1962) and others. Networking, advocating, negotiating support, buffering, assessing, and sharing information are included. Networking serves several functions for the team; the alliances built via networking facilitate the gathering of information necessary for the team's functioning as well as the dissemination of information about the team. Advocating for the team is a specific element of networking by which the team leader serves as the defender of the team as well as its public relations officer. Online newsletters, blogs,

and other publicity activities (e.g., press conferences) inform key stakeholders of team successes and ensure that the necessary team resources are maintained. Buffering entails "taking a hit for the team" on occasion, but also includes protecting team members from potential distractions in the environment. Assessing environmental indicators of the team's effectiveness is essential to gauge the success of the team in the eyes of customers, suppliers, and other key stakeholders. For instance, owners and coaches pay attention to ticket sales and luxury box attendance, among other things. Lastly, sharing relevant environmental information involves a filtering process related to buffering. The team leader conveys mission-relevant information while protecting the team from the inevitable noise in the environment. Many a postevent press conference has been conducted by owners or coaches to defuse volatile situations created by internal and external controversies.

Team Effectiveness

The last element of Hill's model is related to the outcomes of the team. In particular, Hill focuses on both performance and development of the team itself. The reason a team exists is to accomplish the task at hand and to improve the "quality of decision making, the ability to implement decisions" (p. 24), with the outcome of teamwork measured by the work completed and the problems solved (Nadler, 1998), Development focuses on the relational side of team outcomes. Ideally, team members should be satisfied with their individual contributions to the team while keeping team goals at the forefront. Feelings of cohesiveness and effectiveness are the focus of the development outcomes of teams.

As we have mentioned before, the environment in which teams operate is constantly evolving and growing increasingly complex. This complexity has been affected by technological advances. Specifically, technology has facilitated the development of geographically dispersed teams that are able to function in a virtual world. Virtual teams, though, create new challenges for team leaders.

LEADING VIRTUAL TEAMS

Managing sport organizations in today's business world will inevitably require connecting team members in multiple regions of the country, if not from multiple countries. Therefore, virtual contact via computers, smartphones, and other technology is simply the way that business gets done. The fact that "*virtual teams* differ from face-to-face teams in terms of coordination, communication, and collaboration" (Malhotra, Majchrzak, & Rosen, 2007, p. 61) has been supported by an extensive body of research (e.g., Bachiochi, Rogelberg, O'Connor, & Elder, 2000; Fiol & O'Connor, 2005; Kirkman, Rosen, Gibson, Tesluk, & McPherson, 2002; Saunders, Van Slyke, & Vogel, 2004). The reliance on communication technology to conduct the team's business changes nearly all of the team leader actions summarized previously in this chapter, some in minor ways and others rather fundamentally. Establishing team norms, managing work, networking, and more team functions are affected by moving the team to a virtual setting. Malhotra et al. (2007) outline six practices of effective virtual team leaders.

Effective virtual team leaders "establish and maintain trust through the use of communication technology" (Malhotra et al., p. 62). This is accomplished by setting norms for information sharing, having virtual get-togethers to reinforce those norms, and communicating progress via the virtual workspace. Effective team leaders also ensure that the suffering (early starts for videoconferences, late calls with clients) of the geographically dispersed is evenly distributed across the team. Effective team leaders also "ensure diversity in the team is understood, appreciated, and leveraged" (p. 62). This requires the maintenance of an online directory of the prominent team expertise and skills, rotation of team members, and the use of online discussion threads to promote expression of diverse opinions.

Effective virtual team leaders also manage the virtual work cycle and meetings. Brainstorming and disagreements can happen *between* meetings via asynchronous discussion threads, but idea convergence and conflict resolution occur *during* virtual meetings. The virtual nature of meetings also affects some basic meeting processes. The start of virtual meetings should be used for relationship building, and during the meetings the leader should check in with everyone to ensure they are engaged in the discussion. At the end of the meeting, the minutes and future plans need to be posted at a common accessible online site. The virtual team leader should also monitor team progress through the use of technology. This involves scrutiny of electronic discussion threads and the use of balanced scorecard measures posted in the team's virtual workspace.

The effective team leader must also "enhance external visibility of the team and its members" (Malhotra et al., p. 62) by reporting to a virtual steering committee of the bosses of team members. Finally, team leaders need to "ensure individuals benefit from participating in virtual teams" (p. 62) by holding virtual reward ceremonies, providing individual recognition at the start of virtual meetings, and ensuring that team members' bosses are aware of these achievements as well.

SUMMARY

Work in teams continues to evolve and, as such, the work of team leaders also continues to evolve. Effective team leaders need to optimize a combination of task-management and people-management skills because there is no one-size-fits-all approach to leading teams to their potential. The type of organization, the type of task(s), and the people involved all have an impact on the approach taken by a leader. Leaders must be wary of the tenets of groupthink, social loafing, and the size of groups. Steiner's Typology of Tasks serves as an important reference to decide whether a team is needed to perform a task or whether an individual working on a task would suffice. Once a team has been formed, Hackman's five preconditions for team success can help leaders start the team process with a good chance at achieving the desired results. Finally, Hill's model for team leadership equips the leader with a roadmap to know which internal and external actions to take to enhance team effectiveness. Taken together, Steiner's, Hackman's, and Hill's suggestions can help teams achieve success, whether it is in the ticket office for a minor league hockey team or in the classroom of your sport finance class.

LEADERSHIP PERSPECTIVE

Rob Crain.
Courtesy of Rob Crain

Rob Crain is the president and general manager of the Scranton/Wilkes-Barre RailRiders. The RailRiders of the International League are the Triple-A affiliate of the New York Yankees. Before coming to the RailRiders, Crain worked as the assistant general manager of the Omaha Storm Chasers.

Q: How do you encourage the involvement of your front office team in decision making that affects the organization?

My job is to lead them to make the decisions on their own, but you give them the direction. So you set the culture of, in my case, how you want the team to be run. What are some of your key talking points? That message goes through the decisions that are made with your executive team.

Q: Do members of your front office team ever work in small groups to accomplish tasks? Do you ever encounter problems with groups not getting along or not working together?

Yes, on both fronts. In minor league baseball there are all these theme nights. What we have done is put together a theme night committee where they brainstorm and come up with new ideas for theme nights, and they figure out a plan for how to sell tickets to them, how to execute them, and all the details going forward. We've also done these for opening day and for big events. You put these smaller committees in with people from all departments, from ticket sales to sponsorship sales to marketing to operations. You put everyone in there because everyone has different ideas. So, what happens in some of these is you get big personalities. The larger personalities almost take over the meeting and it's basically all their ideas, and it gets away from the team aspect you are trying to get. So, what you've got to do sometimes is step in and ensure that everyone's ideas are being heard and being considered. You have to set that tone with your smaller groups. Some people take offense if you don't like their ideas or don't think their idea can work. That's just a part of it because not all ideas can be used. You have to manage that process with people's feelings. They are still encouraged to throw out another idea next time because next time might be the big one that is able to be a part of that discussion and then be executed at a game.

Q: Sport management students are often asked to work in groups to complete assignments. Why do you think the ability to work in groups is such an important skill for the professional workplace in sport?

You work in a group no matter what. You always have to work with people of different personalities, of different backgrounds, of different ethnicities. Each person looks at the world differently. It's important that people in groups can work cohesively and that everyone shares ideas because where I think companies go wrong is that they separate themselves into these silos. In my world, ticketing only worries about ticketing things, marketing only worries about marketing things, sponsorships only worry about sponsorships, operations only worries about operations. But if you don't intertwine those, you don't work in groups and you don't work together, then you are really setting yourself up for failure. So, the ability to work in groups and the ability to really hear and understand other folks' ideas and seeing how they can be implemented, you have to be able to do that in business. And it doesn't matter if you are in sport or accounting firms, you are always working with other folks. To be able to work in groups is a must.

Q: How do you guard against groupthink—or the idea that group members simply want to unite behind a decision that they think their leader wants? In other words, how do you encourage group members to be honest and suggest ideas that might put them at odds with other people they work with and organization leaders?

I ask them directly. One of the things I think leaders need to be able to do is ask direct, blunt questions. Literally ask, "Do you agree with this? Yes or no? If yes, why?" Then a lot of times leaders can find out if they are just BSing you or not. I think being more blunt in business is one of the things you have to be able to do. People get "PC" and don't want to ask the wrong thing, but we're all here for one goal no matter what the goal is. You really have to ask them, "OK, why? Why do you agree with it? Why don't you agree with it?" And the leader has to take the attitude that just because it's your idea, it's not the only idea. I think leaders, including myself, struggle with that every single day. There are ways to get around it, but I think the thing you have to do is ask blunt questions and ask, "Do you agree with that or not?" It's OK to not agree with me. And then once you set the bar and a leader communicates, "OK, here is an idea" not "Here is a directive," then they are all on the same plane together.

Q: Have you ever seen a situation where individual goals of group members take precedence over the group's collective goal or power dynamics derailed a group project? If so, what happened?

You see it a lot. People get very defensive of their area. If they are in tickets, they want to make sure that everything they are doing is based around tickets, and they are almost myopic. "This is a ticket thing and it does not matter how it affects sponsorships or operations." That can go into any of the departments. And that can derail things. You don't get exactly what you are looking for because one person or one person in a department tries to make it all about that one specific thing, ticket or operations. It is the leader's job to ensure that this is not the case. The leader has to be mindful of all the departments, all of the folks that are in that discussion and make sure what is being done is best for the team and not what is best for one department.

KEY TERMS

groupthink

Hill's model for team leadership

social facilitation

social loafing

task typology

team effectiveness

virtual teams

DISCUSSION QUESTIONS

1. How would you describe team effectiveness for the front office staff of a Major League Baseball team? What conditions are necessary to achieve team effectiveness?
2. Have you seen evidence of groupthink in group projects you have worked on in a class? Cite a specific example. Using the tenets of groupthink mentioned in the chapter, which characteristics of groupthink were most prevalent in the example you cited?
3. Using Hackman's five conditions for team effectiveness, suggest which conditions are crucial for a "street team" of marketers that has been organized to come up with a marketing campaign for a new WNBA team moving to Austin, Texas.
4. The authors suggest the growing prominence of virtual teams. What methods, in general, can a leader use to make virtual teams succeed when half the team works in New York and the other half works in Hong Kong?
5. Looking at Hill's model and internal leadership actions specifically, which task or relational actions seem most important when a general manager has six employees working in her box office and three of them are fresh out of college?

For a full suite of assignments and additional learning activities, use the access code found in the front of your book. If you do not have an access code, you can obtain one at **www.jblearning.com**.

REFERENCES

Abraham, P. (2012, October 3). Bobby Valentine says Red Sox coaches were disloyal. Retrieved from http://www.boston.com/sports/2012/10/03/bobby-valentine-says-red-sox-coaches-were-disloyal/s4Fbb3ETulUojnKlqA7QMP/story.html

Allport, F. H. (1920). The influence of the group upon association and thought. *Journal of Experimental Psychology, 3*, 159–182.

Associated Press. (2012, August 26). Adrian Gonzalez 'excited' for Dodgers. Retrieved from http://espn.go.com/mlb/story/_/id/8302934/josh-beckett-adrian-gonzalez-packed-gone-boston-red-sox-dodgers-blockbuster-trade-looms

Bachiochi, P. D., Rogelberg, S. G., O'Connor, M. S., & Elder, A. E. (2000). The qualities of an effective team leader. *Organizational Development Journal, 18*(1), 11–27.

Burke, C. S., Stagl, K. C., Klein, C., Goodwin, G. F., Salas, E., & Halpin, S. M. (2006). What type of leadership behaviors are functional in teams? A meta-analysis. *Leadership Quarterly, 17*(3), 288–307.

Burwitz, L., & Newell, K. M. (1972).The effects of the mere presence of cofactors on learning a motor skill. *Journal of Motor Behavior, 4*, 99–102.

Edes, G. (2012, July 16). Bobby V puts onus on Kevin Youkilis. Retrieved from http://espn.go.com/boston/mlb/story/_/id/8168192/boston-red-sox-bobby-valentine-blames-kevin-youkilis-poor-relationship

Fiol, C. M., & O'Connor, E. J. (2005). Identification to face-to-face, hybrid, and pure virtual teams: Untangling the contradictions. *Organization Science, 16*(1), 19–32.

Fraser, C. (1971). Group risk-taking and group polarization. *European Journal of Social Psychology, 1*, 493–510.

Hackman, J. R. (2002). *Leading teams: Setting the stage for great performances.* Boston, MA: Harvard Business School.

Hackman, J. R., & Walton, R. E. (1986). Leading groups in organizations. In P. S. Goodman (Ed.), *Designing effective work groups* (pp. 72–119). San Francisco, CA: Jossey-Bass.

Hamilton, J. (2013, June). The Darko ages: How magical thinking and racism produced the NBA's most notorious draft bust. *Slate.com.* Retrieved from http://www.slate.com/articles/sports/sports_nut/2013/06/darko_milicic_draft_how_magical_thinking_and_racism_produced_the_nba_s_most.html

Harrison, I. (2012, September 15). Bobby V: Weakest roster in September. Retrieved from http://espn.go.com/boston/mlb/story/_/id/8379248/weakest-roster-red-sox-history-bobby-valentine

Hill, S. E. K. (2012). Team leadership. In P. G. Northouse (Ed.), *Leadership: Theory and practice* (6th ed., pp. 287–318). Thousand Oaks, CA: Sage.

Janis, I. L. (1972). *Victims of groupthink.* Boston, MA: Houghton-Mifflin.

Johnson, D. W., & Johnson, F. P. (2000). *Joining together: Group theory and group skills* (7th ed.). Boston: Allyn and Bacon.

Kerr, N., & Tindale, R. (2004). Group performance and decision making. *Annual Review of Psychology, 55*, 623–655.

Kerr, N. L., & Tindale, R. S. (2011). Group-based forecasting: A social psychological analysis. *International Journal of Forecasting, 27*, 14–40.

Kirkman, B. L., Rosen, B., Gibson, C. B., Tesluk, P. E., & McPherson, S. O. (2002). Five challenges to virtual team success. *Academy of Management Executive, 16*(3), 67–79.

Komaki, J. L., Desselles, M. L., & Bowman, E. D. (1989). Definitely not a breeze: Extending an operant model of effective supervision to teams. *Journal of Applied Psychology, 74*, 522–529.

Kozlowski, S. W., Gully, S. M., McHugh, P. P., Salas, E., & Cannon-Bowers, J. A. (1996). A dynamic theory of leadership and team effectiveness: Developmental and task contingent leader roles. In G. R. Ferris (Ed.), *Research in personnel and human resources management* (Vol. 14, pp. 253–305). Greenwich, CT: JAI Press.

Larson, J. R. (2010). *In search of synergy in small group performance.* New York: Psychology Press.

Latané, B., Williams, K., & Harkins, S. (1979). Many hands make light the work: The causes and consequences of social loafing. *Journal of Personality and Social Psychology, 37,* 822–832.

Liden, R. C., Wayne, S. J., Jaworski, R. A., & Bennett, N. (2004). Social loafing: A field investigation. *Journal of Management, 30*(2), 285–304.

Locke, E. A., & Latham, G. P. (2006). New directions in goal-setting theory. *Current Directions in Psychological Science, 15*(5), 265–268.

Malhotra, A., Majchrzak, A., & Rosen, B. (2007). Leading virtual teams. *Academy of Management Perspectives, 21,* 60–70.

McDonald, J. (2012, June 22). David Ortiz tired of negative reports. Retrieved from http://espn.go.com/boston /mlb/story/_/id/8082136/david-ortiz-fed-reports-turmoil-boston-red-sox-clubhouse

McGrath, J. E. (1962). *Leadership behavior: Some requirements for leadership training.* Washington, DC: U.S. Civil Service Commission, Office of Career Development.

Michaels, J. W., Blommel, J. M., Brocato, R. M., Linkous, R. A., & Rowe, J. S. (1982). Social facilitation and inhibition in a natural setting. *Replications in Social Psychology, 2,* 21–24.

Mueller, J. S. (2012). Why individuals in larger teams perform worse. *Organizational Behavior and Human Decision Processes, 117,* 111–124.

Murnighan, J. (1981). Group decision making: What strategies should you use? *Management Review, 25,* 56–62.

Nadler, D. A. (1998). Executive team effectiveness: Teamwork at the top. In D. A. Nadler & J. L. Spencer (Eds.), *Executive teams* (pp. 21–39). San Francisco, CA: Jossey-Bass.

Salas, E., Dickinson, T. L., Converse, S. A., & Tannenbaum, S. I. (1992). Toward an understanding of team performance and training. In R. W. Sweeney & E. Salas (Eds.), *Teams: Their training and performance* (pp. 3–29). Norwood, NJ: ABLEX.

Saunders, C., Van Slyke, C., & Vogel, D. (2004). My time or yours? Managing time visions in global virtual teams. *Academy of Management Executive, 18*(1), 19–31.

Silvia, S., & Neslin, L. (2012, September 11). How the 2012 Red Sox unraveled. Retrieved from http://www .bostonglobe.com/sports/2012/09/11/how-red-sox-unraveled/sX2wPnh3Pt4uB0pKuTesoN/story.html

Steiner, I. (1972). *Group process and productivity.* New York: Academic Press.

Triplett, N. (1898). The dynamogenic factors in pace-making and competition. *American Journal of Psychology, 9,* 507–533.

Wagner, J. A. (1994). Participation effects on performance and satisfaction: A reconsideration of research evidence. *Academy of Management Review, 19,* 312–330.

Weber, B., & Hertel, G. (2007). Motivational gains of inferior group members: A meta-analytic review. *Journal of Personality and Social Psychology, 93,* 973–993.

Zaccaro, S. J., Rittman, A. L., & Marks, M. A. (2001). Team leadership. *Leadership Quarterly, 12,* 451–483.

Zajonc, R. B. (1965). Social facilitation. *Science, 149,* 269–274.

Zenger, J., Musselwhite, E., Hurson, K., & Perrin, C. (1994). *Leading teams: Mastering the new role.* Homewood, IL: Business One Irwin.

CHAPTER 12

SHEPHERDING SPORT FOR DEVELOPMENT ORGANIZATIONS

Jennifer Bruening
Nadia Moreno
Brooke Page Rosenbauer

CHAPTER OBJECTIVES

- Recognize how Sport for Development and Peace (SDP) programs use sport to bring together different genders, ethnicities, religions, abilities, or political systems.
- Describe the various classifications of SDP programs.
- Demonstrate an understanding of SDP programs based on sport as a distraction or diversion, and using sport as a platform.
- Describe the key skills for leaders of SDP programs.
- Demonstrate an understanding of the importance of program quality, monitoring, and evaluation of SDP programs.

CASE STUDY

University of Connecticut's Husky Sport

In the spring of 2002, Dr. Jennie Bruening came to the University of Connecticut (UConn) as a professor in the Sport Management program. One of Dr. Bruening's objectives was to engage students at UConn with children in Hartford, Connecticut. Dr. Bruening had studied the lives of African American female college athletes and learned the importance of mentorship in helping them participate in sports outside of those stereotyped to Black athletes (Bruening, 2005; Bruening, Pastore, & Armstrong, 2008). Dr. Bruening sought out key partnerships to help her develop this objective. She met with community leaders throughout Hartford, and one specifically

(continues)

encouraged her to recognize the potential for UConn students to volunteer and serve as role models for children in Hartford. This key partner, Chris Doucot, codirector of the Hartford Catholic Worker, noted that many of the children living in Hartford do not have connections to college students in their community. As Dr. Bruening learned more about the sport and physical activity aspects of the Saturday program at the Catholic Worker House, she recognized the potential of a great partnership, and the Sport Hartford program officially began (Husky Sport, 2013).

Further partnerships were forged with members of the UConn athletic department to facilitate the involvement of student-athlete volunteers for physical activity programming and nutrition lessons with the children in Hartford. During a meeting in which Dr. Bruening was promoting Sport Hartford to student-athletes, she mentioned the nutrition component of the program that followed an urban health model used at Northeastern University. A fellow faculty member from UConn who was attending that meeting encouraged her to reach out to a colleague in the Nutritional Sciences department, because there was a potential funding opportunity available to help support the currently unfunded Sport Hartford program.

Following a series of meetings with Dr. Ann Ferris, now director of UConn Center for Public Health and Health Policy, Dr. Bruening became a partner on a grant that would support the program. In an effort to align the Sport Hartford program with other programs funded through the grant, the name was changed to Husky Sport. The renamed Husky Sport program received funding to provide nutrition education, in addition to physical activity programming, to children in Hartford.

As the program has grown, from one afterschool program for girls and volunteer activities with Catholic Worker House on Saturdays, to a boys afterschool program, and then a teen program for those children growing out of the afterschool program, Dr. Bruening has had to continue to forge partnerships and find additional funding to help support the growth of the Husky Sport program. Some of the major challenges that Dr. Bruening faces as she looks to the future of Husky Sport are the challenges of growing a sustainable program, working with multiple partners, and seeking out financial resources to support the program.

Questions for Discussion

1. As a leader of the Husky Sport program, Dr. Bruening has had to forge multiple partnerships to help grow and sustain the program. What challenges do leaders face when having to work with multiple partners?

2. When considering the power dynamics associated with Sport for Development and Peace programs, what must Dr. Bruening and the staff at Husky Sport consider when working with the children of Hartford?

3. After reviewing the chapter, would you consider Husky Sport to be an SDP program that uses sport as a platform, sport as a hook, or sport as a distraction? Provide support for your answer.

4. What recommendations would you provide to Dr. Bruening in regard to how best to measure and evaluate the impact that Husky Sport has on its participants?

INTRODUCTION

Sport can play a role in improving the lives of individuals, not only individuals, I might add, but whole communities. I am convinced that the time is right to build on that understanding, to encourage governments, development agencies and communities to think how sport can be included more systematically in the plans to help children, particularly those living in the midst of poverty, disease and conflict.

—Kofi Annan (United Nations, 2002, para. 6)

The statement by Kofi Annan, former secretary-general of the United Nations (UN), speaks to the power of sport to function as a tool for positive social change for individuals and communities. The UN has been a key organization in the growth in understanding of the power of sport as a developmental and peace-promoting tool. In 2001, the UN created a new position, Special Adviser to the Secretary General on Sport for Development and Peace. And in 2003, the United Nations Task Force on Sport for Development and Peace concluded that "sport offers a cost-effective tool to meet many development and peace challenges, and help achieve [the UN's Millennium Development Goals]" (UN Inter-Agency Task Force on Sport for Development and Peace, 2005, p. 1). Annan played a critical role as he encouraged leaders of all sorts to consider the potential of sport more systematically because sport can provide the "information, skills, personal and social resources, and support needed to make key life transitions successfully" (Sport for Children and Youth, n.d., p. 80) for groups and even societies (Welty Peachey & Cohen, 2012).

In this chapter, we will highlight *sport for development and peace (SDP)* organizations from around the world to demonstrate how they use sport to bring together different genders, ethnicities, religions, abilities, or political systems "based upon opportunities to foster trust, obligations, redistribution and respect for sport" (Jarvie, 2007, p. 422). SDP comes alive through deliberate programming in response to the social needs of both individuals and communities. You will see how sport has the capacity to transform individuals through physical, emotional, psychological, and social development while simultaneously playing an integral role in community development. The United Nations and its partners, such as national governments, the International Olympic and Paralympic Committees, nongovernmental organizations, and corporations have recognized the value of sport and have come together to think strategically about sport for development and peace. And as you know, leaders of organizations are charged with this strategic thinking.

SPORT FOR DEVELOPMENT AND PEACE PROGRAMS

Although there are at least 500 registered SDP organizations throughout the world (IPSD, 2011, in Welty Peachey & Cohen, 2012), other tallies find closer to 1,000 (Lyras & Welty Peachey, 2011). Even with the support of the United Nations, SDP is still in its relative infancy.

Sport for development and peace initiatives vary in size, scope, and focus, but all use sport to promote social change (Darnell, 2012; Welty Peachey & Cohen, 2012). Several authors have attempted to classify SDP programs due to this variance. The United Nations (2003) identified three broad areas of focus for SDP programs: social issues, health and education, and economic development. Some examples of these categories are included in **Table 12.1**.

In addition, Levermore (2008) devised the following seven categories that center on the developmental outcomes desired by a program: conflict resolution, cultural understanding, infrastructure development, educational awareness, the empowerment of marginalized groups, encouragement of physical activity and health, and driving economic development. Some examples of these categories are included in **Table 12.2**.

TABLE 12.1 Focus Areas for SDP Programs

Focus Area	Sample Program
Social issues	Soccer for Peace: www.soccerforpeace.org
Health and education	Grassroot Soccer: www.grassrootsoccer.org
Economic development	Upper Nayach Training: www.karibuafrikakenya.org

In this chapter, while acknowledging the validity of both the United Nations' and Levermore's approaches to classifying SDP programs, we have focused on the use of sport as the means of classification and devised four categories for SDP initiatives: *sport as distraction/diversion*, *sport as a platform*, *sport as a right*, and *sport as a hook* or teaching tool (Green, 2008; Le Menestrel, Bruno & Christian, 2002; Perkins & Noam, 2007). We will focus on the continued emergence of sport for development and peace organizations and the different tools needed by leaders for these organizations to carry out their missions. In order for these nonprofits to operate quality programs, gain credibility, and make an impact on participants, leaders have to be creative with what are often small budgets. As the power of sport as a developmental tool and instrument of peace continues to be understood by a larger audience, we see these organizations as possible destinations for graduates of sport management programs. In order to provide more information for these future managers and leaders, we provide a history of sport for development and peace, speak to the potential power dynamics at work in SDP organizations, and then move on to examine the types of sport for development and peace programs and the roles of leaders in these programs. We conclude by highlighting the elements of quality programs and the role of monitoring and evaluation.

History

The concept of sport for development and peace can trace its origins to the spirit of *Olympism*, which can be defined as follows:

> . . . [the] philosophy of life, exalting and combing in a balanced whole the qualities of body, will and mind. Blending sport with culture and education, Olympism seeks to

TABLE 12.2 Development Outcomes for SDP Programs

Development Outcome	Sample Program
Conflict resolution	Football 4 Peace: www.football4peace.eu
Cultural understanding	Exchange programs: www.exchanges.state.gov/sports
Infrastructure development	Good Sports: www.goodsports.org
Educational awareness	America SCORES: www.americascores.org
Empower marginalized groups	League of Dreams: www.ourleagueofdreams.com
Encourage physical activity/health	A World Fit for Kids: www.worldfitforkids.org
Drive economic development	Alive and Kicking: www.aliveandkicking.org

Source: Data from Levermore, R. (2008). Playing for development: Outlining the extent of the use of sport for development? *Progress in Development*, 8(2), 183–190.

create a way of life based on the joy found in effort, the educational value of good example and respect for universal fundamental ethical principles. (International Olympic Committee, 1994, p. 10)

SDP has strong roots in European culture as well. Victorians led the way in understanding that sport was a means by which to learn discipline and develop strong character. Originally, sport was viewed as a luxury or escape from work, but soon it became more organized, institutionalized, and competitive (Coakley & Pike, 2009; Guttman, 1978). Then, as the 1900s began, working-class citizens around the globe began to ask for safe spaces for recreation as they recognized sport and physical activity offered positive outcomes for both adults and children beyond what had been thought by previous generations (Ingham & Hardy, 1984). Expanding one's ability to function within a team and exhibit tolerance of others was seen as a desired impact (Darnell, 2012). In contemporary times, sport has grown to be seen as a means to build human agency and social equity, and, as a result, foster a strong and civil society (Harris, 1998).

One prime example of using sport to build human agency and social equity was the work of Sir Ludwig Guttman, a German neurologist, who practiced at Stoke Mandeville Hospital in England. In 1948, while the Olympics took place in London, Guttman hosted the precursor to the Paralympics. The Stoke Mandeville Games provided the opportunity for wheelchair-bound athletes to build strength and self-respect (O'Hare, 2012). The next major addition to SDP occurred when youth development and education, a focus of many SDP programs today, was formalized by the United Nations Educational, Scientific and Cultural Organization (UNESCO) in 1952 (UNESCO, 1952). Soon thereafter, the UN Declaration of the Rights of the Child (United Nations, 1959) stated: ". . . the child shall have full

opportunity for play and recreation" (para. 14) and reinforced that society as a whole should support this fundamental right.

More recently, many organizations and policy makers have paved the way for a sport for development and peace approach and, as a result, programs have emerged. Leaders of physical education and sport organizations and government offices worldwide have emphasized the importance of access to sport for all, in particular women and children. Other stakeholders in SDP who have established a presence in recent years are mega sport organizations. England's Football Association (FA), the National Basketball Association (NBA), and the Fédération Internationale de Football Association (FIFA) are three prime examples with programs like Just Play, Basketball without Borders, and Football for Hope (Darnell, 2012; Millington, 2010). In addition, transnational organizations such as the International Olympic Committee (IOC) reinforce the spirit of Olympism mentioned earlier in its most current charter, which states that Olympism in action serves to "build a better world" through the development of programs "that provide concrete responses to social inequity" (Darnell, 2012, p. 6).

It is important to note the growth in state and national governments' involvement in SDP policy and programming. Huish (2011) examined the role of the Cuban government in supporting the training of professional coaches across the southern hemisphere as a form of sport-based solidarity. Canada's Ministry of Heritage and its Youth Employment Strategies support the SDP internship program organized by Commonwealth Games Canada (Darnell, 2012). However, the UN has remained the main force behind international SDP efforts. The General Assembly created and passed the World Fit for Children resolution, calling for all (i.e., public and private sectors) to recognize sport and recreational opportunities as a fundamental human right.

POWER DYNAMICS OF SDP

Issues of development give cause for further consideration. Darnell (2012) states that sport is not a "benign social institution"; rather, sport reflects the power dynamics of the larger society. Sport has been positioned by some to provide a "level playing field" (Lapchick, 1996) devoid of the inequalities found in other social institutions. However, an understanding of the potentially hegemonic nature of sport is critical in leading SDP organizations and efforts. As such, leaders who develop and advocate for a commitment to analyzing the ways in which power operates within sport demonstrate that the conferring of positive social change implies a power dynamic. The professed need for development, also known as benevolence or stewardship, can, if not intentionally addressed, foster a power relationship. A dynamic in which the providers of the sport program perceive themselves as the helpers and those receiving the program as needing help can be established. This provider/receiver relationship can cause more harm than good, if not checked, because providers and receivers do not engage in shared decision making in which the opinions of both groups are taken into account (Darnell, 2012).

With knowledge of the inherent power structure of sport at hand, leaders can better examine research around SDP programs. These programs have been found to provide children marginalized by factors such as poverty, gender, disability, ethnic and/or cultural origins, and conflict with a multitude of benefits such as adult role models, opportunities to build self-esteem and self-confidence, means by which to develop social and communication skills, chances to develop leadership skills that can extend beyond sport contexts into education and career, and alternatives to delinquency, criminal gangs, and armed conflict (Sport for Children and Youth, n.d.). SDP programs that combine sport with other activities, such as academic enrichment, community engagement,

and the development of critical thinking skills, increase overall benefits for participants. Most SDP programs provide open opportunities, thus increasing participation by those often excluded; when leaders facilitate this inclusion with a critical social consciousness, meaning they are aware of the experiences of marginalized groups and can include individuals from these groups in a positive way, sport for development program cultures have the capacity to build emotional safety and promote personal development (Bailey, 2006; Linver, Roth, & Brooks-Gunn, 2009; Peck, Roeser, Zarrett, & Eccles, 2008; Zarrett et al., 2009). Sport is uniquely suited for this type of barrier-breaking role because it is predominantly motivated by the fun, friendship, and social aspects associated with sport activities and club membership (Spaaij, 2011). SDP brings people together to watch, play, learn, and compete through sport or sport-based activities in order to promote interaction and inclusion of individuals. "[S]port is well-positioned to play a role in fostering the inclusion of newcomers by breaking down barriers and encouraging cross-cultural understanding" (Winnipeg Community Sport Policy, 2012, p. 3). In fact, the contribution of sport has been shown to align with all of the United Nation's Millennium Development Goals, which are to eradicate extreme hunger and poverty; achieve universal primary education; promote gender equality and empower women; reduce child mortality; improve maternal health; combat HIV/AIDS, malaria, and other diseases; ensure environmental sustainability; and develop a global partnership for development (United Nations Development Programme, 2000).

SPORT AS A DISTRACTION/ DIVERSION

The first type of sport for development and peace program is one that uses sport as a distraction or diversion. In these types of program, sport is utilized as a replacement for deviant behaviors, because participating in sport is a more socially desirable behavior (Green, 2008). Diversionary programs attempt to provide youth with positive activities to distract them from delinquency and crime, and/or from spending time with peers who might encourage that type of behavior (Burrows, 2003). Programs also focus on exposure to protective factors such as promoting wellness, social bonding, working with adult mentors, opportunities to be involved and to lead, building social skills, and the use of recognition and positive reinforcement (Burrows, 2003; Henley, Schweizer, de Gara, & Vetter, 2007). By encouraging more socially acceptable values and behaviors, sport as distraction/diversion programs can address and even prevent youth delinquency and crime (Ewing, Gano-Overway, Branta, & Seefeldt, 2002; Green, 2008).

True diversionary programs do not have sport skill development as the primary goal; rather, they provide a combination of social and emotional interactions with peers and mentors, as well as the sport experience, which characterizes them as sport as diversion/distraction programs. In designing and managing sport for diversion/distraction programs, leaders must understand the context and be sensitive to the experiences and needs of the youth involved. Van Standifer, the founder and director of Midnight Basketball, did just that. As a town manager in Prince George's County, Maryland, in 1986, Standifer studied police reports to find clues to what would assist in crime reduction during the hours when most crimes occurred, 10 p.m. to 2 a.m. What he found was that crimes during these hours were committed almost exclusively by young men ages 17–22. He decided, again through his understanding of the youth involved, that basketball would be the most effective tool to attract the target audience. But he knew basketball alone would not curb crime. So he developed educational and employment workshops that players had to attend in order to play in the league. In doing so, he partnered with law enforcement officers for support, local businesses for sponsorship, and political leaders to help provide positive media coverage (Association of Midnight Basketball League Programs, 2013). Research has shown programs need to be paired with wider offerings of other anti-crime initiatives and a publicized media link (Green, 2008). Today there are at least 20 active chapters of Midnight Basketball across the United States, and even more cities have borrowed from the general concept of Midnight Basketball. Police calls reporting juvenile crime drop by as much as 55% during the summer when Phoenix basketball courts and other recreation facilities are kept open until 2 a.m. Norfolk, Virginia, saw a 29% drop in crime in targeted neighborhoods and a city-wide reduction in violent crime after police, human services agencies, and local citizens partnered to start new youth athletic leagues. Crime rates plummeted 24% after a late-night recreation program was started in Cincinnati, Ohio. Overall, urban midnight basketball leagues have been proven to reduce neighborhood crimes (Hartmann & Depro, 2006; Mendel, 2000). Community leaders need to be able to spot trends in crime rates and juvenile delinquency and build programs that combat these social ills, just like Van Standifer did.

SPORT AS A PLATFORM

Perhaps the most famous example of sport as a platform is the image of Black Olympians Tommie Smith and John Carlos raising their gloved fists from the medals podium at the 1968 Mexico City Olympics as a symbol of protest against the racial discrimination in the United States. The Olympics have also been a platform to call attention to other social injustices. Dating back to World War I, boycotts of and suspensions from Olympic Games have provided countries opportunities to protest wars, military conflicts and invasions, and apartheid (Hums, Wolff, & Mahoney, 2008; Masteralexis, Barr, & Hums, 2011). But beyond individual actors and countries, SDP organizations have also harnessed the power of sport to achieve their objectives. They have used, and continue to use, sport as a platform.

Another example is the Guerreiras Project (GP), a Brazil-based multimedia initiative that uses soccer as a platform to stimulate gender dialogue, empower female players, challenge discrimination, and promote social justice. The project is composed of four parts. GP Multimedia uses stories, still photos, sound, and film from women's soccer to prompt reflection about gender norms. The GP Community Campaign involves professional female soccer players in Brazil in community workshops where they share their own sport experiences in an effort to encourage women and girls to participate in sport, and by doing so, challenge prejudice and gender and racial stereotypes. GP Gender Research uses ethnographic and experiential approaches to shed a feminist perspective on gender and sport, particularly in light of the growing economic benefits to those who "feminize" the women's game. And lastly, GP Gender Dialogues is a partnership with a London-based organization, The People Speak, using soccer as a tool to bring about discussion on gender norms in sport and society (Guerreiras Project, n.d.).

Not unlike Midnight Basketball, the Guerreiras Project is the creation of an individual leader. Caitlin Davis Fisher moved to Brazil from the United States to play professional soccer. (See the Leadership Perspective section at the end of this chapter for an interview with Caitlin.) She quickly realized that women's soccer and women's soccer athletes were not treated the same way as their male counterparts. In talking to her teammates about the stereotypes and prejudice they faced, Fisher decided to conduct research of women's soccer for the Fédération Internationale de Football Association (FIFA) while she continued to play professionally in Sweden and the United States. With her former teammates, Fisher developed the Guerreiras Project. Through the use of educational opportunities, both formal academic programs and life experiences, as well as the understanding of the life experiences of others, she recognized an opportunity to share her knowledge with others. Fisher's organization challenges gender norms in both sport and society as a whole through the lens of soccer. Like Van Standifer, Fisher recognized that sport as a context could be used to develop individuals in some manner. In her case, it is the development of awareness.

SPORT AS A RIGHT

SDP leaders believe in social inclusion, providing opportunities for all to participate in sport regardless of culture, gender, race, nationality, religion, ability, or class. Typically, SDP leaders bring sport to marginalized societies (Kidd, 2008) and underserved or at-risk populations (Green, 2008). Two groups that tend to be a focus of many SDP efforts are young girls and women. Girls, particularly those from low-income and rural communities, face more barriers to sport participation than boys because they often have responsibilities in the home and tend to be subject to restrictive gender conventions (Lee & Macdonald, 2009).

Mathare Youth Sports Association (MYSA) (www.mysakenya.org) was founded in 1987 by UN advisor Bob Munro. From its simple beginnings with Bob refereeing pickup youth soccer games in the slums of Mathare, just outside Nairobi, Kenya, in exchange for the children picking up trash around the area where they played, MYSA has grown to 25,000 members. The organization, now run entirely by adults who grew up as participants in the program, operates a program that uses soccer as a method of inclusion in an attempt to create safe spaces for girls and young women and to assist with school retention (Brady, 2005).

The Mathare Youth Sports Association has grown to 25,000 members and relies on past participants to lead the organization.
© MYSA SHOOTBACK

SPORT AS A HOOK

Perkins and Noam (2007) state that in SDP programs "the sport skill was a secondary goal to the life lessons being learned . . . but sports are the hook that entice young people to participate . . ." (p. 76). Sport is the vehicle through which youth learn larger life lessons and skills. In many cases, sport is what attracts participants to a program or a location where they can receive other services. The most successful programs are those where sport is not the intervention, although the physical activity and lessons learned through sport are of benefit, but in which sport becomes integrated into the intervention (Green, 2008).

Founder and director of GOALS Haiti, Kona Shen, spent many years studying, visiting, and working in Haiti before starting the organization in 2010. She was struck by the Haitian people. It was through playing soccer while there that she

made friends, learned Creole, and was hosted by multiple families during her trips to Haiti. Participants in GOALS Haiti engage in soccer, education, community service, and local capacity development. GOALS uses soccer as a fun and exciting hook for children who are also involved in community work to address environmental issues in Haiti and provides educational seminars to assist them in achieving academically (Can Soccer Save the World, 2012).

Sport can also be a hook for adults. Street Soccer USA (SSUSA), founded in 2005 by Lawrence Cann, forms partnerships with other community social service providers to help affect positive life changes among its homeless participants in 20 U.S. cities. Sport serves as a hook to get homeless individuals back into society's mainstream. Homeless individuals play on soccer teams coached by volunteers and participate in local soccer leagues in each city. SSUSA has three goals:

(1) build community and trust through sports, transforming the context within which homeless individuals live from one of isolation, abuse, and marginalization to one of community, purpose, and achievement; (2) require participants to set 3-, 6-, and 12-month life goals; and (3) empower individuals by marrying clinical services to sport programming and providing access to educational and employment opportunities (SSUSA, n.d.). Each summer, SSUSA stages the SSUSA Cup, a national tournament that brings teams together from its 20 U.S. locations. The tournament, which began in 2006, serves as an incentive for participants to keep striving to achieve their life goals. A team from the SSUSA Cup is selected every summer to compete in the Homeless World Cup.

Skills Needed by Field Leaders

The next several sections of the chapter rely mostly on the observations and experiences of the three practitioners who have written this chapter and the comments of other selected practitioners. Shepherding SDP organizations takes leaders who care deeply about their organization's cause, have a deep desire to serve others, can operate with few resources, and are adept at developing multiple sources of funding. Leaders in the SDP field must be like soccer midfielders: They need to have a good vision of the entire field and know when to get back on defense and how to thread together passes and move the team forward. In order to orchestrate a successful play, they must know the strengths, weaknesses, and preferences of the individual players as well as the chemistry of the team on the field. When necessary, they must be willing to step up and take a strike.

In order to achieve success in the SDP world, three key skills are necessary for leaders: managing stakeholders, building a winning team, and understanding how to use sport as a tool for development

with the goal of improving social or economic outcomes, not for the sake of sport, which focuses on winning championships and trophies. If one overarching skill were to be gleaned out of these three, it would be communication. Effective communication—listening and speaking—is the primary tool used to keep the different stakeholders within the SDP arena and improve and expand programs. No one player's skill set can ever float an entire team; a true leader can mobilize people from all walks of life for a common cause.

Stakeholder Management

SDP is a complex environment with many players. The increased attention on SDP programs has led to an influx of stakeholders, including but not limited to multilateral organizations such as the World Bank; international development agencies such as the U.S. Agency for International Development (USAID); major and small donors and foundations; local governments; nongovernmental organizations (NGOs) and community-based organizations (CBOs); sport organizations, leagues, and federations; and individual scholars, coaches, athletes, philanthropists, students, and everyday citizens. Balancing these stakeholders in successful partnerships and alliances is a difficult juggling act. As such, *stakeholder management* is a key skill for SDP leaders. In projects small and large there are always a variety of stakeholders, including the program beneficiaries and their community, the donors, local governments and businesses, and the media, to name a few. Stakeholder management refers to the juggling act that occurs in balancing the expectations and objectives of the internal and external players involved in an initiative. It is important to garner support from different types of stakeholders, but they often come to the table with different—even conflicting—objectives or expectations for the project. It is important to build positive relationships with stakeholders to ensure community support and longevity of the project.

In the increasingly competitive horizon of SDP, where programs battle for funds and credibility on the international stage, the leaders of these organizations must combine short-term thinking and long-term vision to manage successful programs on the ground while continuing to break ground through new partnerships for future sustainability.

Aside from external stakeholders such as the private sector and donors, it is very important for an SDP leader to have excellent communication skills with the internal team. Communicating respectfully, by listening to the concerns and opinions of primary stakeholders—the participants— is the only way to successfully navigate the complex environment of SDP. A leader must see him- or herself as a member of the team and, through trust, empathy, and good listening, draw from the knowledge and experiences of everyone touched by the program.

Choosing a Winning Team

Any coach or manager knows that a crucial element to success is the ability to choose a winning team. Similarly, SDP leaders must be able to identify the right facilitators, coordinators, coaches, and administrators who bring the creativity, motivation, and flexibility necessary to operate in an environment characterized by low resources and limited training opportunities. Considering that SDP programs typically work with "disadvantaged" or "high risk" youth populations, positive mentors are one of the most important determinants of success; those facilitators, coaches, teachers, and coordinators who have daily contact with the youth participants can change a young person's path by providing emotional support and encouragement. A perfectly designed program can quickly go off track if the facilitation and daily interaction with youth is not positive. Youth model the behaviors of adults around them, and coaches or facilitators in a sporting environment have an even greater mystique or ability to influence.

Using Sport as a Tool for Development

SDP leaders must find the careful balance between those who understand the coaching or sporting side of SDP and those who understand the programmatic side. Sometimes, program leaders are too focused on sport or, an opposite extreme, too focused on the educational or social outcomes. Everyone on the team has to buy into the concept of SDP and have an unwavering dedication to balancing both sides. A final characteristic of a successful SDP leader is the ability to successfully utilize sport as a *tool* for development with the understanding that sport is a means to the end, not the end itself. In other words, SDP programs are not about winning tournaments or trophies. They are about leveraging the "magic" of sport to reach "unreachable" youth and adults to impart valuable skills and knowledge that youth and adults can use to empower themselves and their communities.

When many people hear about SDP programs, they are automatically drawn to the sporting aspect and assume the main objective is to impart technical sporting skills. As explained already, however, most programs utilize sport as a teaching tool to inspire and engage youth that might not have joined a social program otherwise. An excellent leader knows the difference between using sport for sport's sake and using sport for something greater. The leader can effectively communicate that vision to others and mobilize a community coalition around the use of sport for a development-related objective.

PROGRAM QUALITY: MONITORING AND EVALUATION

During the past decade, the heightened attention on SDP has increased not only the flow of donor funding, but also accountability and expectations for demonstrated impact and results. How does a leader demonstrate the impact of a program to their stakeholders? How does a leader gauge program progress? How does a leader determine if the program is achieving expectations? This is possible through *monitoring and evaluation (M&E)*, which consists of collecting information as the program progresses (monitoring) and assessing the information (evaluation). The central purpose of an M&E system is to determine the quality of a program's implementation—does it reach its objectives, to what extent is it successful, and why—and to apply these lessons internally, to improve the program, or externally, to replicate the results in other programs.

Program Quality

Like most nonprofit organizations, SDP programs involve a painstaking process to become established and effective. It takes far more than simply tossing a ball onto a field or throwing money at a group of disadvantaged children to achieve positive impact. There is a significant amount of work that goes into creating an organization that can have an impact and be sustainable over time. In the SDP field, there needs to be constant innovation and research to assess what is successful and what needs improvement.

Monitoring and Evaluation

Why is monitoring and evaluation important? Although some major, multilateral donors such as the World Bank have been slow to jump onto the SDP bandwagon, other entities such as USAID and its Australian counterpart, AUSAID, have become some of the biggest supporters of SDP programs throughout the world. These entities, like many other major agencies and foundations, require a high level of accountability to justify their investment. Many require in-depth logistical frameworks, extensive indicators, frequent reports on results, and sometimes expensive impact evaluations. Although some of the pressure for M&E comes from international funding organizations, the importance of M&E is universal. Diana Cutaia, director of Sport-Based Initiatives at Wheelock College in Boston, said:

> While invaluable in impact, SDP programs still struggle to obtain the financial resources in an ever growing pool of NGOs addressing important societal issues. M&E allows these programs to identify where they are having the greatest success and where they are least effective. This provides funders with tangible evidence of impact and ensures that the organization is effective in achieving its desired outcomes. (D. Cutaia, personal communication, September 7, 2012)

As Cutaia states, in addition to accountability, M&E can also provide the information that programs need to make adjustments and improvements. A well-oiled M&E system can alert a program when something is not working because it has a strong learning component, or feedback loop. If too much time elapses between implementation and evaluation, a program will not have the chance to review strengths and weaknesses. If the feedback loop is effective, however, a program will review data throughout implementation and respond to the preliminary results. In the case of Grassroot Soccer, which integrated an online database called Salesforce, an upgraded M&E system led to operational and cultural program improvements. According to Tommy Clark, CEO and founder of Grassroot Soccer:

> Since adopting Salesforce for M&E in 2009, Grassroot Soccer has grown into a world leader in the field of sport-for-development. Our system has, without question, created a culture of transparency, accountability, and data-driven decision that lends us undeniable credibility and fosters all kinds of growth. (Vera Solutions, n.d.)

Clark's comment demonstrates M&E is not just about collecting and reporting data. It is about using data effectively to improve program delivery and build a better path to pursuing an organization's mission.

Speaking of an organization's mission, the first step in successful M&E of SDP programs is to determine the ultimate objective. It is helpful to classify the program first as either "Sport Plus" or "Plus Sport" (Coalter, 2008). Sport Plus programs are focused more on the sporting component than development and often work toward removing barriers to sport participation, training coaches, developing basic sporting skills, or advocating for the right to recreational activities. Plus Sport programs focus more on development objectives such as reducing HIV/AIDS, increasing educational outcomes, or providing employment opportunities. It is important to note that sometimes the boundary between these distinctions is blurry, but it is a helpful starting point to developing an M&E system.

Once the objective of a program is identified, it is important to develop the logical framework that outlines the outcomes a program strives to reach and the steps that will be taken to get there. These steps are called *indicators*, and will form the basis of the monitoring component of M&E. During the course of the program, it is important to collect information related to the indicators in order to measure achievement. Indicators are *measurable* benchmarks and should be clearly defined. Examples could include participant attendance, school retention rates, or number of mentors trained. It is important to measure these indicators against a baseline or existing data in order to measure change. Although the compilation of information can often be tedious, time consuming, and difficult with limited access to human resources, it creates an important feedback loop that allows an organization to improve implementation.

After a program's objective and the indicators to measure are defined, the third step is to create

tools to collect the information. There are endless ways to collect information during the M&E process. Generally, information is split into two groups: quantitative and qualitative. It is a good idea to have a balanced mix of both types of data. *Quantitative* information is composed of numerical data that answer the questions of how many and how much: numbers, percentages, rates. Quantitative data can be measured through various tools such as questionnaires and surveys. We know that numbers do not tell the whole story, however. *Qualitative* data can provide a deeper perspective on how or why a program works or doesn't work. Qualitative data can be collected through interviews, testimonials, focus groups, or a new tool called Most Significant Change, which focuses on an individual's personal transformation during a program.

The *evaluation* component of M&E is often more difficult, especially for organizations with less experience or capacity. The gold standard of impact evaluation is the experimental design, which involves a control group and a longitudinal design. Few SDPs can afford to undergo such an evaluation, which is why little research exists to provide a credible argument for the strength of SDP programs versus traditional development programs. Although many can attest to the "magic" of sport and the value that sport brings to development programs, it is difficult to articulate and measure the impact in academic terminology. In addition to *summative* evaluations, which are done at the end of a program, it is important to conduct *formative* evaluations, or ongoing assessments that can help a program determine if it is on track to achieving its goals.

One of the foremost researchers on M&E of SDP programs, Fred Coalter, argues that although *outcome-led* M&E is important, such a focus on evaluation and final results does not tell the whole story and does not necessarily assist in building the capacity needed to help the SDP reach maturity and credibility. Coalter (2008) argues that *process-led* or *formative* M&E can lead to improvements of organizations because it focuses on learning from a program's experience rather than just reporting on it. The reality is that many of the organizations have turned to SDP as a cost-effective way to reach "unreachable" youth and do not have the capacity, training, or resources to meet the M&E expectations of donors. With limited training, resources, and capacity, smaller organizations struggle with M&E requirements and run the risk of losing funding or not being able to obtain it in the first place.

Even with limited budgets, a number of SDP organizations have integrated M&E into their programming to satisfy donor requirements and improve their own capacity. Grassroot Soccer "uses the power of sport to educate, inspire, and mobilize communities to stop the spread of HIV" (Grassroot Soccer, n.d.). Its M&E focuses on the pre- and postprogram knowledge tests of its youth participants, program attendance, and coach and participant demographics. The coaches who work directly with the youth are involved not only in implementing the program, but also in monitoring results. Because they are aware of the results of the tests, they are able to adjust the way the curriculum is facilitated to improve youth learning and retention. As mentioned by Clark of Grassroot Soccer, the use of technology in the M&E system has increased the organization's capacity to provide essential information to donors and make better decisions about the curriculum and program implementation.

The Caribbean Sport and Development Agency (www.ttaspe.org), one of the most prolific Caribbean SDP organizations, coaches its local implementing partners in a variety of data collection tools including questionnaires, interviews, surveys, Most Significant Change stories, case studies, and impact assessments. As an umbrella organization, its goal is not only to be accountable to donors and improve capacity, but also to engage in advocacy for the SDP field to better inform practitioners, policy makers, and donors. With an extensive and diversified armory of qualitative and quantitative data about the impact of its programs, the Caribbean Sport and Development Agency (formerly the Trinidad and Tobago Alliance for Sport and Physical Education or TTASPE) has paved the way for future SDP organizations. It is continuing to address gaps in research and capacity to ensure that SDP organizations have the tools, resources, and knowledge to maximize their impact.

SUMMARY

This chapter outlined the purpose and history of global Sport for Development and Peace (SDP) organizations to demonstrate how they use sport to bring together different genders, ethnicities, religions, abilities, or political systems. Additionally, we defined and gave examples of SDP programs that use sport as a distraction/diversion, sport as a platform, sport as a right, and sport as a hook as the different approaches implemented in SDP. Finally, we outlined issues in SDP for leaders to be aware of as well as the skills necessary for leaders to operate quality SDP programs. We firmly believe that SDP is strongest with deliberate programming aligned with the social needs of both individuals and communities. Sport has the capacity to transform individuals through physical, emotional, psychological, and social development while simultaneously playing an integral role in community development.

LEADERSHIP PERSPECTIVE

Caitlin Fisher of Guerreiras Project is a writer/ researcher, activist, and athlete. She helped to found the Guerreiras Project as she listened to the stories her teammates shared about the struggles, prejudice, and stigma surrounding women's futball (soccer) in Brazil (http://guerreirasproject .wordpress.com).

Caitlin Fisher.
Courtesy of Caitlin Fisher

Q: Within this chapter, communication is identified as one of the most important skills necessary for effective leadership of Sport for Development and Peace (SDP) programs. Can you provide insights into or examples of effective communication you have used within your program (Guerreiras Project)?

It is helpful to go back to the start of this project, in 2010. We wanted to explore the issues of prejudice and wanted to use the tools we had to better understand the issues of prejudice as we were experiencing them. We utilized documentary filmmaking as our tool of communication and showcased that film around the World Cup in Germany in 2010. We wanted to communicate what we were experiencing in Brazil, the gender discrimination we were experiencing as women's futballers, to a wider audience and in particular our peers (other women's futball players). So in regard to communication, our question was, how do we speak to a wider audience? How do we get other peers on board to help support our mission? How do we get our message out there? How do we build a team and then position ourselves for funders and donors? We had to communicate our message, our values, and our mission. This is incredibly challenging. But we needed to understand that we are not a sport organization, we are a gender justice organization using sport as a vehicle to communicate our message.

Q: What skills do you look for when seeking partners and/or volunteers to work in the GP Community Campaigns? Why are these skills important to the success of the GP Community Campaigns?

We seek out others who identify with our message. We need partners who can help us to implement. I presented some of this work at the Gender Institute in London to see if this resonated with others doing work around issues of gender discrimination. I had many people say, "How can I help you and how can I support you?" We receive that type of feedback from so many people who want to be a part of our team. Our message back is, please come on board and let's do this together. We need our partners and volunteers to take ownership of this and take a piece of this and make this better. We have recognized the need to provide more communication to our volunteers. We have to provide them the leadership necessary to help our volunteers know how to help us carry out the tasks to meet our mission. We want our organization to evolve organically.

Q: How do you handle issues of power (with those developing the programs and those participants in the programs) when developing and implementing the GP Community Campaigns?

As a leader of this organization, I have been reluctant to step forward. We want a horizontal structure within our organization. However, I recognize that everyone I am working with sees me as a leader, but it is difficult for me to embrace this because we have many founders of this organization. This will continue to be a challenge for our organization, because we will need to have formal titles if we are to be recognized and supported. We call ourselves a collective and our mission is to address gender issues through futball (soccer). Within the community, we want to be role models by sharing our stories. When we go out to tell our stories and share our photos we are also listening and asking questions, and trying to really understand our partners. We do not make any assumptions regarding what our partners will need. As we went out and started telling our stories and sharing photos we realized that it was really powerful. Parents and coaches were calling us back and asking us to come back to work in the community. How we work with groups in the community is the same exact approach that we use in our own group. Knowing that we have as much to get from people in the community as they are able to get from us. We listen to the people in the community, ask questions, and do not assume anything.

Q: Can you discuss the importance of measuring and evaluating the impact of the GP Community Campaigns? How have you used these findings to help enhance or develop new programs?

Measuring and evaluating our program is a huge, huge challenge for us. We need to be able to measure what we do in very direct terms, but how do you measure empowerment? It is understandable that funding agencies want us to measure our impact and we respect that. We are now trying to work from traditional standards of measures/indicators; however, we want to think "outside the box" in terms of measurement and evaluation. We are constantly coming back to the question, "Are we embodying this using our voices?"; therefore, we need to constantly keep these measures at the heart of what we do. Our voices are key tools for change. We keep asking, "How can we use these voices/stories? What is in our heart?" to measure the impact of our program.

Q: Going forward, can you highlight one or two of the most significant challenges you will face as one of the leaders of Guerreiras Project? How do you anticipate addressing these challenges?

Our biggest challenge will be to develop a formal organizational structure, yet still remain an agile and fluid organization that is able to be nimble. We are resisting becoming an NGO [nongovernmental organization]. We are very reluctant to do this and are challenging the existing structures and systems, believing there is a better way to do things. But it is so hard to do this within the current structure in which we operate.

We don't want to be an NGO. We want to be in-between, which allows us to move in between systems and structures. As an organization we want to be able to do what we love without being constrained by organizational structure. This is disconcerting for many, but this is what we want to do. We want to operate in this space. I would like students to hear about projects and case studies and really know that there are alternative ways of doing things. It has taken us a long time to realize that there doesn't have to be a cookie cutter approach to doing sport for development. In our program, we are using gender as our lens to help develop more sustainable ways of thinking and relating and doing. We see gender as the lens to uproot some very deep-seated beliefs and look for alternative systems of being and relating and doing with each other.

KEY TERMS

indicators
monitoring & evaluation (M&E)
Olympism
qualitative
quantitative
sport as a hook

sport as a platform
sport as a right
sport as distraction/diversion
sport for development and peace (SDP)
stakeholder management

DISCUSSION QUESTIONS

1. Why is it important for leaders of SDP programs to develop inclusive programs using a critical social consciousness?
2. What are some of the challenges faced by leaders developing and implementing SDP programs?
3. What are the important skills necessary to successfully lead an SDP program? Provide an example of a leader from an SDP who demonstrates these skills.
4. If you are leading an SDP program, describe why it is of utmost importance to maintain program quality and monitor the performance of the program. Finally, explain how you would evaluate an SDP program and why this is also of significant importance when leading an SDP program.
5. Research current Sport for Development and Peace programs and present a list of five programs using a Sport Plus model and five that are using a Plus Sports model. Describe the differences and also the potential overlaps of these program models.

For a full suite of assignments and additional learning activities, use the access code found in the front of your book. If you do not have an access code, you can obtain one at **www.jblearning.com**.

REFERENCES

Association of Midnight Basketball League Programs. (2013). History. Retrieved from http://amblp.com/basketball/history

Bailey, R. (2006). Physical education and sport in schools: A review of benefits and outcomes. *Journal of School Health, 76*(8), 397–401.

Brady, M. (2005). Creating safe spaces and building social assets for young women in the developing world: A new role for sports. *Women's Studies Quarterly, 33*(1/2), 35–49.

Bruening, J. E. (2005). Academic stereotypes of African American female student-athletes: A qualitative study. *Academic Athletic Journal, 18*(1), 22–35.

Bruening, J. E., Pastore, D. L., & Armstrong, K. L. (2008). Factors affecting the sport participation of African American females. *The ICHPER-SD Journal of Research, 3*(1), 12–21.

Burrows, M. (2003). *Evaluation of the youth inclusion programme: End of phase one report.* London: Youth Justice Board.

Can Soccer Save the World. (2012). Goals Haiti named best new project at Beyond Sport Summit. Retrieved from http://cansoccersavetheworld.com/2012/news-goals-haiti-named-best-new-project-at-beyond-sport-summit/

Coakley, J., & Pike, E. (2009). *Sports in society: Issues and controversies.* Columbus, OH: McGraw-Hill Higher Education.

Coalter, F. (2008). *Sport-in-development. A monitoring and evaluation manual.* London: UK Sport.

Darnell, S. (2012). *Sport for development and peace: A critical sociology.* London: Bloomsbury.

Ewing, M. E., Gano-Overway, L. A., Branta, C. F., & Seefeldt, V. D. (2002). The role of sports in youth development. In M. Gatz, M. Messner, & S. Ball-Rokeach (Eds.), *Paradoxes of youth and sport* (pp. 31–47). Albany: State University of New York Press.

Grassroot Soccer. (n.d.). Mission and vision. Retrieved from http://www.grassrootsoccer.org/what-we-do/mission-and-vision

Green, B. C. (2008). Management of sports development. In V. Girginov (Ed.), *Sport as an agent for social and personal change* (pp. 129–147). Oxford, England: Elsevier.

Guerreiras Project. (n.d.). Retrieved from http://guerreirasproject.wordpress.com

Guttmann, A. (1978). *From ritual to record.* New York: Columbia University Press.

Harris, J. C. (1998). Civil society, physical activity, and the involvement of sport sociologists in the preparation of physical activity professionals. *Sociology of Sport Journal, 15*(2), 138–153.

Hartmann, D., & Depro, B. (2006). Rethinking sports-based community crime prevention: A preliminary analysis of the relationship between Midnight Basketball and urban crime rates. *Journal of Sport & Social Issues, 30*(2), 180–196.

Henley, R., Schweizer, I. C., de Gara, F., & Vetter, S. (2007). How psychosocial sport and play programs help youth manage adversity: A review of what we know and what we should research. *International Journal of Psychosocial Rehabilitation, 12*(1), 51–58.

Huish, R. (2011). Punching above its weight. *Third World Quarterly, 32*(3), 417–433.

Hums, M. A., Wolff, E. A., & Mahoney, M. (2008). Sport and human rights. In J. Borms (Ed.), *Directory of sport science* (5th ed., pp. 469–480). Champaign, IL: Human Kinetics.

Husky Sport. (2013). History. Retrieved from http://huskysport.uconn.edu/about/history

Ingham, A., & Hardy, S. (1984). Sport, structuration and hegemony theory. *Culture and Society, 2*(2), 85–103.

International Olympic Committee. (1994). Olympic charter. Retrieved from http://www.olympic.org/Documents/olympic_charter_en.pdf

International Platform on Sport and Development. (2011). All organisations. Retrieved from http://www.sportanddev.org/en/connect/organisations/organisations_list/

Jarvie, G. (2007). Sport and national identity in the post-war world. *Nations and Nationalism, 13*(1), 159–161.

Kidd, B. (2008). A new social movement: Sport for development and peace. *Sport in Society, 11*(4), 370–380.

Lapchick, R. (1996). Race and college sports: A long way to go. In R. E. Lapchick (Ed.), *Sport in society* (pp. 5–18). Thousand Oaks, CA: Sage.

Lee, J., & Macdonald, D. (2009). Rural young people and physical activity: Understanding participation through social theory. *Sociology of Health and Illness, 31*(3), 360–374.

Le Menestrel, S., Bruno, M. L., & Christian, D. (2002). *Sports as a hook: An exploratory study of developmentally focused youth sports programs*. Washington, DC: Academy for Educational Development.

Levermore, R. (2008). Playing for development: Outlining the extent of the use of sport for development? *Progress in Development, 8*(2), 183–190.

Linver, M. R., Roth, J. L., & Brooks-Gunn, J. (2009). Adolescents' participation in organized activities: Are sports best when combined with other activities? *Developmental Psychology, 45*(2), 354–367.

Lyras, A., & Welty Peachey, J. (2011). Integrating sport-for-development theory and praxis. *Sport Management Review, 14*, 311–326.

Masteralexis, L. P., Barr, C. A., & Hums, M. A. (2011). *Principles and practice of sport management* (4th ed.). Sudbury, MA: Jones & Bartlett Learning.

Mendel, R. (2000). What works in the prevention of youth crime? Retrieved from http://www.cyc-net.org/cyc-online/cycol-0500-mendler.html

Millington, R. S. (2010). *Basketball with(out) borders: Interrogating the intersections of sport, development, and capitalism* (Master's thesis). Queen's University, Kingston, Ontario, Canada.

O'Hare, M. (2012, August). The history of the Paralympic games. Retrieved from http://sport.uk.msn.com/paralympics2012/the-history-of-the-paralympic-games-53?page=5#image=1

Peck, S. C., Roeser, R. W., Zarrett, N., & Eccles, J. S. (2008). Exploring the roles of extracurricular activity quantity and quality in the educational resilience of vulnerable adolescents: Variable- and pattern-centered approaches. *Journal of Social Issues, 64*(1), 135–155.

Perkins, D. F., & Noam, G. G. (2007). Characteristics of sports-based youth development programs. *New Directions for Youth Development, 115*, 75–84.

Spaaij, R. (2011). *Sport and social mobility: Crossing boundaries*. New York: Routledge.

Sport for children and youth: Fostering development and strengthening education. (n.d.). Retrieved from http://www.righttoplay.com/International/our-impact/Documents/Final_Report_Chapter_3.pdf

Street Soccer USA. (n.d.). "We believe that ending homelessness is a team sport." Retrieved from http://www.streetsoccerusa.org/about-us/Mission

United Nations. (1959, November). Declaration on the rights of the child. Adopted by UN general assembly resolution 1386 (XIV) of 10 December 1959. Retrieved from http://www.un.org/cyberschoolbus/humanrights/resources/child.asp

United Nations. (2002). "Right to play belongs to everyone," secretary-general tells Olympic aid forum [Press release]. Retrieved from http://www.un.org/News/Press/docs/2002/sgsm8119.doc.htm

United Nations. (2003). *Sport for development and peace: Towards achieving the millennium development goals*. Report from the United Nations Inter-Agency Task Force on Sport for Development and Peace. Geneva, Switzerland: United Nations.

United Nations Development Programme. (2000). The millennium development goals: Eight goals for 2015. Retrieved from http://www.undp.org/content/undp/en/home/mdgoverview.html

United Nations Educational, Scientific and Cultural Organization. (1952). Records of the general conference, seventh session, Paris 1952, resolutions. Retrieved from http://unesdoc.unesco.org/images/0011/001145/114587E.pdf

United Nations Inter-Agency Task Force on Sport for Development and Peace. (2005). Sport as a tool for development and peace: Towards achieving the United Nations millennium development goals. Retrieved from http://www.un.org/sport2005/resources/task_force.pdf

Vera Solutions. (n.d.). Grassroot soccer. Retrieved from http://www.verasolutions.org/our-clients/

Welty Peachey, J., & Cohen, A. (2012). Sport for social change and development. In G. B. Cunningham & J. N. Singer (Eds.), *Sociology of sport and physical activity* (2nd ed., pp. 191–211). College Station, TX: Center for Sport Management Research and Education.

Winnipeg Community Sport Policy. (2012). Retrieved from http://canadiansportforlife.ca/sites/default/files/resources/WPG%20COMMUNITY%20SPORT%20POLICY%20Jan%206,%202012.pdf

Zarrett, N., Fay, K., Li, Y., Carrano, J., Phelps, E., & Lerner, R. M. (2009). More than child's play: Variable- and pattern-centered approaches for examining effects of sports participation on youth development. *Developmental Psychology, 45*(2), 368–382.

ADDRESSING THE GENDER GAP IN SPORT

Heidi Grappendorf

CHAPTER OBJECTIVES

- Demonstrate an understanding of the historical overview of women's leadership in sport.
- Recognize the significant influence of Title IX legislation on women and leadership in sport in the United States.
- Demonstrate an understanding of the reasons for the continued underrepresentation of women in leadership in sport.
- Describe strategies to address the persistent gender gap in sport leadership positions.

CASE STUDY

Few Women Leaders in Olympic Leadership

The 2012 London Summer Olympics were dubbed the "Year of the Women" by several media outlets, including *The New York Times*, because for the first time ever, Saudi Arabia, Qatar, and Brunei sent female athletes to the Olympic Games (Longman, 2012). However, despite these claims, not every country participating in the Summer Olympics sent female athletes to the Games. What is increasingly evident is that wealthy countries (e.g., the United States) are able to send a large delegation of male and female athletes, but developing nations continue to struggle to even field a team of athletes and will only bring a small contingent of athletes. Overall, women have failed to exceed 45% of participants at any Olympic Games (Smith & Wrynn, 2013).

(continues)

When considering leadership in the Olympic movement, women continue to be underrepresented at all levels. The International Olympic Committee (IOC) requested that by 2005 women be provided with at least 20% of the leadership opportunities in international sport organizations. However, even the IOC failed to meet its own threshold until 2012. Twenty-two of the 106 members of the IOC are women, allowing the organization to meet the more than 20% threshold (20.8%) for the first time ever. There are other firsts for women within leadership at the IOC—there are now 3 female members on the 15-member IOC Executive Committee (20%) and 1 female vice president of the IOC Executive Committee (25%) (Smith & Wrynn, 2013). This is progress for women in leadership positions within international sport; however, there is much work to be done. At the national level, men continue to dominate leadership positions for National Olympic Committees. All-male leadership teams constitute the majority (85.3%) of National Olympic Committees. Only 14.1% of countries have male/female leadership teams, and only one country (Zambia) has an all-female leadership team. The International Paralympic Committee (IPC) has set a threshold of 30% for gender equity in its leadership structures; however, it has not met that threshold, because only 3 of the 15 members of the IPC are female (20%). Only 19 of 175 National Paralympic Committees have female presidents (10.9%) (Smith & Wrynn, 2013).

Despite the increase in the number of U.S. women competing in the Olympics, the National Governing Bodies (NGBs) of U.S. Olympic teams continue to be dominated by men. There are only six women in leadership positions out of a total of 58 U.S. NGBs. There are 23 all-male leadership NGBs, but there are no all-female leadership teams. The underrepresentation of women in leadership within the Olympic movement is a problem that will not be addressed by merely setting quotas for leadership, as evidenced by the IOC's inability to meet its own quota until 7 years after the deadline. In the United States, where the passage of Title IX has led to significant increases in sport participation opportunities for girls and women, women are not gaining access to leadership positions within sport, including within the Olympic movement.

As you will read in the chapter to follow, there are a myriad of reasons for the underrepresentation of women in sport leadership. As a leader for the next generation of sport organizations, you will be faced with the challenge of ensuring gender equity in leadership positions at all levels of sport. If women are competing in greater numbers in sport, in particular in the United States, why are there so few women leading the organizations for which these female athletes are representing the United States on the international stage of competition?

Questions for Discussion

1. The IOC has set requirements for a minimum number of women to hold leadership positions on the committee, but failed to meet its own requirements for several years. What other steps, in addition to setting a quota, should the IOC take to be sure more women are holding leadership positions within the Olympics?

2. As you will read in this chapter, there are a myriad a reasons why women continue to be underrepresented in leadership positions in sport organizations. If you were a member of the IOC, how would you instruct the leaders of National Olympic Committees that have no

female leadership (the majority) to begin to include women on their committees? Provide two potential options.

3. In the United States, the 2012 Summer Olympics team was composed of more female athletes than male athletes for the first time ever. Discuss why it is important for women to also be equally represented in leadership positions within the U.S. Olympic Committee (USOC) and within leadership positions for U.S. NGBs.

4. If you were a member of the USOC, what specific steps would you recommend to help increase the number of women in leadership positions for U.S. NGBs?

INTRODUCTION

Despite the increasing numbers of girls and women participating in sport, women's representation in sport leadership positions has been limited. Like many other traditionally male-dominated fields, the farther up one looks into the higher administrative and leadership ranks, the less women there are. There is a long and storied history of women's efforts and struggles to gain a place in the decision-making and leadership positions in sport. Although women continue to make progress and obtain leadership positions in all realms of sport, there is still a vast underrepresentation of female sport leaders at the high school, college, and professional levels. Efforts by researchers examining the reasons for underrepresentation and suggestions to increase the number of women in sport leadership, as well as actions of female leaders and policy makers, has led to some progress by women moving into the upper echelons of sport leadership. However, increasing the number of women in sport leadership remains a work in progress, and a gap remains regarding the number of women in sport leadership jobs.

This chapter begins with a historical overview, followed by a section on the influence of Title IX. Furthermore, information on the reasons why this underrepresentation has persisted is offered. The chapter concludes with a discussion of some prominent female sport leaders and some suggested strategies to address the persistent gender gap in sport leadership positions.

HISTORICAL OVERVIEW

Women in sport leadership have a storied past that has included conflict and debate regarding their roles and abilities to lead. Following the Civil War, there was great demand from women to participate in physical education and sport. Due to this demand, a need arose for women to oversee physical education and sporting opportunities for women. Thus, some of the first leadership ideals for women in sport developed during this time from those involved with sporting opportunities and later with competitions related to intercollegiate participation (Rintala, 2001; Swanson & Spears, 1995).

While male students were often in charge of competitions for male students, female physical educators were responsible for the organizing and oversight of sporting opportunities for women. This was true at both the interscholastic and collegiate levels (Swanson & Spears, 1995). These female physical educators had their own ideas as to how sport should be organized for women, and they worked tirelessly toward the values they held. Those women leading physical education and women's sport rejected the competitive and commercial male model of sport and emphasized cooperation, academics, and physical activity. Female physical activity leaders also had to be very sensitive to the ongoing evolvement of women's roles and the societal expectations of women (Rhode & Walker, 2007). These activities were organized for fun, enjoyment, social interaction with other women, and health (Boutilier & San Giovanni, 1983). It is important to note that female physical educators organized opportunities for women to participate, but—unlike men's sports—they did not receive any financial backing. In 1892, the first women's intercollegiate athletic competition took place when Senda Berenson, a physical education teacher at Smith College, organized and adapted the rules of basketball for women. As the opportunities expanded for women to participate in sport throughout the late 1800s, the philosophical divide between men's and women's sports and those leading each widened (Rintala, 2001).

The Intercollegiate Athletic Association was created in 1905–1906 to oversee men's sports only. This organization changed its name to the National Collegiate Athletic Association (NCAA) in 1910 (Chepko & Couturier, 2001). Regarding women's participation in sport, female physical educators recognized a need to organize and develop a governing body for women's participation in sport as well. During the early 1900s, as female physical educators were trying to figure out and support a governing body, the American Physical Education Association (APEA) created a Standing Committee on Women's Athletics. The APEA has gone through many changes over the years, and is currently known as the American Alliance for Health, Physical Education, Recreation and Dance (AAHPERD) (Hult, 1991). In 1928, the APEA went through more reorganization, which led to the formation of the National Section on Women's Athletics (NSWA). This organization merged with the Women's Division of the National Amateur Athletic Federation (NAAF) and became the National Section on Girls' and Women's Sports (NSGWS). In 1958, NSGWS

became part of AAHPERD and was known as the Division for Girls' and Women's Sports (DGWS). In 1974, when AAHPERD restructured, DGWS became the National Association for Girls and Women in Sport (NAGWS) (Hult, 1991).

At the college level, as women's sports continued to grow, there was a recognized need to organize and structure as well. In 1967, the Commission for Intercollegiate Athletics for Women (CIAW) was founded as a volunteer organization to encourage development of sport programs for all (Hult, 1980). In 1971, due to the continued growth of intercollegiate sports for women, female physical educators established the *Association for Intercollegiate Athletics for Women (AIAW)* (Hultstrand, 1993; Swanson & Spears, 1995), an outgrowth of the CIAW. The AIAW was created by women because they believed women had been deprived of the sporting learning experience, and they believed there were better approaches than the men's model in the NCAA (Uhlir, 1987). The AIAW accomplished many things for women's athletics, but one of the greatest contributions the AIAW had was related to its role in helping get Title IX passed.

TITLE IX

Female leaders, and particularly the AIAW, played a significant role in getting Title IX passed in 1972. *Title IX* states: "No person in the United States shall, on the basis of sex, be excluded from participation in, be denied the benefits of, or be subjected to discrimination under any educational programs or activities receiving federal financial assistance" (Office for Civil Rights, 1979, para. 3). Despite the fact that girls and women were playing sport, and women were involved in the oversight of women's participation in sport, Title IX is a significant piece of legislation to note because it was an indicator of how far women's sport had grown and evolved. With Title IX, a piece of federal legislation mandated opportunity for women in sport. However, despite the fact that it contributed to more girls and women participating in sport and it required that administrators and leaders in sport treat women's sport equitably, no one predicted the decline of women in sport leadership to come.

Opportunity for women in sport has increased since the time of this Smith College basketball game in 1903; equitable treatment for men's and women's sport was mandated in 1972 by the passage of Title IX legislation.
© Katherine Elizabeth McClellan/Smith College Archives

STATUS OF WOMEN IN SPORT LEADERSHIP

To gain a broad understanding of the situation for women in sport leadership, it is important to examine the available data. In other words, it is necessary to look at the number of women currently holding leadership positions within sport, as well as the history of representation of women in these positions.

High School

If there has traditionally been an overlooked area of study of women in leadership, it has occurred at the high school level. Unlike intercollegiate athletics, where Acosta and Carpenter (2012) have longitudinally provided status updates and data on the numbers of women in leadership, there is no similar study that tracks this information at the interscholastic level.

Research by the National Federation of State High School Associations (2012) does indicate there are more females participating at the high school level than ever before. However, as noted by the Women's Sports Foundation (n.d.), 80% of all coaches at the high school level are male. Regarding athletic directors, Whisenant (2003) noted in data from 22 of 50 state high school athletic associations that of the 7,041 athletic directors only 899, or 13%, were female. Lovett and Lowry (1994) found in Texas that only 2% of athletic directors were women. Ultimately, although more females may be playing sports, they are likely to be participating in programs led by men.

In one of the limited studies conducted regarding females and high school athletics, Whisenant, Miller, and Pedersen (2005) found that job descriptions and job qualifications relating to football may prevent women from applying for jobs. If a qualification for athletic director includes having been a football coach, then women would almost certainly be excluded from being considered for an athletic director position. Whisenant et al. (2005) found this in 17% of job descriptions for athletic director in Texas.

College

In their 2012 study, researchers R. Vivian Acosta and Linda Carpenter found the highest-ever participation on intercollegiate teams by women. Despite the tremendous participation opportunities, there has unfortunately been a downside to Title IX. One of the unintended consequences or backlash effects of Title IX has been a decline in the number of women in leadership positions, particularly in coaching and administration at the intercollegiate level. Prior to Title IX being passed, women coached more than 90% of female teams and more than 90% of women's athletic programs had a female athletic director. As **Table 13.1** indicates, Acosta and Carpenter (2012) found only 42.9% of female teams being coached by females. Additionally, as **Table 13.2** indicates, only 21.3% of athletic directors are women, compared to over 90% of the administrators who headed women's programs in 1972 (Acosta & Carpenter, 2012).

Professional Sport

Like interscholastic and intercollegiate sport, women are underrepresented in the leadership ranks of professional sport. Although there are growing opportunities for women in women's professional sports with the expansion of leagues such as the Women's National Basketball Association (WNBA), the Women's United Soccer Association (WUSA), and Women's Professional

TABLE 13.1 Percentage of Female Head Coaches for All Divisions, in All Women's Sports

Year	Percentage of Head Coaches
1972	90+
1978	58.2
1988	48.3
1998	47.4
2008	42.8
2010	42.6
2012	42.9

Source: Data from Acosta, R. V., & Carpenter, L. J. (2012). Women in intercollegiate sport: A longitudinal, national study thirty-five year update, 1977–2012. Retrieved from http://acostacarpenter.org/AcostaCarpenter2012.pdf

TABLE 13.2 Percentage of Female College Athletic Directors

Year	Percentage of All Divisions
1972	90.0+
1980	20.0
1988	16.1
1998	19.4
2008	21.3
2010	19.3
2012	20.3

Source: Data from Acosta, R. V., & Carpenter, L. J. (2012). Women in intercollegiate sport: A longitudinal, national study thirty-five year update, 1977–2012. Retrieved from http://acostacarpenter.org/AcostaCarpenter2012.pdf

Soccer (WPS), there is still a lack of women in sport leadership because few women's leagues have survived and most professional sports are traditional male sports.

The University of Central Florida's Devos Sports Business Management Program publishes the Racial and Gender Report Card. The report card examines the racial and gender hiring practices of Major League Baseball (MLB), Major League Soccer (MLS), the National Basketball Association (NBA), the National Football League (NFL), and the Women's National Basketball Association (WNBA) as well as college athletic departments (Lapchick, 2012a). Notorious for lower grades, the NFL in 2012 received a C+ for its hiring practices related to gender. On the other hand, the WNBA has regularly been the leader for all professional sports when it comes to diversity and gender hiring. The NBA received an A– for 2012 whereas MLB received a C+. In 2010, when the last study was done, MLS received a B– for gender hiring practices. Similar to what Acosta and Carpenter do with their studies of intercollegiate athletics, the

University of Central Florida publishes its report card to indicate areas of improvement, stagnation, and regression in the racial and gender composition of professional and college sport personnel and to contribute to the improvement of integration in front office and college athletics department positions (Lapchick, 2012a).

REASONS FOR UNDERREPRESENTATION OF WOMEN IN SPORT

Women in sport leadership have and continue to face barriers that have limited them in attaining positions in the upper echelons of sport organizations. A significant amount of research has been done examining these reasons as well as reasons for the continued underrepresentation of women in sport leadership. The research that has addressed the underrepresentation of women in sport leadership has been extensive and explored a variety of causes. Potential barriers examined include stereotypes, discrimination, hegemony, and societal views about women's capabilities to lead in a traditionally male-dominated area. However, as noted by Shaw and Hoeber (2003), the reasons for the lack of women seen in leadership positions are "overwhelming" (p. 348). It would be impossible to list all of the reasons noted in the research regarding the lack of women in sport leadership. Everything from social forces and phenomena, to structural forces, to psychological reasons have been identified and are further noted next.

Cunningham (2007) identified three categories to explain the underrepresentation of women in sport leadership: (1) stereotypes, (2) structural forces, and (3) personal characteristics. Stereotypes affect people's beliefs about women's abilities to lead and what roles they are capable of being successful in. Structural forces are those that constrain or prevent women from advancing in athletics and can include the lack of social networks, discrimination, or the hours and days associated with careers in sport. Lastly, personal characteristics, although influenced by stereotypes and structural forces, include things such as attitudes and intention to move up, or the decision to leave one's career.

Stereotyping has been shown to impact women in leadership and in sport leadership. Stereotypes, prejudice, and discrimination based on stereotyping have been explored as one mechanism accounting for inequity in the workforce for women (Sigleman & Tuch, 1997; Steinbeck & Tomaskovic-Devey, 2007). Prejudice can arise from perceptions regarding the characteristics of members of a social group (e.g., emotional) and the requirements of the social roles that group members occupy (e.g., caretakers, leaders, subordinates) (Eagly & Karau, 2002; Garcia-Retamero & López-Zafra, 2006, 2009; Heilman, Wallen, Fuchs, & Tamkins, 2004). A high potential for prejudice exists when perceivers hold a stereotype about a social group that is incongruent with the attributes that are thought to be required for success in certain classes of social roles. As an example of this potential for prejudice, when compared to women, men are perceived to have the stereotypical characteristics of successful managers (Schein, 2001).

When considering *gender equity* in management, *role congruity theory* has been applied to explain the lack of women in leadership positions through examination of gender role stereotyping and lack of fit for leadership roles. Gender expectations (e.g., being aggressive, self-confident, and dominant for men; being nurturing, affectionate, and weak for women) impact whether women and men are perceived to successfully fulfill their stereotypical gender roles. When evaluators review the qualifications of women for management positions, they are often influenced by stereotypical gender role expectations (Eagly & Karau, 2002). Role congruity theory then posits that a prejudice exists against women in management and leadership because leadership ability is more generally ascribed to men (Eagly & Karau, 2002). Hence, women may be disadvantaged in obtaining management and leadership positions because of the perception that they do not possess the requisite skill set to lead effectively. Additionally, even if women are in leadership positions, they may not be evaluated as favorably as men if they are perceived as violating gender norms attributed to women (Eagly & Karau, 2002). Burton, Grappendorf, Henderson, and Dennis (2008) applied this perception to sport and found male athletes benefit most and have been evaluated as more competent for upper-level positions when compared to male nonathletes, female athletes, and female nonathletes with identical educational backgrounds.

At the structural level, the concept of *homologous reproduction*, which is the tendency to hire those most like ourselves, has been cited as a reason for underrepresentation of women in sport leadership (Knoppers, 1994; Stangl & Kane, 1991). Homologous reproduction would suggest that typically, because White males are in the top leadership positions in sport at the high school, college, and professional levels, they would then tend to also hire other White males. The theory of homologous reproduction would contend that people tend to feel comfortable and can identify with others most like themselves (Knoppers; Stangl & Kane), so when it comes to making a hiring decision they are often biased in whom they select. Homologous reproduction is not necessarily blatant and overt discrimination because the hiring manager may not even consciously be aware of this tendency.

Hegemony, which can be defined as the power and dominance of one group over another, has also been well documented (Coakley, 2007; Sage, 1998; Whisenant et al., 2005) and could also be identified as a structural barrier. Hegemony, for example, could include men having power over women. A component of hegemony would be the

resistance to giving up the dominance the group possesses. As applied to sport, men are in power positions in leadership and, thus, are in a position to exert control.

Stroh, Langlands, and Simpson (2004) examined the *glass ceiling effect*, which refers to an invisible, but real barrier that prevents women from moving upward in administration. The glass ceiling effect literally refers to women that may be able to see those above them but face barriers that prevent them from reaching and attaining higher ranking positions.

Acosta and Carpenter (1988) note a variety of reasons that may lead to the underrepresentation of women in sport leadership: (1) lack of support systems for women, (2) failure of the "old girls' network," (3) female burnout, and (4) failure of women to apply for job openings. Although this was a study done over 25 years ago, the research related to these categories continues. It is noteworthy, however, that in this study Acosta and Carpenter pointed out the underrepresentation of women at the individual level, focusing on what women could do to alleviate the situation.

Shaw and Frisby (2006) suggested examining reasons for underrepresentation of women in sport leadership in a different way than previous research. The researchers noted that it was important for researchers to challenge power structures within sport organizations and to go beyond three dominant frameworks that have been utilized to examine gender issues in organizations. The three frameworks they believed researchers need to move beyond were (1) fixing women, (2) valuing femininity, and (3) creating equal opportunity. Shaw and Frisby suggested examining practices about assumptions regarding men's and women's roles in organizations. To address this, Burton, Grappendorf, and Henderson (2011) studied how individuals perceive male and female candidates' potential success for specific positions in athletic administration. They found that female candidates were evaluated as significantly less likely to be offered the position of athletic director when compared with the male candidate.

The aforementioned reasons for the underrepresentation of women in sport leadership are far from an extensive list. However, they may provide some insight into helping further the understanding of some of the complex and complicated issues that have impacted the lack of women in sport leadership.

Women of Color: Double Jeopardy

Women of color have traditionally found it difficult to move into leadership positions in professional and collegiate athletics; hooks (1981) asserted that "When Black people are talked about the focus tends to be on Black men, and when women are talked about the focus tends to be on White women" (p. 7).

According to Abney (1988), several Black women working in intercollegiate athletic departments recalled being excluded from participating in events, from leadership positions, and from membership on key committees. Many noted the double burden of racism and sexism. Alexander (1978) described this *double jeopardy* (Beale, 1979) as a hindrance to Black women in gaining access to formal networks (e.g., educational training) and informal networks (e.g., social relationships) that can enhance career advancement and help Black women break through the glass ceiling (Abney, 2000; Knoppers, Meyer, Ewing, & Forrest, 1991). Although not highly documented, anecdotal evidence suggests that other women of color face similar hindrances. As a result, women of color continue to face significant underrepresentation in sport leadership positions in college. The 2011–12 NCAA Race and Gender Demographics Report shows that 199 of the 1,044 athletic director positions at predominantly White institutions (PWIs) (19%) were held by women; of those 199, just 13 (6.5%) were occupied by women of color. Specifically, there were five Black, one American

Indian, two Asian, three Hispanic, and two biracial women athletic directors. Women of color held 59 associate athletic director positions out of 2,106 (2.8%), and just 5.2% of all senior woman administrator posts (Irick, 2012). Unfortunately, these percentages do not represent major progress, because since 2008, the number of female athletic directors of color has remained consistently between 11 and 13, with a slight increase in the number of female associate athletic directors of color.

Women of color are similarly represented in low percentages in collegiate head coaching positions. In 2007, the Black Coaches and Administrators (BCA) started issuing a report on the status of women of color in head coaching basketball positions. The number of women hired into head coaching positions in Division I basketball has increased slightly since 2006; however, the number of females of color hired into women's head basketball positions has not shown significant improvement although hiring practices have been more inclusive. In its 2012 report card, the BCA noted that of the 25 openings in summer 2012, 12 positions were filled with women; 4 of those 12 hires were Black women and 1 was Latina (Associated Press, 2012). Still, with more and more women of color playing collegiate sport, it is troubling that more of these women are not ascending to higher levels in athletic administration and coaching after their playing days are over.

At the professional level of sports, the WNBA is the most diverse professional sport league. The number of women of color in ownership positions or part-ownership positions in the WNBA has increased in recent years. In 2006, Sheila Johnson became the first Black woman to hold any ownership in a WNBA team; in 2012, Laurel J. Richie became the WNBA's president, thus becoming the first female of color to become president of a professional sport league (Lapchick, 2012b). In 2012, 42% (5 out of 12) of the head coaches of the WNBA were women, with women of color holding two of the head coaching positions. Other women of color, however, have very little to no representation in ownership, staff, and head coaching positions.

NOTABLE FEMALES IN SPORT LEADERSHIP

There have been women who have worked diligently advocating for women in sport leadership and those who have broken into the ranks of sport leadership at all levels. These women have worked diligently in their own spheres to help women advance in the sport realm. Some have led as athletes, coaches, advocates, researchers, or administrators. What has been evident is their influence on and impact for females in sport leadership as well as interest in sport leadership in the future. To highlight a few:

> **Billie Jean King** was a professional women's tennis player who infamously beat Bobby Riggs in the "Battle of the Sexes," and in doing so helped break down stereotypes and perceptions of female athletes. King later started the Women's Sports Foundation (WSF), a leading advocacy and educational organization (Spencer, 2000).
>
> **Pat Summitt** is a former University of Tennessee women's basketball coach who has 1,098 victories, 8 national championships, 18 Final Fours, and 16 conference titles to her credit. When Summitt retired in 2012 she had won more games than any other basketball coach in NCAA history. She is credited with being a pioneer, an inspiration, and a leader for 38 years as a basketball coach and leader of athletes (Zinser, 2012).
>
> **Linda Carpenter** and **R. Vivian Acosta** are two professors and researchers who

have been tracking the numbers of women in leadership positions, as well as participation numbers over the past 35 years. They have arguably provided the most comprehensive look at the status of women in sport leadership positions over the years. Their longitudinal tracking of the numbers of women in leadership has brought awareness and insight to the ongoing issue of the underrepresentation of women as leaders (Hums & Yiamouyiannis, 2007).

Anita DeFrantz is the senior member of the International Olympic Committee (IOC) for the United States. She was only the fifth woman ever named to hold a seat on the 93-member IOC. DeFrantz is both the first African American and the first American woman to serve on the committee (Dwyre, 2012; Hums & Yiamouyiannis, 2007).

Donna Lopiano was the chief executive officer of the Women's Sports Foundation from 1992–2007. Lopiano is known as an advocate for and expert on women's sport and has been named to "Most Powerful Women in Sports" lists over the years. She also served as the women's athletic director at the University of Texas at Austin for 18 years. She is well-respected in the sport world and recently started Sports Management Resources, a consulting company (Hums & Yiamouyiannis, 2007).

Val Ackerman was founding president of the WNBA. When she resigned as president, she was named the first female president of USA Basketball in 2005. Both men's and women's basketball have garnered gold medals in both Olympic games since her taking the reins (O'Connor McDonogh, 2010).

Strategies to Increase Women in Sport Leadership

Although there are numerous barriers to be overcome for women to achieve equitable representation in sport leadership, research has been done regarding strategies to overcome underrepresentation. Researchers have focused on various tools, strategies, and methods to assist women in moving into the ranks of sport leadership.

Grappendorf, Burton, and Lilienthal (2007) recommended for women to (1) get an education in sport management or a business-related area, (2) get involved in networking activities, (3) build networks, (4) get involved with national organizations, (5) gain knowledge of career paths and key positions that lead to leadership positions, (6) be willing to self-promote, and (7) get a mentor. Grappendorf et al. also note that it is not just important for women to take steps to attain leadership positions in sport. They recommend that it is crucial to educate those involved in the hiring process. This education would include disseminating information to those hiring (often men) regarding recruitment, evaluation, supervisor support, discrimination, stereotypes, and biases that could occur. In other words, it is important to look at strategies not just at the individual level to increase the representation of women in sport leadership, but also at the organizational and structural levels.

In a study funded by the NCAA, Drago, Hennighausen, Rogers, Vescio, and Stauffer (2005) studied why women were underrepresented in the leadership ranks of coaching and athletic administration. In the Coaching and Gender Equity (CAGE) Project report they recommended: (1) increasing the number of women in the pipeline; (2) formalizing the hiring practices, decision-making processes, training and development, and career paths of women; (3) making the environment for coaches and administrators more welcoming and flexible in response to family commitments; and (4) providing a more inclusive environment for women.

It is important to note that strategies to address the underrepresentation of women in sport leadership are not just women's issues. In other words, both men and women need to be educated about issues and barriers that impact women so that more leadership opportunities and positions can be filled.

Summary

One may have thought that Title IX would increase not only the number of women participating in sport, but also the numbers in leadership. However, clearly this has not occurred, and the numbers of women in leadership at the high school, college, and even professional levels have not improved. More women participating in sport has not led to more women in leadership in sport. Women continue to be under-represented in the ranks of sport leadership. At all levels, including the high school, college, and professional ranks, women continue to struggle with issues and barriers that have limited their leadership opportunities. It is important not only to continue to track these numbers, but also to continue to examine the reasons why the underrepresentation persists. Finally, it is essential that strategies and tools be developed for women, and that the education and training of those responsible for hiring or already in leadership positions continue.

LEADERSHIP PERSPECTIVE

Beth Bass has served as the chief executive officer of the Women's Basketball Coaches Association (WBCA) since 2001. She is only the second person to hold that position within the WBCA. Prior to her position at the WBCA, Beth worked as a marketing executive for Nike and for Converse.

Beth Bass.
Courtesy of Beth Bass

Q: What do you believe are the most important skills necessary for women aspiring to be in leadership positions in sport organizations?

The skills that I believe are most important for women aspiring to be a leader are the same skills that you learn when you are an athlete playing a team sport. I believe that playing a team sport, not necessarily an individual sport, is so important. The skills you learn as an athlete competing in a team sport are very similar to the skills you will need to be a good leader. This is especially true given the male-dominated sports industry. Boys grow up and are socialized into playing team sports. They take those skills with them and apply them to their adult work lives. So much of the corporate world, including the sports industry, works like a team sport. As girls are now playing more team sports, they are also becoming prepared to work in the corporate world.

In addition, I believe that women have to be confident and demonstrate emotional intelligence. Women seem to have a natural aptitude to be more emotionally intelligent, which can benefit them as leaders.

Q: Can you describe what you perceive to be the most significant challenges women face when striving for leadership positions in sport organizations?

I believe one of the most significant challenges women face is in regard to the hiring process for leadership positions. These positions are very "costly" positions, meaning a lot of financial, emotional, and physical work is put into hiring for leadership positions. When people hire for these positions, because of the high costs associated with them, they tend to go to their natural comfort zone. That is, when hiring for leadership positions, leaders usually will hire those that look like them. They tend to look to their comfort zone, and hire those they feel comfortable with, those who are similar to them. Men make up the majority of those in leadership positions in sport organizations, so therefore the majority of those hired are also men. Another challenge in the hiring process is that so many leadership positions are filled by word of mouth. If you are connected to people in leadership positions, you will learn about those positions. Therefore, it is so important for women to get a "foot in the door" in a sport organization. That is most important. Once you are hired, you have to work hard. Unfortunately, women have to be twice as good as men, and for minority women it is even more challenging. When you are hired, you need to know your role, make yourself valuable, be a team player, and outwork your peers.

Once you are in leadership positions you will always have to prove yourself. Being a leader is a constant learning process. As women we need to demonstrate vulnerability when leading women, but not necessarily when leading men. As a leader you have to constantly keep learning and seeking to improve. You have to be nimble enough to be relevant as a leader. As the sport industry is constantly changing, leaders need to constantly be innovative and always changing.

Q: What can current leaders in sport do to help more women rise to leadership positions in the field?

Women in leadership positions, and men, have to be mentors. You have to be a mentor that speaks the truth and will give back. Leaders can give back by creating opportunities through internships. When providing these opportunities, be committed to getting a diverse pool of applicants for those positions. Leaders have to work on breaking down barriers to entry in the sports industry. We have to continually work on mentoring, providing internships, and having a diverse hiring pool. This takes effort on the part of leaders; it takes effort to hire outside of your comfort zone and mentor those who are different from you.

Q: What strategies would you suggest women utilize if they aspire to leadership positions in sport? Will these strategies be different than those you would provide to men aspiring to leadership positions in sport? If so, can you elaborate on why that would be the case?

I would tell women that if you aspire to a leadership position in sports then you have to outwork other people. You have to volunteer for as many positions as possible to gain experience and to enhance your resume. Remember that no job is too big or too small for you to do well. Enrich your skill set by doing those internships, even if those are unpaid positions. Each work opportunity you take is an opportunity to build relationships and enhance your network.

In whatever position you take, look at what is required to get noticed and do it. Be the best you can be at your job. It is also important to recognize the person who gave you the opportunity and do everything you can to show that selecting you for the position was the right decision.

I also encourage women to make sure they get mentors that don't look like them and to break the mold of only working with those that are similar to them. I encourage women to find male mentors, and for Black women to meet with and seek out White men as mentors. Seek out someone different from you that can serve as your mentor. Ask those mentors who are different than you to be honest with you and ask how you can better communicate with those who are different from you. By doing this I believe we are breaking the glass ceiling both ways.

When women are in leadership positions, it is also important to hire with intuition and fire with compassion. Women should not be afraid to show more feminine characteristics, like compassion, and to be proud of those feminine qualities. Balance those feminine characteristics with those characteristics learned when you were a competitive athlete. Use all of your skills when in a leadership position.

Overall, I'm encouraged by the future for women in leadership in sport. I am encouraged that young boys and girls are playing sports together and don't think about gender when playing together. I believe that those experiences in youth sport will translate into the work world, so that as adults, they won't see any difference between working with men and women.

KEY TERMS

Association for Intercollegiate Athletics
    for Women (AIAW)
double jeopardy
gender equity
glass ceiling effect

hegemony
homologous reproduction
role congruity theory
Title IX

DISCUSSION QUESTIONS

1. If you were hiring for an open position for athletic director at the high school level, how would you avoid the perception that homologous reproduction may influence your selection of a candidate for that position?
2. Consider Cunningham's three categories to explain the underrepresentation of women in sport leadership: (1) stereotypes, (2) structural forces, and (3) personal characteristics. Research how one of the major professional sports leagues (NFL, NBA, NHL, MLB, or MLS) attempts to address the lack of women in leadership positions within its own league.
3. Describe the concept of the glass ceiling and how this concept can help to explain why there are so few women in athletic director positions in Division I FBS and FCS universities.
4. Considering the challenges women face in obtaining leadership positions in sport organizations, how would you mentor young women graduating with sport management degrees regarding strategies to advance to leadership positions in sport organizations?
5. Research a woman serving in a leadership position for a major professional sport organization and provide details about her education and career path. How has her experience in the field of sport been influenced by Title IX?

For a full suite of assignments and additional learning activities, use the access code found in the front of your book. If you do not have an access code, you can obtain one at **www.jblearning.com**.

REFERENCES

Abney, R. (1988). The effects of role models and mentors on career patterns of Black women coaches and athletic administrators in historically black and historically white institutions of higher education. *Dissertations Abstract International, 49*(11), 3210. (UMI No. 8903907).

Abney, R. (2000). The glass ceiling effect. In D. Brooks & R. Althouse (Eds.), *Racism in college athletics: The African-American athlete's experience* (2nd ed., pp. 119–130). Morgantown, WV: Fitness Information Technology.

Acosta, R. V., & Carpenter, L. J. (1988). *Perceived causes of the declining representation of women leaders in intercollegiate sports—1988 update* (unpublished manuscript). Brooklyn College, Brooklyn, NY.

Acosta, R. V., & Carpenter, L. J. (2012). Women in intercollegiate sport: A longitudinal, national study thirty-five year update, 1977–2012. Retrieved from http://acostacarpenter.org/AcostaCarpenter2012.pdf

Alexander, A. (1978). *Status of minority women in the Association of Intercollegiate Athletics for Women* (unpublished master's thesis). Temple University, Philadelphia, PA.

Beale, F. (1979). Double jeopardy: To be Black and female. In T. Cade (Ed.), *The Black woman: An anthology* (pp. 90–100). New York: New American Library.

Boutilier, M. A., & SanGiovanni, L. (1983). *The sporting woman*. Champaign, IL: Human Kinetics.

Burton, L., Grappendorf, H., & Henderson, A. C. (2011). Perceptions of gender in athletic administration: Utilizing role congruity theory to examine potential prejudice against women. *Journal of Sport Management, 25*(1), 36–45.

Burton, L. J., Grappendorf, H., Henderson, A. C., Field, G. B., & Dennis, J. A. (2008). The relevance of intercollegiate athletic participation for men and women: Examination of hiring preferences to entry level management positions based on role congruity theory. *International Journal of Sport Management, 9*, 175–192.

Chepko, S., & Couturier, L. (2001). From intersection to collision: Women's sports from 1920–1980. In G. Cohen (Ed.), *Women in sport: Issues and controversies* (pp. 79–110). Oxon Hill, MD: American Association of Health, Physical Education, Recreation and Dance.

Coakley, J. (2007). *Sport in society: Issues and controversies* (9th ed.). Boston, MA: McGraw-Hill.

Cunningham, G. B. (2007). *Diversity in sport organizations.* Scottsdale, AZ: Holcomb Hathaway.

Drago, R., Hennighausen, L., Rogers, J., Vescio, T., & Stauffer, K. D. (2005). CAGE: The coaching and gender equity project. Retrieved from http://www.epi.soe.vt.edu /perspectives/policy_news/docs/CAGE.doc

Dwyre, B. (2012). Anita DeFrantz is still pulling an oar for the Olympic movement. Retrieved from http://articles .latimes.com/print/2012/aug/08/sports/la-sp-oly- dwyre-defrantz-20120809

Eagly, A. H., & Karau, S. J. (2002). Role congruity theory of prejudice toward female leaders. *Psychological Review, 109*, 573–598.

Garcia-Retamero, R., & López-Zafra, E. (2006). Prejudice against women in male-congenial environments: Perceptions of gender role congruity in leadership. *Sex Roles, 55*, 51–61.

Garcia-Retamero, R., & López-Zafra, E. (2009). Causal attributions about feminine and leadership roles. *Journal of Cross-Cultural Psychology, 40*, 492–509.

Grappendorf, H., Burton, L. J., & Lilienthal, S. (2007). *Strategies for improving opportunities for women in sport management positions.* In M. Hums, G. Bower, & H. Grappendorf (Eds.), *Women as leaders in sport: Impact and influence* (pp. 299–320). Oxon Hill, MD: American Association of Health, Physical Education, Recreation and Dance.

Heilman, M. E., Wallen, A. S., Fuchs, D., & Tamkins, M. M. (2004). Penalties for success: Reactions to women who succeed at male tasks. *Journal of Applied Psychology, 89*, 416–427.

hooks, b. (1981). *Ain't I a woman: Black women and feminism* (Vol. 3). Boston: South End Press.

Hult, J. (1991). The governance of athletics for girls and women: Leadership by women physical educators, 1899–1949. In J. S. Hult & M. Trekell (Eds.), *A century of women's basketball: From frailty to final four.* (pp. 53–82). Reston, VA: American Association of Health, Physical Education, Recreation and Dance.

Hult, J. S. (1980). The philosophical conflicts in men's and women's collegiate athletics. *Quest, 32,* 77–94.

Hultstrand, B. J. (1993). The growth of collegiate women's sports: The 1960's. *Journal of Physical Education, Recreation, and Dance, 64,* 41–43.

Hums, M. A., & Yiamouyiannis, A. (2007). Women in sport careers and leadership positions. In M. A. Hums, G. G. Bower, and H. Grappendorf (Eds.), *Women as Leaders in Sport: Impact and Influence* (pp. 1–24). Oxon Hill, MD: American Association of Health, Physical Education, Recreation and Dance.

Irick, E. (2012). 2011–12 NCAA race and gender demographics report. Retrieved from http://web1 .ncaa.org/rgdSearch/exec/main

Knoppers, A. (1994). Gender and the coaching profession. In S. Birrell & C. L. Cole (Eds.), *Women, sport and culture* (pp. 119–133). Champaign, IL: Human Kinetics.

Knoppers, A., Meyer, B. B., Ewing, M., & Forrest, L. (1991). Opportunity and work behavior in college coaching. *Journal of Sport and Social Issues, 15*(1), 1–20.

Lapchick, R. E. (2012a). 2012 racial and gender report card. Retrieved from http://www.tidesport.org /racialgenderreportcard.html

Lapchick, R. E. (2012b). The 2012 Women's National Basketball Association racial and gender report card. Retrieved from http://www.tidesport.org/RGRC /2012/2012_WNBA_RGRC.pdf

Longman, J. (2012, July 13). Before games, wins for women. Retrieved from http://www.nytimes.com/2012/07/14 /sports/olympics/before-london-games-wins-for-women.html?_r=0

Lovett, D., & Lowry, C. (1994). "Good old boys" and "good old girls" clubs: Myth or reality? *Journal of Sport Management, 8,* 27–35.

National Federation of State High School Associations. (2012). High school sports participation reaches all-time high. Retrieved from http://www.nfhs.org /content.aspx?id=7495

O'Connor McDonogh, M. (2010). Women as leaders in professional sport. In K. O'Connor (Ed.), *Gender and women's leadership: A reference handbook* (pp. 869–875). Thousand Oaks, CA: Sage.

Office for Civil Rights. (1979). *A policy interpretation: Title IX and intercollegiate athletics.* Retrieved from http:// www.ed.gov/about/offices/list/ocr/docs/t9interp.html

Rhode, D. L., & Walker, C. J. (2007). Gender equity in college athletics: Women coaches as a case study. Retrieved from http://law.bepress.com/cgi/viewcontent. cgi?article=9336&context=expresso

Rintala, J. (2001). Play as competition: An ideological dilemma. In G. L. Cohen (Ed.), *Women in sport: Issues and controversies* (pp. 37–56). Oxon Hill, MD: American Association of Health, Physical Education, Recreation and Dance.

Sage, G. H. (1998). *Power and ideology in American sport: A critical perspective* (2nd ed.). Champaign, IL: Human Kinetics.

Schein, V. E. (2001). A global look at psychological barriers to women's progress in management. *Journal of Social Issues, 57,* 675–688.

Shaw, S., & Frisby, W. (2006). Can gender equity be more equitable?: Promoting an alternative frame for sport management research, education, and practice. *Journal of Sport Management, 20,* 483–509.

Shaw, S., & Hoeber, L. (2003). "A strong man is direct and a direct woman is a bitch": Gendered discourses and their influence on employment roles in sport organizations. *Journal of Sport Management, 17,* 347–375.

Sigleman, L., & Tuch, S. A. (1997). Metastereotypes: Blacks' perceptions of Whites' stereotypes of Blacks. *Public Opinion Quarterly, 61,* 87–101.

Smith, M., & Wrynn, A. (2013). *Women in the 2012 Olympic and Paralympic Games: An analysis of participation and leadership opportunities.* Ann Arbor, MI: SHARP Center for Women and Girls.

Spencer, N. E. (2000). Reading between the lines: A discursive analysis of the Billie Jean King vs. Bobby Riggs "Battle of the Sexes." *Sociology of Sport Journal, 17,* 386–402.

Stangl, J. M., & Kane, M. J. (1991). Structural variables that offer explanatory power for the under representation of women coaches since Title IX: The case of homologous reproduction. *Sociology of Sport Journal, 8,* 47–60.

Steinbeck, K., & Tomaskovic-Devey, D. D. (2007). Discrimination and desegregation: Equal opportunity progress in U.S. private sector workplaces since the Civil Rights Act. *Annals of the American Academy of Political and Social Science, 609*(1), 49–84.

Stroh, L. K., Langlands, C. L., & Simpson, P. A. (2004). Shattering the glass ceiling in the new millennium. In M. S. Stockdale & F. J. Crobsy (Eds.), *The psychology and management of workplace diversity* (pp. 147–167). Malden, MA: Blackwell.

Swanson, R., & Spears, B. (1995). *The history of sport and physical education in the United States.* Burr Ridge, IL: McGraw-Hill.

Uhlir, G. A. (1987). Athletics and the university: The post-woman's era. *Academe, 73*(4), 25–29.

Whisenant, W. A. (2003). How women have fared as interscholastic athletic administrators since the passage of Title IX. *Sex Roles, 49,* 179–184.

Whisenant, W. A., Miller, J., & Pedersen, P. M. (2005). Systematic barriers in athletic administration: An analysis of job descriptions for interscholastic athletic directors. *Sex Roles, 53,* 911–918.

Women's Sports Foundation. (n.d.). Coaching—Do female athletes prefer male coaches: The Foundation position. Retrieved from http://www.womenssportsfoundation .org/home/advocate/foundation-positions/equity-issues/do_female_athletes_prefer_male_coaches

Zinser, L. (2012). Summit stepping down as Tennessee coach. Retrieved from http://www.nytimes.com/2012/04/19 /sports/ncaabasketball/pat-summitt-stepping-down-as-tennessee-womens-coach.html

CHAPTER 14

LINGERING ISSUES IN RACE AND LEADERSHIP

Jacqueline McDowell
Algerian Hart
Emmett Gill

CHAPTER OBJECTIVES

- Understand the historical implications of prejudicial attitudes and discrimination that still impact sport leadership in the 21st century.
- Describe how stereotypes manifest themselves into prejudicial biases that can limit leadership avenues for minority groups in the United States.
- Recognize situations of race underrepresentation in leadership within sport organizations.
- Identify and understand the different leadership issues from league to league in professional sport and from professional sport to collegiate sport.

CASE STUDY

Mentor Leadership

"Each one, teach one" is a widely understood phrase that denotes the moral obligation of passing on your knowledge to others. Nobody understands this practice better than former National Football League (NFL) coach Tony Dungy, who is widely regarded as a "mentor leader." In 2007, Dungy, who coached both the Tampa Bay Buccaneers (1996–2001) and the Indianapolis Colts (2002–2008), became the first Black man to coach a team to a Super Bowl victory. Two seasons later, Mike Tomlin of the Pittsburgh Steelers, a Dungy protégé, became the second Black man to coach a team to a Super Bowl victory. In the 2007 Super Bowl, won by Dungy's Colts, the losing coach was Lovie Smith of the Chicago Bears. Smith is also a Dungy protégé. The meeting was only the second

(continues)

time in the four major sports that the championship had both teams led by a Black head coach/manager. The first meeting was in 1975 when Al Attles's Golden State Warriors defeated KC Jones's Washington Bullets in the National Basketball Association (NBA) Finals (Associated Press, 2007).

In addition to Smith and Tomlin, who both served as assistant coaches to Dungy, Herm Edwards, Leslie Frazier, and Jim Caldwell also served as assistant coaches under Dungy. They all went on to become head coaches. In Dungy's book, *The Mentor Leader: Secrets to Building People and Teams That Win Consistently*, Caldwell wrote in the book's foreword:

> After the 2005 season, I had a few NFL teams contact me about their head coaching positions. . . . In order to prepare myself for future opportunities and the possibility of one day leading an NFL franchise, I asked Tony if he would mind if I came into his office periodically to ask him a question or two about the role of head coach. He was always so gracious, and he agreed enthusiastically to my request. (Dungy, Caldwell, & Whitaker, 2011, p. viii)

Research has shown mentorship is needed to help young Black coaches move into leadership positions. In a study of Black female assistant coaches in college basketball, 9 of 10 coaches interviewed for the study said at least one important mentor had assisted them during their careers (Borland & Bruening, 2010). C. Vivian Stringer, who has coached the Rutgers University women's basketball team since 1995 and was mentored by former Temple coach John Chaney, has been instrumental in helping young Black women get their start in college basketball on the court, next to her on the bench, or on the benches at other universities. Dungy and Stringer appear to have been cut from the same cloth. Dungy pointed out in his book that "leadership is not an innate, mystical gift; rather, it is learned ability to influence the attitudes and behavior of others" (Dungy et al., 2011, p. xv). Dungy insists that once a leader becomes a leader, he or she then needs to teach others, thus empowering them to reach their full potential.

As this chapter will illustrate, people of color have not been afforded the same opportunities as their White counterparts in competing for leadership positions in professional and collegiate sport. The reasons, of course, are many, but it boils down to someone above them who holds the power to hire and fire giving them an opportunity to display their skills. Leaders like Dungy employ servant leadership—he calls it mentor leadership—whereby they become intensely interested in the development of followers and empowering them. Dungy has spread the roots of his "coaching tree" far and wide and now it is up to each one of his mentees to use Dungy's model to teach others.

Questions for Discussion

1. Why are coaches like Dungy and Stringer so important to the progress of racial equality and diversity in coaching ranks? What do they offer young people looking to become coaches?

2. Give some thought to whether you currently have or have had a mentor. If so, how has that mentor helped you? If not, how would a mentor be helpful to you in the near future as you pursue your chosen career?

3. Other than it being only the second time two Black head coaches have met in the title game of a major professional sport, why was the Smith/Dungy meeting in the Super Bowl significant?

4. At the end of the of the summer 2013, there were just four minority coaches in the NFL: Tomlin, Frazier in Minnesota, Marvin Lewis in Cincinnati, and Ron Rivera in Carolina. Does the NFL have a problem in regard to representation of head coaches who are racial minorities? Why or why not?

INTRODUCTION

In every organization there is a person at the top who oversees and guides the organization in the best direction. These leaders are essentially individuals who have the ability to understand their own times, who express or articulate programs or policies that reflect the perceived interests and desires of particular groups, and who devise instruments or political vehicles that enhance the capacity to achieve effective change. In very limited ways, leaders imprint their personal characteristics or individual stamp on a given moment in time. Leaders do make history, but never by themselves, and never in ways that they fully recognize or anticipate.[1]

In a commencement speech delivered to Knox College in 2005, U.S. Senator Barack Obama said:

> The true test of the American ideal is whether we're able to recognize our failings and then rise together to meet the challenges of our time. Whether we allow ourselves to be shaped by events and history, or whether we act to shape them. Whether chance of birth or circumstance decides life's big winners and losers, or whether we build a community where, at the very least, everyone has a chance to work hard, get ahead, and reach their dreams.

In 2008, Obama became the 44th "Leader of the Free World"—becoming the first Black American[2] to hold the most prestigious leadership position in the nation. President Obama has an exceptional educational background and was admitted into Occidental College and Columbia University, and he earned his Juris Doctorate from Harvard University Law School. Moreover, he was the first Black American to serve as president of the *Harvard Law Review*. Prior to his ascension into the U.S. presidency, he was elected to the Illinois State Senate and the U.S. Senate. With these great accomplishments and his historic achievement, many people see this as evidence that the United States is in a postracial era, in which all Americans, regardless of race, can attain prestigious leadership positions if they take advantage of educational resources and work hard (Jimenez, 2011; Rachlinski & Parks, 2010).

A Black American may hold the most prestigious position in the nation, but are we in a post-racial era? As evidenced in a lot of the rhetoric surrounding President Obama's campaigns and elections (Hehman, Baertner, & Dovidio, 2011; Piston, 2010; Rachlinski & Parks, 2010), prejudicial attitudes and discrimination still persist in U.S. society. Progress has been made, and

---

[1] Portions of the introductory paragraph were generated from ideas espoused by Dr. Jack Thomas, president of Western Illinois University, in December 2012.

[2] President Obama would be considered biracial because he has a White mother and a Black Kenyan father, but in the racial understanding of U.S. society, many people consider a person with "one drop of Black blood" to be Black (Hickman, 1997; Ho, Sidanius, Levin, & Banji, 2011).

many people of color[3] have made notable accomplishments, but there are still barriers and obstacles that prevent all Americans from getting ahead and reaching their dreams. In many organizations, people of color still struggle to obtain and retain leadership positions and are disproportionally concentrated in lower service positions.

The sport industry is no exception; a *black-bottomed pyramid* exists in that people of color are represented more at the bottom of the pyramid as athletes than in top leadership roles in sport organizations (Shropshire, 1996). Discussions about the low representation of people of color in leadership positions have lingered for years and have many people inquiring as to when the conversations will cease and whether progress is being made. Defining progress is subjective, and "we are not going to be able to paint, in advance, a statistical picture of success" (Shropshire, 2004, p. 194); despite difficultly in objectively defining progress, in this chapter we provide evidence that progress is being made, but equity and parity have not been reached and persistent discriminatory and nondiscriminatory behaviors continue to affect people of color's opportunities in sport leadership positions.

Accordingly, this chapter focuses on the underrepresentation of men and women of color in front office (e.g., managers/general managers, athletic directors, owners) and head coaching positions in college and professional sport organizations—with a particular focus on American football, baseball, and basketball. In sport organizations, *underrepresentation* has been determined by comparing the number of people of color in leadership positions to U.S. Census demographic percentages (e.g., Race and Gender Report Cards) or to their representation as student-athletes (e.g., Black Coaches and Administrators Reports). However, unlike most industries that use specific geographic locations to determine underutilization, we contend that a local or regional labor market is not appropriate when determining underrepresentation of people of color in sport leadership positions. Moreover, extant sport research suggests that players are the most plausible labor force for determining underutilization (Cunningham & Sagas, 2002; Everhart & Chelladurai, 1998). Hence, in this chapter we define underrepresentation based on demographic comparisons between leadership and playing positions; however, we challenge readers to critically assess the limitations and strengths of both methods for claiming underrepresentation.

Based on this working definition of underrepresentation, Hispanics/Latinos, Asians, and Native Americans would not be referred to as being underrepresented in sport leadership positions because the reference group—their representation as athletes at the college and professional levels—has traditionally been very low, with the exception of Hispanic/Latino baseball players in Major League Baseball. As a result of not being deemed underrepresented in leadership positions, the experiences of these racial groups are often neglected in research, mass media, and *social justice* efforts. According to Chideya (1999), "In the basest and most stereotypical terms, White Americans are considered 'true' Americans; Black Americans are considered inferior Americans; Asians and Latinos are too often considered foreigners; and Native Americans are rarely thought of at all" (p. 7). These sentiments ring true as dominant discourses on race and sport focus primarily on "Americans" —White and Black—and the experiences of Asians, Latinos, and Native Americans are often neglected. This *binary* racial thinking has served to exclude and marginalize the experiences of these racial groups.

In this chapter we center on the experiences of Black Americans, Hispanics/Latinos, Asians, and

---

[3] The expression "persons/people of color" has recently emerged as a preference over using non-White and minority to refer to Native Americans and Americans of African, Asian, or Hispanic descent. In this chapter we have chosen to use this expression because it is more inclusive, whereas the expression "non-White" defines people by what they are not and the term "minority" can convey inferiority and subordination (Clark & Arboleda, 1999; Safire, 1988).

Native Americans in sport leadership positions. In order to obtain a more accurate understanding of people of color's current experiences and opportunities in sport, a broader understanding of current and socio-historical leadership barriers is needed. Hence we first present an overview of educational and socio-psychological barriers to leadership attainment, followed by a discussion of the current status of people of color in sport leadership positions. This chapter concludes with a review of current social justice efforts to increase the representation of people of color in sport leadership positions.

HISTORICAL AND CURRENT LEADERSHIP BARRIERS

The United States has a remarkable history that has situated it as one of the most powerful nations in the world, but this history is tainted with the forced servitude of Africans, Native American genocide, Chinese exploitation, segregation of Whites and "colored" individuals, and subordination of women. These historical events have influenced people of color's current experiences, opportunities, and access to power, and subsequently have shaped the way they are evaluated as leaders. For example, an Ivy League education has been viewed as a key to President Obama's success (Dierenfield &White, 2012); however, compared to White Americans, people of color have higher school dropout rates and hold significantly fewer higher education degrees. These negative trends can be explained by numerous individual, community, and societal factors, and also by the lingering effects of historical race relations in the United States.

Prior to the Civil War, education of Black Americans was virtually nonexistent, and after slavery was abolished, segregation laws prevented many from attending public institutions (Harris, 1956; Thomas, 2005). It would not be until 1823, 181 years after the first White college graduates, when Alexander Lucius Twilight would become the first Black person to earn a bachelor's degree from a U.S. college (Middlebury College). He would later become the first Black American elected to public office as a state legislator. It would take another 39 years, however, before a Black woman, Mary Jane Patterson, would earn a similar degree.

Similar to Black Americans, Mexican Americans were exposed to inferior public schools with poorly trained teachers and segregated facilities or classrooms (San Miguel, 1987; Verdugo, 2006). School segregation was challenged in the 1940s in the *Mendez v. Westminster* and *Delgado v. Bastrop Independent School District* federal court cases; it was determined that segregation of students of Mexican descent into separate schools and classrooms was unconstitutional (Vélez, 1994; Verdugo, 2006). Black Americans, however, did not receive the same benefits of the law until 1954, when the *Brown v. Board of Education* Supreme Court case declared "separate educational facilities are inherently unequal" and unconstitutional for *all* Americans. Integration, however, does not necessarily mean equal opportunity because resistance and curriculum and educator deficiencies continued.

Native Americans likewise faced many barriers to obtaining quality education. Children were forced to go to boarding schools—separating them from their reservation and family, and forcing them to abandon tribal mores and their native languages (U.S. Senate, 1969). In the 1960s Native Americans gained autonomy to make educational decisions and choices, but earlier coercive practices instilled in many a mentality that "school is the enemy" (U.S. Senate, 1969, p. 9).

Explicit structural barriers to education may have been removed, but as noted by former U.S. President Lyndon B. Johnson in a commencement address at Howard University in 1965:

> You do not wipe away the scar of centuries by saying: Now you are free to go where you want, and do as you desire, and choose the leaders you please. You do not take a person who, for years, has been hobbled by chains

and liberate him, bring him up to the starting line of a race and then say you are free to compete with all others, and still justly believe that you have been completely fair. (Johnson, 1965)

Internal (controllable) and external (uncontrollable) barriers and constraints still persist today to limit people of color's attainment of quality education and subsequently their leadership opportunities.

In addition to the role that education plays in leadership attainment, implicit and explicit stereotypes and discrimination limit leadership opportunities. *Stereotypes*, manifested into prejudicial thoughts, along with discriminatory behaviors coalesce in work environments creating a figurative glass ceiling that inhibits increased *diversity* among leadership positions (Thomas, 2005). Black Americans, Hispanics, and Native Americans, for instance, are more likely than other racial groups to be perceived as lazy, incompetent, and having a lower work ethic and ambition than White Americans (Devine & Elliot, 1995; Dixon & Rosenbaum, 2004; Fiske, Cuddy, Glick, & Xu, 2002; Smith, 1990)—all of which are characteristics deemed antithetical to leadership (Lord, Foti, & de Vader, 1984; Rudman & Glick, 1999). In contrast, Asians and Asian Americans are often deemed "model minorities" and are stereotyped as being smart and gifted in math and science. These stereotypes may appear to be positive; however, they result in Asians' leadership opportunities being limited because "those who are oriented toward the math and sciences are rarely presumed to have a comparably high level of people skills and leadership abilities" (Thomas, 2005, p. 79). Also, many Asians are stereotyped as having presumed language barriers, so when hiring managers see names on resumes that allude to Asian national origin, biases can affect the hiring decision.

Leadership then becomes defined by more than just qualifications and characteristics—it becomes defined by race and ethnicity. These views and stereotypes are implanted throughout society and organizations through various socializing agents (e.g., family, friends, and media) that consciously and subconsciously implant racialized thoughts into people's heads. Explicit verbalization and consciously applying racial stereotypes has lessened over the years; still, implicit stereotypes that function outside of a person's conscious awareness still linger, affecting decision makers' attitudes and behaviors (Banaji & Greenwald, 1995).

HISTORICAL AND CURRENT BARRIERS IN SPORT LEADERSHIP

Deep-Rooted Barriers in Baseball

Stereotypes and prejudices that exist in the larger society spill into organizations and interfere with people's ability to obtain and retain leadership positions. The infamous statement made by Al Campanis in 1987—40 years after Jackie Robinson broke the color line in a Brooklyn Dodgers uniform—clearly illustrates the pandemic nature of societal stereotypes. Specifically, in an interview with Ted Koppel, former Los Angeles Dodgers general manager Al Campanis stated that the low number of Black managers in baseball (or as pitchers, catchers, or football quarterbacks) was because they were thinking positions and Black people lacked the ability to adequately fill those positions. He emphatically stated, "No, I don't believe it's prejudice. I truly believe that [African-Americans] may not have some of the necessities to be a field manager or perhaps a general manager" (Hoose, 1989). In striving to discount the role of prejudice in hiring decisions, Campanis inadvertently reinforced that hidden prejudicial attitudes play a significant role. In response, Frank Robinson, Major League Baseball's first Black manager, acknowledged the hidden prejudicial view that Blacks are acceptable on the field, but not in the front office:

> Baseball has been hiding this ugly prejudice for years—that Blacks aren't smart enough to be managers or third-base coaches or part of the front office. There's a belief that they're fine when it comes to the physical part of the game, but if it involves brains they just can't handle it. Al Campanis made people finally understand what goes on behind closed doors: that there is racism in baseball. (Wilhelm, 1987)

Following the interview, Campanis was immediately fired with promises from the league regarding improved advancement opportunities for Black players. The fulfillment of those promises has been sparse.

In the 21st century there have been slight increases in the number of Black American players, coaches, and team vice presidents, but the number of Black managers and general managers has been on the decline (Lapchick et al., 2013). As of 2012, only one Black owner and five Black managers and general managers have been hired since Campanis's statement, and those hirings were often short-lived with only two of the five general managers lasting for more than 1 year (Lapchick et al., 2013; Zirin, 2012). Research suggests that persons of color need higher qualifications to obtain similar jobs as White Americans. With the demise of the Negro Leagues and the shifting cultural significance from baseball to basketball in Black communities, a significant increase in the number of Black managers is uncertain, as the number of Black American players and programs to encourage children to play baseball are disappearing.

Historically, Native Americans and Latinos were allowed to play professional baseball, so some Black Americans would try to pass as these racial groups in order to play or manage the game (Shropshire, 1996). However, despite having an earlier entry into professional baseball, Native Americans' representation in Major League Baseball (MLB) leadership positions is negligible (Lapchick et al., 2013). As of 2007, 50 verifiable full-blooded Native Americans have played Major League Baseball (Baseball Almanac, 2013), but none has become a manager. In contrast, Latinos represent the largest minority group (27.3%) of players, but the majority of these players have been recruited from outside the United States—which does not translate into increased leadership opportunities given that the majority of coaches and managers are U.S.-born. Currently, Latinos hold three managerial positions in MLB (Lapchick et al., 2013), and in 2003, Arturo Moreno, a Mexican American, became the first Latino owner of *any* major sport league when he purchased the Anaheim Angels (Shaikin, 2003).

Arturo Moreno, a Mexican American, became the first Latino owner of any major sport league when he purchased the Anaheim (now Los Angeles) Angels.
© Paul Connors, File/AP Images

Are these statistics a byproduct of prejudicial attitudes and discrimination or people of color not having the "necessities" to lead professional baseball teams? The centrality thesis of stacking—the discriminatory assigning of players of color to noncentral outfield positions—has been a popular explanation for the *glass ceiling* in baseball (Loy & McElvogue, 1970), because the majority of MLB managers have been found to have infield experience. Evidence supporting or refuting the occurrence of this phenomenon, however, has been mixed. Multiple factors, working conjointly—such as the uncertainty thesis of discrimination, which contends that "positional segregation is due to a form of racial discrimination that becomes effective when it is difficult to measure performance" (Lavoie & Leonard, 1994, p. 141); the centrality hypothesis of stacking; social closure; personal choices; and human capital differences—may provide a more accurate holistic picture of what occurs in baseball (Sack, Singh, & Thiel, 2005). Furthermore, Rimer's (1996) investigation of MLB managers' qualifications suggests that players of color are being held to higher standards to obtain similar jobs as White managers. Specifically, Black Americans and Latinos had more MLB playing experience and a longer tenure in the league before they were given the opportunity to trade in the title of player for that of manager.

Implicit Biases in National Football League Leadership

In 1988, sentiments expressed about Blacks in baseball possessing inferior leadership skills would be repeated by late CBS Sports commentator Jimmy "the Greek" Snyder when he espoused that Blacks were better athletes than Whites because they are offspring of slaves that were bred to be big and strong (Goodwin, 1988). He further expressed his concern with Black Americans obtaining coaching positions: "If they take over coaching, like everybody wants them to, there is not going to be anything left for White people." Unfortunately, these explicit sentiments about protecting prized coaching positions from Blacks or that they were

more suited to be players and not managers are not antiquated or held by a few people.

A 2002 report released by lawyers Johnnie Cochran and Cyrus Mehri posited that Black coaches were being discriminated against in the hiring process, faced increased criticisms and judgments for mistakes, and "are the last hired and the first fired." In response to Cochran and Mehri's report, the NFL instituted the Rooney Rule, which requires each NFL team to interview at least one minority candidate when interviewing for head coaching vacancies (see "Social Justice Efforts" later in the chapter for more information), but this diversity hiring policy is constantly criticized and violated. Outcries about the inefficiencies of the Rooney Rule and discrimination prevail in the media. A recent report sanctioned by the NFL found that coaches of color are not getting second chances as head coaches, coordinators, or college head coaches (Harrison, 2013). It was recommended that efforts be made to increase coaches' social networks, and the NFL should increase transparency in the hiring process and institute an incentive and disincentive model for diversity efforts. Recent research also suggests that the Rooney Rule's focus should be on positional and coordinator positions (Madden & Ruther, 2011; Solow, Solow, & Walker, 2011).

These diversity efforts will spur social change, but do not necessarily change persons' prejudicial attitudes and stereotypes. A recent analysis of more than 600 sport news articles, representing all National Collegiate Athletic Association (NCAA) Division I colleges, suggests that "goal-based stereotyping may systematically bias leader evaluations against Black leaders, in part explaining the glass ceiling faced by Black leaders in organizations" (Carton & Rosette, 2011, p. 1153). Mainly, the analysis found that if a Black quarterback had a good performance it was because of athleticism (e.g., physical ability, strength, speed, and agility), but if the performance was poor, evaluators highlighted his lack of competence (e.g., determination, analytical ability, intelligence, and decisiveness), not athleticism. These findings were not obtained for White quarterbacks. This suggests that beliefs of Black Americans' diminished leadership capabilities still prevail.

These biases and stereotypes are manifested in more implicit ways and are evident in hiring trends in sport leadership positions. For instance, in 1922 Fredrick "Fritz" Pollard was the first Black to be hired as an NFL head coach, but it took 68 years after his hiring before another Black American would gain the same opportunity. Between 1921 and 2012 only 17 Black Americans had been hired for more than 400 NFL head coaching openings (Lapchick, 2012); and as of 2012, there have been only three Latino and no Native American or Asian head coaches in NFL history. History was made in 2012 when Shahid Khan, a Pakistani American, became the majority owner of the Jacksonville Jaguars—making him not only the first Asian owner of color, but also the first owner of color of an NFL franchise (Lapchick, Costa, Sherrod, & Anjorin, 2012). Moreover, it is often reported that "there has never been a president/CEO of color in the NFL" (Lapchick, Costa, et al., 2012, p. 8), but in 1920 Jim Thorpe, a Potawatomi, was the first commissioner/president of the American Professional Football Association (later renamed the National Football League). This historic achievement has essentially gone unmentioned in sport research, thus supporting Chideya's (1999) statement about the invisibility of Native Americans. This oversight could be due to the fact that in 1920 the NFL had a different name. Regardless, Thorpe's accomplishment should not be overlooked in sport history.

Diversity in the National Basketball Association

The National Basketball Association (NBA) has been heralded as having the most racial diversity in leadership positions out of any professional sport league. In 2012, there were more head coaches of color than White head coaches. Black Americans are by far the largest racial group represented. They entered into leadership positions starting in 1966, 16 years after the NBA integrated, when Bill Russell was hired to coach the Boston Celtics. As of 2012, there have been 60 Black NBA head coaches (Gray, 2012). In that same year, Black Americans held 13% of all president and CEO positions for NBA franchises, and 23% (7 of 31) of general manager positions (Lapchick et al., 2012). In December 2002, a significant milestone was achieved when Robert Johnson become the principal owner of the Charlotte Bobcats (Rhoden, 2006). This historic moment was "heralded as one of the most significant milestones since Jackie Robinson desegregated MLB" (p. 247), because he was the first Black American majority owner of a professional sport franchise (Powell, 2008; Rhoden, 2006). Robert Johnson's hiring opened the door for other Black owners, such as Shawn "Jay-Z" Carter, Fred Jones, Earl Stafford, and Dr. Sheila Johnson. In contrast to other professional sport organizations, Black Americans are increasingly being provided opportunities to shatter the glass ceiling in the NBA and showcase their talents on and off the court.

In the 21st century, progress that is being witnessed for Black Americans is starting to become evident for other people of color—albeit on a smaller scale. As noted in **Table 14.1**, in the 21st century Latinos and Asian Americans have started making inroads into NBA head coaching positions (Lapchick, Lecky, & Trigg, 2012). Native Americans' presence and power in the NBA and other sports is also becoming increasingly known. Native Americans traditionally invest in the gaming industry, but more recently have used money earned from gaming to promote boxers (e.g. Sycuan Ringside Promotions, Seminole Warriors Boxing), develop golf courses, sponsor NASCAR races, and buy basketball franchises (Boeck, 2007). For example, the Mohegan tribe purchased the WNBA's Connecticut Sun in 2003

TABLE 14.1 **Firsts in Sport Leadership Positions* (partial list)**

20th Century

Year	Name	Minority	Position
1920	**Jim Thorpe**	**Native American**	**NFL commissioner**
1921	**Fritz Pollard**	**Black**	**NFL football coach (Akron Pros)**
1938	Miguel "Mike" Angel Gonzalez	Hispanic*	MLB manager (St. Louis Cardinals)
1951	Al Lopez	Latino**	MLB manager (Cleveland Indians)
1962	John Jordan "Buck" O'Neil	Black	MLB coach (Chicago Cubs)
1966	Bill Russell	Black	NBA head coach (Boston Celtics)
1967	Tom Fears	Hispanic	NFL coach (New Orleans Saints)
1970	Will Robinson	Black	NCAA Division I basketball coach (Illinois State University)
1972	Wayne Embry	Black	NBA general manager (Milwaukee Bucks)
1975	Frank Robinson	Black	MLB manager (Cleveland Indians)
1977	Bill Lucas	Black	MLB general manager (Atlanta Braves)
1979	Willie Jeffries	Black	NCAA Division I-A head football coach (Wichita State University)
1988	Dick Versace	Hispanic (Puerto Rican)	NBA coach (Indiana Pacers)
1989	**Art Shell**	**Black**	**NFL coach of the modern era (Los Angeles Raiders)**
1989	**Bertram Lee, Peter Bynoe, Arthur Ashe, and Ron Brown**	**Black**	**Managing general partners of major sport franchise (Denver Nuggets)**
1990	Barry Alvarez	Latino	NCAA Division I football coach (University of Wisconsin–Madison)
1995	Ted Nolan	Native American	NHL coach (Buffalo Sabres)

21st Century

Year	Name	Minority	Position
2002	**Robert L. Johnson**	**Black**	**Majority owner of a U.S. major sport league team (Charlotte Bobcats, NBA)**
2002	Ozzie Newsome	Black	NFL general manager (Baltimore Ravens)
2002	Omar Minaya	Latino	MLB general manager (Montreal Expos)
2003	Arturo "Arte" Moreno	Hispanic	MLB team owner (Anaheim Angels)
2008	**Erik Spoelstra**	**Asian American**	**NBA head coach (Miami Heat); first Asian American head coach in any Big Four professional sport**
2008	Don Wakamatsu	Asian American	MLB manager (Seattle Mariners)

TABLE 14.1 Firsts in Sport Leadership Positions* (partial list) (Continued)

21th Century

Year	Name	Minority	Position
2010	**Rich Cho**	**Asian**	**General manager in major men's professional sport league (Portland Bobcats)**
2011	Norm Chow	Asian American	Division I football coach (University of Hawaii)
2011	O. B. Osceola, Jr.	Native American (Seminole)	NASCAR team owner (Germain-Osceola Racing)
2012	**Shahid Khan**	**Pakistani American**	**Owner, NFL franchise (Jacksonville Jaguars)**
2012	Earvin "Magic" Johnson	Black	Owner, MLB franchise (Los Angeles Dodgers)
2012	Caleb Canales	Latino	NBA head coach (Portland Trailblazers)

*Bold text indicates first person of color to hold that position.
*Hispanic is used for persons whose ancestry is from Spanish-speaking countries (Spain and Spanish-speaking Latin American countries).
**Latino is used for persons of Latin American origin (Central and South America, and Spanish-speaking Caribbean Islands).

and has also used gaming dollars to sponsor Matt Kobyluck, a Busch East Series auto racer (Boeck, 2007). Also, in 2005, the Yakama Nation purchased the now-defunct Yakima Sun Kings, a minor league basketball team in the Continental Basketball Association.

NCAA COLLEGE SPORTS

Racial occupational stratification would predict that minority groups would have higher representations in lower positions of a hierarchy, but college sports' brand equity is starting to surpass that of professional sports. This has resulted in people of color facing increased challenges and barriers to obtaining leadership positions. The "black-bottomed pyramid" (Shropshire, 1996) is evident for people of color, whereas White Americans are disproportionately represented in more powerful leadership positions in intercollegiate athletics. As

noted in Table 14.1, in 1979 Willie Jeffries was the first Black American to be hired as a head coach of an NCAA Division I-A team, but since then only 41 (out of more than 183 vacancies) have been hired to coach at the highest level of collegiate football (Anjorin, & Nickerson, 2012). During the 2012–13 academic year, among the Football Bowl Subdivision's (FBS's) 120 institutions, there were only 14 Black American, 2 Latino, and 2 Asian head football coaches.

These dismal numbers do, however, represent progress. As shown in **Table 14.2**, progress in hiring Black coaches as head coaches of NCAA FBS and Football Championship Subdivision (FCS) football programs has been made. Prior to 2008 (with 2006 as an exception), it was common for Black and other coaches of color to obtain only one or two of the open head football coaching positions. Many speculate that this positive hiring trend is partially attributed to the success of two Black NFL football coaches—Lovie Smith

TABLE 14.2 **Black Coaches and Administrators Reports: Division I Head Coaching Football Positions**

Year	Total Open Positions	White Coaches Hired	Black Coaches Hired	Other Minorities Hired
2004	28	27	1	0
2005	30	28	2	0
2006	26	22	4	0
2007	35	33	1	1
2008	31	27	3	1
2009	32	27	5	0
2010	34	26	8	0
2011	29	22	7	0
Total	245	212	31	2

Source: Data from Black Coaches and Administrators, http://bcasports.org

and Tony Dungy (see this chapter's case study)—in leading their teams to the Super Bowl in 2007. Unlike the positive trajectory witnessed in the hiring of Black coaches, only three Latinos and two Polynesians have been hired as head coaches in FBS schools and one Native American hired as head coach of an FCS school (Lapchick, Anjorin, et al., 2012; Lapchick, Farris, & Rodriguez, 2012).

Public debate in the media and sport research suggests racial stereotyping and discrimination are still prevalent in limiting opportunities for coaches of color. In fact, in 2008, Charles Barkley publicly opined that race was the "No. 1 factor" for Gene Chizik to get the head football coaching position at Auburn over Turner Gill (Schlabach, 2008). Informal and prejudicial hiring mechanisms, such as homologous reproduction, the tendency to hire those similar to ourselves, pressures from boards of trustees and boosters, lack of formal interviews and search committees, and designations of successors for head coaching positions, have also been suggested as prominent factors contributing to limited opportunities for coaches

of color in Division I football. Researchers have also suggested that the black-bottomed pyramid in collegiate football is a result of discriminatory stacking of Black athletes in running back or wide receiver positions, in contrast to quarterback and offensive line positions—positions that are viewed as a pipeline to coordinator positions (Anderson, 2008; Finch, McDowell, & Sagas, 2010).

Men and women's collegiate basketball also has a history of inequitable hiring practices for coaches of color. Following the integration of college teams, Black players quickly became the dominant demographic group on the court. Many of these players were recruited from Black high schools, but the upward mobility of the Black college coaches from historically Black colleges and universities (HBCUs) that trained these players did not transpire. In 1970, Will Robinson became the first Black American to lead a major college program as a coach instead of a player. Since Robinson's hiring, the number of Black coaches has steadily been on the rise, but their continued low representation as coaches in comparison to their high representation as players suggests that some Black Americans have shattered the glass ceiling but for many others, biases and discrimination in the hiring process prevent them from moving up.

In 2012, the inaugural Black Coaches and Administrators (BCA) Division I men's basketball hiring report card reported 20 open head coaching positions, for which 7 Black Americans were hired—bringing the number of Black coaches to 29 of 120 positions at the BCS schools (Laucella, 2012). The report indicated that the majority of the universities have good to excellent hiring practices, but in contrast to hiring trends in football, the number of coaches of color has gradually declined since 2008, despite a steady rise in players of color. This negative hiring trend is evident in women's Division I basketball as well. The access to athletics has been extended to Black female athletes, but not to Black women in coaching and administration (Hattery, 2012). Moreover, as of 2012, Hispanic, Asian, and Native American coaches have yet to break into the highest levels of college basketball.

Racial demographics in athletic director positions parallel those of head coaching positions. As recently as 2010, over 90% of athletic directors were White (Irick, 2011). Furthermore, a person of color has never held the title of commissioner for a BCS conference—the most powerful and influential positions in college sport. Moreover, recent NCAA reports indicate that Black men and women hold approximately 9% of athletic director positions whereas Hispanic/Latino men and women account for approximately 2% and Asians and Native Americans have less than 0.5% combined representation at all three division levels (Irick, 2011). In 2012, there was a slight increase in the number of Latinos and Asians in key leadership positions at FBS schools and conferences. In general, past diversity hiring trends have shown minimum improvement or "remained stagnant" (Lapchick, Farris, et al., 2012).

Research suggests that discrimination, perceived human capital deficiencies, and occupational segregation, or the disproportionate number of people of color working in academic support positions and not athletic director pipeline positions (e.g., donor relations, business operations, and marketing), has a substantial effect on the number of people of color attaining athletic director positions (Cunningham, 2012; McDowell & Cunningham, 2007; McDowell, Cunningham, & Singer, 2009). Findings of a study conducted by McDowell, Cunningham, and Singer (2009) found that career preferences, working in conjunction with structural limitations such as discrimination, informal hiring practices, and lack of career role models and social networks, contributed to occupational segregation.

SOCIAL JUSTICE EFFORTS

As highlighted in this chapter, lingering issues in race and professional and collegiate sports persist, but the concerns are increasingly being addressed by advocacy groups and governing organizations, in particular in sports where a large percentage of participants are racial minorities. Internal and external diversity efforts are resonating within sports and among states with prominent football teams.

The Rooney Rule

On September 30, 2002, Johnnie L. Cochran, Jr. and Cyrus Mehri issued a landmark report, *Black Coaches in the National Football League: Superior Performance, Inferior Opportunities*, revealing the National Football League's (NFL) Black head coaches are held to a higher standard when compared to their White counterparts. *Superior Performance, Inferior Opportunities* supported the notion that Black American males are denied opportunities for NFL head coaching positions. The report raised awareness of the disparate

NFL team hiring practices, and as a result the league formed a diversity committee headed by the Pittsburgh Steelers owner Dan Rooney. In 2003, the NFL diversity committee announced a plan including minority training and development programs, internships, and the implementation of the *Rooney Rule*, which requires NFL teams to interview at least one candidate of color for open head coaching positions (Holder, 2012; National Football League, 2002; Nichols, 2008; Thornton, 2007). In 2009, Rooney requirements were strengthened to apply to all senior NFL football operations position searches, regardless of a team's racial/ethnic diversity (Brandt, 2011).

Black NFL coaches have successfully demonstrated their leadership capabilities and a Black head coach or general manager has participated in four of the last six Super Bowls (Holder, 2012; Wells, 2011). Still, a struggle characterizes professional football diversity efforts, as some NFL owners and general managers circumvent the Rooney Rule. In 2003, the NFL fined the Detroit Lions $200,000 for failure to interview a Black candidate for the team's vacant head coaching job. The Lions fired Marty Mornhinweg and immediately hired former San Francisco 49ers head coach Steve Mariucci. Detroit's leadership said they attempted to interview Black candidates, but the candidates withdrew citing the inevitability of Mariucci's hiring (Associated Press, 2003). The granting of coaches of color "token" interviews is in direct opposition to the intent of the Rooney Rule. Other avoidance strategies include head coaches who name a successor before their imminent retirement and the lack of transparency in the hiring process.

Despite concerns the Rooney Rule amounts to affirmative action, the NFL continues to form relationships with diversity advocates and the Fritz Pollard Alliance to help promote inclusion in NFL hiring. NFL teams must request permission to interview external candidates, positioning the commissioner to monitor the demography of team hiring processes. Still, one prevailing issue is the dismal number of Black NFL offensive and defensive coordinators because serving as a coordinator typically leads to a head coaching opportunity (Johnson, 2012). In the midst of lingering issues, Richard Lapchick, director of The Institute for Diversity and Ethics in Sport (TIDES), believes the Rooney Rule has been enormously successful (Holder, 2012).

The Robinson Rule

There are meaningful efforts by the *Black Coaches and Administrators (BCA)* organization, the NCAA, and *The Institute for Diversity and Ethics in Sport (TIDES)* to increase racial diversity in sport administration and coaching in revenue-generating sports. The BCA was formed in part to assist persons of color aspiring to have a career in sport through education and professional development. Over the BCA's 20-year history, one of its most meaningful contributions has been the BCA Football Hiring Report Card, developed in 2004 in conjunction with TIDES. The report card grades FBS schools based on who is on the search committee, who is interviewed, the length of the process, and whether a school sought assistance from the BCA in the hiring process (Lapchick, 2012). The BCA also has discussed pursuing Title VII under the 1964 Civil Rights Act as another remedy, and last resort, to produce diversity and inclusion (Duru, 2008; Gordon, 2008; Moye, 1998; Nichols, 2008). The Civil Rights Act of 1964 prohibits both intentional and unintentional employment discrimination practices that have the effect of discriminating on the basis of race, religion, sex, or national origin. Increased diversity efforts appear necessary considering the low percentage of Black FBS coaches (15%) compared to NFL coaches of the same race (24%); however, the NCAA recently scaled back its inclusion efforts.

In 2005, the NCAA created the Office of Diversity and Inclusion (ODI) to increase representation among women and people of color in collegiate sports. ODI, led by former DHL executive Charlotte Westerhaus, was charged with developing and implementing strategies, policies, and programs to promote empowerment, diversity, inclusion, and accountability. There were tangible outcomes of BCA, TIDES, and ODI efforts, such as the 27 ethnic minorities who were interviewed for 22 Division I head football coaching vacancies in 2008 (Carey, 2009). The issue remains on the NCAA's radar according to current association president Mark Emmert, who said: "The fact we have to grow diversity among the coaching ranks is self-evident" (Johnson, 2010). However, in a move to restructure the NCAA, the Office of Diversity and Inclusion was eliminated in 2010 (Woods, 2010). The new diversity structure involves a joint inclusion oversight panel that consists of presidents and the chairs and vice chairs of the Minority Opportunities and Interests Committee (MOIC) and the Committee on Women's Athletics (CWA) to oversee diversity-related strategic initiatives.

Recently, advocates and legal scholars have lobbied for extending the Rooney Rule to college football (Lapchick, 2009; Nichols, 2008). Lapchick has proposed "The Robinson Rule," named after legendary former Grambling University head football coach Eddie Robinson (Harrison, Lapchick, & Jansen, 2009). Eddie Robinson, the winningest coach in Division I-AA football, was never offered a Division I-A (now FBS) head coaching position. The need for the Robinson Rule in college football may be increasing because at the conclusion of the 2012 season, two Black FBS coaches were fired, dropping the percentage of Black FBS head football coaches to 17. The 2012 firing of one Black head coach, Jon Embree, raised the issue of ethnic minority retention and rehiring (Henderson, 2012). Only 1 of 41 Black coaches fired from FBS head coaching positions were rehired to lead an FBS program (ESPN, 2012). This was Tyrone Willingham, who left Notre Dame in 2004 and became head coach at the University of Washington. Former Colorado football head coach Bill McCarty said: "I believe Black men have less opportunity, shorter time if you will" (Henderson, 2012). The recent reversal in ethnic minority hiring and retention demographics has led state governments to explore Rooney-like requirements in collegiate football (Lapchick, 2009).

Oregon House Bill 3118

Change via advocacy groups and the NCAA is not the sole avenue for diversity and inclusion. Collegiate sports are a part of the social fabric of state-run colleges and universities and, thus, state government is increasingly involved in the industry. The state of Oregon has developed and implemented social policy that encourages diversity and inclusion in FBS head coach hiring (Lapchick, 2012). Oregon House Bill (HB) 3118 states: "Each institution under the jurisdiction of the State Board of Higher Education shall interview one or more qualified minority applicants when hiring a head coach or athletic director" (Bachman, 2012). HB 3118 was enacted in September 2009 after Oregon state representative Mitch Greenlick (D-Portland) drafted HB 3118 at the request of Sam Sachs, a college football minority rights activist, as a measure to slow down and open up a process deemed as quick and secretive (Bachman, 2012). HB 3118 covers six state universities: Oregon, Oregon State, Portland State, Eastern Oregon, Western Oregon, and Southern Oregon (Bachman, 2012). The bill has been received favorably, and as noted by Rob Cashell, the Eastern Oregon athletic director, the bill might help because it might "strengthen our pool of candidates" (Bachman, 2012, para. 11). Still, HB 3118 also states: "It is an affirmative defense claim of a violation of this paragraph that the institution, in good faith, was unable to identify a qualified candidate who was willing to interview for the position" (Bachman, 2012). Although

HB 3118 accounts for one of the challenges of the Rooney Rule—reactions to token interviews—it does not provide a solution, only relief, to universities. Florida, Alabama, and New Jersey have explored similar legislation, but no other state has adopted head coaching diversity legislation (Crabbe, 2012).

WOMEN OF COLOR IN SPORT

Few organizations have advocated for women of color in sport participation and administration like the Black Women in Sport Foundation (BWSF). Tina Sloan-Green, a founder of BWSF, shares her views in the "Leadership Perspective" at the end of the chapter. Women of color in sport face two daunting issues—limited post–Title IX participation of female athletes of color in sport and the subsequent lack of women of color in sport administration and coaching. As such, the BWSF is focused on grassroots efforts to spur girls and women of color's involvement in sport. In particular, the foundation emphasizes programming aimed at increasing participation of women of color in the female prep sports including soccer, volleyball, and lacrosse. The BWSF Next Step Forum has served as a space and a tool to discuss barriers and facilitators to the participation of women in sport as athletes, coaches, and administrators (BWSF, n.d.). One issue believed to restrict the hiring of female athletic directors is their ability to navigate the BCS football culture.

SUMMARY

Even in the dawn of a new era of access and proven success there continues to be concerns about Black leadership across the sporting industry. This chapter highlights some of the lingering issues related to race in professional and collegiate sport and asserts that progress toward equal opportunities has been made, but racism still prevails in limiting the opportunities of persons of color to achieve sport leadership positions. As noted by Rosellini (1987), "The new-fashioned racism is like a chill breeze that sneaks through the dugout late in the season, creeping among the stands, nosing into stadium offices, wandering unexpected and unwanted across the field. It is so subtle, yet systematized." These words were in reference to the racism that persists in MLB, but are also reflective of other sport organizations, associations, and departments.

We live in a global community that is becoming increasingly intertwined and interdependent. Demographic, cultural, technological, and economic changes are compelling us to live and work with a wide variety of people. To survive and thrive in this modern society means to understand that each of us is mutually connected to the other. Thus, it is in our best interest to embrace diversity, develop cultural competencies, increase leadership capacities, and create inclusive spaces as a means of fully utilizing all human resource potential.

LEADERSHIP PERSPECTIVE

Tina Sloan-Green.
Courtesy of Tina Sloan-Green

Tina Sloan-Green is a founding member of the Black Women in Sport Foundation and a professor emeritus at Temple University.

Q: You were one of the founding members of the Black Women in Sport Foundation in 1992. In the past 21 years, how have you seen the situation change (or not change) for Black women striving for leadership positions in sport?

You have the statistics, I'm sure—the statistics as far as collegiate administration is concerned. With regard to high school statistics, they are not normally recorded by race. In Pennsylvania, we are trying to get schools to record student sport participation, coaches, and sport administrators by race and gender. I think the critical element is starting early on, especially for people of color. You usually have to have an interest in sport in order to get involved in the business, especially in nontraditional sports. I have seen a lot of progress, especially in some high-profile positions, but I also see the historically Black schools still being a major player in producing people that are qualified for these positions. Although you are seeing more Black women in the field, you are also seeing them exit. The statistics also need to show retention rates. I think this is really critical. Equity really doesn't exist in the male-dominant sports like basketball and track and field. It seems like the numbers should be greater in those areas. In the WNBA, have the number of Black female coaches increased proportionately to the athlete participation rate? On the collegiate level, we have seen an increase. Dawn Staley is an example. But some people are getting the job and then leaving. They are getting a chance, but after they leave they may not get another job in coaching or administration.

Q: What do you perceive as the most stubborn obstacles facing Black women in achieving leadership positions in sport?

What is critical here is access to opportunity, your access to sports. When you are young and you have access to lacrosse, field hockey, and tennis, the networking starts early. It is the old girls' and old boys' networks that most of the time get you the job. If you're not part of that network or you don't know how to access that network, your chances of getting an interview are going to be slim.

Q: Is it time for NCAA member schools to enact some sort of mechanism—like a Rooney Rule—to make sure minority candidates are represented in the interview/hiring process?

I think people of color are treated as "tokens." If the institution is serious about hiring a person of color and they go out and search, they need to be strategic. There are people who have jobs and others just coming into the system who are not really trying to apply. They don't want to be merely tokens. Search firms can locate the right people, but you have to have the right search firms. Some search firms are money-makers, and they'll get someone in there, but, oftentimes, it's not a long stay at all. I don't have much faith in a Rooney Rule. My conversations with knowledgeable people lead me to believe it has not been that successful. I mean, yes, you get the interview but then what? Oftentimes, people interview you to get information about your program for self-interest. I think people are getting more sophisticated about the use of their time and their energy. In reality, when people hire for high-level positions, they or their associates know you. The applicants must also know people who are not of color. You really have to be known. An internship is a good way to display your work. This is a look-and-see opportunity for employers. They can observe how you fit into the system and how you relate. There are so many subtle observations added to the equation.

Q: You mentioned networking in an earlier answer. Are there any other obstacles that you think are out there and how can Black women overcome these obstacles?

Again, the biggest obstacle to me is access to the workplace written rules and the unwritten rules and access to the sport. Then you also need access to mentors, people who recognize that you have talent and are willing to help you along. Most people who advance have this and it could be a person of color or a White person that is in the network. In predominantly Black schools, sometimes you get greater access because they often give women more responsibilities in administration as well as membership on the management team. The woman might not be the head athletic director, but she might be the associate, assistant, or assistant to the AD. Another obstacle in Division I jobs is that they want administrators with football experience. So you have to be at a school that has football. A good thing about some of the historically Black schools is they do have football, so female administrators can get that experience. I think, too, you need to have a terminal degree. Many modern-day athletic directors have law or MBA degrees. For many who are just starting their careers, how are they going to afford that MBA or that law degree? And how many internships and/or scholarships are offered in law or MBA programs? Sport management is good, but some find that when they go through sport management programs they are still not qualified for Division I positions. My advice to the young is, if they want to go Division I, don't go into sport management. You need to pursue a terminal degree in law or business to be in the mix. Another thing students can do is volunteer . . . sometimes this is a way you can get into the real mix, especially people of color. Sacrifice is necessary, especially when you are young. Volunteer to give out programs or be an usher at athletic events. Make sure the athletic administrators know your name. When you negotiate for a job these days, you need the services of a lawyer or an agent to help you negotiate a 3- to 5-year contract. I think this is critical. Also, in that negotiation, make sure there is a support system included, which is a must in regards to retention. When you go into these situations, often they don't want you there anyway. You're a first or a second and there is not even subtle racism, there is overt racism. When you are hired into a situation where you are going to be a pioneer, you have to have someone in that system that is going to be a support system for you. Negotiate that ahead of time or don't take the job. Some people are bounced out after 2 years. Once you are bounced out, it is hard to recover and get another job in the field. Regardless, you have to remain squeaky clean because we stick out like a sore thumb. Within this modern-day workplace, you have to understand the environment and what you can't do and what you can do.

Q: What advice would you give a Black female student-athlete who hopes to work her way up to an athletic director position someday after her playing days are over?

I would tell them to start the process when they are athletes, when they are participating in sport. Start looking at what is happening behind the scenes. Don't just concentrate on playing, concentrate on what drills are being done and who is distributing the meal money and, also, try to get involved with the athletic director. If they want someone to come to an event and greet people, be that greeter. You not only want to get to know your coach, but you want the athletic director to know you. You want the senior women's administrator to know you. Let them know that you are interested in an internship somewhere. Ask, can you help me? Establishing a personal relationship early on as an athlete or as a sport management major is important. As a former coach, I looked differently at those athletes who were assertive and said to me, "I want to be a coach. Can you help me?" You look at them differently because it is rare that student-athletes start thinking like this early on. Also, I think internships are critical. Even internships that don't pay money might be the best internships. It's hard to get a Division I internship but Division II, Division III sometimes are better because you get to do a lot of stuff that you wouldn't normally do if you were Division I. You might get closer to the athletic director in that type of environment than you would Division I. . . . I tell young people they have to love the work, not just like it. A career and a job are two different things. In a career, you enjoy coming to work, you enjoy doing what you are doing. The money is important, but the job satisfaction is more important. Young people need to really stay in touch with people, especially in this age of social media. Don't just write your former teammates, coaches, or athletic director when you need something. Stay in touch. That personal touch is so important.

KEY TERMS

binary
black-bottomed pyramid
Black Coaches and Administrators (BCA)
diversity
glass ceiling
Rooney Rule

social justice
stereotypes
The Institute for Diversity and Ethics
   in Sport (TIDES)
underrepresentation

DISCUSSION QUESTIONS

1.   Chideya (1999) states: "In the basest and most stereotypical terms, White Americans are con-
     sidered 'true' Americans; Black Americans are considered inferior Americans; Asians and
     Latinos are too often considered foreigners; and Native Americans are rarely thought of at all."
     Do you agree with this statement when it comes to sport leadership? Why or why not?

2.   Other than the examples mentioned in the chapter, what other social justice initiatives
     should the NCAA and professional sport leagues undertake to ensure diversity in leadership
     positions?

3.   What stereotypes in sport can be attached to Black Americans? Latinos? Asians? Native
     Americans? List some for each group. How do these characteristics affect these groups' ability
     to obtain leadership positions in sport?

4.   Why do you think there has been more racial diversity seen in sport leadership positions
     in the NBA versus MLB and the NFL? Although not discussed in this chapter, why is there
     such a lack of diversity in player participation in the National Hockey League (NHL) and the
     Professional Golfers' Association (PGA)?

5.   Given that there is a large percentage of Black players evident on the football fields and bas-
     ketball courts of Division I schools—much higher than the percentage of Blacks in the U.S.
     population—why don't these high percentages translate into higher percentages of Blacks in
     leadership positions such as coaches and athletic directors at Division I schools?

For a full suite of assignments and additional learning activities, use the access code found in the front of your book. If you do not have an access code, you can obtain one at **www.jblearning.com**.

REFERENCES

Anderson, D. (2008). Cultural diversity on campus: A look at intercollegiate football coaches. *Journal of Sport and Social Issues, 17*(1), 61–66.

Associated Press. (2003, July 25). Lions Millen fined $200k for not interviewing minority candidates. Retrieved from http://archive.is/v4Ji

Associated Press. (2007, February 4). Dungy becomes first Black coach to win Super Bowl. Retrieved from http://sports.espn.go.com/nfl/playoffs06/news/story?id=2754521

Bachman, R. (2012). Affirmative action college football coaches: Bill would require Oregon universities to interview at least one minority football coach candidate. Retrieved from http://www.minorityjobs.net/article/1536/Bill-would-require-Oregon-univesities-to-interview-at-least-one-minority-football-coach-candidate-Affirmative-action-college-football

Banaji, M. R., & Greenwald, A. G. (1995). Implicit gender stereotyping in judgments of fame. *Journal of Personality and Social Psychology, 68*, 181–198.

Baseball Almanac. (2013). American Indian baseball players. Retrieved from http://www.baseball-almanac.com/legendary/american_indian_baseball_players.shtml

BCASports. (n.d.) Black Coaches and Administrators. Retrieved from http://bcasports.org

Black Women in Sport Foundation. (n.d.). Next step program. Retrieved from http://blackwomeninsport.org/next-step-program

Boeck, G. (2007, February 23). Native American athletes face imposing hurdles. Retrieved from http://usatoday30.usatoday.com/sports/2007-02-21-native-american-cover_x.htm

Borland, J., & Bruening, J. E. (2010). Navigating barriers: A qualitative examination of the under-representation of Black females as head coaches in collegiate basketball. *Sport Management Review, 13*(4), 407–420.

Brandt, A. (2011, January 5). The Rooney Rule: An analysis. Retrieved from http://www.nationalfootballpost.com/The-Rooney-Rule-an-analysis.html

Carey, J. (2009, July 24). New Oregon law requires minority interviews for coaching positions. Retrieved from http://usatoday30.usatoday.com/sports/college/football/2009-07-23-collegiate-rooney-rule_N.htm

Carton, A. M., & Rosette, A. S. (2011). Explaining bias against black leaders: Integrating theory on information processing and goal-based stereotyping. *Academy of Management Journal, 54*(6), 1141–1158.

Chideya, F. (1999). *Color of our future.* New York: William Morrow.

Clark, C., & Arboleda, T. (1999). *Teacher's guide for in the shadow of race: Growing up as a multiethnic, multicultural, and "multiracial" American.* Mahwah, NJ: Lawrence Erlbaum Associates.

Crabbe, N. (2012, June 27). Bill may require more minority coaches. Retrieved from http://www.ocala.com/article/20100627/ARTICLES/100629694#gsc.tab=0

Cunningham, G. B. (2012). Occupational segregation of African-Americans in intercollegiate athletics administration. *Wake Forest Journal of Law and Policy, 2*(1), 165–178.

Cunningham, G. B., & Sagas, M. (2002). The differential effects of human capital for male and female Division I basketball coaches. *Research Quarterly for Exercise and Sport, 73*, 489–495.

Devine, P. G., & Elliot, A. J. (1995). Are racial stereotypes *really* fading? *Society for Personality and Social Psychology, 21*(11), 1139–1150.

Dierenfield, B., & White, J. (2012). *A history of African-American leadership.* Harlow, UK: Pearson Education Limited.

Dixon, J. C., & Rosenbaum, M. S. (2004). Nice to know you? Testing contact, cultural, and group threat theories of anti-Black and anti-Hispanic stereotypes. *Social Science Quarterly, 85*, 257–280.

Dungy, T., Caldwell, J., & Whittaker, N. (2011). *The mentor leader: Secrets to building people and teams that win consistently.* Carol Stream, IL: Tyndale Momentum.

Duru, N. J. (2007). Fritz Pollard Alliance, the Rooney Rule, and the quest to level the playing field in the National Football League. *Virginia Sports and Entertainment Law Journal, 7*, 179–197.

Everhart, C. B., & Chelladurai, P. (1998). Gender differences in preferences for coaching as an occupation: The role of self-efficacy, valence, and perceived barriers. *Research Quarterly for Exercise and Sport, 69*(2), 188–200.

ESPN. (2012) FBS leadership, coaches remain mostly white, male. Retrieved from http://sports.espn.go.com/espn/wire?section=ncf&id=8687377

Finch, B., McDowell, J., & Sagas, M. (2010). An examination of racial diversity in collegiate football. *Journal for the Study of Sports and Athletes in Education, 4*(1), 47–58.

Fiske, S., Cuddy, A., Glick, P., & Xu, J. (2002). A model of (often mixed) stereotype content: Competence and warmth respectively follow from perceived status and competition. *Journal of Personality and Social Psychology, 82*(6), 878–902.

Goodwin, M. (1988). CBS dismisses Snyder. Retrieved from http://www.nytimes.com/1988/01/17/sports/cbs-dismisses-snyder.html

Gordon, H. (2008). Robinson Rule: Models for addressing discrimination in the hiring of NCAA head football coaches. *Sports Lawyers Journal, 15*, 1–19.

Gray, G. (2012). NBA black head coaches 2012. Retrieved from http://blackathlete.net/2012/11/nba-black-head-coaches-2012/

Harris, R. (1956). The Constitution, education, and segregation. *Temple Law Quarterly, 29*(4), 409–433.

Harrison, C. K., Lapchick, R. E., & Jansen, N. K. (2009). Decision making in hiring: Intercollegiate athletics coaches and staff. *New Directions for Institutional Research, 144*, 93–101.

Harrison, K. (2013). Examining coaching mobility trends and occupational patterns: Head coaching access, opportunity and the social network in professional and college sport. *NFL Diversity and Inclusion, Coaching Mobility, Volume 1.* Retrieved from http://usatoday30.usatoday.com/sports/nfl/2013-05-28-nfl-diversity-report.pdf

Hattery, A. J. (2012). They play like girls: Gender and race (in) equity in NCAA sports symposium: "Losing to win: Discussions of race and intercollegiate sports." *Wake Forest Journal of Law and Policy, 2*(1), 247–266.

Hehman, E., Baertner, S., & Dovidio, J. (2011). Evaluation of presidential performance: Race, prejudice, and perceptions of Americanism. *Journal of Experimental Social Psychology, 47*, 430–435.

Henderson, J. (2012, November 27). Bill McCartney takes to airwaves to blast Colorado firing Jon Embree. Retrieved from http://www.denverpost.com/cu/ci_22076669/bill-mccartney-blast-colorado-firing-jon-embree

Hickman, C. (1997). The devil and the one drop rule: Racial categories, African Americans, and the U.S. Census. *Michigan Law Review, 95*, 1161–1265.

Ho, A., Sidanius, J., Levin, D., & Banji, M. (2011). Evidence for hypodescent and racial hierarchy in the categorization and perceptions of biracial individuals. *Journal of Personality and Social Psychology, 100*, 492–506.

Holder, S. F. (2012, January 19). NFL's Rooney Rule has boosted minority coaches and general managers. Retrieved from http://www.tampabay.com/sports/football/bucs/nfls-rooney-rule-has-boosted-minority-coaches-and-general-managers/1211219

Hoose, P. (1989). *Necessities: Racial barriers in American sports.* New York: Random House.

Irick, E. (2011). Race and gender demographics: 2009-10 NCAA member institutions' personnel report. Retrieved from http://www.ncaapublications.com/productdownloads/2010RaceGenderMember.pdf

Jimenez, L. (2011). Are we in a post-racial America? *Profiles in Diversity Journal.* Retrieved from http://www.diversityjournal.com/4493-are-we-in-a-post-racial-america

Johnson, G. (2010, June 23). Emmert: Well-being of student-athletes the ultimate priority. *NCAA News.* Retrieved from http://fs.ncaa.org/Docs/NCAANewsArchive/2010/aWide/emmert_well_being_of_student_athletes_the_ultimate_priority.html

Johnson, L. B. (1965, June 4). "To fulfill these rights": Commencement address at Howard University. Washington, DC.

Johnson, R. S. (2012, January 13). Modify the Rooney Rule. Retrieved from http://espn.go.com/espn/commentary/story/_/id/7450944/modify-rooney-rule-include-nfl-hires-offensive-defensive-coordinators

Lapchick, R. E. (2009, May 22). Oregon hears call to action. Retrieved from http://sports.espn.go.com/ncf/columns/story?id=4199225

Lapchick, R. E. (2012, January 9). College athletics shows diversity progress, room for improvement. Retrieved from http://www.sportsbusinessdaily.com/Journal/Issues/2012/01/09/Opinion/Richard-Lapchick.aspx?hl-Richard+lapchick&sc=0

Lapchick, R., Anjorin, R., & Nickerson, B. (2012). Striving for sustained positive change: The Black Coaches and Administrators (BCA) hiring report card for NCAA FBS and FCS football head coaching positions (2011-12). Retrieved from http://www.tidesport.org/Grad%20Rates/BCA/2012%20BCA%20Football%20Report%20Card.pdf

Lapchick, R., Bernstine, C., Nunes, G., Okolo, N., Snively, D., & Walker, C. (2013). The 2013 racial and gender report card: Major League Baseball. Retrieved from http://www.tidesport.org/RGRC/2013/2013_MLB_RGRC_Final_Correction.pdf

Lapchick, R., Costa, P., Sherrod, T., & Anjorin, R. (2012). The 2012 racial and gender report card: National Football League. Retrieved from http://www.tidesport.org/RGRC/2012/2012_NFL_RGRC.pdf

Lapchick, R., Farris, M., & Rodriguez, B. (2012). Mixed progress throughout collegiate athletic leadership: Assessing diversity among campus and conference leaders for Football Bowl Subdivision (FBS) schools in the 2012-13 academic year. Retrieved from http://www.tidesport.org/RGRC/2012/2012_D1_Leadership_Report.pdf

Lapchick, R., Lecky, A., & Trigg, A. (2012). The 2012 racial and gender report card: National Basketball Association. Retrieved from http://www.tidesport.org/racialgenderreportcard.html

Laucella, P. (2012, November 15). BCA hiring report card for NCAA Division I men's college basketball head coaching positions. Retrieved from http://www.sportsjournalism.org/wp-content/uploads/2012/11/FINALBCApdf.pdf

Lavoie, M., & Leonard, W. (1994). In search of an alternative explanation of stacking in baseball: The uncertainty hypothesis. *Sociology of Sport Journal, 11*, 140–154.

Lord, R. G., Foti, R. J., & de Vader, C. L. (1984). A test of leadership categorization theory: Internal structure, information processing, and leadership perceptions. *Organizational Behavior and Human Performance, 34*, 343–378.

Loy, J., & McElvogue, J. (1970). Racial segregation in American sport. *International Review of Sport Sociology, 5*, 5–24.

Madden, J., & Ruther, M. (2011). Has the NFL's Rooney Rule efforts "leveled the field" for African American head coach candidates? *Journal of Sports Economics, 12*, 127–142.

McDowell, J., & Cunningham, G. B. (2007). The prevalence of occupational segregation in athletic administrative positions. *International Journal of Sport Management, 8*, 245–262.

McDowell, J., Cunningham, G. B., & Singer, J. N. (2009). The demand and supply side of occupational segregation: The case of an intercollegiate athletic department. *Journal of African American Studies, 13*, 431–454.

Moye, J. (1998). Punt or go for the touchdown: A Title VII analysis of the National Football League's hiring practices for head coaches. *UCLA Entertainment Law Review, 6*, 105.

National Football League. (2002). NFL clubs to implement comprehensive program to promote diversity in hiring. Retrieved from https://www.nfl.info/nflmedia/News/2002News/NFLDiversityProgram.htm

Nichols, M. J. (2008). Time for a Hail Mary? With bleak prospects of being aided by a college version of the NFL's Rooney Rule, should minority college football coaches turn their attention to Title VII litigation? *Virginia Sports and Entertainment Law Journal, 8*, 147.

Piston, S. (2010). How explicit racial prejudice hurt Obama in the 2008 election. *Political Behavior, 32*, 431–451.

Powell, S. (2008). *Souled out? How blacks are winning and losing in sports*. Champaign, IL: Human Kinetics.

Rachlinski, J., & Parks, G. (2010). Implicit bias, election '08, and the myth of a post-racial America. *Cornell Law Faculty Publications*, Paper 178.

Rhoden, W. (2006). *Forty million dollar slaves: The rise, fall, and redemption of the Black athlete*. New York: Three Rivers Press.

Rimer, E. (1996). Discrimination in Major League Baseball: Hiring standards for Major League managers, 1975-1994. *Journal of Sport and Social Issues, 22*, 118–133.

Rosellini, L. (1987). Strike one and you're out. *U.S. News & World Report, 103*, 52–58.

Rudman, L. A., & Glick, P. (1999). Feminized management and backlash toward agentic women: The hidden costs to women of a kinder, gentler image of middle managers. *Journal of Personality and Social Psychology, 77*, 1004–1010.

Sack, A., Singh, P., & Thiel, R. (2005). Occupational segregation on the playing field: The case of Major League Baseball. *Journal of Sport Management, 19*, 300–318.

Safire, W. (1988, Nov. 20). On language; people of color. *The New York Times*. Retrieved from http://www.nytimes.com/1988/11/20/magazine/on-language-people-of-color.html

San Miguel, G. (1987). *Let all of them take heed, Mexican Americans and the campaign for educational equality in Texas, 1910-1981*. Austin: University of Texas Press.

Schlabach, M. (2008, December 16). Lobbying for Gill, alum Barkley says Auburn should have hired black coach. *ESPN.com*. Retrieved from http://sports.espn.go.com/ncf/news/story?id=3770769

Shaikin, B. (2003, May 16). Moreno dream comes true: He becomes the first Latino owner of any major sports after baseball approves his purchase of the Angels for $183.5 million. *Los Angeles Times*. Retrieved from http://articles.latimes.com/2003/may/16/sports/sp-angelsale16

Shropshire, K. (1996). *In Black and White: Race and sports in America*. New York: New York University Press.

Shropshire, K. (2004). Minority issues in contemporary sports. *Stanford Law and Policy Review, 15*, 189–215.

Smith, T. W. (1990). Ethnic images. *GSS Topical Report No. 19*. Chicago, IL: National Opinion Research Center.

Solow, B., Solow, J., & Walker, T. (2011). Moving on up: The Rooney Rule and minority hiring in the NFL. *Labour Economics, 18*, 332–337.

Thomas, K. M. (2005). *Diversity dynamics in the workplace*. Belmont, CA: Thomson Wadsworth.

Thornton, P. K. (2007). The legacy of Johnnie Cochran, Jr.: The National Football League's Rooney Rule. *Texas Southern University Law Review, 33*(1), 77–81.

U.S. Senate. (1969). Committee on Labor and Public Welfare. *Indian education: A national tragedy—A national challenge* (Kennedy Report) (S.Rpt. 80). Washington, DC: Government Printing Office.

Vélez, W. (1994). Educational experiences of Hispanics in the United States: Historical notes. In F. Padilla (Ed.), *Handbook of Hispanic cultures in the United States: Sociology* (pp. 151–159). Houston, TX: Arte Publico Press.

Verdugo, R. (2006). *A report on the status of Hispanics in education: Overcoming a history of neglect*. Washington, DC: National Education Association of the United States.

Wells, B. (2011, February 6). Super Bowl 2011: Notice how no one made a big deal Steelers coach Mike Tomlin is Black. Retrieved from http://www.stampedeblue.com/2011/2/8/1981752/super-bowl-2011-notice-how-no-one-made-a-big-deal-steelers-coach-mike

Wilhelm, M. (1987, April 27). In America's national pastime, says Frank Robinson, White is the color of the game off the field. *People Weekly, 27*(17), 46.

Woods, D. (2010, September 17). Diversity officer Westerhaus one of 17 employees laid off by the NCAA. Retrieved from http://usatoday30.usatoday.com/sports/college/2010-09-17-ncaa-layoffs_N.htm

Zirin, D. (2012). 25 years since Al Campanis shocked baseball: What's changed and what hasn't. Retrieved from http://www.thenation.com/blog/167400/25-years-al-campanis-shocked-baseball-whats-changed-and-what-hasnt

CHAPTER 15

POSITIONING THE ORGANIZATION THROUGH BRANDING

John F. Borland
Sungho Cho

CHAPTER OBJECTIVES

- Establish why leaders of sport organizations must understand the process of branding as it relates to consumer behavior and implications for the organization.
- Explain the process of branding and provide a historical background of branding practices.
- Explain the importance of building a brand internally.
- Understand the prevalence of corporate social responsibility and its effects on brand identity.

CASE STUDY

Branding the 2012 London Olympics

Few brands have stood the test of time like the Olympics. Results of a survey conducted by Sponsorship Intelligence following the 2012 London Olympics showed that when compared to other "global cultural, entertainment or sporting events, the Olympic Games has the highest appeal and awareness ratings among the respondents as a whole, and specifically among young people aged eight to nineteen" (Olympic Movement, 2013, para. 3). The first modern Olympic Games was created in 1896, but the Latin Olympic motto—Citius, Altius, Fortius (Faster, Higher, Stronger)—was not introduced until 1924. The famous, five intertwined circles known as the Olympic rings were not designed until 1912, years after the start of the modern Olympics (Kennedy, 2012). Along

(continues)

with these symbols grew history and traditions that continue to have global significance. Despite challenges, controversies, scandals, and consumerism, the brand remains strong. How has this brand remained and persevered through the 30th games of the Olympiad?

Shortly after the announcement that London would be the host city for the 2012 Summer Olympics, Parliament passed the London Olympic Games and Paralympic Games Act 2006 in an effort to begin the organization necessary to prepare for the Olympics. The act covered four main areas: (1) the establishment of the Olympic Delivery Authority (the Games organizing committee), (2) the formation of an Olympic Transport Plan (an organizing committee to develop a transportation strategy), (3) Secretary of State regulation of advertising near the Games, and (4) Secretary of State regulation of street trading near the Games. In particular, this act gave power to Games organizing committee (London Organising Committee of the Olympic Games) and the Secretary of State to regulate trade and punish violators with respect to the Olympic Games. In trying to protect the Games' image, the London Organising Committee of the Olympic Games (LOCOG) assigned a reported 300 brand enforcers to monitor and regulate, among other things, improper use of logos, symbols, and words such as "2012," "Twenty Twelve," "gold," "bronze," or "medal," as well as misspelled words like "Olympix" (Olson, 2012).

Ambush marketing is another issue Olympic organizers must fight. Ambush marketing is a method used by nonofficial sponsors to attempt to benefit financially by associating themselves with an event without paying for sponsorship. In Atlanta in 1996, Nike handed out swoosh banners for patrons to wave at competitions and built a large Nike center overlooking the Olympic Stadium. Nike was not an official sponsor of the Games, but many thought the company was. Only a handful of sponsors, which pay a large sponsorship fee, get to use the word "Olympic" and the five rings in their advertising (Sauer, 2002).

Shortly before the London Games, as well as during, there was a public response to these attempts to protect the Olympic brand. New reports highlighted strict enforcement of the London Olympic Games and Paralympic Games Act 2006 (Segal, 2012). Some criticized the law for being too narrowly focused and too broadly enforced. "I have said to LOCOG and the IOC, 'I think you're scoring an own goal here,'" said Michael Payne, author of *Olympic Turnaround* (Carne, 2012, para. 3). "The controls and measures have gone too far when it is starting to suffocate local street traders" (Carne, 2012, para. 4).

The 2014 Winter Olympics in Sochi, Russia, is not immune to these highly protective measures of securing the Olympic image. A controversial painting depicting the Olympic rings as nooses led to the firing of a prominent museum curator. Russian censors removed both the painting and the curator from the museum and have accused the painter of illegally using the Sochi/Olympic symbols without permission (Kovalyova, 2013).

The Olympic rings remain one of the most recognizable symbols in the world. The image has had a storied past, yet today still captures the essence of the product: Citius, Altius, Fortius. As stated by the founder of the modern Olympics, Baron de Coubertin, "These three words represent a programme of moral beauty. The aesthetics of sport are intangible" (de Coubertin, 1895, p. 89).

Questions for Discussion

1. Why have leaders of Olympic Host Committees, including the London Olympic Committee Organising the Games (LOCOG) and the Russian Olympic Committee, worked so hard to protect the Olympic brand?
2. Have the stringent protections put in place led to a negative impact on the Olympic brand? Why or why not?
3. How will future leaders of Olympics organizing committees be impacted by lessons learned in protecting the brand during previous Olympic Games?
4. How can Olympics organizing committees prevent ambush marketing?

INTRODUCTION

If you are reviewing this chapter before class begins, look around briefly at your classmates and observe what they are wearing. If they are sport management majors like you, you are likely to see a wide array of clothing adorned with sport company names, logos, colors, and even phrases. Adidas, Under Armour, Nike, Reebok, a Livestrong bracelet or two, names of colleges, sports teams, and player jerseys will undoubtedly be well represented in the wardrobes of your peers. Some questions you might ask are: How does a person choose to express loyalty to one sport outfitter over another? One sport team over another? Executives in sport apparel companies and sport organizations are always thinking about cultivating loyalty and transforming consumers into more than one-time buyers. Leaders want lifetime consumers, so they continually consider how to add value to their products and their organization's reputation with consumers and employees.

This chapter explores branding in the context of leadership. We begin with working definitions of *brand*, *branding*, *brand schema*, and *brand equity*. The chapter then briefly narrates a historical background of branding practices and why strong leadership is crucial for the successful building of

a brand's identity. Transformational leadership, creating raving fans of brands, and organizational alignment will be discussed as important leadership qualities, as will the importance of building brands from the inside out. Finally, a discussion of corporate social responsibility and its influence on brand identity and loyalty is discussed.

WHAT IS A BRAND?

A *brand* is defined as an "identifying mark, symbol, word(s), or combination of same that separates one company's product or service from another firm. . . . Brand is a comprehensive term that includes all brand names and trademarks" (Imber & Toffler, 2000, p. 68). Brands have long been thought to have appeal as marketing tools. As Mollerup (1998) notes, trademarks have existed for at least 5,000 years, establishing the distinguishing character of something, whether to confirm social identity (e.g., heraldic marks), to denote ownership (e.g., farmers marking their cattle), or to certify origin (e.g., ceramic marks). Although the literal name of a brand might be the most salient and recognizable form, other informational cues designating the origin of goods or services are also the subject matter of brands. For instance, "Patriots" as the business name of the NFL franchise in New England is just one form of the team brand. Other cues representing the team are also under the umbrella of the Patriots brand family, such as Minutemen, its throwback logos, the design of player uniform, the cheerleading squad's choreographed performance, Gillette Stadium, and even the combination of navy blue, red, and silver if used in the context of football. These various forms of the Patriots' brand individually or collectively indicate the source of the goods and services produced, sold, or endorsed by the organization (i.e., live or televised games, sponsored events or products, team apparel, memorabilia, and accessories). In fact, the primary function of all brands is signaling where goods or services are from. Smith (2009) provides a more holistic definition, noting that a brand

> is, or should be, no less than the DNA of the organization, the fundamental building block and expression of its existence. In an ideal world, the customer should be able to experience any customer process, talk to any employee, examine any product and the essence of the brand should come through. (p. 99)

The signaling function of a brand ultimately purports to distinguish its goods or services from competitors' products. After repetitive exposure to marketing messages or direct consumption experience, consumers may develop some stereotyped images of different brands associated with their products or services (e.g., "Reebok sneakers are innovative," "The Masters golf tournament is elite," "Titleist products are for serious golfers," "Nike products have wholesome images"). According to consumer psychology, such stereotyped brand images are referred as brand schemata (Gwinner & Eaton, 1999). When a consumer develops and maintains a *brand schema* that is well connected to positive psychological valences—for instance, "Under Armour is reliable, and it symbolizes a type of person I want to be"—he or she is more

likely to purchase an Under Armour product without any further information search and processing. That is, a strong brand schema would facilitate the product search and decision-making process because it likely reduces the need for a time-consuming thought process to compare and analyze all identifiable benefits and shortcomings of each available product or brand.

Branding

Branding, the managerial and leadership process behind creating and sustaining brands and perceptions about brands, was not discovered by a single scholar nor devised by a group of ingenious entrepreneurs. Ever since human civilization first developed, primitive forms of systemized manufacturing and merchandising have existed. The grotesque shape and superior quality of the Saracen scimitar swords during the Crusades symbolized the advanced smelting technology of Damascus in the 12th century and terrified European knights who faced them. The psychological effects of the swords on European soldiers were identical with the mental state that modern branding practices attempt to establish in consumer minds, that is, solid stereotypical beliefs—although modern branding practices are hoping for positive reactions to brands rather than fearful ones. Likewise, French wineries in earlier centuries also tried to guarantee the authenticity and consistent product qualities by labeling the corks and bottles with unique cachets. Although such primitive forms of branding were popular even in the pre-industrial era, they were not strategically implemented and rarely were practiced consciously. Branding was not crystalized until after mass consumer markets matured in the 19th century (Aaker, 1991). As branding practices became competitive, advanced brand management tactics were devised and employed. Eventually, the so-called *era of branding* arrived in the 20th century. Sport teams and athletes, political parties, and pop stars all consider themselves brands. As demand for sport and leisure services has increased in recent years, brands play an increasing role in a world in which consumers are becoming more difficult to please.

From an organization's perspective, branding entails the execution of coordinated marketing initiatives to establish strong brand equity in a target market that is consistent with long-term goals. Under this definition, branding is not a stand-alone business activity separated from other business functions of the organization. Rather, the entire process of branding must be aligned with the organization's long-term strategy. Thus, leaders of sport organizations must understand the process of branding in terms of relevant consumer behavior as well as the organization's future direction. They must understand not only how effective branding efforts would likely elicit positive consumer reactions and establish desirable brand images in the marketplace, but also why branding efforts must be implemented in accordance with the organization's long-term plans. Branding involves both external and internal dynamics around an organization, and these dynamics occur concurrently because both employees and consumers must be made aware of an organization's branding efforts. As for the external dimension, branding is a consumer-oriented effort to create desired brand equity in a targeted market. *Brand equity* refers to the knowledge about brands that comes to exist in and persist in consumers' minds in the forms of brand awareness and images (Keller, 1993). This created knowledge is developed through the recognition of a set of intangible assets and liabilities that may positively or negatively affect the perceived value of a given product or product line of the brand (Aaker, 1991). *Brand knowledge* in consumers' minds would be activated and influenced by their brand choice when effective marketing signals trigger the stored information. For example, Reebok attempts to build strong brand awareness and desirable brand images associated with its new product line, Zigtech, so that consumers would recognize Zigtech more easily and perceive

the brand as the one closely connected to what they want to be. Once successfully developed, a positive brand schema of Zigtech significantly affects consumers' decision-making process when they choose a pair of sneakers.

The definition of branding also indicates that various internal mechanisms and dynamics within the organization might be involved. Branding needs consistency, control, and coordination within the organization. Consumers usually develop a significant level of brand awareness and well-configured brand images only after interacting with a variety of marketing antecedents for a substantially long period of time (e.g., direct consumption experience, peer pressure related to goods consumption, after-sales services, media advertisements, word of mouth, spokespersons, and perceived characteristics of branding company). Building brand equity in the market requires consistent marketing signals disseminated by various channels for a long period of time, so carefully designed strategic and tactical plans must be formulated and systematically implemented by an organization. Branding must be conducted as coordinated efforts of different organizational units. In addition, a control system must evaluate the performance of each organizational unit and provide feedback.

For example, a football gear brand, Riddell, may want to enhance its safety-oriented brand image in response to player safety issues recently raised by many experts in the field and lawsuits. One of the company's branding initiatives might be the launching of Riddell Revolution, which adopts a newly developed concussion reduction technology. Under the branding plan, different units would need to perform various yet coordinated tasks to disseminate consistent marketing messages by using various channels of communication. The marketing unit would highlight how effectively the helmet would protect football players from multiple concussions by monitoring each impact on them. The unit would employ various communication methods such as celebrity testimonials, sponsorship, social networking, and traditional media ads. The public relations department may organize a series of community events where the product is introduced and tried. The same unit may circulate media releases in order to emphasize the innovative preventive monitoring technology.

Finally, a more holistic way to think of branding—and a line of thinking that leaders should take to heart—comes from Deming (2007). He noted that branding is the construction of a feeling around an organization's brand and all the tangible (products) and intangible (organization's core values) things that go with it. "You feel trust, loyalty, comfort, love, need, desire, and happiness for brands because of beliefs derived from very precise experiences" (p. 10). Deming notes that customers can construct strong feelings about brands through excellent customer service whereby interactions between them and employees are memorable and satisfying. Aaker and Joachimsthaler (2000) noted a loyal customer base can influence others to buy as well.

BRAND EQUITY'S PSYCHOLOGICAL VALUE

In addition to knowledge collected about a brand, brand equity can also be seen as the increased or decreased value of products or services that are attributed to the psychological properties associated with the brand. Brand equity materializes when some source identifiers of a brand (e.g., brand name, logo, catch phrase, unique features of goods or services) clearly represent the brand identity in the market. Burton snowboards might have to sell its products at significant discounts if the company is suddenly not allowed to use its brand name and logo. The brand name and logo trigger a strong value in the mind of a prospective buyer. Without the power of the iconic swoosh logo, it would have been harder for Nike to expand its business to the golf equipment industry. Keller (1993) attempted to further crystallize the sphere of brand equity by focusing on the psychological

values associated with a brand, the so-called *consumer-based brand equity*. The central idea of his framework reflects how lay consumers psychologically value the various attributes of a brand as a whole in terms of brand loyalty, brand awareness, perceived quality of products, and relevant brand associations. Therefore, Keller's brand equity (1993) refers to a set of psychological properties in consumers' minds that are likely established by the whole organizational performance encompassing past and present branding efforts. In sum, brand equity is an intangible psychological value of a brand in consumers' minds that would likely affect future performance of the branding company.

When considering psychological value, it would be instructive to consider the recent past histories of the Big Four North American professional sports leagues. The National Football League (NFL) had a difficult beginning to the 2012 football season. The league used replacement referees for the first 7 weeks of the season, including the preseason. Fans and players complained frequently about the quality of the officiating. Commissioner Roger Goodell acknowledged "you're always worried" about the perception of the league (Associated Press, 2012, para. 16). "Obviously, this has gotten a lot of attention. It hasn't been positive, and it's something that you have to fight through. . . . We always are going to have to work harder to make sure we get people's trust and confidence in us" (Associated Press, 2012, para. 17). Goodell appears to acknowledge the NFL's brand took a hit. Worse, the league, while negotiating a new contract with the regular referees, was not adding value for consumers. In addition to the replacement referees, the league has contended with issues surrounding concussions and new rules to protect players that not all fans and players were happy about.

The NFL is not alone. Other professional leagues have suffered brand damage for issues specific to their leagues. When it seemed like Major League Baseball (MLB) had gotten a grip on steroid usage, reports surfaced during 2013 about several players' connection to Biogenesis, an anti-aging clinic. MLB suspended Ryan Braun for 65 games for his alleged involvement with performance-enhancing drugs dispensed at the clinic. Although other leagues have suffered work stoppages, the National Hockey League (NHL) seems to have suffered this problem more frequently, with three such stoppages in the past two decades. The 2012–2013 campaign consisted of a 48-game season that was delayed 4 months due to an extended lockout. In the National Basketball Association (NBA), the past 10 years have seen an ugly brawl between two teams that included fans and players fighting, and an officiating scandal involving a referee accused of making in-game calls that would affect the point spread of games. In Europe, some Black players on football clubs, including AC Milan and FC Basel, have endured "monkey chants" from fans. The Union of European Football Associations (UEFA) is grappling with what to do to stem the racism. If the acts continue, it could hurt the brands of teams who do not do enough to control their fans.

Brand Loyalty and Evangelism

In the case of professional leagues, fans' loyalties are divided among the teams and not necessarily devoted to the league or governing bodies themselves. In fact, NBA Commissioner David Stern, as a representative of the league, is often roundly booed when he steps to the podium at the NBA Draft every summer. When individual teams or leagues suffer indignities that can harm their brands, fans tend to forgive and forget and continue to purchase products associated with their brands. Commissioners and other league officials, however, seem to bear the brunt of bad league publicity because they act as enforcers. *Brand loyalty* is defined as a "degree to which a consumer repeatedly purchases a brand" (Imber & Toffler, 2000, p. 70). The repeated purchases here are influenced by various factors such as attitude toward brand, peer pressure, and interpersonal relationship with salespersons (Imber & Toffler, 2000). Attitude toward brand is a critical element for the purpose of branding because it is a learned predisposition (Kiesler, Collins, & Miller, 1969) that might not change easily. Once a consumer develops a positive or negative attitude toward a brand based on some marketing antecedents (e.g., satisfactory or dissatisfactory consumption experience, advertisement, or celebrity endorsement) it will be invariant for a long time, sometimes for the entire lifespan of the person.

Petty and Cacioppo (1981) discuss the formation of this consistent trait, explaining that an attitude is an enduring affective state that is established because of a long-term interrelationship between a person and an object. If a person's affective responses toward an object become relatively continuous and stable, the resulting configuration of the pattern is understood as an attitude. An attitude is differentiated from a momentary feeling or an emotional status quo in terms of its relative continuity. For instance, a consumer who has developed a positive attitude toward Adidas would likely be a loyal consumer making repeated purchases for a substantial period of time. Brand leaders ultimately want products to become a meaningful part of a customer's life or self-concept (Aaker & Joachimsthaler, 2000) so that they will become evangelists for the brand. Deming (2007) describes *brand evangelists* as raving fans of brands and "the brand is now part of their belief system because of the unique interpersonal experiences they have with that brand" (p. 11). Sport brands lend themselves to these unique interpersonal experiences because of the genuine and personal connections we form with teams and athletes we root for (e.g., "We won," rather than "The Red Sox won") and the sport apparel we wear to make ourselves better athletes or, at least, look the part.

To distinguish between brand loyalty and evangelism, brand loyalty entails our personal satisfaction with a brand and the likelihood we will buy repeatedly; evangelism occurs when we let everyone else know about our personal satisfaction and recommend that others adopt our purchasing behavior. Evangelism is loyalty taken to a new level.

BRAND LEADERSHIP

Research shows leaders decisively influence the overall performance of their organizations (Aronson, Reilly, & Lynn, 2008), and achieving loyalty to brands is a key performance indicator. Given the complexity of tasks involved with branding, a systematically designed management structure with an efficient coordination system is necessary. Aaker and Joachimsthaler's (2000) model of brand leadership in **Table 15.1** serves

as a contemporary paradigm that views brand building as more of a leadership function than a management concern. The model consists of three areas that show this evolution: (1) an emphasis on strategic, rather than tactical, management; (2) organizations should move from a limited to a broad strategic focus; and (3) brand identity—not just sales and revenue—should be a driver of strategy. Starting with a focus on more strategic thinking, the title *brand manager* has been given much higher status in an organization and can often be a chief executive officer (CEO). This brand manager assumes control of brand strategy, making sure it aligns with the organization's vision. Furthermore, the brand manager focuses on building brand equities (long term) rather than simply building brand image (Aaker & Joachimsthaler, 2000).

TABLE 15.1 Brand Leadership: The Evolving Paradigm

	The Classic Brand Management Model	The Brand Leadership Model
From Tactical to Strategic Management		
Perspective	Tactical and reactive	Strategic and visionary
Brand manager status	Less experienced, shorter time horizon	Higher in the organization, longer time horizon
Conceptual model	Brand image	Brand equity
Focus	Short-term financials	Brand equity measures
From a Limited to a Broad Focus		
Product-market scope	Single products and markets	Multiple products and markets
Brand structures	Simple	Complex brand architecture
Number of brands	Focus on single brands	Category focus—multiple brands
Country scope	Single country	Global perspective
Brand manager's communication role	Coordinator of limited option	Team leader of multiple communication options
Communication focus	External/customer	Internal as well as external
From Sales to Brand Identity as a Driver of Strategy		
Driver of strategy	Sales and shares	Brand identity

Source: Data from Aaker, D. A., & Joachimsthaler, E. (2000). *Brand leadership* (p. 8). New York: The Free Press.

For instance, the brand manager of a baseball team might recommend to the team's community relations director that she make consistent efforts every season to partner with community organizations for player appearances and group sales discounts, rather than making these efforts sporadically. Inconsistent efforts may build brand image for a short time, but it will not build brand loyalty for the long haul.

The second rung of the Aaker and Joachimsthaler's (2000) brand leadership ladder—from a limited to a broad focus—concerns the growing complexity of multiple products, many brands, multiple communication efforts, and a global perspective. Nike lends itself as an example that has grown from a limited focus (only producing track running shoes) to a company with multiple products (golf clubs, jerseys, shorts, cricket shoes, skateboard shoes, shoes for many other outdoor activities, an iPod companion that measures running or walking pace, sport watches, and, of course, other apparel besides shoes). Given the number of products Nike has in its brand portfolio, the company can target several consumer markets, from serious athletes to athletes who play popular sports, athletes who participate in niche sports, and regular people looking to improve their athletic fitness. The Nike brand will be perceived differently by these markets. "Life is a sport, make it count" is a brand message that might appeal to serious athletes; "I'm what's next" might appeal to a youth market. Nike has gone from "Just do it," to multiple brand messages. Nike's brand building has a global perspective because the firm wants to manage its products across multiple markets in multiple countries. Finally, Nike's brand leaders have used an assortment of communication strategies, including sponsorships, athlete endorsers, social media, publicity, promotions, and transformational leadership of employees within the organization.

The final perspective in Aaker and Joachimsthaler's (2000) brand leadership ladder is a focus on brand identity as a driver of strategy, rather than simply analyzing sales numbers. *Brand identity*, the researchers say, is the cornerstone of brand strategy. When you think of Nike, what words come to mind? Phil Knight? Oregon? High performance? Air Jordan? Mia Hamm? Sweatshops? "I Can"? "Just do it"? A strong brand should have a set of associations the brand strategist seeks to create or maintain (Aaker & Joachimsthaler, 2000). A brand with a strong identity is clear about what the brand represents; those involved with the brand—whether they are consumers, athlete endorsers, or employees—should know what the brand embodies. It is a leader's job to oversee the process that makes this brand identity clear for stakeholders.

Qualities of Brand Leaders

The research on leadership qualities needed in organizations that place a premium on brand management prominently mentions three areas that leaders should consider: transformational leading, the understanding that memorable relationships forged with customers drive brand loyalty, and the importance of creating alignment between internal and external stakeholders.

Transformational leadership was mentioned earlier in the discussion of Aaker and Joachimsthaler's (2000) brand leadership model with regard to it being instrumental in internal communication. Transformational leaders involved in brand-building activities constantly communicate brand values by presenting a promising vision of ideal service and recognizing employees' needs via coaching and support to subsequently reach customers' expected outcomes (Herold, Feder, Caldwell, & Liu, 2008; Liao & Chuang, 2004. To foster an organizational brand climate, transformational leaders hope organizational members will share transformational leaders' behavioral patterns, which could influence employee climate perceptions and ultimately the overall service environment (Hackman, 1992; Herold et al., 2008; Liao & Chuang, 2004 Schneider, 1983). Transformational leaders motivate followers to achieve an organization's desired results through critical thinking, intellectual stimulation, individualized consideration, inspirational motivation, and charismatic style (Asree, Zain, & Razalli, 2010; Scott-Halsell, Shumate, & Blum, 2008).

Although followers are benefiting from transformational experiences, leaders must also consider the experiences of customers. Deming (2007) points out the importance of creating relationships with customers by delivering unique experiences. Typical service exchanges between customers and employees meet the customer's standard expectation and should be the bane of any organization hoping to build brand loyalty. If you have just purchased a new pair of running shoes and the sole begins to rip after your first week of using them, you will not be happy. You will likely take them back to the store and complain. You might get an apology and an offer to replace the shoes. However, this is not likely to make you feel any better about the store or the brand given that the shoes did not work out in the first place. But, if the sales representative apologizes sincerely, takes the time to ask questions about how the shoe ripped, replaces the pair, and then gives you a $100 gift certificate for a future purchase, this interaction rises to the level of what Deming might term a unique experience. By asking questions about the shoe and showing concern for the previous poor experience, the sales representative is tapping into a customer's "sweet spot" (Aaker & Joachimsthaler, 2000). Delivering a unique experience enables employees to learn from individual customers in face-to-face interactions, which can be even more valuable than learning about customer groups through marketing research done remotely on a computer.

Branding is an ongoing interaction and negotiation of values among the internally held identity, the identity-defining brand, and the identity as perceived by the stakeholders (Urde, 1994). The core values and promises bridge the internal and external sides of the corporate brand, thus ensuring identity congruence. The desired image of the organization can be communicated conventionally through an integrated communication mix (Christensen, Firat, & Torp, 2008). In whatever ways the image is communicated, there needs to be a well-orchestrated and aligned strategy among all stakeholders. Alignment is the ability to have multiple stakeholders in agreement about vision, strategies, business practices, and resources in building a brand. Furthermore, alignment is having customers and employees agree on what the identity of a brand is. Leaders must monitor the alignment between departments and key stakeholders in an organization. A new general manager for a minor league baseball team may see the need to bring more families to the ballpark. Before this rebranding effort can take place, all departments—ticketing, sponsorships, marketing—must understand that a family-friendly ball team is the branding goal. The team will try to acquire family-friendly sponsors, families will be targeted by marketers when the team is promoted in the months before the season, and the box office will consider reduced ticket rates for young children. Sometimes, alignment does not happen. The Women's United Soccer Association (WUSA), which operated from 2000 to 2003, folded after losing $100 million. Lack of alignment about the league's identity might have been one of the culprits. O'Connor McDonogh (2011) learned through interviews with WUSA leaders that they felt one of the reasons the league failed was because there were conflicting brand messages sent out to key external stakeholders because internal stakeholders were not sure of the league's identity:

> It seemed to many of the WUSA leaders interviewed indicated the league could not decide if it was a professional sport organization or if it was a goodwill or philanthropic organization promoting women's

team sports. Both players and team leaders spoke of moving between both identities as they sold sponsorships, reached out to various fan bases, and made pleas to local and national media outlets for increased promotion and recognition. (O'Connor McDonogh, 2011, p. 161)

WUSA leaders noted there was an internal struggle about the league's brand identity. Was the league to serve as a role model for young girls or was it to provide the best women's soccer in the world? "Without a clear, cohesive message being sent internally, the league could, in turn, not send a clear message externally" (O'Connor McDonogh, 2011, p. 162).

The Women's United Soccer Association (WUSA) operated from 2000 to 2003 and folded after losing $100 million.
© Grant Halverson/AP Images

Internal Brand Building

Internal brand building, the process of aligning staff's behavior with a brand's identity, reduces the gap between the desired brand identity and that perceived by the company's stakeholders (see, e.g., Balmer & Soenen, 1999; Harris & de Chernatony, 2001; Urde, 1994). Before leaders can communicate to customers the attributes of a brand, communication must take place internally with employees and managers. Not sharing brand expectations with employees before launching an advertising campaign can lead to overpromising and underdelivering if employees are not prepared (Smith, 2009).

In reality, the brand/employee fit process begins when prospective employees walk through the door for an interview. Vallaster and de Chernatony (2005) noted that this interviewing perspective—of finding the best fit—is not necessarily formalized but is done intuitively. A general manager (GM) of a snowboard firm noted that although the firm's brand values were not written down, it seemed well understood that the company was looking for individuals active in sport. Thus, the GM contended, brand image seems to "preselect" potential staff (i.e., a strong brand triggers identification and commitment with the company) (Vallaster & de Chernatony, 2005). Given the importance of selecting the right individuals in the screening process, human resources managers also need to be aligned with an organization's brand identity (see, e.g., Blumenthal, 2004; Schultz, 2003), given their position on the front lines of hiring. Apart from customers, the main external stakeholders are prospective organizational members. A strong and well-known brand facilitates recruitment, thus potentially having impact not only on sales and market share, but also on securing key resources—in particular for organizations competing for a highly qualified workforce (Karreman & Rylander, 2008).

Ultimately, organizations hope employees will become "citizens" of the brand so they can also serve as evangelists (Deming, 2007). Burmann and Zeplin (2005) consider brand-citizenship behavior as resulting from a strong, emotionally characterized desire to fulfill the corporate brand's promise. For this to occur there must be a moral and emotional bond between the organization and employees that goes beyond a "normal" relationship. Employees need to have a particular feeling of belonging to an organization. Such identification is strongly related to internalization. Through internalization, employees incorporate the core values of a brand into their own value system (Burmann & Zeplin, 2005) and therefore are "more likely to work toward the success of the organization, because in doing so they are behaving in a manner consistent with their own values" (Meyer & Allen, 1991, p. 76). Employees develop an inner conviction that the corporate brand's promise is important and adds value to the consumers (de Chernatony & Segal-Horn, 2001; Thomson, de Chernatony, Arganbright, & Khan, 1999).

Once new employees begin work, they must be exposed to "brand training that will emotionally engage managers and employees and equip them with the knowledge, attitude, and skills to deliver the brand promise" (Smith, 2009, p. 110). Professional development seems to be managed more in line with the defined brand values. In a sports shoe–producing company, for example, employees visited the production process as part of their training to see the cumbersome process it takes to produce even a single shoe. Training and workshops were considered useful tools to enhance employees' understanding of the brand identity. Such two-way communication encourages the audience to participate, which facilitates the development of intuitively lived brand-committed behavior (Ballantyne, 2003; Harris & de Chernatony, 2001; Tosti & Stotz, 2001).

CORPORATE SOCIAL RESPONSIBILITY

Organizational philosophy as well as the characteristics of a company as perceived by employees and consumers in various public relations activities affect the organization's brand image. So if an organization is considered a good citizen in the marketplace by consumers, this can affect perceptions of its brand. In relation to the role of public relations in marketing initiatives, what the primary role of private business entities is in society has been controversial. Conservative economist Milton Friedman (1970) argued that profit maximization to serve shareholder interests is probably the only social obligation imposed on private companies. Thus, other obligations not legally mandated or directly related to shareholder interests would be unfair as well as detrimental to society in general (Friedman, 1970). But this thinking is outdated. Other scholars claim companies must take on more *corporate social responsibility (CSR)* because companies operate their business for the sake of all stakeholders, rather than exclusively for the shareholders with direct financial interests (Babiak & Wolfe, 2006). Scholars also agree firms should be expected to advance corporate behavior "to a level where it is congruent with the prevailing social norms, values, and expectations of performance" (Sethi, 1975, p. 62). In addition to honoring their legal and economic duties, firms need to meet ethical and discretionary responsibilities to society, such as environmental excellence or the well-being of employees and people in general (Carroll, 1979). Based on the work of Kotler (1997), a CSR brand is defined as being a stakeholder-based, strategically integrated orientation toward ecological and social well-being; at the heart of CSR brands lies a socially responsible dimension intended to differentiate a firm's products or services from those of competitors. Patagonia is a leading outdoor clothing and gear firm with a brand strongly positioned on CSR. Its mission to "build the best product, do the least harm, use business to inspire and implement solutions to the environmental crisis" (Patagonia, n.d., para. 1) runs through all of Patagonia's organizational aspects and brand relationships (Maignan, Hillebrand, & McAlister, 2002; York, 2009).

Companies involved with more community-related activities likely perform better than others

(Carroll & Shabana, 2010), presumably because they can establish positive attitudes toward their brands in the competitive market environment partly driven by contemporary consumers who are much more concerned and informed on community issues than their grandparents were. Various CSR initiatives have been implemented by professional sport leagues (e.g., NFL Play 60, PGA First Tee program, NHL Hockey Fights Cancer, NBA Cares). Such CSR activities intend to establish positive brand images while helping communities near where the industry operates. Barcelona FC affected perceptions about its brand when the soccer club formed a partnership in 2006 with UNICEF and pledged $10 million over 5 years to help fight human immunodeficiency virus (HIV) and acquired immune deficiency syndrome (AIDS) in Africa and Latin America. In addition to the funding, the club featured the UNICEF logo on its jerseys, the first sponsorship placement in the club's 107-year history (UNICEF, 2006).

Branding research points out potential benefits arising from CSR, primarily through the link to consumers' and other stakeholders' positive product evaluations or the brand evaluations, choices, and recommendations that derive from an association with specific CSR initiatives (Klein & Dawar, 2004; Sen & Bhattacharya, 2001; Sen, Bhattacharya, & Korschun 2006). Thus, linking CSR to a brand can be fundamental for the development of the brand's values and personality (Kitchin, 2003; McElhaney, 2008).

For leaders, positioning brands (corporate or product) according to CSR typically entails a "significant strategic shift in the way the organization thinks about itself and its activities, including communications with [a wider range of] internal and external stakeholders" (Polonsky & Jevons, 2006, p. 346). In a global context, stakeholders from different cultures and geographical areas demand strategic consideration if the organization hopes to develop a socially responsible business orientation (Carroll, 2004) and brand image.

Research suggests CSR brand leadership, aimed at building assets that will result in long-term profitability (Aaker & Joachimsthaler, 2000), must be supported by and inextricably linked with action; there must be "a long-term commitment to CSR activities, which must be supported at the senior management level, taking into consideration the issues that are salient to the brands' stakeholders. . . ." (Polonsky & Jevons, 2006, p. 342). In that perspective, prior research also suggests that firms should follow specific managerial approaches to connect CSR efforts to a brand strategy: knowing themselves, finding a good CSR–brand strategy fit, being consistent, simplifying, working from the inside out, knowing customers, and telling a good story (McElhaney, 2008).

SUMMARY

This chapter was intended to give the upper-level sport management student an introduction to brands, branding, and the leadership issues revolving around brand building. Given the growing emphasis on service in the sport industry, it is imperative that future sport leaders understand the importance of excellent customer service and how such service can lead to brand loyalty. The creation of brand loyalty can lead to the creation of brand evangelists who can tout brands for organizations. Word of mouth, after all, is still a powerful marketing tool.

Another important takeaway from this chapter is the contemporary leadership paradigm with regard to organizations and brand leadership. To build brand loyalty, leaders must think strategically and with a broad focus. Visionary thinking is a must for leaders. Organizations cannot only get caught up in quarterly sales and revenues. The building of brand identity and loyalty has to be a consistent discussion among an organization's key internal stakeholders. This discussion needs to take place before any of the employees can deliver the kind of customer service that will enable a customer to walk away with the same perceptions of a brand that the employees and leaders have.

Finally, the chapter closed with a discussion of corporate social responsibility. More organizations are engaging in CSR, and this shows the shift organizations have had in thinking strategically about their brands. Research indicates that these organizations are viewed more favorably. Consistent CSR efforts are needed to build brand loyalty, but organizations need to select the correct CSR initiatives for the organization.

LEADERSHIP PERSPECTIVE

Kirsten Suto Seckler is Vice President of Branding and Communications for Special Olympics.

Kirsten Suto Seckler.
Courtesy of Kirsten Suto Seckler

Q: Special Olympics has a strong brand that is recognized globally. Can you describe how leadership within the Special Olympics has supported the development of the brand?

Special Olympics has a strong brand in the United States, with a 95% favorability rating. We are continuing to improve our brand recognition outside of the United States. As our organization has evolved we have experienced rapid growth in the last 13 years. In 2000, we served 1 million athletes in 150 countries, with 75% of our work occurring inside the United States. Special Olympics today serves over 4 million athletes in nearly 180 countries. We are a sport organization, but we also are providing health, education, and community building, and 75% of our work now takes place outside of the United States.

As a result of this growth we sought to conduct work on brand alignment. We conducted this work with input from our Special Olympics athlete leaders, family leaders, and all relevant stakeholders. We synthesized this work across the organization. As a global nonprofit organization, our mission and our brand lives and breathes at the local level. When conducting our brand realignment we knew that we needed all voices to be contributing to this realignment and that all voices were aligned with our brand.

We conducted our brand realignment in four stages. We wanted to be sure our brand was reflecting our evolution as an organization.

The first stage was discovery. We spent a significant amount of time in this stage carefully examining how our brand is being represented at all levels of the organization. We conducted this work through multiple focus groups, surveys, and in-depth discussions. We concluded this stage at our 2011 World Games where we could speak with many constituents from nearly everywhere in the world.

The second stage was definition. We gathered all information from the discovery phase to synthesize and define our brand. We developed a solid brand model based on our guiding idea, personality, and the benefits provided by our organization. We also wanted to be sure that all of the work we did in developing our brand had a home within our organization and this was defined through a brand architecture.

The third stage was the development stage. During this stage we developed our brand guidelines, tools, and resources that will be available to everyone in the organization, from our volunteers at the local level all the way up to those working within the Special Olympics organization.

We are now in the on-going stage, the fourth stage, which is brand management. This is where we conduct message training and storytelling regarding the brand. In addition, we will market our brand in such a way that we can build understanding throughout the world.

Q: What skills are required of leaders to help facilitate a strong brand?

Leaders must be both storytellers and story doers. Leaders need to understand the brand inside and out. It is important for leaders to get out in the field and have a deep understanding of the organization's constituent groups and how those groups connect with your brand. Leaders must also not only speak to the brand, they must live the brand. Being authentic is such an important part of facilitating a strong brand. When leaders are really living the brand, that is much more powerful than merely speaking to the brand.

Q: How does leadership influence the maintenance of a brand in the sport industry?

Leadership influences the maintenance of the brand by being sure that all stakeholders in the organization are staying on message. Leaders influence maintenance of the brand by representing the brand in a way that is growing the brand.

Leaders must be authentic to the brand and to the brand promise. Again, authenticity is so important, especially in the sport industry. Leaders must consider their constituent groups (including fans) and recognize that fans are authentic and will know when leaders are not being authentic to the brand.

Q: Has Special Olympics developed a unique branding strategy that is perhaps different from other branding strategies for organizations in the sport industry? How does leadership within Special Olympics help facilitate this strategy?

Our organization is unique in how we developed our branding strategy as we adopted a brand democracy. We are a sport organization that is also a nonprofit, making us a different entity than most sports brands. As a nonprofit sport organization we had to take a different approach. We don't have the resources to police our brand, but we do have a network of passionate supporters who act as our brand ambassadors. To help support this network of brand ambassadors we created tools to support the brand. We empowered our ambassadors to use our tools and resources to support our brand. We created an open brand website that contains tools/templates with our brand information. We want our coaches and volunteers to be able to use these brand tools, so we made a lot of materials available as Word documents. This open brand website allows our brand ambassadors to use these tools and also helps us to maintain brand consistency. This strategy is very different than how most sport organizations would manage their brand strategies. However, because of the type of organization that we are, and how we are structured, serving nearly 180 different countries, we must do things in a different way from other sport organizations.

Q: Do you have recommendations for best practices in supporting a strong brand in the sport industry?

One best practice I have observed is, again, being authentic to your brand. Knowing your fans and demonstrating authenticity to the brand resonates with your fans.

Another way to demonstrate authenticity is to be philanthropic in the community. Leaders can show that their organizations are not there merely to collect money from the community, but that their organizations also want to contribute money and do "good" within the community. It is important for sport organizations to embrace their communities and care about their communities.

KEY TERMS

brand

brand equity

brand evangelist

brand identity

branding

brand knowledge

brand loyalty

brand manager

brand schema

consumer-based brand equity

corporate social responsibility (CSR)

DISCUSSION QUESTIONS

1. What sport brands are you most loyal to? Pick at least two. What arguments would you make to friends to get them to try these particular brands?
2. What activities seem most important for leaders to engage in when building a brand?
3. Suppose you are the general manager for a Single-A, short season, minor league baseball team that is moving from Oneonta, New York, to Norwich, Connecticut. (This actually happened by the way.) If you had a year before the new season started, what steps would you take to build the brand internally and externally?
4. The National Football League has embarked on a new initiative, NFL Evolution (www .nflevolution.com). Why would the leadership within the NFL want to engage in this initiative as a potential way to enhance and/or change the brand of the NFL?
5. Why are transformational leaders such a good fit for organizations that care intimately about building brands?

For a full suite of assignments and additional learning activities, use the access code found in the front of your book. If you do not have an access code, you can obtain one at **www.jblearning.com**.

REFERENCES

Aaker, D. A. (1991). *Managing brand equity: Capitalizing on the value of a brand name.* New York: The Free Press.

Aaker, D. A., & Joachimsthaler, E. (2000). *Brand leadership.* New York: The Free Press.

Aronson, Z. H., Reilly, R. R., & Lynn, G. S. (2008). The role of leader personality in new product development success: An examination of teams developing radical and incremental innovations. *International Journal of Technology Management, 44*(1), 5–27.

Asree, S., Zain, M., & Razalli, M. R. (2010). Influence of leadership competency and organizational culture on responsiveness and performance of firms. *International Journal of Contemporary Hospitality Management, 22*(4), 500–516.

Associated Press. (2012, September 27). Roger Goodell apologizes to fans. Retrieved from http://espn.go.com /nfl/story/_/id/8431573/roger-goodell-apologizes-fans-replacement-refs

Babiak, K., & Wolfe, R. (2006). More than just a game? Corporate social responsibility and Super Bowl XL. *Sport Marketing Quarterly, 15*(4), 214–222.

Ballantyne, D. (2003). A relationship-mediated theory of internal marketing. *European Journal of Marketing, 37*(9), 1242–1260.

Balmer, J. M. T., & Soenen, G. B. (1999). The acid test of corporate identity management. *Journal of Marketing Management, 15,* 69–92.

Blumenthal, D. (2004). For the end of brand balderdash— And the beginning of a real future. *Journal of Brand Management, 11*(3), 177–179.

Burmann, C., & Zeplin, S. (2005). Building brand commitment: A behavioral approach to internal brand building. *Journal of Brand Management, 12*(4), 279–300.

Carne, L. (2012, July 22). Olympic "brand police" score own goal. Retrieved from http://www.couriermail.com.au /sport/olympic-brand-police-score-own-goal/story-fncvmu49-1226431864720

Carroll, A. B. (1979). A three-dimensional conceptual model of corporate performance. *Academy of Management Review, 4*(4), 497–505.

Carroll, A. B. (2004). Managing ethically with global stakeholders: A present and future challenge. *Academy of Management Executive, 18*(2), 114–120.

Carroll, A. B., & Shabana, K. M. (2010). The business case for corporate social responsibility: A review of concepts, research and practice. *International Journal of Management Reviews, 12(1)*, 85–105.

Christensen, L. T., Firat, A. F., & Torp, S. (2008). The organisation of integrated communications: Toward flexible integration. *European Journal of Marketing, 42*, 423–452.

de Chernatony, L., & Segal-Horn, S. (2001). Building on services characteristics to develop successful services brands. *Journal of Marketing Management, 17*(7/8), 645–669.

de Coubertin, P. (1895). *Olympism: Selected writings* (Vol. II). Lausanne, Switzerland: International Olympic Committee.

Deming, S. (2007). *The brand who cried "wolf": Deliver on your company's promise and create customers for life.* Hoboken, NJ: John Wiley & Sons.

Friedman, M. (1970, September 13). The social responsibility of business is to increase its profits. *The New York Times*, pp. 122–126.

Gwinner, K. P., & Eaton, J. (1999). Building brand image through event sponsorship: The role of image transfer. *Journal of Advertising, 28*(4), 47–57.

Hackman, J. R. (1992). Group influences on individuals in organizations. In M. D. Dunnette & L. M. Hough (Eds.), *Handbook of industrial organizational psychology* (Vol. 3, pp. 99–267). Palo Alto, CA: Consulting Psychologists Press.

Harris, F., & de Chernatony, L. (2001). Corporate branding and corporate brand performance. *European Journal of Marketing, 35*(3/4), 441–456.

Herold, D. M., Fedor, D. B., Caldwell, S., & Liu, Y. (2008). The effects of transformational and change leadership on employees' commitment to a change: A multilevel study. *Journal of Applied Psychology, 93*(2), 346–357.

Imber, J., & Toffler, B. (2000). *Dictionary of marketing terms.* Hauppauge, NY: Barron's Educational Series.

Karreman, D., & Rylander, A. (2008). Managing meaning through branding—The case of a consulting firm. *Organization Studies, 29*(1), 103–125.

Keller, K. L. (1993). Conceptualizing, measuring, and managing customer-based brand equity. *Journal of Marketing, 57*(1), 1–22.

Kennedy, P. (2012, June 11). Who made the Olympic rings? Retrieved from http://www.nytimes.com/2012/07/15 /magazine/who-made-the-olympic-rings.html

Kiesler, C., Collins, B., & Miller, N. (1969). *Attitude change.* Hoboken, NJ: Wiley & Sons.

Kitchin, T. (2003). Corporate responsibility: A brand extension. *Journal of Brand Management, 10*(4/5), 312–326.

Klein, J., & Dawar, N. (2004). Corporate social responsibility and consumers' attributions and brand evaluations in a product-harm crisis. *International Journal of Research in Marketing, 21*(3), 203–221.

Kotler, P. (1997). *Marketing management* (7th ed.). Upper Saddle River, NJ: Prentice Hall.

Kovalyova, A. (2013, June 21). Russian censors target Olympic-themed art ahead of Sochi 2014. Retrieved from http://worldnews.nbcnews.com /_news/2013/06/21/19058345-russian-censors-target-olympic-themed-art-ahead-of-sochi-2014?lite

Liao, H., & Chuang, A. C. (2004). A multilevel investigation of factors influencing employee service performance and customer outcome. *Academy of Management Journal, 47*(1), 41–58.

Maignan, I., Hillebrand, B., & McAlister, D. (2002). Managing socially responsible buying: How to integrate non-economic criteria into the purchasing process. *European Management Journal, 20*(6), 641–648.

McElhaney, K. (2008). *Just good business: The strategic guide to aligning corporate responsibility and brand.* San Francisco, CA: Berret-Koehler.

Meyer, J. P., & Allen, N. J. (1991). A three-component conceptualization of organizational commitment. *Human Resource Management Review, 1*(1), 61–89.

Mollerup, P. (1998). *Marks of excellence: The history and taxonomy of trademarks.* London, UK: Phaidon Press.

O'Connor McDonogh, M. (2011). *The case of the Women's United Soccer Association: Explaining the rise and fall of a social movement organization* (unpublished doctoral dissertation). University of Louisville, Louisville, KY.

Olson, P. (2012, July 19). The army and "brand police" swoop on London Olympics. Retrieved from http://www.forbes.com/sites/parmyolson/2012/07/19/the-army-and-brand-police-swoop-on-london-olympics

Olympic Movement. (2013). The Olympic brand maintains its global strength and recognition. Retrieved from http://www.olympic.org/news/the-olympic-brand-maintains-its-global-strength-and-recognition/190770

Patagonia (n.d.). Our reason for being. Retrieved from http://www.patagonia.com/us/patagonia.go?assetid=2047

Petty, R. E., & Cacioppo, J. T. (1981). *Attitudes and persuasion: Classic and contemporary approaches*. Dubuque, IA: William C. Brown.

Polonsky, M., & Jevons, C. (2006). Understanding issue complexity when building a socially responsible brand. *European Business Review, 18*(5), 340–349.

Sauer, A. (2002). Ambush marketing: Steals the show. Retrieved from http://www.brandchannel.com/features_effect.asp?pf_id=98

Schneider, B. (1983). Interactional psychology and organizational behavior. In L. L. Cummings & B. M. Staw (Eds.), *Research in organizational behavior* (pp. 1–31). Greenwich, CT: JAI Press.

Schultz, D. E. (2003). So you want to be a branding guru? *Marketing Management, 12*(2), 8–9.

Scott-Halsell, S., Shumate, S. R., & Blum, S. (2008). Using a model of emotional intelligence domains to indicate transformational leaders in the hospitality industry. *Journal of Human Resources in Hospitality and Tourism, 7*(1), 99–113.

Segal, D. (2012, June 24). Brand police are on the prowl for ambush marketers at London Games. Retrieved from http://www.nytimes.com/2012/07/25/sports/olympics/2012-london-games-brand-police-on-prowl-for-nike-and-other-ambush-marketers.html?pagewanted=all&_r=0

Sen, S., & Bhattacharya, C. B. (2001). Does doing good always lead to doing better? Consumer reactions to corporate social responsibility. *Journal of Marketing Research, 38*(2), 225–243.

Sen, S., Bhattacharya, C. B., & Korschun, D. (2006). The role of corporate social responsibility in strengthening multiple stakeholder relationships: A field experiment. *Journal of the Academy of Marketing Science, 34*(2), 158–166.

Sethi, S. P. (1975). Dimensions of corporate social performance: An analytical framework. *California Management Review, 17*(3), 58–64.

Smith, S. (2009). Brand experience. In R. Clifton (Ed.), *Brands and branding* (pp. 96–111). New York: Bloomberg Press.

Thomson, K., de Chernatony, L., Arganbright, L., & Khan, S. (1999). The buy-in benchmark: How staff understanding and commitment impact brand and business performance. *Journal of Marketing Management, 8*(15), 819–835.

Tosti, D. T., & Stotz, R. D. (2001). Brand: Building your brand from the inside out. *Marketing Management, 10*(2), 28–33.

UNICEF. (2006, September). Sport for development: Football club Barcelona. Retrieved from http://www.unicef.org/sports/index_40934.html

Urde, M. (1994). Brand orientation—A strategy for survival. *Journal of Consumer Marketing, 11*, 18–32.

Vallaster, C., & de Chernatony, L. (2005). Internationalisation of services brands: The role of leadership during the internal brand building process. *Journal of Marketing Management, 21*(1/2), 181–203.

York, J. G. (2009). Pragmatic sustainability: Translating environmental ethics into competitive advantage. *Journal of Business Ethics, 85*(1), 97–109.

CHAPTER 16

Leading Athletes with Disabilities

Mary A. Hums
Eli Wolff
David Legg

CHAPTER OBJECTIVES

- Demonstrate an understanding of the history of the development of disability sport.
- Understand the influence of leaders making key contributions to disability sport.
- Recognize and highlight current issues facing leaders in disability sport.
- Describe the necessary skill set for leaders in disability sport.

CASE STUDY

Special Olympics Unified Sports

Special Olympics Unified Sports is a component of Special Olympics that partners an equal number of individuals with and without intellectual disabilities on teams for sport training and competition (Special Olympics, 2012). Special Olympics Unified Sports is recognized globally as an iconic program promoting social inclusion that focuses on integrating Special Olympics athletes and athlete partners of similar ages and abilities on the field of play. The objectives of Unified Sports are to promote social engagement and development for both Special Olympics athletes and athlete partners. When playing sports together, as teammates or coparticipants, athletes are recognized alongside partners as contributors and are received with acceptance and respect on the field of play. Through this program, Special Olympics athletes develop a sense of belonging, interact meaningfully with others, and forge lasting and mutually rewarding relationships. Unified Sports

(continues)

incites changes in attitudes and aids in community building through coparticipatory experiences between individuals with and without intellectual disabilities while broadening the relevance and impact of the Special Olympics movement.

There has been an abundance of research to demonstrate the benefits of Special Olympics Unified Sports programs, including enhanced social inclusion for athletes (friendships, improved social networks) (Dowling, McConkey, Hassan, & Menke, 2009), improved physical fitness (Wilski, Nadolska, Dowling, McConkey, & Hassan, 2012), skill development (Castagno, 2001), and improved self-efficacy (Dowling et al., 2009). Despite the research and noted benefits associated with participation in Unified Sports programs, as of 2012 only 60% of Special Olympics programs were currently offering some type of Unified Sports programming.

Michael Mudrick and Raymond Cotrufo, graduate students at the University of Connecticut, carried out a project for the Special Olympics to help develop an operations manual to support implementation of Unified Sports programs in the United States and internationally. While developing this manual, they uncovered several challenges regarding why only 60% of Special Olympics programs were providing Unified Sports programming. In their discussion with leaders of Special Olympics programs there were three issues that appeared to represent the most significant perceived challenges to implementing Unified Sports. The first challenge that many leaders discussed was the lack of financial resources available to support Unified Sports. Many leaders described having limited financial resources to support current Special Olympics programming and therefore felt they did not have the resources necessary to expand programming into Unified Sports. Included in this concern was the perception that using what are already limited financial resources on programming that benefits non–Special Olympics athletes was counter to their goals as leaders of Special Olympic programs. A second concern, also reflective of issues regarding funding, was that even if funding were provided through the federal government, through programs like Project Unify (www.specialolympics.org/Sections/What_We_Do/Project_Unify/Project_Unify.aspx), that money could be lost at a future time, leaving the program unfunded but already established.

One of the most challenging concerns raised by leaders of Special Olympics programs was the loss of a special, exclusive space for Special Olympics athletes to compete with their fellow Special Olympians. For many parents, especially those with older (adult) children, including non–Special Olympic athlete partners is concerning. There is a concern that there could be a potential of limiting access to Special Olympics programming for Special Olympics athletes, because there would be more partner athletes (non–Special Olympics athletes) participating in Special Olympics programming through Unified Sports. Included in that is a perception that resources will be shifted from Special Olympics athletes to support Unified Sports programming. Resources (including travel funding and coaching) and participation opportunities are offered to Special Olympics athletes and partner athletes within the Unified Sports program model. Leaders do not want to take away opportunities or resources from Special Olympics athletes.

As Mike and Ray continued their work, discussions with other leaders within the Special Olympics community revealed a changing attitude among parents of younger Special Olympics athletes. These leaders reported that parents of the younger generations of athletes were interested in more inclusive opportunities for their sons and daughters. Many of these younger athletes are attending inclusive schools and have lived their lives in more inclusive environments. Having the opportunity to engage in sports with athlete partners is appealing to both the Special Olympics athletes and their parents. Furthermore, many leaders also described the importance of inclusion as a potential area of growth for the Special Olympics movement. They cited the increased exposure Special Olympics receives when athlete partners become involved in Unified Sports. This exposure leads to more volunteer participants in other Special Olympics events, increased engagement by schools and community groups, and increased funding and sponsorship by athlete partners and businesses.

Questions for Discussion

1. If you were recently hired as chief executive officer of a Special Olympics organization that did not have a Unified Sports program, based on the information included in the case study, would you make the decision to start Unified Sports? Provide support for your answer.

2. When deciding upon implementation of a Unified Sports program, one of the concerns leaders voiced centered around the issue of funding. How would you try to address this issue while attempting not to compromise funding for your existing Special Olympics programs?

3. How would you address a parent's concern regarding the potential for decreased opportunities for Special Olympics athletes?

4. What suggestions would you make to help other leaders of Special Olympics programs implement Unified Sports programs? What support would leaders need from the national and international leaders of the Special Olympics?

INTRODUCTION

When people talk about diversity in sport, most often the dialogue revolves around race and gender. Only recently has disability found a voice at the table. Now, with the rapid growth of the *Paralympic Games* and the recent ratification of the United Nations Convention on the Rights of Persons with Disabilities, people with disabilities in sport are beginning to be recognized and valued. This chapter will provide a brief history of the development of disability sport, including information about some leaders in disability sport. Then it will discuss several timely and sometimes controversial issues facing people in leadership positions in sport for people with disabilities.

Disability sport refers to sport that is competed in or participated in specifically by people with disabilities. Examples of major events in disability sport include the Summer and Winter Paralympic Games, the *Deaflympics*, and *Special Olympics*. But disability sport is not limited to events such as these; it also encompasses grassroots-level activities such as adaptive physical education, participation by people with disabilities in community or recreational sport, and physical activity for children with disabilities. This chapter, however, will focus mainly on major events such as the Paralympic Games, present information about some leaders in disability sport, and highlight current issues these leaders face.

HISTORY OF THE PARALYMPIC GAMES

This section recounts some of the historical steps along the way in the founding of the Paralympic Games. Following World War II, Sir Ludwig Guttmann at Stoke Mandeville Hospital in England established what we now refer to as the Stoke Mandeville Games, which ultimately morphed into the Paralympic Games. In the aftermath of World War II, the hospital served scores of disabled veterans. Guttmann believed strongly in the positive impact of sport in making people "whole" again. Yes, the people at the hospital needed physical and occupational therapy, but they were mainly young, physically active people, and sport and physical activity were important to them. The first competition in 1948 involved 16 men and women who competed in archery. Interestingly, today we see sport used in the rehabilitation of injured war veterans in programs such as the Warrior Games and Wounded Warrior Project. Following the slow and deliberate growth of the Stoke Mandeville Games in the 1950s, Sir Ludwig contacted the International Olympic Committee (IOC) with hopes of organizing the Stoke Games in Rome to coincide with the IOC's hosting of the 1960 Summer Olympic Games. The IOC leadership agreed, and wheelchair events were held for 400 athletes from 23 countries. These events are now viewed as the founding Paralympic Games. At these Games, Pope John XXIII declared Guttmann ". . . the de Coubertin [the founder of the modern Olympic Games] of the paralyzed" (Steadward & Foster, 2003).

Summer Paralympic Games followed in Tokyo coinciding with the Olympic Games. In 1968, the Paralympic Games were held in Tel Aviv while the Olympic Games were held in Mexico City. In the 1970s, both Games were held in the same countries—Munich (Olympic) and Heidelberg (Paralympic), Germany, in 1972 and Montreal (Olympic) and Toronto (Paralympic), Canada, in 1976. In 1980, Olympic Games were held in Moscow while Paralympic Games were hosted in Arnhem, the Netherlands. A small profit was garnered at these Games, which allowed the creation of a secretariat to help manage the burgeoning movement and Games (Steadward & Foster, 2003).

In 1981, four international sport organizations representing athletes with spinal injuries, cerebral palsy, amputations, and visual impairments determined there was a need to coordinate Games and thus, in 1982, they created the International Coordinating Committee Sports for the Disabled (ICC). This came about, in part, because of IOC President Juan Antonio Samaranch's request to correspond and collaborate with only one umbrella organization as opposed to the four mentioned already along with Deaf Sport and the Special Olympics (Robert Steadward, personal communication, 2012). In 1983, the new group met in Lausanne, Switzerland, where it was reaffirmed that there needed to be one voice. In fall 1984, Dr. Robert Steadward, a university professor leading the growth of disability sport in Canada, circulated a proposal worldwide recommending a new organizational structure and democratically elected governance and asked that other nations and disability sport organizations consider submitting alternative proposals. The ICC secretariat helped plan and organize an event in March 1987 where representatives could debate and discuss these various proposals. Here, disability sport leaders spent a day presenting a variety of proposals in 15- to 20-minute sessions. The following 2 days were spent sifting through the various ideas. From these 23 resolutions, the following stood out as most essential (Steadward & Foster, 2003):

- Change the structure of the existing organization.
- Include national representation as well as regional and athlete representation.
- Reduce the number of classifications.

- Implement a functional classification system.
- Develop a structure by sport and not by disability.
- Work toward integration with the International Olympic Committee and other international sport federations.

It is also important to note that two demonstration status events had been staged in the Olympic Games for athletes with a disability in 1984. At the Winter Olympic Games in Sarajevo alpine events had been held, and in Los Angeles during the Summer Games, events for wheelchair athletes on the track had been held. The demonstration events for the Winter Games were last contested in 1988 in Calgary; the wheelchair track events continued until 2008 in Beijing (Legg, Fay, Hums, & Wolff, 2009).

The IOC was hesitant to upgrade the events from demonstration status to full medal status, a request that was submitted every Games until a decision was made to finally cancel the demonstration status events in 2008. During this time, Steadward and Samaranch agreed that the Olympic Games were perhaps getting too large and the IOC members were not prepared to consider further integration of the two Games. What they did agree to, however, was that all bidding cities for Olympic Games also had to bid for Paralympic Games (Robert Steadward, personal communication, 2012).

In Seoul, the practice of hosting the Paralympic Games after the Olympic Games using many of the same facilities was initiated. It was not until 2000 that an official agreement was reached between the International Olympic Committee and the International Paralympic Committee (created in 1989) in which a bidding city had to agree to host both Games. Beijing then was the first Summer Games that required a bid city to host both. Winter Games began in 1976 with a similar pattern, with Games being held in the same city starting in 1992 at Albertville, France.

Since 1988, the Olympic Games and Paralympic Games merged perhaps organically. Most, but not all, host cities typically had one host organizing committee that organized both Games. Other subtle changes also took place, such as in Vancouver 2010 where "Paralympic" was included in the official name of the host organizing committee, a joint marketing agreement with the host National Paralympic Committee was created, and a member from the National Paralympic Committee was named to the organizing committee's board of directors (Coward & Legg, 2011). Other new initiatives in Vancouver that were echoed by London in 2012 included creating a separate countdown clock for the Paralympic Games, and flying the Olympic and Paralympic flags side by side. For the London 2012 Games, the logos for the Olympic and Paralympic Games were essentially the same, with the only difference being the five rings and the three *agitos*. The agitos (Latin for "I move") for the Paralympic Games are three asymmetrical crests used to symbolize movement. As of 2012, the Paralympic Games include 21 sports for the summer games and 5 sports for the winter games (see **Table 16.1**). As noted earlier, this cooperation will continue for the near future because the IOC and IPC have signed a cooperation agreement until 2020 ensuring the Paralympic Games will be held in the same city as the Olympic Games. This agreement extends the practice of "one bid, one city" to the PyeongChang 2018 Winter Games and the Tokyo 2020 Summer Games.

INFLUENTIAL LEADERS IN DISABILITY SPORT

It is important to highlight people who are leaders in the arena of disability sport. The odds are that most of you may not be aware of these names because they are not necessarily names we read about in traditional sport management textbooks.

TABLE 16.1 Sports of the Summer and Winter Paralympic Games

Summer	Winter
Archery	IPC alpine skiing
IPC athletics	Biathlon
Boccia	Cross-country skiing
Canoe	IPC ice sledge hockey
Cycling	Wheelchair curling
Equestrian	
Football (five a side)	
Football (seven a side)	
Goalball	
IPC wheelchair dance sport	
Judo	
IPC powerlifting	
Rowing	
Sailing	
IPC shooting	
Sitting volleyball	
IPC swimming	
Table tennis	
Triathlon	
Wheelchair basketball	
Wheelchair fencing	
Wheelchair rugby	
Wheelchair tennis	

Source: The International Paralympic Committee, www.paralympic.org

They are not nearly as visible in the media as leaders in the Olympic movement. This section mentions some of the men and women who have helped move disability sport forward.

Robert Steadward served as founding president of the International Paralympic Committee (IPC), holding the office from 1981 to 2001. A Canadian, Dr. Steadward led the IPC through a series of organizational transitions and was pivotal in its growth as a major international multisport governing body. These transitions included the coming together of different disability groups to form a common umbrella organization; the founding of the *International Paralympic Committee*; the securing of a site for the IPC Headquarters in Bonn, Germany; and ongoing negotiations with international sponsors and the International Olympic Committee leading to the agreement whereby host cities would bid for both Games. The IPC grew to over 175 members during his term (Canadian Paralympic Committee, n.d.). He also served on the IOC's Commission on Ethics and Reform. He is a recipient of both the Olympic Order and the Paralympic Order in honor of his lifetime contributions to these organizations.

Sir Phil Craven, current president of the IPC, represented Great Britain in wheelchair basketball in five consecutive Paralympic Games. He became the president of the IPC in 2001, following Steadward to become just the second person to hold that office (Dugan, 2012). He is also a member of the IOC and a board member of the London Organising Committee of the Olympic and Paralympic Games (LOCOG). Sir Craven was bestowed his title MBE (Member of the Most Excellent Order of the British Empire) in 2001 in honor of his service to wheelchair basketball, and he was knighted in 2005 for his service to Paralympic sport. During his tenure, the Paralympic Movement has grown to over 200 members, and the worldwide coverage of the Summer Paralympic Games has expanded, with close to 4 billion people watching the London 2012 Games (Davies, 2012).

London Paralympic Games.
© Sebastian Widmann/AP Images

Ann Cody is currently the Director of Policy and Global Outreach for BlazeSports America, an organization devoted to promoting sport and physical activity for children with disabilities. Cody is a recognized leader in the fields of disability sport and human rights and was pivotal in the development of the IPC's Committee on Women (Sportanddev, n.d.). She serves on the IPC Governing Board and is the highest-ranking U.S. citizen and highest-ranking woman in the IPC worldwide. She is also a Paralympic Gold Medalist in Athletics and competed on three U.S. Paralympic teams (Basketball, 1984; Athletics 1988, 1992) (BlazeSports, 2012). The "Leadership Perspective" feature for this chapter includes Cody's thoughts about disability sport.

Baroness Tanni Grey-Thompson represented Great Britain in five Paralympic Games in the sport of Athletics, winning 11 gold medals along the way (Tanni, n.d.b). Although her success on the track is unprecedented, her contributions beyond the field of competition are equally valuable. A director of UK Athletics, she is also a member of Transport for London and a tireless international advocate for the rights of people with disabilities. In 2010, she took the title Baroness Grey-Thompson of Eaglescliffe in the County of Durham (Tanni, n.d.a).

Although the leaders mentioned all have direct ties to the Paralympic movement, others have made contributions to disability sport in other ways. Kirk Bauer has been in the service of Disabled Sport USA since 1982, over half of those years as executive director. An amputee from an injury in the Vietnam War, he was awarded a Bronze Star and a Purple Heart during his time in the service. Perhaps first among Bauer's many accomplishments and contributions was the 2003 establishment of the Wounded Warrior Disabled Sport Program. This program offers instruction in over 20 sports for wounded servicemen and servicewomen in the U.S. military (Disabled Sports USA, 2011). A number of veterans who have gone through the program have represented the United States in the 2008 Beijing, 2010 Vancouver, and 2012 London Paralympic Games.

Another organization active in providing opportunities for people with disabilities to practice sport is the Special Olympics. The Shriver family is behind the Special Olympics, although it should be noted that the Shrivers first noticed the work done by Frank Hayden, a Canadian who had identified fitness gaps between people with disabilities and those without disabilities (Department of Kinesiology and Community Health, n.d.). In the 1960s, Eunice Kennedy Shriver saw how unfairly people with intellectual disabilities were treated and decided to do something about it (Special Olympics, n.d.b). What started as a summer camp program rapidly grew, and with the support of the Shriver family, Special Olympics was born and gained momentum. The first Special Olympics World Summer Games were held in Chicago in 1968 and the first Special Olympics World Winter Games followed in 1977 in Steamboat Springs. The 2011 Summer Games, which took place in Athens, Greece, drew over 7,000 participants from 170 countries. Special Olympics continues to be a global advocate for people with disabilities. Today, Special Olympics touches the lives of more than 3.5 million people with disabilities in 170 countries (Special Olympics, n.d.b).

Although the most recognizable disability sport organizations are the International Paralympic Committee and Special Olympics, we would be remiss in not mentioning the world of Deaf Sport, whose showcase event is the Deaflympics. The international governing body for Deaf Sport is the Comité International des Sports des Sourds, CISS (International Committee of Sports for the Deaf,

ICSD). The ICSD was the first international sport organization founded for people with disabilities. It was the brainchild of Eugène Rubens-Alcais of France and Antoine Dresse of Belgium, who saw the need for competition for the deaf (Ammons, 1990). The first Deaflympics, then called The Silent Games, were held in Paris in 1924, and the first Winter Deaflympics followed in 1949 in Seefeld, Austria. Today, the ICSD membership includes 104 national deaf sport federations (International Committee of Sports for the Deaf, 2012). Deaf athletes also compete at different levels, including intercollegiate sport in the United States. Gallaudet University, the world's only university specifically designed to meet the needs of deaf and hearing-impaired students, offers a 15-sport program (Gallaudet University, 2012).

All of the people described in this chapter, and many more whose names are not mentioned here, are leaders in disability sport. Their vision and dedication created opportunities for people with disabilities around the world to be active. But it was not without struggles and challenges. Many of the challenges these leaders faced remain even today. The next section of this chapter highlights some of the issues people working in the management of disability sport face today.

CURRENT ISSUES FACING SPORT LEADERS WORKING IN DISABILITY SPORT

Just as in any segment of the sport industry, sport managers in disability sport face numerous challenges. If these managers want to truly be leaders, they will need to step up and respond to these challenges using a global view for solutions. Some of these issues will challenge sport managers to exhibit good leadership skills, particularly including (1) being proactive vs. reactive, (2) showing flexibility, (3) being resourceful, (4) being open to change, and (5) taking initiative (Holden

Leadership Center, 2009). Although some of the following issues are unique to disability sport, others tie directly to other segments of the sport industry.

Technology

Although technology impacts many aspects of sport, from lighter racing bicycles to new materials in running shoes to swimsuits with less drag, one could argue that the industry segment where technology has had the greatest impact is in disability sport. World records continue to be shattered at the Paralympic Games in events such as downhill skiing and track and field, often as the result of newer and increasingly high-tech equipment. Improved racing chairs, mono-skis, and competition-level prosthetics are being developed on a regular basis.

The person who brought the issue of technology to the forefront was double below-the-knee amputee sprinter Oscar Pistorius, who represented South Africa at the 2012 London Olympic Games. The first amputee to compete in the Olympic Games, Pistorius raced in both the 400-meter individual race and the 4×100-meter relay team. His participation raised the discussion about whether his prosthetic legs gave him an advantage over the other competitors. In an interesting twist, during the 2012 Paralympic Games, when Pistorius was beaten at the tape by Brazilian sprinter Alan Fonteles Oliveira, Pistorius claimed his opponent had an advantage because of the length of his carbon fiber blades (Brown, 2012).

Rapidly changing technology also raises a larger question facing sport managers across the industry, particularly those working for sport governing bodies. Whenever a type of technology/equipment is devised that can be used by athletes, not just by athletes with disabilities, three questions need to be addressed:

1. Is the technology/equipment safe?
2. Is the technology/equipment affordable?
3. Is use of the technology/equipment fair?

For example, someone could design a baseball outfielder's glove with a chip in it that could somehow track the speed and flight pattern of a fly ball. The glove would likely cost upwards of $500. Let's say a state high school athletics association was approached about allowing this glove to be used in school competition. In addressing the questions listed, one could likely argue that the glove is safe for the user and his or her teammates. However, with the price tag involved, it is certainly not affordable for general use. For example, students in more affluent high schools might be able to afford to purchase the glove, whereas those from poorer school districts would not. This leads to the third question. Given the advantage in tracking the fly balls people using the gloves would have, is it fair to sanction it for competition? The premise of these three questions can also be applied in the case of Pistorius. After consideration by the Court of Arbitration for Sport (CAS), sport managers had to be flexible in deciding how to best facilitate Pistorius's participation as he pursued his goals.

One other question arises here: Why is it that in sport, when people with disabilities become more gifted or talented than able-bodied people, there is an uproar? In other areas such as education or the arts, successful people with disabilities are celebrated rather than questioned. Take the case of Adrian Anantawan. Born without a right hand, an adaptive device allowed him to become a renowned professional violinist. "He is now enrolled in the Harvard Graduate School of Education Arts in Education Program, with the goal of helping other disabled students in their artistic and creative development" (Harvard Gazette, 2012, para. 1). According to the founder of Gimp, the dance group for people with disabilities, "The goal is to honor each person's really specific ways of moving, really specific, unique personalities" (Kilgannon, 2009, para. 6). Yet in sport, we find resistance, as Pistorius did when wanting to compete in the Olympic Games or when wheelchair racer Tatyana McFadden wanted to compete on the same track at the same time as able-bodied high school runners. Perhaps there is something about the nature of sport, and those who organize it, that lends itself to this unique phenomenon.

Media Coverage

Media coverage of disability sport, in particular the Paralympic Games, is lacking. Media coverage of the Paralympic Games has evolved over time. Schantz and Gilbert (2001) concluded the quality and quantity of the print media coverage of the 1992 Atlanta Summer Paralympic Games was of a low standard. Since the 1992 Games there has been a sharp increase in the number of accredited media covering the Games (Brittain, 2010), but the coverage is not uniform around the world. Coverage of the 2012 London Games was quite competitive in Great Britain. The Beijing Paralympic Games in 2008 brought in a record number of viewers. In the United States, NBC has never broadcast the Paralympic Games live. IPC President Sir Philip Craven was quoted saying he was "very disappointed" there would only be 5.5 hours of Paralympics coverage (not live) broadcast in the United States, where NBC owns the rights to broadcast the Olympic Games (Associated Press, 2012b).

The 2012 London Paralympic Games delivered the largest television audience of any Paralympic Games (Mackay, 2012). This is not the case in the United States, however, where events received minimal coverage and were not broadcast live on network television. NBC chose not to be the rights holder for the Paralympic Games in the United States (Associated Press, 2012a). This angered some fans, particularly given that a number of the U.S. athletes are military veterans, and they see these Wounded Warriors as national heroes (DeWind, 2012). International viewers tuned in; the British Broadcasting Corporation (BBC) estimated the peak number of viewers for the Paralympic Games Opening Ceremonies at

11.2 million (BBC, 2012). The London Organizing Committee for the Olympic Games announced it had 90 global broadcasters, which would bring in $16 million. Comparatively, NBC paid $4.38 billion for its rights for the Summer and Winter Olympic Games through 2020. In Britain, Channel 4 planned to show 150 hours of the games, and 350 hours more online (Associated Press, 2012a).

In London, Channel 4 was given the rights to cover the Paralympic Games, marking the first time that the contract for the Olympic and Paralympic Games was split. This allowed Channel 4 to put together a unique and extensive advertising campaign in the run-up to the Games. Channel 4 scheduled 400 hours of coverage, built up profiles of British Paralympic athletes, and highlighted disability transport problems in London. Social media became a prominent presence at the Paralympic Games with organizations such as Channel 4, Around the Rings, and the IPC, as well as numerous athletes such as the United States' Josh George who also blogged for the *New York Times*, tweeting about the Paralympic experience. The London Paralympic Games were an online success; there were close to 9 million views of videos featuring London 2012 sporting action or ceremonies uploaded to www.youtube.com/paralympicsporttv, a 130% growth of IPC's official Facebook group, and four-figure growth of athlete Facebook fan pages (IPC, 2012). Rachael Latham, an ex-Paralympian and current broadcaster, explained that Channel 4 also made social media a large part of Paralympic Games coverage (Stewart-Robinson, 2012). Sport managers here showed great resourcefulness in utilizing the most up-to-date methods of communicating information about the Paralympic Games.

Many countries were not able to watch any of the Paralympic Games live on local television, so the IPC established an Internet-based broadcasting system called ParalympicSport TV, which provided full coverage of the games (British Library Board, n.d.). The video was available at the IPC website and featured three channels in English and one in Spanish. In addition, a new technology feature called Smart Player allowed viewers to call up different sports, on-screen statistics and results, and other information. Twitter played an active role as well, as numerous athletes, National Paralympic Committees, and media outlets tweeted events as they happened and offered their opinions and experiences for their followers to share. To recognize those in the media who have covered the Paralympic Games in an extraordinary fashion, the IPC has established its Paralympic Media Awards. There are four categories: broadcast, written (print and online), photo, and radio. Recent award winners include Sky Sport New Zealand and also the *Vancouver Sun* newspaper with coverage by writer Gary Kingston, whom the CPC nominated for the award (IPC, n.d.).

Sponsorship

People around the world can name at least a few of the International Olympic committee's worldwide partners—the corporations who are part of the TOP (The Olympic Partners) program. These companies include global brands such as McDonald's, Visa, and Coca-Cola. But what about corporate sponsorship of the Paralympic Games?

The IPC currently has four Worldwide Partners—Visa, Atos, Samsung, and Otto Bock—and one International Partner—Allianz. A number of companies, such as Proctor and Gamble, Coca-Cola, and McDonald's, not only have sponsored the Olympic Games, but also have extended their sponsorship to the Paralympic Games. Some companies, such as J Sainsbury, a U.K. supermarket chain, have been able to negotiate Paralympic Games–only sponsorship deals, flying a bit under the strict IOC guidelines related to Olympic sponsorship (Gillis, 2011). Both the IPC and its sponsors have shown great initiative in pursuing new deals and innovative ways to provide sponsorship support for the Paralympic Games.

The London 2012 Paralympic Games saw its sponsorship go a little more mainstream

(Arthur, 2012). Some corporations linked the Olympic and Paralympic Games and sponsored both. In a *Wall Street Journal* article, Gillis (2011, para. 3) stated, "Today, endorsement opportunities for elite disabled athletes like (Great Britain's) Baroness Grey-Thompson are no longer solely a matter of altruism. For reasons ranging from growing crowds to greater exposure, the Paralympic Games has turned into a fully fledged marketing opportunity."

When discussing sponsorship in disability sport, the discussion cannot be limited to the Paralympic Games. Another major force in the disability sport arena is Special Olympics. A visit to the Special Olympics International website indicates 31 sponsors, including well-known companies such as Hilton, ESPN, Coca-Cola, and Wal-Mart (Special Olympics, n.d.a). Here in the United States, Special Olympics has been named the nation's Most Credible Charity, and polls indicate people would be likely to purchase products from companies that sponsor Special Olympics (Special Olympics Kentucky, 2012).

Inclusion

The issue of *inclusion* has been a hot topic in disability sport. There are various definitions, interpretations, and perspectives about the inclusion of people with disabilities in sports. For example, Nixon (2007, p. 417) defines inclusion as, "the final stage of integration of people with disabilities in a sport competition or organization, in which they are involved, accepted, and respected at all levels of the competition or organization."

The authors of this chapter have focused their work over the years on looking at inclusion frameworks and models for individuals with disabilities in the sporting environment. The authors have also investigated inclusion from comparative, historical, social justice, and human rights perspectives to examine disability in sport in context with opportunities for women in sport and race and ethnic minorities in sport. This section discusses the inclusion model sport managers can use called the "Criteria for Inclusion," and will also present the framework of universal design and its application to the realm of disability sport. The authors will then discuss inclusion within the Olympic and Paralympic movements, and finally examine inclusion from the perspective of Article 30.5 in the United Nations Convention on the Rights of Persons with Disabilities, which outlines the right to sport for all persons with disabilities.

CRITERIA FOR INCLUSION

One strategy for examining inclusion is to be able to establish an assessment of sport organizations to see how well sport managers provide service and deliver opportunities to individuals with disabilities. The Criteria for Inclusion (Wolff, Hums, & Fay, 2000) provide a framework to be able to research and study all areas and aspects of a sport organization to determine where there is progress toward inclusion and where invisibility and exclusion are still evident. The Criteria for Inclusion outlines nine areas of assessment to consider for a full evaluation of a sport organization (Hums, Moorman, & Wolff, 2009; Wolff et al., 2000). Each area and examples for each area are included here:

1. Funding/sponsorship (budget distribution to athletes with disabilities in the organization, sponsorship money designated to people with disabilities)
2. Media/information distribution (use of images of athletes with disabilities, advertising events for people with disabilities)
3. Awards/recognition (awards such as ESPN's ESPY for Best Male and Best Female Athlete with a Disability)
4. Governance (people with disabilities in governance structure of the organization)
5. Philosophy (disability mentioned in mission statement)
6. Awareness/education (educating organizational members about disability)

7. Events/programs (including athletes with disabilities in events, such as racers using wheelchairs in a marathon)
8. Advocacy (taking an active role in promoting sport for people with disabilities)
9. Management (employing people with disabilities as sport managers)

UNIVERSAL DESIGN

In the United States, we are used to seeing how the Americans with Disabilities Act has opened up physical access to buildings, including sport facilities. Our neighbors to the north in Canada do not have a similar federal act, and only Ontario, the largest province, has a specific piece of legislation. The Accessibility for Ontarians with Disabilities Act hopes to improve accessibility standards to all public establishments by 2025. But the "bricks and mortar" of a building are only part of the way leaders can think about making sport facilities truly accessible for all. The term *universal design* was coined by the architect Ronald L. Mace to describe the concept of designing all products and the built environment to be aesthetic and usable to the greatest extent possible by everyone, regardless of their age, ability, or status in life (Human Centered Design, n.d.). Universal design has not been extensively applied to the realm of disability sport, but we believe that the assessment elements of universal design, similar to the criteria for inclusion, offer a useful framework to consider inclusion in sport at the present as well as possibilities for the future. The Institute for Human Centered Design (2012), an international nonprofit based in Boston, Massachusetts, articulates the five dimensions for examining universal design as follows:

1. Built environment (indoors and outdoors)
2. Information environment (print materials, way-finding/navigation and signs)
3. Communication environment (telephone, web, and multimedia)

4. Policy environment (evidence of policies that impact equality of experience)
5. Attitudinal environment (staff or administrative behavior or beliefs)

According to Wolff, Hums, and Fay (2012, p. 2):

> Through a review of sports organizations from the perspective of Universal Design, it is possible to gather information and data to be able to provide an in-depth review and assessment. The Universal Design review process allows "user-expert" consumers to be able to identify the gaps, barriers, and challenges as well as the strengths and models of success. The assessment is a way to further articulate and define inclusion in concrete terms and to be able to help others understand what is and what is not working smoothly.

Using universal design allows sport managers to be ahead of the game in providing access for all people. When they do so, they take the role of leaders by being proactive in promoting inclusion in the sport industry through quality customer service and policy development.

THE RIGHTS OF PERSONS WITH DISABILITIES

From 2003 to 2006, the United Nations, governments, and civil society drafted the United Nations Convention on the Rights of Persons with Disabilities (CRPD). The CRPD is a legally binding document that articulates and defines the rights that people with disabilities have in all aspects of life, including in sport and recreation. The authors of this chapter contributed to the drafting process, serving as the coordinators and facilitators for drafting Article 30.5. This article, or section of the Convention, specifically addresses the right to sport, recreation, leisure, and play for individuals with disabilities. Through the process, the International Disability in Sport Working

Group (IDSWG) was formed by international disability sport and disability rights organizations. These groups then worked together to finalize the text for Article 30.5, which offered a shared view on the significant elements defining inclusion and the right to sport for all persons with disabilities (IDSWG, 2007).

Significantly, Article 30.5 articulates inclusion in mainstream and disability-specific settings, representing the view that individuals with disabilities should be able to have access to and reach their potential in all sporting settings and environments. Furthermore, Article 30.5 specifically addresses venues, services, and also activities in the schools. Along the lines of universal design, Article 30.5 sets out an ideal standard for what inclusion can and should look like in sport, recreation, and play for people with disabilities around the world. Access to sport does not only happen on the playing fields, but also takes place in all aspects of the sporting culture, such that we are working toward building an inclusive sporting environment.

The text of Article 30.5 states (United Nations, n.d., p. 23):

> 5. With a view to enabling persons with disabilities to participate on an equal basis with others in recreational, leisure, and sporting activities, States Parties shall take appropriate measures:
>
> (a) To encourage and promote the participation, to the fullest extent possible, of persons with disabilities in mainstream sporting activities at all levels;
>
> (b) To ensure that persons with disabilities have an opportunity to organize, develop and participate in disability-specific sporting and recreational activities and, to this end, encourage the provision, on an equal basis with others, of appropriate instruction, training, and resources;
>
> (c) To ensure that persons with disabilities have access to sporting, recreational, and tourism venues;

(d) To ensure that children with disabilities have equal access with other children to participation in play, recreation and leisure, and sporting activities, including those activities in the school system;

(e) To ensure that persons with disabilities have access to services from those involved in the organization of recreational, tourism, leisure, and sporting activities.

SUMMARY

As evidenced by this chapter, disability sport is alive and growing. Millions of spectators, viewers, and participants make this a vibrant segment of the sport industry. Sport is something that makes all of us more fully human, and sport, recreation, and play are essential for fully realizing the promise of human rights (Hubbard, 2007).

Sport managers working in disability sport need to put into action some basic leadership skills, including (1) being proactive vs. reactive, (2) showing flexibility, (3) being resourceful, (4) being open to change, and (5) taking initiative (Holden Leadership Center, 2009). Using these skills to address specific issues will help move disability sport forward as a strong segment of the sport industry.

Why is it important for future sport managers and leaders in the sport industry to have an understanding of sport for people with disabilities within the sport? Well, that same question was asked "back in the day" when women and African Americans wanted access to sport, wasn't it? Just as women and racial/ethnic minorities have become a force in the sport industry, so, too, we see the same happening with disability sport. In years to come, you will look back on reading this chapter and realize that reading this put you "ahead of the game."

LEADERSHIP PERSPECTIVE

Ann Cody.
Courtesy of Ann Cody

Ann Cody is the Director of Policy and Global Outreach for BlazeSports America, an organization whose mission is to provide all children and adults who have physical disabilities the chance to play sports and live healthy, active lives. In her role, Cody develops relationships with major national and international partners, shapes the organization's policy efforts, and supports the organization's sport development initiatives overseas. She is a Paralympic gold medalist in Athletics and competed on three U.S. Paralympic Teams (Basketball, 1984; Athletics, 1988, 1992).

Q: What can leaders in disabled sport do to help generate more media interest in and subsequent public interest in sports involving athletes with disabilities?

I believe one critical piece is developing viable broadcast rights holders for the Paralympic Games in the U.S. market. Millions and millions of people enjoy broadcast television coverage of the Paralympic Games in more than 100 countries and territories. U.S. coverage of the Paralympic Games has been sparse because the Paralympic property has not been developed enough to generate advertising revenue for broadcasters—until now. The 2012 Paralympic Games in London set new broadcasting records reaching 39.9 million people in the United Kingdom alone. That is over 69% of the U.K. population. Like most people, I've been frustrated with the lack of television coverage we've had here in the United States, especially the Games coverage for London. The United States looks to countries like Australia, Germany, and the United Kingdom to understand how they built interest in Paralympic broadcasting. The U.S. Olympic Committee (USOC) is diligently working to ensure there is high-quality broadcast coverage for future Paralympic Games. Given the USOC's commitment to secure rights holders, I'm confident we will emerge with a better situation in the future. Social media platforms just exploded during and leading up to the 2012 Paralympic Games. The International Paralympic Committee's (IPC's) Facebook following increased by 350% and there were 82.1 million views of its pages. Twitter followers grew by 50%. Paralympic organizations and athletes took to social media in the absence of more traditional media coverage. This medium enabled us to reach and attract new and younger followers. The stories of Paralympic athletes also resonate with young people.

Q: Discuss the influence of technology on participation for athletes with disabilities because technology to improve performance seems to be a prevalent topic these days.

As a wheelchair racer, technology is an important part of my sport, and the rules of the sport dictate the specifications for building racing wheelchairs. The diameter and number of wheels, length of the racing chair, and prohibition of components used solely for aerodynamic purposes define what equipment is allowed to be used in competition. Each sport utilizes equipment of a specific nature, and Paralympic athletes modify or adapt the equipment to their unique needs. Every sport on the Olympic program also relies on technology to one degree or another, whether its sports equipment or the way sports are measured. The International Paralympic Committee has a policy on sports equipment that recognizes that human performance must be the driving factor in sport performance, not the equipment. Additionally, the policy dictates that sports in the Paralympic Movement have a responsibility to support the development of universally available high-standard sports equipment. With this in mind, sport federations for wheelchair basketball, wheelchair tennis, and wheelchair racing have been working with developers of adapted equipment, such as Motivation (www.motivation.org.uk), a nonprofit organization in the United Kingdom, to design lightweight sport wheelchairs at a reduced cost. This helps ensure that high-performance sports equipment is available to athletes in emerging countries.

Q: One of the questions posed by the authors of this chapter is: "Why is it that in sport, when people with disabilities become more gifted or talented than able-bodied people, there is an uproar?" How would you answer this question?

We see this at every level of sport. There is a perception that people with disabilities cannot be better athletes than nondisabled people. This myth is perpetuated by a lack of awareness and information. The reasonable accommodations and/or adapted sports equipment we use tend to raise suspicions, and it magnifies what makes us different. Educating people about athletes with disabilities, the equipment we use, and the rules modifications that are sometimes necessary will help mitigate these long-held misconceptions.

Q: How can the disability sport movement *continue* to be a movement? What does *full integration* mean to you? What would that look like?

Full integration is a process. We see it occurring at various stages here in the United States and abroad. For example, the U.S. Olympic Committee (USOC) is responsible for preparing and sending athletes and teams to the Paralympic Games. A number of USOC athlete services and programs support both Paralympic and Olympic hopefuls. These hopefuls live and train alongside each other at Olympic and Paralympic training centers. Several national governing bodies, such as the U.S. Tennis Association, have responsibility for developing athletes with disabilities as well as athletes without disabilities. We may also see sports like wheelchair basketball open their rosters to people without disabilities, creating reverse integration. This practice is used in some leagues today. At the local level, it makes sense to integrate athletes with disabilities into their local club or high school sport whenever possible. We see this occurring in sports like swimming, track and field, tennis, and wrestling where athletes are categorized by age, gender, and weight. Integration of athletes in these sports and programs will occur over time and where practical. Athletes with disabilities may require some specialized instruction in sport-specific movements such as how to push a racing wheelchair or run with a prosthetic blade. This expertise is becoming more accessible to local athletes and coaches thanks to technology and the Internet. Organizations like BlazeSports and U.S. Paralympics provide training and education for coaches and recreation professionals to promote access and opportunities.

Q: What are the most significant challenges facing leaders in disability sport as we look to the future?

We must build a sports infrastructure that supports and develops athletes at both ends of the spectrum if we hope to regain our status as a leading sports nation. This requires us to make sport for people with disabilities a priority, which entails eliminating barriers to full participation and investing resources in athlete and sport development. On the global front, we must aid emerging countries in developing sport for persons with disabilities. At the 2012 Paralympic Games in London, 46 nations entered only one athlete in the competition, and women athletes made up just 35% of the total number of athletes. Addressing these disparities must continue to be a focus of our leaders. As the prominence of disability sport increases we should anticipate that new challenges will arise. Endorsements from sponsors, financial rewards for performance, and greater media exposure will be welcome resources to disability sport. We are well-served to recognize the challenges and responsibilities these resources will bring our sports and athletes.

KEY TERMS

Deaflympics
disability sport
inclusion
International Paralympic Committee

Paralympic Games
Special Olympics
universal design

DISCUSSION QUESTIONS

1. Several major challenges for leaders in disability sport were discussed in this chapter. Consider one of those challenges and discuss how you would address that challenge if you were working within disability sport.
2. Media coverage of disability sport is lacking in the United States when compared to other countries. As a leader in this field, how would you try to generate greater media interest in disability sport?
3. Consider the Criteria for Inclusion as outlined by Wolff, Hums, and Fay (2000). How would a director of a city Parks and Recreation Department adopt those criteria within the sports program supported by the department? Discuss at least three of the nine Criteria for Inclusion in your answer.
4. Research the concept of universal design and how it has been applied to sports facilities. Discuss how a sport facility, using universal design principles, can improve access for athletes with disabilities. Use examples from actual sports facilities to support your answer.
5. As we witness more athletes with disabilities competing with athletes without disabilities, some will question the influence of technology on fostering participation of those athletes with disabilities. As a leader within the sports industry, how would you address this question?

For a full suite of assignments and additional learning activities, use the access code found in the front of your book. If you do not have an access code, you can obtain one at **www.jblearning.com**.

References

Ammons, D. (1990). Unique identity of the World Games for the Deaf. *Palaestra, 6*(2), 40–43.

Arthur, D. (2012, August 28). Brand power: Why sponsoring Paralympians allows everyone to strike gold. Retrieved from http://theconversation.edu.au/brand-power-why-sponsoring-paralympians-allows-everyone-to-strike-gold-7549

Associated Press. (2012a, August 23). Full TV coverage for Paralympics, just not in US. Retrieved from http://sports.espn.go.com/espn/wire?section=oly&id=8295913

Associated Press. (2012b, August 27). Paralympics to be broadcast in more than 100 countries after the new deals following Olympics. Retrieved from http://summergames.ap.org/article/more-100-countries-broadcast-paralympics

BlazeSports. (2012). Ann Cody among 40 women honored for impact during 40 years of Title IX. Retrieved from http://www.blazesports.org/2012/05/ann-cody-among-40-women-honored-for-impact-during-40-years-of-title-ix

British Broadcasting Corporation. (2012). Paralympics opening ceremony attracts 11 million. Retrieved from http://www.bbc.co.uk/news/entertainment-arts-19408222

British Library Board. (n.d.). The media and the Paralympics. Retrieved from http://www.bl.uk/sportandsociety/exploresocsci/sportsoc/media/articles/paramedia.html

Brittain, I. (2010). *The Paralympic Games explained*. London, UK: Routledge.

Brown, O. (2012, September 2). Oscar Pistorius stunned as he is beaten into second place by Brazilian Alan Oliveira in T43/44 200m. Retrieved from http://www.telegraph.co.uk/sport/olympics/paralympic-sport/9516463/Oscar-Pistorius-stunned-as-he-is-beaten-into-second-place-by-Brazilian-Alan-Oliveira-in-T4344-200m.html

Canadian Paralympic Committee. (n.d.). Former IPC President Robert Steadward to be inducted into Alberta Hall of Excellence. Retrieved from http://www.paralympic.ca/news-and-events/press-releases/former-ipc-president-dr-robert-steadward-be-inducted-alberta-order

Castagno, K. S. (2001). Special Olympics Unified Sports: Changes in male athletes during a basketball season. *Adapted Physical Activity Quarterly, 18*, 193–206.

Coward, D., & Legg, D. (2011). Vancouver 2010. In D. Legg & K. Gilbert (Eds.), *Paralympic legacies* (pp. 131–142). Champaign, IL: Common Ground.

Davies, G. A. (2012, May 3). Sir Philip Craven receives Lifetime Achievement Award at Sport Industry Awards. *The Telegraph*. Retrieved from http://www.telegraph.co.uk/sport/olympics/paralympic-sport/9242746/Sir-Philip-Craven-receives-Lifetime-Achievement-Award-at-Sport-Industry-Awards.html

Department of Kinesiology and Community Health. (n.d.). Frank J. Hayden, MS '58, PhD '62. Retrieved from http://kch.illinois.edu/Alumni/Hayden.aspx

DeWind, D. (2012). U.S. military finish proudly in the 2012 London Paralympics. Retrieved from http://themoderatevoice.com/159245/u-s-military-finish-proudly-in-the-2012-london-paralympics

Disabled Sports USA. (2011). Our staff. Retrieved from http://www.dsusa.org/about-staff.html

Dowling, S., McConkey, R., Hassan, D., & Menke, S. (2009). A model for social inclusion? An evaluation of Special Olympics Unified Sports Programme. Annual Special Olympics Symposium, Berlin, Germany.

Dugan, E. (2012, August 26). Sir Philip Craven: Meet a real straight-shooter. *The Independent*. Retrieved from http://www.independent.co.uk/news/people/profiles/sir-philip-craven-meet-a-real-straightshooter-8081245.html

Gallaudet University. (2012). Gallaudet athletics. Retrieved from http://www.gallaudetathletics.com/landing/index

Gillis, R. (2011, January 23). Paralympic gold lures sponsors. *Wall Street Journal*. Retrieved from http://online.wsj.com/article/SB10001424052748703398504576099680221267872.html

Harvard Gazette. (2012, November 7). One-handed violinist makes beautiful music. Retrieved from http://news.harvard.edu/gazette/story/multimedia/one-handed-violinist-makes-beautiful-music

Holden Leadership Center. (2009). Leadership characteristics. Retrieved from http://leadership.uoregon.edu/resources/exercises_tips/skills/leadership_characteristics

Hubbard, A. (2004). The major life activity of belonging. *Wake Forest Law Review, 39*(1), 217–267.

Human Centered Design. (n.d.). Ron Mace. Retrieved from http://humancentereddesign.org/adp/profiles/1_mace.php

Hums, M. A., Moorman, A. M., & Wolff, E. A. (2009). Emerging disability rights in sport: Sport as a human right for persons with disabilities and the 2006 UN Convention on the Rights of Persons with Disabilities. *Cambrian Law Review, 40*, 36–48.

Institute for Human Centered Design. (2012). Universal design. Retrieved from http://humancentereddesign.org/universal-design

International Committee on Sports for the Deaf. (2012). ICSD facts. Retrieved from http://www.deaflympics.com/icsd.asp?icsd_facts

International Disability in Sport Working Group. (2007). Sport in the Convention on the Rights of Persons with Disabilities. Retrieved from http://assets.sportanddev.org/downloads/34__sport_in_the_united_nations_convention_on_the_rights_of_persons_with_disabilities.pdf

International Paralympic Committee. (n.d.) The IPC—Who we are. Paralympic media awards. Retrieved from http://www.paralympic.org/TheIPC/HWA/AboutUs

International Paralympic Committee. (2012). London 2012 Paralympic Games prove to be online success [Press release]. Retrieved from http://www.paralympic.org/news/london-2012-paralympics-prove-be-online-success

Kilgannon, C. (2009, March 17). Confronting disability with modern dance. *New York Times*. Retrieved from http://cityroom.blogs.nytimes.com/2009/03/17/confronting-disability-with-modern-dance

Legg, D., Fay, T., Hums, M. A., & Wolff, E. A. (2009). Examining the inclusion of wheelchair exhibition events within the Olympic Games, 1984-2004. *European Sport Management Quarterly, 9*(3), 243–258.

Mackay, D. (2012, November 22). London 2012 Paralympics watched by billion more TV viewers than Bejing 2008. Retrieved from http://www.insidethegames.biz/paralympics/summer-paralympics/2012/1011836-london-2012-paralympics-watched-by-billion-more-tv-viewers-than-beijing-2008

Nixon, H. L. (2007). Constructing diverse sports opportunities for people with disabilities. *Journal of Sport and Social Issues, 31*(4), 417–433.

Schantz, O., & Gilbert, K. (2001). An ideal misconstrued: Newspaper of the Paralympic Games in France and Germany. *Sociology of Sport Journal, 18*, 69–94.

Special Olympics. (n.d.a). Meet our sponsors. Retrieved from http://www.specialolympics.org/meet_our_partners.aspx

Special Olympics. (n.d.b). Our history. Retrieved from http://www.specialolympics.org/history.aspx

Special Olympics. (2012). Special Olympics Unified Sports quick reference guide. Retrieved from http://resources.specialolympics.org/uploadedFiles/special-olympics-resources/Topics/Unified_Sports/Files/4.18-SO%20Unified%20Sports%20Qk%20Ref%20Guide_09%2020%2012.pdf

Special Olympics Kentucky. (2012). Corporate giving: Special Olympics is good business. Retrieved from http://www.soky.org/corporate.htm#.UEUHTkxHsmU

Sportanddev. (n.d.). Ann Cody. Retrieved from http://www.sportanddev.org/en/connect/userprofile.cfm?user=2988

Steadward, R., & Foster, S. (2003). History of disability sport: From rehabilitation to athletic excellence. In R. D. Steadward, G. D. Wheeler, & E. J. Watkinson (Eds.), *Adapted physical activity* (pp. 471–496). Edmonton, Alberta, Canada: University of Alberta Press.

Stewart-Robertson, T. (2012, August 14). Channel 4 gives blanket coverage to Paralympics, while NBC falls short. Retrieved from http://www.pbs.org/mediashift/2012/08/channel-4-gives-blanket-coverage-to-paralympics-while-nbc-falls-short227.html

Tanni. (n.d.a). Present day. Retrieved from http://www.tanni.co.uk/biography/presentday/

Tanni. (n.d.b). Sporting career. Retrieved from http://www.tanni.co.uk/biography/sportingcareer/

United Nations. (n.d.). *Convention on the Rights of Persons with Disabilities*. Retrieved from http://www.un.org/disabilities/convention/conventionfull.shtml

Wilski, M., Nadolska, A., Dowling, S., McConkey, R., & Hassan, D. (2012). Personal development of participants in Special Olympics Unified Sports teams. *Human Movement, 13*, 271–279.

Wolff, E. A., Hums, M. A., & Fay, T. (2012). *Access and inclusion in sport for people with disabilities: Article 30.5, Universal Design and a call to action*. Boston, MA: Institute for Human Centered Design.

CHAPTER 17

LEADERSHIP ON A GLOBAL SCALE

James J. Zhang
Kenny K. Chen
Jay J. Kim

CHAPTER OBJECTIVES

- Develop a philosophy of leadership to achieve organizational objectives in a globalized sport marketplace.
- Understand the evolvement, meaning, and complexity of leadership and leadership theories applicable in international sport management.
- Describe global sport leadership competencies and their applications in multicultural contexts.
- Recognize various training approaches and activities that organizations may adopt to develop global sport leaders.

CASE STUDY

Under Armour's Global Strategy

It began as a frustration on the football field: an uncomfortable, sweat-saturated cotton shirt on the back of Kevin Plank, then captain of the University of Maryland football team. From this frustration came an underdog sport performance apparel company that now tangles with the largest sport apparel manufacturers in the world. With its global marketing strategy released to investors, Under Armour is poised to spring onto the world stage (Rutter, 2013).

(continues)

In 1996, Plank graduated from University of Maryland with a bachelor's degree in business administration. Using seed money from a college business selling roses for Valentine's day, Plank began researching fabrics with the properties he felt were important for his vision of a performance garment (Dessaur, 2009). With his connections in football, Plank had a network of people who were eager to test his products with the possibility of discovering something that would enhance their performance. Plank combined his passions for business and performance, resulting in a successful enterprise. "It did not matter what we were doing . . . Kevin was always the most competitive one in the group," says Andy Kish, friend and director of manufacturing in Asia for Under Armour (Dessaur, 2009, para. 17).

Plank took his Baltimore-based sportswear company, Under Armour, Inc. (NYSE: UA) public in 2005 (Dessaur, 2009). With more than 2,000 employees worldwide (Dessaur, 2009) and revenues around $1.5 billion annually (*Bloomberg Businessweek*, 2013), Under Armour has grown into a whole new market segment called "performance apparel." Plank credits the success of the company to a few pivotal turning points. The first was getting selected for a product placement deal in Oliver Stone's *Any Given Sunday*, while at the same time investing his newly founded fledgling company's last $25,000 in an *ESPN The Magazine* advertisement (Dessaur, 2009). Both strategies paid dividends and launched the company toward success.

In the second quarter of 2013, Under Armour detailed an aggressive plan with a focus on revenue generation and expansion. Specifically, Under Armour plans to double its revenue in 3 years to $4 billion by, among other things, placing emphasis on global expansion (Trefis Team, 2013). Currently, only 6% of Under Armour's revenue comes from foreign markets. To put this in perspective, Nike's market revenue outside the United States is about 58% (Rutter, 2013). In 2012, Under Armour activated a jersey sponsorship deal with north London soccer club Tottenham Hotspur. The company also plans on expanding heavily in Brazil to capitalize on the 2014 World Cup and 2016 Olympic Games held in that country. Furthermore, analysts suggest that Under Armour will focus on regions including Asia (China, Korea, and Japan), Europe (United Kingdom, France, and Germany), Australia, and Latin America (Brazil, Mexico, Argentina, and Chile) to expand (Trefis Team, 2013). The company has proceeded internationally with caution. In the company's 2012 annual report, Plank notes the company continues to believe that its strength remains in the United States, and this core business gives the firm the opportunity and patience to make the right decisions abroad. While rival Adidas spends more than $100 million on a top-tier Olympics sponsorship, Plank said, "One of the worst things we can do is get caught up in a game of keeping up with the Joneses" (Sharrow, 2012, para. 4). Plank added that the company's expectation is to be a global brand. In the meantime, Under Armour plans to capitalize on currently unrealized markets, including women's business, youth, footwear (Trefis Team, 2013), and a new market segment, fitness technology, with its Armour39 fitness monitoring system.

Questions for Discussion

1. As described in the chapter, to be an effective global leader one must be self-reflective and open to change. In your view, has Kevin Plank demonstrated that he could be an effective global leader? If so, how? If not, what does he need to change?

2. What considerations must a leader keep in mind when trying to expand a business to a new country?
3. What social, cultural, and political concerns must a leader be aware of when expanding to Asia? Latin America? Europe?
4. How can the Global Leadership Triad (discussed later in this chapter) be applied to Under Armour?

INTRODUCTION

Due to a growing interest in leisure activities, the adoption of healthy lifestyles, the augmentation of sport competitions and events, the evolution of sport media technology, and most importantly, the globalization of the sport marketplace, the sport industry has shown rapid growth and become one of the largest industries in North America. The growth trends of sport on other continents and in other regions resemble those observed in North America, although North America remains the world's largest market; the estimated size of the sport business industry in North America has risen sharply in recent years, from $213 billion at the end of the 1990s to more than $425 billion in 2010 (Plunkett Research, 2010). Sport leagues, teams, and events have played an integral part in forming part of the cultural and economic bases for many communities and have become one of the most popular leisure and entertainment options in North America. Spectator sports, in particular, have shown healthy growth over the last two decades, and the revenue produced by spectator sports has shown a 5–6% annual growth rate in recent years (Crawford, 2008; Zhang, Cianfrone, & Min, 2011). These increases are expected worldwide as emerging middle classes in developing nations become potential customers for multinational sport firms.

As this chapter will demonstrate, global leadership competencies are an important consideration for the 21st-century sport leader. Sport organizations are routinely looking beyond their local and domestic markets to sell products and spread their influence, and these organizations need leaders with a worldview. The chapter begins with a discussion of the globalized sport marketplace to ground sport management students in a global perspective that few have probably considered. The discussion then moves to the importance of adopting a global perspective in leadership and management tasks as organizations move away from domestic targets and into domestic *and* global marketplaces. Needed leadership competencies are suggested for the global sport leader to give sport management students some ideas about skills they should consider developing, particularly if they will pursue, or are already pursuing, an advanced degree. Finally, the contributors give several concrete suggestions about how potential leaders can develop these competencies. This chapter is key in that it should allow students to consider a global leadership perspective rather than an ethnocentric one.

THE GLOBALIZED SPORT MARKETPLACE

The 21st century has seen an increase in the growth of a free flow of capital, ideas, people, goods, and services that lead to the interaction, exchange, and integration of economies and societies. *Globalization* has resulted in companies, organizations, and even countries forming links and partnerships through trade, investment, and activities that strive for border-transcending competitiveness (Hill & Vincent, 2006). In fact, globalization has benefited the sport industry in a number of ways, including but not limited to: (1) the spread of sports throughout the world; (2) diversity in the origins of athletes participating in many of the professional and amateur leagues around the world; (3) an increasing number of countries participating in international sporting events; (4) an increasing number of athletes participating in a diverse range of sports, often crossing gender and religious lines and climate barriers; and (5) increased opportunities in sport participation and also employment for athletes, coaches, and leaders (Thibault, 2009).

For a variety of reasons, such as seeking access to new markets, development of new customers, enhanced marketing opportunities, sport and brand growth, acquisition of resources, and profit generation, increasingly more professional and amateur sport leagues and teams, sporting goods manufacturers, sport service companies, and other sport organizations seek to compete in the international marketplace than ever before. Sport organizations on every continent are embracing a global vision as their domestic target markets become saturated. For many sport organizations, globalization is the result of stagnant or declining home markets. Many sport managers believe that the potential for long-term growth and stability can be realized through international operations (Walker & Tehrani, 2011). For instance, in addition to developing international broadcasting programs and conducting exhibition games, the National Basketball Association (NBA) has developed and launched such programs as Basketball Without Borders, which is aimed as a synergistic approach for youth development through basketball and grassroots expansion of NBA markets (Means & Nauright, 2007). Manchester United, in an effort to conduct grassroots promotion of soccer, has in recent years opened soccer schools or soccer summer programs in Asian and North American countries (Hill & Vincent, 2006), where soccer training, academic learning, and character building are integrated into their curriculum.

Youth participating in a soccer training program.
© Jorge Felix Costa/ShutterStock, Inc.

According to Rowe and Gilmour (2010), Asia has become a prime target market for the expansionary strategies of some of the world's most powerful professional sport leagues, teams, manufacturing companies, and media corporations. The influence of transnational broadcasters in Asia and the intensive marketing efforts of Western sport organizations provide European- and American-based sport leagues, such as the English Premier League and the National Basketball Association, with a significant advantage within the market. Sport consumers in Asia tend to develop a predisposition of choosing globally marketed Western sport leagues, teams, stars, and licensed products over those made in Asia. At the same time, the popularity of Western sport leagues has led Asian corporations, such as Samsung, Air Asia, Chang Beer, Emirates Airlines, Malaysia Airlines, Li-Ning, and Tiger Beer, to sponsor Western leagues such as the Premier League and the NBA in order to attract customers within Asia, devoting little of their promotional budgets to local Asian professional clubs. There are concerns among Asian countries that this could negatively impact the development of domestic leagues and sports.

Although international sporting events have been ongoing since the late 19th century, the past two decades have marked the rapid rise of a globalized sport production and consumption trend, due in part to the advancement of modern technology. In an era of a globalized sport marketplace, sports have become a commodity to meet the needs of commerce (Gupta, 2009). In recent years, international elements have risen to a greater diversity in sport production, coverage, and consumption. Technological changes have transformed broadcasting revenues, creating more sport entertainment options for fans and more revenue streams for organizations than ever before. Shifts in technology, transportation, and communications are creating a world where anything can be made and sold anywhere on the face of the earth. Financial investment has moved with great speed, creating new stadiums, teams, and merchandising opportunities. There has been an escalated increase in North American–based organizations becoming multinational (Pfahl, 2011). With today's *globalized economy*, geographical and cultural boundaries are continuously being transcended. Many nations and regions have strategically developed and adopted a comprehensive plan to use sporting events and sport participation as catalytic agents to transform communities, revitalize the urban environment, improve public infrastructure, project a destination image for tourism and business, enrich the residential quality of life, nurture an active lifestyle, enhance societal harmony and solidarity, and promote interorganizational collaborations and work efficiency (Zhang et al., 2011). Events are also used to build the global brands of cities and countries. Consider the Beijing Olympics. The 2008 Olympic Games served as an opportunity to upgrade the country's image in the eyes of Westerners and display China's national brand. Beijing welcomed the world with its "One World, One Dream" theme and adroitly utilized the Olympics to brand itself as a harmonious, nonthreatening world power (Bu, 2009).

GLOBAL EMPHASIS ON LEADERSHIP AND MANAGEMENT

Leadership has vital significance for future global business applications. In the past, with U.S. industry at the center of the world's economy during the industrial age, the emphasis was on self-sufficiency in every sort of enterprise—education, business, or government. Business and government at that time called for a command and control or highly directive style, with one-way, top-down communication. It was a management style appropriate to the mass production of work calling for job specialization, and it helped the United States survive a depression and help win two major wars by teaching people discipline, courage, dominance, and self-preservation. As U.S. industry continues on the global path, openness to diversity will be a necessary prerequisite for successful competition and partnership with others around the world. Understanding of the interdependent nature of the team experience, along with associated characters and leadership skills such as self-sacrifice and cooperation, are needed to be successful in global business (Jenkins, 2005). The international nature of modern sport requires sport organizations to modify their management practices in order to remain effective and competitive in a border-transcended marketplace. Differences in such areas as culture, religion, tradition, politics, law, policy and regulation, communication, language, technology, and environment in global, national, regional, and local communities make this task a challenging one. Over the spectrum of global and local, sport organizations must make efforts to establish a brand success in local markets while identifying ways in which to increase an international presence. Sport managers responsible for making the strategic, cultural, political, and economic decisions for sport organizations must be prepared for the challenges of the new sport landscape. They must be equipped with knowledge, skills, abilities, and worldviews that are inclusive yet can differentiate cultural and other related elements (Means & Nauright, 2007; Pfahl, 2011).

Theories and Best Practices

Within sport management, leadership plays a vital role in establishing a new culture, developing new directions, mobilizing change, creating opportunities, and motivating organizational members. Leadership is an important process of directing the members of the organization toward achieving the stated objectives. When the stated objectives are global in nature rather than solely domestic, leadership needs to convince followers to adapt to a wider worldview. According to Morrison (2000), global leadership can learn a great deal from theories and best practices that were derived in domestic settings. The vast majority of leadership models generated in the United States have functioned relatively well in helping leaders operate in a domestic context. These models have generally focused on the adoption of hierarchical command and structures. Stoner, Freeman, and Gilbert (1995) explained that due to the influences of research beliefs and methods that are dominant in behavioral sciences, instead of trying to figure out who effective leaders are, leadership studies have been devoted to determining what effective leaders do in terms of delegation, communication, motivation, and completion of tasks.

Researchers have long realized that leadership techniques that best contribute to the attainment of organizational goals might vary in different situations or circumstances; however, global situations or circumstances have seldom been the focus of study. Nevertheless, the primary belief that the match between leadership style and the situation determines leadership effectiveness can be reasonably applied to global settings. Traditionally, the contingency considerations in domestic settings have been focused on such factors as task requirements; peer expectations and behaviors; employee characteristics, expectations, and behaviors; and organizational culture (Stoner et al., 1995; Zhang, Jensen, & Mann, 1997). Contingency considerations have led to the formulation of matching theory (Fiedler, 1967), where effective leadership can only be achieved by matching the manager to the situation (which is characterized by task structure, leader–member relations, and position power) or matching the situation to the manager, such as the Situational Leadership Model (Hersey & Blanchard, 1977), which is formed on the principle that effective leadership style varies with the readiness of employees (which is characterized by desire and goal for achievement, willingness to accept responsibilities, and possession of task-related knowledge, ability, skill, and experience), and the Path-Goal Leadership Model (Evans & House, 1971), which emphasizes the leader's role in clarifying for subordinates how they can achieve high performance and its associated award.

Generally speaking, the aforementioned contingency theories focus on the micro-perspectives of different situations or circumstances. When the organizational culture is embedded in a global setting, it would be further complicated by the cross-cultural environment that is influenced by the local religion(s), values, norms, beliefs, tradition, habits, politics, law, policy and regulation, communication, and language. In recent decades, some countries, regions, and/or organizations have made concerted efforts to send large groups of students to study in the developed Western, English-speaking countries. The reasons for globalizing higher education institutions are complex, one of which arguably is economic (Tomkovick, Al-Khatib, Baradwaj, & Jones, 1996; Yang, 2003). The United States, with more than 671,000 international students, is by far the largest host country and home to more than a quarter of the world's foreign students (Fischer, 2009). English-speaking nations, such as the United States, the United Kingdom, Australia, Canada, and New Zealand, remain the largest international education destinations, hosting more than 50% of foreign students in the world (Marginson, 2006). Conceivably, in these situations or circumstances where so many personnel have had Western educations and/or professional experiences, the behavior leadership theories derived in the United States may have a greater applicability; conversely, in situations where foreign persons have had little exposure, contact, and work relationship with Western people there is a much greater challenge when adopting leadership guidelines presumably effective in the United States.

New Markets, New Challenges

To achieve *global reach and influence*, North American sport organizations are increasingly embracing a global vision as their U.S. target markets have become saturated, and they are selling products far beyond their initial focused markets. A globalized marketplace has brought increased complexity in organization operations in terms of interdependence, ambiguity, and multiculturalism. Unlike domestic settings, global leaders have to face greater challenges in such areas as connectedness, boundary spanning, ethical standards, dealing with tension and paradoxes, and understanding diverse cultures (Mendenhall, 2013). Traditional leadership models derived in the United States have not been designed for broader, international applications. Due to differences in cultural norms and a variety of other factors, domestic leadership models from one part of the world generally do not work well in other parts of the globe. Leadership models developed in Europe, Asia, and Latin America are often different than those adopted in the United States. Leadership models differ because values, ethics, beliefs, perceptions, and attitudes vary from culture to culture, country to country, and even

region to region. The importance of such variables as relationships,. short-term profits, hierarchies, employment security, diversity, and risk may also be different. If U.S. businesses cannot integrate a global perspective into leadership practices, their capability of competing in the globalized marketplace may be hampered tremendously. For an organization to maintain its competitive edge in a global setting, its leaders must develop competencies that overcome cultural, national, and regional differences and embrace the best practices in varying parts of the world (Morrison, 2000; Yeung & Ready, 1995).

GLOBAL SPORT LEADERSHIP

More and more, leaders of sport organizations, such as Nike, Adidas, Under Armour, and the Ladies Professional Golf Association (LPGA) are confronted by a *globalized sport industry*, in which organizational leaders must see their firms as international businesses looking to tap into any market, whether it is in South America, North America, Europe, or Asia. There has been a blurring of geographical borders worldwide, and many businesses have been willing to set up distribution systems in areas where people have disposable income, no matter whether it is in Springfield, Massachusetts, or Hamburg, Germany. Fairley and Lizandra (2012) identified several characteristics of sport globalization, and we suggest leaders might find four of these developments important. First, countries compete against one another in international competition; leaders of sport apparel firms see these competitions (World Cups, Olympics) as opportunities for sponsorships that encompass a global reach because the TV-viewing audience is global. Second, the international broadcasting of sport competition and events has increased; executives of media organizations such as ESPN know their media outlet can grow its influence worldwide, giving it the opportunity to set up television networks in other countries (e.g.,

ESPN Deportes) and allowing businesses to run advertisements on these international networks. Next, individuals compete alongside players from different countries in organized leagues; leaders of the Major League Soccer (MLS), Major League Baseball (MLB), and English Premier League franchises should consider international players for their rosters. When the Los Angeles Galaxy added David Beckham to its roster, not only did the team improve, but Beckham fans in England followed the Galaxy so the team increased its fan base. When Ichiro Suzuki joined the Seattle Mariners, the Mariners used it as an opportunity to engage Japanese American fans in Seattle. Finally, sport is used as a social tool; sport for development and peace (SDP) organizations operate throughout the world under similar principles, so SDP leaders can operate in different countries.

Given these examples, leaders need to consider global strategy, or the idea that their organization must create products, services, and philosophies that generate the same demand anywhere in the world (Fairley & Lizandra, 2012). Some products, like golf, do not differ significantly whether they are played in Scotland or South Korea. The LPGA has taken advantage of the worldwide interest in golf by becoming a world tour. In 2013, the LPGA had tour stops in Australia, Thailand, Singapore, China, Canada, and France as well as several in the United States. Nike sells more of its products overseas than it does in the United States (Fairley & Lizandra, 2012). Team ownership is also reaching across the pond. Boston Red Sox owner John Henry also owns Liverpool FC (a soccer team). Stan Kroenke, who owns the Denver Nuggets and Colorado Avalanche, is also the major stakeholder in the famed Arsenal soccer club. English soccer fans have treated this "intrusion" of U.S. ownership cautiously. In addition, the Brooklyn Nets are owned by Russian businessman Mikhail Prokhorov.

Sport leaders like Prokhorov, Henry, Kroenke, LPGA Commissioner Michael Whan, and Nike's Phil Knight are global leaders, and their organizations need to hire other leaders who possess critical thinking skills in understanding societal and global concerns, generating ideas, and seeking effective solutions. Sport managers that work for global firms need to have effective problem-solving abilities, human resource talents, knowledge in law and regulatory procedures, and sensitivity to diversity and cultural issues. As sport organizations are increasingly becoming market-driven, it is imperative for professionals to possess expertise in marketing, budgeting, and financial management (Zhang et al., 2011). This would seem to indicate that obtaining an advanced degree beyond a bachelor's degree is important for anyone who wants to be involved in international sport business.

Competencies

A sense of value is important for effective leadership. Values are inherently laced through all facets of the leadership process, whether it is about retaining and motivating people, servicing customers, or maintaining brand integrity (Jayne, 2008). Both individual and collective values are essential to successfully compete in the global business environment now and in the future (Jenkins, 2005). Value is an "enduring belief that a specific mode of conduct or end-state of existence is personally or socially preferable to an opposite or converse mode of conduct or end-state of existence" (Rokeach, 1973, p. 5). A set of values allows people to connect themselves with society because they help individuals evaluate and understand interpersonal relationships and guide the individuals' adaptation to the surrounding world. Values are also conceptualized as criteria used by individuals to evaluate, select, and justify their actions (Grunert-Beckman & Askegard, 1997).

Communication is essential for carrying out the basic leadership component through interpersonal relations and exertion of influences. Communication is a constant process of sharing, learning, and understanding of oneself and others, particularly those who are different from oneself, which is needed when trying to understand global citizens. Most interpersonal social exchange occurs through language. Many languages exist around the globe, with English being the most often adopted international language. Nonetheless, one of the most significant barriers to effective organizational operations in a globalized market environment is that of communication, and more specifically, language. By not understanding another person's language, the communication process can be easily interrupted or interfered with by variables within and beyond a communication context. Language is associated with power in the sense that language can be used to persuade, inspire, enlighten, or coerce others. To a great extent, cultural elements are created, shared, and passed on over generations through language. Often, media coverage or arguments can be used to perpetuate one belief or another. In the world of sport, communication and language are key points to effective leadership performance (Pfahl, 2011). This communication is particularly effective when attempting to sell products in foreign markets. To succeed around the world, global sports are compelled to accommodate the local (Maguire, 1999). An understanding of *glocalization*, or how organizations can adapt their marketing and business practices to fit with local cultural conditions, tastes, and practices (Matusitz & Leanza, 2009), is a form of business communication leaders must hone.

The small collection of competencies discussed thus far—values, communication, understanding local cultural conditions, critical-thinking skills, an attention to diversity—serve as a model for leaders to follow. But we are only scratching the surface here. Although it would be unrealistic to have a global leadership model that can be adopted in all situations or circumstances involving international sport operations, some generalizable competencies can be identified. Brake (1997) believed that highly functional, global leadership is the starting point for an organization

and its leaders to adopt a global perspective, and proposed a competence model, the *Global Leadership Triad*. The triad serves as an addendum to the aforementioned competencies. The model consists of three dimensions: (1) business acumen, (2) relationship management, and (3) personal effectiveness. Business acumen contains ingredients such as adaptability, entrepreneurial spirit, professional expertise, stakeholder orientation, and organizational astuteness (Brake, 1997). These competencies would be possessed by someone who has experience working for an organization that is beholden to a number of clients and both internal (followers, managers, leaders) and external stakeholders (customers, suppliers, politicians, media). These universal business skills are appropriate in any global context. Relationship management consists of change agentry, community building, conflict management, cross-cultural communication, and influencing (Brake, 1997). These competencies equip leaders with the ability to function in global contexts other than their own, but can certainly be practiced at home. Cross-cultural communication is of special interest here. The global leader must become a student again and learn as much as possible about the countries and communities where his or her organization wants to conduct business. Conflicts are likely to occur as a new company is likely to be perceived as an intruder rather than a change agent. Finally, the last part of the triad involves personal effectiveness, and this area includes competencies such as accountability, curiosity and learning, improvisation, maturity, and agile thinking (Brake, 1997).

At the center of the triad is the transformational leader-self, created through self-reflection, personal mind management, and openness to change (Brake, 1997). In any situation or circumstance, international or domestic, global or local, any restructuring and repositioning of an organization requires strong leadership in the top or key positions in order to change goals and processes, improve efforts and the performance level of organization members, and attain stated objectives.

Those who guide their organizations to transform into innovative and profitable enterprises are called transformational leaders. Transformational leadership is important for global leadership in that it emphasizes a visionary process via conducting comprehensive analysis of market conditions and resources available. The process is usually implemented by articulating the vision, convincing the members, expressing confidence, empowering the members to be innovative and creative, and focusing on emotions, values, goals, needs, higher order of motivations, confidence, and self-esteem (Stoner et al., 1995). Plausibly, many new initiatives in a global context would generally demand transformational leadership. In the case of the Global Leadership Triad, a leader or a leadership team also needs to first transform themselves through regular personal reflections, analysis, adjustment, adaptation, and control of personal cognitive and affective orientations, and embracing of change.

There are stronger and weaker characteristics that come through in each individual and necessarily contribute to his or her leadership style. In other words, the style of leadership in any particular position can change and adapt; so, to some extent, a leadership style needs to be circumstantial. Global leaders who live and work outside their own country will need to adapt to different businesses and broader cultures. The global context sometimes can mean being slow to push ideas or opportunities; otherwise, cultural differences could lead to misunderstandings or missing out on opportunities (Jayne, 2008). A leader's global mindset has two components: (1) emotional intelligence and (2) intellectual intelligence. *Global emotional intelligence* involves *cultural acumen* and self-management, and it is composed of cross-cultural self-awareness, understanding, adjustment, and effectiveness. These components form the basis for global behavior skills and global managers' leadership styles. *Global intellectual intelligence* entails both business acumen and the ability to manage paradoxes (e.g., local vs. global,

individual vs. team, stability vs. change, centralization vs. decentralization).

There are five steps to managing paradoxes: (1) identifying competitive forces, (2) analyzing the pros and cons of competing forces, (3) seeking win–win solutions, (4) embracing contradictions, and (5) building systematic procedures to regularly deal with paradoxes (Rhinesmith, 2003). Black, Morrison, and Gregersen (1999) identified three distinct characteristics of effective global leaders: (1) demonstrating savvy in global business and organizations, (2) exhibiting character in emotional connections and personal integrity, and (3) embracing duality in the ability to manage uncertainty and to balance the often-powerful tensions between globalization and localization pressures. A leader's inquisitiveness is the glue to integrate and unify these three factors, which motivates a leader to eagerly ask questions about new cultures, industry conditions, market environment, customer values, and microeconomics. Jokinen (2004) also highlighted the importance of a leader's inquisitiveness as a necessary global leadership quality. Similarly, Bird and Osland (2004) developed a pyramid model with five layers of *global leadership competencies*: (1) global knowledge, (2) threshold traits (integrity, humility, inquisitiveness, and resilience), (3) global mindset (cognitive complexity and cosmopolitanism), (4) interpersonal skills (mindful communication, building trust, and multicultural teaming), and (5) system skills (ethical decisions, influencing stakeholders, leading change, spanning boundaries, and architecting and building community).

Strategies and Processes

The flexible and adaptive leadership theory (Yukl & Mahsud, 2010) expects leadership behavior to change over time and across situations in order to adapt to various and changing circumstances. To be flexible and adaptive, a leader working in the international sport business setting is expected to willingly and effectively take on new responsibilities, deal with crises, balance competing values, and transition into new roles. Goldblatt (2005) explained the differentiations of leadership as a concept between Eastern and Western cultures. Between the two, there are significant differences in seniority vs. professionalism, obedience vs. breakthrough opportunities, tradition vs. flexibility, autocratic vs. democratic, and leader power vs. integrated system. According to Van Der Wagen (2001), at times global sport business leaders need to manage diverse, long-term, and even temporary workforces. When group members display a wide range of individual differences, particularly in language and culture, a few strategies can be used to enhance communications with individuals: (1) identify the specific information needs of group members, (2) use plain English, (3) develop subteams by individual familiarity and bonding, (4) utilize graphics, (5) rotate roles among group members, (6) be fair and equal to individual group members, and (7) develop group identity.

It is necessary to note there are contrasting differences between long-term (e.g., employees in the NBA Asia Office) and short-term (temporary employees working at an international sporting event) teams. Long-term team members tend to have a greater commitment to the organization's mission, focus on career development within the organization, and seek intrinsic motivation. To lead such a group, a leader or a leadership team needs to focus on making decisions by seeking consensus, establishing group cohesion over time, empowering group members through proper delegation and job enrichment, promoting lifelong learning, and conducting positive performance management. Short-term team members tend to commit to the task, have no career or organization orientation, and pay more attention to tangible rewards. To lead them, a leader or a leadership team may be expected to make decisions and solve problems, delegate limited responsibilities, offer financial incentives, and offer positive references.

Leadership effectiveness is predicted based on both cognitive and behavioral knowledge and skills. Normally, people first think and then act. In global settings, leaders often have to use cognitive and behavioral knowledge and skills simultaneously. Bird and Osland (2004) proposed the Effective Cycle Model, which describes three key steps that effective global leaders take to carry out a know–feel–do process: (1) perceive, analyze, and diagnose to decode the situation; (2) identify options for effective managerial actions and choose a feasible course of actions; and (3) uphold the behavioral repertoire and flexibility to act appropriately in the given situation and circumstance. Osland (2013) explained that global leaders work with colleagues from other countries; interact with business partners, vendors, and clients from other countries; supervise employees of different nationalities; develop strategic plans on a global basis; and communicate effectively in diverse cultural settings. Global leadership effectiveness can be predicted by high-contact leadership development activities, which can be moderated by the personality characteristics and cultural experiences of the leader. High-contact leadership development activities may include a wide range of training and preparation programs, such as structured leadership rotation programs, short-term expatriate assignments, and sitting in global meetings. Key personality characteristics affecting the effectiveness of global leadership usually include extraversion, flexibility, openness to experiences, motivation to learn, respect for others, sensitivity, and conscientiousness. Cultural experiences, both organization-initiated and nonwork experiences, predict dynamic cross-cultural competencies in terms of tolerance of ambiguity, cultural flexibility, and reduced ethnocentrism.

Based on Scott and Lane's (2000) organizational identity construction (OIC) framework and on stakeholder theory (Clarkson, 1995; Freeman, 1984), Parent and Foreman (2007) proposed and examined the applicability of the OIC procedure within organizing committees of major sporting events. In the OIC model, organization identity refers to all central, enduring, and distinct elements that define the organizing committee. There are three types of identity referents: (1) the nature of the event (e.g., an Olympic Games versus an NCAA men's basketball tournament), (2) the context of the event (i.e., the context or setting in which the event takes place), and (3) the key individuals or actors (i.e., individuals considered to be leaders of the organizing committee). Parent and Séguin (2008) adopted the OIC model and conducted a case analysis of a leadership process for the Montreal 2005 FINA (Fédération Internationale de Natation) World Championships.

In 2001, FINA chose Montreal, Canada, to showcase its world championships. For the city, Montreal 2005 was the largest gathering of young athletes since the 1976 Olympic Games. The event hosted more than 2,000 athletes from 160 countries in the disciplines of swimming, diving, synchronized swimming, water polo, and open water swimming, along with 1,000 team officials and 300 competition officials. It also involved 2,500 volunteers, 160,000 spectators, more than 1 billion television viewers worldwide, and a media contingent of more than 1,300 journalists. However, during the preparation stage, the organizing committee experienced three leadership changes, which resulted in a major change of direction and almost losing the opportunity to host the event. On January 19, 2005, FINA decided to withdraw the championships from Montreal, following a number of problems in the areas of leadership and finance. The mayor of Montreal and other key leaders quickly took over the command and created a new organizing committee in an effort to save the event. Under the new leadership and with new paid staff and volunteers, FINA handed the event back to Montreal on February 10, 2005.

Temporary organizations, such as Montreal 2005, usually rely on few formal employees during the initial stage of the organizing process. Thus, having the right kind of leader(s) in place is essential because most decisions usually rest among a few key individuals. This historical case helps highlight the importance of leadership and the leadership group.

Cultural Dilemmas

Sport managers worldwide share similar tasks, challenges, and problems; however, they differ in how they resolve them. These universal differences emerge from the relationships they form with other people and their attitudes toward issues in the organizational environment. Essentially, sport managers are concerned about social processes by which they get involved in reconciling seven fundamental cultural dilemmas in order to perform planned tasks and achieve stated objectives. These dilemmas are the following:

1. *Universalism* (rules, codes, laws, and generalizations) vs. particularism (exceptions, special circumstances, unique relations)
2. *Individualism* (personal freedom, human rights, competitiveness) vs. communitarianism (social responsibility, harmonious relations, cooperation)
3. Analyzing (facts, reductive analysis, units, specifics) vs. integrating (patterns, relationships, synthetic, rational)
4. Neutral (interactions are objective and detached from emotions) vs. affective (expression of emotions is acceptable)
5. Achieved status (what you have done, your track record) vs. ascribed status (who you are, your potential and connections)
6. Time as sequence (time is a race along a set course) vs. time as synchronization (time is a dance of fine coordination)
7. Inner-directed orientation (conscience and convictions are located inside) vs. outer-directed orientation (examples and influences are located outside)

A leader's knowledge of the cultural meaning of sport in a particular country would equip him or her with a valuable tool in managing the cultural diversity of their own workforces and developing appropriate cross-cultural skills needed for operating international events, marketing campaigns, sponsorship deals, and joint ventures (Girginov, Papadimitriou, & De D'amico, 2006).

GLOBAL LEADERSHIP DEVELOPMENT

Approaches that organizations adopt to develop global leaders usually involve altering existing traditional leadership development protocols by incorporating a global perspective (Oddou & Mendenhall, 2013). A combination of global leadership talent, training, and experience tends to form effective leadership competencies that are fundamental for organizational success in global settings. Global leadership is a nonlinear, personal transformation process that requires engrained changes in one's competency, expertise, and worldview through experiential learning over time. Undoubtedly, an individual's background can serve as a foundation for developing global leadership, which would likely include one's family background involving intercultural experiences in mixed culture marriage and bilingual parents; early education involving international schools, overseas summer camps, and international travel; later education involving international exchange programs, language learning, and interacting with people of international background; and family support for being adaptable, adventurous, and mobile. In addition, acquiring an internship with an organization, such as Octagon (see the Leadership Perspective later in this chapter), could serve as an international experience depending on assigned duties and the department in which you work. However, not all effective global leaders have international

backgrounds. In such cases, leaders are highly intelligent, quick learners and have developed cognitive and social flexibility. In addition to the personal background, organizations can play a key role in transforming and developing an individual into a global leader through training, transfer (international assignments), teamwork, and travel. A critical factor in global leadership development is access to high-level challenges. Although not guaranteed, frequent access to the "right" kinds of challenges would likely help develop solid global leadership competency. Organizations need to ensure that prospective global leaders are provided with transformational experiences in their development process. The transformational process may include, but is not limited to, cultural exposure, global education (e.g., courses, seminars, coaching, mentoring), job novelty in terms of multicultural components, global experiences, participating in decision making, interpersonal encounters, and preparing for challenges (e.g., simulations, case analyses, workshops). Although organizations cannot force individuals to develop and transform, they can develop an organizational culture and policies that would help enhance global leadership development. Organizations should be both intentional and collaborative about leadership development. Themes and lessons an organization can choose for global leadership training may include such activities as the following (Osland & Bird, 2013):

1. Learning about different cultures and learning to deal with cultural issues
2. Learning to run a business, both local and global
3. Learning to manage others
4. Learning to deal with problematic relations
5. Learning about the personal qualities required of a leader
6. Learning about self and career

7. Providing foundation assignments, major line assignments, short-term experiences, and/or perspective experiences
8. Providing and interpreting feedback on development, performance, and outcomes
9. Providing incentives and resources to hold people accountable for achieving developmental goals
10. Providing emotional support to the individual and family members

Information exchange with others and personal work experience play important roles in global leadership training in addition to classroom settings, so experiential learning should be an integral part of global leadership development. Experiential education involves giving individuals exposure to actual business operations in geographically dispersed, culturally diverse, and functionally different operations. Through such experiences, a network can be developed and information can be exchanged. Based on the rigor of experiential learning opportunities, there could be three levels of activities, which are explained in **Table 17.1**.

Conceptually, an individual needs to go through a process of contrast, confrontation, and remapping or replacement in order to reach the desired outcome of global leadership development. Contrasting geographical, cultural, and functional differences would help an individual to confront the dissimilarities, reformulate perceptions and beliefs, and adopt a new or an altered set of leadership attitudes and behaviors. Interestingly, global leaders need to be aware that a superficial addition to their "mental maps of the world" is not as efficient as actually replacing the mental maps with more sophisticated ones. This dynamic process for an individual's global transformation may be referred as "unfreezing → changing → freezing." The Ulysses Program conducted by PricewaterhouseCoopers (PwC), a global accounting, marketing, and event management firm that managed the 2013 World University Games (i.e., the 27th Universiade) held in Kazan, Russia, is a standardized, crucible program for global leadership competency training. This program assigns three to four trainees into a group and sends the group to a developing country or countries for 2 months to work on challenging assignments with local and international partnership organizations. Throughout this service learning program, team members receive individualized coaching on how to approach leadership, cope with leadership challenges, deploy their expertise, and learn global leadership skills. Essentially, the team is being forced to resolve tensions and paradoxes in the new, unfamiliar environment; deal with a new cultural environment to accomplish their project task; and cope with adversity and the emotional burdens that accompany the adversity. The crucible experiences can be powerful vehicles for the development of global leadership competencies in the areas of cultural

---

TABLE 17.1 **Experiential Education for Global Leadership**

Beginning Level	Lectures, self-study, cultural briefing, films, books, and seminars
Intermediate Level	Role playing, case analysis, cultural assimilator training, language training, global virtual teams, global taskforces, global project teams, and international exposure trips
Advanced Level	Strategic international business travel, planned field experiences, sophisticated simulations, and international assignments

intelligence, intercultural competence, cultural tolerance, openness to diverse cultural norms and practices, nonjudgmental behavior, cosmopolitan thinking, managing complexity, self-reflection, self-awareness, and abilities to reconcile global and local imperatives. For an organization to become a globally integrated enterprise, all employees need to have varied exposure, training, and experience to enhance their knowledge and skills to work in a global context. Depending on an individual employee's responsibilities and their proximity to the leadership functions in the client-facing roles that are of a global impact, he or she is provided with different levels of global training, experience, and development (Oddou & Mendenhall, 2013).

SUMMARY

In this chapter, an attempt was made to illustrate the market and organizational environments that lead to the increasing demand for global sport leadership, identify global sport leadership competencies from recent research inquires, and discuss avenues for global sport leadership development. The concept of global sport leadership is still an emerging area of study, so it is reminiscent of the stages of domestic sport leadership studies that started by examining leadership traits and subsequently evolved with more complex theories, guidelines, and best practices. Accordingly, the content of this chapter represents initial insights, conceptualizations, and inquiries regarding global sport leadership. Expectedly, the chapter helps stimulate more comprehensive and sophisticated inquiries and investigations.

Global sport leadership is a multifaceted phenomenon; logically, the competencies associated with effective leadership are multifaceted. Few people possess all the competencies, attributes, and behaviors. Leaders usually possess a combination of some of these. A question remains on which competencies, attributes, behaviors, and their combination would work in certain global sport situations and circumstances. More empirical studies, simplification studies, and/or longitudinal studies are needed to verify the discussed suppositions, presumptions, and preliminary research findings that have mainly been generated from philosophical, historical, qualitative, and/or small-scale empirical analyses or investigations. Expanded empirical evidence is very much needed to identify antecedents and consequences of effective global sport leadership.

Regarding training of new global leaders in sport organizations, Danylchuk (2011) highlighted the importance of, need for, and procedures to incorporate international components into teaching and learning curriculums of sport management. Typically, this has been done through "add-on approaches" such as readings, textbooks, films, videos, case studies, and guest lecturers, or devoting a session to an international topic in classrooms. A more in-depth approach might entail the addition of one or more international courses within the curriculum or the requirement of students to attend an internationally oriented course from other academic areas of studies, such as international relations/affairs and global studies, European studies, Asian studies, international business, and/or international development studies. From the perspective of students, opportunities for international learning experiences may be achieved by participating in international dual-degree programs, study abroad programs, intentional cooperative programs, international internships, and international service learning programs.

Those sport organizations that seek to compete globally must recognize that entry into the global marketplace requires substantial commitment to the planning, investing, organizing, leading, and monitoring process of organizational operations. A strategic plan along with clearly articulated goals and objectives serve as the cornerstone of a successful global expansion; to develop and implement such a plan, effective leadership is crucial. With more concerted efforts to understand the concept and application of global sport leadership, policies, regulations, best practices, and training programs can be formed to develop leadership skills, guide leadership functions, and ultimately, ensure the high achievement level of sport organizations that provide goods and services in a border-transcending, continent-transcending, and culture-transcending market environment and climate.

LEADERSHIP PERSPECTIVE

John Shea.
Courtesy of John Shea

John Shea is Executive Vice President for Consulting for Octagon Americas. With 19 years of experience, John has excelled as one of the industry's most accomplished leaders. In 2008 and 2009 he was awarded the SportsBusiness Journal's *"Forty Under 40" recognition.*

Q: What are the unique challenges with respect to leading groups on an international basis?

I think understanding cultures and acknowledging that different countries conduct business in different ways is a very important part of what I do. The way we treat a business in the United States is different than how we treat a business in Brazil, for instance. As we enter new markets, the discipline of sports marketing is often not quite as advanced as it is in the United States, so we identify the skill sets that people have and then offer new training programs to help round out their skills. However, there are many similarities that exist across businesses, and we find that these similarities allow us to develop best practices. I've found that our most effective marketers are able to adapt our methodologies and best practices to a local market's ways of doing business. Although we can't automatically implement a U.S.-centric process and mindset in a local market, similarly someone who is only capable of taking a local approach to business will have a hard time finding success at our company.

Language can certainly be a barrier when working in different countries, without a doubt, but the way we handle that is by having skilled people with respect to language on both sides of the business equation. We are fortunate that most of the countries that we are moving into have strong English language skills. Still, I slightly adapt the way I speak to people who are not native English speakers to ensure they understand me clearly. This small gesture goes farther than you might think.

I don't think there is any road map, or book, or clear way to identify the different ways to conduct business in new places or with new people without sitting down face to face and going through the process of getting to know a person and their approach to business. That said, being a part of a large multinational company, we have access to great resources and people who have led business ventures all over the world, and this gives us an advantage as we develop our business in new countries. Like many companies, we have identified Brazil as an emerging market and purchased a small, four-person agency (B2S Marketing) to help establish Octagon. During my trips to Brazil, I have met many great people and found them to be a smart, talented, and proud group of people. Many are looking to the World Cup and Olympic Games as a way to celebrate and further introduce their culture to the world. From a business standpoint, we have been able to integrate the best practices from around the world to help grow a small Brazilian agency of four people into an agency of more than 50 people in a 2-year period. I am very proud to say that this group of like-minded and service-oriented people could work in any Octagon office. I attribute this to finding great people with similar characteristics yet with diversity of thought, diversity of experiences, and diversity of cultures. When you introduce a common goal to people with these kinds of backgrounds you can realize great results.

Q: What skills are required of a leader with respect to leadership in the international community?

Leaders must have a vision for their business. In doing so, they must be available and visible to their employees and clients, set clear objectives, be accountable, and be great listeners and communicators. I believe these skills apply to all realms of leadership, not just business.

Respect is not granted to leaders, it is earned. Our business is a hands-on business. Our leaders share many of the same jobs on a day-to-day basis as everyone else in the organization. One of the things I firmly believe in is not asking someone to do something that I have not done in the past or that I am not willing to do. Hard work is an expectation of all. This helps to develop respect throughout the organization. Having said that, years of experience in the sports industry carries some weight with people in countries where the sports market isn't as mature. However, that can only take you so far. Leading by example continues to be my approach in the United States and abroad. Hiring great people and letting them do their job is a successful philosophy. We hire good people who are good at their jobs and help position them to succeed.

My experiences have proven that good ideas come from everywhere and everyone within an organization.

Q: What ways/techniques have you developed in having to work in an international setting?

Being available is important when working in an international business setting. Having to account for time changes and geography challenges is part of this environment. Communication in this sense is essential. In today's day and age, communication and availability are made easier through technology. Technology offers us the ability to communicate effectively across time zones and geographies in real time.

Awareness of situations, awareness of cultural differences, and awareness of the business landscape of a particular country, like laws or business practices, is extremely important. International business requires a degree of sensitivity to situations, to people and cultures. That sensitivity needs to be part of a leadership culture, and training helps to reinforce this throughout an organization.

Q: Do you have any best practices for leading in sport business on an international scale?

Be a good listener, which might sound counterintuitive. When you listen more than talk, you learn a lot about the individual or an issue. You then get to apply your expertise drawing from past experiences. I like to process as much information as possible on a topic prior to making a decision or formulating a plan. That's important when interacting with people from other countries. Give them the opportunity to not only explain the issue, but also the cultural context around that issue, before providing feedback.

Be solutions-oriented. Identifying problems is not particularly difficult; identifying the solution is often the real challenge. This is where great people separate themselves from the pack.

Identify and communicate goals. Whether for individuals, teams, or organizations, establishing goals and a strategy provides a clear roadmap for success along with accountability.

KEY TERMS

cultural acumen
global emotional intelligence
global intellectual intelligence
globalization
globalized economy
globalized sport industry

global leadership competencies
Global Leadership Triad
global reach and influence
glocalization
individualism
universalism

DISCUSSION QUESTIONS

1. Consider recent global initiatives by U.S.-based professional sport organizations (National Football League [NFL], NBA, MLB, National Hockey League [NHL], or MLS). Describe one of those major global initiatives and discuss three major leadership challenges associated with that initiative.
2. As described in the Global Leadership Triad model developed by Brake (2007), to be an effective global leader one must be self-reflective and be open to change. Consider your own values and communication styles and describe how those will help you develop skills as a global leader. What challenges do you recognize you will face based on your values and communication style that may hinder your leadership development?
3. If you were responsible for setting up a new player development program for MLB in South America, describe the process of leadership training you would plan for the senior management team that would be responsible for managing the new program.
4. Imagine you have obtained an internship working for a team in the English Premier League. What steps should you consider so that you can immerse yourself in the experiential learning process while working for a top international sport organization?
5. Describe two challenges that leaders of major sport organizations must face when attempting to implement a new marketing plan within a global context.

REFERENCES

Bird, A., & Osland, J. (2004). Global competencies: An introduction. In H. W. Lane, M. L. Maznevski, M. E. Mendenhall, & J. McNett (Eds.), *Handbook of global management* (pp. 57–80). Oxford, England: Blackwell.

Black, S., Morrison, A., & Gregersen, H. (1999). *Global explorers: The next generation of leaders.* New York: Routledge.

Bloomberg Businessweek. (2013). Under Armour Inc-Class A (UA:New York). Retrieved from http://investing .businessweek.com/research/stocks/financials /financials.asp?ticker=UA

Brake, T. (1997). *The global leader: Critical factors for creating the world class organization.* Chicago, IL: Irwin.

Bu, T. (2009). Beijing Olympics: A new brand of China. *Asian Sport Science, 5*(3), 84–90.

Clarkson, M. B. E. (1995). A stakeholder framework for analyzing and evaluating corporate social performance. *Academy of Management Review, 20,* 92–117.

Crawford, G. (2008). *Consuming sport* (2nd ed.). London: Routledge.

Danylchuk, K. (2011). Internationalizing ourselves: Realities, opportunities, and challenges. *Journal of Sport Management, 25,* 1–10.

Dessaur, C. (2009). Team player. *Bethesda Magazine.* Retrieved from http://www.bethesdamagazine.com /Bethesda-Magazine/March-April-2009/Team-Player/

Evans, M., & House, R. J. (1971). A path-goal theory of leader effectiveness. *Administrative Science Quarterly, 16,* 321–339.

Fairley, S., & Lizandra, M. (2012). International sport. In L. P. Masteralexis, C. A. Barr, & M. A. Hums (Eds.), *Principles and practice of sport management* (pp. 187–217). Sudbury, MA: Jones and Bartlett Learning.

Fiedler, F. E. (1967). *A theory of leadership effectiveness.* New York: McGraw-Hill.

Fischer, K. (2009). Number of foreign students in U.S. hit a new high last year. *Chronicle of Higher Education.* Retrieved from http://chronicle.com/article/Number- of-Foreign-Students-in/49142

Freeman, R. E. (1984). *Strategic management: A stakeholder approach.* Boston, MA: Pitman.

Girginov, V., Papadimitriou, P., & De D'amico, R. L. (2006). Cultural orientations of sport managers. *European Sport Management Quarterly, 6,* 35–66.

Goldblatt, J. (2005). *Special events: Event leadership for a new world* (4th ed.). Hoboken, NJ: John Wiley & Sons.

Grunert-Beckman, S. C., & Askegaard, S. (1997). Seeing with the mind's eye: On the use of pictorial stimuli in values and lifestyle research. In L. R. Kahle & L. Chiagouris (Eds.), *Values, lifestyles, and psychographics* (pp. 161–182). Mahwah, NJ: Lawrence Erlbaum Associates.

Gupta, A. (2009). The globalization of sports, the rise of non-Western nations, and the impact on international sporting events. *International Journal of the History of Sport, 26,* 1779–1790.

Hersey, P., & Blanchard, K. H. (1977). *Management of organizational behavior: Utilizing human resources* (3rd ed.). Upper Saddle River, NJ: Prentice Hall.

Hill, J. S., & Vincent, J. (2006). Globalization and sports branding: The case of Manchester United. *International Journal for Sport Marketing and Sponsorship, 2,* 213–230.

Jayne, V. (2008). Kiwi style: Going global. *New Zealand Management, 55,* 21–25.

Jenkins, W. (2005). The pitch for a new leadership metaphor. *Human Resource Planning, 28*(1), 19–20.

Jokinen, T. (2004). Global leadership competencies: A review and discussion. *Journal of European Industrial Training, 29,* 199–216.

Maguire, J. (1999). *Global sport: Identities, societies, civilizations.* Cambridge, MA: Polity Press.

Marginson, S. (2006). Dynamics of national and global competition in higher education. *Higher Education, 52*(1), 1–39.

Matusitz, J., & Leanza, K. (2009). Wal-Mart: An analysis of the glocalization of the cathedral of consumption in China. *Globalizations, 6*(2), 187–205. doi:10.1080 /14747730902854158

Means, J., & Nauright, J. (2007). Going global: The NBA sets its sights on Africa. *International Journal of Sports Marketing and Sponsorship, 3,* 40–50.

Mendenhall, M. E. (2013). Leadership and the birth of global leadership. In M. E. Mendenhall, J. S. Osland, A. Bird, G. R. Oddou, M. L. Maznevski, M. J. Stevens, & G. K. Stahl (Eds.), *Global leadership* (2nd ed., pp. 15–32). New York: Routledge.

Morrison, A. J. (2000). Developing a global leadership model. *Human Resource Management, 39,* 117–131.

Oddou, G. R., & Mendenhall, M. E. (2013). Global leadership development. In M. E. Mendenhall, J. S. Osland, A. Bird, G. R. Oddou, M. L. Maznevski, M. J. Stevens, & G. K. Stahl (Eds.), *Global leadership* (2nd ed., pp. 229–253). New York: Routledge.

Osland, J. S. (2013). An overview of the global leadership literature. In M. E. Mendenhall, J. S. Osland, A. Bird, G. R. Oddou, M. L. Maznevski, M. J. Stevens, & G. K. Stahl (Eds.), *Global leadership* (2nd ed., pp. 54–93). New York: Routledge.

Osland, J. S., & Bird, A. (2013). Process models of global leadership development. In M. E. Mendenhall, J. S. Osland, A. Bird, G. R. Oddou, M. L. Maznevski, M. J. Stevens, & G. K. Stahl (Eds.), *Global leadership* (2nd ed., pp. 111–126). New York: Routledge.

Parent, M. M., & Foreman, P. O. (2007). Organizational image and identity management in large-scale sporting events. *Journal of Sport Management, 21,* 15–40.

Parent, M. M., & Séguin, B. (2008). Toward a model of brand creation for international large-scale sporting events: The impact of leadership, context, and nature of the event. *Journal of Sport Management, 22*(5), 526–549.

Pfahl, M. E. (2011). Key concepts and critical issues. In M. Li, E. W. MacIntosh, & G. A. Bravo (Eds.), *International Sport Management* (pp. 3–29). Champaign, IL: Human Kinetics.

Plunkett Research. (2010). *Sports industry trends and statistics.* Rockville, MD: Market Research.

Rhinesmith, S. (2003). Global leadership and global emotional intelligence. In M. Goldsmith, V. Govindarajan, B. Kaye, & A. A. Vincete (Eds.), *The many facets of leadership* (pp. 215–228). Upper Saddle River, NJ: Prentice Hall.

Rokeach, M. (1973). *The nature of human values.* New York: Free Press.

Rowe, D., & Gilmour, C. (2010). Sport, media, and consumption in Asia: A merchandised milieu. *American Behavioral Scientist, 53,* 1530–1548.

Rutter, T. (2013). Will a new global strategy lift Under Armour stock? Retrieved from http://www.fool.com/investing/general/2013/06/03/will-a-new-global-strategy-lift-under-armour-stock.aspx

Scott, S. G., & Lane, V. R. (2000). A stakeholder approach to organizational identity. *Academy of Management Review, 25,* 43–62.

Sharrow, R. (2012). Under Armour CEO Kevin Plank 'prudent' on the Olympics. Retrieved from http://www.bizjournals.com/baltimore/news/2012/07/24/under-armour-ceo-kevin-plank-patient.html

Stoner, J. A. F., Freeman, R. E., & Gilbert, D. R. (1995). *Management* (6th ed.). Englewood Cliffs, NJ: Prentice Hall.

Thibault, L. (2009). Globalization of sport: An inconvenient truth. *Journal of Sport Management, 23,* 1–20.

Tomkovick, C., Al-Khatib, J., Baradwaj, B. G., & Jones, S. I. (1996). An assessment of the service quality provided to foreign students at U.S. business schools. *Journal of Education for Business, 61*(3), 130–135.

Trefis Team. (2013). Under Armour can flex various muscles for growth. Retrieved from http://www.trefis.com/stock/ua/articles/192921/under-armour-can-flex-various-muscles-for-growth/2013-06-27

Van Der Wagen, L. (2001). *Event management for tourism, cultural, business and sporting events.* Sydney, Australia: Pearson.

Walker, S., & Tehrani, M. (2011). Strategic management in international sport. In M. Li, E. W. MacIntosh, & G. A. Bravo (Eds.), *International sport management* (pp. 31–51). Champaign, IL: Human Kinetics.

Yang, R. (2003). Globalisation and higher education development: A critical analysis. *Revue Internationale de l'Education, 49*(3–4), 269–291.

Yeung, A., & Ready, D. (1995). Developing leadership capabilities of global corporations: A comparative study in eight nations. *Human Resource Management, 34,* 529–547.

Yukl, G. A., & Mahsud, R. (2010). Why flexible and adaptive leadership is essential. *Consulting Psychology Journal, 62,* 81–93.

Zhang, J. J., Cianfrone, B. A., & Min, S. D. (2011). Resilience and growth of the sport industry in North America. *International Journal of Asian Society for Physical Education, Sport, and Dance, 9,* 132–139.

Zhang, J. J., Jensen, B. E., & Mann, B. L. (1997). Modification and revision of the Leadership Scale for Sport. *Journal of Sport Behavior, 20*(1), 105–122.

CHAPTER 18

REAL WORLD APPLICATIONS AND CAREER PATHS

Tim Liptrap

CHAPTER OBJECTIVES

- Recognize the importance of taking on leadership roles, regardless of how small, while at school, work, home, or an internship site, or on sport teams.
- Identify leadership and experiential opportunities at school, work, home, or an internship site, or on the field of play.
- Discuss the ethics, professionalism, and maturity required at work and internship sites.
- Understand how to network with individual leaders to seek a mentorship or future opportunities.

CASE STUDY

The Internship Dilemma

It was the week prior to Spring Break in March 2012, and junior sport management student Michael Minor was wrestling with a decision that could change the course of his career path for years to come. He explained to his advisor that he had two internship opportunities on the table and had to make a decision by April 1, which was less than 2 weeks away. It was apparent to the advisor that the decision was difficult because both internships offered excellent opportunities for his leadership development, but one internship site had a perceived stronger brand in the marketplace than the other.

(continues)

Both internships would start June 1 and continue through the end of the fall semester of his senior year, at which time he would return to campus to complete his degree. Both internships would require him to move away from home and school; the money for rent, food, and living expenses were about the same and each internship site was willing to provide a small weekly stipend to help offset expenses.

Michael was offered an internship opportunity at a Worcester, Massachusetts–based not-for-profit agency that supports cancer research. In the internship he would help organize events for both fund- and friend-raising. These events—walks, runs, bikes, and golf and basketball tournaments—were particularly attractive to Michael because they involved event management, which was the type of work he wanted to become involved with as a career. In the position he would have a leadership role in each event, travel throughout New England, and work alongside a well-known event planner. Michael also had an emotional interest in the cause, being that the disease had affected his immediate family in multiple ways.

The second opportunity was to be a ride operator at a nationally known theme park (Disney World). The theme park was different from the cancer agency in that it has a well-defined internship training program in place and works with thousands of students each year. Michael went through three interviews, which included a phone screen, a Skype interview, and a final phone call with a placement officer. He felt he was competing with many other students for the same position, which gave him a sense of accomplishment when he was offered an internship. In this position Michael would be trained in the particulars of the ride he would work on, visitor safety, extensive customer service, leadership, and, in addition, he would be exposed to other student interns from around the world. In his conversation with his advisor, Michael felt that being a ride operator was not for him, but he was willing to consider this unique opportunity because it was with Disney in Florida.

Prior to the meeting with his advisor, Michael developed a SWOT (strengths, weaknesses, opportunities, threats) analysis for both positions. The strengths of Disney were the brand name and the training program for customer service and leadership, along with the opportunity for growth at the end (potential employment). The strengths of the not-for-profit agency included the event management skills, being able to do a "little of everything," having a professional mentor in the field, traveling throughout New England, and the opportunity to develop his leadership skills.

The weakness of the Disney program was focused around the type of work he would be doing as a ride operator. He did not think the title or the work were what he wanted to have on his resume, and he was afraid of being pigeonholed in one area and not being able to work in other parts of the business. The weaknesses of the agency were that the operation was small (less than 10 people), he found the office culture "stuffy," and there was little potential to be employed later on.

The opportunity for employment at Disney and its related companies (ABC, ESPN) seemed more extensive than that of the agency, but learning to run events in a nonprofit agency could open doors into the not-for-profit world. Not-for-profits employ 12 million people per year, or 9% of the workforce (University of Wisconsin-Madison, n.d.). Michael's parents were leaning toward Disney because the brand name and logo would be with him the rest of his career. They felt the Disney name would initiate a conversation with potential recruiters and employers.

Knowing Michael from his classroom experiences, his advisor thought Disney might be a better experience overall for him. The advisor believed going away for an internship would allow Michael to focus on the internship and not his family or social life. By doing so, Michael could focus more on the task at hand—his career. In comparison, the not-for-profit agency was located within a 2-hour drive of his family home in Connecticut, and he would have been encouraged by his family and friends to come home on a regular basis, including some nights and most weekends.

Questions for Discussion

1. What is the value of a brand name on your resume? Would you be willing to forego experiences in exchange for being associated with a larger brand name?
2. What differences in training could Michael receive in a larger organization versus a smaller one?
3. Do you agree with his advisor's suggestion to focus solely on his career during an internship experience?
4. If you were Michael, which internship would you have chosen, and why? Which internship seemed to give Michael the better chance to develop and display leadership skills?

INTRODUCTION

This chapter seeks to help students develop leadership skills, both while they are in school and during their first years in the workplace. The chapter begins with thoughts and research on how to build leadership skills, differentiating some of the core leadership skills from the top-level competencies. The author then recommends several ways to take advantage of opportunities on campus or in nearby communities. He touches on the importance of itemization, which is the act of identifying the skills you are developing and then connecting them to your leadership development.

The importance of internships cannot be understated, and the chapter spends a fair amount of time discussing how to search for internships, how to apply for them, and how to conduct yourself at an internship interview and at a site after you have received the position. Furthermore, the chapter makes clear why internships are important for young people. For many students, internships and other practical experiences open up opportunities for networking and acquiring mentors, concepts that are also covered in the chapter. Finally, the author gives advice on how to initially build leadership skills after a graduate has landed that first job.

The information in this chapter is of great value to upper-level undergraduate students and graduate students who are getting ready to make their way into the workplace. It should get them thinking about which leadership skills they already possess and which ones they need to acquire to be a successful professional in the sport industry.

BUILDING LEADERSHIP SKILLS

Sport teams, sponsors, agencies, and other related businesses are looking for new and energized leaders. A study conducted by the National Association of Colleges and Employers (NACE) found employers hiring a new employee are looking for leadership skills that include communication, teamwork, problem solving, decision making, and the ability to influence others. In the same study, it was found that 95% of employers believe work experience should factor into a hiring decision (NACE, 2012).

The youth unemployment rate at the national level for the 18–29 age group in February 2013 was reported at 13.1% (MyCommNet, 2013). Employers, professors, and college students understand that college students need to develop their skills and experience to compete in the job market. Older adults who have been laid off and out of work for an extended amount of time are taking open positions that otherwise would have been made available to recent college graduates. Workers older than 55 took 58% of all new jobs between July 2011 and July 2012, according to the Center for Economic and Policy Research (Kavoussi, 2012).

For new graduates to stand out in a competitive marketplace, they must be able to demonstrate leadership skills and highlight practical experience. In addition to maintaining a strong GPA (3.0 or higher), undergraduate students should engage in extracurricular activities such as participating on a sport team, volunteering for projects, organizing events, leading a club, running for office, or managing a group or team. By doing so, students will be able to practice leadership skills introduced in coursework.

College students are improving upon their leadership activities every day. By accomplishing tasks such as homework, written papers, and tests on a regular basis, it could be argued students are developing strong time management, communication, and problem-solving skills, which are all traits of a good leader. This is true, but it is hard to demonstrate in an interview with future employers how these skills are a benefit.

Students may also find other leadership opportunities outside the college campus. Leadership activities can take place in a hometown, high school, church, work, or recreational program. Undergraduate students are encouraged to volunteer for projects that will help build their leadership capabilities, skills, and experience during both their winter and summer breaks. Even if a leadership experience happens outside the academic campus, it can still be included on a resume or in a leadership portfolio.

A resume acts as a sales brochure highlighting the student's specific job positions, responsibilities, dates served, awards, activities, and skill sets. A resume gives enough information to warrant an employer to conduct a screening interview, generally over the phone. If a candidate makes it to the next round or the second interview, then a leadership portfolio should be brought along as well. A *leadership portfolio* is a compilation of work examples, projects, spreadsheets, and writing samples that can be used to demonstrate a candidate's leadership ability and other skills. A leadership portfolio can be as simple as a three-ring binder with relevant materials enclosed, or to the more extreme, elevator pitch videos, individualized websites, or sales videos posted online.

The *elevator pitch* is a one-minute sales pitch students craft as a branding message about themselves. Information about how to tailor the your elevator pitch to try and obtain an employment position can be found here (http://www.forbes.com/sites/nextavenue/2013/02/04/the-perfect-elevator-pitch-to-land-a-job/), Other examples can be found on YouTube with a simple search for "elevator speeches."

The Four Cs

In its 2012 Critical Skills Survey, the American Management Association found "the ability to think critically, solve problems, innovate, and collaborate are highly valued at every level within the organization" (PR Newswire, 2013, para.1). Additionally, three out of four managers and executives of the 768 surveyed said the four Cs of *critical thinking, communication, collaboration,* and *creativity* will become ever more important in the fast-paced, competitive global economy. By understanding what is needed in the workforce prior to graduation, a student can build these skills before leaving campus, or early on in a career.

The top-level competencies of critical thinking, communication, collaboration, and creativity are developed in individuals through experiential learning. *Experiential learning* simply means students need to gain "real world" work experience as part of the learning process. Experiential learning is instrumental in acquiring the four Cs. But prior to developing expertise in the four Cs, young leaders must develop competencies in core skills first. The core skills associated with strong leadership include the individualized development of analytic skills, communication, delegation, interpersonal skills, organizational skills, problem solving, strategic planning, time management, tactfulness, and teamwork.

SKILLS IN ACTION

To illustrate common skills associated with strong leadership, this chapter will use an example of a college student who is volunteering to manage a local Little League team, and how the day-to-day tasks can build leadership skills. The team has 11 players, 1 head coach (the college student), 2 assistant coaches, and parents who are actively involved in their children's athletic development.

- *Analytic skills:* These competencies are numerically or statistically based and are used to problem solve. As a coach, data such as player statistics, errors, runs batted in (RBIs), and times at bat could be used to develop a stronger team or try to create a competitive advantage.
- *Communication skills:* These competencies include speaking capability, written communication, presenting, and listening (Robles, 2012). A coach's communication skills are imperative because he or she will speak with players, parents, and league officials. Understanding how to use words and body language to communicate helps the coach transmit a correct message to the parents.

- *Delegation skills:* This denotes the coach assigning work to be completed by others. Delegating work to assistant coaches and volunteer parents displays leadership capabilities.
- *Interpersonal skills:* The ability to be sociable, nice, personable, patient, friendly, and nurturing; showing a sense of humor and empathy; and exhibiting self-control (Robles, 2012) are important traits for leaders. As a coach, strong interpersonal skills help build rapport and trust among players and parents.
- *Problem-solving skills:* These are methods and techniques used to develop and find solutions for problems. As a coach you will need to manage problems as they arise without getting frazzled by the situation.
- *Strategic planning skills:* This area of the skills set helps an organization focus on producing effective decisions and actions that create value (Bryson, 2004). As a coach, you will need to plan the team lineups, player positions, and batting order, while maintaining fair amounts of playing time and the desire to produce both fun and wins.
- *Time management skills:* These competencies are used in balancing multiple tasks at once and making the most out of available time. As a coach, time management skills come into play when the team is practicing at multiple stations, and the coach is in charge of the processes.
- *Teamwork skills:* These include being cooperative, getting along with others, and being agreeable, supportive, helpful, and collaborative (Robles, 2012). Leaders must encourage players on teams to work together, trust each other, and support each other.

By itemizing the tasks done on a baseball field— or any other practical experience—students can demonstrate how the projects they engage in have transferable skills to any type of leadership role. This itemization should be done before composing a resume so skills can be mentioned within bulleted job duties or in an overview at the top of a resume.

LEADERSHIP OPPORTUNITIES ON CAMPUS

During college, it is a good idea to take advantage of the opportunities made available at your institution. Many classes in sport management programs are now programming experiential-learning opportunities into the curriculum so students will experience a classroom assignment in a "real work" environment. In addition, these assignments provide an opportunity for students to begin building their resumes while in school. Springfield College in Springfield, Massachusetts, utilizes approximately 80–100 sport management students every January to staff the Spalding Hoophall Classic, sponsored by the Basketball Hall of Fame. This national high school basketball showcase is a 5-day event during which undergraduate students work as ushers, security personnel, liaisons to teams, and supervisors. Upper-level sport management students serve as supervisors while freshmen and sophomores perform liaison, security, ushering, and media check-in duties. The tournament provides a perfect marriage of curriculum with student leadership development. Although faculty members are present at the tournament to answer questions, the student supervisors are in charge of various leadership duties, such as scheduling shifts, delegating, mentoring younger students, and helping provide an exemplary customer service experience to the many players and coaches who have traveled to Springfield. As younger students show proficiency in ushering, security, liaison, and media check-in tasks, they are afforded opportunities to become supervisors at future tournaments.

Faculty members mentor upper-level sport management students during the Spalding Hoophall Classic at Springfield College.
Photo provided by John Borland, courtesy of Springfield College

Not all sport management or business programs have these experiential-learning opportunities available, so students may need to initiate an opportunity if one is not readily available. Ideas and examples of leadership opportunities students can develop for themselves on campus include: take classes in leadership and leadership development; participate in case-study competitions; become a team captain in either a varsity sport or intramurals; actively participate in your Student Government Association (SGA); take a leadership role in Greek life; become a student club president; volunteer to run an event for either student activities or athletics; ask your professor for extra leadership-based projects; volunteer at a local Boys and Girls Club; coach youth sports; volunteer to take the leadership role when working on group projects; become a resident assistant; or work as an orientation leader and/or give campus tours for your admissions office. The opportunities are there; students need to seek them out and get involved.

Student-Athletes

Student-athletes may have difficulty finding the time to volunteer for additional projects outside of the classroom or on the sport field. Many student-athletes dedicate 20–30 hours a week to their sport and simply do not have time (Brown, 2011). To gain leadership skills, student-athletes are encouraged to take on leadership roles within teams on which they play. A leadership role on a sport team may include a position as team captain, co-captain, or team manager.

Students who take on leadership roles within sport teams are shown to have similar skills to those of others who do not participate in sport but volunteer for other activities. Leadership skills such as communication, coordination, and problem solving are developed among these athletes as they are involved in scheduling, organizing, and managing team events (Tanguay, Camp, Endres, & Torres, 2012).

Volunteering

Volunteering at events is a good way for college students to learn about the business of running professional events. The Fiesta Bowl, Federation Cup (women's tennis), Chicago Marathon, and Deutsche Bank Championship are examples of events that look for volunteers to run the event prior to and on game days. The Nichols College Sport Management program views volunteer experiences as an integral part of students' development before looking for a job. Volunteering is important because it:

- Builds students' professional experience
- Provides exposure to the inner workings of events
- Allows for networking with professionals in the sport industry
- Provides support to a local charity event
- Teaches how to work and manage volunteers
- Makes classroom learning more relevant

If your academic program does not encourage volunteering at events, it is recommended that students locate all the major sport, recreation, and entertainment events held in the general geographic vicinity of their hometowns and reach out to offer their time, experience, and skill.

Now that this chapter has discussed the development of leadership skills and places on and off campus where these skills can be obtained, **Tables 18.1** and **18.2** provide a summary of leadership competencies that can be developed based on the event, activity, or project a student is engaged in.

INTERNSHIPS

Ryan and Krapels (1997) define *internships* as "learning opportunities that improve job selection and provide low-cost, nearly risk-free, hands-on job training to prospective employees,

TABLE 18.1 **Leadership Skills by Event, Project, or Activity**

	Analytic	Communication	Delegation	Interpersonal	Organizational	Problem Solving	Strategic Planning	Time Management	Tactfulness	Teamwork
Athletic team manager	x	x	x	x	x	x		x	x	x
Campus tours		x		x	x	x		x	x	
Case study competitions	x	x	x	x	x	x	x	x	x	x
Classes in leadership development		x		x	x	x	x	x	x	
Coaching youth sports	x	x	x	x	x	x	x	x	x	x
Event or student activities		x	x	x	x	x	x	x	x	x
Group projects		x	x	x	x	x	x	x	x	x
Leadership-based projects		x	x	x	x	x	x	x	x	x
Leadership position in Greek life		x	x	x	x	x	x	x	x	x
Orientation leader		x		x	x	x		x	x	x
Resident assistant		x	x	x	x	x		x	x	x
Running a radio show		x		x	x	x		x	x	
Special event or tournament for athletics	x	x	x	x	x	x	x	x	x	x
Student-athlete		x	x	x	x	x		x	x	x
Student club president	x	x	x	x	x	x	x	x	x	x
Student Government Association (SGA)	x	x	x	x	x	x	x	x	x	x
Team captain, either varsity or intramural		x	x	x	x	x		x	x	x
Volunteering at a Boys and Girls Club		x		x	x	x		x	x	x

while at the same time, interns contribute real, productive work" (p. 126). Internships and other experiential opportunities (hands-on work) allow students to build leadership skills and professional skills, and apply their academics to real world situations. Experiential-learning opportunities within companies or schools go by many names, which can include co-opportunities (co-ops), internship, externship, volunteerism, student teaching, or a practicum. For the purpose of our discussion, all of the above will be known as an internship.

Educators find that exposing students to real world experiences such as teaching, management issues, and leadership and administration will provide for an easier and more successful transition for them into the workforce (Turner, 1993). According to Eyler (2009) "Experiential education [internships], which takes students into the community, helps students both to bridge classroom

TABLE 18.2 Leadership Skills by Academic Event, Project, or Activity

	Analytic	Communication	Delegation	Interpersonal	Organizational	Problem Solving	Strategic Planning	Time Management	Tactfulness	Teamwork
Solving case studies	x	x	x		x	x				
Working with databases	x				x	x				
Developing Excel workbooks	x				x	x				
Group project		x	x	x	x	x		x	x	x
PowerPoint presentation	x	x			x					
Giving a presentation/speech		x	x	x	x			x	x	
Reflection paper		x			x	x				
Research paper	x	x			x	x		x		
Simulation game	x		x	x	x	x	x	x		
Creating and conducting survey analysis	x	x	x	x	x	x	x	x	x	x
Volunteering at an event		x		x	x	x		x	x	x

study and life in the world and to transform inert knowledge into knowledge-in-use" (p. 24). In a practical application, an internship is often an organized work situation where a student, receiving little or no money, will volunteer their time at a professional sport organization and receive college credit in his or her academic program. In exchange for their time and energy, students will receive practical hands-on education that may lead to enhanced job skills, leadership skills, and/or future employment.

The National Association of Colleges and Employers (2012) reported that 61.2% of full-time internships have led to a full-time employment offer. This reinforces the fact that internships and volunteer experiences are vital in finding a leadership position in sport, and setting oneself apart in the competitive job market.

For many students, the internship is their first experience in an office atmosphere. In addition to learning specific tasks, students are exposed to a unique organizational culture, which includes the leadership hierarchy, team dynamics, office politics, dress codes, deadlines and timelines, and practical lessons in management.

The length of an internship is dictated by one of two things, generally the amount of credits that a student needs to earn and the team or company the student works for. A full-time internship may require between 10 and 60 hours a week or 100 to 450 hours in the semester. But some organizations might ask a student to work longer than the school requires, given the events or activities the organization has planned during the intern's time with the organization. For example, an intern for a minor league baseball team might start in January to begin promotions for a new season but is often asked to stay during the summer season to assist with game operations.

Who Does an Internship?

Those generally in the college-age group secure internships. Students from any major who are willing to create an experiential education for themselves are encouraged to complete an internship. As the economy has changed, a new trend has emerged in that older generations of employees, not just college-age students, are looking for internships. In a recent trend explained by Cohen (2012), *returnships* (a term trademarked by Goldman Sachs) are internships for those professionals who are resuming a career after a hiatus from work, such as a job layoff, raising a child, or taking time to take care of a sick parent. Companies such as Goldman Sachs, Sara Lee, and Sikorsky Aircraft offer short experiences to those who have been out of work and are trying to break back into the marketplace.

How Do You Find an Internship?

Internships are experiential education opportunities and can be found using a variety of methods. In today's world, it is easy to find internship listings on the Internet, through job search engines, or in specialized locations for internships like portals, such as Teamworkonline.com. Students' first step should be to talk to their professors, along with their career services office. Depending upon the size of a school, there may even be an office dedicated to internships and other practical experience opportunities. Some academic programs have internship coordinators.

Internship seekers who are unsure of the type of internship, place of internship, or desired area in which they would like to use their time should start backward. First, identify the geographic location in which you would like to conduct an internship. Second, identify the team or organization for

which you would like to work. Third, identify the type of work that you would like to do, such as game-day operations, marketing, finance, sales or sponsorship, ticketing, coaching, or public relations. Do not apply only for your dream internship. Be sure to apply for several internships. Having to pick between two or three options can be difficult, but it is better than having no options at all. **Table 18.3** gives examples of the types of companies, events, and leagues that offer internships. This is not an exhaustive list, just examples. Most teams post their current available internships on their websites.

Do not wait until the last minute to begin the internship search. A 6-month window is preferable to do the search. Job postings may not be up when the student is ready to apply, but at least students can identify sites where they would like to apply and possibly talk to others who have worked at these sites.

APPLYING FOR AN INTERNSHIP

Applying for internships takes preparation and planning. Students should have resumes and sample cover letters ready several months before they need to send out applications. These resumes and cover letters need to be vetted by both a student's career services office and the student's academic advisor. Furthermore, different cover letters and resumes need to be sent out for different job postings because each internship site is looking for different skills and competencies. Students must tailor their resumes, cover letters, and portfolios to different work sites.

The companies looking for interns for the summer, fall, or spring will indicate the position title, job description, hours, location, and other information in a job posting. These postings can usually be found on company websites. When applying for a position, students may need to

TABLE 18.3 Internship Site Examples

Potential Internship Site	Website
Anheuser-Busch	www.buschjobs.com/Careers
Cape Cod Baseball League	http://capecodbaseball.org/teams/players
Disney Professional Internships	http://disneyinterns.com
ESPN	http://espncareers.com/campus/internships.aspx
International Management Group	www.imgworld.com/careers/internships-usa.aspx
Ladies Professional Golf Association	http://golfjobs.lpga.com/teamwork/jobs/
Live Nation	http://concerts.livenation.com/careers
Major League Baseball	www.mlb.com/careers
Major League Soccer	http://www.mlssoccer.com/jobs
NASCAR	www.employment.nascar.com/#/internship
National Basketball Association	www.nba.com/careers/internship_program.html
National Collegiate Athletic Association	www.ncaa.org
National Football League	www.nfl.com/careers/internships
National Hockey League	http://hockeyjobs.nhl.com/teamwork/jobs
National Recreation and Park Association	www.nrpa.org
NBCUniversal	www.nbcunicareers.com/internships
Nike	http://nikeinc.com/pages/internships
Octagon	www.octagon.com
PGA Tour	www.pgatour.com/company/internships.html
Royal Caribbean Cruises	https://jobs.rccl.com
SMG Worldwide	http://smgworld.com/jobs/
Tough Mudder	http://toughmudder.com/were-hiring
Under Armour	www.underarmour.jobs/internships.asp
U.S. Golf Association	www.usga.org
U.S. Olympic Team	www.teamusa.org/Careers/Internship-Program.aspx
U.S. Rugby Association	www.usarugby.org/careers
U.S. Sailing	http://home.ussailing.org
U.S. Tennis Association	www.usta.com

upload a resume, cover letter, and potentially a short video about themselves.

Getting Hired

Bryant Richards, the director of corporate governance at Mohegan Sun Casino in Uncasville, Connecticut, asks this question of all potential interns: "What can you bring to the table that somebody else cannot?" Richards wants to know what skills, talents, and uniqueness interns have that others do not possess, and he wants to know about students' willingness to work hard (Bryant Richards, personal communication, 2013).

Richards explained how the expectations of supervisors are relatively low for interns at many sites in the hospitality and sport industries. He said, "In many cases, it does not take much for a manager to say, 'Wow,' when it comes to interns." If a student can create a "Wow" from each of the manager(s) that oversee internships, it is more likely he or she will get better opportunities and increased responsibilities than the other interns.

In getting hired for an internship, students generally have one shot at impressing a corporate recruiter, the department head, or a manager. In many cases, the key it is how students present and represent their skills and talent. By the time an applicant has been invited onto the property, the person in charge of hiring has done background research on the applicant. They have Googled you, checked your Twitter feed, searched for you on Facebook, and have made calls to your professors.

Many of the hiring managers understand the academic programs from which interns have come. They may work with the professors there, look at the courses students have taken, and, in some cases, have helped build the projects students do in class. Richards said that during the interview process he looks for internship candidates to demonstrate their leadership potential, which can be illustrated by past experiences on their resumes. Richards said his organization also looks for transferable skills that Mohegan can

work with because of the industry training interns will receive.

Richards said that many times it is the simple things that occur during the internship interview that make the difference. Did an applicant show up on time? How did he or she treat the receptionist? Is the student dressed for the position? Is the student prepared for the position? Did the student do their homework on the company?

Richards said his organization seeks interns with burgeoning leadership skills, and he identifies these by looking for leadership roles that can be demonstrated by the students. Those roles could be in one's community, being an resident assistant, working in the admissions office on campus, or working in other team-like environments that put the students into situations where they need to work together and make judgments quickly.

Richards pointed out that organizations, unlike academic programs, do not accept "C" work. Although a professor may accept work late with a points deduction or grade assignments on a sliding scale, this situation does not exist in the workplace. Students need to get the job done right the first time. In the workforce, it is not OK to get a 70 on a document that is turned in to a supervisor. Getting a 70 on a work project means that the boss will have to redo it, and it also shows that the student did not have the skill or desire to complete work with high standards (Bryant Richards, personal communication, 2013).

"You're Fired"

Donald Trump is well known for his trademarked line, "You're fired." Similar to what happens on his reality TV show, it is possible to be fired as an intern. It does not happen very often, but to protect yourself from being fired, you should understand the rules of employment at your internship site. Sport management professor Timothy Liptrap from Nichols College, who publically speaks on the use of social media, tells a story about one of his junior sport management students who was released from his internship with an NFL team due to a Twitter post. After his first day of work, the student was so excited that he Tweeted about his day. In reality, it was not a significant post, but the student violated the NFL team's social media policy by putting the team name in a Twitter post without permission. Another student took an internship with the New York Knicks and shortly after he started, the student decorated his cubicle with Boston Celtics banners, flags, and pictures. The student was not fired, but he did receive a warning from his supervisor. As an intern, you must know that work policies are different than those of your college. Liptrap and Richards of Mohegan Sun recommend these tips for interns:

- Be the first one in the office every day and the last to leave.
- Show up on time.
- Dress appropriately for the position.
- Do what you say you are going to do.
- Try to solve a problem (before you ask your boss for help).
- Identify problems that your boss may not have noticed yet.
- Respect the culture of the office.
- Have loyalty to the company.
- Do it right the first time.
- Do not embarrass the college, your professor, or yourself.
- Do not embarrass your manager or boss.
- Plan ahead on projects.
- Act professionally at all times.
- Shake hands well and firmly, and make good eye contact.
- Have conversations with people of all different backgrounds.

NETWORKING AND RELATIONSHIP BUILDING

It has often been said in the sport industry—and probably by your professors—that finding a job comes down to whom you (or your relatives) know or, as others say, who knows you. Many young college graduates have proven this theory wrong by working hard at internships and showing off their skills, talents, and experiences. In other words, they have made themselves indispensable to organizations. This is not to say that whom you know is not important, because it is. Having a large network of friends, business colleagues, and friends of friends has opened doors to opportunities for many people, young and old.

Networking Tools

Susan Adams, the author of *Me 2.0: 4 Steps to Building Your Future*, has created a list of what she believes to be the six most important *networking* tools newly graduated college students should use to get their first job out of college (Adams, 2012). Her list includes:

1. Create a LinkedIn profile.
2. Establish a presence on WordPress or through your own blog.
3. Get an internship as early as possible.
4. Get creative about finding a mentor.
5. Use your school's career services office.
6. Join a professional development or industry-specific group.

Networking cannot wait until after school, however. It should start when a student begins school. Getting to know professors, setting up "job shadows" at nearby organizations, attending conferences such as baseball's Winter Meetings, attending lectures on campus given by leaders, and volunteering at events and then offering your services again after the event is over to an organizer are all part of networking activities that students can pursue in school. Furthermore, at internship sites, students often make the mistake of only getting to know their supervisors. Getting to know everyone in the building and finding out their paths to their current jobs is a strategy students should employ.

Mentoring

Relationship building can also be accomplished through acquiring a mentor; furthermore, if the mentor is a leader, this can be a way for a student to model leadership behavior and build leadership skills. A mentor could be one of your parents, a coach, an employer, a professor, or a friend whom you admire for their accomplishments. According to Holland, Major, and Orvis (2012), a mentor is a seasoned professional or peer who provides guidance, encouragement, and social support to help a mentee succeed in their social life, job, or career. Having a mentor aids in a student's personal and career development—in particular, when enhancing a student's leadership skills. Goulet (2011) found that there is a correlation between *mentorship* and leadership, "particularly after practicing leadership through challenging experiences, developing leaders benefit from the mentoring a more experienced person can offer" (p. 51).

In addition to developing leadership skills, acquiring and working with a mentor may lead to increased income at work. It was found that young professionals who have had a positive mentor have earned more than $7,000 a year more than their peers who did not (Fried, Lim, Mangla, Rosato, & Wang, 2013).

Finding a Mentor

A young professional may need to take a proactive approach when developing a relationship with a potential mentor. It is not uncommon to have multiple mentors for different life stages or phases within a career. Your first career mentor should be one whom you admire, respect, and believe can help you reach your next goal.

Mentorship should be seen as a two-way street. In the corporate world, the next level past mentorship is called sponsorship. A mid-level to senior-level leader in a company will sponsor a younger employee and help them with their career decisions and leadership development, and position them for success. This model and sponsorship would consider the mentee as a protégé. In a study of 4,000 sponsors and protégés, sponsors indicated that the most successful protégés are those who demonstrate trust and show loyalty. When the potential sponsors were asked about what it takes to be successful protégés, 62% said protégés should "assume responsibility and be self-directed," 39% said they should "deliver 110%," and 34% said protégés should "offer skill sets and bring a perspective different than mine" (Hewlett, Marshall, & Sherbin, 2011, p. 133).

Getting Started at Your First Job

Essentially, college serves as a minor league. You make mistakes and grow at the same time. You gather practical experiences to put on your resume; you develop networks and acquire mentors. Once you walk across that stage and grab your diploma, and unless you have aspirations to complete a graduate degree, you have graduated to the professional ranks.

Once you start your first job you are naturally nervous and intimidated by the people around you. You may not be quite sure about the work you need to do and how your supervisor perceives you. You may also be concerned about not embarrassing yourself. A common sense model that works in the sport industry has five basic premises; these premises are:

1. Be proactive in your work.
2. Listen more than you speak.
3. Communicate.
4. Keep up with industry trends.
5. Take responsibility for your actions.

Let's step through this model with an example. You have just started a ticket sales job at a professional basketball team. Your supervisor has been in the business for well over 20 years and has a great track record at the team and within the industry. She has an extensive network of other business professionals, as well as those in the league. As you start your first week of work you are learning that the hours are extensive, your boss is very particular, the expectations on you are extreme, and you need to make your sales quota each month.

Be proactive in your work. Chances are your manager is busy with work, her bosses, and other employees. You'll become a model employee if you provide your boss information she needs when she needs it without her having to ask you for it. Be proactive and help your boss in her job, and you will be recognized for it later on. For example, if your boss is going to a meeting with her supervisor and needs Excel spreadsheets from you, be sure to give them to her *before* she needs them.

Listen more than you speak. In your first few months at a new position it is imperative that you listen to others. Although you may have a strong opinion on how the work should be done, it might be offensive to those who have worked there for years if you try to make changes without listening and understanding the process within the office. If you argue with your boss over the way work should be completed, keep in mind you are perceived as being new to the office and "wet behind the ears." A helpful tip would be to take notes as you are shown a new method, process, or work that is required of you.

Communicate. Do not be afraid to ask questions and communicate with your supervisor. Many managers and supervisors would like to see you ask questions because it indicates that you are interested in the work. Asking questions helps you understand what is being presented and shows that you are trying to give your best to the project at hand.

Keep up with industry trends. Show your leadership as you build knowledge in your field. A mistake that many professionals make is not taking time to keep up with changes in the industry. Ask your manager and fellow employees what they read to keep up with industry knowledge. To become an expert in your area it has been shown that you will need to devote more than 10,000 hours of deliberate practice to your trade (Ericsson, Prietula, & Cokely, 2007). It has been shown "consistently and overwhelmingly, experts are always made, not born" (p. 5), and deliberate practice was a key to their success. Your deliberate practice can start your first day at work, by reading the *SportsBusiness Journal*, in-house training manuals, and current news about your industry for an hour a day. By doing so, you will become knowledgeable in the industry and a resource in the office.

Take responsibility for your actions. Be willing to take responsibility for your actions, either good or bad. The sport industry is a small industry, and people are well connected and know each other. Build your reputation on honesty, and that brand will stay with you the rest of your career. When you are with your boss and she asks you a question, answer regardless of whether it has negative consequences—but do it with diplomacy.

This common sense model of the five premises will help you develop a foundation of being a respected leader in the sport industry.

Going back to the example of your new job in ticket sales, you will find that in order to sell tickets and gain respect from your peers and supervisor, you will need to build trust and influence. Dr. Robert Cialdini, the author of *Influence: The Psychology of Persuasion*, encourages young leaders to consider how their actions in the workplace influence those around them. Cialdini's rules, as described by Barbara Kaufman (2011), are simple:

- Tell the truth, and be consistent in your explanations; inconsistency breeds distrust.
- Encourage others to "speak truth to power'" and tell you the truth, no matter how unpalatable.
- Set a good example by admitting your mistakes and developing a culture that expects others to be accountable for and learn from their mistakes.
- Follow through on promises and commitments.

Summary

Students have the opportunity to gain leadership skills in a variety of settings prior to completing their first internships or getting their first entry-level positions. Those leadership opportunities can be gained inside and outside the classroom. Students can take up positions of leadership in student clubs, in volunteer organizations, on intercollegiate or club sports teams, and in Greek life, to name a few. Leadership skills can be developed and refined in this setting and should be included on students' resumes when applying for internship positions. Students should recognize that a first internship can be used as a platform to showcase work skills and also provide the best opportunity to learn from other professionals in the organization. At a student's first internship, he or she can also begin to develop leadership skills in a work setting. Finally, students should seek mentors and develop a network of professional contacts that will help support leadership development.

LEADERSHIP PERSPECTIVE

Carol Stiff.
Courtesy of Carol Stiff

Carol Stiff is Vice President, Content Program and Integration, espnW at ESPN, where she has worked for over 20 years. During that time she has worked in the programming department that shepherded the relationship between the NCAA and ESPN to broadcast the women's college basketball tournament. In her newly created role at ESPN she is now focused on integrating the content and stories from the comprehensive multiplatform espnW initiative and elevating its presence across ESPN.

Q: Considering your own experiences, what opportunities helped you most develop your leadership skills as a young professional? How did you create those opportunities?

I really developed my leadership skills as an athlete, playing on teams, and later as a coach. As a player, coach, and now as a leader, I have learned that each person on the team has a skill and that each person has a role. I have used those lessons throughout my career. As I have reinvented myself and developed new leadership skills over the years, I have taken advantage of new opportunities while working at ESPN—such as working on the V Foundation, which is the ESPN foundation of choice. I worked to develop "V Week" in early December, when we ask our viewers to donate to the foundation. I have also taken the opportunity to work on espnW, work on developing our social networking and digital space, and work with the Kay Yow Cancer Fund. As I have taken on new roles, I have learned to further develop my leadership skills.

Q: Early in your career, how did you begin to develop your professional network? As your career has advanced, how has your approach to networking changed? What advice would you give students regarding how to go about developing their professional networks (in particular, early in their careers)?

I believe that relationships are so important in helping to develop your leadership skills and to advance your network. I have learned that you have to make hard decisions and that you have to make personal connections. You need to be able to pick up the phone and have difficult conversations with people; you need to make those "hard calls."

Q: What role have mentors played in helping you develop your leadership skills throughout your professional career? In particular, how were mentors influential in the early stages of your career?

I have had both male and female mentors throughout my career. My first mentor was a woman working in sports information. She was a trailblazer and navigated the waters of dealing with men in sport media. She really pushed against stereotypes, and she has pushed hard for diversity. I learned through her and through other mentors how to best handle situations as a leader. I still maintain contact with my mentors. Early in my career I went to my boss and talked about problems, but I also provided solutions to those problems. As a leader, I want people to come to me with both the recognition of problems and potential solutions to those problems.

Q: What advice would you give to students regarding selection of their first internship experience/entry-level position? What should students consider when selecting an internship/entry-level position that will best help them to develop their leadership skills?

You need to build your own brand. That means that once you leave your house know that you are representing yourself and your family. Do not embarrass yourself or damage your brand. Always conduct yourself in a professional manner. Always be prepared. You have to listen, listen, listen, and listen. Practice those listening skills. When you cut someone off during a conversation, you are not listening to what that person is saying. Gain as much experience as possible, and ask a lot of questions. In all of your work, go beyond the call of duty and beyond what is asked of you.

You should always be prepared and remember that you don't know it all. Look to your leaders for feedback and be humbled at times.

Finally, the most important advice I would give to students is to practice ethical behavior at all times. You need to recognize ethical boundaries and stay within those boundaries.

Q: What advice would you provide to a student regarding how to begin developing leadership skills during his or her first internship experience?

You should be resourceful and listen to feedback. Then, ask questions to get the facts and then make a decision. An important aspect of leadership is to gather as much information as possible regarding what works and what didn't work. An important aspect of leadership is being willing to share knowledge with others and to also be willing to learn from others.

KEY TERMS

collaboration   internship
communication   leadership portfolio
creativity   mentorship
critical thinking   networking
elevator pitch   returnships
experiential learning

DISCUSSION QUESTIONS

1. As noted in the chapter, undergraduate students can begin to develop leadership skills while in school. Consider your experiences outside the classroom. What leadership skills have you learned and developed from those out of class experiences? What skills do you need to still develop?

2. If you were composing an elevator pitch, what would you be likely to include?

3. What activities can you become involved in while you are at school that can help you to develop your leadership skills?

4. After reading this chapter, it should be apparent how important internships have become. What kind of work would you like to pursue? Which organizations would you like to pursue?

5. Identify a person in your life whom you would consider a mentor. What have you learned from this mentor in regard to leadership skills?

For a full suite of assignments and additional learning activities, use the access code found in the front of your book. If you do not have an access code, you can obtain one at **www.jblearning.com**.

REFERENCES

Adams, S. (2012). 6 things you must do to get your first job after college. *Forbes*. Retrieved from http://www.forbes.com/sites/susanadams/2012/11/12/6-things-you-must-do-to-get-your-first-job-after-college

Brown, G. (2011). Second GOALS study emphasizes coach influence. *National Collegiate Athletic Association*. Retrieved from http://www.ncaa.org/wps/wcm/connect/public/NCAA/Resources/Latest+News/2011/January/Second+GOALS+study+emphasizes+coach+influence

Bryson, J. M. (2004). *Strategic planning for public and nonprofit organizations: A guide to strengthening and sustaining organizational achievement*. San Francisco, CA: Jossey-Bass.

Cohen, C. (2012). The 40-year-old intern. *Harvard Business Review, 90*(11), 21–23.

Ericsson, K. A., Prietula, M. J., & Cokely, E. T. (2007). The making of an expert. *Harvard Business Review, 85*(11), 147.

Eyler, J. (2009). The power of experiential education. *Liberal Education, 95*(4), 24–31.

Fried, C., Lim, P., Mangla, I., Rosato, D., & Wang, P. (2013). Building wealth: Best moves if you're 35 to 44. *Money, 42*(4), 68.

Goulet, L. (2012). Leadership is everybody's business. *T+D, 66*(8), 48–53.

Hewlett, S., Marshall, M., & Sherbin, L. (2011). The relationship you need to get right. *Harvard Business Review, 89*(10), 131–134.

Holland, J. M., Major, D. A., & Orvis, K. A. (2012). Understanding how peer mentoring and capitalization link STEM students to their majors. *Career Development Quarterly, 60*(4), 343–354.

Kaufman, B. (2011). Leadership strategies: Build your sphere of influence. *Business Strategy Series, 12*(6), 315–320. doi: http://dx.doi.org/10.1108/17515631111185950

Kavoussi, B. (2012, July 6). Jobless youths left behind as older workers fill more openings. *Huffington Post*. Retrieved from http://www.huffingtonpost.com/2012/07/06/jobs-young-people_n_1654367.html

MyCommNet. (2013, February 1). Millennial jobs report: Youth unemployment reaches 13.1 percent. *PR Newswire*. Retrieved from http://plp.acc.commnet.edu:6018/ps/i.do?id=GALE%7CA317172410&v=2.1&u=22522&it=r&p=GPS&sw=w

National Association of Colleges and Employers. (2012). Internship and co-op survey. Retrieved from http://www.naceweb.org/research/intern-co-op/2012-survey/

PR Newswire. (2013, February 13). American Management Association survey reveals that more than half of executives admit their employees are "average" at best. Retrieved from http://www.prnewswire.com/news-releases/american-management-association-survey-reveals-that-more-than-half-of-executives-admit-their-employees-are-average-at-best-191016351.html

Robles, M. M. (2012). Executive perceptions of the top 10 soft skills needed in today's workplace. *Business Communication Quarterly, 75*(4), 453–465. doi:10.1177/1080569912460400

Ryan, C., & Krapels, R. H. (1997). Organizations and internships. *Business Communication Quarterly, 60*(4), 126–131.

Tanguay, D. M., Camp, R. R., Endres, M. L., & Torres, E. (2012). The impact of sports participation and gender on inferences drawn from resumes. *Journal of Managerial Issues, 24*(2), 191–206.

Turner, E. T. (1993). On the spot: Spontaneous learning. *Journal of Physical Education, Recreation and Dance, 64*(8), 9–11.

University of Wisconsin-Madison. (n.d.). What are nonprofit jobs and how do I find them? Retrieved from http://careers.ls.wisc.edu/documents/What_are_Nonprofit_Jobs_and_How_Can_I_Find_Them_August_2010.pdf

ABOUT THE CONTRIBUTORS

Peter Bachiochi, PhD

Peter Bachiochi is a professor of psychology at Eastern Connecticut State University, where he teaches courses in Industrial and Organizational Psychology at the undergraduate and graduate levels. He worked for four years at IBM in their HR research group as a survey specialist and internal consultant. He provides survey consulting services to several nonprofit organizations. His research interests include minority employee recruiting and retention, student engagement and retention, affirmative action, job satisfaction, and team leadership. He has published and presented on these topics extensively. He is an ad hoc reviewer for the *Journal of Business and Psychology.*

Blair Browning, PhD

Blair Browning is an assistant professor in the Department of Communication at Baylor University. He teaches courses in leadership and conflict management, as well as small group communication. His research interests center on interim and transitional leadership, the influence of social media with regard to communication and sport, and communication pedagogy. His work has appeared in outlets such as *Human Relations, International Journal of Sport Communication, OD Practitioner*, and *Communication Teacher*. He received the prestigious Collins Outstanding Professor Award at Baylor in 2012.

Jennifer Bruening, PhD

Jennifer Bruening has been a part of the Sport Management program at the University of Connecticut (UConn) since January 2002 after spending eight years as an athletic administrator and volleyball coach at Kenyon College in Ohio, including two years as athletic director. She serves as director of the Laboratory for Sport Management at UConn. Dr. Bruening's research line has focused primarily on barriers and supports for women and minorities in sport. She is a research fellow with Northeastern University's Center for the Study of Sport in Society and the North American Society for Sport Management. Dr. Bruening is also the program founder and director for Husky Sport, a program that provides mentors (UConn students) as planners of sessions at community sites in Hartford, CT, that emphasize exposure and access to sport and physical activity, and advocate good nutrition and healthy lifestyles.

Kenneth K. Chen

Kenneth K. Chen is a PhD candidate of Sport Management in the Department of Kinesiology at the University of Georgia (UGA). He teaches the Introduction to Sport Management course and is a teaching assistant for several other undergraduate courses in sport management. His research interests focus on examining sport consumer behavior from the perspectives of consumer demand and event operations, especially in the context of professional and intercollegiate sports. He has served as the student manager of the International Center for Sport Management (ICSM) at UGA and is a frequent reviewer for *Sport Management Review* and other academic journals.

Sungho Cho, JD/PhD

Sungho Cho is an assistant professor of sport management in the School of Human Movement, Sport, and Leisure Studies at Bowling Green State University. He teaches courses in legal aspects of sport and governance of sport organizations at the undergraduate and graduate levels. His research interests focus on use of social science methods in trademark litigation and multivariate analysis of sport-related case law. As an attorney, Dr. Cho mainly practices in the area of business incorporation and trademarks. He is a member of the New York and Connecticut state bar associations.

Zachary J. Damon, MBA

Zachary J. Damon is a doctoral student in the Sport Management Department at Texas A&M University. He is a teaching assistant for the Diversity in Sport and Sociology of Sport classes, helping to oversee course management and maintenance. Damon uses current leadership theories to focus his research on leadership in sport, including emerging sport contexts that have potentially vital impacts on their communities and members.

Wendi Everton, PhD

Wendi Everton is a professor of industrial and organizational psychology in the Department of Psychology at Eastern Connecticut State University. She teaches courses in statistics, research methods, and psychology of work, including a course in groups and teams. Her research interests focus on the perceptions of fairness in a wide variety of organizations, including academic and sport organizations.

Emmett Gill, PhD

Gill is an assistant professor at the North Carolina Central University (NCCU) Department of Social Work and the director of the Student-Athletes Human Rights Project (SAHRP), an organization dedicated to social justice for student-athletes. Prior to working at NCCU, Dr. Gill worked as an assistant professor at Rutgers and at the U.S. Military Academy Center for Enhanced Performance, where he supervised men's and women's basketball student-athletes with academic and athletic performance enhancement. Dr. Gill's scholarship focuses on the intersection between social work and collegiate athletics. His latest work, Integrating Sports into Social Work Education, will appear in the *Journal of Social Work Education.*

Heidi Grappendorf, PhD

Heidi Grappendorf is an assistant professor at the University of Cincinnati in Sport Administration. Before this, Dr. Grappendorf held positions at North Carolina State University, Texas Tech University, Salem State University, and Webber International University. Her research involves the underrepresentation of women and diversity in leadership. Her interests include the lack of women and diversity in sport, as well as Title IX. She has given many national and international presentations, authored journal articles and works in numerous publications, and written several book chapters. She has served as vice president of research for the National Association for Girls and Women in Sport (NAGWS), was on the executive board of the Research Consortium and the editorial board of *Women in Sport & Physical Activity Journal*, and was co-chair of the North American Society for Sport Management Diversity Committee.

Meg G. Hancock, PhD

Meg G. Hancock is an assistant professor of sport administration in the Health and Sport Sciences Department at the University of Louisville (UL). She teaches courses in organizational behavior, sport management and leadership, and sport management principles at the undergraduate and graduate levels. Dr. Hancock's research interests include gender and diversity in the workplace, sport management education, and sport for development. Prior to UL, she worked as an assistant athletic director followed by a stint as assistant dean of first-year students and director of orientation at Dartmouth College.

Maylon T. Hanold, EdD

Maylon T. Hanold is an instructor in the Sport Administration and Leadership master's program at Seattle University. She teaches courses in sport leadership, sport management and organizations, human resources, sport sociology, and sport ethics. She researches sport cultures and sport leadership with a focus on the intersections between attitudes, beliefs, and actions. In her current research, Dr. Hanold examines the various ways that values are articulated and how those inform how ultrarunners experience their bodies. In leadership, she has explored ways in which bodily critical self-awareness can lead to more inclusive ways of leading and more inclusive perceptions of competent leaders.

Algerian Hart, PhD

Algerian Hart serves as graduate program coordinator for the Sport Management program and assistant professor in the Department of Kinesiology at Western Illinois University. A former world-class athlete and coach, Dr. Hart has served the collegiate athletic community as a recognized NCAA speaker for hazing as well as drug and alcohol awareness. His research interests include international approaches to sport leadership, the value of diversity in sport history, and the plight of NCAA-governed student-athlete matriculation. He teaches courses in sport leadership, financial issues in sport, sport organizational behavior, and sport governance and policy.

Larena Hoeber, PhD

Larena Hoeber is an associate professor of Kinesiology and Health Studies at the University of Regina. She teaches courses on volunteer management, diversity, and sociology of sport at the undergraduate level, and qualitative research methods at the graduate level. Her research agenda focuses on the use of organizational culture to understand and critique the functioning of amateur sport organizations, the understanding of socio-cultural issues within sport, and the employment of a variety of qualitative research methods. Her specific research interests are in the areas of organizational culture and values, diversity-related issues, innovation, and volunteerism. Dr. Hoeber has published her research in the *Journal of Sport Management; Sport Management Review; Qualitative Research in Sport, Exercise and Health; Gender, Work & Organization; Sex Roles; European Sport Management Quarterly*; and *International Journal of Sport Management and Marketing*. Dr. Hoeber served as the 2013–2014 NASSM president.

Orland Hoeber, PhD

Orland Hoeber is an associate professor in the Department of Computer Science at the University of Regina. Although his primary research interests are in the domains of information visualization, geo-visual analytics, and web search interfaces, Dr. Hoeber also has interests in the process of innovation and the use of novel computer technology to support the collection and analysis of data in business and academic research contexts. He is a principal investigator, co-investigator, or collaborator on multiple research grants from both the Natural Sciences and Engineering Research Council of Canada (NSERC) and the Social Sciences and Humanities Research Council of Canada (SSHRC).

Mary A. Hums, PhD

Mary A. Hums is a professor of sport administration at the University of Louisville. She was the 2009 NASSM Earle F. Zeigler Lecturer, was an Erasmus Mundus Visiting International Scholar in Belgium, and represented the United States at the International Olympic Academy in Olympia, Greece. Dr. Hums worked the Paralympic Games in Atlanta, Salt Lake City, Athens, and Vancouver, as well as the Olympic Games in Athens. She also served as athletic director at Saint Mary-of-the-Woods College. She is the author/editor of five books and numerous articles and book chapters. Dr. Hums has given more than 150 presentations both domestically and abroad. She earned her PhD from Ohio State University, an MBA and MA from the University of Iowa, and a BBA from the University of Notre Dame. Dr. Hums contributed to Article 30.5 of the United Nations Convention on the Rights of Persons with Disabilities and is a Research Fellow at the Institute for Human Centered Design. She is an inductee to the Indiana ASA Softball Hall of Fame.

Jay J. Kim

Jay J. Kim is a doctoral student in the Sport Management and Policy program at the University of Georgia. As a graduate assistant, he has taught various undergraduate basic physical education courses such as soccer, racquetball, and bowling. Drawing theories from sport marketing, media, and technology, his research interests focus on the technological and psychological factors that affect sport consumer behavior. He has presented at international and national conferences.

David Legg, PhD

David Legg is a professor in the Department of Physical Education and Recreation at Mount Royal University in Calgary, Canada. He is actively involved as an educator, researcher, and volunteer in sport management and adapted physical activity. In 2004, Dr. Legg was a visiting professor at Dalhousie University in Halifax, Canada, and in 2008–2009 at Deakin University in Melbourne. As a volunteer, Dr. Legg is the president for the Canadian Paralympic Committee, leadership team member for Canadian Sport for Life, and board member for the Toronto 2015 Pan Parapan American Games.

Ming Li, EdD

Ming Li is a professor of sports administration and interim executive director of the Center for International Studies at Ohio University. His research interests are in financial and economic aspects of sport and management of sport business in a global context. He has published a number of textbooks in sport management, including *Economics of Sport, Research Methods in Sport Management*, and *International Sport Management*. He previously served on the editorial board of the *Journal of Sport Management* and is currently a member of the editorial board of *Sport Marketing Quarterly*. Dr. Li is also past president of the North American Society for Sport Management (NASSM).

Timothy Liptrap, EdD

Timothy Liptrap is an associate professor and chair of the Sport Management program at Nichols College in Massachusetts. His research interests are in social media, marketing, youth sports and leadership development. Professionally, he was a vice president of World TeamTennis, was the national marketing manager of the United States Tennis Association, and was named one of the 40 Under Forty in the tennis industry.

Kevin McAllister, EdD

Kevin McAllister is an assistant professor of sport management and recreation in the Department of Health, Physical Education, and Recreation at Springfield College. In addition to teaching undergraduate courses in sport governance and customer service, Dr. McAllister serves as the graduate coordinator of the Sport Management and Recreation program and teaches several graduate courses, including budgeting in sport and recreation, event management and planning, legal issues and social issues, and policy for sport organizations. Before receiving his master's and doctorate degrees at Boston University, Dr. McAllister worked as executive director for the U.S. Rugby Football Foundation and as a service manager for the Marriott Corporation. Dr. McAllister has served in leadership positions for a number of community boards and commissions.

Jacqueline McDowell, PhD

Jacqueline McDowell is an assistant professor in the Department of Recreation, Sport, and Tourism at the University of Illinois at Urbana-Champaign. Dr. McDowell's research focuses on issues of diversity and inclusion in intercollegiate athletics. Her primary research interest is investigating the organizational experiences of women of color who serve in athletic administration and coaching positions and exploring how they negotiate their race and gender identities in the workplace. She is also interested in exploring the outcomes of diversity management strategies and the effectiveness of diversity initiatives in sport organizations. She teaches courses in sport ethics, human resource management, and intercollegiate athletics management.

Nadia Moreno, BA

Nadia Moreno is a sport for development officer for the A Ganar Program. Led by Partners of the Americas, A Ganar is a youth workforce development program that utilizes soccer and other team sports to help youth in Latin America and the Caribbean, ages 16–24, find jobs, learn entrepreneurial skills, or reenter the formal education system. Moreno is a graduate of Emory University with a degree in political science and sociology. Prior to joining A Ganar, Moreno worked with Soccer in the Streets (Atlanta, Georgia) and Fundacion Fundem (Bogota, Colombia). She has extensive experience in sport and community outreach work. Moreno is a firm believer in the power of sport to change lives.

Mauro Palmero, PhD

Mauro Palmero is an assistant professor of sport management in the Department of Kinesiology Sport and Recreation Department at East Tennessee State University. He teaches courses in legal issues, sport marketing, and facilities management at the undergraduate and graduate levels. His research interests focus on risk management, facilities and event management, and sport consumer behavior. Dr. Palmero serves as reviewer for the *Journal of Sport*.

Brooke Page Rosenbauer, MS

Brooke Page Rosenbauer is the senior technical coordinator for sport for development at Partners of the Americas. Focusing specifically on the Caribbean region, she coordinates the A Ganar youth workforce development program, which uses a sport-based employability curriculum to reduce youth unemployment. Previously, Rosenbauer directed the Lose the Shoes campaign for Grassroot Soccer's HIV/AIDS awareness and prevention program and has more than 10 years of youth coaching experience. She is the 2008 Harry S. Truman Scholar for the state of Vermont and holds an MS in International Health Policy and Management from the Heller School of Social Policy and Management at Brandeis University in Boston.

Jimmy Sanderson, PhD

Jimmy Sanderson is an assistant professor in the Department of Communication Studies at Clemson University. His research interests center on the influence of social media on sports with an emphasis on sports media, sports organizational management, and athlete-fan communication and interaction. His work has appeared in outlets such as *Communication Quarterly, International Journal of Sport Communication, Journal of Computer-Mediated Communication*, and *Western Journal of Communication*. He is also the author of *It's A Whole New Ballgame: How Social Media is Changing Sports*. He serves on the editorial board of the *International Journal of Sport Communication*.

Pete Schroeder, EdD

Pete Schroeder is an associate professor of sport management and chair of the Department of Health, Exercise, and Sports Sciences at the University of the Pacific. He earned his doctorate from the University of Missouri in Leadership and Policy Analysis and a BS in exercise science at Truman State University. Dr. Schroeder has conducted award-winning research on organizational culture in university and college sport and has published research in *Sport, Education and Society; Journal of Sport Behavior; Journal of College Student Development;* and *Journal of Issues in Intercollegiate Athletics*. In addition, he has presented research on international labor migration and sport management pedagogy.

Janelle E. Wells, PhD

Janelle E. Wells is an assistant professor in the Department of Sport Management in the College of Education at Florida State University. After receiving her BBA and MBA in management and prior to earning her doctorate, Dr. Wells worked in the private sector and coached collegiate volleyball. She has taught Human Resource Management in Sport, Administration in Sport and Physical Activity, Introduction to Business Statistics, Sport and Society, and Introduction to Sport Management. Her research interests focus on the career development of sport leaders and the impact of leaders on employee selection, turnover, organizational change, and performance.

Jon Welty Peachey, PhD

Jon Welty Peachey is an assistant professor in the Department of Recreation, Sport, and Tourism at the University of Illinois at Urbana-Champaign. Before that, he worked in the Department of Health and Kinesiology at Texas A&M University, where he taught courses in management of sport organization, facility and event planning, sport finance, and organizational behavior at the undergraduate and graduate levels. His research agenda centers on sport for development and social change, organizational change, and developing effective and inclusive leadership strategies for sport organizations. Prior to his work in academia, Dr. Welty Peachey worked as a senior administrator in the international sport field for a decade.

James J. Zhang, PhD

James J. Zhang is a professor in the Department of Kinesiology at the University of Georgia. His primary research interests are applied measurement and/or applied studies examining sport consumer and organizational behaviors. He has studied sport leadership with a focus on formal and informal leadership associated with athletic program management. He publishes frequently in sport management journals and presents regularly at academic conferences. Dr. Zhang recently served as the president of the North American Society for Sport Management (NASSM).

INDEX

Note: Page numbers followed by *f*, or *t*, indicate material in figures, or tables, respectively.